THE FIRST
POLITICAL ORDER

THE FIRST
POLITICAL ORDER

*How Sex Shapes Governance
and National Security Worldwide*

VALERIE M. HUDSON
DONNA LEE BOWEN
PERPETUA LYNNE NIELSEN

Columbia University Press
New York

Columbia University Press
Publishers Since 1893
New York   Chichester, West Sussex
cup.columbia.edu

Library of Congress Cataloging-in-Publication Data
Names: Hudson, Valerie M., 1958- author. | Bowen, Donna Lee, 1947- author. |
    Nielsen, Perpetua Lynne, author.
Title: The first political order : how sex shapes governance and national security
    worldwide / Valerie M. Hudson, Donna Lee Bowen, Perpetua Lynne Nielsen.
Description: New York : Columbia University Press, 2020. |
    Includes bibliographical references and index.
Identifiers: LCCN 2019028604 (print) | LCCN 2019028605 (ebook) |
    ISBN 9780231194662 (cloth) | ISBN 9780231550932 (ebook)
Subjects: LCSH: Sex discrimination against women—History. |
    Sex role—History. | Women's rights—History. | Social structure—History. |
    National security—History.
Classification: LCC HQ1237 .H93 2020 (print) | LCC HQ1237 (ebook) |
    DDC 305.4209—dc23
LC record available at https://lccn.loc.gov/2019028604
LC ebook record available at https://lccn.loc.gov/2019028605

Cover design: Catherine Casalino
Frontispiece: Statue of grieving woman holding an ouroboros, Verano Cemetery, Rome, Italy.
Photograph by Douglas Keister.

CONTENTS

PART III: CHANGE

ACKNOWLEDGMENTS

Given the wide-ranging nature of this book, we have many individuals and organizations to thank.

First, we would like to thank our sponsors. In the first place, this includes the U.S. Department of Defense, which provided funds for our data collection and scalings through the U.S. Army Research Laboratory and the U.S. Army Research Office via the Department of Defense's Minerva Research Initiative under grant number W911NF-14-1-0532. Hudson would also like to thank the Andrew Carnegie Corporation for their supportive fellowship in the social sciences, which allowed her release time to write. The authors gratefully acknowledge the support of the Compton Foundation and are deeply appreciative for their unfailing enthusiasm and support for our work. At Brigham Young University, we would like to thank the David M. Kennedy Center for International Affairs, the College of Family, Home, and Social Sciences, the Department of Political Science, the Department of Geography, the Department of Statistics and the Women's Research Initiative for their support. At Texas A&M University, we would like to thank the Department of International Affairs, as well as The Bush School of Government and Public Service within which that department is housed, for their support. The views expressed herein are our own and do not represent the views of these organizations.

Without the student coders and scalers of The WomanStats Project, this research could not have taken place, and we are so very grateful to those who worked with us from 2014–2018 on the project. We especially thank Lauren Eason, as well as Arielle Newman and Natalie Romeri-Lewis, for their assistance as program coordinators. Meghan Blizinski is owed a special thanks for transforming our references into endnotes. A very special acknowledgment must be given to Kaylee Hodgson for her yeoman's work on the multivariate modeling and logistic regression analyses. Hodgson went above and beyond the call of duty and should be considered a secondary author on chapter 7.

There are many researchers whose work has inspired our own. Indeed, they may or may not even know how much their work meant to us. We would include in this group scholars such as Ariel Ahram, Victor Asal, Elin Bjarnegard, Mary Caprioli, Mounira Charrad, Andrea Den Boer, Cynthia Enloe, Patricia Gowaty, David Jacobson, Ann Jones, Mary Hartman, Theodore Kemper, Gerda Lerner, Erik Melander, Rose McDermott, Robin Morgan, Susan Moller Okin, Carole Pateman, Malcolm Potts, Peggy Reeves Sanday, Barbara Smuts, Rebecca Solnit, Gloria Steinem, Ann Tickner, Jacqui True, Mark Weiner, and Richard Wrangham.

Patricia Gowaty, Dan Reiter, Alison Brysk, and Khandis Blake are endeared to us forever for reading the entire final draft of the manuscript—you cannot know how much your enthusiasm and support bolstered our spirits! We also thank the two anonymous reviewers who each offered excellent advice for improving the draft. A special shout-out goes to Caelyn Cobb of Columbia University Press who saw the promise of this book, and who also provided extremely helpful editorial advice throughout the process.

We also thank Laurie Weisler, Tiffany Huff, and Carina Alleman (and her redoubtable assistants) for their support, without which we would have spent far more time on administration and bibliographic formatting than on writing. And we thank Marijke Breuning, without whose initial encouragement of our work, we might never have reached this point. We also thank Michael Geary, who unfailingly and swiftly fixed any glitches with our online database and map generator that hindered our progress—even while on vacation!

Finally, we would like to thank our families who made this work so meaningful to our lives. Hudson would like to thank her husband David, and children Joseph, John, Thomas, Jamison, Rose, and Eve. Ariel, if you had been here, I am sure you would have helped us write this book. Bowen thanks her husband Jim. Nielsen is immensely grateful for her five children: Marc, George, Cinta, Brian, and Rebekah.

June 2019
Proverbs 8: 2–4, 36

THE FIRST
POLITICAL ORDER

INTRODUCTION

A light went on for one of our coauthors, Valerie Hudson, one spring day more than a decade ago when she had the opportunity to have lunch with one of the first female Afghan ministers of parliament (MPs). As Hudson chirped about the growing empowerment of women in Afghanistan, as evidenced by the fact that her guest was university educated and an MP, the MP stopped her: "Valerie, I could go home today, and my husband could divorce me by simply saying the phrase 'I divorce you' three times. If he did, I would lose custody of my children and would have nowhere to live. Even if he does not divorce me, I may have little say in when and to whom my children are married. How empowered am I really, Valerie?" Hudson was pulled up short. Although she was used to assessing women's empowerment through indicators such as educational attainment and political participation, she clearly had failed to consider something prior to and much deeper than these things. In a sense, this entire book emerged from that conversation of more than a decade ago.

In his 2015 study, *Sapiens: A Brief History of Mankind*, historian Yuval Noah Harari notes that throughout human history, the hierarchy "of supreme importance in all known human societies" is the hierarchy of sex. "People everywhere have divided themselves into men and women. And almost everywhere men have got the better deal."[1] So why is this the case, not just in one or two cultures, but almost universally? Why would men get the better deal not just in one place, but most everywhere? And why would this system be so stubbornly persistent, from the dawn of history even into the twenty-first century?

We aim to answer these questions in this book. Building upon, but then extending, decades of scholarship, we explain the causes of women's systematic subordination as an outcome of human societies' dependence on men to defend their physical security. In particular, we uncover a deeply male security dilemma that guides the choice of security provision mechanism within most human societies even to this day. That preferred means is the male fraternal group. Men seeking their own security attempt to construct strong male-bonded alliances, typically based on patrilineal (agnatic) relationships, and these alliances strive for security through dominance. Of course, women have historically been an irreplaceable support to this security provision mechanism, as it is they who biologically reproduce the group, providing brothers and sons for this male alliance. The fraternity's dependence on women, we argue, leads to the necessity for men to control them. We analyze an interlocking set of eleven practices—remarkable in their consistency across space and time in human history—that simultaneously strengthen the patrilineal–fraternal alliance structure, while profoundly subordinating women. We demonstrate that these practices remain common in today's world and that they cross geographic regions, ethnic groups, religious groups, and language groups.

This socially constructed system of male security alliances, united through agnatic kinship networks that have safeguarded their physical and social repro-duction over millennia, is what we term in this book the Patrilineal/Fraternal Syndrome. We call it a syndrome because we identify a set "of symptoms that characterize a particular social condition," which leads to "a predictable, characteristic pattern of behavior." A syndrome is often associated with a pathological condition, which is what we believe the Patrilineal/Fraternal Syndrome produces.

Through the set of practices that make up the Patrilineal/Fraternal Syndrome, control over women has solidified the subordination of women throughout human history and around the world. Although male willingness to utilize physical force, which is used universally to dominate women, is a critical factor, the Syndrome encodes more systematic means of female control that make day-to-day use of such violence less necessary, such as early marriage for girls, polygyny, differential inheritance rights for men and women, and other mechanisms we will detail. Furthermore, it is important to recognize that women may very well consciously support this Syndrome to ensure their own security and perhaps even augment their status in a world of men who are prepared to use violence against them. We suggest that this system of control begins at the most intimate level—the relationship of husband and wife—and from that point radiates through the extended family, through societies, and through nation-states, and ultimately has the ability to cross borders and desta-bilize regions. Denial of equal participation in family decision making, unequal access to resources, asymmetrical use of violence in the home, and unequal status in common law all help create the schoolhouse that ensures the perpetuation of the Syndrome through time.

We document the creation and maintenance of this universal Syndrome, but our purpose does not end there. We theorize that the Syndrome actually—and ironically—heightens the insecurity and instability of the group. That is, despite the fact that reliance on male-bonded alliances was chosen for its presumed ability to provide security, it ultimately subverts that aim. The heart of this book, therefore, is our empirical documentation of the negative impact this system has on women, children, men, and nation-states. We find through rigorous cross-national empirical analysis that the search for security through a male-based fraternity that strongly subordinates women, pushed to its logical end, has serious and negative ramifications for the security, stability, resilience, prosperity, health, and happiness of the collective as well as negative security effects regionally and even internationally. Our empirical results strongly suggest that for peace, stability, security, and resilience to obtain, the Syndrome must be disrupted and dismantled. For example, every unit increase in our scale measurement of the subordination of women (see chapter 3) increases a state's chances of being fragile by 2.3 times. Every unit increase results in a 3.5 greater chance that a nation-state's government will be autocratic, less effective, and more corrupt, and a 1.57 greater chance the nation will be unstable and violent. Every unit increase in the subordination of women gives a nation 1.5 times the chance of experiencing poverty and 1.8 times the chance of experiencing food insecurity (see chapter 7 and appendix III for details). It appears as if the surest way to curse one's nation is to subordinate its women.

The informal social organizations that best mirror the patrilineal/fraternal kinship networks we study are tribes and clans. Although some might think of clans and tribes as being prevalent today only in the least developed countries, that is untrue. Agnatic kinship groups are power brokers in many different types of countries, rich and poor, developed and less developed, democratic and autocratic. Most people recognize that tribal societies exist in countries such as Afghanistan and South Sudan, but the power of agnatic kinship groups is also strong in countries such as India, Qatar, and Indonesia. Other countries are in transition to either greater or lesser reliance on such networks, such as the Philippines, Tunisia, and China.

For a man, status and success in this type of social environment stem from being the protector of his family and also his kinship group. For example, reflecting this worldview, a popular Pakistani tribal proverb states, "a man's gun is his jewelry." In contrast, women's role in these types of societies is to reproduce the agnatic kinship group. Although women may have great pride in their tribal affiliation, they are rigorously governed by expectations of honorable behavior as defined by obedience, modesty, and chastity. As the group is all-important, the effort of all members is required to secure group strength, defend group property, and reproduce the group. Individual subordination to the group is expected, but if flouted, will be punished by expulsion or death.

As some societies began to slowly and fitfully move beyond male kinship groups as the most important security provision mechanism, observers began to note the emergence of two different approaches to societal organization where once there had been only one. For example, nineteenth-century legal scholar Sir Henry Sumner Maine seized on this difference. He described one type of society as being "status societies," which in his view were more traditional societies in which family, clan, and tribal identities were the basis of social organization. Status societies, according to Maine, emphasize the needs and customs of the whole, the larger group at the expense of individual members who are expected to sublimate personal needs. In these societies, states may be absent or weak, and individuals rely on their kinship group to pursue their interests as well as their security.[2]

In contrast, Maine also identified a second category of states whose governance is based on contracts between rulers and the ruled that grant and enforce rights of the individual as well as safeguard the nation. Such systems, according to Maine, often feature rights of personal freedom, free markets, and restrictions on state authority, all of which are supported by government institutions subject to laws and regulations and are applied equally. Women and minorities specifically benefited from these developments as they claim rights established to belong to individuals.[3]

Maine's status societies are analogous to the societies we identify as encoding the Patrilineal/Fraternal Syndrome. As we have noted, such societies have developed a web of practices to ensnare women as permanent subordinates. We find not one practice, but a combination of practices that interlock to provide a perfect straitjacket of female subordination. The eleven practices we focus on in this volume include physical violence against women, patrilocal marriage in which brides move to their husbands' family compounds, early marriage for girls, personal status laws that benefit men and grant women few rights in the family, laws and traditions restricting women from owning property, practices of dowry and brideprice, son preference and sex ratio alteration, cousin marriage, polygyny, sanction/impunity for the killing of women, and the treatment of rape as a property crime against men. In the Patrilineal/Fraternal Syndrome, all of these practices are interrelated in a vicious cycle, seemingly without beginning or end, like an ouroboros, that is, the mythical snake of antiquity eternally swallowing its tail.

Breaking the links of the Syndrome through such developments as later marriage of girls, formation of nuclear families in their own domiciles (neolocal marriage), and the abandonment of practices such as polygyny has historically created an observable division between what Maine termed status and contract societies. In part III of this volume, in which we undertake the subject of change, we argue that much can be learned from these historical and even contemporary efforts to move beyond fraternity as the security provision mechanism of the society. Some of these efforts have been hugely successful; others have been dismal failures. Analysis of these cases provides the foundation for contemporary applications and recommendations in the final chapter of our book.

Our study is designed to identify practices and methods of informal social organization that subordinate women and benefit men, not to demonize men as a sex. Many, perhaps most, men have chosen a more peaceful and egalitarian relationship with women and are strong advocates of women's rights. Furthermore, although we document the actions of men in the social practices that we detail, as noted previously, these practices can be maintained only through the acquiescence, and in many cases the active collusion, of women. Thus, when women search for additional wives for their sons or value their daughters less than their sons, they become complicit in propagating the Syndrome. We agree that women have far less power than men in household decisions, but it must be acknowledged that some women have been instrumental in furthering practices that harm women, just as others have actively worked to abolish such practices. In sum, men are not devils and women are not angels in the story we tell in this book.

✳ ✳ ✳

This has been a long-term project. To formulate and support our argument both theoretically and empirically, we delved into the disciplines of history, anthropology, sociology, evolutionary biology, and political science, seeking insight on the subordination of women and the effects of that subordination on the group. As we worked out the means by which women are controlled, we discovered that many of the variables we thought to be critically important, such as prevalence of patrilocal marriage, were not objects of current cross-national study. More bluntly put, there wasn't any data. To undertake this research project, we were going to have to compile that data. We could not have done so without the help of our sponsors, particularly the Minerva Initiative of the U.S. Department of Defense. With that crucial support, we led our teams of student coders in compiling and then scaling the empirical data necessary to investigate our arguments. Finally, we performed extensive statistical analyses to evaluate our assertion that the subordination of women undermines national security and stability.

Our academic home for this research is The WomanStats Project (woman-stats.org), which holds that "The fate of nations is tied to the status of women." To demonstrate the linkage, WomanStats has assembled data on every country with a population greater than 200,000, currently 176 nations. Coders who are graduate and undergraduate students at Brigham Young University (BYU), Texas A&M University (TAMU), the University of Kent, Ankara Social Sciences

University, and the Universidad del Rosario have been tasked with researching open sources for data on more than 350 different variables that detail the situation of women country by country. The superb student researchers at BYU and TAMU were those who compiled the empirical data for this book. The WomanStats database allows researchers access to both qualitative and quantitative data on women's worldwide situation, plus cross-national univariate and multivariate scales as well as analysis and mapping of the data. All of the data compiled for our analysis as well as maps and other materials are freely available on our website, representing our contribution to any who are interested in these topics.[4]

This book, the culmination of that massive data collection effort, is divided into three sections. Part I introduces what we term the "first political order," the order of authority in the household that forms the basis for community and state actions. Part I also presents our theoretical framework concerning the male security dilemma and its resolution through fraternal alliances. We extend that framework by delineating the specific means that subordinate the interests of women to that of the fraternal alliance. We define and explicate the Patrilineal/Fraternal Syndrome and explain how it manifests historically and in the modern day.

Chapter 1 defines the options for household authority relations, laying out the sexual political order that we believe is determinative of the wider political order. Here, we explore the first political order in the title of this work. The chapter surveys the works of philosophers and theorists seeking to answer how the subordination of women produces a given political order. Chapter 2 outlines our theoretical framework and introduces our definition of the Patrilineal/Fraternal Syndrome. As agnatic kin groups coalesce to counter threats of violence from other groups, they strategically utilize practices designed to concentrate authority, reproductive rights, and property in male hands. We define how the Syndrome operates through these component practices, and note, in a preliminary way, implications for the organization and behavior of the nation-state. We suggest that the tragedy of great power politics actually derives from the tragedy of the Syndrome. Chapter 3 lays out the contemporary prevalence of the Syndrome. The introduction to the chapter details our construction of the Syndrome index and our methods in determining its prevalence and intensity in countries worldwide. We then examine the eleven components of the Syndrome and trace how each plays its role in the subordination of women, even in today's world.

Part II further develops our theoretical framework, by positing in detail the causal mechanisms through which the Patrilineal/Fraternal Syndrome produces negative consequences for governance, security, and stability within a society. Chapter 4 examines the consequences of the Patrilineal/Fraternal security order for state governance and national security and discusses the ways the Syndrome undermines state stability and resilience as well as furthers conflict. Chapter 5 takes up three of the mechanisms by which the Syndrome obstructs marriage markets, which obstruction in turn deepens national instability: these three mechanisms are alteration of sex ratios, polygyny, and brideprice or dowry. This chapter explores the impact of such obstruction not only on individual women and men but also on the larger society and on the stability and security of the nation-state. Chapter 6 examines the variety of consequences, outside of security and governance, that the Syndrome visits upon societies. These consequences affect families, communities, and states across a range of dimensions, including health, demographics, food security, economic performance, environmental protection, educational investment, and social progress. Human, economic, and environmental security are all undermined by reliance on male fraternities for security.

Chapter 7 introduces the empirical analysis designed to test the propositions proposed in chapters 4, 5, and 6. The chapter first notes which additional factors, such as urbanization, may influence, contextualize, or compete with the Syndrome as possible explanations of these nation-state outcomes, and these then serve as control variables in our models. The remainder of the chapter is the heart of our analytical work—that is, we present the results of our multivariate modeling. We divide our empirical analysis into nine dimensions of nation-state outcomes and explore the relationship between outcome variables in each dimension and a model incorporating the Syndrome and our seven control variables. The dimensions are as follows:

1. Political Stability and Governance
2. Security and Conflict
3. Economic Performance
4. Economic Rentierism
5. Health and Well-Being
6. Demographic Security
7. Education of the Population
8. Social Progress
9. Environmental Protection

Each dimension contains dependent variables that together grant insight into the impact that the Syndrome has on the overall stability and security of the nation-state, its people, and its environment. Although some familiarity with quantitative analysis is helpful for getting the most from these empirical results, we have streamlined the presentation of the results for the sake of the reader. (Most of the technical details and tables for the multivariate analyses are provided in appendix III, with summary tables and extensive comments throughout chapter 7 that will guide the general reader.) We have provided visual aids such as scatterplots showing the relationship between the Syndrome and specific outcome variables in our large N analysis. In addition, where possible, we computed odds ratios through logistic regression analysis, analyzing how each unit of additional intensification of the Syndrome affects the outcome variables. Appendixes I–V provide additional information, and our full replication dataset and ancillary files can be found online (see appendix III for details on locating the online information).

Part III considers the possibility of change. In particular, it identifies meaningful distinctions among Post-Syndrome, Transition, and Syndrome societies, and it notes that nation-state outcomes for Transition nations are intermediate between the other two types of society. In other words, we show that even a partial dismantling of the Syndrome's components offers salutary effects for the nation-state. Chapter 8 examines the first political order from a historical perspective to shed light on what specific changes to the Syndrome have allowed states to move away from the centrality of male fraternity, and as a result, to create and maintain rule of law and individual rights. We highlight in this chapter the work of scholars such as Jack Goody, John Hajnal, Mary Hartman, and others who have written on the revolutionary adjustments made over human history to counter Syndrome practices, such as neolocal marriage and the abolition of polygyny and cousin marriage. Positive cases, such as post-Roman northwestern Europe, are examined, but we also examine cases in which change failed, such as in Soviet Central Asia during the early part of the twentieth century. This historical backdrop, plus a look at cases in the modern era, such as South Korea, help us to understand what works to facilitate change and under what conditions.

Chapter 9 ponders the question of what can be done to limit the Syndrome's influence today. It suggests and evaluates specific policies and approaches that can make a difference in diminishing the grasp that the Patrilineal/Fraternal Syndrome has on societies. It also suggests when other policy initiatives, such as democratization, are likely to fail as a result of the Syndrome status of the target nation.

Before moving to the first chapter, we invite the reader to turn to the illustration in the frontispiece. If you examine the seated figure, you will note that the woman with hooded face and dejected posture is holding a snake in her right hand. On closer examination, you can see that it is not just an ordinary snake but rather an ouroboros, the serpent who has swallowed its tail, thereby forming a continuous unit, a circle that in classical imagery reflects infinity. We see the Patrilineal/Fraternal Syndrome as best symbolized by this archetype, a phenomenon also without beginning or end. The ouroboros is destined to live on eternally—no wonder the hooded female figure is so sorrowful.[5] Unlike the classic ouroboros, however, we find that the Syndrome can be disrupted and dismantled through concerted, focused efforts. We write this book to aid those efforts and pray they may be successful. Otherwise, the Syndrome, which has plagued humankind for millennia, will continue to cause immeasurable grief for us all far into the future.

PART I

THE FIRST POLITICAL ORDER

CHAPTER 1

THE FIRST POLITICAL ORDER IS THE SEXUAL POLITICAL ORDER

Confronted with the obvious, generally accepted, but frequently ignored fact that babies come out of females and female genitals differ from male genitals, people seek to solve the puzzle of sex differences by sorting out how and why the differences came about, what is to be done about the differences, and how the two kinds of people resulting from the differences are to relate to one another and to their environment.

—Peggy Reeves Sanday

Many impressive tomes have been written about the origins of political order, from Aristotle to Francis Fukuyama.[1] Very few of these works recognize that an intimate relationship may exist between the political order between men and women, on one hand, and the political order that develops within the nation-state, on the other.[2] Indeed, for the majority of such works, one looks in vain in the final index of the volume for the entries "women," "woman," or even "female." Still fewer contemplate a relationship between these two political orders and the resulting stability and resilience of the nation-state. This book probes both propositions.

Gender performance varies widely across cultures. What does not vary is that roughly half of the population of a given human collective has the potential to be mothers (and not fathers) and the other half to be fathers (and not mothers) and that children require the interaction of both a mother and a father to be brought into being and thus are all of "mixed" heritage.[3] This sexual parameter of human life, we argue, sets the stage for the origin of all politics.

Add to these foundational sexual facts the differential upper-body strength between men and women (termed "human sexual dimorphism"), differential bodily and time investment in reproduction, and readily observable anatomical differences and the political game is already afoot. Men and women are the originary "Others" for each other, and the politics between them will profoundly influence the socialization of the children born to them—and the larger society that forms as a result. Historian Karen Offen notes that "'Biology' may not be destiny, and indeed it may also be socially constructed, but physicality does pose constraints as well as opportunities. Difference does not, of necessity, imply dominance—or subordination."[4] Offen is suggesting that the political choices catalyzed by sexual difference need not result in female subordination, and we agree with that assertion. Unfortunately, they often do in practice, or to quote Yuval Noah Harari, "One hierarchy . . . has been of supreme importance in all known human societies: the hierarchy of gender."[5]

Dimensions of the First Political Order

To "see" the first political order—the sexual political order—consider the foundational societal decisions arising from the manner in which these two halves of any human collective relate. The first political order can be understood as having four dimensions, all of which are inherently political. We might conceive of a continuum between two polar extremes along which human societies might be arranged according to how they structure male–female relations, as shown in the following figures.

Four Political Dimensions of the First Political Order

1. Status in the context of difference: Will these two groups engage each other as equals, or as subordinate and superordinate?

Unequals ⬌ Equals

2. Decision making in the context of difference: Will decisions in the society be made by one group or by both groups?

One group ⬌ Both groups

3. Conflict resolution in the context of difference: If the two groups disagree, how is that disagreement to be resolved? Can one group be coerced to provide what is required for group survival and persistence against their will?

Violent coercion ←——————————————→ Nonviolent resolution

4. Resource distribution in the context of difference: With regard to resources necessary for survival and persistence, such as food, land, weapons, children, and wealth, which group will control these resources, or will control be shared?

Resources controlled by one group ←——————————————→ Resources controlled by both groups

To explore how determinative of the wider political order the first political order (i.e., the *sexual* political order) is, it is useful to conduct a thought experiment. Consider what type of society is formed when the answers to these four questions all appear on the *left*-hand side of the continuum.

One group, let's call it A, is superordinate over the other (B) and makes all important decisions for the collective. The second group, B, may be ignored or punished if it protests this arrangement. A strives to monopolize and control all resources necessary for survival and persistence, including land, wealth, and children. B can be coerced into providing what the first group needs through physical violence until acquiescence is obtained. B becomes, in essence, another resource controlled by A, a resource from which rents, such as productive and reproductive labor, are extracted by coercion and subordination.

If that were the structure of male–female relations—if this was the *sexual* political order established—how would that shape the development of the collective's *societal* political order? We argue that, in this case, the groundwork will have been laid for an inequitable political order ruled by monopolistic rent seekers prepared to ensure the continued flow of their rents through exploitation, corruption, and violence. Worse yet, such societal arrangements would seem "natural and right" given the original choices made with regard to the First Other—that is, the first B—woman. For good reason, evolutionary biologist Patricia Gowaty has asserted, "Women's oppression is the first, most widespread, and deepest oppression . . . Sexist oppression is fundamental to—is 'the root' of—all other systems of oppression."[6]

Furthermore, in such a context, it would seem unremarkable to use physical violence if necessary to effect that subordination. Gowaty continues, "The antithetical icon of autonomy for many women is rape. . . . The insight that violence against women is sexy (turns men on) provides a powerful proximate analysis that explains what many of us know in our guts—sexuality is the fulcrum of subordination/domination."[7] Philosopher Kate Manne states it simply: "She will give, and he will take, in effect; or else she may be punished."[8]

And All the "Others"

An unsurprising consequence is that all "others" in the society—those of different ethnicity, religion, and ideology—thus also tend to be relegated to the same lower status accorded to females. In a sense, these others are "feminized" because their status, agency, and so forth correspond more to that of women in society than to that of men. Historian Gerda Lerner states that "the precedent of seeing women as an inferior group allows the transference of such a stigma onto any other group which is enslaveable."[9] Another way of putting it, as anthropologist Richard Alexander and coauthors suggest, is to see "culture as a gigantic metaphorical extension of the reproductive system."[10]

In a sense, the sexual system represented by the left-hand side of the four political continua is, at its core, *authoritarian* in nature. We see, with philosopher Sylviane Agacinski, that "the question of the duality of the sexes was political from the start . . . traditional injustices connected to sexual difference are reproduced in the spheres of political, social, economic, and family life."[11] We should not be surprised, then, if societies based on such a sexual system are at once both violent and fragile. She continues, "Isn't the other sex, for each, the closest face of the *stranger*? . . . The way we think the *other* sex determines the way we think the *other* in general."[12] Agacinski is asserting that how men treat women will come to be the founding template for how all minorities and out-groups will be treated. Indeed, the very act of male–female sexual intercourse will be interpreted in such a culture as supporting this treatment, or as the sociologist Theodore Kemper puts it, "sexual occasions are themselves importantly dominance or eminence encounters . . . there can be a dominance encounter even at the core of intimate interaction,"[13] or as philosopher Michel Foucault suggests, sexual behavior is "an especially dense transfer point for relations of power."[14] Anthropologist Peggy Reeves Sanday concurs, suggesting an alignment of "social relations of male dominance and female subordination with sexual relations of male aggression and female passivity or masochism."[15] Politics' deepest roots may well be found in our interpretation of the act of heterosexual intercourse.

In our thought experiment, we might also imagine a sexual political order based on the options presented on the *right*-hand side of the political continua, although it is challenging to find historical examples. In this alternative order, men and women would stand as equals even in the context of their sexual difference, decisions for the collective would be made jointly and without coercion, conflicts would not be decided by violence or the threat of violence against females, and resources would be frankly shared between the sexes. According to Sanday, some indigenous cultures come close to that ideal type, which she terms "diarchy," and those cultures are characterized by significantly less violence and rent seeking as well as far greater stability and resilience in the face of environmental challenges (we return to these observations in later chapters).[16] If such an alternative sexual political order were in place, Agacinski argues, the broader societal political order would change as well and new vistas would emerge: "the masculine monopoly on political power comes to an end and the time for a mixed democracy opens before us . . . the more a civilization establishes sexual equality, the more it respects individuals."[17]

The Sexual Order and the Political Order: Mill, Engels, Lerner, and Pateman

The idea that the sexual order and the political order are linked is not new, by any means. For example, Karen Offen notes Montesquieu's observation that "under despotic governments, women were 'in servitude,' an 'object of luxury' while under republics, 'women are free by the laws and restrained by manners.'"[18] In the past, the sexual order was seen as dependent on the political order (e.g., "better" governments treat women "better"), but the present work considers the reverse proposition: that the broader political order is, in the first place, deeply molded by the sexual political order. In other words, "better" government is not in the offing, nor can it be, if women are subordinated.

If this is true, the character of relations between men and women in any society is critically important in shaping that society's structures and processes. More specifically, it is important because the answers to the four dimensions given above concerning the first difference—that is, the nature of the sexual political order—may work to normalize inequity, violence, authoritarianism, and a parasitical and monopolistic rent-based economy within the broader societal political order. This, too, is not a new idea: from Friedrich Engels in the nineteenth century to Carole Pateman, Gerda Lerner, and Peggy Reeves Sanday in the twentieth, a handful of political philosophers, historians, and anthropologists have explored these foundational linkages. We will examine but a few major works here, noting that we would have reviewed other work as well, if space had permitted.[19]

A number of famous thinkers have lamented the subordinate place of women even in polities that called themselves democracies, the most celebrated being John Stuart Mill, who, writing in 1861, asserted that "from the very earliest twilight of human society, every woman (. . . owing to her inferiority in muscular strength) was found in a state of bondage to some men. Laws and systems of polity always begin by recognizing the relations they find already existing . . . and convert what was a mere physical fact into a legal right [and] give it the sanction of society."[20] Because Mill felt this conversion from physical right to legal right was unmindful, he concluded that the disconnect between the status of women and democracy remained unrecognized within the broader society.

Mill opined that because women will always be inferior in physical strength in relation to men, unlike other groups that contest societal status, women's subordination

> would be the very last to disappear. It was inevitable that this one case of a social relations grounded on force would survive through generations of institutions grounded on equal justice, an almost solitary exception to the general character of their laws and customs; but which, so long as it does not proclaim its own origin, and as discussion has not brought out its true character, is not felt to jar with modern civilization, any more than domestic slavery among the Greeks jarred with their notion of themselves as a free people.[21]

The remedy appeared to Mill, then, to be some type of morally based discussion or deconstruction of the subordination of women to bring it into line with democratic principles. Thinkers could lead the way, according to Mill, for "every step in [human] improvement has been so invariably accompanied by a step made in raising the social position of women, that historians and philosophers have been led to adopt their elevation or debasement as on the whole the surest test and most correct measure of the civilization of a people or an age."[22]

There is nothing wrong with this approach, and to read Mill's *The Subjection of Women* even today is an inspiring undertaking. What we lack in Mill (or William Thompson, or Anna Wheeler, or Mary Wollstonecraft, or others), however, is an understanding of how the subordination of women *produces* a particular type of polity and a particular type of state behavior. It is not that there is a disconnect, à la Mill, but rather that there is a deep "connect."

The earliest writer who we believe makes this connection is Friedrich Engels, who wrote *The Origins of Family, Private Property, and the State* in 1884. Engels's inspiration came from Marx, who had written that "the modern family contains in germ not only slavery (*servitus*), but also serfdom. . . . It contains in miniature all the contradictions which later extend throughout society and its state."[23] Engels describes how wives were little more than slaves in most ancient households, calling them "his [the patriarch's] chief female domestic servant."[24] Wives possessed few rights and labored under a double standard of behavior between men and women in which women could be killed for daring to do things that men felt they were entitled to do, such as promiscuity and polygamy. Although there might be rhetoric against these things generally, Engels notes, "in reality this condemnation never falls on the men concerned, but only on the

women; they are despised and outcast, in order that the unconditional supremacy of men over the female sex may be once more proclaimed as a fundamental
law of society."[25]

But stepping back, what Engels offers that differs from thinkers such as Mill
is the link from these domestic arrangements to the larger society. For example,
Engels opines that "the Greeks themselves put the matter quite frankly: the sole
exclusive aims of monogamous marriage were to make the man supreme in the
family, and to propagate, as the future heirs to his wealth, children indisputably
his own."[26] Thus, to Engels, the form of household relationships and the form of
economic power were integrally linked; the former made possible a particular
form of the latter. Engels asserts that the family "is the cellular form of civilized
society, in which the nature of the oppositions and contradictions fully active
in that society can be already studied. . . . The modern individual family is
founded on the open or concealed domestic slavery of the wife, and modern
society is a mass composed of these individual families as its molecules."[27]

Furthermore, according to Engels, there were echoes of that household
slave economy in the larger state. As such, the state becomes a machine for
"bleeding its subjects," militarized to provide order and protection, but "its
order was worse than the worst disorder," and it was "crippled by extortion"
and immense societal inequality "by giving one class practically all the rights
and the other class practically all the duties."[28] How could it be otherwise,
asserts Engels, given the nature of the household "molecules" that make up the
state's society?

Engels, in the end, does not give us much more than this, but if we skip
forward approximately 100 years, political philosopher Carole Pateman
fills in the blanks in her classic work *The Sexual Contract*, first published in
1988.[29] Pateman believes that "marital domination is politically significant,"
for it means that the original contract—which is the *marital* contract—is "an
exchange of obedience for protection," creating "civil mastery and civil subordination."[30] What Pateman is calling the original contract, we are calling the
first political order: both concern the relationship between the two halves of
humanity, and both are prior to and foundational for the relations that men
establish among themselves in the more widely considered social contracts
discussed by Locke, Hume, and others. Pateman asserts, "Sexual difference
is of fundamental significance for political order,"[31] and Lerner extends this
insight: "Men learned to institute dominance and hierarchy over other people
by their earlier practice of dominance over the women of their own group."[32]
(Indeed, Lerner argues that slavery was based on the template of male treatment of women in their own group.[33])

Pateman does not emphasize father right, as Engels did, but rather fraternal right: "Women are subordinated to men *as men*, or to men as a fraternity.
The original contract . . . creates modern *fraternal patriarchy*."[34] This fraternal

right is in turn based on what she terms "the male sex-right" in the conjugal contract: "The original political right is a man's right to have sexual access to a woman's body so that he could become a father. . . . The law of male sex-right extends to all men, to all members of the fraternity."[35] This fraternity is not politically neutral: "They also have a common interest *as men* in upholding the terms of the sexual contract, in ensuring that the law of male sex-right remains operative."[36] More specifically,

> Contract is seen as the paradigm of free agreement. But women are not born free; women have no natural freedom. The classic pictures of the state of nature also contain an order of subjection—between men and women. . . . Sexual difference is political difference; sexual difference is the difference between freedom and subjection. Women are not party to the original contract. . . . Women are the subject of the contract. The (sexual) contract is the vehicle through which men transform their natural right over women into the security of civil patriarchal right.[37]

This originary contract has major implications for the polity created within the society, according to Pateman. For example, she argues that "modern patriarchy is fraternal, contractual and structures capitalist civil society."[38] In particular, "Once woman has been enslaved and families formed, men held both the concept of slavery and the means to extend their mastery beyond the household: 'he found himself free to limit and to conquer other human beings; and he is fully secure in that his "wife"—that is to say, his female slave—would roast his meat and attend to any other of his needs.'"[39] Pateman is suggesting that economic relations within a society based on the syndrome of the subordinative first political order on the left-hand side of our four spectra cannot help but be exploitative and predatory in nature: "Conjugal relations are part of a sexual division of labor and structure of subordination that extends from the private home into the public arena."[40] Marriage arising out of a very different first political order—for example, based on the right-hand side of the four spectra—would be a very different relationship from what Pateman describes, and therefore, would create a very different economic system.

Furthermore, Pateman suggests that the nature of the original contract begins to contaminate contracts about nonsexual matters within the larger society, not just in economics but also in politics. For example, "The employment contract creates the capitalist as master; he has the political right to determine how the labour of the worker will be used, and—consequently— can engage in exploitation."[41] The parallels to the marriage contract become striking. Although conceived by classic political philosophy as the foundation of freedom, contract becomes, over time, something far more closely related to the nature of the sexual contract, which is subordinative and by no means an expression of freedom. What is contracted is an exchange of some type of support or protection, however piecemeal or even insincere, for almost full subordination and submission. Pateman explains, "Contract theory . . . justified subjection by presenting it as freedom."[42] This is highly ironic for men. Commenting on nineteenth-century political theorist William Thompson's reflections on the matter, Pateman states, "Thompson . . . suggests that without the sexual contract, men would not have entered the social contract and created the state; men's conjugal mastery looks as if it 'compensate[s] them for their own cowardly submission almost everywhere to the chains of political power.'"[43] By insisting on the first subordinative political order in regard to women, men prime *themselves* to be subordinated. The polity created by such societies will tend toward autocracy, and the type of "democracy" found in such societies will be found to have a subordinative core of gross inequality.

Nevertheless, if female subordination is viewed as natural or as divinely mandated, it may be difficult to even conceive of a society that does not have this inequality at its core. Indeed, according to Pateman, even John Locke found the subjection of women through the sexual contract to be completely natural: Locke felt Eve's subjection "can be no other subjection than what every Wife owes her Husband . . . [Adam has] a Conjugal Power . . . the Power that every Husband hath to order the things of private Concernment in his Family, as Proprietor of the Goods and Lands there, and to have his Will take place before that of his wife in all things of their common Concernment."[44]

As Pateman points out, this original contract between men and women is clearly not envisioned as one made between equals: "if one party is in an inferior position [such as a wife or woman], then he or she has no choice but to agree to disadvantageous terms offered by the superior party."[45] Indeed, Pateman goes so far as to say,

> If some individuals are assumed by nature to be significantly stronger or more capable than others, and if it is also assumed that individuals are always self-interested, then the social contract that creates equal civil individuals or citizens, governed by impartial laws, *is impossible*; the original pact will establish a society of masters and slaves [for] the strong can present the contract as being to the advantage of both; the strong no longer have to labour and the weak now can be assured that their basic needs will be provided for. . . . [And] when the strong coerce the weak into the slave contract, the obvious objection is that it is not really a "contract": the coercion invalidates the "agreement." [emphasis added].[46]

And where did this concept of "slave" even originate? Commenting on Lerner's classic work *The Creation of Patriarchy*, alluded to previously,

Pateman notes, "Slavery came about because an example of subordination and 'otherness' had already been developed. Women were already subordinated to the men of their social groups . . . so men 'learned that differences can be used to separate and divide one group of humans from another.' . . . The first slaves were *women*."[47] No wonder, then, that the idea of contract—twisted because of the nature of the marital contract under a subordinative first political order—is used to justify the notion that someone is free to be alienated from his or her own freedom. Lerner writes, "Civil slavery becomes nothing more than one example of a legitimate contract. Individual freedom becomes exemplified in slavery."[48]

From this analysis we see that a society's understanding of ethics is molded—and may be warped—by the nature of the first political order. As Pateman notes, "Ethical life depends upon marriage because marriage is the origin of the family. In the family, children learn, and adults are continually reminded of what it means to be a member of a small association."[49] When what marriage means is a natural subjection based on difference, the ethics of dealing with all others who are different in society—by race, creed, class, or language—become stamped with that same subordinative character. After all, Pateman explains, "sexual difference is political difference, the difference between mastery and subjection,"[50] and Lerner adds, "sexual dominance underlies class and race dominance [for] men had learned how to assert and exercise power over people slightly different from themselves in the primary exchange of women. In so doing, men acquired the knowledge necessary to elevate 'difference' of whatever kind into a criterion for dominance."[51]

Even with the expansive vision provided by these thinkers, however, the full logic of how choices made on the left-hand side of figure 1.1 *arise* and *persist*, and conversely, how a society may begin to *transition* toward the right-hand side of the continuum, is not easy to tease out from this literature. At some point, terms like "patriarchy" and "hegemonic masculinity" become too vague to assist in that critical analytical task.[52] Furthermore, the *full societal consequences* of veering to the left or to the right side of these political continua have not been adequately explored. What, precisely, are the ramifications of choosing the left-hand poles representing male dominance for the governance, stability, resilience, and security of the society? These theoretical and empirical tasks are the focus of the present volume, and they are of absolute importance in understanding and alleviating insecurity and instability at the individual, societal, national, and international levels.

CHAPTER 2

THE OLDEST SECURITY
PROVISION MECHANISM

*I have a friend whose family tree has been traced back a thousand years,
but no women exist on it. She just discovered that she herself did not exist,
but her brothers did. . . . Go back more generations and hundreds, then
thousands [of women] disappear.*

—Rebecca Solnit

Genealogical invisibility is but one example of how a societal
emphasis on the male bond distorts reality, laying the groundwork for insecurity and instability. In this volume, we propose a
theoretical framework suggesting that a sexual political order exists that crosses
space and time in its manifestation, an order that is focused on building fraternity through the systematic subordination of women and that often uses
patrilineality to facilitate the creation of that fraternity. We refer to this order in
terms of what we argue is an interlocking pattern of institutions, processes, and
norms that enforce it.[1] More specifically, we refer to this interlocking system
as the Patrilineal/Fraternal Syndrome. This Syndrome embodies the left-hand
side of the four political continua illustrated in figure 1.1, and we assert that this
societal structuration requires—and can be identified by—the frank subordination of female interests to that of the fraternal alliance. Furthermore, we argue
that the instantiation of this Syndrome through specific and nearly universal

enforcement practices has profound direct and indirect effects on a society's levels of stability, resilience, and security, mediated by the type of societal political order that emerges from this first sexual political order.

To identify this Syndrome at work in the contemporary world and study its effects, we further assert it is most useful to view the Syndrome as being promulgated, in the first place, as a *security provision mechanism*. In other words, we propose the Syndrome's existence is justified by its practitioners by the need to provide physical security for group members from external or out-group threats, which, in the view of its practitioners, necessitate the creation of a strong fraternity that is typically deemed incompatible with equality between men and women.

More justifications are always available for this sexual order than the need to meet external or out-group threats. When individual men subordinate women in their household, they receive tangible and quite personal goods and services, including sexual services; services to maintain the household, such as water, fuel, and food gathering; elder care for the man's parents; and bearing and rearing of children.[2] Deprivation of such expected goods and services is a strong goad for maintaining the first sexual political order, whether or not external threats exist. Justification on the basis of out-group threat, however, seems foundational in the rise of the order subordinating women, even though that rise is shrouded in antiquity.

Scholarly work, including that of Gerda Lerner, Peggy Reeves Sanday, and Richard Wrangham, among many others, provides suggestive evidence for this stance; we know that violence and conflict arose quite early in human history, as did slavery, and human sexual dimorphism has been a constant during recorded history.[3] The continual threat of violence, perpetrated almost exclusively by men, has indelibly shaped humankind.[4] Indeed, new research has shown that human male genetic diversity collapsed in the Neolithic era around 5000–7000 BCE, almost to the point at which one would think there was one man per seventeen women. Biologists Tian Chen Zeng, Alan J. Aw, and Marcus W. Feldman present findings that suggest warfare between groups of genetically related males was the cause. They note,

> If the primary unit of sociopolitical competition is the patrilineal corporate kin group, deaths from intergroup competition, whether in feuds or open warfare, are not randomly distributed, but tend to cluster on the genealogical tree of males. . . . Extinction of whole patrilineal groups with common descent would translate to the loss of clades of Y-chromosomes. Furthermore, as success in intergroup competition is associated with group size, borne out empirically in wars as "increasing returns at all scales", and as larger group size may even be associated with increased conflict initiation, borne out in data on feuds, there

may have been positive returns to lineage size. This would accelerate the loss of minor lineages.[5]

Throughout history, then, humans have sought security in the face of such potentially existential threats. Furthermore, the fact that Zeng and collaborators find this genetic collapse for men and not for women suggests the existential threats may have been felt most keenly among men. Additional research by geneticist Inigo Olalde and colleagues finds a similar collapse of male lines on the Iberian Peninsula between 2500 and 2000 BCE. At this time, nearly all Y-chromosomes were replaced by those from males of Russian steppe ancestry, whereas local female ancestry did not collapse.[6] These historical findings suggest, then, that the security dilemma is, first and foremost, a *male* security dilemma.

We propose that there are two primary security provision mechanisms among humans and that one is extremely old—that is, the Patrilineal/Fraternal Syndrome—whereas the other is relatively new. The relatively new mechanism is what we now know as a "state," meaning a centralized governing authority with a monopoly on the use of force and legitimated more or less by the consent of the governed. In contrast, the old mechanism for providing security for individuals and groups is the *extended male kin group*, sometimes called clans or tribes or lineages. Legal scholar Mark S. Weiner comments, "For most of human history, the primary institutions of legal and social order have been kin groups . . . The origin of the lineage form of political organization lies deep in human history, in the transition between the Paleolithic and Neolithic eras."[7] He further explains that "a state protects its citizens; clan members protect their cousins . . . These groups [clans] are highly cohesive, and they provide many tangible benefits to their members, including the physical and material security that comes with solidarity and the dignity that accompanies an unshakable feeling of personal belonging."[8] This form of security provision mechanism may resemble, but is not identical to, clientelism, patronage, and similar systems.[9] Rather, as political scientist Kathleen Collins defines such clan groups, they are "informal organization[s] comprising a network of individuals linked by kin-based bonds [that] are both vertical and horizontal, linking elites and nonelites, and they reflect both actual blood ties and fictive kinship."[10]

Historically, states arose by utilizing the more ancient governance structure of clans to govern far-flung territories. Although some people might consider that modern, developed, democratic states are the antithesis of clans,[11] it is also true that states never could have originally emerged without cooperating with and using clan governance structures to rule (and in many countries, they still do). As anthropologist Steven Caton notes about primitive states, clans and tribes were "responsible for collecting taxes, conscripting young men into the state's army, and implementing policies; in short, [they were] the state's indirect ruler. However, the [tribal] elite also acted to safeguard the interests of its constituents in the face of encroaching state power; and having been elevated to power by the state . . . could become its potential enemies . . . Tribes and the state have never lived in isolation from each other but have always been interdependent."[12] The sociocultural anthropologist Lois Beck is even more eloquent on this point: "tribes and states . . . did not function as two separate, opposing systems. They represented alternative polities, each creating and solving political problems for the other."[13]

Indeed, anthropologist Richard Tapper argues that the first states emerged in cases in which one tribe ruled over and by means of other tribes. In the next stage in the evolution, a nontribal entity would rule with the support of tribes, and in the final stage, a state would attempt to eradicate tribes and claim nationality for all.[14] In a sense, then, clans and states are not necessarily opposed, and in many if not most states, they will coexist, although some states are no longer reliant or coopted by these kin networks. As we shall see, we assert that for states still reliant on kin networks, the horizon is far more limited in terms of the provision of public goods, including human rights and national security, than states that are not so reliant (we more fully explore this in part II of this volume).

Despite the existence of states no longer reliant on extended kin networks, these networks are still powerful worldwide. Kathleen Collins states, "Clans are not pre-modern phenomena, but socially embedded identity networks that exist in many societies and states, even in the twentieth and twenty-first centuries."[15] We further posit that even in the twenty-first century, when seemingly non-network-reliant states fail to provide security for groups and individuals within the society, these groups and individuals are poised to naturally and swiftly fall back on the ancient security provision mechanism of extended male kin groups for that security. This means that the relevance of kin networks can easily resurge in the face of exigency. As political scientist Edward Schatz notes, "We should not hastily conclude that clan politics will shortly fade away under the pressures of market-style urbanization and industrialization,"[16] for as political scientist Bassam Tibi explains, "nation-states have failed to cope with the social and economic problems created by rapid development because they cannot provide the proper institutions to alleviate these problems. Because the nominal nation-state has not met the challenge, society has resorted to its pre-national ties as a solution."[17]

In other words, the Patrilineal/Fraternal Syndrome, as we define it, is alive and well, for it can provide the physical and economic security that many nation-states are incapable of providing. Furthermore, when such networks resurge, the problems associated with that security provision mechanism resurge as well. As Schatz points out, "For many populations across Central

Asia, the Caucasus, the Middle East, Africa, and Southeast Asia, clan politics propels real-world challenges to governance, economic performance, and, in some cases, stability."[18]

Furthermore, we assert that some present-day "states" are actually a façade behind which extended kin groups hold true power. Mark Weiner comments:

> Across the world today, naturally, the rule of the clan is a great deal more than a romantic memory. In highly tribal societies like Yemen, semi-autonomous tribal regions like Waziristan, weak states like Kenya or South Sudan, and even in the midst of more advanced democracies such as India and the Philippines, it is a basic fact of life. . . . Likewise, the principles of clannism influence nations that long ago ceased to be organized along tribal lines but that still afford a prominent role to lineage or ethnicity, such as Bosnia, or that hold patriarchal family authority in especially high regard, such as Egypt or China.[19]

Clan networks—not to be confused with non-kinship-based networks and thus by nature more situationally defined patrimonialism[20], patronage, or clientelism[21]—may flourish in the absence of state authority or in the presence of a state. Clans may undergird state rule or may profoundly weaken it depending on their interests.

This would be purely academic were it not for the fact that the choice of security provision mechanism determines, in large part, the horizon of possibility for things that the majority of human beings value deeply: democracy, human rights, rule of law, peace, and prosperity. We argue that although states not reliant on clan networks may or may not provide these goods, they are *capable* of producing them. In contrast, in part II of this volume, we argue that governance by extended male kin groups, whether embedded in state structures or not, is generally *incapable* of providing these goods.

It is our contention that reliance on extended male kin groups for security always produces a dysfunctional, corrupt, violent destiny for any society. The primary reason it does so is due to the character and structure of the first sexual political order. When that first order, encompassing as it does the two halves of the human race, is predicated on violence, predation, oppression, coercion, and exploitation experienced by one half at the hand of the other half (to which it has given birth, ironically enough[22]), the die is cast. It would take an extraordinary assault on the components of that subordinative first political order for society to escape its fate. Weiner notes "the anti-individualism of the rule of the clan burdens each and every member of a clan society, but most of all it burdens women. The fate of women lays bare the basic values of the rule of the clan, and as outsiders, citizens of liberal states often find their own values clarified when they confront the lives clans afford their female members."[23]

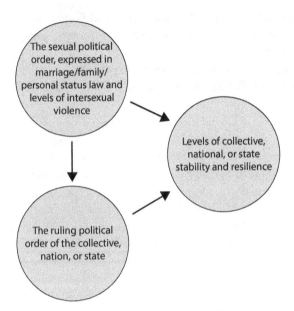

FIGURE 2.1 The Two Orders' Effects

Figures 2.1 and 2.2 present the highest level abstraction of our argument. We offer these visual aids because what is depicted, in large measure, has been made invisible in existing theoretical work on the development of political order. We felt we must foreground these links to be able to see them at all. We encounter feedback loops at every turn, so a more elaborate diagram would feature those connections as well (which we show in figure 2.2).

Before proceeding with this larger argument linking choice of security provision mechanism to group outcomes in part II, we must pause to explicate *how* the security provision mechanism that is the male-bonded kin group arises and persists over time and space. Rather than discuss terms we feel are more vague, such as "patriarchy" or "hegemonic masculinity," we are much more interested in the *specific means* by which the subordinative sexual order is implemented and enforced.[24] This will aid in our understanding of the linkages between certain practices and their rationale, on one hand, and their consequences and the possibility for change, on the other. It will also enable us to see the Syndrome as it manifests across space and time in different contexts, as it will enable us to see similarity in means of implementation and enforcement. Examining this Syndrome of interlocking practice-based components will illuminate not only how the Syndrome functions to provide perceived security and actual insecurity but also how it persists and is replicated through time. This examination reveals the Syndrome's dual character as, in the first place,

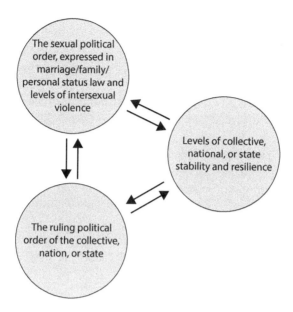

FIGURE 2.2 The Two Orders, with Reciprocal Influences

reflecting a particular sexual political order, as well as, in the second place, creating the larger societal political order *in that first order's image*.

The clearest way to "see" the structure of these relationships between men and women, we assert, is to examine law and customs about their interaction, especially those governing marriage. Marriage or its equivalent represents, if you will, *the first social contract* struck within any human society, indelibly shaping the evolution of the larger political order.[25] This was recognized even in ancient history, with Confucius noting, "This ceremony [marriage] lies at the heart of government."[26] Evolutionary biologist and psychologist David Barash updates this principle, asserting, "The husband-wife sociosexual contract is thus the governmental social contract writ small."[27] In this same vein, international relations scholar Rose McDermott and colleagues explain that "scholars of international relations tend not to recognize marriage as a fundamentally political institution; in fact, marriage is the single most universal of political institutions, existing as the bedrock of family structure, and thus the foundation of national political unity, in essentially every country in the world."[28]

The characteristics of the marriage contract as enshrined in law and custom—and enforced through coercion if necessary—will be, we argue, a strong determinant of societal governance, stability, resilience, and security observable at the nation-state level of analysis. This is so because this sexual order cannot persist unless it is reproduced, which explains the deep importance attached by the clan to biological reproduction as the fountain of social reproduction.[29] How the society forms households that produce the next generation matters deeply, and only if that household formation is structured consonantly will the subordinative first sexual political order be recreated from generation to generation.

To keep the fraternity of the first sexual political order alive, it must be birthed in a way that facilitates its ongoing re-creation. In practice, this often means a focus on agnatic lineage. Although we will delve more deeply into the subject in the following sections, in essence, fraternity is created from a deep sense of belonging to that agnatic line, or what would be termed "patrilineality." As sociologist Mounira Charrad perceptively observes about the function of patrilineality in creating fraternity: "The socially meaningful ties unifying the network thus bind men together and bypass women."[30] Thus, clans can reproduce themselves only in a relatively exclusionary manner emphasizing the male line or else the fraternity will wither. Consider the following assertions by clan scholars:

- "The most powerful metaphor of exclusion was the clan."[31]
- "[Tribes] invoked genealogies to define and maintain their exclusivity, and their lineages were often highly endogamous."[32]
- "The clan is the basis of a strong, but narrow and exclusivist social organization."[33]

We argue that clan exclusivity can be reproduced only by restricting the agency of clan women in marriage, or as Charrad explains, "The central questions [for clans] concern procedures for marriage, rights and obligations of each spouse, polygamy, conditions for divorce, custody of children, and inheritance."[34] Arguably the most vulnerable family members in status societies are the women whose role it is to reproduce the patriline, because the subordination of female interests, reproductive or otherwise, is how patrilineal clans are formed in the first place. Schatz is correct when he states, "Whether clan divisions persist or not hinges on identifiable mechanisms of identity reproduction."[35] Identity reproduction will thus mirror the character of biological reproduction.

Female subordination, specifically in marriage, thus is the basis not only of biological reproduction but also of identity reproduction for agnatic clans. Patrilineal authority must define the parameters of marriage choice for women to strengthen the male kinship bond, or else the clan as a demarcated group will disappear. Lerner expands this idea by suggesting that "the 'exchange of women' is the first form of trade, in which women are turned into a commodity and are 'reified,' that is, they are thought of more as things than as human beings.

The exchange of women . . . marks the beginning of women's subordination. It in turn reinforces a sexual division of labor which institutes male dominance . . . men became the reifiers because they conquered and protected."[36]

This suggests, then, that to "see" the security provision mechanism choice made by a society, one should examine the situation of women at the household level. That is, reliance on extended male kin networks may be concealable, or as Schatz puts its: "While kinship divisions often remain below the researcher's field of vision (since they are less observable than other identity categories to which states give positive sanction), they may be more politically important than more visible divisions . . . the most important inherent quality of clan divisions [is] their concealability . . . like watching bulldogs fight under a carpet."[37]

What is not concealable, however, is the subordination of women. Therefore, observation of household-level phenomena is key to lifting that carpet under which the bulldogs fight, we assert, because it is the site of identity reproduction. Schatz extends the point by commenting, "Groupness does not survive merely by definition; rather it survives (if and when it does) because of identifiable *mechanisms of identity reproduction* [emphasis added] . . . If we can identify the mechanisms of identity reproduction, we gain exceptional purchase on both identity persistence and identity construction."[38] "Consequently," and hopefully, as Schatz also asserts, "if such mechanisms are disrupted or changed, we can expect concurrent changes in the shape, meaning, and salience of associated group identities."[39]

Where, then, should we look to gain the sight we need?

The Patrilineal/Fraternal Syndrome

Western language can be an impediment when discussing a syndrome-like phenomenon, for the cultural style of language is quite linear, implying a starting point leading to subsequent points, leading to an ultimate point. Truly, however, this ancient syndrome we describe is more of an ourobouros, and we feel it is futile to denote its beginning and end in such a linear manner (figure 2.3). The characteristics of the sexual political order that we describe— these mechanisms of identity reproduction—hang together in such an integral fashion that it is almost impossible to put forward a sequence to them, which is why we refer to them as a "syndrome." Even so, the linear language of our culture is all we coauthors have, and so we warn the reader not to focus on the sequence we outline, but rather to focus on the interlocking nature of these phenomena. In other words, notice how well these things fit together, and how they prop each other up in an almost seamless fashion.

FIGURE 2.3 An ouroboros, an archetypal image of a snake eating its own tail

Human Sexual Dimorphism

Because we do need a starting point, let's start with sexual dimorphism—that is, the different body structure between men and women—in humans. The upper-body strength, height, skeletal mass, and muscle mass of human males of a given human collective is—on average—significantly greater than that of human females of the same group.[40] Barash comments, "when fat is discounted . . . men are 40 percent heavier [than women], with 60 percent more muscle mass and a whopping 80 percent more muscle in their arms."[41] This means that human males can, if they so choose, rather effectively physically coerce human females of their group, on average, even if women also display aggression.[42] We argue that it is this choice to use the capability for effective physical coercion of women by men as a result of sexual dimorphism that lies at the heart of the Syndrome's sexual order.[43] Indeed, Patty Gowaty suggests,

"Female-male competition over control of female reproduction is an untested, viable alternative to the male-male competition explanation for "males larger" in sexually dimorphic species."[44]

Questions of status, decision-making, and resource access can be "resolved" fairly definitively by men in regard to women through the use or threat of violent coercion. Rebecca Katibo, married as a child in South Sudan, puts it simply, "In my husband's house everything is by force—there is no request. If I refuse there will be a problem. My husband will beat me."[45] As economists Jean Dreze and Reetika Khera express, "One can argue that . . . the subjugation of women is intrinsically based on violence or at least the threat of it,"[46] or as primatologist Richard Wrangham suggests in his book with Dale Peterson, "Patriarchy has its ultimate origins in male violence."[47]

This predisposition for male-on-female violence is commonly enacted; men are overwhelmingly the perpetrators of violence in their communities. As military historian Azar Gat notes, "Perpetration of serious violence and crime is in fact the most distinctive sex difference there is, cross-culturally."[48] Barash adds that "the male-female difference in perpetrators of violent crime is about 10 to 1, consistent across every state in the United States, and true of every country for which such data are available . . . The overwhelming maleness of violence is so pervasive in every human society that it is typically not even recognized as such; it is the ocean in which we swim."[49] Wrangham and Peterson note that female behavior among most primate groups, including humans, revolves around their need to protect themselves and their children "against this one terrible threat that never goes away,"[50] or as anthropologist Barbara Smuts puts it, "in many primates, hardly an aspect of female existence is not constrained in some way by the presence of aggressive males."[51] Reproductive scientist Malcolm Potts, writing with journalist Thomas Hayden, observes, "For female chimpanzees, the most practical strategy for survival is usually to join the troop of males that is most successful at killing its neighbors and expanding its territory. Human females through history have been confronted with similar choices."[52] The battering that women suffer from the men with whom they live is the price paid for such protection, and occurs "in species where females have few allies, or where males have bonds with each other."[53]

Why is human male dominance so much more pervasive and elaborate than male dominance in other primate species, then? Smuts theorizes the differences have to do with how effective or ineffective female resistance to control by men is within a given collective. The more ineffective that resistance, the deeper and wider will be male dominance—and social structures and processes that systematically decrease the effectiveness of female resistance, in general, will be chosen by men for just such purposes. We submit that these structures and processes are, in the first place, what we call the Patrilineal/Fraternal Syndrome.

That is, given the background threat of male violence, more effective and less costly means of sexual coercion could be developed that did not require constant one-on-one violence. Indeed, Smuts argues that "gender ideology" was the first product of human speech.[54] Men created codes of conduct for women, including marriage patterns, which would favor their interest in male control over any female autonomy interests. Furthermore, women can easily be coerced to adopt and enforce such codes: "women's adoption of cultural values that appear to go against their own interests may in fact be necessary for survival."[55] Over time, the ideology is naturalized; political scientist Francis Fukuyama observes, "Many women in traditional societies accept and even celebrate their subordinate position to men; while the norm legitimizing patriarchy may have been rooted in coercion, it was not always seen as coercive."[56]

Although battering or its threat may bring reproductive rewards for men, its use also guarantees primary access for the batterer to *all* useful resources, even the most basic. Indeed, philosopher Kate Manne has proposed that women are tagged as "givers" within human societies, and when women fail to give or are perceived as not giving enough, they will be punished. In her words, the giver or woman "is then obligated to offer love, sex, attention, affection, and admiration, as well as other forms of emotional, social, reproductive, and caregiving labor . . . A man may be held to be entitled to lay claim to them from some women. Moreover, if he is not given his due, he may then be permitted to take such goods, that is, to forcibly seize them from her with impunity."[57] This asymmetrical support relationship between men and women, ultimately based on the threat of physical coercion or other punishment such as abandonment, can be found worldwide, and often in day-to-day living. In many societies even to this day, for example, women are expected to eat last after men and boys have eaten, and to eat less, especially less protein. Men may feel entitled to rape their wives, or take an additional wife without their current wife's consent, or to be unfaithful to their wives with impunity. Women may need the permission of their father or husband to even leave the house, whereas men enter and leave as they please.

Furthermore, male-coded privileges in such an asymmetrical support relationship are out of bounds for women; privileges such as "leadership, authority, influence, money,"[58] or whatever societies may deem valuable, from land to gold to livestock to children. The threat of physical violence in a sexually dimorphic context means, perforce, that men will ensure themselves greater access to and control over all such resources compared to women. Thus, in many societies in which male battering of women is normalized, we also find tremendous economic inequality between men and women, with women prohibited, for example, from holding land or property in their own name. Even children become an asset subject to seizure; women in numerous cultures automatically lose custody of children upon their divorce.

Such economic dependency and emotional vulnerability are purposefully created to ensure women's compliance. In particular, it is after the development of agriculture and animal husbandry, in which land and animals belonged exclusively to men, that the complete economic dependence of women could be effected.[59] As Smuts notes in a survey of empirical results, the lower the share of female contribution to subsistence, the higher the level of wife beating and rape within the society.[60] Anthropologist Barbara D. Miller concurs, observing that "human gender hierarchies are one of the most persistent, pervasive, and pernicious forms of inequality in the world. Gender is used as the basis for systems of discrimination which can, even within the same household, provide that those designated 'male' receive more food and live longer, while those designated 'female' receive less food to the point that their survival is drastically impaired."[61]

The Logic of Security for Men: Male Fraternity

Even in a context in which the use of physical violence between the sexes is normalized, men find the game of politics does not end there. As Hobbes commented on the state of nature "red in tooth and claw" in chapter 15 of *The Leviathan*, "there is no man who can hope by his own strength, or wit, to defend himself from destruction, without the help of confederates." That is, a man will need to ensure his safety in regard to *other men* who are similarly prepared to use violence, because these other men also have been socialized to see violence as effective for men in relation to women within their own households. Sanday observes, "By displaying their ferocity against women, men show other men that they are capable of violence and had better be treated with respect and caution,"[62] or as the feminist activist Robin Morgan expresses it, "whatever cruelties men visit upon one another they have first tested and refined on women."[63] Because of the threat of violence that underlies the first political order, men ironically create a vicious security dilemma for themselves with respect to other men.

This security dilemma creates a male need for confederates, as Hobbes put it, and also for signaling a deterrent message. With respect to deterrence signaling, the need is addressed by the concept of "honor," which legal scholar Ivan Perkins defines as "the proud, aggressive, forceful, physical, anger-laced, testosterone-based, masculine demand for respect."[64] "Honor" functions as a signaling mechanism between men in the quest for male security in such societies; it denotes that men are ready to use violence against anyone, male or female, insider or outsider, who seeks to curtail their prerogatives.[65] Sociologist David Jacobson notes "if women in these tribal societies are the promise of reproduction of family and culture, men are the bedrock of security. The honor of virginity and fidelity is matched by the honor of the martial courage of men."[66]

Deterrence signaling aside, the key problem for men in this context, then, is finding male allies, for a lone man in the context of many men socialized to use physical violence through household-level use of male-on-female coercion cannot but be profoundly insecure no matter how much signaling he undertakes. The importance of this task in the lives of each man in such societies cannot be overstated; men desperately seek a way to feel and to be more secure within a *group of men*. This, almost above all, drives male behavior. As security studies scholar Stephen Rosen argues, unless a sense of security can be achieved,

> men with individual predispositions to engage in dominant behavior, when placed among other high-testosterone men, would perceive the behavior of their companions as challenges [which] would tend to keep testosterone levels high, and levels of dominant behavior high. Even without an initial population of high-testosterone males, if set in motion, this cycle of interaction could drive up levels of dominant behavior and keep them high.[67]

Political scientists David Johnson and Bradley Thayer add that among such male leaders, "the very acquisition and exercise of power itself is known to inflate dominance behavior further . . . we may expect sometimes to observe power-maximizing behavior whether or not it is a good strategy."[68]

Therefore, to relieve their constant anxiety about this need for security, men seek a regularized security provision mechanism. In other words, they seek to establish a male-based alliance that persists over time without the need for constant re-creation. As Smuts notes, "Male reliance on alliances with other males in competition for status, resources, and females is a universal feature of human societies."[69] They need a trustworthy fraternity, for men can feel secure only if the men within the group are not liable to suddenly turn on them. That is, any male allies must be men who will find it to their advantage not to be disloyal; they must be dependable allies. The male alliance must create an in-group in which each man feels their individual physical safety becomes a group interest.[70]

Historically, this existential conundrum for men has been resolved through kinship ties. Male kin, bonded by blood ties, become preferred alliance partners, for biologists tell us, "the more closely related individuals are, the more willing they are to take risks for one another."[71] As sociologist Ivan Ermakoff explains,

> In environments that lack the stabilizing effects of well-functioning legal settings, interpersonal commitments are constantly undermined by the possibility of defection and betrayals. By contrast, because of the normative underpinnings of kinship, and because of the density and the mutual dependence inherent to family relations, family ties bring with them the

promise of interpersonal commitment. They maximize the cost of defection for potential defectors and are better suited to the goals of maintaining supervision and enforcing sanctions than ties of friendship or relations of personal exchange.[72]

Kin networks afford the kind of power—and security—that lone males lack. Gottschall notes, "might is determined not only by one's physical prowess, but by the number, age range, and sex ratio of the kin network."[73] Larger kin networks, it follows, are better suited to exercise influence in a given community. In a fascinating empirical study of Viking-era Icelandic histories in the journal *Evolution and Human Behavior* that bears out these propositions, anthropologists Markel Palmstierna, Anna Frangou, Anna Wallette, and Robin Dunbar find that despite the finite amount of land on the island nation, "not a single close biological relative ($r \geq 0.125$) was killed in a dispute over land in any of the sampled sagas . . . the wider kin circle acts as a lineage-based alliance for protection."[74] They also find that killers in the Norse sagas were significantly more likely to come from larger kin groups than their victims.

Male-bonded kin groups are ubiquitous in human history. Richard Wrangham and Dale Peterson note that out of "4,000 mammals and 10 millions or more other animal species" only two species (humans and chimpanzees) live in "patrilineal, male-bonded communities wherein females routinely reduce risks of inbreeding by moving to neighboring groups [to mate]. . . . with [these communities having] a system of intense, male-initiated territorial aggression, including lethal raiding into neighboring communities in search of vulnerable enemies to attack and kill. . . . *The system of communities defended by related men is a human universal that crosses space and time*" [emphasis added].[75] While noting this universality in human systems, they also note that "we quickly discover how odd that system really is, [making] humans appear as members of a funny little group that chose a strange little path."[76]

One's male kin can provide a robust physical security provision mechanism for the group's men, or as the old Bedouin saying goes, "I against my brothers. I and my brothers against my cousins. I and my brothers and my cousins against the world." Weiner comments,

> In tribal societies the bonds of kinship are exceptionally strong. Members of a lineage possess powerful feelings of fellowship with each other—and under the principle of unilineal descent the lines and boundaries of solidarity are exceedingly clear. At the same time, members of distinct lineage groups that are related through a common ancestor will share strong feelings of *opposition* to any group to which they have mutual reason to be hostile. In theory each lineage group will join with all the other lineage groups to which it is related to fight against an enemy common to them all.[77]

Thus, while it is entirely possible to create a fraternal alliance among men who are not kin or only fictive kin, such as in military units or criminal gangs,[78] and these non-kin-based fraternities may also engage in Syndrome practices, the most reliable form of fraternity for men is produced, historically speaking, by kinship.[79]

Furthermore, kinship allows specifically for control of younger men by older men, otherwise the generational divide would threaten to tear apart the fraternity, diminishing its usefulness as a security provision mechanism for men. As Fukuyama comments, "Broadly speaking, the central problem that any society faces is controlling the aggression, ambition, and potential violence on the part of its young men, directing it into safe and productive channels. In most human societies, this job almost always falls to the older men in the community, who seek to ritualize aggression, control access to women, and generally establish a web of norms and rules to constrain young men's behavior."[80]

In addition to providing security, however, it is easy to see how *predation* arises as a collective strategy for powerful male kin networks. Such a network could not only protect its members but also *take* from nonmembers. Anthropologist Luke Glowacki and colleagues found that in the traditional pastoralist societies they studied, men with more social connections went on more cattle raids against neighboring groups.[81] The male alliance can take assets useful for survival and increased dominance, such as food, land, other valuables, from out-group populations. Journalist Brooke Adams notes, "men killed each other less frequently where such [fraternal] agreements were in force—they could now take their collective capacities for violence and begin to project them outward, onto other groups, subject populations and civilizations."[82] Thus, there appears to be strong selection in humans and chimpanzees for aggression: "Although warfare is a high-stakes collective action problem, warriors are willing to participate because over evolutionary time the dividends have tended to outweigh the costs."[83] After all, the idea that women owe men goods and can be justifiably harmed if they demur[84] provides a robust template for a more general strategy of extortion, predation, and plunder by men, and suggests that other things (e.g., the earth) or other human groups may easily come to be seen in the same light as women.

Team aggression, which is pronounced among chimpanzees and is echoed among their human cousins, is facilitated by men staying in the collective while women leave for other troops through exogamy, because exogamy of females ensures the men in such groups are all blood relatives.[85] Exogamous marriage produces patrilocal marriage, in which wives move to their husbands' households. Marvin Harris suggests the logic at work linking exogamy, patrilocality, and warfare:

The practice of patrilocality . . . clearly reflects the influence of internal warfare since success in war depends on the formation of combat teams, of men who have trained together, trust each other, and have reason to hate and kill the same enemy. Combat teams that meet these criteria consist of co-resident fathers, sons, brothers, uncles, and paternal nephews. To remain together after they get married, these paternally related males must bring their wives to live with them rather than go off to live with their wives' families.[86]

Exogamy and the Patriline: Cementing Fraternity

Let us explore this last observation further. For a male kin network to provide the sought-after physical and material security, the extended kin group must solve the social cooperation dilemma facing all human (and primate) collectives. As we have discussed, the first priority in managing group security requires managing male propensity for risk-taking, violence, and aggression—and harnessing these forces for pro-group ends, lest these propensities destroy the group.[87] As the aforementioned fraternal alliances develop among male kin, a hierarchical ranking of men within the group—a male dominance hierarchy—is increasingly selected as a way to dampen male–male competition within the group (although such competition can never completely be eliminated).

The threat of such competition is real. As Stephen Rosen notes, "Members of high-testosterone groups that have not established a stable status hierarchy are even more likely than isolated high-testosterone individuals to engage in dominant behavior."[88] But with a stable male dominance hierarchy in place, dominant men police nondominant men, corralling their propensities to better ensure the interest of the larger male kin group, which may be defined in terms of their personal interests.

This structure is clearly observable in several primate species, such as chimpanzees, and it is also observable in humans. As Johnson and Thayer comment,

As Johnson and Thayer comment, a species that lives communally could have two broad forms of social organization:

> The group can accept organization with some centralization of power (dominance hierarchies), or it can engage in perpetual conflict ("scramble competition"), which incurs costs in terms of time, energy, and injuries, as well as depriving the group of many benefits of a communal existence, such as more efficient resource harvesting. Among social mammals, and primates in particular, dominance hierarchies have emerged as the primary form of social organization.[89]

Within such a kin-bonded male dominance hierarchy, inter-male competition and hostility—although present—can be dampened.[90] As Rose McDermott and colleagues note,

Even though victory in competition tends to lead to higher testosterone levels and dominance displays among [male] victors across numerous contexts, this reaction is muted when the defeated party is considered part of the in-group. Aside from the obviously stabilizing effect this has on intra-group relations, this muted testosterone response mitigates the prospect of anger turning into hatred and, therefore, helps to mitigate the perceived need among the defeated for revenge against in-group members.[91]

Johnson and Thayer add, "A dominance hierarchy is created competitively, often violently, and is maintained forcefully, but it can serve to prevent or reduce conflict within a group because it establishes a pecking order that is generally respected." It is respected for it benefits both elites and nonelites, providing "an organized social structure [that] can help promote the harvesting of resources, coordinate group activity, and reduce within-group conflict."[92] In a sense, these dominance hierarchies tamp down the effects of anarchy within the group, while potentially maximizing violent competition between groups.

Relatedly, although dominant men police lower-ranking men, all men police women. Indeed, the deal struck for the lower-ranking men to submit to the male hierarchy is that in addition to being able to share in the benefits of the male alliance, they will be able—even encouraged—to enjoy and display dominance against "others," with the first Others being women. Interestingly, researchers have found that it is lower-ranking men who are the most active and most brutal at policing women who push back against subordination, for they feel the most threatened by any rise in women's status.[93] As evolutionary biologists Michael Kasumovic and Jeffrey Kuznekoff comment, "the increase in hostility towards a woman by lower-status males may be an attempt to . . . suppress her disturbance on the hierarchy to retain their social status," and also to maintain the boundary between those who have the perceived right to dominate (i.e., men) and those who do not (i.e., women).[94] The bargain appears to be that men agree to be ruled by certain other men in return for all men ruling over all women.

Furthermore, predation and plunder of out-groups not only are useful as economic strategies but also become an expedient means of maintaining harmony in the context of hierarchy among men in a group. To maintain elite male privilege without engendering rebellion in the ranks, it may be necessary to provide booty and plunder for nonelite men within the group. Anthropologist James Boone, in describing the mechanisms of expansionist warfare, explains that such warfare assists elites in maintaining control:

Among competitive human groups, dispersion resulting from subordination effects can take the form of direct aggression against neighboring groups. Controlling individuals or coalitions can be expected to encourage subordinates in this activity when the alternative is having the competition directed against themselves. In this sense, expansion would not be due directly to a desire by the controllers to accommodate general population pressure per se, but rather to direct the competition of close subordinates against other groups. I suggest that this is an important factor in generating expansionist warfare among early states.[95]

As we have noted, throughout history, we find evidence that human groups have typically established hierarchical fraternal alliances, usually based around patrilines. Indeed, anthropologists William T. Divale and Marvin Harris note that "patrilineality occurs five times more frequently than matrilineality," and our theoretical framework helps explain why.[96] (Note that matrilineality says little about female power in a society, for as they also observe, "In matrilineal societies no less than in patrilineal societies, males dominate the allocation of domestic resources, labor, and capital.")[97]

The genetic imperative for exogamy, recognized at least thirty-four thousand years ago, provides a natural springboard for the development of such patrilineal norms, with its accompanying patrilocal marital residence.[98] That is, although patrilineal groups have strong endogamous predispositions[99]—which explains why close cousin marriage is often associated with patrilineality—the genetic costs of endogamy become plain over time, forcing exogamous marriage.[100] As we have seen, the logic of the fraternal alliance as the security provision mechanism of groups will ensure that men stay in the collective, while women marry "out" of it exogamously. In other words, to comply with the genetic demands of exogamy in a way that preserves resources and alliances for men, female children will be made to leave upon marriage, and male children will stay.[101] Postmarital residence determines comparative power, for "postmarital residence is closely associated with control over access to, and the disposition and inheritance of, natural resources, capital, and labor power."[102]

Furthermore, as Weiner notes, exogamy can be an asset to a male kin group in search of alliance partners, for it "creat[es] a network of political alliances that contribute to social integration and stability in a given geographic area. The norm of exogamy also provides the basis for a lean anthropological definition of a clan, a term for which there are many conceivable meanings, namely: the largest group of lineage members to whom principles of exogamy apply. If as a Nuer man you are allowed to marry a Nuer woman, then by definition the woman is not a fellow clansman."[103] This understanding is echoed across time and space. Economists Tanika Chakraborty and Sukkoo Kim note that in northern India,

> At the clan level, marriages between the families of the same maximal lineage can threaten the political balance within the clan because these families can use

marriage to build a more powerful political coalition. By requiring women to marry outside their *gotra* or *sapinda* and by requiring them to marry outside the villages of the maximal lineages, the northern system insured the political stability of the maximal clan lineage by significantly reducing the bargaining power of women.[104]

Anthropologist Corina Knipper and colleagues at the Max Planck Institute have found that as early as the end of the Stone Age, women were traveling a considerable distance (literally hundreds of miles) to marry patrilocally.[105]

In this exogamy-of-females context, a more structured patrilineality thus often develops as a strategy for men to more reliably husband both male allies and resources in the context of out-group women providing children for the group. Friedrich Engels noted the importance of this development in world history, stating, "The establishment of the exclusive supremacy of the man shows its effects first in the patriarchal family . . . [in] the organization of a number of persons, bond and free, into a family under paternal power for the purpose of holding lands and for the care of flocks and herds."[106] That this strategy was found, in general, to be effective is demonstrated by the high percentage of cultures that anthropologists have found to be patrilineal in nature. As we have noted, the vast majority of lineage-based groups trace descent through the patriline, practice patrilocality, and inherit land and property through the patriline.[107] The agnatic lineages thus become the "basic political building-blocks" of these societies.[108]

Once patrilineality is enshrined as the security provision mechanism for the group, many ancillary customs will naturally arise. Inheritance only through the patriline from father to son is one such custom, ensuring that the men of the kin group maintain control over resources that are key to ensuring goods, such as survival, security, and reproductive success. Another custom is stripping women—even those born to the patriline—of any meaningful property rights. Land and livestock are conceptualized as male-only resources, and other rights, such as the right to conclude contracts, may also be invested in men alone. Men—and not women—must control the clan's assets, whether these are children or land or cattle, or the power of the clan will dissipate. For example, Fukuyama observes, "While widows and unmarried daughters may have certain inheritance rights, they are usually required to keep the lineage's property within the agnatic line."[109] The marriage of a daughter thus becomes a type of disinheritance: early legal systems, such as Roman law, included the maxim, "*Mulier est finis familiae* . . . none of the descendants of a female are included in the . . . family relationship."[110]

These twin strategies of cementing male control over group resources through differential inheritance and property rights become the hallmarks of patrilineality, even when state law or, less frequently, religious law inveighs against such a practice. Anthropologist Jack Goody gave an example of the Bedouin:

> Women are not permitted to inherit. Bedouin are aware that in dispossess-
> ing women of inheritance they are contravening the law [of Islam], but to
> do otherwise would result in an uncontrolled alienation of property . . . if
> [women] inherited as wives and daughters, an uncontrolled run on corporate
> resources would ensue. This would be serious enough if only mobile prop-
> erty were involved, but if land was threatened in this way, also, the entire
> basis of corporate life would collapse [for the] group *is a corporation of males.*
> [emphasis added].[111]

Historian Adrienne Edgar similarly chronicles how in Soviet-era Turkmenistan, the customary code called *adat* was held to supersede Islamic law,
especially as it provided fewer inheritance rights for women than Islam.[112]
In addition to keeping resources in the hands of men, as noted, effecting the
complete economic dependence of women ensures female compliance with
male demands.

Extending the logic of this male-kin-based security system, patrilineality
also implies, or even fairly demands for its efficacy, the norm of patrilocal
marriage. Men, their kin, and their goods stay together—it is women who
typically are made to move to the household of the groom's family to effect
human exogamy. As anthropologist Monica Das Gupta puts it, "Thus it is that
only men constitute the social order, and women are the means whereby men
reproduce themselves."[113]

Smuts suggests that the more ineffective female resistance is, the more effective male dominance will be, and says that men will select for social structures
and processes that tend to render female resistance ineffective. Smuts hypoth-
esizes that several near-universal social structures and processes in traditional
human societies preclude effective female resistance. Not surprisingly, first and
foremost is patrilocality, which deprives a woman of female kin networks that
could potentially prohibit sexual coercion. Evolutionary psychologist Anne
Campbell claims this arose fairly early in human history, with hunter-gatherer
societies adopting patrilocal mating patterns in which women left their natal
families to mate with men outside their kinship system, thereby weakening
women's natal bonds.[114] This is the first example Smuts offers of how "male
aggression has influenced not only female behavior but also the form of the
social system itself."[115] Patrilocality undercuts female resistance to this emerging sexual order by making female solidarity much more difficult to attain
than male solidarity.

Patrilocal marriage has historically been far more common than matrilocal or neolocal marriage, being found in approximately three-quarters of

human groups.[116] Patrilocality and patrilineality reinforce fraternity as the security provision mechanism for the group, or as Divale and Harris explain, threat "leads to the establishment of, or reinforces the prior existence of, solidary groups of males who have a joint interest in the exploitation and defense of a common territory. Patrilocality is the cross-generational objectification of these male-centered interest groups; and patrilineality is the appropriate kinship ideology for enhancing the sentiments of solidarity within the co-resident core of sons, fathers, and brothers."[117]

Defense of the patriline's territory—its "patrilocale," if you will—is the first order of business. As economist Avraham Ebenstein notes:

> The strength of patrilocal norms is . . . intimately related to the fertility of land to support a dense population, as is found in many fertile areas of China and India. Patrilocal norms will also emerge in response to intensive agriculture as a result of the increased importance of local defense when land is valuable. Since intensive agriculture requires repeated cropping of land, it generates a fixity of settlement that necessitates defense of one's land. Attacks by nomads and groups looking to expand their territory would have led to both the need for sons for defense and also patrilocal norms, as these sons would need to remain nearby for defense. Therefore, rigid patrilocality and having a history of clan-based conflict are likely to be correlated.[118]

Subordination and Devaluation of Female Life

We argue that patrilocal marriage has even a more important effect. It tends to produce a profound devaluation of daughters and a deep suspicion, bordering on animosity, toward wives. As Sanday puts it, "Cross-cultural research demonstrates that whenever men build and give allegiance to a mystical, enduring, all-male social group, the disparagement of women is, invariably, an important ingredient of the mystical bond . . . The degradation of women [is] a prerequisite for masculinity . . . Compassion for women implies castration."[119]

Daughters in such cultures are often considered not to be kin, but rather merely guests who will leave the family within a dozen years or so. They are considered burdens, like "watering a plant in another man's garden," as the Indian saying goes. They may not even be reckoned in the family's genealogy, as noted in this chapter's epigraph, although they are full siblings of their brothers who may be prominently featured in the family lineage. The birth family considers that the girl's "true" family is her future husband's family.

Her future husband's family, however, is quite unlikely to view her as family, either. She comes from another kin group, and thus represents a threat to the established social order within the home; in some cases, wives may come from subjected groups, so that men marry the women of their enemies, and the resulting marriage is viewed as more than a figurative conquest. As Sanday notes, "Wives are treated as if they were enemies."[120] Anthropologist Charles Lindholm offers the following observation from the Swat Pukhtun of northern Pakistan:

> Relations between husbands and wives tend to be warlike. Even in sex, tenderness is said to be absent . . . The problem of sexual relationships is understandable given the ideology that all women are, in themselves, repulsive and inferior, and have the potential to shame men. The repulsiveness of women is linked to the conundrum they pose in the social structure as the foci of the contradiction between the necessity of exchanging women and the social ideal of the self-sufficient [patrilineal] family. Also linked is the prevalence of homosexuality among the men, who find a relationship with a boy less demanding and more pleasurable than with a woman. Yet, though women are despicable, men know they cannot survive without them. A woman can chase her husband from the house by simply refusing to cook for him. Women are powerful, despite the ideology of their inferiority. This ambiguity further stirs the disgust of the Pukhtun . . . A woman not only exposes the contradictions of the patrilineal pose of splendid male isolation and domination, but she is also in herself a contradiction, embodying both weakness and strength.[121]

New brides, even if from a friendly group, will almost always occupy the lowest rung on the hierarchy within her husband's family. The full weight of the male-imposed sexual political order, including violent coercion, lack of decision-making power, and lack of access to resources may be quite explicit within families with respect to wives and daughters.

It goes without saying that the devaluation of daughters and wives is matched by open son preference in patrilineal societies. Passive or active female infanticide can not only be found in the history of *all* geographic regions but also—augmented by the technology enabling sex-selective abortion—in at least nineteen nation-states today.[122] Public health economist Priya Nanda and colleagues found a strong link between gender unequal attitudes and son preference, finding that "a comprehensive study of several thousand men and women across seven states in India shows that combining two vectors of masculinity—controlling behavior and traditional gender attitudes—predicts both son preference and intimate partner violence."[123]

A cascade of effects emanates from this devaluation of female life in the patrilineal kin group context. Age of marriage for girls will be depressed, as natal families attempt to rid themselves of burdensome daughters as quickly as possible. At the same time, the rights of wives in marriage will be severely circumscribed. Wives may have virtually no right to divorce, whereas husbands may divorce at will for no cause. Wives may have no access to their children after divorce. Marital property may default to the groom's surviving brothers and parents upon his death. Crimes such as adultery may be punished by death if committed or suspected on the part of a wife, but may incur no punishment at all if committed by a husband. Husbands may have the right to control the movements of their wives, even whether they may go to school, visit relatives, work, or leave the house for any reason. Husbands may control any property belonging to the wife, such as her wages, or her dowry. Goody asserts, "The presence of strong patrilineal groups [is] directly linked to the weak nature of the conjugal bond, to the prevalence of polygyny, the ease of divorce, and more generally the low position of women."[124] Physical battering of wives may not even be considered a criminal act in such contexts, but rather as a property right held by men.

Ironically, in these societies where it is seen as so important to control women to reap reproductive and productive benefit, women may be seen as burdens. As Rebecca Solnit notes, "Patriarchy—meaning both male domination and societies obsessed with patrilineal descent—has, in many times and places, created many versions of dependent, unproductive women, who are disabled by dress or body modification, restricted to the home, and limited in their access to education, employment, and profession by laws and customs backed by threats of violence. Some misogynists complain that women are immobile burdens, but much misogyny has striven to make women so."[125] Women's voice in such societies is purposefully suppressed; they are generally excluded from household and larger group decision-making. In addition to this state of affairs within the household, Goody also notes that patrilineality entails "separation of the sexes and exclusion of women from public life."[126]

Two Paths, One End

Interestingly, this sexual order can evolve in a couple of different, but ultimately parallel, directions, depending on whether women's labor is considered essential for food production (in which case brideprice will be established), or not (in which case dowry will be established). That is, no matter which of these two paths is taken, assets will be exchanged upon marriage, for as Divale and Harris argue, "Almost all cases of brideprice and dowry are associated with patrilocal, patrilineal systems."[127] What Divale and Harris mean by these terms is that in the case of brideprice, assets flow from the groom to the bride's father upon marriage; in the case of dowry, assets flow from the bride's father to the groom upon marriage.

These alternatives depend on how valued women's productive (not reproductive) labor is. If women's labor is seen as valuable, such as we see in Sub-Saharan Africa where women do the lion's share of agricultural labor in societies that are primarily agricultural, we often see polygyny, or the practice of men having several wives, and brideprice together, with little alteration of normal sex ratios. As Goody puts it, "Bridewealth and polygyny play into each other's hands."[128] In these cultures, a father finds himself in possession of a valuable commodity— the productive and reproductive capabilities of his daughter, who will gain for him a brideprice. One's daughters thus become goods on which one may gain a handsome profit, so even though they are less valued in familial terms than sons, one will not see passive or active female infanticide. At the same time, men with greater wealth will be in a position to purchase more laborers, and thus polygyny will become a predisposition of those with means.[129]

In contrast, if women's labor is *not* considered valuable, a second type of marital system may develop, in which the woman's family may have to pay the groom's family a dowry to take her off their hands. Faced with the loss of what is typically a substantial amount of money for an individual who is not even considered a real part of the family and who is moving away in patrilo-cal marriage, the temptation will be strong to alter sex ratios to dispense with unwanted daughters through female infanticide or its contemporary alternative of sex-selective abortion. In this case, hypergyny, in which brides marry upward in the social hierarchy as a result of their relative scarcity, becomes the societal tendency.

These two paths suggest to anthropologist Stanley Jeyaraja Tambiah that, "Bridewealth and dowry have different potentialities in the way they can link up with the politico-economic institutions of the society in which they are found."[130] Goody explains the alternative trajectories in this way: "Bridewealth is more commonly found where women make the major contribution to agri-culture, whereas dowry is restricted to those societies where males contribute most . . . dowry tends to be found with monogamy, bridewealth with general polygyny."[131]

Both paths—dowry/sex-ratio alteration and polygyny/brideprice—are but variants of the same male-imposed sexual political order of the society. Anthropologist Joseph Manson and colleagues explain it eloquently: "Human females are often subject to unusually intense male coercion as a result of uniquely elaborate male-male cooperation to control their sexuality and male control of resources."[132] The subordination of women in each marriage system is actually quite similar in its effects on their daily lives.

Seeing How the Syndrome Components Interlock

Stepping back to view the entire picture (figure 2.4), all the sequelae we have discussed reinforce the entire Syndrome. Once set in motion, the pieces inter-lock closely and support each other in a never-ending cycle of the serpent devouring its tail. If a group chooses the male-bonded kin group as its security

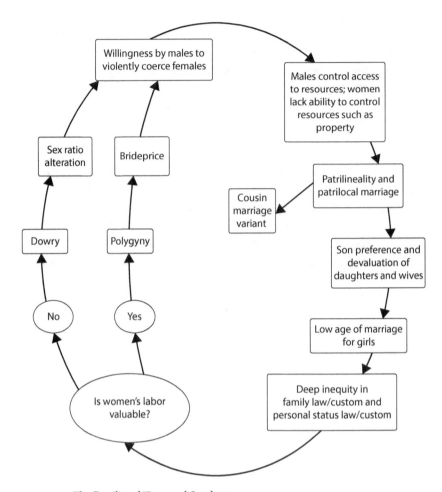

FIGURE 2.4 The Patrilineal/Fraternal Syndrome

provision mechanism, then male control of resources, patrilocal marriage, lack of women's property rights, and devaluation of female life click together like a bracelet of magnetic beads. What kind of women the Syndrome produces is easily understandable and will be explored more fully in the next chapter. What has been less discussed, we believe, is what kind of men the Syndrome produces. We turn to John Stuart Mill for a cogent description:

All the selfish propensities, the self-worship, the unjust self-preference, which exist among mankind, have their source and root in, and derive their principal nourishment from, the present constitution of the relation between men and women. Think what it is to a boy, to grow up to manhood in the belief that without any merit or exertion of his own, though he may be the most frivolous and empty or the most ignorant and stolid of mankind, by the mere fact of being born a male he is by right the superior of all and every one of an entire half of the human race . . . People are little aware, when a boy is differently brought up, how early the notion of his inherent superiority to a girl arises in his mind; how early the youth thinks himself superior to his mother, owing her perhaps forbearance, but no real respect; and how sublime and sultan-like a sense of superiority he feels, above all, over the woman [he marries]. Is it imagined that all this does not pervert the whole manner of existence of the man, both as an individual and as a social being?[133]

As Valerie Hudson and Patricia Leidl wrote in *The Hillary Doctrine*, this warping of the human souls of males is tragic for the men involved and tragedy-producing for women.[134] Journalist Ann Jones perceptively notes that those "in charge"—overwhelmingly men—are profoundly, and thus humiliatingly, dependent on those who are "not in charge," that is, women.[135] It is not the powerful who are indispensable, but the powerless. In traditional societies, it is primarily women who till the soil, provide for a man's next meal, and give him his very future in the form of children, even though he too often deems the women in his life to be inferior beings.

Indeed, a man knows that his very existence originates from what he may consider to be the deformed and unclean body of an inferior, a woman. Furthermore, his cherished customs and values and beliefs would simply evaporate if that inferior woman refuses to cooperate in socializing his children to accept his belief system, or if she is persuaded by other ways and other beliefs. It is an awful psychological state to find oneself in—to *feel* oneself as powerful and entitled to be so, but also simultaneously *know* one is powerless. It is a recipe for the deepest shame and humiliation and thus for the cruelest abuse based on the fear that those who are inferior will not forever accept that status.

Thus, one can argue that an overwhelming imperative to contain and ultimately obliterate female agency lies at the very core of the Patrilineal/Fraternal Syndrome. Men know that a woman who is left to her own devices and is free of fear is also more likely to reject his need of her, whether that need be for temporal sustenance, for children, for socialization of the young, or even for sex. Indeed, a woman's sexual autonomy may threaten his very self. He may be the rapist, but she is to blame. He wants her, but he loathes that he wants her and he hates her even more for not wanting him. Furthermore, he hates that he desires a body that he considers so polluted, one that bleeds and is so very unlike his own. Fraternal love is rather to be preferred, for it carries with it no such inherent threat.[136]

Although women fear that men will kill them, men fear that women will humiliate them by repudiating their control, which casts into doubt men's "manhood." Even today, many courts consider humiliation a mitigating factor when men beat or murder women. This control can be subtle or overt, but it is woven into the daily lives of women. While working in Cote d'Ivoire and

Liberia, Jones gave cameras to the women and asked them to record the scenes of their daily life:

> Wives were told every day to do things they didn't have the time or strength to do, let alone the inclination. Failure brought punishment. When the women began to bring in their photographs, I learned that men routinely beat their wives for their failure: to produce dinner on time, wash the clothes, sell tomatoes, stay at home, go to the field to work. The list was endless. Men also beat their wives for small acts of assertion; going to visit a neighbor, answering back, being tired or "lazy." Men referred to wife beating as "education." Men said that educating a wife in proper conduct was a great and tiring responsibility . . . This was another reason the women wanted education: to relieve men of the duty of beating them. Annie . . . said she enrolled in a literacy course for precisely that reason, but every day her husband ripped the latest exercise from her notebook and used it as toilet paper. Kebeh . . . said that when she disobeyed her husband's order to give up her literacy class, he got out his gun . . . and tried to kill her. Annie and Kebeh reached the same conclusion . . . "He doesn't want me to be educated," Annie said, "He'd rather hit me." What emerged from these massed photos was a bigger picture, a broader definition of gender-based violence. For village women gender-based exploitation, enforced by violence, seemed to be life itself—a life that requires relentless forced hard labor *because they are women* [emphasis in original]. Here was the perfect political economy of misogyny: gender-based servitude. Women labored. Men profited. . . . For some women, it seemed, the difference between peace and war was not what was done to them, but which men did it.[137]

This deep pathology of male resentment is literally surreal. For, literally, to despise women is to despise your own life; to attack women is to attack your own life. You can beat her, rape her, kill her, control her, but you will always need her. That need means that in actuality you are not powerful and she is not powerless. She is not, in the end, "yours."

Pace John Mearsheimer,[138] the tragedy of great power politics has *nothing* on the tragedy of this sexual political order. Indeed, we would argue that the tragedy of great power politics actually *derives* from the tragedy of the Syndrome. That is, the subordinative, exploitative, predatory, and violent first sexual order cannot but reproduce itself at the community, national, and international levels of analysis.

But *how* does this happen? *How* do the practices of the Syndrome create this insecurity and instability? We will first take a closer look at each of the component parts of the Syndrome in comprehensive fashion in the next chapter, and then in part II examine in detail the overall and specific effects of the Syndrome on the societies in which it is encoded.

CHAPTER 3

ASSESSING THE PATRILINEAL/ FRATERNAL SYNDROME TODAY

We know better than to repeal our masculine systems.

—John Adams

The Patrilineal/Fraternal Syndrome we have described, so ubiquitous throughout recorded human history, is alive and well today. In many nations, reliance on male-bonded kin groups for security remains the norm. Indeed, nations might be placed along a spectrum according to how important this security provision mechanism remains, or as Mark Weiner notes, clan societies "range from stateless societies known as 'segmentary lineage systems' to modern societies in which a weak state has difficulty containing the forces of clannism. In some circumstances, they even exist in developed, centralized states."[1] In other words, just because a nation is democratic or authoritarian, rich or poor, or located in a particular region, may not be sufficient to tell us the predominant security provision mechanism in use by its citizens.

To probe whether reliance on extended male-bonded kin groups as a security provision mechanism is linked to worse outcomes for nation-states, we first must define how we gauge this degree of reliance. This is not a straightforward task; each nation's situation is nuanced and complex, having its own idiosyncratic history, its own mixture of subnational groups, and its own contemporary trajectory. Thus, the attempt that follows should be viewed for what it must be at this stage: a first step that cannot do justice to all of the observable complexity and particularity of the nations of the world. Even so, the theoretical framework laid out in the first two chapters of this volume tell us where to start: with the situation, status, and security of women. To gauge reliance on male-bonded kin groups as the predominant security provision mechanism, we look for evidence of the Syndrome components outlined in figure 2.4 in chapter 2.

Many countries, even in the twenty-first century, have a fairly intact Syndrome-based society, meaning that the primary mechanism of security provision in the society is the patrilineal kin network.[2] Weiner explains that plenty of seemingly modern states are, in fact, "founded on informal patronage networks" and "traditional ideals of patriarchal family authority."[3] In these states, "government is hijacked for purely factional purposes and the state, conceived on the model of the patriarchal family, treats citizens not as autonomous actors but rather as troublesome dependents to be managed. Clannism is the rule of the clan's historical echo [and] often characterizes rentier societies."[4]

Reliance on male-bonded kin networks as the predominant security provision mechanism within states may be open and overt, such as in contemporary Afghanistan or South Sudan, but this reliance may be present even in countries with centralized states. For example, Weiner argues:

> A form of clannism likewise pervades mainland China and other nations whose political development was influenced by Confucianism, with its ideal of a powerful state resting on a well-ordered family, and where personal connections are essential to economic exchange . . . Likewise, the principles of clannism influence nations that long ago ceased to be organized along tribal lines but that still afford a prominent role to lineage or ethnicity, such as Bosnia, or that hold patriarchal family authority in especially high regard, such as Egypt.[5]

In addition, some countries are transitioning back to this reliance on male kin networks as the primary security provision mechanism after having moved away from that reliance in earlier time periods—we see this phenomenon in the post-Soviet Caucasus, for example. Explaining this regress toward the older security provision mechanism, the United Nations Development Program (UNDP) notes about that region,

> Clannism flourishes, and its negative impact on freedom and society become stronger, wherever civil or political institutions that protect rights and freedoms are weak or absent. Without institutional supports, individuals are driven to seek refuge in narrowly based loyalties that provide security and protection, thus further aggravating the phenomenon. Partisan allegiances also develop

when the judiciary is ineffective or the executive authority is reluctant to implement its rulings, circumstances that make citizens unsure of their ability to realize their rights without the allegiance of the clan.[6]

In contrast, other societies are gradually moving away from the full Syndrome, such as we have seen in South Korea's dismantlement of the patrilineal *hoju* system.[7] Even in these latter societies, however, we still see some of the fundamental components present, meaning that it remains possible for the Syndrome to resurge in the future if conditions are right. For example, although Latin American countries in the contemporary era do not practice brideprice or dowry, the foundation of high levels of violence against women, even to the point of widespread femicide, combined with highly inequitable family law and property ownership, as well as greater human capital investment in sons, remains and continues to undermine national outcomes. Indeed, these factors of widespread, normalized violence against women along with inequity in family and personal status law are reservoirs for Syndrome resurgence in many countries that have moved away from the full-blown Syndrome.

Wherever we find a fuller expression of the Patrilineal/Fraternal Syndrome, we know that extended male kin groups have substantial power within society. This explains why more general indicators of gender inequality within a society are insufficient for our purposes. Indicators such as female literacy, or the representation of women in parliament, for example, do not tap into the reproduction of clan exclusivity. As another example, high female labor force participation may exist even in a society encoding most of the Syndrome. As the political scientist Lindsay Benstead notes, it should trouble us that Libya ranked so well on the UNDP's Gender Inequality Index compared with its neighbors in the Middle East and North Africa (MENA) region.[8] The dimensions of that index, examining health, labor force participation, and political participation, are not tapping into the proximate mechanisms of household-level disempowerment of women. Even maternal and infant mortality rates are insufficient for our purposes, because it is entirely possible to encode the Syndrome and yet deploy the nation's resources to significantly lower those rates, as we see in the Gulf states. The prevalence of child marriage for women, the prevalence of patrilocal marriage, and other indicators of such household-level disempowerment of women can better inform us whether the reproduction of male kin group exclusivity is taking place.

In this chapter, we first provide a global overview of the Syndrome and then explore each of its components in greater detail. In this broad chapter, we focus first on how each of these control mechanisms subverts the position of women. Then in part II of this volume, we propose and then test a theoretical framework linking the degree to which a nation encodes the Syndrome to worse nation-state-level outcomes on a variety of dimensions of national security, stability, and resilience.

An Overview of the Incidence of the Syndrome Today

As outlined in chapters 1 and 2, we first identified the following eleven variables (see figure 2.4):

1. prevalence of male willingness to use physical coercion against women, which includes both levels of violence against women, and degree of sanction/impunity for such violence, to wit—
   a. overall level of violence against women;
   b. societal sanction for the murder of women; and
   c. whether a rapist can escape punishment by offering to marry his victim (indicating that female security is but a property right belonging to males);
2. prevalence of patrilocal marriage;
3. prevalence of cousin marriage;
4. preference for sons, including sex ratio abnormalities;
5. age of first marriage for girls in law and practice;
6. overall inequity in family law/practice favoring males;
7. prevalence of brideprice and dowry;
8. prevalence of polygyny in law and practice; and
9. property rights of women in law and practice.

We then developed a scale of how closely a society came to a complete incarnation of the Patrilineal/Fraternal Syndrome using these eleven variables. We first approached construction of this scale through an exploratory factor analysis of the eleven components of the Syndrome, and followed with the creation of a combinatorial algorithm to produce the scale. Appendix I provides a full description of each of the eleven variables used to create the Syndrome score, the results of our exploratory and confirmatory factor analyses justifying the combination of these variables into the Syndrome scale, the algorithm used to combine subcomponent score, and Cronbach's alpha measuring reliability of the scale, as well as specifies coverage of countries and time periods. The appendix also provides the Syndrome scores for 176 countries (all those with a population of at least two hundred thousand) for the time period from 2010 to 2015. We call this overall index the Patrilineal/Fraternal Syndrome scale. This scale ranges from 0–16, with 16 being interpreted as meaning the society fully encodes the Patrilineal/Fraternal Syndrome as its security provision mechanism, and 0 meaning that the society is free of Syndrome practices.

With this scaling in hand, we produced a map (figure 3.1) showing the 176 countries in our analysis. Mapping sixteen colors is not realistic, so for the map's five legend colors, the cut-points we selected as inductively sound were [0,1,2], [3,4,5], [6,7,8,9], [10,11,12], [13,14,15,16]. For a dichotomous measure (Syndrome/non-Syndrome), then we propose that 0–5 would be considered

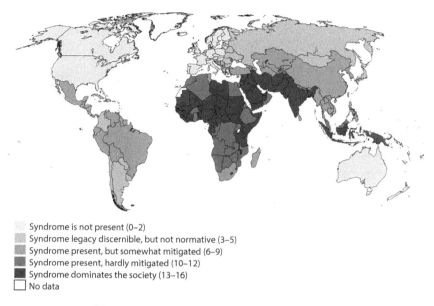

Syndrome is not present (0–2)
Syndrome legacy discernible, but not normative (3–5)
Syndrome present, but somewhat mitigated (6–9)
Syndrome present, hardly mitigated (10–12)
Syndrome dominates the society (13–16)
No data

FIGURE 3.1 Map of the Patrilineal/Fraternal Syndrome Scale, scaled 2017

as, generally speaking, non-Syndrome societies, and 6–16 would be considered, generally speaking, Syndrome societies. Furthermore, we suggest that scores of 6–9 indicate that a society is in clear transition, with either directionality of transition possible. We will utilize this trichotomy [0,1,2,3,4,5], [6,7,8,9], [10,11,12,13,14,15,16] in subsequent chapters as we explore the dynamics of change.

The map clearly shows the full spectrum of degree of reliance on male-bonded kin groups in the world today. Many nations lack the components of the Syndrome almost entirely, and yet in quite a few nations, the Patrilineal/Fraternal Syndrome remains the most dominant security provision mechanism in the society and nearly all components of the Syndrome can be found. Furthermore, even today, quite a few nations in the medium-gray or transitional portion of the map experience legacy effects from earlier, fuller instantiation of the Syndrome.

The complete range of data from 0 to 16 is evident in the scale scores, with South Sudan being the lone country scaled as instantiating the fullest version of the Syndrome in the present time period at a scale point of 16. The histogram in figure 3.2 shows that countries cluster into roughly three categories of severity when it comes to the Syndrome's enactment: we interpret these three categories as indicating non-Syndrome, Transition, and Syndrome societies.[9] In the final chapter, we discuss the dynamics of change and evaluate the case

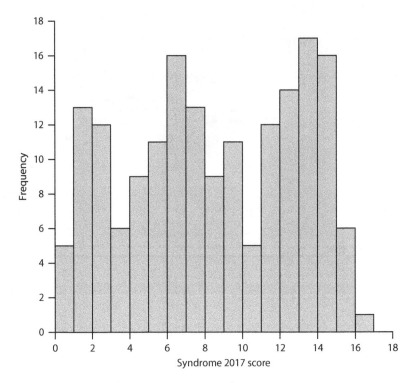

FIGURE 3.2 Histogram of Syndrome Scale scores for 176 countries

of those middle countries transitioning between the two extremes: Under what conditions do these nations move away from the fuller Syndrome? Under what conditions do these nations regress toward the fuller Syndrome? What are the policy implications of the answers to these questions?

If we use a dichotomous approach, with countries scoring 5 and under deemed as no longer encoding the Syndrome, and with countries scoring 6 and above as fundamentally rooted in the Syndrome, then 56 countries are presently scaled as non-Syndrome, and 120 are scaled as Syndrome-based countries. Syndrome-based countries thus outnumber non-Syndrome countries by more than two to one. If we look only at the high-scoring countries, for which almost the full complement of Syndrome variables is evidenced (i.e., scale points 13–16), 40 countries in our sample of 176 nations currently meet that description. The Syndrome is clearly still very much with us even in the twenty-first century.

In terms of geographic distribution, the high-scoring countries are located in a belt across sub-Saharan Africa, the Middle East, West Asia, and South Asia, extending into Indonesia. Transition countries, or countries in the middle-scoring cluster of nations, show great geographic diversity, with such nations spread across all continents except for the island continent of Australia. Non-Syndrome countries are generally found in that set that might be called the member nations of the Organization for Economic Cooperation and Development (OECD).

Construct Validity Checks

Is the Syndrome scale measuring what we hope it measures? That is, does it possess "construct validity"? To assess construct validity, we examined the correlations between our Patrilineal/Fraternal Syndrome scale and two scales that measure the degree to which clans and tribes dominate society. We also looked at two oft-used measures of the overall situation of women. We would hope to see strong positive correlations, as the Syndrome score gauges both clan governance as well as women's status. The Syndrome scale, however, measures both of these concepts in different ways from these other scales. The clan scales we examine, for example, emphasize variables other than whether women are controlled in marriage and are insecure; furthermore, the two scales of women's overall situation in society that we use for the construct validity check do not focus on women's household-level disempowerment as the Syndrome scale, but focus instead on women's economic, education, and political participation.

The two scales we selected for this construct validity check are a tribalism scale created by David Jacobson[10] and a clan governance scale created by Weiner,[11] each of which represent independent approaches.[12] The purpose of each scale is to gauge the degree to which extended kin networks dominate the politics of a nation-state. The bivariate correlation (N = 155) between the Syndrome scale and Jacobson's tribalism scale was 0.487, which was significant at the 0.001 level, and that between the Syndrome scale and Weiner's clan governance scale (N = 160) was 0.489, which again was significant at the 0.001 level.

We selected two scales of women's overall situation in society for this construct validity check: the Global Gender Gap Index (GGI, 2016) of the World Economic Forum, and the Gender Inequality Index (GII, 2015) of the UNDP. In the GGI, a higher score is better, whereas in the Syndrome scale, a higher score is worse. Thus, we would expect a strong negative correlation between these two scales and that is what we find: the correlation between the Syndrome scale and the GGI (N = 144) is −0.670, significant at the 0.001 level. The bivariate correlation between the Syndrome scale and the GII (N = 155) was 0.800, significant at the 0.001 level.

All of these correlations are comparatively strong, significant, and in the anticipated direction. We conclude that the Syndrome scale has construct validity as a measure that seeks to capture the degree of reliance on male-bonded kin groups within a society based on a women's situation in marriage and on their personal status and security, which in turn is reflective of the overall levels of gender inequality within a society. Because we feel the Syndrome, reflecting the first political order, is the wellspring of both of these societal-level phenomena, in a theoretical sense, we feel justified in using the Syndrome to explain the presence of clan governance and the level of gender inequality, rather than the other way around.

Before we can discuss the consequences of the Syndrome for the outcome measures of interest concerning governance, security, stability, and resilience of the nation-state in part II of this volume, we must first set the stage to see those connections by examining how each component of the Syndrome affects the lives of those who experience it, especially the women themselves. As we come to understand those experiences, we will establish the theoretical groundwork on which to put forward a variety of propositions linking the Syndrome variables to the state-level outcomes of national security, stability, and resilience.

The Individual Components of the Syndrome Today

Jacobson rightly notes that "traditional (and especially tribal) patriarchy, the rule of men, . . . tends to be in the mold of vitriolic hostility to women's rights."[13] In this section, we detail how each component of the Syndrome affects the lives of women and girls as well as the pertinent effects on men and boys. The picture is unrelievedly tragic. Jacobson may be right when he suggests that it is the treatment of women and girls that represents the deepest "global fissure" in the world today,[14] deeper than ethnicity or religion or ideology. As he puts it, "This is the first global struggle over the nature of the self . . . A critical issue is 'self possession,' or who owns and controls one's body, especially when it comes to women: is it the individual herself or the community[?] Women are now at the heart of the world's most dangerous quarrel."[15]

We argue that the tragic consequences of women's subordination are not confined to women, but extend to all men, all children, and all nations in which the Syndrome organizes society. In this chapter, we explore the effects of the Syndrome on women and girls, and to a lesser extent men and boys, but in part II, we explore the wider national-level effects, demonstrating that the Syndrome affects virtually all aspects of the nation-state's situation, including political, economic, and security dimensions.

What follows is an overview of each of the eleven subcomponents of the Patrilineal/Fraternal Syndrome scale, emphasizing how each means of control functions to support the male-bonded kin group, and how each undercuts the position of women and girls.

Brideprice and Dowry[16]

Some people who live in the Western hemisphere might be surprised to learn that the practices of brideprice and dowry are prevalent in the early twenty-first century. The societies that maintain these practices represent almost half of the world's countries, and account for far more than half the world's population—indeed, more accurately, almost three-quarters of the world's population—and span a wide range of regime types, including communist one-party rule in countries such as China.[17] Brideprice, or payment from a groom to the bride's family, is far more common than dowry, or payment from the bride's family to the groom, in today's world. David Barash finds that two-thirds of societies in the Ethnographic Atlas practice brideprice, with only a few, largely South Asian societies practicing dowry today.[18]

Several patterns can be seen in figure 3.3: a regional pattern, an economic pattern, and a cultural pattern. Jack Goody noted in 1974 of the former that "the data shows the dominance of bridewealth in all continents except America."[19] In the modern day, we would include Australia, Europe, and other cultures such as Japan. As for the economic pattern, setting aside the Americas for a moment, we also see that more developed countries do not practice brideprice. As anthropologists Alice Schlegel and Rohn Eloul note, "Absence of marriage transactions, beyond the small gifts that usually accompany the establishment of social bonds everywhere, is itself of interest, as it implies that property, and

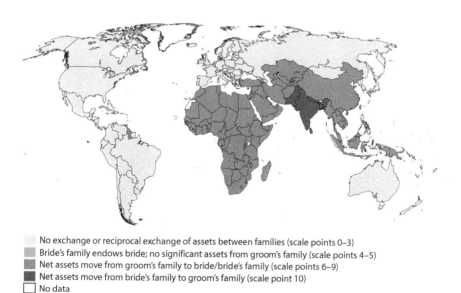

No exchange or reciprocal exchange of assets between families (scale points 0–3)
Bride's family endows bride; no significant assets from groom's family (scale points 4–5)
Net assets move from groom's family to bride/bride's family (scale points 6–9)
Net assets move from bride's family to groom's family (scale point 10)
No data

FIGURE 3.3 Map of Brideprice/Dowry/Wedding Costs, scaled 2016

the reallocation of labor or status, either are not critical issues for those house-holds or are not negotiated through marriage."[20]

Finally, with regard to ethno-religious patterns, predominantly Christian cultures appear less likely to practice brideprice in the contemporary era. There are reports of Christian missionaries inveighing against the practice during the colonial period, likening it to slavery.[21] The case of sub-Saharan Africa deserves special mention: although sub-Saharan Africa has a strong Christian presence, Christians account for only about 38 percent of the population, and Christian families often find it difficult to part ways with the larger culture on this practice.[22] In this area, therefore, one can find substantial representation of Christians in countries where brideprice is prevalent. Although this and other regional, economic, and cultural exceptions exist, brideprice is a dominant practice in much of the world. Indeed, those living in countries without this practice may underestimate the prevalence and importance of this custom.

Our own scaling of brideprice/dowry finds a roughly equal bimodal distri-bution, shown in the histogram in figure 3.4, among the nations of the world.

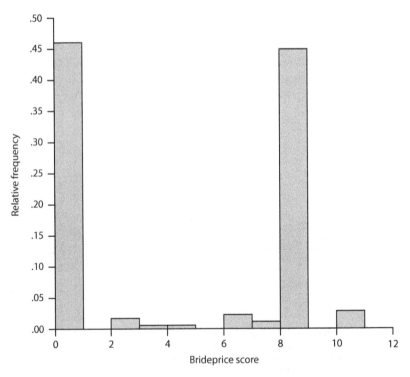

FIGURE 3.4 Histogram of Brideprice/Dowry/Wedding Costs Scale
(*Note*: 0 indicates no brideprice, dowry, or obligatory wedding costs)

As noted earlier, however, about three-quarters of the world's population lives in countries that still practice brideprice/dowry.[23] Although there are profound consequences of brideprice/dowry for societal stability, which will be explored in the next chapter, we confine this discussion to an examination of the effects of this practice on women.

The natural consequences that grow out of this system are deeply detrimental to the status of women, despite the fact that the practice is often justified as a protection to women in case they are divorced by their husbands. In addition to patrilocal marriage and lack of property rights, brideprice/dowry societies are characterized by arranged marriage in the patriline's interest, relatively low age of marriage for girls, profound underinvestment in female human capital, intense son preference, highly inequitable family and personal status law favoring men, and chronically high levels of violence against women as a means to enforce the imposition of the patrilineal system on often recalcitrant women. Consider the findings of a Tanzanian women's organization following an extensive survey that "due to brideprice," women suffer "insults, sexual abuse, battery, denial of their rights to own property, being overworked and having to bear a large number of children."[24] One female assembly member in Ghana noted that "some of the young men who were able to afford the items [in the brideprice] treated their wives as 'slaves' or 'properties' they had acquired with their wealth because of the huge sums they spent."[25] Psychiatric researcher Susan Rees and her colleagues, studying brideprice in Timor-Leste, find strong associations to intimate partner violence (IPV) against women, women's anger and mental distress, and a deep feeling of injustice among women whose marriages involved the payment of brideprice.[26]

An IRIN report relays that "Women also complained of some men's tendency to reclaim the brideprice when marriages broke up, saying fear of this outcome forced women to cling to their marriages even when abused."[27] An article from a Ghanaian newspaper concurs: "Women who wanted to divorce their husbands because of ill treatment were made to return the exact dowry collected before the marriage, and since most families are not able to refund the items, the women are left to suffer in the marriage."[28]

Journalist Marc Ellison tells the story of Grace in rural Tanzania, who refused to marry an older man, and then was abducted at age twelve and forcibly married to him so that her father could obtain the negotiated brideprice. The human toll for these girls is catastrophic: Grace was beaten and raped every day for eleven months until her husband died in a motor accident, leaving her penniless and with a baby. In Grace's case, the brideprice was in cows, and she comments, "Bitterness still fills my heart when I look at them [the cows]; Given what I went through, I wish I had been born a cow. That day felt like the end of everything."[29] Ellison notes that in Grace's region of Tanzania, almost 60 percent of girls are married as children, and it gives pain to note that the motto of the men in her ethnic group is "alcohol, meat, and vagina," naming the three things to which every man is entitled. Of course, that "vagina" is attached to a real, living human being.

As noted in chapter 2, two variants of the Syndrome also demand our attention, particularly given their effects on the status of women overall. First, where women's work is valued in the productive labor of the society, such as farm labor, brideprice and polygyny are often prevalent. Given that marriage is patrilocal and inheritance effected through the patriline, buying or exchanging women between descent groups becomes essential, and brideprice becomes the reimbursement to the family who invested the resources necessary to raise the girl to puberty. Richer men within the kin group can afford to pay the brideprice for more than one wife, and thus they ensure for themselves even greater returns on investment than those who cannot. As Schlegel and Eloul note, in such societies "the powerful man does not keep his wealth, but distributes it to acquire wives and in-laws."[30] This brideprice-with-polygyny-for-the-rich system is by far the most prevalent variant of patrilineality. Goody finds that 78 percent of the patrilineal cultures he has studied practice brideprice, and a further 6 percent practice bride-service, a variant thereof.[31]

The second, less frequent variant of dowry occurs in cases in which women are not valued for their productive labor; women are seen as a burden, and those who give the bride must be prepared to compensate the groom and his family for their assumption of this burden through payment of a dowry. Goody explains, "Bridewealth is more commonly found where women make the major contribution to agriculture, whereas dowry is restricted to those societies where males contribute most; this is the difference between hoe agriculture and the use of the plough, which is almost invariably in male hands."[32] Furthermore, one can also find societies in which dowry is practiced in higher socioeconomic classes, but brideprice is practiced among the poor. In such societies (and India is one), dowry among the rich becomes, in anthropologist John McCreery's words, "a means of social mobility in stratified societies where men use rights over women, like other property, to compete for higher status."[33] In contrast, among the poor, especially in cases in which dowry has caused sex ratio alteration, the poor must pay for a bride.

The practice of brideprice differs from that of dowry in its effects on the status of women; tellingly, dowry is more often associated with female infanticide and sex-selective abortion, for families can be bankrupted by daughters whose dowries they must pay. The negative consequences of dowry on the lives of women are well-known. Demographer P. N. Mari Bhat and public health expert Shiva Halli write that in India, the "amount of dowry demanded has grown to a size that threatens the destitution of households with many daughters,"[34] with up to two-thirds of total household assets going toward one daughter's dowry in some places. Furthermore, they note that "while a large dowry does raise the prestige of the bride among her affines, more importantly, a small one can make her life miserable in the new home. The number of instances of such harassment that lead to either the suicide or murder of the helpless woman is increasing rapidly, and these cases frequently make newspaper headlines."[35]

The effects of brideprice, in contrast to that of dowry, are less well recognized. In patrilineal systems, obligatory brideprice becomes a tax on young men, payable to older men. The young man's father and male kindred may help him pay that tax, but the intergenerational nature of the tax should not be overlooked, especially in the case of poor young men whose father and kin may not be of much assistance for any number of reasons. Brideprice can be costly: in a recent article, the regional brideprices in Afghanistan ranged from a low of 100,000 afghanis to a high of 3 million afghanis (between $1,450 and $45,000). Furthermore, even though such a brideprice may be considered a *mahr* or dower that is supposed to be the property of the bride, this almost never occurs. This is a brideprice that almost always goes to the girl's father or brother. As one man from Ghazni said,

> On the day of my engagement in 2011, my father and brothers decided on a sum of 800,000 Pakistani rupees [about US$9,230] to be given as *mahr* to my future wife. The money was paid directly to her brother and after the wedding, when I asked my wife about the *mahr*, she told me that she did not receive a penny of the 800,000 [Pakistani] rupees. Instead, she told me that her brother had used the money to arrange the marriage of his son.[36]

Marriage is often delayed for men as they often must migrate to earn these sums, and marriage is often quite early for women as male relatives want the brideprice to pay for their own wedding costs, which means the age gap between spouses can be quite large.

The impact of wedding costs, even apart from brideprice or dowry, must also not be overlooked. In a recent *New York Times* article, Joseph Goldstein tells the tale of a thirty-one-year-old groom in Afghanistan who was a car salesman. On top of the brideprice, he was also expected to pay for a wedding that would feed well over six hundred people—most of whom he did not even know. The cost of his wedding was $30,000, and he would have to take out loans that would take him years to repay. When Afghanistan was considering a cap on the number of wedding guests at five hundred people (which bill passed in 2015), one young man expressed to Goldstein, "I demand that the president sign this law," said Jawed (twenty-four years old), who sells fabric in a small stall in an underground shopping mall. "I beg him to sign this law as soon as possible so people like me can get married soon."[37]

Brideprice has caused problems throughout Afghanistan's history. Valentine Moghadam notes,

> way back in 1978, the new left-wing government in what was then the Democratic Republic of Afghanistan decreed a limit to brideprice (*walwar*). This was one of the reasons for the tribal-Islamist uprising that began in the summer of 1978 (another was compulsory schooling, especially for girls). Stupidly and tragically, the DRA reforms were denigrated as "Sovietization" by outside detractors, including those in Human Rights Watch (like Jere Laber).[38]

The problem is so serious that several state governments have gotten involved in limiting these egregious wedding costs. For example, Tajikistan recently passed a law that allows the government to seize excess wedding items, such as food, and imposes a $4,000 fine for offenders. Tajik officials may be fired if they are found holding outsize weddings.[39] The Saudi government has also been proactive, as well, in attempting to limit wedding costs.[40]

Why marry at all, then, if the brideprice is exorbitant? The logic of patrilineality demands marriage. As Farea Al-Muslimi comments about Yemen, "as soon as a young person reaches puberty, their only concern becomes marriage."[41] A man's place in the agnatic lineage is only assured if he maintains that patriline into the future. Without a son, there is no one to inherit his position and his wealth, which will then devolve to his brothers and cousins. Without a son, there will be no one to take care of him in old age or to perform requisite religious rituals for his soul. If a man breaks the patrilineal chain, he cannot be regarded as an honorable part of the lineage group. For example, Monica Das Gupta notes about Korea,

> [Ancestors] who died unmarried or without male descendants are filled with resentment and can create all kinds of problems for their siblings and other kin. It is apparent that there is much pressure from a wide range of family members to ensure that each individual performs their filial duties of marrying and bearing sons quickly, and caring for their ancestors.[42]

Therefore, even if brideprice or dowry is high, young men will strive mightily to marry and produce sons. Important in understanding the consequences of brideprice is the evidence that brideprice acts as a *flat* tax—for the most part, brideprice is the same "going rate" within the society. The brideprice is nudged slightly upward or downward at the margin according to the status of the bride's kin, but it is not affected greatly by the status of the man responsible for paying it. If the cost of brideprice rises, it will rise for every man, rich or poor. The flat-tax nature of brideprice is independent of geographic region; studies conducted in Afghanistan, China, and Kenya found that regardless of socioeconomic class, young men are expected to pay the same price to get married.

The tendency toward a consistent brideprice is easily understood. Goody suggests, "in bridewealth systems, standard payments are more common; their role in a societal exchange puts pressure towards similarity."[43] The reason for this is that men pay for their sons' brideprices by collecting the brideprice for their daughters. This is another force pushing down girls' age of marriage. In a given family, unless it is very wealthy, daughters in general must be married off first so that the family can accumulate enough assets to pay the sons' brideprices. Quoting anthropologist Lucy Mair, Goody remarks, "'when cattle payments are made, the marriage of girls tends to be early for the same reason that that of men is late—that a girl's marriage increases her father's herd while that of a young man diminishes it' . . . Men chafe at the delay, girls at the speed."[44] If brideprice were variable within a society, families could not count on the brideprices brought in by their daughters to be sufficient to fulfill the obligation they owe their sons. Thus, over time, a fairly consistent brideprice emerges for the community at any given time, although the actual cost may trend upward or downward over time depending on local conditions.

Indeed, many accounts suggest that men are sensitive to any new trends in brideprice, and the societal brideprice level is easily pushed upward. Quoting Mair again, Goody notes "Every father fears being left in the lurch by finding that the bridewealth which he has accepted for his daughter will not suffice to get him a daughter-in-law; therefore he is always on the lookout for any signs of a rise in the rate, and tends to raise his demands whenever he hears of other fathers doing so. This mean in general terms, that *individual* cases of over-payment produce a *general* rise in the rate all around."[45] This is true even in the case in which governments try to cap brideprices to stop this inexorable inflation; for example in Niger, even though the government has placed a cap of 50,000 CFA francs on brideprices, in practice families pay far more than this amount.[46] (The attempt to cap brideprice can be a catalyst for rebellion, as we saw in the case of the attempted reforms in the Democratic Republic of Afghanistan in the 1970s, which was a catalyst for insurgency.) Poorer men who must delay marriage to save up enough to marry may find that brideprices have also risen over time, making their endeavors to "catch up" impossible in the end; this phenomenon also has been noted in China.[47]

Exigency plays a role in the sudden rises and sudden falls of brideprice. Brideprice can collapse precipitously in times of exigency—for example, Yemen's civil war has caused just such a collapse. Before the civil war, a brideprice of 1 million Yemeni rials was standard (about $4,650). After the war was underway, the going price dropped to about 300,000 Yemeni rials. Although some families never considered marrying their daughters for such a low price, and refused to have them married as a result, other families were concerned whether their daughters would be able to marry at all and took the lower price.[48] When they took the lower price, they lowered the price for all, causing on overall collapse in price. Steep inflation in brideprice can also occur as a result of exigency, for example, from abnormal sex ratios. *The Economist* reports that brideprice in rural China has increased dramatically over the past decade, from about 3,000 yuan to more than 300,000 yuan as a result of the increasing scarcity of brides.[49]

As noted, brideprice is associated with early age of marriage for girls, because that practice ensures that men may accumulate capital to purchase wives. Women's economic value as wives, when added to their value as marriageable daughters, allows for the accumulation of wealth to bring in more wives. As a result, the sale of daughters tends to take place as early as practicable, pushing down the age of marriage for girls. As Goody remarks, "Polygyny . . . is made possible by the differential marriage age, early for girls, later for men. Bridewealth and polygyny play into each other's hands . . . the two institutions appear to reinforce each other."[50] We have already noted that this polygynous tendency will be exaggerated in societies in which women perform a substantial proportion of productive labor, such as farm labor. Buying additional wives is thus one route to increased wealth through accumulating a larger labor force. Polygyny is also a marker of higher status within the society, and is sought after for display of that higher status, as well, even in societies in which women's labor is not valuable (such as in the United Arab Emirates).

Given the social utility and centrality of marriage in these patrilineal contexts, brideprice is not a luxury tax affecting the budgets of the elite, but rather it is more akin to a regressive tax that disproportionately affects the poor and middle class. This places a heavy economic burden on young men—particularly in situations of economic stagnation, rising inequality, or brideprice inflation. A summary of the average brideprice from a number of different periods and countries found that the burden equated to as much as twelve to twenty times the per capita holdings of large livestock or two to four times gross household income.[51] We will explore the societal effects of such a strain in chapter 5 of this volume.

Polygyny

Polygyny, that is having formal or recognized marriages with two or more women, is not uncommon in today's world (figure 3.5). Indeed, Rose McDermott and Jonathan Cowden suggest that it exists "in more than 83 percent of 849 cultures worldwide," and note that "everywhere the practice is more widespread among high-status, high-wealth men."[52] Polyandry, virtually never practiced in human societies, is a practice of the very poor and is usually fraternal,

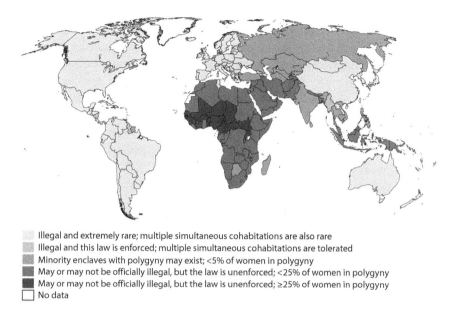

Illegal and extremely rare; multiple simultaneous cohabitations are also rare
Illegal and this law is enforced; multiple simultaneous cohabitations are tolerated
Minority enclaves with polygyny may exist; <5% of women in polygyny
May or may not be officially illegal, but the law is unenforced; <25% of women in polygyny
May or may not be officially illegal, but the law is unenforced; ≥25% of women in polygyny
No data

FIGURE 3.5 Map of the Prevalence and Legal Status of Polygyny, scaled 2016

that is, where brothers share a wife because they are too poor to afford the brideprices required for each one to marry separately. It is telling that even in cultures with traces of polyandry, rich men will still take multiple wives.

Although most prevalent in Sub-Saharan Africa and Islamic-majority countries, polygyny in some areas is creeping back in after decades of suppression, such as in post-Soviet Central Asia or in areas with high numbers of widows because of warfare.[53] Polygyny is easily effected by wealthy elites in brideprice societies. As Goody notes, "Bridewealth [i.e., brideprice] and dowry have different potentialities in the way they can link up with the politico-economic institutions of the society where they are found. Bridewealth can neatly tie in with polygyny."[54]

Polygyny serves two distinct functions. It is most widely known today as a marker of elite status, as only the wealthy will be able to afford to pay multiple brideprices. Polygyny also cements more than one political alliance among the various leaders of male kin groups. Such marriage alliances are more durable and more likely to deter internecine conflict than those not sealed by marriage and offspring.[55] Anthropologist Thomas Barfield notes, "marriage ties created patterns of alliances that crosscut the seemingly rigid set of patrilineal relationships within a conical clan. For this reason, polygynous marriages by tribal rulers were common."[56]

Status is also displayed in the formation of these alliances; for example, social anthropologists Madawi Al-Rasheed and Loulouwa Al-Rasheed observe that when the house of Saud won out over the Rashidis, they smoothed relations by marrying Rashidi women in polygynous circumstances, but they never allowed Saudi women to marry Rashidi men, for "wife-givers" are in status inferior to "wife-takers."[57] As a status marker, polygyny is an effective means of raising one's status even when one's birth status is not extraordinary. As Goody notes, brideprice has "a leveling function,"[58] by which he means that as long as a man has the requisite assets, in many cases he can marry a comparatively high-status woman regardless of his own family's social standing.

This type of elite polygynous marriage as a status marker can occur in various types of economic systems. Polygyny, however, takes on a special cast in societies in which agriculture is the primary source of wealth and in which women are the primary agricultural laborers. In such societies, polygyny arises as an effective means of improving the rate and the absolute amount of wealth accumulation for a subset of men. Goody notes, "Polygyny is found where women make a substantial contribution to productive activity, especially to cultivation."[59] Marrying more women increases the amount of land that can be profitably cultivated, and surplus income can even be used to marry additional wives.

The effects of polygyny on women and their children are as profound as those of brideprice and dowry. Unless the family is so wealthy that resources are bounteous, polygyny significantly depresses investment in women and children beyond the initial investment in the acquisition of the wives involved. Numerous studies have demonstrated that significantly less attention is paid to the health (physical and mental), nutrition, and education of women and children in polygynous households.[60] Richard Alexander notes that a man may trade off investment in his offspring for the ability to purchase additional wives as a reproductive strategy.[61]

McDermott and Cowden find a statistically significant relationship between the legality and prevalence of polygyny within a country, on the one hand, and what they call "an entire downstream suite of negative consequences for men, women, children, and the nation-state," on the other.[62] Their data analysis points to a significant relationship between polygyny and unequal family law, higher birth rates, rates of primary and secondary education for both male and female children, HIV infection, low age of marriage for girls, high maternal mortality, lower life expectancy, higher levels of sex trafficking, and higher levels of domestic violence. The evolutionary psychologist Satoshi Kanazawa has also found lower age of menarche.[63] Other experts have pointed to psychological harms for women and children in polygynous marriages, including anxiety and depression.[64] This anxiety and depression may not only be felt by women (and their children) already in polygynous relationships but also by women (and their children) currently in monogamous relationships, who must worry about whether their husband and father will take additional wives. In a cross-cultural sample, Barash finds that 90 percent of polygynously married women reported sexual and emotional conflict, particularly involving children and the allocation of resources within the household.[65]

McDermott and Cowden also note that polygyny often creates a class of unmarriageable young men. In the polygynist communities in the western United States and Canada among the Fundamentalist Church of Jesus Christ of Latter-Day Saints (FLDS), a group splintered off from the Mormon Church that still practices polygyny, they are called the "Lost Boys," for they are thrust out of their communities.[66] For wealthy men to have many wives, a sizeable number of young men must have none. As we detail in chapter 5, this may catalyze instability and even conflict. In addition to the substantial risk of being crowded out of the marriage market, Barash notes that sons in polygynous cultures are affected in other ways, as well. For example, sons often are socialized to be highly competitive and aggressive in polygynous cultures.[67]

Polygyny reliably produces harms for children. We have noted McDermott and Cowden's findings on lower rates of primary and secondary education for girls and boys, but the literature finds consistent underinvestment overall in the children of polygynous unions. The evolutionary biologist Joseph Henrich asserts that "polygynous men invest less in their offspring both because they have more offspring and because they continue to invest in seeking additional wives. This implies that, on average, children in a more polygynous society will receive less parental investment."[68] Henrich and his coauthors cite several studies showing that in both West Africa and East Africa, children in polygynous households had significantly higher death rates and significantly poorer nutrition than children in monogamous households.[69] For example, among the polygynous Dogon tribe of Mali, a child born to a polygynous family is seven to eleven times more likely to die early than one born to a monogamous couple; among the Temne of Sierra Leone, the mortality rate among children born into polygyny was found to be 41 percent, compared with 25 percent for those born into monogamy.[70] Fascinatingly, they also note that the survival rates among nineteenth-century Mormon children in Utah were actually lower for wealthier families that practiced polygyny than for poor families that did not. Even among the modern FLDS, rampant child labor, malnourishment, physical abuse, and inbreeding all take a tremendous physical and emotional toll.[71] Because of all of these demonstrable harms, Canada has upheld the constitutionality of a ban on polygamy in both 2011 and 2018.[72] We outline additional consequences of polygyny in chapters 4 and 5 as we trace the effects of the Syndrome's components on the larger social order.

Patrilocality

Patrilocality is a natural extension of the logic of patrilineality as a system of security provision (figure 3.6). Male blood relatives stay together to provide the requisite fraternal alliance, and it is women who must move to bring about the needed exogamy that will prevent genetic disaster. Women move out of their natal home and go to live with their husband's kin group. In some cases, they may never see their birth family again.[73] Economist Louise Grogan estimates that at least 70 percent of human societies practice patrilocal marriage.[74]

Avraham Ebenstein argues that the logic of patrilocality reaches its zenith when the chief inheritable asset is land. He asserts:

> The adoption of patrilocal norms serves to keep the son close for defense, to provide him wealth to support one or more wives, and to care for his elderly parents in their old age . . . and sons need their fathers' land. Often, this implicit barter will be further reinforced by religious norms that develop to enforce the agreement, such as Confucianism's focus on filial piety, or the need for a son to pray for the dead in Hinduism. . . . The elders become the holders of capital, and can exchange this for their children's labor, mediated through a norm of coresidence.[75]

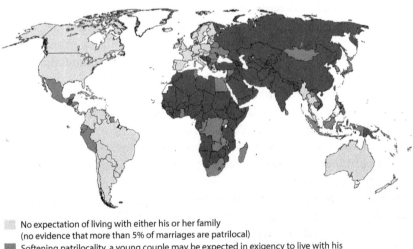

　No expectation of living with either his or her family
　(no evidence that more than 5% of marriages are patrilocal)
■ Softening patrilocality, a young couple may be expected in exigency to live with his
　family; more than 5%, but less than or equal to 20% of marriages are patrilocal
■ Strong presence of patrilocality; young couples are expected to live
　with the husband's family; greater than 20% of marriages are patrilocal
☐ No data

FIGURE 3.6 Map of the Prevalence of Patrilocal Marriage, scaled 2016

Although inheritable land drives patrilocal norms in some cultures, it is also true that nomadic tribes often practice patrilocality as well, and for many of the same reasons, such as defense by the extended male kin group. We suggest it is necessary to examine the prevalence of brideprice in connection with patrilocality, for the need to produce brideprice also fuels the need to consolidate (as versus disperse) patriline assets, and again this favors patrilocal norms.

As with brideprice or dowry and polygyny, the effects of patrilocal marriage on women are detrimental. Patrilocality typically cuts off a woman from sources of kin support that may serve to protect and sustain her. In fact, her birth family may come to see investment in her as a daughter as meaningless, for she will soon depart from their midst to join her husband's family.[76] We find proverbs from all over the patrilocal world that demonstrate this attitude: "Raising a daughter is like watering a plant in another man's garden," "A daughter is a thief," "A daughter is but a houseguest." This may help explain other norms, such as differential feeding practices for daughters and sons, and differential investment in health and education.

Once this "outsider" reaches her new home with her husband's family, she is likely to face more differential treatment—as well as suspicion and perhaps even abuse. This predisposition actually may be augmented by the payment of brideprice, which may be taken by some to mean that the girl has been bought, and thus she has the status of a chattel. As Xie Lihua of *Rural Women's Magazine* in China put it, "there's a saying among men: 'marrying a woman is like buying a horse: I can ride you and beat you whenever I like.' Men feel that 'I've spent money on bringing you into my family, so I have the right to order you around.' And a man will beat a woman if she has a mind of her own."[77]

In addition to physical consequences, there are also profound psychological consequences for the woman. Where, exactly, is her home, that is, her place of safety and acceptance? It appears not to be either in her parents' home or in her in-laws' home. What is her central love relationship? It is not to be found in her birth family, and it is not with her husband. Rather, her only lasting love relationship is with her son, if she produces one, which accounts for the deep tension between mother-in-law and daughter-in-law when that son marries. It also accounts for intensified son preference; as Grogan notes, "Sons are the key intergenerational link where women move to their husband's natal residence upon marriage."[78]

Furthermore, the patrilocal nature of marriage puts the woman at risk should she be widowed or divorced. A widow may be subject to levirate marriage (marriage to her dead husband's brother or other near kin), or she simply may be ousted from the household by her in-laws and left to forage for herself. She may not be able to inherit as a widow from her husband in some cultures, with all his property reverting to the patriline. A woman who is divorced may also lose custody of her children, because they are considered to be affines of her husband's family, and she may not be able to return to her birth family, either, leaving her without a place to live.

Although urbanization attenuates patrilocality, the practice can return after decades of more neolocal marriage norms. For example, Grogan notes that after the fall of the Soviet Union, economic shocks and rising instability catalyzed a return to a patrilocal marriage norm in nations such as Tajikistan.[79] Again, we see that reversion to the security provision mechanism of the Patrilineal/Fraternal Syndrome as the result of exigency will also cause a regress in the situation of women at the household level.

Son Preference and Sex Ratios

A discussion of son preference and sex ratios naturally follows from a discussion of brideprice, polygyny, and patrilocality (figure 3.7). Son preference follows from patrilineality as one more logical extension. From all that we have learned, it is clear that the "true members" of a kin group are the males in the patriline, and for a man to continue that kin line is obligatory for him to have full standing in the group and to be able to pass an inheritance to his own posterity and not to his brothers. That means he must have a son; a daughter will simply not suffice. Although daughters may be valued for their instrumental usefulness in bringing in a brideprice, or for their productive or reproductive

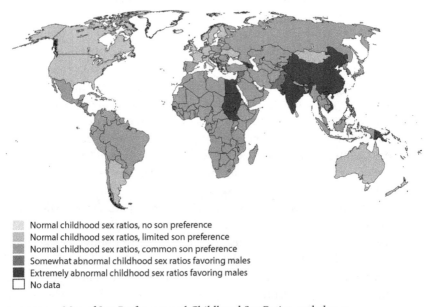

Normal childhood sex ratios, no son preference
Normal childhood sex ratios, limited son preference
Normal childhood sex ratios, common son preference
Somewhat abnormal childhood sex ratios favoring males
Extremely abnormal childhood sex ratios favoring males
No data

FIGURE 3.7 Map of Son Preference and Childhood Sex Ratios, scaled 2015

labor, only sons have existential value and thus merit sustained investment in their nutrition, health care, and education. Only sons are a bridge to the future for a patriline; only sons bring to their fathers a permanent standing in the lineage group.

Intense son preference can lead to high fertility and high maternal mortality rates in some societies. One Afghan woman was interviewed by the Afghan Women's Writing Project in the Herat Maternity Clinic, and offered her story:

> First I talk to a woman who tells me about her life with tears pouring from her eyes. Wounds on her face show she has recently been beaten. She cannot tell me much, she is afraid and cannot say her name to me, but she talks about her life. She does not tell her age; she says only that she was the youngest in her family. She is pregnant with her ninth child. She has eight children who are all girls, and in three months her next child will be born. She says her husband's family forced her to continue to become pregnant to give birth to a boy and she says this time she knows she will have a son because the pregnancy feels different from the other times. All of her children were born at home and she came to the clinic only because of bleeding. Her husband had beaten her. She says if she does not bear a son her husband will end their marriage and will abandon her with her daughters.[80]

Part of the calculus of son preference is that because of patrilocality, only sons provide old age insurance for elderly parents. Daughters will be leaving to live with their husband's family, but sons will stay and are responsible for the care of elderly parents. As Das Gupta notes, "Son preference is found in certain types of cultures, that is, patrilineal cultures . . . [where] daughters are formally transferred on marriage to their husband's family and can no longer contribute to their natal family. This drastically lowers the value of daughters relative to sons, reducing parents' willingness to invest in raising girls."[81]

Thus, we are not surprised to find that patrilocal norms are strongly associated with abnormally high sex ratios favoring males.[82] That is, these norms incentivize both the bearing of sons and the prevention of the birth of daughters either through female infanticide or sex-selective abortion. Ebenstein notes this connection, stating

> parents abort girls because of patrilocality: [patrilocality] is the single common factor across countries with high sex ratios, and as such, should be viewed as the primary factor in explaining the phenomenon. Patrilocality is the single feature common to the social norms of Christians in Armenia, Muslims in Azerbaijan, Hindus in India and Buddhists in China—all live with their sons when they are old . . . every country with abnormally high sex ratios at birth in the samples has a high proportion of elderly living with sons.[83]

Ebenstein shows empirically that even when controlling for measures of gender equity, such as education and employment rates, groups where sons live with their parents have higher sex ratios. His analysis is revealing; he finds that even where women are not otherwise disadvantaged in education or employment, such as in Armenia or China, if the elderly typically coreside with sons, high sex ratios are manifest.[84]

Armenia is a telling case in Ebenstein's view, because sex ratios in that country were absolutely normal until the collapse of the Soviet Union. Ebenstein notes that after that event, "Parents realized that old age support would be provided by the family rather than the state."[85] He found that, consequently, sex ratios rose to 53.1 percent male among lower-income Armenians. He posits that this socioeconomic class began to demonstrate son preference to ensure care later in life because they could rely on neither their savings nor the state to provide it. "The Armenian experience documents the dangers facing policymakers when social protections are removed among parents who have access to sex selection technology," he explains.[86]

Armenia is not the only post–Soviet era nation seeing a resurgence in male-skewed sex ratios. Azerbaijan, Georgia, Montenegro, and Albania all have seen increased sex ratios, with Georgia clocking in at an estimated 122 boys per 100 girls born in the 2000–2005 period.[87] The birth sex ratio in Armenia hit 114.4 in 2011, and Azerbaijan's was 115.5.[88] Furthermore, political scientist Andrea Den Boer also notes excess female mortality in the first few years of life, as well, indicating passive infanticide of girls. (Ironically, the chronic housing shortage in the Soviet Union contributed to the continued cultural practice of patrilocality in this region, according to Den Boer.)

Patrilineal societies typically fuse religious belief with the importance of the patriline, and therefore it is not unexpected to find religious or quasi-religious beliefs supporting son preference. For example, in China, Das Gupta notes,

> It is believed that one's own soul and that of one's male ancestors need to be cared for by male progeny, without which the dead will become what in China is called "hungry ghosts." No pension plan can cover care in the afterlife. Angering the ancestors through unfilial acts can bring their wrath down on you in this life, bringing supernatural sanctions and bad luck. Not bearing a son is a major dereliction of filial duty.[89]

Sex ratio alteration is a telling indicator of women's disempowerment at the household level. Economist Andrew Francis notes that "the incidence of selective abortion, infanticide, and neglect [of females] is inversely related to women's intra-household bargaining power. Empowering women, wives and mothers, reduces the number of 'missing' women."[90] Indeed, the fact that it is often mothers-in-law who most directly pressure daughters-in-law to get rid of female offspring is a testament to just how disempowered women are, indicating that only the birth of sons lifts a woman's status in the home, even among other women.

The toll on women's health of son preference can be appalling; public health expert Narjis Rizvi and colleagues conducted thirty focus groups of 250 women in Pakistan, finding that many of the women indicated that they "continue bearing children until the family has at least one son; she sometimes delivers 7 or more daughters in order to accomplish the objective. . . . Except the post-delivery period in case of the male baby, when higher allowances are given so that the boy can be breastfed, generally meager nutritional allocation and repeated pregnancies make them malnourished."[91]

Interestingly, unless other Syndrome components are present to prevent it, masculinized sex ratios can actually increase women's bargaining power within the home. That is, in a context in which potential wives are relatively scarce, if women are relatively free to choose whether to marry and have access to divorce, custody, and property rights in marriage, empirical research suggests that, once married, they are able to bargain for greater investment in the children of the marriage (e.g., greater number of years of schooling) as well as ensure lower rates of infanticide, sex-selective abortion and neglect of daughters, and achieve lower total fertility.[92] For example, in China, one young man interviewed by the *China Youth Daily* noted, "In my hometown, the status of the wife and her mother-in-law has reversed, especially in a family with bad finances. The mother-in-law needs to treat the wife carefully in order to avoid the wife leaving the family. It's not the wife that the mother-in-law truly cares about, it's [the brideprice]."[93] In most Syndrome-encoded societies, however, this situation rarely occurs. Indeed, one could propose that the interlocking straitjacket of the Syndrome purposefully serves, among many other things, to effectively insulate men and their patriline from any such development.

Abnormal sex ratios play havoc with brideprice, as we discussed earlier. As one Chinese matchmaker put it, "The scarcity of marriageable women makes men like a starving man—all food is delicious to them."[94] As brideprice rises beyond the reach of many men, they may seek divorced women or women with mental or physical disabilities, for the brideprice will be considerably lower for these women. Families with several sons may be able to fund only the marriage of the eldest. One family in Hubei, China, with four sons, decided that the four brothers would have to jointly raise enough money for the eldest to marry and that the rest would probably have to forgo any hope of marrying at all.[95]

Abnormal sex ratios are not a thing of the past; indeed, they are spreading. In 1990, five nation-states had abnormal sex ratios in early childhood (ages birth to four years old); now there are nineteen (twenty-one, if you include Hong Kong and Macau). In 1990, the phenomenon was confined to Asia, but now the countries with abnormal sex ratios across ages birth to four years old include many outside that continent, including Albania, Armenia, Azerbaijan, China, Hong Kong, Macau, Egypt, Fiji, Georgia, India, Kosovo, Kuwait, Lebanon, Montenegro, Philippines, South Sudan, Sudan, Taiwan, Macedonia, Vanuatu, and Vietnam.[96] Expatriate communities may also create enclaves of higher sex ratios; for example, in Canada, Indian-born women with two daughters have a birth sex ratio for their third child of 196 boys per 100 girls.[97]

Migration can create age-cohort pockets of abnormal sex ratios,[98] as has been noted in Sweden after the mass migration of 2015, subsequent to which the sex ratio of sixteen- and seventeen-year-olds in Sweden rose to 123 males per 100 females, far surpassing the sex ratio of China for the same age cohort (117:100). Furthermore, historical path dependencies may be at work—for example, researchers have tied modern West African polygyny to a legacy of abnormal sex ratios resulting from slavery, where about two-thirds of those exported as slaves from West Africa were male.[99]

The devaluation of female life, expressed most starkly in female infanticide and sex-selective abortion, is interwoven with the history of female subordination stretching back millennia. As Gerda Lerner notes, "One of the first powers men institutionalized under patriarchy was the power of the male head of the family to decide which infants should live and which infants should die. This power must have been perceived as a victory of law over nature, for it went directly against nature and previous human experience."[100] Indeed, as the current estimate of the number of missing women in Asia alone rises inexorably toward two hundred million,[101] it is astonishing that the world considers this toll, which dwarfs that of any war, so unremarkable—and so unrelated to national and international security. In part II, we explain how wrong that mind-set proves to be.

Low Age of First Marriage for Girls

Estimates are that almost five million girls are married annually at younger than sixteen years of age (figure 3.8).[102] These young girls are, for the most part, not marrying men of the same age: the average difference in age is six years, with the husband being substantially older. In Niger, for example, 59 percent of child brides married a man at least ten years older; the corresponding figure for Bolivia was 46 percent. The United Nations Population Fund notes that 19 percent of young women in developing countries become pregnant before the age of eighteen, and 95 percent of those births occur within marriage. Furthermore, 2 million of the 7.3 million births every year to adolescents are to those who are younger than age fifteen—in some countries, that represents 10 percent of under-fifteen girls.[103]

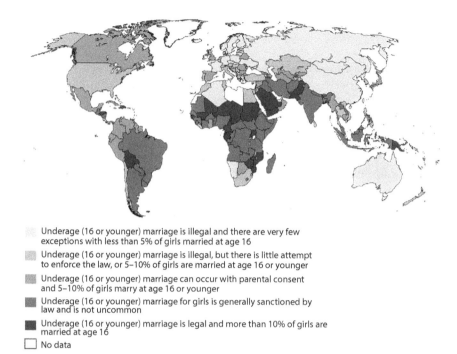

Underage (16 or younger) marriage is illegal and there are very few exceptions with less than 5% of girls married at age 16

Underage (16 or younger) marriage is illegal, but there is little attempt to enforce the law, or 5–10% of girls are married at age 16 or younger

Underage (16 or younger) marriage can occur with parental consent and 5–10% of girls marry at age 16 or younger

Underage (16 or younger) marriage for girls is generally sanctioned by law and is not uncommon

Underage (16 or younger) marriage is legal and more than 10% of girls are married at age 16

No data

FIGURE 3.8 Map of Age of Marriage for Girls in Law and Practice, scaled 2015

Patrilineality tends to be associated with a low age of marriage for girls, even child marriage. This is largely because daughters hold less value compared with sons in patrilineal culture; daughters marry exogamously and therefore are not considered full members of the kin group, but they must be fed, clothed, and housed before marriage; preserving the sexual purity of daughters becomes more onerous to the family with each year past puberty; and daughters may bring in a good-size brideprice upon marriage, which subsequently could be used to contract marriages for the men of the family. Child marriage for girls minimizes expenditures and expedites income that may be needed to pay for the marriages of the more important sons. In addition, child marriage for girls may reduce threats to the family's honor (and hoped-for brideprice) by reducing the time period in which she is vulnerable to sexual predation.

Exigencies also increase the rate of child marriage for girls. Whether as a result of natural disaster or conflict, crisis will push down the age of marriage as families are scrambling for resources and are willing to marry off girls in exchange. In addition, in desperate situations caused by having to flee conflicts, families may feel completely unable to protect their girls from sexual predation, and marriage may seem the best way to preserve their honor. This dynamic is playing out as we speak among refugees from the Syrian conflict. Save the Children reports,

> Child marriage existed in Syria before the crisis—13 percent of girls under 18 in Syria were married in 2011. But now, three years into the conflict, official statistics show that among Syrian refugee communities in Jordan . . . child marriage has increased alarmingly, and in some cases has doubled. In Jordan, the proportion of registered marriages among the Syrian refugee community where the bride was under 18 rose from 12 percent in 2011 (roughly the same as the figure in pre-war Syria) to 18 percent in 2012, and as high as 25 percent by 2013. The number of Syrian boys registered as married in 2011 and 2012 in Jordan is far lower, suggesting that girls are, as a matter of course, being married off to older males.[104]

The same phenomenon is observable in Yemen's civil war, as well, and Oxfam has asserted that girls as young as three years of age are being married off to obtain brideprice to feed the rest of the family.[105]

Interestingly, a new exigency for modern parents is that educated girls may refuse to marry a partner they deem unacceptable, or they may refuse to marry at all. Marrying daughters off early may prevent such insubordination from occurring. Louisa Chiang notes, "Reversing a long-running trend, some rural families now marry off their daughters earlier, enticed by the high brideprice and concerned that older, more educated daughters are likely to leave or are harder to dictate marriage terms to."[106] The highly masculinized sex ratio pushes down the age of marriage for women, as witnessed by the resurgence of early marriage in China despite laws against such practices.[107]

Another type of family exigency is debt or blood debt; in certain cultures, girls may be "gifted" to pay such a debt. In Afghanistan the tradition is known as *baad,* and it is estimated that more than 10 percent of marriages in that country stem from the practice. The Afghan Penal Code supposedly prohibits *baad,* but only for women over eighteen years old and widows. Virtually all those given in *baad* are young girls, however.[108]

The effects on girls of child marriage are devastating. We will argue in later chapters that the effects on the broader society are equally devastating. For the girls, however, gender and foreign policy expert Rachel Vogelstein notes they are "forced to leave their families, marry against their will, endure sexual and physical abuse, and bear children while still in childhood . . . it is tantamount to sexual slavery."[109] Woe unto the girl who wishes to escape her fate:

> A child bride's instinct to run away is often met with horrific consequences. If a child bride leaves her husband's home, she risks retaliation from both her husband's family and her birth family. For the bride's family, having a

daughter that has run away from her husband's home brings shame onto the entire family. The bride's virtue is automatically called into question, and she is labeled as promiscuous and disobedient. Ultimately, the perceived shame for the birth family will become unbearable, until finally, a male in the family will seek to bring back the family's honor by killing the source of the pain: the young bride . . . Thirteen-year-old Yemeni child bride Ilham Mahdi al Assi died tragically three days after her wedding in April, after she was tied down, raped repeatedly and left bleeding to death. Another recent example is 12-year-old Fawziya Abdullah Youssef, also a Yemeni child bride, who died after three days of excruciating labor pain because her body wasn't developed enough to give birth.[110]

Child marriage clearly does not serve the interests of the girls involved in terms of their physical health, opportunities for education, or level of safety within the household. As a United Nations Children's Fund report summarizes, "Child marriage is a violation of human rights, compromising the development of girls and often resulting in early pregnancy and social isolation. Young married girls face onerous domestic burdens, constrained decision-making and reduced life choices."[111]

One of the most important feedback loops with in the Syndrome is between child marriage, brideprice or dowry, and violence against women. Vogelstein reports:

Data from India show that girls married at age eighteen or older are more likely to repudiate domestic violence, whereas those married under the age of eighteen are more likely to have experience with physical or sexual abuse. Girls married as children are also more likely to be physically abused not only by their husbands, but also by their family members and in-laws. Wide disparities in age and power between husband and wife, as well as marital financial transactions such as dowry and brideprice, can exacerbate social norms that sanction violence."[112]

Child marriage produces many cascading effects on human and economic security, which we detail in chapter 6. World Bank economist Quentin Wodon summarizes them here:

By curtailing education, increasing fertility, and limiting opportunities for employment, child marriage contributes to poverty. The practice is also associated with a higher risk of intimate partner violence and other forms of violence, which may lead to severe injuries and even death, as well as losses in earnings and out-of-pocket costs for healthcare. Next, child marriage is associated with higher risks of . . . maternal mortality and morbidity . . . malnutrition and depression [and] poor sexual and reproductive health outcomes including through sexually transmitted diseases. The practice also has consequences for children in terms of infant mortality, low birth weight, and stunting. Finally, child marriage also leads to losses in empowerment and decision-making as well as participation more generally.[113]

But these statistics may obscure the sheer enormity of the human cost.[114] As Stephanie Sinclair, the award-winning photographer whose photos of child brides put a shocking face to these statistics, reflects,

> I first encountered child marriage in Afghanistan in 2003. I was horrified to learn that several girls in one province had set themselves on fire. After some investigation, it became apparent that one of the things propelling these girls to commit such a drastic act was having been forced to marry as a child. They told me they'd been married at 9, 10, 11—and in their misery [they] had preferred death over the lives they were living. . . . Every girl I met, in each country, completely broke my heart—particularly the ones married to much older men. The more I pursued the phenomenon, the more the issue continued to unravel before me. The trauma these girls carry with them into adulthood is utterly palpable when speaking with child marriage survivors about their experiences. These heroic women live their lives just like anyone else, but if they're comfortable enough to discuss their past with you, the toll taken by such an intense childhood trauma becomes very, very clear. Then you take the experiences of the relative handful of girls and survivors I've met and then realize . . . with child marriage occurring in more than 50 countries worldwide, how many more girls are living a similar hell, day in and day out. The numbers are staggering! At least 39,000 girls married every day—that's one girl every two seconds! Every day that goes by, an incomprehensible number of girls' lives have been forever changed.[115]

And not for the better. As one health-care worker put it in Morocco, "This type of marriage is child rape; that is to say, her life has been raped by means of this marriage."[116] The incidence of child marriage is falling worldwide, except in Latin America where rates are rising.[117] Even so, gains have been painfully slow. For example, a legal change in Morocco designed to reduce the number of girl-child marriages has unintentionally increased the number.[118] Furthermore, as noted by Vogelstein, "The failure of some governments to implement systems of birth and marriage registration also makes it easier to avoid compliance with minimum age of marriage laws."[119] As we have seen, any type of exigency may catalyze child marriage for girls, for the Patrilineal/Fraternal Syndrome rigidly encodes their lower value as well as their higher risk to family honor. In November 2014, the Human Rights Committee of the United Nations General

Assembly adopted by consensus a resolution calling on all nations to end child marriage and forced marriage. The resolution had 118 sponsors from across all continents—but the map at the beginning of this subsection tells the true tale.

Cousin Marriage

Cousin marriage is common in some patrilineal societies as a way to keep assets within the family—that is, so that brideprice or dowry does not leave the family when a woman marries (figure 3.9).[120] Reciprocal exchange of daughters between kin, or "bride exchange," with marriage often to one's father's brother's daughter, often occurs in this context to maintain roughly equal status between the cousins' families, for in patrilineal societies, as Goody explains, "[There is a] strong tendency for the wife-receiving group to rank the higher."[121] Reciprocal exchange of women within the kin group prevents this status difference from emerging.

Anthropologist Bernard Chapais and others believe cross-cousin marriage developed early in human society, perhaps even in the prelinguistic era. Interestingly, he posits its rationale is the construction of what he terms "affinal brotherhood," that is, linking a brother (and his father) through the brother's sister to her husband, maintaining affinity across the branches of the patriline. This brotherhood-through-marriage permits "male pacification,"

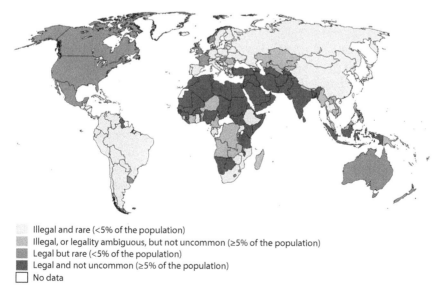

Illegal and rare (<5% of the population)
Illegal, or legality ambiguous, but not uncommon (≥5% of the population)
Legal but rare (<5% of the population)
Legal and not uncommon (≥5% of the population)
No data

FIGURE 3.9 Map of Prevalence and Legality of Cousin Marriage, scaled 2016

by which Chapais means reduction in competition and violence between men "connected" by women.[122] This brotherhood then forms the basis of the larger community, the agnatic tribe, whose boundaries are circumscribed by how far across the genealogical tree one may marry.

The presence of cousin marriage is a tip-off that patrilineality is present, for without patrilineality, there would be no incentive for it, especially given the genetic risks that are disproportionately present in cases in which cousin marriage is practiced. One Egyptian pediatrician asserts that 90 percent of the genetic diseases seen in children in that country are the result of consanguineous marriage, and include microcephaly, cystic fibrosis, thalassaemia, and previously unseen disorders.[123] In the United Kingdom, where it is estimated that 60 percent of couples of Pakistani heritage are in consanguineous marriages, the death rate attributed to inherited disease was thirty-eight times that of reference couples.[124] In Egypt, about 40 percent marry cousins, and rates are similar for Jordan and also the Gulf states. Iran's rate of cousin marriage is approximately 37 percent.[125] Across the MENA region as a whole, up to 50 percent of marriages may be consanguineous.[126] The toll of misery from genetic disease is appallingly high in all these countries.

Even so, in Saudi Arabia, there is a saying concerning cousin marriage that, "a piece of fabric remains beautiful only if the additional fabric attached to it is from the same kind."[127] Abdul Al Lily describes how some Saudi tribes will reject marriage proposals from nonfamily members and even will decide on marriage partners from among the cousins for a child at the time of their birth. Oftentimes even an ominous genetic test result between cousins may not preclude the marriage.[128]

Cousin marriage not only is prevalent in MENA but also is practiced among some groups in South Asia. Hanan Jacoby and Ghazala Mansuri reference a 2004–2005 survey in the Pakistani provinces of Sindh and Punjab, finding that more than three-quarters of women had married a blood relative, typically a cousin.[129] It is also not uncommon for cousin marriage to be reciprocal, that is, female cousins are exchanged between kin so that no money or assets need change hands, and even the women's inheritances are kept within their birth families. (Sometimes such a "swap" can even take place between families that are not kin, although our scale of cousin marriage does not capture that practice.) "Swapping" women can sometimes be risky, however, because if one of the marriages ends in divorce, the other couple may be forced to divorce, as well—even if they are happy together—for reasons of honor.[130] If one wife is killed through domestic violence, the other may be killed, as well, in retribution. An additional catalyst besides preservation of patriline assets is the often-fierce rivalry between male cousins, which this type of marriage is meant to ameliorate.[131]

In historical Europe, as well, patrilineal elites often sought special dispensation from the Catholic Church to marry cousins, again to conserve status and assets through endogamy. However, cousin marriage violated the Church's ban on incest—defined as marriage or sexual relations within four to seven degrees of separation, depending on the time period examined. Goody explains that "property was key" to understanding these marriages, which often took place among elites and nobles.[132] Indeed, he further suggests that in the context in which land is the key asset, cousin marriage in the context of patrilineality will almost always develop, noting that "the possession of livestock does not lead to quite the same pressure for status preservation and endogamy as occurs in systems of intensive farming."[133]

Cousin marriage may ameliorate some of the emotional distance between a bride and her natal family, offering a sense of bilaterality and perhaps providing stronger protections for the bride. Harming a bride from a nonrelated family is one thing, but harming a bride from your uncle's family is quite another. Tanika Chakraborty and Sukkoo Kim propose that "women's bargaining position seems to be higher in societies where cross-cousin marriages are allowed than in societies that restrict marriages to non-kin. Because women marry into familiar kin networks rather than to strange families, they are likely to have more allies. Women's property rights are positively correlated with marriages in which women are in close proximity to their natal home, which is often the case in cross-cousin marriages."[134]

Unfortunately, this proposition may not hold in real life. For example, despite the authors hearing from numerous interviewees in societies that practice endogamy that the practice offers physical protection for the bride, it is also true that economist Alberto Alesina and coauthors find that "being from an ethnicity that was traditionally endogamous is positively associated with violence experienced, increasing the likelihood of ever being victim of violence by 6.9 percentage points, a 26 percent increase over the mean. This is accompanied by a positive and significant effect on the reported male acceptability of violence towards women."[135]

In sum, then, the practice of cousin marriage produces not only avoidable devastating genetic consequences, but also firmly asserts the patriline's interest over that of the woman involved. She may have little say in whom she marries and may have very little chance of escaping an abusive marriage because it has been arranged by the entire kin network in its own strategic interest. Lerner describes the logic of cousin marriage well when she writes,

> The "exchange of women" . . . is always preceded . . . by the indoctrination of women, from earliest childhood on, to an acceptance of their obligation to their kin to consent to such enforced marriages. [Quoting Levi-Strauss] "The total relationship of exchange which constitutes marriage is not established between a man and a woman . . . but between two groups of men, and the woman figures only as one of the objects in the exchange, not as one of the partners . . .

This remains true even when the girl's feelings are taken into consideration, as, moreover, is usually the case. In acquiescing to the proposed union, she precipitates or allows the exchange to take place; she cannot alter its nature."[136]

Inequity in Family Law and Practice

In their work analyzing responses from the World Value Survey, political scientists Ronald Inglehart and Pippa Norris uncovered an unusual finding: there was little cross-national variation in the degree to which survey respondents valued democracy and democratic institutions. "With the exception of Pakistan, most of the Muslim countries surveyed think highly of democracy: In Albania, Egypt, Bangladesh, Azerbaijan, Indonesia, Morocco, and Turkey, 92 to 99 percent of the public endorsed democratic institutions—a higher proportion than in the United States (89 percent)."[137] Rather, the most extreme differences in attitudes that they found concerned the role and place of women in society:

> Huntington is mistaken in assuming that the core clash between the West and Islam is over political values. At this point in history, societies throughout the world (Muslim and Judeo-Christian alike) see democracy as the best form of government. Instead, the real fault line between the West and Islam, which

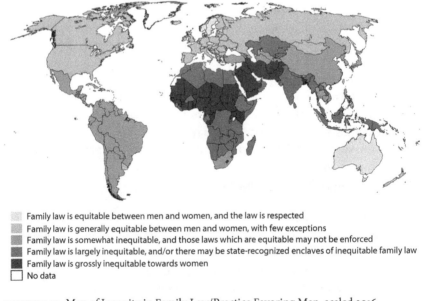

Family law is equitable between men and women, and the law is respected
Family law is generally equitable between men and women, with few exceptions
Family law is somewhat inequitable, and those laws which are equitable may not be enforced
Family law is largely inequitable, and/or there may be state-recognized enclaves of inequitable family law
Family law is grossly inequitable towards women
No data

FIGURE 3.10   Map of Inequity in Family Law/Practice Favoring Men, scaled 2016

Huntington's theory completely overlooks, concerns gender equality and sexual liberalization. In other words, the values separating the two cultures have much more to do with *eros* than *demos*.[138]

What Norris and Inglehart mean by *eros* is what we have referred to as the first political order, or the sexual political order. Although Norris and Ingelhart focus on "the West and Islam," the issue is much more complex than such a binary comparison would indicate. Instead, we argue that their survey results reveal evidence that the Syndrome runs much deeper than political preferences; it is a deep structural element of every society. The world may be becoming more homogenized with regard to certain attitudes, such as attitudes toward democracy, but it is definitely not homogenized with regard to choices about the first political order.

An excellent indicator of the Patrilineal/Fraternal Syndrome's sexual political order is in the *structural control* offered men by family law systems.[139] As Weiner expresses it, "the role of women in clan societies is to physically reproduce the clan itself, and this role shapes all the legal rules affecting them, from their ability to sue or be sued to their property rights."[140]

Family law refers to the statutory and customary law that regulates marriage and parenthood, and to a great extent, it speaks to how a given state or society views the relations between men and women and subsequently, the families that form from their union. It establishes the legal order that defines how individuals and kin-based groups, whether families or tribes, relate to each other and the rights they hold as part of a family under the state. A state's legal authority establishes practices that reproduce and govern family entities, but it is also true that social, community, and religious practices set up norms that govern family relations as well. A back-and-forth relationship exists between these two sources: although norms influence laws, laws also indisputably have an impact on norms.

According to our theoretical framework, the male-bonded kin group made family law *in the image of its own patrilineal/fraternal interests.* Consider the remarkable convergence of family law throughout both time and space in human history: adultery considered a much greater crime for women than for men; female infanticide as a historically sanctioned practice in virtually all human cultures, polygyny being legal but non-fraternal polyandry proscribed; divorce being easy for men and nearly impossible for women; male-on-female domestic violence and marital rape not recognized as crimes; a common legal sequel to rape being the marriage of the victim to the rapist; the legal age of consent and of marriage being years younger for women than for men; and inheritance of resources preferentially allocated to males. Still other practices that are an expression of physical and sexual dominance of men over women, such as infibulation, chastity belts, *droit de seigneur*, and gender-based dress codes that inhibit the mobility of women, are also under-standable in this light.

The convergence in family law systems, expansively defined, through time and space, leads us to the conclusion that the formation of family law is at least in part the result of highly ranked men in all cultures having originally created family law through their political power and having created it in the image of male reproductive interests situated in the patrilineal/fraternal framework.[141] Lerner points out that this explicit inequity in family law is apparent even in the earliest recorded legal system, the Code of Hammurabi.[142] Consider Lerner's observation that in ancient Sumerian, "the word 'marriage' is different for man and woman. A man 'takes a wife,' but a woman is described as 'entering a man's house.'"[143] Even today, as the writer Al Lily notes, in Saudi Arabia, "wedding invitations display only the groom's name and the name of the bride's father."[144] Control over women by men, baldly put, is at the foundation of historical family law because of humanity's common reliance on the Patrilineal/Fraternal Syndrome as a security provision mechanism.[145] Political scientists Mala Htun and Laurel Weldon express it well:

> Family law—also called personal status law—is one of the central institutions of gender. It molds social identities and distributes rights and responsibilities, forging relations of power between men and women, parents and children, brothers and sisters. These status differences are consequential not just for the private sphere but also for public opportunities. Family laws shape the capacity of a citizen to own, inherit, and manage property; to work outside the home; her freedom to marry, divorce, and remarry; and her or his relationship with children. Most modern family law emphasizes patriarchy and other forms of male dominance. It tended (and still tends) to maximize men's power over women and limit the latter's ability to make decisions and take independent action. Classical Islamic law, the Napoleonic Code, Anglo-American common law, and the customary law of many sub-Saharan African groups and indige-nous peoples of the Americas all upheld the notion that men were in charge of family life: they controlled property, were the legal guardians of children, and had the right to restrict their wives' public activities. Women were obliged to obey their husbands, had limited access to divorce, and, in many traditions, fewer inheritance rights than men.[146]

It is possible even today to find full structural control in the patriline's interest, as shown by the map in figure 3.10; however, some countries have made sustained and consistent departures from inequitable family and per-sonal status law. For example, in many societies, it is as straightforward for a woman to obtain a divorce or to inherit from her parents as it is for a man. As Inglehart and Norris have argued (from survey results), so we argue (from our theoretical framework), that the key cultural differences between human societies may have less to do with ethnic and religious differences, and more to do with whether the society has chosen to continue with the patrilineal/fraternal security provision mechanism, or whether the society purposefully acts to mitigate that heritage. Family and personal status law offers a particularly insightful view of which path a society has taken to this point. As seen in chapter 1 and 2, overt physical dominance by males is typically buttressed by the creation of structural means to more easily ensure male control over females and thus over families. We should expect that inequitable family law systems and high levels of violence against women would be highly correlated, and indeed, that is exactly what we find.[147]

Remember that judicial structures—whether formal or informal—are typically male dominated. In more developed countries, judges and police are still primarily male; in less developed countries where village elders and councils informally adjudicate cases, these bodies are also usually exclusively male. For example, in India, village councils have doled out misogynist rulings time after time, prompting the Supreme Court of India to declare these councils should be illegal. For example, the *Washington Post* reports,

> In 2014 . . . a clan council in the state of West Bengal ordered the gang rape of a woman as punishment for her relationship with a man outside her tribal community—with a leader allegedly urging the council to "go enjoy the girl and have fun," according to a police complaint . . . Women are forced to retrieve a coin from a vat of boiling oil to prove their purity. One woman was forced to walk, scantily clad, through the forest while the panchayat members threw balls of dough straight off a fire at her back . . . Women typically receive the harshest punishments.[148]

Oftentimes, these informal judicial structures attempt to stop victims from accessing the formal state-run system. One leader of a clan council stated, "We say, 'Let's not go to the courts; let's resolve it,'" he said. "We encourage them to go back to the police if a [complaint] has already been filed and say, 'I was not in a right state of mind; I want to take back my statement.'"[149]

In addition, with respect to the status of women, customary law often trumps formal national law.[150] Indeed, in most states, where family law practice diverges from state family law, we typically find that the state stands mute and does not intervene. This may even be codified; in certain African states, for example Zambia and Botswana, formal laws may contain a clause at the end that explicitly states that where tribal and customary practices clash with state law, practice will supersede law. In Ethiopia, the legal marriage age is eighteen, but it is not uncommon for parents to contract marriages for their much younger daughters, including girls as young as seven, and the state does little to nothing to interfere.[151] In Utah, Texas, and Arizona, as well as in British Columbia in Canada, breakout polygynous religious factions marry girls at young ages. In response, Utah and Arizona set the legal marriage age at eighteen and require parental consent for girls ages sixteen to seventeen years old. In Utah, girls of fifteen years not only need parental consent but also consent from the Juvenile Court, which must rule whether the marriage is voluntary and in her best interest. Arizona requires a court order as well as parental consent for girls fifteen years or younger.[152] Despite these laws, many girls are still married in private religious ceremonies at ages as young as twelve.[153] Polygyny is illegal in the United States and Canada, but nonetheless is practiced widely enough in some states that observers would be forced to conclude that these states do not prioritize enforcing laws against polygamy.

In addition, parallel systems of family and personal status law may be indulged to keep the peace, but this choice also has political consequences. Suad Joseph, a scholar of gender and the Middle East, writes here about Lebanon, but she could also be writing about other states with multiple family law systems:

> That there is no civil family law in Lebanon further throws the citizens back onto their religious/ethnic affiliation and their families. The state defers marriage, divorce, child custody, and inheritance to the courts of the eighteen legally recognized religious sects. The religious clerics tend not only to encourage intra-sectarian marriages, as much as possible, but to reinforce the patriarchal familial structure in general. Thus, the state and religious institutions both rely on and work to construct family systems to keep individuals within their family structures. Political familism has a religious cosponsor.[154]

With this perspective in mind, the news that Iraq is considering formal establishment of sectarian family law is troubling. A proposed bill would consult the appropriate religious jurors according to the *husband's* faith.[155] In Lebanon, a similar provision led to religion-shopping on the part of men looking for the best personal outcome for themselves.[156] According to the Human Rights Watch, the gauntlet for women is daunting:

> Evangelical, Sunni, and Maronite courts alike dismiss evidence of abuse; while in Shia and Sunni divorce, women must prove the abuse "exceeds her husband's legal authority to discipline his wife." Catholics will not annul a marriage for abuse. In April 2014 Lebanon passed a landmark Law on Protection of Women and Family Members from Domestic Violence—but it is undercut by an exemption for personal status law and does not include marital rape.[157]

And, of course, these family sectarian courts are staffed almost exclusively by male judges.

Furthermore, the case of "borrowed law" adds an additional layer of complexity in the legal arena. For example, at independence, the North African countries of Morocco (1956), Algeria (1962), and Tunisia (1956) had the option to follow the French model of codified law or to return to the traditional system of Muslim religious courts. Each country saw a necessity for reform, and sought political consensus that allowed them to codify family law with some reforms (specific to each country) while still reflecting their Muslim heritage. At the same time, France, their colonial power, had yet to reform the Napoleonic Code of 1804, which had established a civil law based on male-dominated families. The North African countries eliminated some of the worst abuses of traditional Islamic law in their codes at that point. But many other problems, resulting in part from the French legacy, remained, which progressive reforms sought to rectify over the coming decades.[158] Htun and Weldon note that in an ironic twist, "Some customary laws in Africa granted women more rights to land than the colonial laws that replaced them . . . Often, colonial rule codified a more uniform and male-dominated version of indigenous practice than the social orders and family forms previously existing."[159]

Both India and Turkey instituted reforms that were influential as other Muslim countries began searching for models. Indian Muslim reformers tried to reform Muslim law to accord to some British standards of human rights resulting in the Muslim Marriage Act of 1939, which regulated family law for India's Muslim population. Turkey, the former seat of the Muslim caliphate, discarded traditional Islamic law and enacted the 1926 Civil Code, modeled after the 1912 Swiss personal status code. Thus, when discussing family and personal status law, it is important to recognize several historical layers of accretion in the law codes of former colonies and other regimes striving to break with the past, which may make reform that much more difficult.[160]

The path of family law reform is filled with zigs and zags, even in the twenty-first century, as may be expected when an issue of identity is involved.[161] For example, change may not always mean greater equity or safeguards for women, but rather the opposite. Following the demise of the Soviet Union, the bias of judges against women claimants when adjudicating divorce cases in Central Asian republics has become far more pronounced.[162] Some of these republics have even attempted to reintroduce legalized polygyny.[163]

This tension between individual rights, as recognized under the Convention on the Elimination on All Forms of Discrimination Against Women (CEDAW) and international human rights law, versus rights of the family and the community, is at its most powerful in issues concerning women and decision-making power within the family unit. It is not only men who may oppose such reforms; women may oppose them as well. For example, the heralded reforms to the Moroccan *mudawana* or family law code were facilitated by organized political action on the part of tens of thousands of Moroccan women and their male allies, which resulted in substantive change. Changes included increased autonomy for women, assertion of the wife's equal responsibility with the husband for maintenance of the family, and an increase in women's rights (e.g., to contract their own marriages, and to place all divorces before a judge). Equally notable was the degree of opposition to the reforms, even among women. Quite a few middle- and lower-class women were reluctant to endorse these reforms: many feared change, and some resented them as an unknown quantity pushed by the West and possibly prejudicial to women's well-being.[164]

Despite increasing international pressure to end legal discrimination against women, demands to be governed by religious or traditional systems of family law have instead increased in recent years. In several Western nations, religious minorities maintain that equal representation under the law is possible only if family law systems are recognized as part of the legal fabric of the country. These proposed enclaves would allow religious courts to rule on issues of family law and would also grant exceptions to rights recognized under each country's legal system.

Historically speaking, the concept of a legal enclave permitting diverse family law systems to coexist with a unified criminal law is not new. Far-flung empires, even more recent ones such as the Ottoman Empire and the British Empire, permitted localized family law systems based on religion and ethnicity. Several countries today, such as India and Bangladesh, maintain such a legal pluralism with regard to family law, with several family law systems being accommodated within the context of a common criminal code.[165] The advantages asserted for legal pluralism include respect for cultural and religious integrity, traditions, and practice, but also the diminishing of conflict among groups by segregating practice along community lines.[166]

Allowing cultural and religious identity to be preserved is a recognized human right: the United Nations in 1992 issued the "Declaration on the Rights of Persons Belonging to National or Ethnic, Religious and Linguistic Minorities" (A/RES/47/135), which in turn cited Article 27 of the International Covenant on Civil and Political Rights, declaring that "States shall take measures to create favorable conditions to enable persons belonging to minorities to express their characteristics and to develop their culture, language, religion, traditions and customs," but in the same breath continues, "except where specific practices are in violation of national law and contrary to international standards."[167] Minority communities, notably Muslims in Western countries, argue that secular countries are negating their religious and cultural traditions by rejecting the practice of their family law systems.[168]

The question of the universality of women's human rights cannot be avoided in this discussion about legal enclaves, however. For example, a 2009 United Nations Economic and Social Council report notes:

> Compatibility between certain individual rights, including freedom to practice a religion or faith or to observe rites, and women's fundamental rights as universal rights poses a major problem. The problem stems from the fact that the right to engage in certain practices injurious to women's health or their position before the law or their status in general is claimed by persons, communities or States pursuing those practices or perceiving them as a component of freedom of religion and as a religious duty by which they and their ancestors have been bound from time immemorial and which in their eyes appear unrelated to issues concerned with the universal protection of women's rights. Universality of the rights of women as individuals thus draws us into a classic yet still topical debate, that of the universality of human rights, and women's rights in particular, in the face of cultural diversity. The issue is a sensitive one since practices or norms that impair the status of women originate, from the standpoint of the discriminator, in what are regarded as deeply held beliefs and, on a practical level, in rules, regulations or values based on or imputed to religion.[169]

This legitimate concern for cultural and religious integrity poses a dilemma. In the West, universal application of law recognizes individuals as the fundamental unit of society with uniform legal rights and obligations. Other cultural and religious traditions, however, may recognize collectives as the basic unit, and these collectives generally privilege senior male members and create mechanisms of structural control of females by males.[170] It is difficult to mesh these two different legal traditions. Furthermore, as religious studies scholar Katherine Young insightfully notes, "When a religion has a predominantly ethnic base, any threat to the family is also a fundamental threat to the religion."[171]

Interestingly, evidence shows that Muslim women living outside of Muslim-majority countries may not in fact support religious law enclaves.[172] Jytte Klausen, author of a study that documented support for application of Islamic law in European countries, states that women "were notably less supportive of legal pluralism and multicultural devolution of authority to Islamic scholars and imams than were the male leaders."[173] This did not mean that the women were not observant Muslims. Although the women overwhelmingly sought freedom to practice their religion, they opposed being governed by religious personal status law. Three-quarters of the women in Klausen's study rejected the proposition that secular law should be changed to devolve authority to religious leaders in matters of personal law, as did half of the men. Klausen emphasizes that this rejection does not reflect levels of religiosity or women's positions on other issues.[174]

Klausen relates an interview with a young British lawyer who stated emphatically her allegiance to shari`a law. When told that even very religious Muslim women did not want imams and shari`a councils to issue binding decisions on family law matters, the woman exclaimed, "But oh no . . . they are right. You cannot trust these matters to imams. That would be terrible for women. We must have professionals make those decisions."[175] The question of whether women from cultures with relatively inequitable family law systems would prefer to be governed by secular family law is an important and underdeveloped area of research, deserving of greater attention by scholars in several social science fields. Legal scholar Robin Fretwell Wilson has offered the formula that parallel systems could be countenanced if and only if government courts are legally obligated to refuse the ruling of religious courts in the event that women, specifically, would be worse off under the religious judgment than a government judgment, concluding, "Society has a stake in the outcome."[176]

We believe Wilson is right: society does have a stake in the outcome, and this volume speaks to the point.[177] The relationship between law and practice is complex, and positive change depends on navigating that complexity. Law cannot dictate practice and often stands impotent before it, but law is nevertheless generally regarded as being a strong normative factor and capable of modifying practice over time, and importantly, of establishing state and community ideals.

In this sense, despite the ingrained nature of practice, contestation over law is often a critical first step in changing practice, although this process is long and complicated. In Uganda, under the Divorce Act, grounds for seeking divorce differ for men and women. For example, a man may obtain a divorce by proving his wife guilty of adultery. A woman seeking to divorce an adulterous husband not only must prove adultery but also must show that the husband committed, rape, bigamy, desertion, or sodomy to obtain a divorce and apply for a divorce settlement. A 2004 court case ruled that grounds for divorce should apply equally to men and women. Although it will take time for the court judgment to be accepted, judges held that the roles of men and women had changed significantly during the past century and the law should reflect this reality.[178]

Nevertheless, family law is a critical hinge point in the transition from the reliance on the Patrilineal/Fraternal Syndrome as the society's security provision mechanism to relinquishing that reliance. Htun and Weldon rightly observe that "as the state strengthens and expands, it often—but not always—seeks to seize control over family law from churches, clans, tribes, and other cultural communities. . . . Transformative state projects seeking to secularize, modernize, and civilize the nation and the polity are often played out on the terrain of the family."[179] We return to this point in part III, in which we discuss the dynamics of change.

Property and Inheritance Rights of Women

Keeping resources within the patriline, as we have seen, requires both that inheritance and property rights favor men and that major economic resources such as land will remain solely within male hands and be passed from male to male within the patriline. Thus, women's property rights in practice (as opposed to formal law) are strongly indicative of whether extended male kin networks play an important role in societal governance (see figure 3.11). As Fukuyama notes, "The ability of women to own and bequeath property is an indicator of the deterioration of tribal organization and suggests that strict patrilineality [has] disappeared."[180]

In societies reliant on the Patrilineal/Fraternal Syndrome as a security provision mechanism, brothers and husbands are the favored property holders, for they are the "true" members of the family, being the expression of the patriline.[181] With regard to brothers, Goody aptly notes, "Inheritance and marriage rules are seen as intimately related, both being linked to the mutual claims of brother and sister."[182] We thus see in many societies that a woman may have a lesser right (or no right) to inherit from her parents so that her brothers may inherit all real property. Given that patrilocal marriage attends this Syndrome, it is sons who will presumably stay and take care of their elderly parents, entitling them and their male descendants to the assets of the patriline.

　Virtually no discrimination is codified in law, and practice follows law
　Virtually no discrimination is codified, and practice tends to discriminate more than law
　Moderate discrimination may be codified in law, and practice follows law
　Moderate discrimination is codified in law, and practice discriminates even more than law
　Significant discrimination is codified in law, and practice follows law
　No data

FIGURE 3.11 Map of Property Rights in Law and Practice for Women, scaled 2017

Goods given by the bride's family at her wedding, or dowry (if that is the custom), are thus considered to be the inheritance of daughters, a type of premortem inheritance. Thus, even when women are given equal inheritance rights by formal law, they may feel they cannot exercise those rights because their brothers will be upset. Should the woman find herself divorced, it may well be these very brothers to whom she would have to turn for help. She cannot afford to anger them by asserting her inheritance rights, and so she will often sign over her land rights to her brothers.[183]

The situation is even more controversial with respect to husbands and their surviving widows. When a man dies, his agnatic kin may lay claim to all his goods, and in some cultures, this means that the widow, and possibly also her children, are left homeless and without any property at all. In other cultures, the children (especially sons) may be kept within the patriline, and only the wife is turned out. In yet other cultures, the dead man's property includes not only all of the man's material possessions, but also his children and even his wife. Women not only may not inherit from their husbands, but also may actually be inherited, usually by a brother of her dead husband, to whom she may owe wifely services, including childbearing.

Thus, a perfect storm can overtake a woman if she is widowed or divorced, given her lack of property rights. In a 2016 article, the *Economist* notes, "In several places custom dictates that only men can inherit land. In Uganda stories abound of widows being turfed off their marital land by in-laws. One woman was thrown out of her home a week after her husband died in an accident; she had refused to marry any of his five brothers, and her children were taken away to a sister-in-law."[184]

Land is especially salient in every discussion of women's property rights, and the thought that women could own land—one of the very foundations of the agnatic identity—would seem outrageous. Das Gupta's observation about Asia holds in other regions, as well: "Patrilineages functioned as corporations. Although land was privately held, people could not sell land inherited from the patrilineage to an outsider, without giving members of the lineage the first right of refusal."[185] Women, notably, are always considered "outsiders" to the patriline.

Thus, it makes sense that, for example, women own only 13 percent of land in India, even though three-quarters of Indian women make their living as farmers.[186] Estimates are that in the MENA region, only 4 percent of women have title to land.[187] Reporter Tina Rosenberg explains,

> The consequences are enormous. Without title, female farmers acting on their own don't have access to credit, subsidies, government programs for seeds, irrigation or fertilizer. They cannot get loans and do not invest to improve their yields. They live in fear that someone more powerful—which is everyone—can kick them off their land. When women's incomes suffer, so

do their children. More than 40 percent of all children under 5 in India are malnourished. And India's agricultural productivity is needlessly diminished. Landlessness also raises the risk of domestic violence.[188]

Indeed, research has shown that women who own land are up to eight times less likely to suffer domestic violence.[189] Furthermore, lack of land rights is associated with higher rates of HIV among women, which is attributed to lower bargaining power within the household for women, hampering them in negotiating safe sex practices.[190]

The lack of property and land rights severely hampers women, not only with regard to household-level bargaining between men and women that in turn affects their children but also as economic actors. Lack of property and land rights cuts a woman off from credit, for she has no real collateral to offer. It may also reduce her ability to live independently, for she cannot sell or lease real property. She may not be able to control how the land is used, or how the proceeds from the use of the land are distributed. In many cultures, political participation may be linked to land rights, as may head-of-household status, which may confer additional rights.[191]

These issues are so sensitive that even where great progress has been made on reform of personal status laws, such as we see in Morocco (2004) and Tunisia (1956 and 2014), the issue of inheritance—especially inheritance of land or other male-coded goods such as cattle—is still off limits in terms of reform, even at the time of this writing.[192]

As alluded to earlier in this subsection, property rights are a pivotal stage in transition away from reliance on the patrilineal/fraternal security provision mechanism. Goody concludes, "We should view the formal rights of women to inherit equally with their brothers both movable and immovable properties as the critical transforming agent."[193] Goody is of the opinion that

> The fact that women are heirs to significant property affects the whole nature of the conjugal relationship . . . leading it. . . . to be associated [with] the concept of "love." Gluckman has argued that "love" serves to separate both spouses from their kin (and kin groups), uniting them in a conjugal team. Such separation is an aspect of love in the modern Western world; if you have to love one woman more than someone else (whether sibling, parent, or partner), then a rationale is established for splitting society into spatially distinct groups based upon monogamous unions.[194]

In other words, women's property and land rights give rise to neolocal marriage, rather than patrilocal marriage, and neolocal marriage is also more resistant to polygyny.[195] In other words, several of the magnetic beads of the Syndrome begin to unlink when women's property rights are established.

Three Indicators of Violence Against Women, and Sanction of Such Violence

Human sexual dimorphism enabling most men to physically coerce most women (as noted in chapter 1), including the ability to impregnate them against their will through rape, is arguably at the heart of the first political order. If coercion and rape of women are given sanction, or at least impunity, within the collective, that choice will reverberate through every societal practice and institution. Indeed, virtually all of the components of the Syndrome, whether lack of property rights for women, son preference, or polygyny, are merely logical extensions of this foundational coercive choice.

Criminologist and gender scholar Hilde Jakobsen rightly proposes that "violence [must be] integrated into social theory in ways that recognize its significance both in maintaining social order and in the very constitution of the social . . . Violence constitutes social order, making and reproducing structures of inequality, [aided by] discourses that authorize violence."[196] "Consent," then, may be a façade behind which coercion hides. In her fieldwork in Tanzania, this was openly explained to Jakobsen as she asked questions about wife-beating.

More specifically, Jakobsen realized the norm underpinning the behavior was that "men should govern, and if they governed rationally, they could legitimately use violence to govern."[197] Her focus groups revealed that "A strategically administered beating could make a wife more governable . . . Steering a wife's choices, then, was a beating's legitimizing goal."[198] Indeed, the focus groups she worked with found it "hilarious or perverse" that a wife could beat her husband for his mistakes and faults, and so "women cannot beat men with the approval with which men can beat women . . . It was husbands, not wives, who should control their spouse by violence if necessary, and it was wives, not husbands, who should submit to this coercive control."[199] Why? The answer was really very simple: "to beat was to censure through violence, and that who censured whom was a question of who ruled whom. The good beating, then, is violence that orders society: supported by a dominant discourse insofar as it enforced a specific power order between husband and wife . . . the perceived social legitimacy of violence is what makes it powerful."[200] With coercion so near the surface, women develop strategies of self-defense that look like acquiescence: "Women's self-censorship is for self-protection . . . Women themselves enforce the norm so that men will not use violence to enforce it. This shows that it is not with full and free consent that women support the norms."[201]

Have any societies *not* made such a coercive choice in its first sexual political order? Peggy Reeves Sanday asserts there have been diarchic societies in which men and women rule together.[202] Usually, a system of checks and balances is in place, such as in societies where women own the land, appoint the male chiefs, and then retain veto power over his decisions. At the household level, men and women share responsibilities and actively cooperate. Men do not segregate themselves into a fraternal order, and sex is not a commodity. Interestingly, in these societies, Sanday asserts the concept of "gang rape" is unheard of.

Even Sanday admits, however, that such diarchic societies have been rare. Rather, what we see today are many societies in which the components of the Syndrome are still pretty much in place to one degree or another, and a few other societies where those components have been largely dismantled. Even in those latter cultures, however, the key reservoir allowing for possible resurgence of the Syndrome lies in the ubiquity of women's physical insecurity. For example, in a phenomenon dubbed the "Nordic Paradox," researchers have observed that Scandinavian countries have a disproportionately high level of intimate partner violence (IPV) compared with the rest of Europe. This is unexpected, for Scandinavian women have gained unprecedented levels of gender equality within their societies.[203] Whether this higher level of IPV stems from a backlash or simply higher reporting rates is unclear.

What is clear, however, is that within virtually all societies, it seems, women's everyday physical insecurity is viewed as completely unremarkable, and in this way, given tacit sanction. Levels of domestic violence, rape, and even domestic murder remain high, even in states that have largely done away with other components of the Syndrome.[204] Phumzile Mlambo-Ngcuka, executive director of UNWomen, has stated that "Violence is the biggest challenge facing women around the world," with "even countries that have the highest indicators on gender equality like Iceland, they still have to confront the issue of violence against women."[205]

In states encoding components of the Syndrome, violence may be endemic. Development scholar Deepa Narayan says of her nation, "India can arguably be accused of the largest-scale human rights violation on Earth: the persistent degradation of the vast majority of its 650 million girls and women." She explains:

> In 2016, the rape of minor girls increased by 82 percent compared with the previous year. Chillingly, across all rape cases, 95 percent of rapists were not strangers, but family, friends, and neighbors . . . Indian government surveys show that 42 percent of girls in the country have been sexually abused . . . Over 50 percent of Indian men and women still believe that sometimes women deserve a beating. One woman is killed every hour for not bringing in enough dowry to a husband.[206]

In South Africa, legal scholar Shima Baradaran found that South Africa is rightly called the rape capital of the world, with a woman raped every twenty-six seconds, and one in three South African women being raped in their lifetime. The norm of violence against women is ingrained in even the youngest in the society. Baradaran tells of a grandmother from the Eastern Cape who recounted that one evening her three-year-old grandson told her, "you better not take your panties off, grandma or I'll rape you in the night."[207] Her informants told her that rape was a form of compensation used by men who felt their status was threatened and thus must be reasserted in a dramatic fashion. Women were perceived as acceptable objects against which violence could be used, and rape was perceived as an act speaking directly to the perpetrator's masculinity.

Masculinity and violence against women was intertwined even when rape was not present; Baradaran found her Xhosa informants joked that "Xhosa men always keep a stick under their pillow, for their wife."[208] Interestingly, Baradaran felt that brideprice played a role in this view of women as objects who could be beaten or used sexually at will: "The Xhosa man pays *lobola* [and] the traditional view of women as property implies that a man may use any means to control his wife as he would his other property."[209] Bride raiding was also traditionally practiced in this culture, and the infidelity of men and lack of emotional attachment to women is highly praised. One convicted rapist summed up his mind-set, "I knew I was hurting her. It gave me power. I was in control."[210]

In our scaling of the Patrilineal/Fraternal Syndrome, we look specifically at three indicators to gain purchase on the level of control-by-coercion of women present in the society: (1) overall prevalence of violence against women, and then two measures of societal attitudes toward such violence, including (2) the existence of widespread sanction or impunity for those harming women under certain circumstances (e.g., honor killings, accusations of witchcraft), as well as (3) the construction of rape as a property crime perpetrated not primarily against a woman but against her male kin. That is, rather than the law recognizing the woman has been physically assaulted, the more important question appears to be restitution of honor to the woman's male kin. Under such a conceptualization, the law will often provide that a rapist may be exonerated if he offers to marry his victim, thus making good the property crime against the victim's male kin—but making the victim's life a double tragedy. The maps for each of these three indicators are presented in figures 3.12, 3.13, and 3.14.

Most important, male fraternity—the end goal of the Patrilineal/Fraternal Syndrome—depends on defining and then subjugating those who are other-than-men, that is, women. Sanday comments on how "abuse of women [is] a means to renew fraternal bonds and assert power as a brotherhood . . . the unstated goal is agreement and fraternal unity."[211] Because the "otherness" is based on sex, sexual aggression—particularly gang rape—becomes the ultimate symbolic display of male dominance. Sanday goes so far as to assert, "I suggest that rape is not an integral part of male nature, but the means by which men programmed for violence and control use sexual aggression to display masculinity

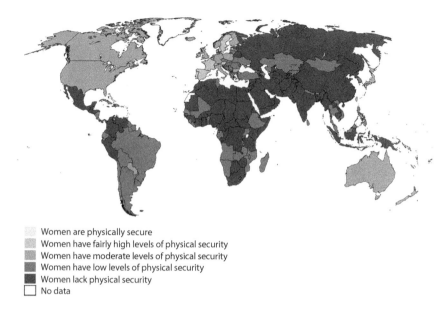

Women are physically secure
Women have fairly high levels of physical security
Women have moderate levels of physical security
Women have low levels of physical security
Women lack physical security
No data

FIGURE 3.12 Map of the Overall Physical Security of Women, scaled 2014

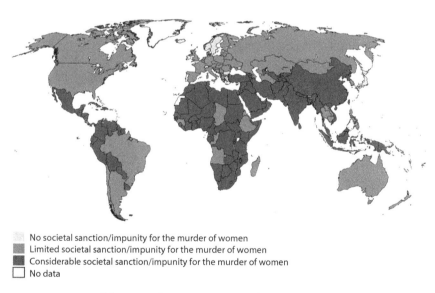

No societal sanction/impunity for the murder of women
Limited societal sanction/impunity for the murder of women
Considerable societal sanction/impunity for the murder of women
No data

FIGURE 3.13 Map of the Societal Sanction/Impunity for the Murder of Women/Femicide, scaled 2016

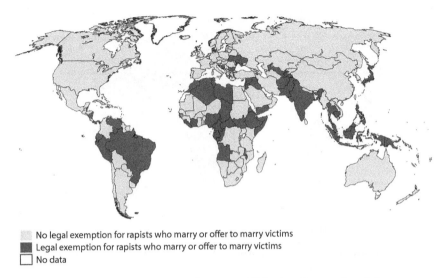

No legal exemption for rapists who marry or offer to marry victims
Legal exemption for rapists who marry or offer to marry victims
No data

FIGURE 3.14 Map of Legal Exemption for Rapists if Marriage Proposed, scaled 2015

and to induct men into masculine roles."[212] As a consequence, love and compassion are reserved for brothers only. Even the "bro talk" about "tits and asses" that accompanies Wall Street financial circles shows how "the bonding . . . goes hand in hand with the objectification of the other sex."[213]

Although men may have depended on women when they were children, they now feel liberated from that dependence on their mothers by becoming dependent solely on the fraternal bond. That bond demands men earn the respect of other men through the repudiation and the subordination of anything female. After all, "Without the fraternity there is no power—there is certainly no power that accrues to the individual male."[214] Dominance carries with it not only a feeling of potency, then, but also a sense of security, while those who are dominated feel fear and depression.[215] Furthermore, even in the context of a male dominance hierarchy in which nonelite males may experience domination, they can always recapture those heady feelings by dominating those who are not part of the fraternity—women, in the first place, but also out-groups. As sociologist Theodore Kemper expresses it, "the dominant are not dependent for their sense of well-being on the voluntary responses of others. The dominant simply take what they want."[216]

That this learned behavior cascades outward can be seen in the interviews Sanday conducted with fraternity members in the United States; one instructive quote from just such a young man states, "The belief that 'no means yes' is not necessarily just a notion of convenience to allow us to push for gratification. It is part of the general cycle of abuse and ignoring the needs of others by which we learn to pursue *all* of our social and sexual goals with other people."[217] Truly, the bootcamp for autocracy is often the relationship between the sexes, or as political scientist Ariel Ahram observes, "Modes of gender domination offer models for domination and marginalization of other groups."[218]

Coercion for the sake of asserting masculinity is a prominent motivation for violence at the level of individual males, but it is also true that the logic holds at the kin group level, as well. The interests of the male kin group must dominate over female interests, but patrilines often find that women—even women born to the patriline—often do not share their interests. Mothers may object to child marriages of their daughters. Sisters may object to a lack of inheritance. Wives may object to male dominance in household decision making, including decisions that bring a new wife into the family. Therefore, in addition to inequities in family law that keep male interests superordinate— such as arranged child marriage, polygyny, and patrilocality—the patriline is also prepared to use physical force to enforce the dominance of its interests over those of women. Thus, we expect that societies reliant on the Patrilineal/ Fraternal Syndrome as a security provision mechanism would tolerate the highest levels of violence against women (even though all societies tolerate a significant level of such violence).[219] That is why even when new laws against violence against women are proposed, such as in Morocco, spousal abuse is often excepted, for the woman is the property, if you will, of the patriline.[220]

To uphold the patriline's interests in cases where childhood socialization is not effective, more coercive means will be unveiled. In Rizvi and colleagues' study, they conducted thirty focus group interviews with 250 women in Pakistan, a country with a high Syndrome score. They found that

> from childhood, girls are informed, taught and trained to believe that only men who are physically powerful and hence mentally competent to make decisions; "*She is counseled, and if this does not work, she is forced through threats and violence to believe that she is an object that has to be operated by a male family member*" [emphasis added]. In cases where women challenge these patriarchal privileges and/or seek to enforce their rights, violence is used as a means to control them.[221]

Moreover, they explain that the types of violence the women in their study were quite varied: "It could be physical ranging from slapping to burning; verbal such as taunting, use of bad language; mental like threats of divorce and actual divorce; and sexual in the form of rape and incest."[222]

Violence against women in the home is endemic in our world. Note, however, that the levels of violence are the highest in those countries encoding more of the components of the Patrilineal/Fraternal Syndrome. The Demographic and

Health Surveys (DHS) ask whether wife-beating is justified. Although data are missing for many countries, the following is a sample of countries with the highest percentages reported among men, with the Syndrome score of the country noted in parentheses (table 3.1).

These are fairly alarming percentages, and it comes as no surprise that these countries also encode for many other components of the Syndrome, as indicated by their scores on that scale. The wide variety of forms of violence against women is also staggering—from estimates that one woman is killed every hour in India because of insufficient dowry,[223] to estimates that up to two hundred women are killed each year as witches in Papua New Guinea[224] (a country where 41 percent of men admitted to having raped a woman who was not their partner, and 13 percent of rapes are committed against girls under the age of seven years old).[225]

It comes as no surprise, then, that societal sanction is often given to the harming or even killing of women, providing impunity for such crimes.[226] Reasons of male honor are often invoked, and these crimes may have deep cultural resonance. As Al Lily explains about Saudi Arabia, "masculinity is measured not mainly according to how muscular and tough a man is, but also according to how jealous and protective he is of his female relatives. The masculinity of a man is questioned if a female relative of his has done anything immoral or culturally inappropriate. His masculinity comes into question if anything bad happens to her, and he could not protect her."[227] In Ecuador, the saying goes, "A man's honor lies between the legs of a woman."[228]

Even in more developed countries, there may be subcultures where male honor is inextricably tied up with female sexual behavior. In Texas (appeal decided 2002), a man was given a four months' sentence for killing his ex-wife due to "sudden passion," while given fifteen years for wounding her lover at the very same time.[229] These crimes are so universal that special terms have been coined to denote them such as "femicide," "honor killings," or "honor suicides" (which are typically forced suicides, and therefore more rightly regarded as murders).

Sanction for a female's killing may extend beyond a woman's sexual behavior to any type of "deviant" woman. As we have seen, if one is regarded as a "witch," one may be killed with impunity in certain cultures. Often perpetrators feel they are undertaking a heroic task. One of a mob who killed a "witch" in Papua New Guinea was quoted as saying, "I see myself as a guardian angel. We feel that we kill on good grounds and we're working for the good of the people in the village."[230]

This idea that the femicide is a virtuous act is common. The brother who kills to cleanse the family honor after his sister has been raped may say, "Yes, she's my sister and I love her, but it is a duty."[231] When this degree of societal sanction for femicide exists, it is clear the interests of the patriline and the fraternity are paramount.

TABLE 3.1 Percent of Men Who Feel Wife-Beating Is Justified

Country (Syndrome Score)	Percent of Men Who Feel Wife-Beating Is Justified (%)
Afghanistan (15)	72
Albania (9)	36
Azerbaijan (8)	58
Bangladesh (14)	36
Burundi (10)	44
Chad (14)	51
Congo (11)	40
Cote d'Ivoire (13)	42
Democratic Republic of Congo (11)	61
Equatorial Guinea (12)	52
Eritrea (12)	45
Gabon (13)	40
Guinea (13)	66
India (14)	42
Kyrgyzstan (9)	50
Laos (8)	49
Lesotho (14)	40
Madagascar (9)	46
Mali (14)	51
Myanmar (7)	49
Pakistan (14)	32
Solomon Islands (13)	57
Timor-Leste (12)	81
Uganda (12)	44
Tanzania (14)	40
Uzbekistan (8)	61
Vanuatu (10)	60

Source: UNICEF (updated 2017).

Even when laws exist to protect women from violence, as they do in almost all modern states, they may seldom be enforced. For example, the State Department's human rights report on Rwanda for 2007 notes that in police stations, the government did not feed detainees awaiting hearings or transfers. Police regularly told victims of violence and rape, especially women, that if they did not provide food to their attacker, they would release him.[232] To make matters worse, a woman often would face sexual assault at the hands of the police when she delivered the food required to keep her rapist in jail.

Another example comes from Algeria. In 2015, all cheered when Algeria passed a new law against domestic violence, providing for up to twenty years' detention for those found guilty of injuring one's spouse, and up to life in prison if the violence resulted in death. The legislation, however, included a clause that the woman could legally "pardon" her attacker, and if she did, he would not be prosecuted.[233] The pressure on the woman to pardon her husband would be immense under such circumstances, thus, in a sense, making the law null and void. Worldwide, according to the World Health Organization, about 40 percent of all murders of women are committed by intimate partners.[234]

Our third and final indicator examines whether a rapist can be exonerated if he offers to marry his victim. When rape is considered a property crime against a patriline, and not a crime against a woman, the society is again foregrounding the interests of the patriline and the fraternity over and against the interests of women. As Yuval Harari observes, "In many societies women were simply the property of men, most often their fathers, husbands or brothers. Rape, in many legal systems, falls under property violation—in other words, the victim is not the women who was raped but the male who owns her."[235] This is linked to the fact that the woman's body is perceived not to belong to her, but to the group. Jacobson suggests, "Virginity reflects a commitment—perhaps a forced commitment—to the community . . . Virginity represents sacrifice of self and body to the larger good, a spiritual virtue, a commitment to social institutions from family to the community."[236]

More specifically, in 2015, 51 countries had laws that exonerate rapists if they offer to marry their victim, usually accompanied by a payment of cash or assets to the father's family.[237] The double trauma caused to such women—rape, then forced to marry your rapist—may be enough to induce suicide. In fact, Morocco changed its law on rape exoneration because of the suicide of Amina Filali, who was only sixteen years old when she swallowed rat poison to escape being married to her rapist.[238] Tunisia and Jordan have followed suit, but as of this writing, such laws were still on the books in countries such as Lebanon, the Philippines, Tajikistan, and several other countries as our map shows.[239] Furthermore, it may be that conceptualizing it as a property crime against men catalyzes rape as a form of plunder during wartime.[240]

All in all, then, any examination of the Patrilineal/Fraternal Syndrome must give an account of the coercion that undergirds its first political order. From that fountainhead of violence come not only the components of the Syndrome but also a cascade of negative effects that sap the stability, resilience, and security of the society.

Concluding Thoughts

We have traversed an immense amount of ground in this chapter. In great detail, we have examined the logic of each subordinative mechanism in the Patrilineal/Fraternal Syndrome, noted its current prevalence worldwide, and assessed its negative effects on the lives of women and girls. We have illuminated how these mechanisms interlock, forming a tightly woven straitjacket constraining women. We noted that this straitjacket can exist even in the presence of high female literacy and with high female labor force participation as well as in the context of relatively high levels of representation of women in the national legislature. We have trained our eyes to see these Syndrome mechanisms at work much closer to home.

It is now time to assess whether the Patrilineal/Fraternal Syndrome not only constrains and harms women, but also constrains and harms the larger society. We argue that what is done to women, ultimately is done to the nation-state. If women are subject to autocracy in their homes, so will the society be subject. If women are terrorized in their homes, so will the society be challenged by terrorism. If women are exploited by corruption in their homes, so will the society be plagued with exploitation and corruption.

In part II, we take an inventory of those negative effects for the larger society of the choice to subordinate women. We first lay out a theoretical framework from which we derive testable empirical propositions linking the presence of the Syndrome to a wide-ranging set of negative outcomes on dimensions of national security and stability. We end part II with a comprehensive empirical investigation of these propositions.

PART II

THE EFFECTS OF THE FIRST POLITICAL ORDER

CHAPTER 4

THE EFFECTS OF THE SYNDROME, PART ONE

Governance and National Security

The issue of justice within households is significant because the family is the first, and arguably the most influential, school of moral development . . . The myriad interconnections between life within the household and life outside of it must be recognized.

—Susan Moller Okin

Reliance on the patrilineal/fraternal security provision mechanism means that one's society is rooted in a fundamentally authoritarian and violent sexual order, and this fact has important consequences for the larger political order, as well as for the stability and resilience of the group or nation-state. We examine those linkages in this chapter. In chapters 5 and 6, we look more specifically at the structural goads catalyzing societal instability created by the Syndrome's predisposition for marriage market obstruction and examine other types of macrolevel consequences, including implications for human, economic, and environmental security. Political scientist Scott Weiner has rightly noted that "the linkage between familial and state-level patriarchy is widely asserted but not well specified . . . These accounts assert that familial patriarchy is 'reproduced' [at the state level] without explaining the mechanisms by which that reproduction occurs."[1] We take up the challenge to specify those links and mechanisms in this part II of the book.

The ancient security provision mechanism of the Patrilineal/Fraternal Syndrome, as specified in part I, does accrue tangible benefits to at least some group members, otherwise, it would not exist or persist or be as ubiquitous as it is across time and cultures. Physical security for individuals in the face of out-group threats is provided by the male kin alliance (although for women, physical security against out-groups does not preclude grave physical insecurity from violence perpetrated by in-group males). Through strong deterrent signaling and the quasi-legal codes that spring up around that signaling, the risk of intergroup violence can be diminished, at least for a time, by male kin alliances. These quasi-legal codes, often referred to as codes of honor, are often harsh toward individuals in an effort to satisfy debts of honor between groups. As Weiner explains: "Collective liability thereby moderates infractions against other clans, enabling kin groups to coexist peaceably despite being autonomous and responsible to themselves alone."[2]

Despite its persistence and prevalence, reliance on the extended male kin group for security "comes with a profound price."[3] We detailed in part I the profound price that women pay. But women are not the only ones who pay. Given the authoritarian and violent nature of its foundational sexual order, we argue the Patrilineal/Fraternal Syndrome breeds a fragile societal peace based on a combination of dominance (sticks) and side-payments (carrots), or as the political scientist Edward Schatz puts it, "clan balancing" and "clan clientelism."[4] Should the effectiveness of either tactic wane, the political order begins to crumble as well, unleashing the violent pursuit of dominance as power is contested within the society—very much like how when women attempt to leave abusive relationships, they find their lives, and the lives of their children, most in peril.[5]

Our overall argument is that reliance on the Patrilineal/Fraternal Syndrome and its subordination of women does not produce healthy, functional nation-states. For example, development expert Clare Castillejo notes the presence of a "mutually-reinforcing relationship between gender inequality and the weak governance, under-development and conflicts that characterise [fragile] states."[6] Because the Syndrome is so prevalent across culture, time, and space, some suggest it must be adaptive. Not so, we assert. As Patricia Gowaty notes,

One cannot assume that because a character is common, it is adaptive and has evolved by natural selection. This point is important to any arguments that assume that all gender differences are adaptive. There are many who argue that because sexual division of labor (and power) is so widespread, it must be adaptive, and, further, it must be genetically based. However, there is no evidence that either statement is correct . . . I find little in the biology of gender differences that requires us to maintain the unequal status of men and women in society. Whatever it is that does account for those phenomena, it is "not in our genes."[7]

Malcolm Potts and Thomas Hayden extend Gowaty's point, suggesting the subordination of women produces unnaturally dysfunctional outcomes: "The proverbial man from Mars—or woman from Venus—would surely find it odd that the members of one sex should behave in this way, hazarding their own lives and inflicting so much pain on others."[8] The polity, in a real sense, may come to resemble the typical Syndrome-based households found within it, in which can be found the almost daily use of dominance, control, extortion, and injustice on a day-to-day basis. When that order is threatened, the polity may be consumed by a paroxysm of violence not unlike a domestic murder-suicide. Let us examine the more specific linkages to state governance, security, and stability in the following sections.

Conceptualizing State Security and Stability

National security can be defined as "a capacity to control those domestic and foreign conditions that the public opinion of a given community believes necessary to enjoy its own self-determination or autonomy, prosperity and wellbeing,"[9] but that "capacity" needs to be further defined.[10]

In its working papers, the Princeton Project on National Security suggests ten key functions of the state that gauge its capacity to ensure state security: a legitimate monopoly on the means of violence, administrative control, sound management of public finances, investment in human capital, the creation of citizenship right and duties, the provision of infrastructure, the regulation of the market, management of state assets, effective management of international relations, and maintenance of the rule of law.[11] Development and foreign policy strategist Clare Lockhart suggests that "a state is fragile . . . where one or more of these functions have really eroded or are not being performed properly."[12] Pertinent to our discussion of Syndrome-based polities, international relations scholar Barry Buzan further points out that national security "presupposes a strong state (where government and society enjoy a high degree of consensual integration)," which means that "the concept of national security is difficult to apply to weak states (low integration between government and society and high levels of coercion) because feuding parts will make their own security claims against each other."[13]

Stable states, then, are states that have moved beyond insecurity by achieving capacity in the provision of state functions, as listed earlier, and that are not significantly regressing on these measures. A stable state, accordingly, is relatively secure, so that when we speak of state stability, inferences about state security can be made as well.

We must remember, as historian Ira Lapidus observes, that "we are dealing with a system involving two types of political and cultural entities [on] the same territory, competing for power and legitimacy."[14] The extent to which male-bonded kin networks or clans degrade state stability is dependent, then, on the degree to which these networks have "captured" state institutions and capabilities. Even in the presence of a functional state government, such capture becomes easier under certain conditions, such as endemic economic shortages and other types of exigency.

Capture mechanisms are plentiful, and include clan-based voting, kin-based patronage, the stripping of state assets (such as oil) by clans in power, and what Kathleen Collins calls "crowding out" participation of nonclan members in formal institutions, such as political parties, the media, or unions by clan mobilization. "By pervading formal institutions . . . clans use the [state's] assets to fortify their group, effectively bankrupting state coffers, decentralizing state power, and creating competing wealth/power centers where they govern through an informal regime of clan bargaining," she explains.[15]

Collins concludes that "clan politics is not democratic. Even if civil and political liberties exist, clan politics creates informal political and economic rules that are not pluralist, equally and fully participatory and representative, or transparently contested. Clan politics therefore undermine formal civil and political liberties."[16]

The tension between the goals of the clans and the state lead many to conclude, as Collins does, that "tribes and states have created and maintained each other in a single system, though one of inherent instability, [and that] tribes have proved an unstable basis on which to build the future of [a] country."[17] In what specific ways, then, might greater reliance on patrilineality and fraternity as a security provision mechanism affect state security and stability? We assert six specific causal pathways in this chapter:

- Force as the preferred means of conflict resolution.
- Autocracy as the preferred regime type.
- Raiding for the rents upon which governance is based.
- Corruption and nepotism integral to governance.
- Impunity instead of the rule of law.
- Chronic fissioning of the group, resulting in annihilative political feuding, terrorism, rebellion, and harsh treatment of out-group members.

Force as the Preferred Means of Conflict Resolution

If the sexual political order is maintained through violence or the threat of violence by men, then the barriers to the use of force as a conflict resolution mechanism will be quite low. Indeed, violence may be the default approach within such a society. For example, the research of international relations scholars Elin Bjarnegard, Erik Melander, Victor Asal, and others empirically demonstrates that the belief that women are men's inferiors is associated with greater hostility toward other nations as well as toward minority groups within one's own nation and is predictive of actual engagement in political violence for both individuals and organizations.[18]

This is to be expected. Psychologists argue that the key to training an individual to become violent both within the family and in peer groups is to demonstrate the functionality of violence. Violence and coercion must "work" for these to be perpetuated. The reactions of parents, siblings, and peers teach individuals to select actions that work and to ignore those that do not. Male children who imitate the violence they observe against women in the home are likely to perpetuate it as long as it gets them what they want. "Events [of male violence against women] operate to glue the male group as a unified entity; it establishes fraternal bonding and helps boys to make the transition to their vision of a powerful manhood—in unity against women, one against the world. The patriarchal bonding functions a little like bonding in organized-crime circles, generating a sense of family and establishing mutual aid connections that will last a lifetime."[19]

Where violence against women is allowed to persist, individuals (especially men) are committing continual, possibly daily, acts of aggression and violence against women, which may not only be applauded by male peers, but for which they are afforded virtually complete impunity. As we have argued in previous work,[20] extrapolating from Patterson's model, the relative rate of reinforcement is a significant predictor for the relative rate of aggressive behavior, and the rate of reinforcement for violence against women is extremely high, resulting in overlearned violent acts that become automatic.[21] This strongly suggests that violence at different levels is connected. States that allow violence against women to persist are allowing men—that half of society that holds both physical and political power—to engage in frequent, even daily, antisocial acts. Theodore Kemper draws the connection for us:

> At the micro level, the powerful control their interpersonal environments through verbal and physical violence, preemptive decisions, reducing others to dependency, and forming coalitions . . . At the macro level, the powerful not only enforce socialization codes and define reality through culture, they also beat, arrest, and imprison opponents; they enforce deference routines by painful sanctions; they compel conformity by inducing fear of punishment; they overcome opponents in direct confrontations and . . . through decrees and by direct exclusion.[22]

The witnessing of violence against women in one's household as a child is particularly significant. Priya Nanda and colleagues found that "rigidly masculine" factors, such as "witness of childhood discrimination and violence against women, lower education, and economic stress" tripled the odds of men committing violence.[23] A 2003 study published in the *Journal of Interpersonal Violence* found that boys who experienced domestic violence in their childhood home were four times more likely to become perpetrators later on.[24] Pamela Shifman of the NoVo Foundation comments, "Violence tends to be first experienced in the home [and] is often the root justifier of all violence."[25]

We underestimate the larger social and political consequences of homes imbued with violence against women. Rose McDermott notes, "Why should we be surprised that children come to believe that might equals right because that is the relationship they see between their mothers and fathers? Children do not outgrow such developmental disturbances. Instead, they carry such a paradigm of inequality and violence into their larger personal, professional, and social lives and seek to re-create hierarchies of dominance that are natural, but also learned."[26] This socialization can be found worldwide, in countries rich and poor; for example, an eleven-year-old Australian boy told his mother, "I'll slit your throat and put a bullet to your brain"—because he had witnessed his father say the same to her.[27]

Political scientist Dara Kay Cohen explains how this takes place, using the example of rape used by rebel and state soldiers during civil war: an individual must be trained to overcome an

> innate hesitation to commit violence, and especially violence that is physically close, such as rape. Once this hesitation is overcome, whether through training that simulates battle or simply through force or pressure to commit violence, violent behavior then tends to lead to more violence. This occurs through one of several processes: desensitization, moral disengagement, or other forms of "dissonance reduction" that allows individuals to justify committing violence they once found repugnant.[28]

That "dissonance reduction" is already primed in the households where women are treated as the inferiors of men and are subject to domestic violence. The same process has been documented in cases of child warriors forced to "commit horrifying acts of violence within their own communities with the intention of breaking the bond between children and their communities."[29]

Even sexism without violence in the home can create a hierarchical order based on sex, justifying such similar hierarchy in social relations outside the home. As one anonymous *New York Times* commenter eloquently put it,

> If kids who grow up seeing sexism, even if subtle, in their own homes as so many do it normalizes the idea that some people are inherently superior to others. I believe this makes prejudice against other groups that are not intimate acquaintances much more likely. After all, if Dad is dismissive of Mom's work,

feelings or ideas, if he neglects or devalues chores our society views as "women's work," kids will pick up on this even if nothing is ever explicitly said. Both boys and girls unconsciously internalize the idea that the women are somehow "less than." If it is normal to treat those you love this way why would you hesitate to treat strangers even worse? If we want a society that does not discriminate against minorities we need to "denormalize" discrimination and prejudice against our own moms and sisters.[30]

What men overlearn with regard to their interpersonal relationships with women will become the toolkit they carry into positions of power in the larger society. For example, Potts and Hayden note, "Once individuals are identified as belonging to an out-group, there seems to be no limit to the human capacity for cruelty."[31] The first out-group for men is always women, and scholars have noted that one of the first signs of dehumanization of a group is its *feminization*. That is why to be called a "woman" is an insult for men across nearly all cultures, and why individuals with highly gender unequal beliefs are so much more hostile to minorities and foreigners—these groups are perceived, socially, as "women."[32]

Sulome Anderson interviewed captured ISIS fighters in 2016, and their comments when she asked about the treatment of women demonstrate how feminization and dehumanization are of a piece. One fighter said, "Women exist to be married and have children . . . Women survive; they do not live." Another, asked how he would feel if his own mother were raped, as he had raped other women, said, "Even if it were my mother, that is Islamic sharia law and I would not mind because it would be for the jihad. We treat women the way we are required to by Islamic law, not human law. This is how they are supposed to live. They are second-class humans."[33] No wonder men are so afraid to be perceived as feminized.

Ultimately, then, the foreign policy of human groups, including modern states, may be more dangerous because of the human male evolutionary legacy to form male-bonded kin groups as a security provision mechanism. Richard Wrangham and Dale Peterson analyze the primate roots of behavior that results when "males hold sway by combining into powerful, unpredictable status-drive and manipulative coalitions, operating in persistent rivalry with other such coalitions":

Unfortunately, there appears something special about foreign policy in the hands of males. Among humans and chimpanzees at least, male coalitionary groups often go beyond defense [typical of monkey matriarchies] to include unprovoked aggression, which suggests that our own intercommunity conflicts might be less terrible if they were conducted on behalf of women's rather than men's interests. Primate communities organized around male interests naturally tend to follow male strategies and, thanks to sexual selection, tend to seek power with an almost unbounded enthusiasm.[34]

A fascinating study by evolutionary psychologist Aaron Sell and colleagues suggests some linkages from male dominance to the use of force as a preferred method of dispute resolution. This research team finds that the physical strength of the survey respondent was a significant predictor of support for the use of force not only in interpersonal conflict, but also in international conflicts.[35] This finding was much more robust for men than for women: strong men were far more prone to anger and to consider themselves entitled to better treatment, and they also were more likely to prevail in conflicts of interest—and thus become leaders. Such men are more likely to experience overconfidence on the eve of aggression, lowering the psychic barriers to aggressive action.[36]

Because we feel the socialization for force as a preferred method of conflict resolution comes from daily experience of the effective subordination of women by men in Syndrome societies, it is worth considering once more the conclusions reached by Bjarnegard and Melander, who found in cross-national analysis that individuals with highly gender unequal beliefs were also far more hostile toward other nations as well as toward minorities within their own society. In additional findings, they note that male survey respondents in Thailand with more highly gender unequal beliefs were also significantly more likely to actually participate in political violence (sociologist Ana Velitchkova notes similar results from Africa).[37] They propose that "patriarchal values lead to othering, and that masculine toughness drives violent aggression, so that honor ideology predisposes men to participate in political violence."[38] Middle East studies scholar Sebastian Maisel notes this dynamic at play in contemporary Saudi Arabia, where "tribal discussion forums frequently report about clashes between young tribal members over issues of honor, pride, status, or genealogies."[39] These observations suggest that Syndrome-encoding societies would be predisposed toward increased levels of conflict within their nation and in relations to other nations.

More specifically, societal expectations of benefits from violence at every level of analysis will almost certainly be higher if men, who dominate political power in every human society, have received both tangible benefit and obvious impunity from committing aggressive acts toward women. Benefit and impunity abound, for as Peggy Reeves Sanday notes, "In an all-male social group, the disparagement of women is, invariably, an important ingredient of the mystical bond, and sexual aggression the means by which the bond is renewed."[40] Indeed, numerous researchers have noted the association between sexism and warfare. Marvin Harris, for example, comments that martial societies "have correspondingly more pronounced forms of male sexism . . . In keeping with this intense pattern of warfare, relations between . . . men and women are markedly hierarchical and androcentric."[41]

Force not only is legitimized in this way but also can become valorized as the preferred conflict resolution mechanism of the society. After all, "the ability to exclude fellow humans from our emotional in-group may well be the trait underlying much of what we call evil . . . and such 'evil' acts have made evolutionary sense for males for many millions of years."[42] In the sexual order of the Patrilineal/Fraternal Syndrome we have explicated, men first learn to practice such emotional exclusion on women.[43]

Numerous recent aggregate statistical findings underscore these conclusions.[44] Political scientists Monty Marshall and Donna Ramsey find a relationship between women's disempowerment and state willingness to use force.[45] International relations scholar Mary Caprioli finds that greater domestic gender equality is correlated with less emphasis by the state on using military force to resolve international disputes.[46] Caprioli and Mark Boyer find that severity of violence used in an international conflict decreases with greater levels of domestic gender equality.[47] Political scientists Patrick Regan and Aida Paskeviciute find that the degree of women's access to political power in a society is predictive of the likelihood of that state engaging in interstate disputes and war.[48] Caprioli and Peter Trumbore find that states with lower levels of gender equality are more likely to be the aggressors and to initiate the use of force in interstate disputes, which has been confirmed in research by David Sobek, Rodwan Abouharb, and Christopher Ingram.[49] Caprioli and Trumbore, as well as Melander, find that states with lower levels of domestic gender equality are more likely to be involved in intrastate conflict.[50] Security studies scholars Cameron Harris and Daniel Milton find that states with higher levels of gender inequality also have significantly higher levels of domestic terrorism.[51] Political violence scholar Victor Asal and colleagues find that states with greater commitment to gender equality show greater predisposition to peaceful strategies of contention, and found the same to be true with ethno-political subnational movements.[52] Caprioli and colleagues find that states with higher levels of violence against women are also less peaceful internationally, less compliant with international norms, and less likely to have good relations with neighboring states and that violence against women is a better predictor of these outcomes than level of democracy, level of wealth, or presence of Islamic civilization.[53] Melander finds men

> who endorse honour ideology tend to view relations with others as a zero-sum conflict rather than a positive sum competition. Consequently, states where honour ideology is strong can be expected to produce and be influenced by more offensive realists, and fewer defensive realists, and therefore power transitions that involve such states will indeed be particularly threatening . . . Those who endorse honour ideology are thus particularly likely to take perceived affronts to their nation personally, and to react with demands for a strong response.[54]

Political scientists Reed Wood and Mark Ramirez demonstrate from a nationally representative U.S. survey that those who have more gender egalitarian attitudes exhibit lower support for the use of force to achieve security objectives, such as ensuring the oil supply and fighting terrorism, except in cases such as those involving genocide or other serious human rights abuses for which support is actually higher.[55] From this body of research, we conclude that a deep connection exists between attitudes toward gender equality and attitudes toward violence, including political violence.

Specific components of the Patrilineal/Fraternal Syndrome may aggravate the predisposition toward the use of force. For example, the typically high fertility rates of Syndrome societies, resulting from the repression of female family planning interests, predispose those societies to conflict: as Anthony Lopez, Rose McDermott and Michael Petersen note, "one of the strongest predictors in explaining the severity of modern wars is the frequency of young males in the relevant populations. As the frequency of young males increases, so does the severity of the war."[56] Furthermore, they note the intersection of male population and marriage market obstruction,[57] a topic that will be explored more thoroughly in chapter 5, by noting that men who are disadvantaged in the marriage market may actively seek heroic success in battle to improve their status.

The most illustrative example of how components of the Syndrome aggravate conflict, however, is that of polygyny.[58] Polygyny produces especially unstable societies, because it means that certain men in the clan will have several mates, whereas others may have none, undermining the solidarity necessary among the men of the group. Interestingly, evolutionary biologist Richard D. Alexander has posited that the first evidence of transition away from a clan-based foundation of society is the prohibition of polygyny: "It is almost as if no nation can become both quite large and quite unified except under socially imposed monogamy. . . . Socially imposed monogamy inhibits the rise of the kind of disproportionately large and powerful lineages of close relatives."[59] Anthropologists also have found significant correlation between polygyny and the amount of warfare in which societies engage.[60] Satoshi Kanazawa suggests that "polygyny may be the first law of intergroup conflict (civil wars),"[61] and James Boone even suggests that polygynous societies are more likely to engage in expansionist warfare to distract low-status males who may be left without mates.[62]

Anthropologist Jillian Keenan, in her work on Burundi, has found that polygyny's linkage to high fertility has fueled bloody land conflicts in that country. Polygynous men may have twenty or more sons who must all be satisfied with a tiny share of a plot of land, causing brother to turn against half-brother, brothers against cousins, sons against fathers, and even wives against husbands. Keenan notes, "within polygamous families, sons born by different mothers fight for finite land. In Muramvya, people speak in low voices about a woman who slit her husband's throat to accelerate a land inheritance for her son." Keenan interviews a nurse working at a family planning clinic: "[Christine] Nimbona says that of the roughly 30 patients she sees each week, 'almost all' cite fears about land resources and potential inheritance conflicts as their reasons for seeking family planning. 'I know that by what I am doing, I am fighting the escalation of violence in my country,' Nimbona says."[63] Not surprisingly, Burundi has the worst ranking on the Global Hunger Index as a result of too little land and too many sons.

Polygyny, however, is but an extreme example. Speaking more broadly, we would expect that states where the structural control of women by men is allowed to persist will exhibit not only higher levels of violence against women but also higher levels of authoritarianism, greater use of force in conflict resolution with resulting higher levels of violence within society, and lower levels of state peacefulness at home and abroad. This is a proposition that has unaccountably received little attention in the field of security studies. Azar Gat notes, "Students of war scarcely think of sexuality as a motive for fighting. The underlying links that connect the various elements of the human motivational system have largely been lost sight of."[64] Wrangham and Peterson elaborate why it is crucial to include a gender lens in explaining violence conflict:

> Humans are cursed with males given to vicious, lethal aggression. Thinking only of war, putting aside for the moment rape and battering and murder, the curse stems from our species' own special party-gang traits: coalitionary bonds among males, male dominion over an expandable territory, and variable party size. The combination of these traits means that killing a neighboring male is usually worthwhile, and can often be done safely.[65]

What evolution has produced in men, generally speaking, is a tendency "to seek power with an almost unbounded enthusiasm" and to engage in "unprovoked aggression."[66] Potts and Hayden observe that "male Homo sapiens . . . have an inherited predisposition to team up with kin—or *perceived kin*—and try to kill their neighbors."[67] Note, then, that nationalist identity can substitute for biological kin ties, as "shared cultural traits functio[n] as cues for kinship."[68]

It is Stephen Rosen who postulates a concrete explanatory linkage between the logic of clan aggression and the logic of state aggression. He notes that particular societal arrangements and cultural beliefs will bring more aggressive men to positions of highest authority:

> Some societies do embody values that reward strong responses to perceived challenges. This means not only that men with a higher predisposition to react

strongly to challenges will be rewarded, but also that, as these men interact with each other, a cycle of reinforcing behavior would emerge . . . The biological argument suggests that, in addition to those cultural factors, the ways in which members of such cultures would tend to interact with each other would produce elevated testosterone levels that would also create a self-sustaining cycle, producing individuals who are prone to [dominance behaviors].[69]

Rosen is explicit in his predictions for such states: "A population of states run by groups of men who are prone to react to perceived challenges by punishing the challenger should see more conflict. Such systems will be prone to war."[70] Dominic Johnson and Bradley Thayer concur:

The pleasure of competition and victory has been widely recognized as a feature of human nature from classical times to the present day, and success in competitive interactions and the domination of others are known to increase testosterone and dopamine responses in men—the so-called victory effect. Such dominance behavior is, we suggest, exaggerated among leaders because they are generally ambitious and competitive, and usually male. Moreover, the very acquisition and exercise of power itself is known to inflate dominance behavior further.[71]

Furthermore, as McDermott notes, Syndrome norms such as endogamy through cousin marriage may potentiate a higher distribution of genes or epigenetic methylation encoding for aggression, and in that way, population genetics can play an important role on societal leadership.[72]

When we step back, we cannot help but notice the dysfunctionality of a state system influenced by evolutionary male behavior. Violence is the constant backdrop of a society of states reliant on the Patrilineal/Fraternal security provision mechanism. Potts and Hayden put it best:

Warfare, terrorism, and their attendant horrors are based on just this sort of inherited predisposition for team aggression which, whatever its origins, has become a horribly costly and counterproductive behavior in the modern world . . . The original survival advantage enjoyed by individual males with a predisposition for team aggression has long since been replaced by a major, verging on suicidal, disadvantage for our species as a whole . . . To a very large extent . . . the natural tendencies of men are not consistent with the survival and well-being of their sexual partners, their children, and future generations to come.[73]

Violence, however, is not all that results from the Syndrome, as we will now explore.

Autocracy as the Preferred Regime Type

The willingness to violently coerce others is not the only template that has been learned under this subordinative first sexual political order. What has also been learned is that the drive for dominance pays outsize rewards to men in terms of resource access. If one can dominate women, one can gain food, care, children, and all manner of productive and reproductive services. Dominance as the key to resource access may be experienced on a daily basis through the interaction between men and women within households, and therefore rule-by-dominance will also be an overlearned behavior. This means that the societies built by male kin groups (i.e., fraternities) will not be predisposed to evolve as democracies, but rather to evolve as male dominance hierarchies in the form of autocracy.

Indeed, political autocracies not only seem natural when women are subordinated, but men actually may feel a vested interest in the acceptance of autocracy at the group level to justify the use of autocracy at the household level. John Stuart Mill observed,

> Whatever gratification of pride there is in the possession of power, and whatever personal interest in its exercise, is in [the case of women's subordination] not confined to a limited class, but common to the whole male sex . . . It comes home to the person and hearth of every male head of a family, and of every one who looks forward to being so. The clodhopper exercises, or is to exercise, his share of power equally with the highest nobleman . . . and everyone who desires power, desires it most over those who are nearest to him . . . in whom any independence of his authority is oftenest likely to interfere with his individual preferences.[74]

Indeed, Mill points out that in Great Britain, the murder of a husband by his wife was deemed by the legal system of the time as *treason*. The parallel between household and state rule was clearly drawn in this way: "not a word can be said for despotism in the family which cannot be said for political despotism . . . The family is a school of despotism."[75]

This suggests it may be difficult to construct a more egalitarian—or more secure—society in which households are profoundly inegalitarian between the sexes. Gloria Steinem asserts, "Political philosophers always have told us that the family is a microcosm of the state. Unfortunately, they did not take the logical next step: only democratic families can produce and sustain a real democracy."[76] This is true even of nation-states where the nominal political system includes procedural democracy. For example, one official in democratic South Africa, accused of domestic violence, stated baldly, "Democracy stops at my front door."[77] Democracy may even facilitate a regression back toward the Syndrome: for example, a recent peaceful democratic transition from autocracy in Gambia has seen a resurgence of female genital cutting and child marriage, as Gambian voters decided democracy means that they now have the freedom return to their patrilineal/fraternal traditions.[78]

Scholars have noted that "the tribe is based upon the legitimation of inequality by ideology."[79] Perhaps that legitimation finds its foundational expression in the subordination of women in marriage at the household level; if so, meaningful democratization cannot take place without change at that foundation. As political scientist Steven Fish states,

> Several leading writers have argued that the repressiveness and unquestioned dominance of the father in the family and of the male in relations between men and women replicate themselves in broader society, creating a culture of domination, intolerance, and dependency in social and political life. . . . Individuals who are more accustomed to rigidly hierarchical relations in their personal lives may be less prone to resist such patterns of authority in politics. The generalization applies to the wielders of authority as much as to the objects.[80]

Gerda Lerner agrees with this view, commenting that "children reared and socialized within such authority will grow into the kind of citizens needed in an absolutist kingship. The king's power was secured by men as absolutely dependent on and subservient to him as their families were dependent on and subservient to them. The archaic state was shaped and developed in the form of patriarchy."[81] Political scientist Ariel Ahram concurs:

> The state operates as a macrocosm of the family, and neo-patriarchy deploys modern techniques of governance to reinforce traditional modes of male domination. . . . Even among Arab regimes that espouse secular, progressive nationalism, to say nothing of the autocratic monarchies like Saudi Arabia, the masculinity of the state is embodied in despotic and arbitrary power over populations.[82]

The parallel between the Syndrome's sexual order and the form of governance in the wider polity has been well understood across the millennia, especially by monarchs. Sociologist Julia Adams, for example, quotes James VI of Scotland who wrote,

> Now a Father may dispose of his Inheritance to his children, at his pleasure: yea, euen disinherite the eldest vpon iust occasions, and preferre the youngest, according to his liking: make them beggers, or rich at his pleasure; restraine, or banish out of his presence, as hee findes them giue cause of offence, or restore them in fauour againe with the penitent sinner: So may the King deale with Subiects."[83]

As Sir Robert Filmer put it, "The first kings were fathers of families."[84]

The leader of the group will need to be dominant, indeed, to deter the aspirations to dominance of his male kin. As we have seen, Barbara Smuts (and others) argues that the establishment of a hierarchy among men of the group was increasingly selected as a way to dampen male-male competition within the kin group.[85] Male dominance hierarchies, however, can create extreme inequality among male allies. Smuts suggests that "the degree to which men dominate women and control their sexuality is inextricably intertwined with the degree to which some men dominate others."[86] Not surprisingly, then, this hierarchical strategy is problematic: psychologists Nicholas Pound, Martin Daly, and Margo Wilson observe that "evidence indicates that relative deprivation (as indexed by income inequality) is typically a more powerful predictor of variation in male violence than other socioeconomic measures such as percent below the poverty line or average income."[87]

The reliance on hierarchies among male kin within the patriline is, thus, a highly paradoxical strategy: in attempting to dampen male-male competition, such a hierarchical structure may instead wind up aggravating it, both within and betwixt groups. Francis Fukuyama notes that, "in tribal societies, justice between individuals is a bit like contemporary international relations, based on the self-help of rival groups in a world where there is no higher third-party enforcer of rules."[88] Although peaceful coexistence and pursuit of well-being is nominally the goal, the means by which clans pursue these goals results in a system of "disequilibrium in equilibrium."[89] As David Jacobson explains, "Balanced opposition is a way to organize society. But it also means that violence, or the threat of violence, is an organizing principle of society— at a basic personal and communal level. Any potential attacker knows he may trigger a formidable collective response . . . The role of violence explains why, in good part, the prowess of males is so valued."[90]

To benefit from this tropism of states' systems of governance paralleling household systems of governance, the authoritarian state may purposefully attempt to formally base its governance on patrilineal lines. China and Korea[91] may be the primary examples here. Monica Das Gupta observes that

> In China and Korea, the state made a concerted effort to propagate Confucian values to reinforce the ruler's authority and build a strong authoritarian state. This involved pressuring and incentivizing people to form themselves into patrilineages, and to adopt elaborate rituals of ancestor worship tying the lineage members together. . . . These authoritarian kinship relationships were mirrored through the political hierarchy, culminating in obeisance to the king. Presented as a civilizing force, this enabled the state to control local societies through lineage organization.[92]

But, as Das Gupta notes, state cooptation of lineages depends on the creation of a supra-lineage, with the state leader as the "father of fathers." In cases in which that is not possible or successful, the tension inherent in the system of male-bonded kin groups will come to the fore once again. How do patriline leaders cope with these constant centripetal forces that threaten to tear the extended kin alliance apart? Only with great difficulty; the "state" seems ready to fly apart at the slightest pressure. Leadership succession is often a catalyst: consider S. J. Tambiah's account of historical Burma: "The curious fact is that succession to the throne was always contentious, and the winner who was rarely if ever the eldest son of the chief wife, usually murdered all his half-brothers and their immediate relatives. . . . The son who most often succeeded was the son who could take and maintain the kingship by force."[93]

Implicit in Tambiah's assertion is that polygyny exacerbates all these authoritarian tendencies. As Robert Wright puts it, "Extreme polygyny often goes hand in hand with extreme political hierarchy, and reaches its zenith under the most despotic regimes."[94] Laura Betzig, in an intriguing empirical study of 186 societies, found "the correlation between polygyny and despotism to be statistically significant."[95]

Sex ratio alteration is also a structural point of instability, one that we explore in chapter 5. Highly masculinized sex ratios may predispose the nation-state in the direction of authoritarianism. As Steven Fish describes:

> Extremely high sex ratios themselves make for a social time bomb and may dim the prospects for popular rule. They may create conditions under which young men are more likely to join militant groups and engage in threatening, anomic behavior that provokes official repression. Late marriages for males, who in some Muslim countries must by custom be economically capable of supporting wives who do not work, may contribute to male aggression and frustration, but sheer numbers exacerbate the problem.[96]

In such a context, authoritarian central rule may seem the only recourse.

In sum, although leaders may attempt to pacify other group members by claiming their rule is legitimate or by divine design, their rule is in reality based first and foremost on the threat of violence, just as is the rule of men over women in the society—and our theoretical framework suggests this is because the former is based on the template of the latter. Authoritarianism backed by the threat of violent coercion is thus mirrored at both levels of analysis—the household and the state.

Indeed, even in an autocracy, it is the male-bonded kin networks within the broader society that ultimately determine the limits of the autocrat's power. We have previously mentioned how nominally democratic governments can be undermined by clan politics, so much so that the term "democracy" seems a sham when the autocracy of clan politics, in fact, has captured the institutions designed to implement democracy. The same can happen in an autocracy as well, in which the "all-powerful" autocrat is not actually very powerful at all. Rather, it is the male-bonded kin networks that run the show. Collins's analysis of post-Soviet states allows us to see the mechanisms involved:

> Clans pervade, transform, and undermine the type and durability of the regime, even while new presidents seek autonomy and regime consolidation, [through] kin-based patronage, asset stripping, and "crowding out" formal institutions through clan-based mobilization . . . Clans use the assets to fortify their group, effectively bankrupting state coffers, decentralizing state power, and creating competing wealth/power centers where they govern through an informal regime of clan bargaining . . . Clans also engage in "crowding out," a process by which they participate politically through their network and effectively crowd out non-clan forms of association or participation. Clans use this mechanism (inclusion of members/exclusion of nonmembers) as a means of low cost mobilization and political participation and competition. Clan elites use the clan to mobilize social support for their agenda and thereby avoid the costs of creating new organizations, such as political parties or unions, that would have broader but less reliable constituencies. . . . By pervading formal regime institutions, clan politics inhibits the agenda of both democratic and authoritarian regimes and prevents their consolidation. Finally, clan politics becomes self-reinforcing; it is a vicious cycle difficult to end without some intervening variable.[97]

Collins concludes that in clan-based societies, "the prospects for democratization look bleak," but it is also true that nondemocratic, authoritarian regimes are also severely compromised by these male kin alliances.[98]

Because the balancing act between clans is such a delicate one, a chronic predisposition to instability is inevitable. To forestall the outbreak of violence, patrilineal leaders may attempt to use rents to appease would-be aspirants for power as a near-term strategy, or, as Schatz puts it "as a whole, society experiences a proliferation of non-productive activities, such as rent seeking."[99] Speaking of the weak post-Qaddafi Libyan government's attempts to co-opt leaders of the rebel militias that are the real force in that society, journalists Scott Shane and Jo Becker record in the *New York Times* the plea of one observer: "'Don't give them salaries for nothing,' Mr. Sagezli recalls begging. 'Giving a commander money means giving strength to the militias, more loyalty for the commander, more armaments and more corruption. They never listened.' Instead, he said, 'the politicians started bribing them to buy loyalty.'"[100] Governance-by-rents is a hallmark of the Patrilineal/Fraternal Syndrome, and it is to that topic that we now turn.

Raiding for the Rents Upon Which Governance Is Based

Rents are valuables obtained through some form of raiding or extortion or direct exploitation (such as digging minerals from the earth), rather than through one's production of them. Indeed, one merely expropriates rents from those who or that which has produced them. The accumulation of wealth and power through obtaining and utilizing rents creates what Jack Goody terms "the predatory economy."[101] That is, dominant economic actors will be in the business of "taking" from others who actually produce value. The parasitical form that this strategy of accumulation takes must not be overlooked, as once more the originary template for the strategy may be found in the character of male–female relations within the society, that is, the first political order of relations between the sexes. As economist Elissa Braunstein states, "there are two ways to make a living—producing things or appropriating what others have produced. . . . Social norms like the sexual division of labor are not simply solutions to the problem of coordinating family production, but rather a way to organize family labor in terms that benefit men."[102]

This is reflected even in colloquial language. One "takes" a wife in many cultures, and sires children "upon her." That "givers" are always coded as inferior to "takers" has deep roots in the subordinative first political order.[103] Goody notes that "the agnatic group has strongly endogamous tendencies . . . to give a wife to another lineage is dishonourable, and the wife-*takers* are superior to the wife-*givers*."[104] Children then belong to the patriline, and not to the mother who physically produced them—she may be the "giver," but her husband and his patriline are the "takers." All her labor, productive as well as reproductive, belongs to her husband and, by extension, his lineage group.

The first rents, then, are extracted from women by men through "implicit intra-household rent agreements."[105] ("Agreement" may not be the right word choice, given what we know of the nature of marriage in Syndrome-encoding societies.) Thus, the fruits of both a woman's productive and reproductive labors are typically expropriated by the patriline in such cultures, whether these fruits are in the form of children or food or domestic service or farm labor. This understanding of the expropriative nature of the male–female relation still finds echoes in laws today; so, for example, marital rape is in many countries considered an oxymoron and is not illegal, for a man has "taken" his wife, and in a sense, "owns" her as property. In other countries, a woman's earnings from participation in the labor force or her dower assets are under control of her husband; in many countries, it is not illegal for a man to physically harm a woman who withholds expected services, such as sexual services or food preparation services. The first rents were arguably expropriated from womankind, then.

The usefulness of a strategy of expropriation and raiding does not remain confined to male–female relations. It cascades outward and becomes a type of broader societal economy. Sociologist Maria Mies argues that the development of at-a-distance weaponry, such as spears, arrows, and atlatls, in the historical evolutionary environment allowed men to more safely expropriate goods and slave labor from other groups, simultaneously providing political power to those who excelled at this task.[106]

Rents are easier to expropriate in cases in which that which is valuable is *alienable* from the producer thereof. Anthropologist Joseph Manson and colleagues note, "The predominance of males in human intergroup aggression leads to the expectation that human societies will be characterized by male philopatry and female transfer [as found in cultures with] patrilocal or virilocal postmarital residence . . . we suggest that the object of intergroup aggression should be predictable by resource alienability—i.e., the extent to which resources can be profitably seized."[107] Or, to put it more colloquially, an Arab proverb states, "Raids are our agriculture."[108] The fundamental activity of high-status actors in this type of economy may thus become "raiding," a form of rent extortion.

The raiding and extortion of rents for the purpose of ruling is a trademark of patrilineal/fraternal networks. Speaking of the tribes of Inner Asia, Thomas Barfield notes that historically the tribes not only raided government assets but also extorted protection money from the government, with the payments amounting to one-third of the annual government payroll.[109] But the cumulative effect was anything but stabilizing: "More destructive was the [tribal] tradition of raising revenue by raiding or extortion . . . For this reason, tribal peoples were perceived as threats not just to the stability of weak dynasties but to the very fabric of government as well."[110]

These rents play an important role in the group's logic of male hierarchy. Despite the inequality between the hierarchy's members, the dispersal of rents and their associated sinecures serve to dampen grievance within the patrilineal network. For example, individuals are typically provided opportunities simply because of their place in the patrilineal clan's hierarchy; "family, relatives, and extended clan fill the power ministries."[111] The placement of such male kin (and, in some cases, female kin) in powerful positions in the formal state government generally solidifies the power of the patrilineal network. Patrilineal interests, and the need for some measure of patrilineal clan balancing to keep the peace, drive political appointments and policy decisions, rendering the political process irrational and incapable of pursuing national interests should they diverge from clan interests.[112]

Historian J. E. Peterson gives a classic example in the Gulf States of the 1970s:

> In 1974, the Al Khalifah [patriline] held six out of the 13 ministerial positions in
> Bahrain, while the Al Thani held nine of the 14 posts in Qatar. The allocation of
> cabinet posts in the United Arab Emirates has been particularly ticklish, since
> there are a number of ruling families to take into account. The ruling fami-
> lies of the seven shaykhdoms had members in 12 of the 28 posts announced
> in December 1973, and in seven of the 23 posts in the cabinet announced at
> the beginning of 1977. The most important posts belong to the Al Nahyan
> of Abu Dhabi and the Al Maktum of Dubai, including Prime Minister and
> Deputy Prime Minister. In Oman, close relatives of the Sultan—known as the
> Al Sa'id—occupied three of the 17 cabinet posts, while other members of the
> ruling family hold an additional two posts.[113]

Because every post has its own particular prestige, as does each tribe, the accounting system becomes quite complex, indeed. Honor offenses can easily arise
from a miscalculation of relative status, with possibly disastrous consequences.

More classic resource-based rents are also in play: patrilineal clans offer
significant and concrete economic benefits to their members. For example,
with regard to the Saudi royal family, one anonymous observer interviewed
by journalist David Kirkpatrick of the *New York Times* has noted "the family
has maintained its unity in part by spreading its top government roles and vast
oil wealth among different branches of the sprawling clan. Most important
was the division of the three main security services, which constitute the hard
power on the ground."[114] Although the prevailing ideology of patrilineality is
one of kinship morality, in patrilineal clans, that ideology is tangibly married to
"shared interest, advantage, and service."[115] As historian Joseph Kostiner puts it,
it is both "blood ties and booty"—or, now, subsidies—that keep clans both an
affective and a rational investment.[116] As Collins explains,

> [Clans] persist over time because they are identity networks with cultural
> capital, rooted in both real kinship and the idea of kinship that incorporates
> one's trusted friends . . . Clan elites can trust the members of their networks,
> and nonelites can rely on clan patrons to assist them in times of need . . . they
> are also rational networks that foster individual survival in an environment
> characterized by failing, inadequate, or repressive formal institutions.[117]

This dynamic does not just afflict weak economies, for as Schatz notes,
"Even in some advanced industrial contexts, the performance of formal,
state-introduced institutions suffers in those areas where kinship networks
remain vibrant."[118] Inevitably, then, patrilineal networks "emerged as distinctly
political, by becoming ensnared with questions of distribution and exchange."[119]

This type of political economy, however, is far from functional, just as the exploitation of women upon which it is patterned is dysfunctional.

This parallel has even been explored in scholarly research. In a fascinating study, international relations scholars You-Ming Liou and Paul Musgrave find that women are more subordinated in economies focused largely on oil rents, and they opine that a "gendered resource curse" is at work in addition to the more conventionally noted "resource curse," which has been used to explain the paradoxical durability of these otherwise dysfunctional regimes that are propped up by oil or mineral rents.[120] Liou and Musgrave assert that these regimes are long-lived not only because they provide rents to tamp down levels of discontent but *also* because they explicitly subordinate women—which pleases the winning male coalitions in the society. These winning male coalitions are none other than the patrilineal/fraternal male-bonded extended kin groups we have been discussing, whose very existence and strength relies on the oppression of women in the interest of the patriline.[121]

The predatory economy at the government level is bolstered by the government's unfailing support of it at the household level, and this is intertwined with the authoritarianism seen at both levels of analysis. Lerner expresses it eloquently:

> *[The] dependence of male family heads on the king or state bureaucracy was compensated for by their dominance over their families* [emphasis added]. Male family heads allocated the resources of society to their families the way the state allocated the resources of society to them. The control of male family heads over their female kin and minor sons was as important to the existence of the state as was the control of the king over his soldiers.[122]

That governance-through-rents is not a solid foundation for good governance is well accepted in economic development circles. Collins notes that, "energy resources appear to be particularly susceptible to clan-based corruption, as the 'resource curse' may foster instability between clans and hinder democratization over the longer term."[123]

Furthermore, although rents may make "sense" to men in societies where the fraternal network is the security provision mechanism, it may not make any sense at all from the standpoint of economic rationality and efficiency. Elissa Braunstein elaborates:

> Male rent-seeking in the family, social norms and legal rules afford men opportunities for individual gain in ways that can lower social efficiency. . . . A division of labor [such as the sexual division of labor] that is initially efficient may . . . facilitate the emergence of hierarchies that subsequently may impede efficient reallocation. In other words, the static efficiency of comparative

advantage given by a particular division of labor can lead to dynamic ineffi-
ciencies through the emergence of hierarchy.[124]

Braunstein goes on to note that hierarchies provide a strong source of vested
interest in the status quo, with those at higher levels "buying off" those at lower
levels. In the case of households, elite males allow nonelite males to control
women. But, she notes, such rent-seeking induces men to expend resources
to maintain their dominance over the source of rents (women), *regardless of
the societal cost*—and this both lowers economic growth as well as lessens
human capabilities overall. Depressingly, Braunstein comments, "If gender
equity means the loss of individual or collective rents, it will be resisted regardless of how seemingly socially efficient the attendant economic prescriptions
appear."[125] No wonder the World Bank finds that countries that subordinate
women also experience subpar economic performance,[126] and no wonder that
recognition of this fact has not led to any overhaul of that subordination.

Corruption and Nepotism Integral to Governance

Our theoretical framework suggests that male-on-female predation leading
to the development of a "predatory economy" also primes a society for corruption. Indeed, in an intriguing finding that parallels this assertion, political
scientist Christopher Butler and colleagues found that "the level of financial
corruption in a political system is robustly associated with the extensiveness of
sexual violence committed by policemen and soldiers." If corruption is defined
as "being willing to use your position or power to your own advantage" in a way
that is "dishonest," "lacking in integrity," "illegal or immoral," then the first corruption may well be found in the first political order of women's subordination
at the household level.[127]

It is important to understand "corruption" for what it really is in the
economics of Syndrome-encoding countries—corruption is the *means of
governance*. Mark Weiner suggests, "What we tend loosely to call corruption
is often the distribution of favors along clan lines."[128] Indeed, garnering assets
for one's clan while "simultaneously doling out to rival clans just enough to
prevent open conflict"[129] is the typical *modus operandi* of clan-based states.
Collins notes about post-Soviet Kyrgyzstan how

> the 1990s privatization of major state assets and key positions in government
> went to insider clans, which became entrenched in power and then resisted
> reform. Realizing that the state was nearing bankruptcy, they demanded
> more assets. These strategies have their limits, however, as dividing shrinking
> resources while maintaining a pact and balance of clans proves increasingly

difficult. . . . As regime durability becomes uncertain, clans strip assets faster, and the regime and state become weaker still. Declining state coffers will likely lead the president to break the pact by excluding clans he can no longer afford to patronize.[130]

Thus, although an informal pact between clans based on clan balancing through corruption is often initially struck to enable some peace and regime durability, these pacts often serve to undermine stability. As Collins suggests, "democracy in a clan-based society has not proven stable; it has quickly deteriorated under the pressure of clan interests. Nor is clan-based autocracy a stable political system over the longer term . . . [clans] undermine genuine economic reform that would threaten their vested interests."[131] Under exigency, these pacts will break down, leading to violent conflict to reconfigure rights to rents. Indeed, Collins asserts that "in anticipation of regime or even state collapse, [clans] may in fact be precipitating that collapse. . . . The informal decentralization of power and assets, potentially including access to arms, among clan elites and along group identity lines, raises the likelihood of clan elites instigating intergroup conflict to defend their interests."[132]

The linkage between corruption and state instability is widely acknowledged. For example, Samuel Mondays Atuobi of the Kofi Annan International Peacekeeping Training Centre notes:

The existence of widespread corruption . . . has a deeply corrosive effect on trust in government and contributes to crime and political disorder. . . . At the extreme, unbridled corruption can lead to state fragility and destructive conflict, and plunge a state into an unremitting cycle of institutional anarchy and violence. Inasmuch as corruption destroys the legitimacy of government in the eyes of those who can do something about the situation, it contributes to instability. [Corruption has] often been cited among the reasons for military takeovers.[133]

Furthermore, as we have seen, in patrilineal clan-based societies, government positions are used in a corrupt fashion to obtain additional assets for the clan and its members, and not to build up the broader society or the institutions of the state, generally speaking. The resources of the government are often viewed as potential booty, which clans feel should be preemptively stripped lest they fall to the control of other clans. In Kenya, a country dominated by clan politics, the colloquial term for this asset-stripping by the clan in power is "eating." As a new clan comes to power, members crow, "It's our turn to eat!"[134] Likewise, Tambiah says that historically, "kinship groups were . . . clusters of relatives associated with such privileged officials. . . . In Burma, an official became a *myo-sa*, the 'eater of the town,' and this entitled him to extract tribute from his domain."[135] In Kazakhstan, Schatz notes, the term is *qanyn tartady*, or "bring in their blood." In stripping state assets, clans "create a wealth and power base largely independent of the state."[136] Fukuyama concludes, "public service is often regarded as an opportunity to steal on behalf of the family."[137]

Clan-based corruption is a horse of a different color than run-of-the-mill corruption. As we have noted, "blood and booty" hold clans together: "booty," or asset-stripping, is *always* the foundation of the economic system created in which patrilineal clans (blood) are powerful, and thus corruption is not an aberration, but rather a built-in feature of the governance system.

Douglass North and his colleagues describe this system as one in which "the political system [is used] to create economic rents; the rents order social relations, control violence, and establish social cooperation."[138] Rather than corruption being seen as an impediment to governance, corruption is often seen as the *very means of governance* and the primary leverage with which to control violence. Typically, economic reform will be a nonstarter in these states because it is largely through rent creation and allocation that "elites create credible incentives to cooperate rather than fight among themselves . . . rents then secure political order."[139] Social anthropologist Ernest Gellner elaborates,

> The chief has to guard against defections among the tribal segments by giving subsidies that can rival those promised by other similar chieftaincies, ever ready to seduce some of his following by offering better terms. All this takes money; so he himself is in the market for the reception of subsidies and arms from outside powers, which in turn are eager to use his strategic position either to ensure their own communications or to undermine the communications and claims of their rivals. . . . Treachery is endemic. . . . Nothing, certainly not death, ever terminates the game; leadership in a segmentary society has a dragon's-teeth quality.[140]

Modern examples of these Games of Clan Thrones abound. For example, Chinese personal and familial relationships have aided lineage groups in accessing business opportunities,[141] and in response to numerous scandals, President Xi Jinping launched a major anticorruption campaign upon taking office, although it is unclear whether even the power of a one-party state can offset that of powerful patrilines.[142] In Saudi Arabia, "The Saudi polity tributarises other clan groups, no longer nomadic, and ties them . . . to the redistribution of Saudi wealth; for plunder is substituted by subsidy and the privilege of citizenship, such as the legal sponsorship of foreign business is akin in many ways to the exaction of protection money. Thus tribalism becomes ascendant."[143] In both China and Saudi Arabia, the need to "cull the number of pigs at the trough" has resulted in dramatic anticorruption campaigns without really attacking the government-by-corruption system itself.[144] In Central

Asia, meanwhile, "presidential appointments and policy decisions are defined or sharply constrained by clan interests and their competition for resources. Clan elites actively engage in nepotism and patronage of their kin and clan network."[145]

Kin-based systems will always provide impunity for corruption, as kin networks are the warp and woof of the economy. Collins notes, "Far from being irrational relics of a bygone age, the informal ties and networks of clan life reduce the high transaction costs of making deals in an environment where impersonal institutions are weak or absent and stable expectations are hard to form." An example is Yemen, a very weak state (so weak that a civil war is now raging). Nadwa al-Dawsari states:

> The strong presence of tribes in Yemen is due to the corruption and weakness of the state institutions there. The tribes in Yemen provide social order outside the formal system. Tribes and tribal law act, in the words of political scientist Daniel Corstange, as "second-best substitutes for an absent or weak state." People approve of the tribes because they provide basic rule of law in the form of conflict resolution and regulation.[146]

Indeed, states may routinely "farm out" such security duties to clans and tribes. As Weiner notes, "the rule of the clan and the state can exist side by side," and we would add that corruption is the lubricant.[147]

Clans, in fact, serve as an alternative to formal market institutions and official bureaucracies. Collins explains, "The particularistic ties and repeated interactions that characterize clans build trust and a sense of reciprocity, enabling the people involved to make contracts that extend over time."[148] This lowering of transaction costs has a steep price, however. As Fukuyama notes, nepotism makes institutions "intolerant, inbred, slow to adapt, and oblivious to new ideas,"[149] or as a recent Arab Human Development Report notes, "Clannism implants submission, parasitic dependence and compliance in return for protection and benefits," and it thereby becomes "the enemy of personal independence, intellectual daring, and the flowering of a unique and authentic human entity."[150] Sociologist Ivan Ermakoff concurs, stating patrilineal/fraternal networks undermine state capacity "by begetting arbitrary power and instability, by undercutting incentives for productive innovations, and by fostering the down-ward fragmentation of spheres of influence."[151] Because no separation exists between what is private and what is public, official state property can easily come to be seen as private property. Furthermore, when you cannot fire employees who are incompetent or venal because they are kinsmen, the liability of this system becomes clear.

Additionally, this culture of relational corruption undermines any sense of common ties through citizenship. Members of the patrilineal/fraternal network may not see themselves first and foremost as the citizens of their nation-state, but rather as members of their clans or tribes. As such, the notion of common sacrifice for the good of the country is attenuated because kin-based patronage networks are the dominant resource allocation mechanisms in society. Note what Weiner says about Indian *jatis*:

> The *jati* system and the extended family in which its values are imbued poses a deep challenge to Indian democracy, a challenge that is characteristic of all societies under the sway of the rule of the clan or of clannism. At its core, the *jati* system is marked by what Ambedkar called an "anti-social spirit"—it lacks a sense of shared, common life. It lacks a belief in the public. Each *jati*, like each *varna*, is confined within itself, its horizon of concern ending at the boundaries of its membership. Caste and family are more important than the nation . . . *Societies founded on kin solidarity lack the common consciousness necessary to pursue truly public ends.* [emphasis added][152]

Thus, patrilineal clan members generally have an instrumental view of formal government: In cases in which the formal government supports the clan's interests—which may be ensured by placing one's own members in governmental positions—the clan can strengthen the central government. In cases in which the formal government opposes clan interests, however, the clan may well seek to undermine the formal government. Seen in this light, many authoritarian regimes are actually not authoritarian at all: the "supreme leader" may lack the real power to govern society and be highly dependent on clan acquiescence, as we see in several post–Cold War Central Asian nations.[153]

In her masterful work on corruption, *Thieves of State*, Sarah Chayes notes that corruption undermines the state in two ways. First, the disgust engendered by a corrupt government breeds rebellion:

> Kleptocratic governance—acute and systemic public corruption—was fodder for an expanding insurgency. . . . Corruption was not solely a humanitarian affair, an issue touching on principles or values alone. It was a matter of national security. . . . Acute government corruption may in fact lie at the root of some of the world's most dangerous and disruptive security challenges—among them the spread of violent extremism. . . . For decades . . . extremism had been the only outlet for people to express their legitimate grievances. . . . Militant extremism [seemed] the only alternative to corruption.[154]

And yet, as Chayes points out, corruption may not so much undermine the government as to be the *purpose* of government. Her epiphany occurred during her time serving alongside the U.S. military in Afghanistan:

What if the Afghan government wasn't really trying to govern? What if it was focused on another objective altogether? What if corruption was central to that objective and therefore to the government's mode of operation? . . . I was often asked, moreover, why it was so hard to find honest people to serve in government. If that government was actually a crime syndicate in disguise, the dearth of good people was no surprise. Mafias select for criminality, by turning violation of the law into a rite of passage, by rewarding it, by hurting high-minded individuals who might make trouble. . . . That was the Afghan government. It was not incapable. It was performing its core function with admirable efficiency—bringing power to bear where it counted. And it was assiduously protecting its own. Governing—the exercise that attracted so much international attention—was really just a front activity.[155]

Chayes reflects on why this realization was so difficult for those from non-patrilineal societies to achieve and decides on two primary reasons: (1) "the notion that an entire government might be transformed into what amounts to a criminal organization, that it might have entirely repurposed the mechanisms of state to serve its ends, is almost too conceptually challenging to contemplate," and (2) "the overwhelming evidence that the market liberalization, privatization, and structural adjustment programs the West imposed on developing countries in the 1990s have often exacerbated corruption, not reduced it [is] hard to process."[156] Societies that have moved away from the Patrilineal/Fraternal Syndrome will find the logic of corruption mystifying in a way that societies still encoding the Syndrome will not.

Chayes notes that kinship is at the heart of this system of corruption that passes itself off as government. Her informants consistently point to the "big families," and the "extended ruling families," whose goal is "the extraction of resources for personal gain, and the softening of the state [that] resulted."[157] The state becomes a "feeding trough," and banks become the piggy banks for these families, issuing loans no one believes will be repaid. She describes the system as "a welfare program to secure obedience," which is in line with our theoretical framework.[158] In an interesting echo of how men create the legal systems that oppress women, the "big families" do the very same. Chayes notes, "The legal system was created by the people who were going to benefit."[159] We raise the possibility that the corruption Chayes notes was learned first in the home, where the extraction of resources (and labor) for personal gain was the practice of one sex in regard to the other. Although a fragile stability can be achieved in the short term, governance by means of corruption is ultimately a recipe for instability and rebellion.[160]

Note that this "welfare system" of corruption and nepotism can, in addition to breeding instability and rebellion, seriously constrain innovation, initiative, and reform: deviants will be radically ostracized, perhaps even killed. Furthermore, the patrilineal/fraternal system is no breeding ground for meritocracy. Indeed, basic competence cannot be assumed of those appointed to office, because they have been appointed because of their lineage position. Indeed, political scientist Bassam Tibi notes that this was one reason why in the historical Middle East those who were outside lineages were brought in to run things: "Men can now be trusted, on the whole, to perform their tasks in bureaucratic organizations without constantly yielding to the temptation to bend the rules so as to favor their own kin . . . Traditional society did not have this advantage; for reliable bureaucratic performance it had to rely on slaves, eunuchs, priests, or aliens."[161] It was these outsiders, with no strong clan ties, whose allegiance to the leader of the country could be somewhat trusted to perform on pain of dismissal. Fukuyama comments, "There appears to be something of an inverse relationship between the bonds of trust and reciprocity inside and outside the family; when one is very strong, the other tends to be weak. . . . What made the Protestant Reformation so important for Weber was not so much that it encouraged honesty, reciprocity, and thrift among individual entrepreneurs, but that these virtues were for the first time widely practiced *outside the family*."[162]

More specifically, it is hard to threaten "pain of dismissal" in a kin-based network system. In this type of societal structure, although individuals are easily replaceable by others in the same lineage, the position may be tied to a certain level of status within the lineage—and woe be it unto anyone who seeks change in those parameters. In the short term, acceding to this system may be stabilizing, but in the long term, it augurs for civilizational stasis and decline. Furthermore, it has dire ramifications for individuals who deviate—even in positive ways—from lineage norms. Jacobson expresses it, "Tribal societies do not afford the relatively easy "exit" from family ties that modern functioning states do from kin dependencies, so to dishonor oneself is to live a life of humiliation and shame. Furthermore, it will be difficult for the dishonored to find partners for any social or economic endeavors."[163]

Clannism traps individuals, and by extension, the entire society, into a straitjacket of corruption, nepotism, and economic underperformance, which in turn stoke grievance and rebellion.

Impunity Instead of the Rule of Law

Another effect on the political order from the ascendance of male dominance hierarchies, as we have seen, is that such patrilineal clan governance lessens an individual's sense of personal accountability under state law. In the larger scheme of things, state law is clearly less important than the law of the patriline and the law governing interpatrilineal group relations, thus undermining any movement toward "the rule of law." As Edward Schatz puts it, "kinship groups inspire irrationality in the legal system."[164]

Again, we assert the template for this hierarchy is the inequitable nature of the original social contract between men and women—what typically is called marriage. Family and personal status law in Syndrome-encoding countries openly demonstrate that all people are not equal before the law, for men and women surely are not. For example, wives may be killed if accused of adultery, but men may not be punished for adultery at all. Husbands may easily divorce their wives, but wives may only with great difficulty divorce their husbands. Husbands have full property and inheritance rights, but wives enjoy very few such rights. Husbands may be excused if they beat their wife, but not if they beat another male. And so on.[165] The pattern is quite clear: impunity for the man and harsh punishment for the woman, simply based on sex difference.

We suggest that the profoundly inequitable nature of family law undermines from the start the very concept of rule of law within the society. As economic historian Douglass North and his colleagues put it, "The law cannot enforce individual rights if . . . every relationship between two individuals depends uniquely on their identity within the [group]."[166] or as Weiner expresses it, "communities governed by the rule of the clan possess a markedly diminished conception of individual freedom. This is because under their legal principles people are valued less as individuals per se than as members of their extended families. The rights and obligations of individuals are fundamentally influenced by their place within the kin groups to which they inescapably belong."[167] This is established at the start, for a male's place in the patrilineal/fraternal group is far, far different from that of a woman's place. A husband who kills an unfaithful wife will walk free, for he killed for honor; a wife who kills an unfaithful husband will be executed as a murderess.

Thus, because the first political order is grounded in women's subordination— a founding template of injustice, if you will—a kin-based system may openly sanction impunity for the guilty as well as punishment for the innocent, which undermines the concept of justice being based in accountability for individual actions before the law. In Iraq, there is a saying, "Support your brother even though he is guilty,"[168] which suggests that tribal law is first and foremost about stability and not about justice.

Weiner highlights a critical distinction between shame and guilt, which illustrates the core problem discussed here: "In shame cultures it is not a person's behavior that creates shame. It is instead the fact that the person's community has witnessed or learned of the behavior. Guilt, on the other hand, is solitary. It stems not from a disapproving community but from a bad conscience."[169] Patrilineal/fraternal syndrome societies are decidedly shame-based, for conscience has already been seared through the foundational order of the coercive subordination of women. In such a context, the rule of law cannot be easily developed, even if the country is nominally a democracy. States in such societies "may have elections, but they do not have extensive systems of rights of rule of law for most citizens."[170]

Interestingly, the linkage we posit between elements of the Syndrome and impunity has long been noted. Laura Betzig, in her classic 1982 article on the subject, notes that

> [Social] rank classically correlates with size and strength of the kin group, and with differences in wealth, [which] consistently determine the asymmetrical application of [legal] sanctions. . . . Conflicts of interest are asymmetrically resolved to the point that one individual may, for example, be killed for coughing in the presence of another, while the other may murder with impunity. Simultaneously, perquisites for third party authorities acting to resolve disputes become substantial, frequently equal to the payment of a brideprice or a bride; and degrees of polygyny increase.[171]

In essence, as Fukuyama comments, "the elevation of family and kinship ties above other sorts of social obligations . . . produces a two-level morality, wherein the level of moral obligation to public authority of all sorts is weaker than that reserved for kin."[172] That this two-level morality is corrosive to the nation-state is readily understandable.

Chronic Fissioning of the Group, Resulting in Annihilative Political Feuding, Terrorism, Rebellion, and Harsh Treatment of Out-Group Members

Perhaps the most troubling effect on political order stems from the fact that male-bonded kin groups fission easily, even chronically. As the famous Bedouin saying, "I against my brothers; my brothers and I against my cousins; my cousins, my brothers, and I against the world," makes plain, groups may fission at the drop of a hat, or an insult. And when patrilineal clans engage in conflict, swift and dangerous escalation often ensues. The threat of the feud—the threat of collective liability for offense—keeps the peace, until one day it doesn't and the apocalypse is unleashed. This is one of the most striking behavioral predispositions of societies governed by patrilineal clans. As Weiner describes it, "Without a larger force to intervene to bring the feud to a close, the exchange of reciprocal violence can be ratcheted up until a community implodes in bloodshed. This outcome is especially likely when the ancient legal tool of feud is conducted with weaponry built for warfare by modern nation states."[173] He justifiably calls these episodes of feuding the "Achilles' heel of clan-based government."[174] North and colleagues note that in these societies, "the threat of violence permeates society . . . everyone must be prepared to be violent, and the military resources of the community are widely dispersed throughout the population."[175] As one shopkeeper in western Afghanistan commented to a reporter, "You must have a gun to stay alive in Ghor. It is more important to have a gun at home than food."[176]

Jacobson concurs:

Tribal societies can display, cumulatively, an unusual degree of personal and social violence. . . . Why would tribes, as a whole, exhibit such violence? We observed earlier that balanced opposition is a way to organize security and served to organize many societies for millennia. This also means that *the threat of violence is an organizing principle of society* [emphasis added]—at both a personal and social level. Such a threat is the very antithesis of the civil, republican form of the modern state, where the state monopolizes violence and social relations are to be conducted on the basis of self-restraint and civility. . . . The blood feud is the ultimate tool of accountability."[177]

Such violence is usually local, but it can broaden quickly to encompass whole peoples, such as the world witnessed in the Rwandan genocide, or can even mutate into global militancies, which, in Jacobson's words, "turn tribal-patriarchal concepts—such as honor, gender, and grievance—into ideological rather than kinship-based concerns."[178] After all, one of the useful characteristics of these lineage systems is that virtually all adult males can be mobilized at a moment's notice.[179] As Weiner notes, "clan societies have the potential to destabilize regions vital to our strategic interests. . . . In addition to being sources of regional instability, clan societies also provide safe-havens for a wide variety of militant groups [which] either belong to a particular clan or who can claim its loyalty."[180]

Thus, although clans are capable of using their influence in a strategic fashion to create temporary peace and stability in place of continual violence,[181] certain behavioral predispositions of clans predictably and chronically undermine the stability and security of their societies. We may remember how Richard Tapper expresses it: "blood descent lead[s] to bloody dissent."[182] The "republics of cousins" (a phrase coined by French anthropologist Germaine Tillion) are always an unstable arrangement. National security researcher Patricio Asfura-Heim notes, "tribes are always in constant competition. They challenge each other, form alliances, and break apart to improve their access to resources. A balance of power among lineages keep the peace by guaranteeing that unjustified attacks will result in retribution and equivalent loss. [The leader] must be prepared to avenge every injury."[183] The tales told by former ambassador and anthropologist Akbar Ahmed in *The Thistle and the Drone* about clans' willingness to perish—and have everyone else perish, too—in pursuit of honorable revenge makes for horrifying reading.[184] The logic of honor can easily outweigh the logic of survival.[185]

It cannot be otherwise, according to Ernest Gellner, because of the vital role of fear in keeping the peace. If there's too much peace, according to Gellner, there's not enough fear:

> So as to work at all, the system also must not work too well. . . . The driving force behind the cohesion of the groups is fear, fear of aggression by others in an anarchic environment. If the balancing system really worked perfectly, producing a kind of perpetual peaceful balance of power at all levels, the society would cease to be anarchic, and fear would cease to be a powerful spring of action. . . . The persistence of a segmentary society requires, paradoxically, that its mechanisms should be sufficiently inefficient to keep fear in being as the sanction of the system.[186]

This means, however, that when the clan balancing act becomes unbalanced, violence is easily unleashed. Collins notes: "Once the balance of clan or patronage power is disrupted and the state breaks down, clan lines become clearly visible, and clan warfare extremely personalistic and vengeful; reestablishing trust and cooperation across clan boundaries becomes very difficult. The kinship element of clan conflicts makes them particularly intractable."[187]

"Intractable" is a word often applied to societies that depend on extended male kin networks for security provision. Schatz similarly notes "strongly drawn blood relationships can make conflict more intractable once it has begun. Descent ideologies are easily mobilized by political actors with narrow goals and agendas, as blood ties are widely understood as immutable."[188] Furthermore, despite the idea that clans unite to face external threat, the rivalries continue even as the fight is enjoined. As Schatz notes about Kazakhstan, even during the most widespread anticolonial rebellion against Russian colonization, the Kazakh leader Kasymov "was unable to keep at bay interclan rivalries."[189] Indeed, the power of the state in relation to the clans is measurable by how well it is able to suppress such feuding, although such suppression also may be quite costly to the society in many ways.[190]

Indeed, the very conception of martial masculine honor breeds subgroups within a patrilineal society that seek greater power by becoming the most "honorable of all"—that is, being the most manly, defined as being the most belligerent, the most ruthless, the most brutal, the most violent,[191] and, we would add, the most oppressive of women. This is but one reason why those who have been made "others" or "out-groups" within a society will receive especially harsh treatment—because the society will "feminize" those others by treating them as women are treated. Minority ethnic or religious groups may thus be seen as legitimate targets of violence and violent expropriation because they occupy the same subordinate status in the society as women.[192] This subordinate status often will be enacted in gendered terms, such as wholesale raiding and rape of the minority group's women, as we have seen with the Yazidi minority in Syria under ISIS. As Ahram perceptively notes,

> By selectively reinforcing, creating, and severing ties of kinship, these violent practices can affect bonds of loyalty and obedience far more substantially than the simple distribution of resource rents . . . for the power to control or manipulate sexual and ethnic identity is a key component of all state power. . . . the modes of hyper-masculine statehood that have emerged in the Arab world provided a blueprint for instrumentalising sexual violence as a tool of state-building.[193]

William Divale and Marvin Harris note this logic of hypermasculinity would make no sense without the overriding concerns inherent in patrilineality: "Frequent warfare is significantly correlated with patrilocal residence, patrilineal inheritance, polygyny, marriage by capture, brideprice, postmarital sex restrictions on women, property rights in women, male secret societies, male age grades, and men's houses."[194] When the Syndrome is encoded as the primary security provision mechanism in society, the logic of hypermasculinity is, unfortunately, all too persuasive.

States often vacillate in the face of alternative no-win options. The male-bonded kin groups are so martial and so prickly that the first temptation is to simply allow them their autonomy and rule the country indirectly through these groups. This has been repeatedly tried historically by both states and colonial powers.[195] However, that temptation is always rewarded with increased conflict and violence, as intertribal conflict then escalates as tribes vie with one another for greater dominance. The alternative temptation for states is to forcibly subjugate the tribes to the power of the state, which, as many states such as Iraq and Pakistan have discovered, results in rivers of blood, vengeance, and misery.[196] We suggest a third, hopefully more effective, and certainly more revolutionary, alternative, which is to break the power of the clans by building equality between men and women (discussed in part III).

Structural goads also are embedded in the Syndrome, which tend toward bloodshed. We touch on these here, including polygyny and altered sex ratios favoring men, and note that chapter 5 contains a more in-depth discussion. Elite polygyny is often the cause of bloody succession fights.[197] As we have seen, in societies with elite polygyny, "the son who most often succeeded was the son who could take and maintain the kingship by force."[198] Sex ratio alteration acts in a similar fashion—for example, among the Yanomamo of the Amazon, "The shortage of women causes sexual frustration and jealousy. Having several wives is the insignia of power and influence, which only increases the level of sexual frustration and the motivation for going to war [among those without wives]."[199]

The literature scholar Jonathan Gottschall notes that Mediterranean society at the time of Homer was similarly riven by violence caused by practices such as polygyny and enacted son preference:

> Homeric society suffered from acute shortages of available young women relative to young men. The institution of slave-concubinage meant that women were not equitably distributed across the circum-Aegean world; they were concentrated in certain communities and, within those communities, in the households of powerful men. . . . This shortage of women, whether it was brought about solely through polygyny or also through differential mortality, created strong incentives for men to compete, as individuals and in groups, not only for direct access to women, but also for the limited funds of social and material resources needed to attract and retain them. . . . While the desirability of peace is obvious, Homeric men—like their fathers and grandfathers before them— feel that they are doomed to perpetual conflict.[200]

Ben Raffield and Mark Collard say much the same about the operational sex ratio in eight-century Viking society, which led to a wave of shipborne raiding activity by young men in search of plunder across more than one continent.[201]

Note, with reference to these cases, that polygyny can coexist side by side with female infanticide, which on its face makes little sense. Divale and Harris attempt an explanation:

> Polygyny stands in mysterious contradiction to the high frequency of the practice of female infanticide. . . . Since women are exploited by men, one would expect girls to outnumber boys just as slaves outnumber masters. . . . [However] a premium survival advantage is conferred upon the group that rears the largest number of fierce and aggressive warriors. . . . Sex, rather than other forms of reinforcement such as food or shelter, is used to condition warlike behavior because sexual deprivation does not lead to the impairment of physical fitness, whereas deprivation of food and shelter would cripple fighting capacity. Furthermore, if women are to be the reward for military bravery, women must be reared to be passive and to submit to the decisions concerning the allocation of their sexual, productive, and reproductive services. Polygyny is the objectification of much of this system of rewards. At the same time, polygyny intensifies the shortage of females created by the postpartum manipulation of the sex ratio, producing positive feedback with respect to male aggressivity and fierceness, and encouraging combat for the sake of wife capture.[202]

We expand on this linkage between marriage market obstruction and political violence in the next chapter.

Exigency and the Syndrome

To summarize, then, the political order produced by the Patrilineal/Fraternal Syndrome tends to produce a dysfunctional, violent, unstable, insecure, authoritarian, corrupt, and frequently bloody society.

Furthermore, these effects will be especially pronounced when asset-stripping or natural disaster has imperiled environmental security, for such insecurity and exigency only deepen the Syndrome. In times of exigency during which the state cannot offer relief, the natural recourse will be toward the male-based extended kin network. Such fraternal networks will resurge even if they had faded in previous time periods. Schatz describes how this occurred in Soviet Central Asia: "By creating a political economy based on endemic shortages, the Soviet state generally promoted tight-knit access networks."[203] In other words, although the Soviets' explicit aim was to destroy the clans, the economic exigencies they caused by their policies only served to make kin groups even more salient.

The 2004 Arab Human Development Report described this linkage as well, suggesting that the inadequate security offered by authoritarian government explains the persistence of the Patrilineal/Fraternal Syndrome. We argue the same can be said of democratic governments that prove unable to safeguard their societies. According to the United Nations Development Program:

> In the absence of a viable civil society that could protect citizens' interests, exposed individual turned their backs on the institutions of civil society and sought the rude shelter of the tribal and clan system, with its feudal and organic bonds. Tribal and clan systems continue to command the devoted allegiance of individuals in such groups through just and unjust causes alike because they are a last recourse for identity, solidarity, security, and self-defense. They represent the sole viable definition of an "us."[204]

The resurgence of the salience and usefulness of these networks simultaneously cause the components of the Syndrome—that is, the mechanisms of women's disempowerment at the household level—to resurge as well. For example, food shortages and drought have exacerbated rates of child marriage in Ethiopia;[205] this same phenomenon is seen in the refugee camps surrounding Syria.[206] As Sanday asserts, there is "a causal relationship between scarce resources and the oppression of women."[207] She offers the example of the Plains Indians as a case in point:

> Before the introduction of the horse, Plains warfare was sporadic and less bloody . . . the introduction of the horse also increased the pressure of the whites on the eastern frontier, setting in motion a chain reaction of tribal

displacements that caused Indian groups to compete for the same resources, leading to constant warfare between these groups. . . . In this setting, the legal position of women became largely that of chattel. Wives were bought with horses and treated like property. Upon marriage a woman passed to her husband's group and the husband had the right to kill or torture his wife. It was also the right of a brother to kill his sister.[208]

On the basis of the case studies in her research, Sanday concludes that

men react to stress caused by food shortage or by the circumstances of migration by banding together, excluding women from male-oriented power ceremonies and by turning aggression against women. . . . Generally, male dominance evolves as resources diminish and as group survival depends increasingly on the aggressive acts of men. Male oppression of women, however, is neither an automatic nor an immediate response to stress. Other solutions to stress are possible.[209]

Possible, yes, but not probable, given the millennia of human socialization within the Syndrome.

It is critical to consider what the Patrilineal/Fraternal Syndrome accomplishes, and for whom, to understand why exigency always increases the salience of the Syndrome. The Syndrome provides security for men and ensures that rents will flow from women to men, while also ensuring that rents will flow from the young to the old. A context of generalized insecurity will thus catalyze a tightening of the Syndrome to keep those rents flowing. In speaking about postconflict societies, political scientist Sheila Meintjes and colleagues note,

In the aftermath [of war], men use violence against women and women's fear of violence to reinforce their hold on women; they compel women to comply because they need to re-establish or preserve control over wealth and resources and, above all, over women's productive and reproductive labor. . . . For the older generation, which depends on the young for survival in old age, it is imperative to re-establish the customary flow of wealth from young to old that obtained before the war. In the context of re-establishing livelihood, the older generation finds it particularly important to control young women. Their sexist view of women as commodities persists. Indeed, their view of sexuality is the first tradition they want to reconstruct, and they may use violence to do so.[210]

War is but one type of exigency that produces such results. Another example can be found in modern-day India, where the environmental disaster of drought has catalyzed higher levels of child marriage, polygyny, dowry deaths, and prostitution. In addition, girls are being pulled from school to help find and haul water.[211] Although polygyny is illegal for almost all Hindus in India, marginalized women agree to become "water wives" to survive. Men demand higher dowries because of lower farm income. Because women are more malnourished than usual, they may suffer violence because they cannot bear children as a result of disruption in their menstrual cycles. As men migrate to gain additional resources, the women and girl children left behind are prey to traffickers. Lawyer and activist Varsha Deshpande explains that, "Women are the most vulnerable during drought because it is their duty to fetch water and provide food for the family. She is the first to wake up, she walks the farthest to fetch water, she eats last—and probably the least—and she sleeps last."[212] Although this exigency hits everyone in the society, because of the subordinative first political order, women's subordination and insecurity are disproportionately deepened.

Indeed, Sanday suggests violent male dominance

> evolves in societies faced with depleting food resources, migration, or other factors contributing to a dependence on male destructive capacities as opposed to female fertility. . . . When people perceive an imbalance between the food supply and population needs, or when populations are in competition for diminishing resources, the male role is accorded greater prestige. Females are perceived as objects to be controlled as men struggle to retain or to gain control of their environment. Behaviors and attitudes prevail that separate the sexes and force men into a posture of proving their manhood [including] sexual violence.[213]

Following Sanday's thinking, we argue in chapter 6 that a co-constitutive relationship exists between the Syndrome and environmental stress and exigency. Environmental stress or exigency deepens the Syndrome, to be sure, but the Syndrome also makes environmental stresses and exigencies far more likely than they otherwise would be. Before undertaking that discussion, we round out this discussion of governance and political stability by examining the special role of the Syndrome's structural predisposition to marriage market obstruction in the emergence of state-level insecurity and instability.

CHAPTER 5

THE TREMORS CAUSED BY OBSTRUCTED MARRIAGE MARKETS

A Closer Look

Without a hedge, the vineyard is laid waste, and without a wife, a man is a hopeless wanderer. Who trusts an armed band of vagabonds? Who trusts a man that has no nest?

—*Ben Sira, 36:30–31*

In Post-Syndrome societies, it is true that marriage may no longer be viewed as an important rite of passage for men. In Patrilineal/Fraternal Syndrome societies, however, the existence of the patriline absolutely depends on the biological reproduction of the group—and that means legitimate male offspring through the patriline are an essential requirement for the group's continuation. The ability to marry and sire legitimate male offspring thus remains a pressing concern for each and every male member of the patriline. Consequently, marriage will remain one of the most important rites of passage for the achievement of manhood within the male dominance hierarchy.

Consider that when ISIS conquered areas within Iraq, one of the first items on the agenda was the procurement of legitimate wives (i.e., not sex slaves). As Patrick Cockburn of *The Independent* reported in 2014 before ISIS's defeat,

In the town of Baiji . . . which is completely under the control of ISIS, residents say they are most frightened by ISIS militants going door to door asking about the numbers of married and unmarried women in the house. "I told them that there were only two women in the house and both were married," said Abu Lahid. "They said that many of their mujahedin [fighters] were unmarried and wanted a wife. They insisted on coming into my house to look at the women's ID cards [which in Iraq show marital status]."[1]

Reports from Mosul in 2014 likewise found reports of women kidnapped from their families and forced into "jihad marriages."[2]

The stipulation that all men must marry and extend the patriline has important consequences for women. Laura Betzig cuts to the chase by asserting that kinship is created "as the result of a [man's] success in obtaining women and having children,"[3] but kinship is also one of the reasons an individual man is more likely to find such success. Reliance on male-bonded kin groups as a security provision mechanism renders the subordination of women persistent because of the patriline's simultaneous need for and exclusion of women. As Fukuyama notes, "In agnatic societies, women achieve legal personhood only by virtue of their marriage to and mothering of a male in the lineage"; that is, women "exist" in these societies only in as much as they create the patriline because patrilines cannot exist without women creating them.[4] He goes on to note, "we should not underestimate the importance of sex and access to women as a driver of political organization, particularly in segmentary or tribal societies that routinely use women as a medium of exchange."[5]

The fierceness and the sensitivity with which the subordinate status of women in clan-based societies is guarded by the men of these societies testifies to the truth of Fukuyama's assertion. Mounira M. Charrad cogently observes, "Women represent a potential source of rupture in the web uniting the men of the patrilineage,"[6] which is why they are so strictly subordinated. This understanding that patrilineal clans can only be formed through the subordination of female interests, especially in marriage and sexual relations, suggests that mechanisms of control over female interests in sex, marriage, and reproduction may in fact be the most visible indicators of patrilineal clan governance. As we argued in part I of this volume, one of the most effective ways of seeing clan-based governance structures is by examining the usually very visible situation of women within the society, and in marriage more particularly. As David Jacobson puts it, "gender is the hinge . . . the role of gender in tribes and tribalism is foundational."[7]

Although the consequences of the patrilineal imperative for women are profound and profoundly negative, as we recounted in chapter 3, the consequences for men are equally profound and also may be quite negative. The inability of a male member of the patriline to marry will engender a deep sense of grievance, and that grievance will extend to the established political order. In this, we again see how tightly intertwined the sexual order is with the political order.

If the societal order is based around the patriline and its accompanying fraternity, and a man for whatever reason cannot assume his place in that patriline, both the psychological cost and the material cost to that man will be immense.

We assert that the patrilineal/fraternal sexual political order tends to catalyze the obstruction of marriage markets, because marriage obstruction has destabilizing effects on the societal political order in addition to those we described previously in this book. The Patrilineal/Fraternal Syndrome creates at least three structural goads that cause this obstruction to occur. The first goad to marriage market obstruction occurs through the elimination of females from the childbearing and future childbearing population as a result of the devaluation of female life. This devaluation is enacted by such phenomena as female infanticide, sex-selective abortion of females, passive and active neglect of females, high levels of violence against females, and high levels of female suicide. These practices serve to significantly alter the sex ratio of a society. The second goad to marriage market obstruction occurs through polygyny, which mimics the effects of a highly masculinized sex ratio by allowing dominant men to accumulate women, whereas nondominant males may face a scarcity of women. In essence, this simulates an altered sex ratio among women of marriageable age. The third goad to marriage market obstruction is through high brideprice and wedding costs that substantially raise the age of marriage for young adult men—or preclude it altogether—due to inability to accumulate the demanded sums. The overall effect of all three structural goads on patriline members is to delay marriage or make it altogether unlikely for a significant percentage of men in the society; in other words, the marriage market in the society cannot clear because it is obstructed. The astute observer cannot but note that the *sexual* order imposed by the Patrilineal/Fraternal Syndrome becomes one of the greatest threats to its preferred *political* order simply because that sexual order is chronically predisposed to marriage market obstruction through one of the three structural goads we have identified. *The system is therefore structured to inevitably destabilize.* We examine these three phenomena in greater detail to identify the sources of predisposition and their effects on the character of grievance that ensues (see figure 5.1).

Before doing so, it is important to disabuse oneself of the notion that if women are in higher demand, then their subordination will be lessened. Take, for example, abnormal sex ratios favoring males. Such sex ratio alteration serves but to amplify the Syndrome we have identified. When women are scarce, women's lives do not, generally speaking, improve in quality. They are more likely to become victims of violent assault, kidnapping, and sale.[8] There may be an accompanying rise in demand for prostitution, with associated impetus for trafficking. Violence against women in domestic settings may be heightened as well, for women are even more tightly controlled. The age of marriage for

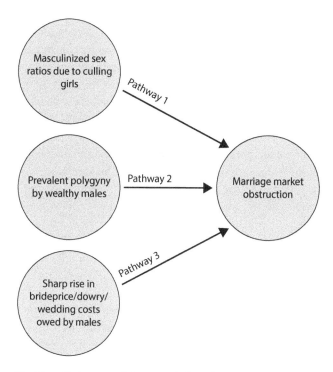

FIGURE 5.1 The Three Pathways to Marriage Market Obstruction

girls may drop even lower than before, as men seek marriage partners among increasingly younger cohorts. Suicide rates among women often rise significantly. All of these phenomena may have ramifications for stability and security of the group, as well. Even as it destabilizes society, the Syndrome becomes even more entrenched and vise-like.

First Structural Goad to Marriage Market Obstruction: Culling Females

As we have noted, in societies where female productive labor is not valued highly and male children are the primary source of economic security for the elderly, female children will come to be seen as unacceptable burdens within their natal family. A family in a Syndrome society may face the prospect of using precious resources to feed, clothe, and shelter its female children, only to export these children to another patrilineal clan at the time of marriage. Furthermore, to the extent that dowry develops within the culture—that is, the payment the natal family must make for the groom's family to agree to take over the burden of caring for the female after marriage—the economic burden may seem immense, even completely unreasonable. In some cultures, the equivalent of a year's income or more is required as a dowry payment, and the demands for dowry "supplements" to ensure the benign treatment of the girl may continue for years. Furthermore, the burden of maintaining a virtuous reputation for the future bride, in many contexts, may be perceived as a heavy burden for her natal family to bear. In this context, raising girls may seem irrational, and ensuring that no daughters are born or survive may seem a reasonable means of coping with the "threat" these daughters pose to the family.

Girls are culled from the population for other reasons as well. In the past, military invaders would forcibly "marry" daughters of local families in order to become their "kin," thereby presumably easing the need to rule by direct military force. The presence of daughters represented, then, a real strategic vulnerability in the face of invasion by out-groups. Similarly, in chronically fragile subsistence societies, such as among the early Australian aborigines or Inuit in the far north, limiting the numbers of those who would bring new mouths to feed into the society seemed imperative.[9] Future mothers, not future fathers, were seen as posing a threat to the survival of the group.

Furthermore, these culling practices often become reified over time, even after the initial catalyst has disappeared. For example, women in modern India are far from unproductive, yet the tradition of dowry persists. Likewise, the notion that the "wife-taker" is superior to the "wife-giver," a relic from the time of the Mughal invasion, is still prevalent. Thus, even in twenty-first-century India, we find social and religious imperatives for hypergyny, where a daughter may be honorably married only to a man who comes from a higher-ranking family than her own. The cost of such a hypergynous marriage may be ruinous, and daughters born to the highest status families may not ever be able to marry at all. This explains why sex ratios among the most educated and wealthiest families in India may actually be worse than those among poor families.[10]

All in all, we can understand why historian William Sumner would assert, "Children add to the weight of the struggle for existence of their parents. . . . Abortion and infanticide are especially interesting because they show how early in the history of civilization the burden of children became so heavy that parents began to shirk it."[11] He's right, but he's missed the gendered aspect—it is first and foremost *female* offspring in these societies who create a perceived burden or threat, and it is first and foremost *female* offspring who are "shirked" by passive or active means of infanticide. This differential treatment stems from the nature of the first political order. Whether we speak of sex-selective abortion, female infanticide, differential feeding practices of sons versus daughters, or refusal to spend resources on the medical care of daughters, the result is that girls will begin to be culled from the group population, and natural sex ratios will become unnatural.

The relationship of these practices to reliance on the patrilineal/fraternal security provision mechanism is unquestionable. The encoding of the Syndrome predisposes the society to devaluing female life. Monica Das Gupta notes,

> The more kinship rules exclude adult daughters from contributing to their parents, the lower the incentives for parents to raise girls. . . . The correspondence between kinship rules and son preference is striking. Within the same country, different levels of permissible contact between daughters and their parents (as documented in ethnographic studies) are mirrored in regional differences in child sex ratios in India, and in regional and ethnic differentials in China. Even within the same culture, variations in kinship system matter—in South Korea, the eldest son is primarily responsible for continuing the family line, and this is reflected in stronger son preference than that expressed by the wives of other sons.[12]

Lest one fall prey to the misconception that culling girls was only a practice of the past, remember that the number of countries with abnormal childhood (age birth to four years old) sex ratios is growing, not shrinking, in the twenty-first century. In 1995, only five countries had abnormal, masculinized sex ratios (not counting Hong Kong). In 2015, there were nineteen (not counting Hong Kong and Macau).[13] The Syndrome's logic is overpowering, even in an age of globalization and international human rights treaties. Over the past twenty years, only one country has seen a reversion from abnormal to normal sex ratios: South Korea. Interestingly, South Korea's success in normalizing its sex ratios has a lot to do with its effective undermining of the dominance of patrilineal clans in its society (discussed further in chapter 8).[14]

A significant imbalance between the number of young adult men and young adult women in society—whether through offspring sex selection, high mortality rates for girls compared with boys or women compared with men, or polygyny—produces obstructions in the marriage market of such societies. There are simply not enough women for each male patriline member to marry and produce offspring. For example, historically among the polygynous Azande in Africa, as Betzig (quoting Johan Lagae) notes, in one locale, for every one hundred adult men, there were twenty-six bachelors, forty-seven men in monogamous unions, eighteen men in polygynous unions of only two wives, and nine men in polygynous unions of more than two wives.[15] These "surplus" men become what in the Chinese vernacular are known as the "bare branches" of their societies; branches of the patrilineal family tree that will never bear fruit. In contemporary India, an estimated 12 percent of young adult men are surplus to the number of young adult women in society, and in China, that figure may be as high as 15 percent.[16] The consequences for a patrilineal/fraternal society in which a substantial percentage of adult men will never marry are both predictable and profound.

First, men with advantages will marry; men without advantages, who are already at risk for antisocial behavior, will not. Indeed, this is the case in all three structural goads we discuss in this chapter—elite men will not suffer from the scarcity of women in their society. But those nonelite men who find themselves pushed out of the marriage market will feel a deep sense of grievance, as well as a determination either to obtain, one way or the other, the advantages that will allow them to enter the market and be successful, or, alternatively, to circumvent or upend the system that relegates them to outsider status.

Thus, we find a variety of fairly predictable strategies being employed by bare branches to better their position, none of which enhance the stability, security, or resilience of their society. The reason is that the one advantage that cannot be taken from bare branches is their comparative physical strength as young adult males and their willingness to use that strength, especially in male-bonded groups and even in illegal or sociopathic ways, to gain what they need to enter the marriage market. It comes as no surprise, then, that masculinized sex ratios correlate with property crime and violent crime rates in numerous empirical studies.

For example, using annual province-level data, economist Lena Edlund and colleagues find that for every 1 percent alteration of the sex ratio in favor of males, there was a corresponding 3.7 percent increase in violent and property crime rates in China. These are not white-collar crimes; these are bare branch crimes—the crimes of "bullies, bandits, and rebels." They hypothesize that high sex ratios create this violent reaction because they act much like polygyny does; the society is "wrecked by the revolt of the mass of inferior men who are condemned to celibacy by it."[17] Other empirical studies have revealed similar results in other nations, such as India and Korea—that is, violent crime increases in tandem with an increase in sex ratios.[18] Jonathan Gottschall senses the ourobouros-like nature of the equation: "Parents bias their investment in favor of males largely because the world is violent; the world is violent largely because parents bias their investment in favor of males."[19]

Crime is not the only trend that corresponds to sex ratios: protests and demonstrations are also increasing in size and frequency. Writing in *The Atlantic*, Alan Taylor notes, "According to research by the Chinese Academy of Governance, the number of protests in China doubled between 2006 and 2010, rising to 180,000 reported 'mass incidents'" in 2010 alone,[20] a figure confirmed by other researchers as well.[21] The types of clashes reported have been serious. For example, in 2011, parts of Inner Mongolia were placed under martial law, and in Guangzhou, after thousands of protesters set fire to cars and attacked government buildings, the police deployed armored vehicles.[22] The 2019 crisis in Hong Kong, which also has highly abnormal sex ratios, is another violent example.

In addition, honor—with its laser-like focus on respect and disrespect—takes on heightened salience in cultures with a sizeable number of bare branches. As sociologists Allan Mazur and Alan Booth explain,

> There may be a general hypersensitivity to insult in any subculture that is (or once was) organized around young men who are unconstrained by traditional community agents of social control, as often occurs in frontier communities, gangs, among vagabonds or bohemians, and after breakdowns in the social fabric following wars or natural disasters. When young men place special emphasis on protecting their reputation, and they are not restrained from doing so, dominance contests become ubiquitous, the hallmark of male-to-male interaction.[23]

These dominance contests catalyze the "risky shift" among groups of young men, that is, the willingness to take greater risks collectively than individually. Thus, the behavior of men in groups—particularly young, single, low-status males—will not rise above the behavior of the worst-behaved individual. Collectively, they will take larger risks and be more violent than they otherwise would be. As one young male gang member in Australia expressed it, "Gang is your best friend. Your whole group, you can do anything. You're happy, you want to do anything. You're not scared of stuff."[24] Fraternity is ever the sturdy friend of risky, violent behavior.

The governing powers of such a society find themselves in quite a quandary. Although they may turn a blind eye to predictable consequences such as the cross-border trafficking of women, they cannot, in general, alleviate the grievances of these young adult men, for even with such trafficking, the sex ratios of the country are likely to remain substantially abnormal. Vice will be winked at by the authorities, but violence will not, for bare branch collectives can at times pose a serious threat to the established order.

For example, the Nien Rebellion in nineteenth-century China originated in a province where, because of grotesquely abnormal sex ratios, 25 percent of men were unable to marry.[25] Sociologist Daniel Little writes, "Families adopted the practice of female infanticide to increase family income and security, but the long-term aggregate result was a skewed demography in which there was a large surplus of young men. These young men became natural recruits for bandit gangs and local militia—thus providing resources for the emergence of collective strategies of predation and protection."[26]

Governments may find they have no choice but to turn to "hard" tactics of authoritarianism, brutally suppressing violence internally, and perhaps exporting the agents of violence to other lands through military campaigns. Sociologist James Boone sums up the situation facing governments in this way:

> Their poor socio-economic position and reproductive prospects make [bare branches] perennial aspirants in large-scale expansionist and insurgent military campaigns through which they might hope to achieve higher positions. . . . A highly competitive, volatile situation [develops] at the societal level with respect to the problem of excess cadet males [i.e., bare branches—ed.]. Rulers must choose between dispersing these individuals, for example, in expansionist campaigns, or facing disorder and overthrow on the home front.[27]

Instability, crime, authoritarianism, and even greater suppression of women attend the development of abnormal sex ratios favoring males, which adds to—and follows logically from—the dysfunctional predispositions created by the Syndrome.

Second Structural Goad to Marriage Market Obstruction: Polygyny

A similar chain of events attends societies that select for prevalent polygyny instead of sex ratio alteration because of the value placed on women's productive labor, as in sub-Saharan Africa. This is so because prevalent polygyny serves as the functional equivalent of an abnormal sex ratio. By marrying multiple women, elite men create an underclass of young adult men who are elbowed out of the marriage market because there are not enough women in that market: these women are alive—unlike societies with abnormal sex ratios—but they have been monopolized by men with far greater resources than these young men. For example, author William Tucker notes that in the 1950s in West Africa, as a result of polygyny, "at least a quarter of the male African population was permanently excluded from marriage, leaving a volatile class of unattached males."[28] This does not bode well for peace within the society. Evolutionary psychologist Joseph Henrich and his coauthors assert, "Faced with high levels of intra-sexual competition and little chance of obtaining even one long-term mate, unmarried, low-status men will heavily discount the future and more readily engage in risky status-elevating and sex-seeking behaviours, [elevating] crime rates, including rape, murder, assault, robbery, and fraud."[29]

The authors go on to note, "Polygynous societies engage in more warfare. . . . When inter-group competition relies on large numbers of highly motivated young men to engage in continuous raiding and warfare to obtain resources, slaves, territory and concubines, groups with greater polygyny may generate larger and more motivated pools of males for these risky activities."[30]

Psychologist David Barash comments, "Like the energy captured in a bow that is drawn back, ready to power an arrow, polygyny generates much of the background tension that erupts into violence."[31]

Even ancient societies realized that polygyny could destabilize their societies. Tucker notes that in ancient Sparta[32] every warrior was guaranteed a wife. This was done purposefully to retain the loyalty of the army, and he provocatively notes,

> The Athenians were the first known urban society in which an alpha male was not allowed to take more than one wife, and was shamed if he divorced. They were also the world's first democratic society. . . . It might not be the case that once a society establishes sexual democracy [among men] it goes on to extend political rights and become democratic. Rather it may be that once the people are given a voice through democracy, they impose monogamy on their rulers. Remember, it is low status men who resist polygamy at the top.[33]

Barash comments that "Monogamy is therefore an equalizing and democratizing system for men . . . [it] may have emerged as a sop to men, reducing the number consigned to frustrated bachelorhood, in a kind of unspoken social bargain whereby powerful men gave up the overt perquisites of polygyny in return for obtaining a degree of social peace and harmony."[34]

Although these same marriage market obstruction patterns and consequences attend polygynous societies as societies in which the sex ratio is altered as a result of the culling of females, the flavor of grievance is somewhat different, and somewhat more intense, than in societies with abnormal sex ratios. When girls are culled from the birth population, it is difficult to blame specific individuals for the dislocations that result. Indeed, many families within the society—perhaps even one's own—may be practicing offspring sex selection. In polygynous societies, however, it is clear to everyone who has unfairly accumulated many wives: wealthy men. Thus, there is a more personal, more specific cause of the grievance in full view in polygynous societies than in abnormal sex ratio societies. One's chances of overcoming this obstruction seem significantly better than in those latter societies—if the collective action problem among one's similarly marginalized fellows could be solved.[35]

So, for example, Barash notes, "the likelihood that a man will kill another man is much higher in societies with large disparities in wealth, situations in which men are particularly pressed to achieve the status needed to acquire and maintain relationships with women . . . polygyny [is] both a manifestation of inequality and a generator of it because it unbalances the sex ratio among marriageable adults."[36] He concludes, "The connection between violence and polygyny is noticeably tight, just like the close coupling between maleness and violence."[37] Interestingly, Barash also notes that men's life expectancies are thus considerably shorter in polygynous societies than in monogamous ones.[38]

No wonder, then, that some studies have shown greater ease of recruitment into rebel groups in polygynous societies. For example, development expert Esther Mokuwa and colleagues demonstrate significantly greater ease of rebel recruitment in areas with higher rates of polygyny within Sierra Leone compared with those areas with lower rates.[39] As noted in chapter 4, anthropologists have found significant correlation between polygyny and the amount of warfare in which societies engage.[40] Some scholars have asserted that polygynous societies are more likely to engage in expansionist warfare to distract low-status mateless males.[41] In other words, polygyny has long been linked to societal instability and lack of resilience in the scholarly literature.

In an interesting study, Rebecca Nielsen finds that during the brutal civil war in Sierra Leone—a culture encoding polygyny and brideprice (and hence marriage market obstruction)—married men tended to join civil militias while unmarried men tended to join rebel groups.[42] The "bet" taken by the unmarried men was that by joining the rebels they would increase their chances of marrying. In areas that experienced low levels of conflict during the civil war, that bet did not pan out. In areas that experienced high conflict, however, the average age of male marriage dropped by seven to fifteen years (from twenty-five to thirty-five down to eighteen to twenty), marriage markets cleared, and most marriages resulted from pregnancy (and thus with a smaller brideprice) than from negotiation with the bride's family before sexual relations. In these high-conflict areas, joining a rebel group did garner tremendous payoffs in the marriage market for the young men who took that bet. Almost certainly, however, nothing changed for the better for the women.

Another relevant case is that of the Vikings. Ben Raffield and Mark Collard posit that the mix of polygyny, concubinage, and rising social inequality in Scandinavia during the late-eighth-century led to the famous Viking raids of this period. They explain:

> With elite men monopolizing an increasing percentage of women, many low-status men would have found it difficult to marry unless they were willing to engage in risky activities to improve their wealth and status. At the same time, elite men were motivated to organize expeditions to acquire plunder and develop their reputations as war leaders. Raiding therefore represented a mutually beneficial means of achieving social advancement, success in the marriage market, and, for elite men, political power.[43]

Jonathan Gottschall argues that the very same dynamic of polygyny and concubinage by elite males drove the wars and conflicts at the heart of Homer's *Iliad*.[44]

Polygyny also provides a standing mechanism for intrafamily resentment and fission. Goody notes that in polygynous societies, "the unit of consumption [is] the children of one mother. This unit, whose existence is dependent upon polygyny, is of central important in the fission of domestic groups."[45] In other words, polygynous patrilines were always on the knife's edge of violent fissioning between the sons of different mothers. Historian Stephanie Coontz notes about medieval Europe that the Church's prohibition of polygyny came as a huge relief to the continent, for when kings married polygynously,

> they left Western European kingdoms vulnerable to the kind of instability and bloodshed [seen] in the Hellenistic dynasties of Asia Minor. . . . Rival heirs from different mothers schemed to further their own ends. Having too many heirs to the throne could be as much of a problem as having too few. . . . The Church's insistence on monogamy and disapproval of divorce [had] the salutary effect of imposing the matrimonial equivalent of an arms limitation agreement.[46]

In a 2018 cross-national study, economists Tim Krieger and Laura Renner have likewise investigated how such polygynous fissioning, pitting elite half-brothers against one another, can lead to political instability.[47]

In addition to intrasocietal grievance and conflict, this lack of resilience in polygynous cultures may manifest in more rigid, and therefore more fragile, governance systems. For example, as we noted, in an intriguing empirical study of 186 societies, Betzig finds the correlation between despotism and polygyny to be .72, significant at the .01 level.[48] Anthropologists Andrey Korotayev and Dmitri Bondarenko obtain similar results.[49] One of the causal mechanisms involved is the creation of a standing pool of marginalized and disaffected young adult men, in reaction to which authoritarianism appears useful as a counterweight. As Robert Wright puts it, "Extreme polygyny often goes hand in hand with extreme political hierarchy, and reaches its zenith under the most despotic regimes."[50] Furthermore, societies practicing polygyny were shown by Rose McDermott and Jonathan Cowden to also demonstrate higher per capita arms expenditures and significantly lower respect for political rights and civil liberties.[51] With the lenses provided by our theoretical framework, we see that it is not only polygyny, but any sustained marriage market obstruction that may well produce this effect.

Even so, polygyny holds a special place in this pantheon of obstructions. In chapter 4, we commented on Richard Alexander's thoughts:

> It is almost as if no nation can become both quite large and quite unified except under socially imposed monogamy. . . . Socially imposed monogamy inhibits the rise of the kind of disproportionately large and powerful lineages of close relatives . . . One of the correlates of the rise of nations, and a function of systems of law, is to suppress the right of responsibility to avenge wrongs done to kin, and to prevent subgroups and clans from attaining undue power.[52]

Thus, in addition to the effects on grievance and conflict, a close relationship exists between polygyny and the type of governance to which the collective can aspire. Meaningful democracy may be out of reach for polygynous societies.

The group also faces economic consequences in the case of prevalent polygyny. Henrich, for example, argues that a higher prevalence of polygyny may reduce national wealth (gross domestic product per capita) for two reasons.[53] First, male economic efforts will be dedicated primarily to obtaining more wives instead of more productive economic investment, and second, there may be an accompanying increase in female fertility.[54] We add that underinvestment in children will also limit economic prosperity across generations. Henrich and his coauthors aver that polygyny also tends to increase the spousal age gap, and increases intrahousehold conflict, which in turn leads to higher rates of child neglect, abuse, accidental death, and homicide. They also propose that

> In the most complex societies, where a society's competitive success is influenced by its economic output, standing armies, innovation rates, trade, division of labour and offspring quality, higher rates of polygynous marriage reduce a society's competitive success. Under these conditions, normative monogamy increases a society's competitiveness because of how it influences crime rates, male motivations, paternal investment, fertility and economic production.[55]

If polygyny produces negative consequences, Henrich and colleagues argue, the reverse is also true: select for monogamy—or ban polygyny—and good things start to happen. For illustration, economist Michele Tertilt has found that banning polygyny "reduces fertility by 40 percent, increases savings by 70 percent, and raises output per person by 170 percent."[56] Peter Turchin points to an interesting paradox: in polygynous societies, men are incentivized to amass wealth, but polygynous societies perform poorly in an economic sense, at least in the African context he has studied. He notes,

> Polygyny should induce males to make greater effort to become rich so that they can afford a wife, and then even richer so they can afford many. If this were so, polygynous countries with hard-working male populations should enjoy greater economic growth than monogamous countries. But the opposite is the case. A comparison of tropical developing countries shows that GDP per capita in monogamous countries is three times higher than in polygamous ones. Differences between individual countries can be staggering. Compare Botswana where polygamy is banned, with Burkina Faso, in which more than half of married women are in polygynous families. Botswana's GDP per capita is 10 times that of Burkina Faso.[57]

McDermott and Cowden similarly note that neither economic development nor increases in female literacy seem to be capable of reducing the prevalence of polygyny.[58] Indeed, economic development may actually spur polygyny among the newly rich, increasing the national prevalence of the practice. Similarly, increases in female literacy seem not to lead to women's emancipation from polygynous marriage norms, as we see in Gulf states with high female literacy rates, for example.

Because polygyny entails, bluntly, reproductive inequality for men, it can only exist in a social system in which inequality is normalized through the first political order. Betzig notes, "Polygyny, or reproductive inequality, requires economic and political inequality: a man with ten times as many women and children must either work ten times as hard to support them, or take what he needs from other men. Across space and time, polygyny has overlapped with despotism, [and] monogamy with egalitarianism."[59] Polygyny requires an enormous amount of stratification and inequality, backed by coercion, to remain even somewhat stable. This can be seen even in U.S. FLDS polygamous communities in which a few elite families dine on lobster, whereas most endure starvation rations.[60]

McDermott and Cowden summarize by noting that the societal choice to embrace and tolerate polygyny or ban it has fateful consequences: "Policymakers would have to change multiple laws across multiple domains to exert as much of an effect on these negative outcomes toward women and children as could be accomplished by the abolition of polygyny. . . . By prohibiting polygyny, we reduce social inequities, violence toward women and children, and the proliferation of single men and the violence they perpetuate, as well as increase political rights and civil liberties for all."[61]

Third Structural Goad to Marriage Market Obstruction: Brideprice, Dowry, and Wedding Cost Escalation

In patrilineal societies, it is common for a man to "buy a wife."[62] Another way to create the functional equivalent of a high sex ratio is a significant escalation in marriage and wedding costs for grooms in brideprice-practicing societies.[63] For example, an entire ethnic group in South Sudan was destabilized by rising brideprices among the group around the time of independence. Cattle theft rose precipitously as desperate would-be grooms sought additional livestock to meet the rising price of brides, and revenge attacks followed these thefts.[64] Jada Tombe, a young man in South Sudan noted, "We risk our lives to raid other communities so we can pay bride price."[65] A U.S. Institute of Peace field study explained: "A government official provided an alternative motive for joining militia groups: 'Some youth are joining the rebels [militias] to loot properties so they can marry.' A recent Norwegian People's aid report supports indications in the authors' interview data that some young men in South Sudan join armed gangs, at least in part, because they believe it will help them pay dowries"[66] (note that they actually mean brideprice, not dowry). Societal stability and resilience are profoundly affected by the existence of a "brideprice economy."

In Libya, those interested in the rebel militias that are the de facto enforcement power in the post-Qaddafi era might think on what the following exchange captured by journalists Scott Shane and Jo Becker might really be saying about the effects of marriage market obstruction:

> Shortly after Colonel Qaddafi was killed, Mr. Sagezli had gathered a group of fighters in Benghazi. A businessman with degrees from Utah State University and the London School of Economics, he knew the rebel militias had been organized along Libya's deepest fault lines: tribal divisions, regional loyalties and differing stances on Islam's proper role. Yet the country could not progress unless the militias were reintegrated into civil society and replaced by a regular army.
> "What do you need?" he asked the fighters. "What are your dreams?"
> Their modest answers surprised and encouraged him.
> "Some were very simple dreams," he said. "Help us get married."[67]

Actually, as we have seen, that's not a very simple dream at all. The Western journalists simply did not understand the significance of the answer. Consider Heather Murdock's analysis of Egypt on the verge of the overthrow of Hosni Mubarak:

> Young men say they want to get married, but can't. They blame the former Hosni Mubarak government for keeping them financially incapable of marriage. They say as long as they have been alive, financial advancement has depended entirely on connections. Without those connections, many young men work ten years or more, just to have enough money to get married. During the 18-days of protests that lead to Mr. Mubarak's resignation, chants of "We want to get married," were heard along with more familiar calls to dissolve the government.[68]

Murdock notes that the average young man in Egypt at the time of the uprising had to delay marriage until his early thirties, for he would need to save thirteen times his annual salary to marry.

In Afghanistan, State Department officials did not understand the importance of the conversations they were having with their Afghan colleagues about brideprice and wedding costs. Following her service in Kabul, Alexandra Tenny, a foreign service officer, related this story about one of her Afghan colleagues in an interview with the authors:

> He was exasperated by the insanely high, and ever rising costs, of weddings in Afghanistan. I really didn't understand what the big deal was. He wanted the government to intervene and thought we in the Embassy should get involved in the conversation. At that time, we, the ever so enlightened American political officers, viewed it through the lens of cultural pressures to put on a good party, as a poverty issue, or discussed it in the terms of women's rights and social issues and cultural norms. We never linked it to national security implications and for me, this research provides the vocabulary necessary. You rightly point out the importance of taking the emotion and moralizing out of it and counting it as an important variable that has a place in the policy conversation. I got a bit exasperated with his insistence on it being a serious issue and showed him research about how many Americans go into extreme debt to have the "dream wedding" making the argument of who are we as foreigners to tell people how to spend their money—I was certainly moralizing.[69]

This wasn't an issue about whether a couple would be releasing doves at their reception; what Tenny's Afghan colleague was trying to get through to her was that this was a security issue about whether would-be grooms would be joining the Taliban to meet brideprice and wedding costs.

Numerous scholars have commented on the destabilizing effects of a "youth bulge" within a country,[70] but the link to marriage market dynamics often is not explored. According to the propositions of this school of research, the "youth bulge" leads to grievance in contexts where the young experience high unemployment and diminished future prospects. What is left unsaid is that the young for whom such grievances may turn explosive are overwhelmingly male. Furthermore, to have a "youth bulge," one must have a high fertility rate, and in only certain countries (i.e., predominantly Patrilineal/Fraternal Syndrome encoding societies) will one find such high fertility rates. If such destabilization is primarily found in these patrilineally organized countries, what is left unseen is that a close relationship exists between young male grievance and obstructed marriage markets in patrilineal cultures.

Such destabilization can lead to the crumbling of democratic institutions. Demographic researcher Hannes Weber, examining 110 countries over the period from 1972 to 2009, found in multivariate modeling that the proportion of young men in a country's population had a strong, significant, and negative effect on indices of democracy.[71] He comments, "Within the observed period of time, full or partial democracies with a share of young men exceeding 19.9 percent of the total adult population [i.e., the median global value] have a probability of 23.1 percent of becoming a dictatorship within the next five years, whereas this probability is 4.6 percent for democracies with less young men."[72] Weber notes that although male young adults (fifteen to twenty-nine years old) express as much support for democracy as any other subpopulation in the World Values Survey, "they express a significantly greater approval of extremist attitudes and readiness to violence and sacrifice, even when education and income levels are held constant. Young men justify political assassinations almost twice as often and support personal violence as a form of political action more than three times as often as the rest of the population."[73] Weber suggests such behavior might catalyze authoritarian response to control the threat and also that as vocal young men become more numerous, the approval of political violence may be contagious within the rest of the population.

The structural goad of brideprice, with its consequence of obstructed marriage markets, may explain the linkage further. As one commentator observed in 2011, "U.S. diplomats identified delayed marriage as a source of discontent in Libya two years ago. Other scholars have called the problem a regional 'marriage crisis,' born out of low incomes, and the high cost of marriage. They point out that in conservative Middle Eastern countries, unmarried young adults are generally denied intimate relationships, and the social status that comes along with being an adult."[74] In other words, the literature on grievance and destabilization is poorer for the omission of the patrilineal-based nature of these societies and thus the role of marriage market obstruction in producing that grievance. Being unemployed is never good, but being unemployed in a society in which you can become an adult man only by marrying and in which marriage requires significant financial resources produces a double dose of vexation and desperation.[75]

Furthermore, rebel and terrorist groups are attuned to this source of discontent, and they openly recruit by promising to solve the marriage asset problem for young men.[76] It is fascinating to see just how many terrorist and rebel groups are so very concerned about the marriage prospects of the young men in their ranks. For example, political scientist Diane Singerman notes, "To mobilize supporters, there were many reports of radical Islamist groups in Egypt in the 1990s arranging extremely low-cost marriages among the group's members."[77] More recently, "Hamas leaders have turned to matchmaking, bringing together single fighters and widows, and providing dowries and wedding parties for the many here who cannot afford such trappings of matrimony."[78] The Syrian government also provides brideprices and weddings for its soldiers, including those who are wounded and those who lost brothers in the civil war.[79] ISIS was well known for providing its foreign jihadis with the opportunity to marry that they may not have had in their home country. In one such campaign, ISIS offered "its fighters a $1,500 bonus to go towards a starter home along with a free honeymoon in their stronghold city of Raqqa."[80] Another report found that "ISIS foreign fighters paid $10,000 dowries to the families of their brides," suggesting that the group was attracting foreign fighters by promising resources (and available women) to marry.[81] Valerie Hudson and Hilary Matfess provide an in-depth case study of Boko Haram's use of brideprice grievance to attract recruits through promises of facilitating marriage through the capture of young women.[82] "In this crisis, these men can take a wife at no extra charge," explained Kaka, a young woman orphaned, captured, and raped by Boko Haram. "Usually it is very expensive to take a wife, very hard to get married, but not now."[83] Matfess met another young woman who told her story:

> Bawagana, a shy 15-year-old living in Sanda Kyarimi camp, one of the official IDP sites, said that a Boko Haram fighter had come to her home in Dikwa, 90 kilometres east of Maiduguri, and asked "Do you love me?"
>
> "Of course I answered, 'no!' " she said, with her eyes fixed on the ground.
>
> "The boy got very angry and said: 'If you do not come with me, I will kill your father, but if you come with me I will let him live.' I followed to save my father."
>
> The boy left 10,000 naira (about $50) on the floor. It was a bride price in Boko Haram's eyes.[84]

Although Boko Haram's founder Mohammed Yusuf helped arrange marriages for struggling young men, after his death, the brideprice has accompanied outright kidnapping of girls. A Human Rights Watch report states that the group would enter villages and "after storming into the homes and throwing sums of money at their parents, with a declaration that it was the dowry for their teenage daughter, they would take the girls away."[85]

This logic applies outside the Nigerian context, as well. For example, commenting on the brideprices offered by ISIS, one commentator stated,

> It's particularly appealing to men, for example, from Gulf countries, who come from a very conservative society where dating is taboo and casual sex is essentially forbidden, and where marriage is off bounds to people who don't have a lot of means. In order to marry, you have to be able to pay a dowry [brideprice], provide for your family, and have a house. Within those strictures you can see how this system, where you can come and essentially buy a poor girl for very little, would be a bonus.[86]

In one of the most poignant testimonies to the havoc created by escalating marriage costs, the sole surviving terrorist from the 2008 Mumbai bombings, Ajmal Kasab, age twenty-one, confessed that he had joined Lashkar-e-Taiba at the urging of his father, who said that by joining, the young man would earn a lot of money, enabling him and his brothers to marry.[87]

In addition to rebel and terrorist groups stepping in to clear marriage markets for young men, we also have the phenomenon of political movements doing the same. In pre-war Yemen in October 2013, for example, two so-called charitable organizations sponsored a mass wedding of four thousand brides and grooms.[88] It was paid for by the Orphan Foundation for Development, an arm of the Muslim Brotherhood, with funding provided by (in 2013) by Qatar's house of Al-Thani. Farea Al-Muslimi comments,

> In Yemen, the wedding of a wealthy young man may cost tens of thousands of dollars because of a social tradition to flaunt one's wealth. Meanwhile, a poor young man may not be able to celebrate his marriage as required by the habits of the region. So charities—often religious associations for social cooperation—specializing in facilitating marriage for young people appeared. They gather money from philanthropists to hold mass weddings for poor young people. . . . Associations such as the Association of Righteousness and Chastity and the Orphan Foundation also have their conditions. The young person who is allowed to join the mass wedding is generally close to the organization's religious and political orientations and those of its financiers.[89]

Similar charitable organizations can be found doing the same in other countries, such as Algeria, India, Lebanon, and Palestine.[90] In Palestine, widows of martyrs may be pressured to marry within the same political organization, and ISIS brides were subject to the same treatment.

States also step in as well, especially for young men at risk for extremism. Historian Robert Lacey recounts the following about Saudi Arabia:

> In fighting its war, the Ministry of the Interior has resorted to a novel tactic—marriage. . . . One cornerstone of the extremist rehab program is to get the "beneficiaries" as they are called, settled down with a wife as soon as possible. The Ministry of the Interior pays each unmarried beneficiary 60,000 riyals (some $18,000), the going rate for a dowry, or bride price. The family arranges a marriage, and whenever he can, Prince Muhammad turns up for the wedding.[91]

Saudi Arabia also has a legal cap on brideprice and wedding costs and is rumored to pay the brideprice for its soldiers.[92] Other states are also in the mass marriage business for low-income couples, such as Indonesia, Taiwan, and Iran.[93] In Iran, the government actually sponsors an online matchmaking service as well (and has even banned vasectomies).[94]

Brideprice inflation is also strongly linked to male labor migration in search of greater resources to marry as well as to the rising age of marriage for men.[95] Historically, as Julia Adams notes, younger sons (whose families may not have been able to accumulate brideprice for more than one or two sons) were often agents of military expansion.[96] Boone, for example, notes the tendency of younger sons during the Middle Ages to join the Crusades, joining themselves as soldiers loyal to younger princes, who themselves felt the same challenges.[97] Similarly, Goody observes about Saharan Africa, "The second of two brothers may have to delay his marriage while waiting for bridewealth cattle. [These second sons often] leav[e] the countryside to swell the growing population of the towns . . . there is a relationship between high bridewealth and labour migration."[98]

In modern days, migration to improve one's luck in the marriage market may involve a new form of crusading, such as becoming a "foreign fighter" for a group that will pay well. It would be interesting to know whether the foreign fighters for ISIS, for example, were primarily younger sons. Unfortunately, sufficient data to test that hypothesis are lacking. Even so, it is worth pondering what Anthony Lopez and his colleagues assert:

> Success in battle may benefit such men in at least two distinct ways. First, men who achieve heroic status through courage on the battlefield, and who may be able to bring benefits back to their community, gain status and wealth that may help them to increase their access and attractiveness to suitable mates. In addition, ancestrally, men were also able to find or kidnap brides from conquered territory, and secure mates in such a fashion. Given these selection pressures acting over human evolutionary history, male psychology should have adapted to implicitly regulate the willingness to engage in collective aggression based on the within-group availability of mates.[99]

Other effects of brideprice have been covered in previous chapters; for example, because girls increase their father's wealth in a brideprice society, while sons diminish it, a higher age of marriage for men is matched by a lower age of marriage for women—the age differential keeps the system afloat, as we saw in chapter 3. As we have previously noted, Jack Goody remarks, "men chafe at the delay, girls at the speed."[100] This relatively high difference in marriage age between men and women is a hallmark of brideprice societies.

Delayed marriage because of the rise in costs for the groom's family has become a new norm in the Middle East. For example, in Egypt, one study documents that families of young adult men must save for five to seven years to pay for their marriages. From 2000 to 2004, wedding costs in Egypt rose 25 percent. As a result, the average marriage age for Egyptian men has risen sharply, from the early twenties to the late twenties and early thirties. In one study, nearly 25 percent of young adult men in Egypt had not married by age twenty-seven; the average age of marriage was thirty-one.[101] In poverty-stricken Afghanistan, wedding costs for young men average $12,000–$20,000.[102] In Saudi Arabia, men usually are unable to marry before age twenty-nine; often they marry only in their mid-thirties.[103] In Iran, 38 percent of twenty-five to twenty-nine-year-old men are unmarried. Across the Middle East, only about 50 percent of twenty-five to twenty-nine-year-old men are married, the lowest percentage for this group in the developing world.[104] Whether in Afghanistan, Iran, Lebanon, or the United Arab Emirates, the exorbitant costs of marriage have delayed the age at which Muslim men marry.

Polygyny, practiced almost exclusively by men with means, has always been a strong contributing factor in the rise of brideprice costs for the rest of the men in society and increases the competition for available women. Polygyny feeds into brideprice in another way, as well: through escalation in the numerical count of wives. As a village elder in South Sudan noted in one field study, "One of the reasons for polygamy is that when you have ten daughters, each one will give you thirty cows, and they are all for [the father]. So then you have three hundred cows. That is why one marries very many wives: so that you can have very many daughters."[105]

The rise in brideprice leads to chronically obstructed marriage markets. Commentators have lamented the emergence of a new class of "old maids" ('unoussa)—young adult men who cannot afford to marry and feel both ashamed and emasculated. One Egyptian commentator notes that these young men are seeking dangerous jobs: "The youth are seeking death. They're already dead at home."[106] Singerman comments, "We can infer that the notion that they are 'already dead at home' refers to both their financial situation, their political exclusion, and their unmarried status."[107] This situation offers terrorist movements an opportunity they have been able to exploit successfully. The journalist Michael Slackman notes, "Here in Egypt and across the Middle East, many young people are being forced to put off marriage, the gateway to independence, sexual activity, and social respect. . . . In their frustration, the young are turning to religion for solace and purpose, pulling their parents and their governments with them."[108] One Egyptian young man states, "Sometimes, I can see how it [frustrated marriage aspirations] does not make you closer to God, but pushes you toward terrorism. Practically, it killed my ambition. I can't think of a future."[109]

In addition to deep grievance that might foster radicalism, outright conflict may be the result, as well. Consider the case of South Sudan, where brideprice has skyrocketed in recent years:

> Emmanuel Gambiri said an educated wife in his cattle-herding Mundari tribe in South Sudan costs 50 cows, 60 goats and 30,000 Sudanese pounds ($12,000) in cash. "At that price, some men who otherwise can't afford a bride turn to stealing livestock in order to buy a wife and gain status," said Gambiri, citing a friend who is now a cattle rustler. A surge in "bride price" has fueled cattle raids in which more than 2,000 people are killed each year. "In his village of Terekeka, in the state of Central Equatoria, Gambiri recalls a time when wives cost as little as 12 cows and tribal chiefs wielded enough power to call the parents and set an affordable bride price.[110]

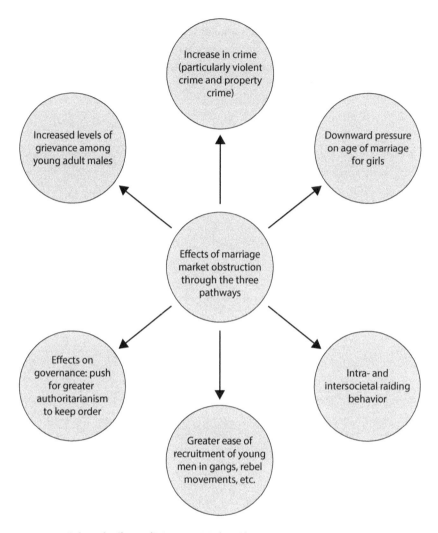

FIGURE 5.2 Selected Effects of Marriage Market Obstruction

In sum, in Syndrome societies based on male kinship as the primary security provision mechanism, marriage markets obstructed by high marriage costs or prevalent polygyny or abnormal sex ratios favoring males can be easily exploited by groups seeking young adult men who are interested in redressing the injustice they feel on a personal level, by force if necessary, and thereby seriously degrading the stability and security of the society. Furthermore, marriage market obstruction also affects governance in the society, pushing it toward greater authoritarianism. Figure 5.2 portrays the relevant effects.

Chapters 4 and 5 have concentrated on the Patrilineal/Fraternal Syndrome's consequences for governance and national security, as well as economic performance. We can broadly group the many other consequences of the Syndrome for nation-states under the concepts of human, economic, and environmental security. It is to those Syndrome effects we now turn in chapter 6.

THE EFFECTS OF THE SYNDROME, PART TWO

Human, Economic, and Environmental Security

Until families are safe and democratic, society will not be. You have to address one before you can the other.

—Pamela Shifman

Although the Syndrome has obvious and direct effects on conventional measures of governance and national security, including violence, instability, regime type, and certain aspects of economic performance (delineated in chapters 4 and 5), a wide variety of other effects of the Syndrome also, perhaps less directly but no less profoundly, affect the security and stability of the nation-state. These might be grouped under the concepts of human, economic, and environmental security, and speak more to the health, demography, social progress, food security, economic welfare, and environmental quality of human life within the nation-state. Although perhaps not traditional security-related variables, the national security establishment of the United States often uses these types of variables to forecast political instability.[1] Figure 6.1 attempts to show how the Syndrome affects societal outcomes other than conflict and governance.

Let us begin at a natural beginning: fertility. *Ceteris paribus*, the more a nation-state is enmeshed in the Syndrome, the higher its birth rate will be.

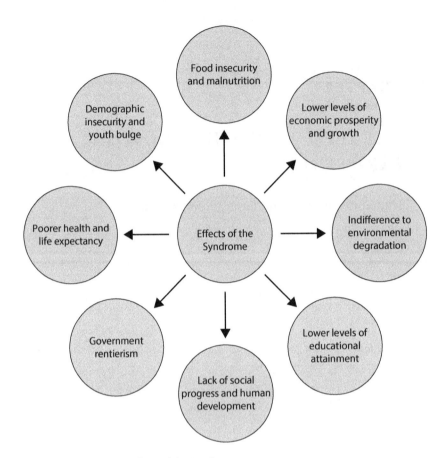

FIGURE 6.1 Ancillary Effects of the Syndrome

This is due to several interlocking reasons. First, in a kin-based power system, kin are power, or as Edward Schatz puts it "if a Kazakh gets rich, he accumulates wives . . . Progeny was a preferred resource, since it produced a web of kin-related supporters who could consolidate authority and provide labor. Material wealth, by contrast, was ephemeral."[2] This worldview emphasizes having a sufficient number of sons for the father to hold a valued place in the patriline and in the larger polity. As Abdul Al Lily explains about Saudi Arabia, "Men are known for liking to have many children. This is because, when one has many children, he becomes powerful. When a stranger attacks a father, all his many sons will protect him."[3]

A second reason explaining the tendency toward higher birth rates is that in societies encoding the Syndrome, the age of marriage for women is depressed, and therefore women have little voice in the affairs of the household, including those concerning family planning. The health effects of a high birth rate for the mother are, if considered at all, of secondary consequence.

Consider the story of Guljan from Afghanistan, a woman interviewed in 2014:

> I am 21 and I have three children. . . . Personally I don't want any more children, but my husband wants one after another. I don't know what he is going to do with all these children. I grew up in a large family and I married into a large family. I don't know about condoms or birth control or other stuff. I just keep delivering children. It seems in our neighborhood families usually have 12 to 13 children. They don't care about other things, they just want their dinner table to be filled with children and that's all. In families where the husband has more wives they'll have even more. If they expect 13 from one wife then more from other wives, the number will be more than 25. If the baby is a boy or girl, for myself it does not matter, but for men, they keep saying it should be boy. Unfortunately, my children are all girls. It absolutely matters to my in-laws. They only want a boy and that's all.[4]

Zarghona, twenty-eight years old and with six children, tells a similar tale:

> Here in Afghanistan having children is not something a woman decides. Whatever men want is what happens. If my husband wants it, I will surely have more children. Most men usually want more than six children, but it will be whatever the man wishes. If in a family where there is only one wife and the man desires to have six children, then you can just imagine if there is more than one wife, then for sure there will be more children—maybe twelve, but sometimes up to twenty children. In Afghanistan men don't think about the future, they just want as many children as possible. They don't worry about how the children live or whether they are healthy or not. I don't know why this is.[5]

Besides the obvious effects on women's health of continual childbearing, it has also been found that, "Household size and the number of births that the woman had are positively correlated with [domestic] violence, probably due to the stress of supporting large families."[6] High fertility rates are not conducive to the national welfare; in the words of Malcolm Potts and Thomas Hayden, "political instability and violence often follow hard on the heels of high birthrates," noting that in 2008, the director of the Central Intelligence Agency asserted that "rapid population growth [was] the number one problem in national security."[7] For example, high birth rates are associated with youth bulges, which, in turn, are associated with higher levels of instability,[8] such as was seen in the Arab revolutions of 2011 and 2012.[9] Economists Noah Bricker and Mark Foley conclude that "historical evidence shows some of the most violent periods of unrest in human history are linked to the presence of large youth cohorts."[10]

It is also true that although virtually all high-fertility societies encode the Syndrome, not all high-Syndrome-encoding societies have high fertility. As Farzaneh Roudi of the Population Reference Bureau notes about the Middle East and North Africa region, "In Bahrain, Lebanon, Iran, Tunisia, and Turkey, fertility rates are now around 2 births per woman. In Yemen, where the risk of maternal death is highest, fertility has declined from an average of 6.5 children to 4.4 children per woman over the past 20 years."[11] But fertility decline has also stalled and even reversed in other nations in the region, such as in Egypt, where the fertility rate has rebounded to the same level as it was twenty years ago.

High birth rates and young age of marriage for girls (not to mention the devaluation of women's lives) are a recipe for high maternal mortality and morbidity rates and high infant mortality rates. Again, it is the case that nearly all high-maternal-mortality-rate countries are also Syndrome countries, although several high-Syndrome-encoding states have relatively low maternal mortality, such as Saudi Arabia. Maternal morbidity is an important issue, with, for example, high rates of fistula reported, especially in child brides who are much more likely to be found in Syndrome-encoding countries.[12] Part of this linkage involves differential feeding practices for male and female members of the household in societies where female life is devalued, which dispropor-tionately increases levels of malnutrition and anemia for women, putting them at risk during pregnancy and childbirth. Another element involves the sheer physical harm caused by childbearing on the bodies of young girls, as Rachel Vogelstein notes:

> Child brides are frequently unable to negotiate sexual relationships with their husbands and lack access to contraception. . . . Girls aged fifteen to nineteen are twice as likely to die from causes related to pregnancy or childbirth than women in their twenties, and girls under the age of fifteen are five times more likely to die. Complications from pregnancy and childbearing are the leading cause of death for girls aged fifteen to nineteen in the developing world. Prolonged or obstructed labor is common for adolescent mothers and can lead to debilitating conditions, such as obstetric fistula . . . and stillbirths and infant mortality are 50 percent more likely when mothers are under the age of twenty, and the risks of prematurity, low birth weight, and childhood malnutrition increase as well.[13]

Undervaluation of female lives may lead to a higher infectious disease burden and lower life expectancy for both men and women in such societies.[14] Vogelstein notes that child marriage puts girls at special risk of AIDS and sexually transmitted diseases, particularly in polygynous cultures where they would usually be married to older husbands.[15] And, of course, HIV can be transmitted to any resulting children. The typically large difference in age between a girl bride and her husband means that "an insurmountable power differential precludes autonomous decision-making" in the home.[16] With little female voice in household affairs in Syndrome societies, men may also demonstrate little constraint on the consumption of masculine-coded commodities, such as alcohol and cigarettes. Furthermore, women may be less educated in Syndrome societies, meaning their ability to properly care for the health needs of their family members—a gendered role typically assigned to women globally—is compromised. As a result, the issues of infant and child mortality are also influenced by women's subordination in Syndrome countries.

The gendered role of caretaking may carry its own risks for women. For example, in the Ebola crisis of 2014 in West Africa, approximately 75 percent of the victims were women, because women were those tasked with caring for ill family members.[17] In the 2005 Asian tsunami, estimates are that four times as many women died compared with men, because they were carrying young children and also, by and large, had not been taught either to swim or to climb trees, as had the men. These disproportionate deaths of women also negatively affect the chance for survival of surviving children as well as cause significant sex ratio imbalances.[18]

Health, sustainable population, and well-being are not the only societal values compromised by the subordinate status of women. Food security in Syndrome countries, where women do the lion's share of agricultural labor (such as in sub-Saharan Africa), is also undermined.[19] As the former president of Ghana John Dramani Mahama stated at a recent agricultural summit, "Africa must achieve food security for its people by increasing agricultural productivity. . . . This cannot be done without the active participation of the African woman."[20]

Many obstacles impede female participation in the agricultural sector. The first is the intense time poverty of most women, especially in the developing world. Women may be responsible for laboring on cash crops, and their income then goes to the male head of household, leaving them less time to cultivate the subsistence crops on which the women and children must depend. Furthermore, assistance and training provided to women farmers may be inferior to that provided to male farmers. Indeed, the Food and Agricultural Organization of the United Nations estimates that if women were given the same agricultural inputs as men, malnutrition would drop by 17 percent globally.[21]

The lack of land rights for women in Syndrome countries also plays a major role in food insecurity. Consider Morocco: as explained by sociologist Zakia Salime, 50.6 percent of agricultural labor comes from women, and 92 percent of those women laborers work in farming. And yet only 4 percent of agricultural land holders are women. Salime notes that "the marginal status of women with regard to land tenure does not reflect the importance of their labor force and knowledge in farming. . . . Women's lack of access to land is certainly the most challenging facet of rural poverty, and the biggest obstacle to sustainable development in the countryside."[22]

As with all things related to the Syndrome, the interlocking effects are multidimensional. Thus, in addition to these links to food insecurity, lack of women's property rights, especially the right to land, has also been linked to higher child morbidity and malnutrition, lower household savings, and lower expenditures on children's education.[23] As agricultural economist Stanley Sharaunga and colleagues observe, gender-sensitive programming can make a real difference in agricultural development outcomes: "women can be empowered through crop management skills, farm financial management skills, improved level of water use security, animal husbandry skills and weed and pest management skills. In the economic arenas, women can be empowered in economic agency, financial capital, human capital, vocational skills and physical capital forms of empowerment."[24]

Ironically, then, even though the Syndrome is designed to maximize resource access by men relative to women, overall prosperity, general speaking, is typically lower in Syndrome countries (as touched on in chapters 4 and 5). It is almost as if gendered relative gains are much more important (if the gains are for men)—or threatening (if the gains are for women)—than absolute gains for everyone in society. The subordination of women and their exclusion from the labor force as well as from the marketplace of ideas profoundly undermines economic growth. A recent study by the consulting firm McKinsey & Co. demonstrates the point well: "A 'full potential' scenario in which women participate in the economy identically to men would add up to $28 trillion, or 26 percent, to annual global GDP by 2025 compared with a business-as-usual scenario. This impact is roughly equivalent to the size of the combined Chinese and U.S. economies today." McKinsey also explored an "alternative 'best in region' scenario in which all countries match the progress toward gender parity of the fastest-improving country in their region," finding that this added as much as "$12 trillion in annual 2025 GDP, equivalent in size to the current GDP of Germany, Japan, and the United Kingdom combined."[25] Absolute gains are sacrificed to maintain greater resource access by men in Syndrome-encoding societies; otherwise, the incentive structure supporting the security provision mechanism of the fraternal alliance would be subverted.

The World Bank corroborated these findings with its own report in 2018, appropriately entitled "Unrealized Potential."[26] The report finds:

- Globally, women account for only 38 percent of human capital wealth versus 62 percent for men. In low- and lower-middle income countries, women account for a third or less of human capital wealth.

- On a per capita basis, gender inequality in earnings could lead to losses in wealth of $23,620 per person globally. These losses differ between regions and countries because levels of human capital wealth, and thereby losses in wealth due to gender inequality, tend to increase in absolute values with economic development. For these reasons, in absolute terms the losses are largest in Organization for Economic Cooperation and Development (OECD) countries.
- Globally, for the 141 countries included in the analysis, the loss in human capital wealth resulting from gender inequality is estimated at $160.2 trillion if we simply assume that women would earn as much as men. This is about twice the value of GDP globally. Said differently, human capital wealth could increase by 21.7 percent globally, and total wealth by 14.0 percent with gender equality in earnings.[27]

Think of the implications: apparently, discriminatory laws and practices concerning women's property rights, land rights, inheritance rights, and access to capital must all be maintained *even if* greater prosperity for all is sacrificed as a result. This is found across all regions, or as the World Bank asserts, "Countries whose laws discriminate against women and do not promote gender equality suffer economically. Previous research tells us that gender gaps in women's entrepreneurship and labor force participation account for estimated income losses of 27 percent in the Middle East and North Africa, 19 percent in South Asia, 14 percent in Latin America and the Caribbean and 10 percent in Europe."[28] The United Nations Population Fund also tallies the economic cost of child marriage, and finds trillions of dollars in loss worldwide. Measuring a mother's foregone annual income over her lifetime, nations such as Guinea have lost 30 percent of annual potential GDP.[29]

Furthermore, this analysis does not consider the economic losses to the state from higher mortality and morbidity, especially of women and their children. We already examined many of the causes of such higher rates of mortality and morbidity, but we cannot overlook domestic violence as a major cause: "Violence perpetrated by men against their female partners is widespread around the world. It is a fundamental violation of women's human rights, and is also a significant public health problem, with significant economic and social costs."[30] Furthermore, higher morbidity rates due to domestic violence may sap budgetary resources from already thinly stretched government coffers. So, for example, CARE International estimated the cost of domestic violence to the nation of Bangladesh as $2.3 billion in 2010, equivalent to 2.1 percent of GDP, and equal to the health and nutrition budget for the entire nation.[31]

In addition to enumeration of losses when women are subordinated, a large body of evidence enumerates benefits when they are not. To offer but one example, when women earn income, a greater proportion is devoted to food and health care for their children.[32] All too often, however, lower female labor force participation, child marriage, lack of women's property rights, lack of educational opportunity for girls, and other constraints imposed in Syndrome countries preclude this greater investment in the next generation, with grave consequences for the future of the nation.

These interrelationships are arguably noticeable in historical analysis as well. For example, Goody suggests that delayed marriage for women in European history was associated with the rise of industrialization on the continent. In other words, he implies that the first anomaly was necessary for the second to occur (a topic we return to in chapter 8):

> The intriguing connection has been made that the late marriage age of European women, combined with the necessity of accumulating property for their marriage, may have been a significant factor in both the supply and the demand for goods in the early stages of industrialization in western Europe. The balancing out has an interesting link with the age of marriage. It has been argued that dowry delays marriage. When the daughter takes her portion, the familial enterprise has to be partly dismembered, whereas the marriage of men affects the fund in a similar way only if the property has to be handed on to the next generation at the time of the marriage.[33]

In a recent article, economic historians James Foreman-Peck and Peng Zhou echo Goody's analysis.[34] They assert that later marriage for girls in historical northwestern Europe with its resulting neolocal marriages was absolutely critical for the type of human capital accumulation that made the Industrial Revolution possible. Such later marriage and neolocality not only allowed for greater female human capital, especially in terms of literacy and education, but also ensured that these women were capable of greater human capital investment in and transmission to their own children, leading to a virtuous cycle of human capital accumulation across the generations. They note that several of the greatest inventors of the Industrial Revolution were taught at home and received no other formal education. Statistically, they find that increased age of marriage was associated with a significantly higher chance of becoming literate for both boys and girls, and with each passing generation, human capital would have accumulated thereby.

In contrast, Syndrome societies may experience gendered educational deficits, which also have far-reaching effects for the nation.[35] For example, child marriage may prevent a girl bride from continuing her education, as many societies do not allow married girls to attend school. Given the emphasis in recent years on the cross-cutting effects of girls' education on many economic development and health outcomes for the society, this is lamentable. Vogelstein states, "Even one year of extra schooling beyond the average can increase women's wages by 10 to 20 percent, and a World Bank study suggests that a one-percentage-point increase in the share of women with secondary education increases a country's annual per capita income growth rate by 0.3 percent. Child survival and immunization rates are also higher for the offspring of educated mothers."[36] Furthermore, education rates for daughters of educated mothers are much higher than that of uneducated mothers, holding the father's education constant.[37] Some Syndrome societies do boast high levels of female education, for example, the United Arab Emirates. Education alone, however, may not be sufficient to see the salutary effects of women's empowerment on the broader society, but it may serve rather effectively to delay age at first marriage for women.[38]

All of this strongly suggests, and is confirmed by empirical analysis, that human security and human development, not to mention economic development, is stunted in Syndrome countries. The Human Development Index (HDI), for example, is strongly and negatively associated with measures of Syndrome dimensions. This is not surprising, because key components of the United Nations Development Program's (UNDP's) HDI include

> achievement in key dimensions of human development: a long and healthy life, being knowledgeable and have a decent standard of living. . . . The health dimension is assessed by life expectancy at birth, the education dimension is measured by mean of years of schooling for adults aged 25 years and more and expected years of schooling for children of school entering age. The standard of living dimension is measured by gross national income per capita.[39]

We have already seen that the Syndrome depresses all of these indicators. It is not surprising that lower HDI correlates with worse outcomes on measures of security and stability.[40]

Similarly, we have noted that Syndrome-encoding countries typically manifest a parasitical rent-based governance structure (see chapter 4). Political elites may be so busy "eating" resources (and stowing them in overseas accounts) that they are not able to invest and conserve them for the long-term benefit of the society. They will be less interested in diversifying their economy, and more vulnerable to global price shocks for the resources from which they create the rents needed to keep peace within the society.[41] Certainly, public goods, such as clean air and water, may well be much lower on the policy agenda of Syndrome countries, and so we would expect to see a higher level of environmental degradation in those countries. Such reckless "eating" of nature's rents also does not augur well for collective stability and security.

The Syndrome produces obvious effects for women (we detailed many of these in chapter 3). Secondary aspects of the Syndrome's effects are also pertinent when examining the negative effects of women's subordination on state-level outcomes. We find that these also interlock, reinforcing one another.

For example, women have far less mobility in Syndrome cultures. Women's freedom of movement is significantly more curtailed in these societies, especially for reasons of safety, but also for issues of honor. This impacts include, for example, women's labor force participation in the formal sector as well as women's access to educational opportunities.

Another dimension of critical importance is the muting of female voice. We know the female voice is distinctly lacking in household decision-making in Syndrome-encoding countries, but such lack of voice at home extends outward to lack of voice in the community and national affairs as well. The political participation of women may be sharply limited or even irrelevant when not limited. This perfect storm of disenfranchisement of women from decision-making at all levels and in all areas, including economic, political, and social, means that women's values, priorities, and concerns will fade from societal discourse. Nowhere is this more tragic than in the inability of mothers to safeguard their children, especially their female children. For example, research shows significantly less investment in children's needs and education in societies with a high prevalence of polygyny.[42] Lack of political power at both the household level and the societal level hamstrings mothers from emphasizing the need for appropriate investment in children—the very future of the collective.

Clare Castillejo contributes a valuable insight by noting the link between group outcomes and women's situation in family and personal status law:

> While women's status within the family is often presented as pertaining entirely to the personal sphere, it has profound implications for broader development and fragility dynamics. Such disempowerment at household level limits women's ability to access services, economic opportunities, or resources such as land; to participate in public life; or to escape abuse. Discriminatory family laws therefore prevent women from contributing effectively to political and socio-economic development and stability, and contribute to . . . population pressures.[43]

Other ancillary effects attend the Syndrome. For example, Syndrome-afflicted societies with substantial marriage market obstruction will see comparatively high levels of trafficking of women and children—a terrible practice that may nevertheless appear economically rational in the context of these obstructed markets. Another example is that suicide rates of women tend to be higher in Syndrome societies. Suicide may often be the last means of resistance available to women caught in the straitjacket of the Syndrome's components, and their stories are heart-breaking.[44]

To summarize, we might consider how each component of the Syndrome relates to outcome variables at the level of the nation-state. Figure 6.2 attempts

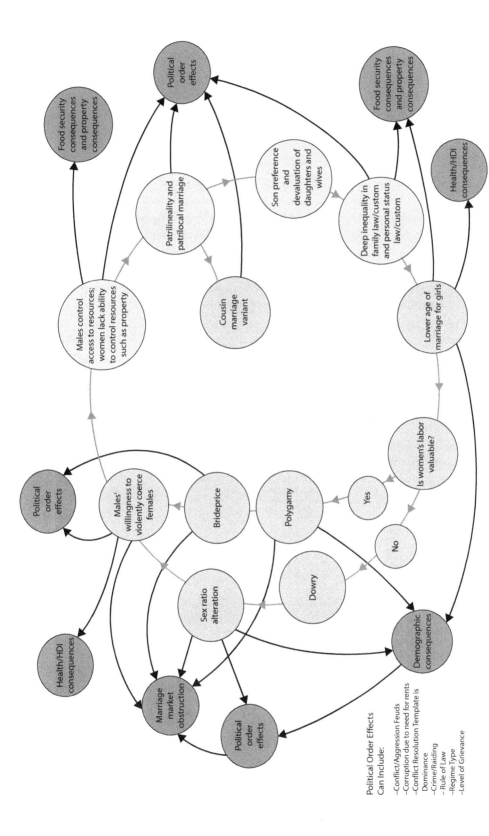

Political Order Effects
Can Include:

-Conflict/Aggression Feuds
-Corruption due to need for rents
-Conflict Resolution Template is
Dominance
- Crime/Raiding
- Rule of Law
- Regime Type
-Level of Grievance

FIGURE 6.2 The Relationship between the Components of the Patrilineal/Fraternal Syndrome and Nation-State-Level Outcomes

to do just that, with the Syndrome depicted as the lighter inner circles, and the various effects on the nation-state seen as the darker outer circles:

To take but one example from this diagram, consider all the many stability-related linkages stemming from just one Syndrome component—child marriage. Vogelstein avers,

> Child marriage perpetuates poverty over generations and is linked to poor health, curtailed education, violence, instability, and disregard for the rule of law. Its effects are harmful not only to girls, but also to families, communities, and economies. . . . The evidence establishing a link between child marriage and ill health, illiteracy, poverty, violence, and instability cannot be ignored. U.S. foreign policy interests in stability and prosperity and U.S. investments in a range of areas—including global health, education, economic growth, and governance—are compromised wherever child marriage endures.[45]

Each component of the Syndrome can be analyzed in a similar fashion. Putting together all that we have learned from chapters 4, 5, and 6, we can now plainly see the causal pathways between the Patrilineal/Fraternal Syndrome and national security and stability outcomes in terms of type of governance, rule of law, corruption, conflict, violence, ill health, economic stagnation and decline, rentierism, youth bulges, abnormal sex ratios, environmental degradation, and a host of national outcomes of significance to both society and the world. With such abundant process-tracing evidence in hand, it is time to ask whether these linkages are also borne out by large-N statistical analysis.

CHAPTER 7

THE EFFECTS BY THE NUMBERS

The Syndrome and Measures of National Outcome

I think the issue of gender relations within the family . . . actually relates to the core of power in society at a broader level. Since the family is the basic unit of society, only if there is justice and democracy within the family can you possibly have justice and democracy in the wider society.

—Ziba Mir-Hosseini

Our goal in this chapter is to assess the relationship between national outcomes and the Patrilineal/Fraternal Syndrome through regression analysis. We comprehensively surveyed outcome variables related to each of the nine dimensions of national stability, security, and resilience we assert are harmed by the Syndrome—that is, Political Stability and Governance, Security and Conflict, Economic Performance, Economic Rentierism, Health and Well-Being, Demographic Security, Education of the Population, Social Progress, and Environmental Protection (described in chapters 4–6). To foreshadow the results presented in this chapter, we echo international relations scholar Rose McDermott's comment about the analysis she conducted on one of the Syndrome components, polygyny: "The findings are clear, consistent, and statistically robust across the board. In fact, the results are the kind of thing most social scientists strive for but almost never find in the course of their careers."[1]

Our analysis raises important questions for the academic fields of international relations and security studies, especially in light of the fact that the U.S. Department of Defense (DoD) paid for this research to be conducted. DoD's investment has yielded a bumper crop of important findings; the question remains whether the academic and policy fields of national security studies are prepared to receive and act on them.[2]

Before laying out our results for each of these nine dimensions of national outcomes, we first discuss the question of causal inference from our regression analysis.

A Note on Causal Inference

Because of the lack of available panel data on the Patrilineal/Fraternal Syndrome, this is a cross-sectional analysis, and some readers might rightfully raise the issues of causality or causal directionality. We remind readers that this stage of our research is still in the exploratory phase. Because of the nature of the statistical methods used, we do not make any causal claims regarding the Syndrome and our dependent variables at present from our statistical analyses, only claims of association. We have, however, identified four reasons to anticipate that further research will advance such claims. First, given the results to be presented in this chapter, we are heartened by the remarkably consistent findings of high significance for the Syndrome in well over one hundred model runs as well as the Syndrome's consistently substantial effect sizes. Second, these consistent, significant, strong findings are buttressed by our extensive theoretical framework for directionality (outlined in part I). Third, we offered process-tracing exploration of the pathways linking the Syndrome with worse national outcomes that also speak to the issue of causal direction (chapters 4–6). Fourth, we found, as it were, dose-dependent effects when comparing Post-Syndrome, Transition, and Syndrome societies, finding that amelioration of some of the Syndrome components also offered significant amelioration of national outcomes (discussed in chapter 9). In the future, as we and others develop longitudinal data showing the progression and regression of Syndrome symptoms and the resulting effects on national outcomes, such data developments will enable the use of causal inference analysis, thus allowing for greater confidence in assessing both causality and causal direction.

Before delving into the details of our regression analysis, a discussion of the contextual variables that modulate the effects of the Syndrome on national outcomes must be engaged. That is, the effects of the Syndrome may be dampened or exacerbated depending on the context in which they are operating in a particular nation-state at a particular time. The identification of such contextual variables then allows for specification of control variables for use in the full regression model.

Contextual Variables and Control Variables

In any empirical investigation, it is important to consider contextual variables in creating a useful empirical model. In studying the Syndrome described in this volume, we have come to the conclusion that several important contextual variables affect the degree to which the Syndrome can self-replicate, as well as the specific course it may take in a given society. We introduced one of those variables in chapter 2—that is, whether women's labor is valuable in agriculture. Two paths diverge from that pivot point: (1) brideprice/polygyny and (2) dowry/ sex ratio alteration variants. These paths do not change the overall effect of the Syndrome, but rather they mold its expression, such as whether sex ratios tend to be normal or abnormal.[3]

With specific reference to national outcomes, we identified at least four contextual variables that are important to our analysis. Before diving into details of the empirical investigation in the next section, we offer a short note on these contextual variables and their intersection with the Syndrome and its effects.

The first contextual variable of importance is a society's degree of urbanization. Patrilines are easiest to cultivate in cases in which physical assets such as land or livestock represent the major source of wealth in the society. When land or livestock are no longer as important, when factors such as higher real estate prices in cities mitigate against extended household coresidence, and when women are more integrated into the formal labor force as a result of urbanization, the character of the Syndrome changes. The government may still be based on male kin alliances, but the expression of the full range of Syndrome phenomena will be constrained.[4] In an urbanized environment, the state has become more of a real, centralized force. Monica Das Gupta perceptively comments that "modern states seek to bring all citizens directly under their rule, and to be the sole source of formal power, including for policing and military defense. This makes them likely to want to undermine traditional organizations with these powers, and clans and lineages are prime examples of independent power bases with considerable potential strength."[5]

Das Gupta also mentions that the urban environment makes other changes in the Syndrome components easier to effect, such as female inheritance. She comments,

> It is far easier to give daughters a share of assets acquired on one's own, and non-farm occupations offer a high potential for acquiring such assets. It is also far easier for women to demand their rightful inheritance in urban areas, where legal resources are close at hand—in contrast to rural areas, where such amenities are distant and instead the woman is surrounded by lineage members hostile to the idea of property passing out of their lineage.[6]

In addition, more secularized norms may develop in urbanized populations, which may dampen the drive for sons. For example, many urbanized families in China no longer place an emphasis on the "incense and fire" funerary rituals that require sons for their performance. In addition, formal labor force participation by women is likely to be higher in urban settings than in rural settings, which may ameliorate the economic prostration of women to a certain extent, as we see in historian Mary Hartman's analysis of northwestern Europe's evolution in the Middle Ages (discussed more fully in chapter 8).[7] Thus, in any empirical investigation of our theoretical framework, we include degree of urbanization as a control variable that mediates the relationship between the Syndrome and the dependent variables we wish to investigate. The precise variable we use is Percent Urban Population, 2015, from the World Bank.

The second contextual variable of importance is whether the society provides a pension system for its elderly. Patrilines retain their visceral relevance even now in the absence of such pensions, as every household must ensure that care for the elderly is provided from within its ranks. Patrilocality ensures that sons (and their wives) will typically stay on-site to provide physical care, and the brideprice fetched for one's daughter may provide enough assets not only for the sons' marriages but also to assist with eldercare obligations. Louisa Chiang notes, "The bridal price in many cases is seen as a retirement fund for the parents of the bride."[8]

When a pension system is created, the relative values of sons versus daughters may change, even fairly swiftly, as has been seen in South Korea over the past quarter century.[9] We take up this discussion in part III.

Furthermore, the effects of pension provision may synergize with those of urbanization, helping to break this association between sons and eldercare as well. Das Gupta notes: "The greater physical mobility of urban industrialized life means that whether people live near their parents is determined by their jobs and personal circumstances, not by their gender."[10] It is also true, however, that declining birth rates may undercut the feasibility of adequate pension provision during the time period in which the proportion of seniors begins to overwhelm the proportion of the working-age population needed to support them. Transition countries such as South Korea are feeling this precise pinch.[11] Right at the historical moment when certain Transition countries might be expected to begin to provide meaningful pension schemes, plummeting fertility may make such initiatives impossible.

Unfortunately for our empirical investigation, extant variables capturing pension coverage would overly constrain our N size. Thus, we did not include an indicator of pensions as a control variable in our multivariate models. We do, however, probe in ancillary analysis both the Syndrome's relationship to pension coverage (in the Social Progress dimension section of this chapter), as well as the specific relationship between pension coverage and sex ratios for that subset of countries for which we have sufficient data (presented in chapter 9).

The third contextual variable of importance in mediating the effects of the Syndrome is the availability and accessibility of mass media that would allow subnational actors or even the government to promulgate new ideas concerning gender equality. Even in cases in which those messages are not always welcome, they are still heard by women and men, girls and boys, alike, perhaps planting the seeds for change.[12] Das Gupta notes that in both China and India, state-supported mass media that positively portrayed women's empowerment has had a demonstrated positive impact on changing attitudes about gender equality and family size in those countries.[13] Given that the rate of access to the Internet is highly correlated with urbanization ($.716, p < .001$), we feel we cannot include this contextual variable separately in the model, but given this high a correlation, urbanization in a sense will serve a proxy for it.

Finally, the fourth contextual variable of importance in understanding Syndrome dynamics is the presence of "shocks" to the society, such as natural disasters, climate change, invasion, and so forth, any of which may profoundly affect the expression of the Syndrome—typically intensifying it.[14] For example, we have noted how polygyny rates, prostitution, rates of child marriage, and dowry deaths have all increased as a result of the devastating drought in India.[15] In times of instability and fear, Syndrome societies deepen their dependence on the patrilineal/fraternal alliance for security. One of the explanations for why the number of countries with abnormal childhood sex ratios favoring males has expanded rapidly since the end of the Cold War lies, as we have seen, in a growing sense of insecurity and threat for many nations. This feeling of insecurity may thrust societies back on a system of security viewed as dependable—or at least more dependable—than the central government, leading to a resurgence of the Patrilineal/Fraternal Syndrome.[16] Das Gupta notes, "The aversion to raising daughters . . . is driven by the fact that girls are seen as a drain on household resources. This is why the proportion "missing" rises when households face a resource crunch—such as the privations of war, a famine, or fertility decline in which total family size drops more quickly than the number of sons desired."[17]

New York Times journalist Steven Erlanger's analysis of the resurgence of the clans in the Gaza Strip is instructive in this regard.[18] Given the pullout of Israeli troops, the split between the Palestinian Authority and Hamas, the high birth rate in Gaza, and the tightening economic sanctions, the sense of exigency is very high. Erlanger comments, "The disintegration of the Palestinian Authority, masked to some degree while Arafat was alive, has meant the reversion of Gazans to seek protection and identity in premodern loyalties and affiliations: the *hamulla*—the clan or tribe—and the mosque."[19] Erlanger quotes Gazan legislator Ziad Abu Amr as saying,

> The Palestinian Authority couldn't fulfill its role in ensuring social transformation. It had no vision for state and society-building, so it had to rely on these traditional clan structures to consolidate its role . . . [In the second intifada] the Palestinian Authority began to disintegrate, and its law and order structures began to disintegrate, and people found protection in parochial affiliations of region, tribe and family. . . . When people have to choose between faction and family, they usually choose family, and why? Because the only solid entity in Palestinian society is the family. The Palestinian Authority and the party can break down.[20]

Power vacuums, then, in addition to more catastrophic events such as natural disasters and war, can lead to a renewed reliance on clans, which inevitably brings with it a greater subordination of women's interests.

Unfortunately for our purposes, we could find no comprehensive indicator of "shock" that would encompass all the many sources of such feelings of vulnerability. The indices we did find included other types of risk, such as inadequate public infrastructure, which were not part of our conceptualization. For example, the World Risk Index from the University of Stuttgart examines poverty, nutrition, public infrastructure, governance, education, investment, and even gender equity.[21] Furthermore, given that most risk indicators include war, we elected to retain conflict-related variables as dependent variables in the model, not as control variables. We therefore leave it to others to probe the relationship between shocks/exigency and the Syndrome when an appropriate variable measuring such shocks has been developed.

Control Variables

The foregoing discussion identified contextual factors that could suggest which control variables would be useful in creating a full regression model for our empirical analysis. Our choice of control variables for multivariate modeling was based on what was *not* identified as a possible ramification or effect of the Syndrome as adumbrated in chapters 4–6. The astute reader will know by this time that our conception of the effects of the Syndrome is quite broad. So, for example, our theoretical framework asserts economic prosperity will be tied to a country's score on the Syndrome scale. (The complete Patrilineal/Fraternal Syndrome scale for all countries in our study is given in appendix I.) As a result, some variables commonly used as control variables in social science research, such as gross domestic product (GDP) per capita, will be reserved for use as dependent variables in our modeling analyses. We do conduct several ancillary analyses of robustness to investigate results when GDP per capita is included in the regression model for other outcome variables.

In the search for additional appropriate control variables beyond percent urban population, we turned to other variables that are not part of the Syndrome scale and that are not hypothesized to be effects of the Syndrome. Our other stipulation was that the bivariate correlation between any two control variables had to be less than .70 to avoid issues with phenomena such as multicollinearity, in which the explanatory or control variables are so highly correlated with one another that one of the variables can be predicted from a combination of the others.[22] This is a problem because one of the regression assumptions is that the predictor variables should be independent; otherwise, problems with model fit and interpretation of the results occur. Furthermore, the variance inflation factors (VIFs), which quantify the severity of multicollinearity, had to be low; all VIFs for our models using these control variables in conjunction with the Syndrome ranged from 1.065 to 1.294, allowing for the retention of all the following variables in the model.[23] The variables chosen to serve as control variables, along with their rationale for inclusion, are as follows:

- Percent Urban Population.[24] As noted earlier, urbanization can weaken the Patrilineal/Fraternal Syndrome's hold over family members by breaking kin ties to land, which in turn undercuts patrilocal marriage. The correlation with the Syndrome is −.496 ($p < .001$), which is not high enough to introduce multicollinearity into our modeling efforts, especially because the VIF used as an indicator of multicollinearity, is a low 1.21. Although Percent Urban Population is partially a function of the wealth of the nation (measures of which are part of our dependent variable set for the economic performance dimension), the bivariate correlation between GDP per capita and Percent Urban Population in our dataset is high, but not overwhelming, at .662 ($N = 168$, $p < .001$), suggesting that with proper precaution, such as examining VIFs, we may use Percent Urban when modeling national wealth. Urbanization is significantly correlated with another control variable, Religious Fractionalization, but the correlation coefficient is only −.260.
- Aggregated Civilization Identification, based on the work of Samuel Huntington.[25] Some, such as Huntington, have controversially opined that it is civilizational identity that drives conflict and instability, and therefore we include an aggregated measure based on Huntington's classification scheme as a control variable for our multivariate modeling. This regionally based variable also addresses Galton's Problem, a known issue in cross-national research. Specifically, we have four categories of civilization: (1) if the nation

belongs to the group of Western/Orthodox/Latin civilizations as identified by Huntington; (2) if majority Muslim; (3) if the nations are identified with Hindu/Sinic/Buddhist civilizations;[26] and (4) African countries without majority Muslim adherents. This variable will be treated as nominal/categorical in the data analysis. An analysis of variance showed that the Syndrome has a significant relationship with our Aggregated Civilization Identification variable ($p < .001$). Because we believe Syndrome and Civilization are conceptually different—one could theoretically see Syndrome components in any civilization given their historical near-universality—we felt it was appropriate to keep Civilization in the model. Indeed, this choice should make it more difficult for the Syndrome to emerge as significant in modeling analysis. Using a one-way analysis of variance (ANOVA) test for continuous variables and a chi-square test for the other categorical variable, we found that Civilization was not significantly correlated with the other control variables included in the analysis.

- Colonial Heritage Status.[27] It is possible that a history of colonization might influence security and stability outcomes, and the presumption is that such a history might negatively affect such outcomes.[28] We developed a dichotomous variable coding whether or not a nation had ever been colonized, with the temporal delimitation being 1700–2017. For full information and Colonial Heritage Status scores, see appendix II, table AII.1. Colonial Heritage Status is not significantly related to the Syndrome score or any of the control variables included in the analysis (tested with two-sample t-tests for equality of means for the continuous variables and a chi-square for the other categorical variable).

- Percent Arable Land.[29] The idea that terrain and land capacity have some bearing on security outcomes is longstanding, manifesting as the study of geopolitics by scholars such as Sir Halford Mackinder and Nicholas Spykman. More recently, an emphasis on the effect of hard-scrabble environments, such as mountains and deserts, on security and stability has been posited.[30] We therefore include in our model a measure of terrain—specifically, the percent of land that is arable (World Bank). This variable is not significantly related to the Syndrome score, nor to any of the other control variables.

- Number of Unique Land Neighbors.[31] Other scholars, for example Harvey Starr, have argued that the number of land neighbors a country has will influence its security and stability.[32] The assumption is that the greater the number of neighbors, the less secure and less stable a nation will be. We include the count of land neighbors as given in Wikipedia. This variable is not significantly related to the Syndrome score, nor to any of the other control variables in the model.

- Ethnic Fractionalization.[33] Population heterogeneity has long been identified as a risk factor for insecurity and instability in national affairs.[34] Although we believe that the Syndrome and Ethnic Fractionalization are linked—that is, lineage groups cannot maintain a separate existence without Syndrome-like tactics—how ethnically, religiously, and linguistically fractionalized a *particular* nation is should be orthogonal to the existence of the Syndrome, and this information may provide additional insight in multivariate modeling. To that end, we used the Alesina group's summary of ethnic, racial, and linguistic fractionalization scores for each country, which the Alesina group simply called "ethnic fractionalization." The correlation between this (summary) ethnic fractionalization indicator and the Syndrome score is .520 ($p < .001$), which suggests that ethnic fractionalization is enhanced in the presence of patrilineal loyalty. This correlation, however, was not high enough to cause exclusion from the model, with the VIF calculated as only 1.29. As noted, this variable is significantly correlated with Urbanization, but the correlation coefficient is a very low −.260, which means that multicollinearity is not a problem.

- Religious Fractionalization.[35] The Alesina group's scores for Religious Fractionalization do not load on the same factor as the other fractionalization scores they developed. We therefore include the religious fractionalization score separately from the aggregated racial/ethnic/linguistic fractionalization score, noting that scholars have long linked this specific type of fractionalization to stability and security outcomes.[36] The Religious Fractionalization score is not significantly related to the Syndrome score, nor to the other control variables.

We now turn to the empirical investigation, in which we explore the proposition that the degree to which a nation-state encodes the Patrilineal/Fraternal Syndrome will be a significant predictor of its state-level outcomes on nine dimensions of security, stability, and resilience.

The Empirical Investigation

We undertook multivariate analysis using general linear models (GLM) and logistic regression analyses, with the purpose of discovering statistically significant relationships pertinent to our hypotheses. We adopt as our level of significance $\alpha \leq .001$, which is a strict standard for social science analysis, meaning the chance is one in one thousand of observing an outcome pattern as extreme or more extreme than what we have observed if a relationship between the explanatory factors and the outcome variable is not actually present. We use this value to guard against an inflated significance level by using a Bonferoni correction, which is one of several methods used to offset the problem of multiple analyses.

Operationalization of Variables

To trace whether the propositions put forward in chapters 4–6 have any empirical support, we must first identify variables to operationalize the concepts we have been discussing. The Syndrome scale was operationalized, coded, and validated in chapter 3 with further detail given in appendix I. We additionally note that the Syndrome score was imputed for four countries whose values were missing for some of the variables used in the Syndrome algorithm, as noted in chapter 3.[37] (The IRMI package in R, a statistical programming language, was used for imputation because of non-random missing ordinal data.) We also operationalized each of the control variables in the section immediately previous. The next step was to conceptualize the variables that would measure pertinent national outcomes.

We identified nine national outcome dimensions for which we would seek measurable indicators. These nine dimensions included the following:

1. Political Stability and Governance
2. Security and Conflict
3. Economic Performance
4. Economic Rentierism
5. Health and Well-Being
6. Demographic Security
7. Education of the Population
8. Social Progress
9. Environmental Protection

In general, and according to propositions elucidated in chapters 4–6, we expect to see worse outcomes in all of these nine dimensions of national security, governance, and stability the higher the score on the Syndrome scale. Our method to ascertain whether these expectations were borne out in empirical analysis was to comprehensively survey outcome variables related to each of the nine dimensions.

In searching for measurable indicators of these nine dimensions, we chose those which are commonly used in the field of International Relations and which we deemed as the most valid indicators of the dimension. In as many cases as possible, we searched for multiple indicators of the same phenomenon, or at least indicators that were fairly close in conceptualization, making it possible to avoid the issues that occur with idiosyncratic operationalizations or poor data quality for particular measures. This redundancy allows us to triangulate our results and have more confidence in the overall trends we see. Some potential variables of interest were excluded because of low N size or correlations > .9 with the other outcome variables in the list of indicators for that dimension (see the endnotes to appendix III). We also used factor analysis to further reduce the number of separate outcome variables (details are given in appendix III).

The Overall Model

After this pruning, we used each of the variables in the final list as a dependent variable in the following GLM:

$$
\begin{aligned}
\text{Dependent Variable or Factor}_i = \beta_o &+ \beta_1 \text{ Syndrome} + \beta_2 \text{ Urbanization} \\
&+ \beta_3 \text{ Type of civilization} + \beta_4 \text{ Colonization status} \\
&+ \beta_5 \text{ Percent arable land} \\
&+ \beta_6 \text{ Number of unique land neighbors} \\
&+ \beta_7 \text{ Aggregated Ethnic Fractionalization} \\
&+ \beta_8 \text{ Religious Fractionalization} + \varepsilon_i
\end{aligned}
$$

Template for Reporting Results

We report our results according to the national outcome dimensions. For each dimension, we first list all the outcome variables we used in the statistical analysis, with supporting documentation provided in appendix III. Next, we provide an overall summary table for the main and ancillary analyses. The dependent variables are listed in descending order of their adjusted R-squared values. For each dependent variable, the significant explanatory variables are listed in descending order of their effect size. Then the results for each of the analyses in the summary table are discussed, and bivariate scatterplots are given for visualization purposes. For the full results tables for the models shown in the summary tables, which full results include parameter estimates, standard errors, p-values, and effect size (partial eta-squared), the reader must refer to appendix III. For ease of reference, we note the specific table number for each result as it appears in that appendix. Additionally, for models for which the Syndrome was significant, we also desired to probe the odds that a worse outcome obtains when the Syndrome is present. Therefore, we transformed the dependent variable into a binary response variable by examining histograms to obtain valid cutpoints for the logistic regression analyses (see appendix IV for full explication).

Appendix III

The full details of our methodological process for these analyses are included in appendix III. In addition to the full results tables, it also includes an alphabetical list of the variables included in the analyses, the variable name, the source from which the variable was obtained, whether the measure is nominal/ordinal/ continuous, the range if applicable, the observation year(s), which directionality the variable takes, the N size, and whether any transformations were used. It also includes a link to the full replication dataset online and other pertinent material posted online.

The Nine Dimensions of National Outcomes

Dimension 1. Political Stability and Governance

In accordance with chapters 4–6, we hypothesize that nations with higher Syndrome scores will have lower levels of political stability, higher levels of corruption, lower levels of democracy and civil rights, and lower levels of government effectiveness and rule of law.

Analyses for the Political Stability and Governance Dimension
We begin our empirical data analysis with the Fragile States Index. This oft-used index measures the vulnerability of a state across a number of pressures that contribute to the risk of the state failing, becoming subject to ethnic tensions, civil war, and the inability to govern capably and transparently. We utilize two variables as ancillary analyses to test the robustness of our initial analysis. The first ancillary analysis uses our Lack of Security, Stability, and Legitimacy factor. Four indicators loaded on this factor. The first indicator is Security Apparatus, a subcomponent of the Fragile States Index, which measures the extent to which the state has a monopoly on the use of legitimate force and can guarantee the physical security of its citizens. The second indicator is State Legitimacy, also a subcomponent of the Fragile States Index, which measures the extent to which citizens believe that a given regime possesses authority or rightful power. The third indicator is the Political Instability Index, which assesses factors that destabilize governments, including the degrees of social unrest, the inability to transfer power following an election, and excessive executive control. The fourth indicator is the Global Peace Index, which measures the country's levels of peacefulness both domestically and internationally. It also assesses societal safety and security, domestic conflict, involvement in regional or international conflict, and militarization within the state. Because the Global Peace Index is widely used, we also include it separately as our second ancillary analysis for the Fragile States Index.

Second, we use our Government System and Effectiveness factor as a main analysis. Five indicators loaded on this factor. The first indicator is the World Bank's Government Effectiveness Index, which includes a wide range of factors that contribute to government stability and resilience. It includes institutional effectiveness; quality of basic services, such as sanitation, education, and health care; and taxation, budgeting, and financial management. The second indicator is the Functioning of Government Index, which measures the ability of government institutions in a given country to function transparently and fairly and their ability to provide needed services to citizens. The third indicator is the Democratic Political Culture Index, which looks at the norms and attitudes regarding what citizens or subjects consider right and authoritative in terms of political regimes and practices. The fourth indicator is Political System Type, which ranks regime types from authoritarian to democratic with two categories of autocracy (i.e., bounded and unbounded) and two of democracy (i.e., ineffective and effective). The fifth indicator is the Equal Protection Index, which measures equal protection under the law for minority ethnic, religious, or other groups. We used two ancillary variables as robustness checks: the World Bank Government Effectiveness Index, which is a component of the previous factor; and Regime Type, which scales political regimes from pure autocracy to minimal democracy with three categories of autocracies (i.e., pure, inclusive, and liberal).

Third, we examine corruption using the World Bank's Corruption Index, which looks at a number of measures of transparency or corruption in state institutions. Examples include corruption among public officials, irregularity in tax collection or public contracts, bribery, and accountability.

Fourth, we look at the World Bank's Rule of Law variable. This well-regarded indicator of the rule of law across nations measures a host of variables that range from extent of types of crime, judicial independence, and protection for private property. We use Private Property Rights in an ancillary analysis. This variable measures the extent to which a citizen may contract openly and legally for property or commercial ventures. The inability to do so demonstrates, for example, judicial ineffectiveness, power held by strong group interests, and presence of state corruption.

Fifth, we use our Lack of Freedom factor on which loaded two indicators: The Press Freedom Index, prepared by Reporters without Borders, which measures freedom of press worldwide that is a major determinant of rights and liberties within a given country; Freedom House's Index of Political Rights, a respected project that measures democratic norms and practice worldwide by surveying competitive elections, the role of parties and interest groups, and the role of the executive.[38] We used two variables for our ancillary analysis: Freedom House's Index of Political Rights and its Civil Liberties Index. The former is a subcomponent of the larger factor. The latter surveys a nation's respect for individual rights, including freedom of speech, press, religion, and respect for judicial process, factors that in the United States would be termed First Amendment rights, freedoms guaranteed citizens under the law.

Sixth, we take up legal and individual means to demonstrate respect and tolerance for the views of others. Freedom to Establish Religion, our main analysis, looks at a state's openness to new expressions of freedom of conscience beyond what is traditionally accepted. For ancillary analysis, we used our Freedom of Religion and Deliberative Component factor. Two indicators loaded on this factor. The first indicator, Freedom of Religion, which guarantees freedom of conscience, is a primary measure of individual rights. The second indicator, the Deliberative Component Index, is a measure of productive dialogue within the political system. It surveys how decisions are reached in a given political system, that is, whether the system is capable of inclusive, respectful, and reasoned dialogue as opposed to coercion to accept a policy advanced by state elites.

Seventh, we look at inclusion of women in government. Our main analysis uses Percent of Seats in Parliament Held by Women, which measures the percentage of seats held by women in legislatures. We use Government Participation of Women in an ancillary analysis. This WomanStats variable looks at women in legislatures and also takes into account the number of ministerial posts held by women for that given year. (A full list of sources for all variables and models by dimension is included in appendix III.)

Model Results

We ran sixteen general linear models under the Political Stability and Governance dimension: seven of these were used in the main analysis and the other nine were used as ancillary analyses. We found that the Syndrome was significant in fifteen of these sixteen models. The only model for which the Syndrome was not significant was for the Freedom of Religion and Deliberative Component factor. Table 7.1 summarizes the GLM results of the seven main analyses and the nine ancillary analyses. We discuss the outcome variables of the seven main analysis in descending order of their R-squared values, which are indicators of the usefulness and explanatory power of the models. For each outcome variable, the significant explanatory variables are listed in descending order of effect size.

In this section, we elaborate on the GLM results of the dependent variables used in the seven main analyses. Full results for each dependent variable are available in appendix III by dimension.

1.1 Fragile States Index

(Higher scores are considered worse.)

The adjusted R-squared is a remarkably strong .744, indicating that the specified model explained at least 74.4 percent of the variability of the Fragile

TABLE 7.1 Summary of GLM Results for the Political Stability Dimension in Descending Order of R-Squared Values

Dependent Variables	Adjusted R-squared (N)	Independent Variables (significant at .001 in descending order of effect size)
1. Fragile States Index (FSI)	.744 (172)	Syndrome Urbanization
Lack of security, stability, and legitimacy factor • *FSI's Security Apparatus* • *FSI's State Legitimacy* • *Political Instability* • *Global Peace Index*	*.605 (158)*	*Syndrome* *Number of Land Neighbors*
Global Peace Index	*.365 (163)*	*Syndrome* *Number of Land Neighbors*
2. Government System and Effectiveness Factor • World Bank Government Effectiveness • Functioning of Government • Democratic Political Culture Index • Political System Type • Equal Protection Index	.565 (158)	Syndrome
World Bank Government Effectiveness	*.612 (176)*	*Syndrome* *Urbanization* *Religious Fractionalization*
Regime Type	*.314 (168)*	*Syndrome*
3. World Bank Corruption Score	.563 (176)	Syndrome Urbanization Colonial Heritage Status

(*continued*)

TABLE 7.1 *(continued)*

Dependent Variables	Adjusted R-squared (N)	Independent Variables (significant at .001 in descending order of effect size)
4. World Bank Rule of Law Score	.561 (176)	Syndrome Urbanization Religious Fractionalization
Private Property Rights	*.513 (170)*	*Syndrome* *Urbanization* *Colonial Heritage Status* *Number of Land Neighbors*

5. Lack of Freedom Factor
  • Press Freedom Index
  • Freedom House Index of Political Rights
	.415 (170)	Syndrome

Freedom House Index of Political Rights	*.426 (176)*	*Syndrome*
Civil Liberties	*.459 (165)*	*Syndrome*
6. Freedom to Establish Religion	.245 (133)	Syndrome Terrain Ethnic Fractionalization

Freedom of Religion and Deliberative Component Factor
  • *Freedom of Religion*
  • *Deliberative Component Index*
	.276 (164)	*Number of Land Neighbors*

7. Percent of Seats in Parliament Held by Women	.116 (172)	Syndrome
Government Participation of Women	*.221 (176)*	*Syndrome* *Muslim Civilization*

Note: Ancillary analyses are in italics.

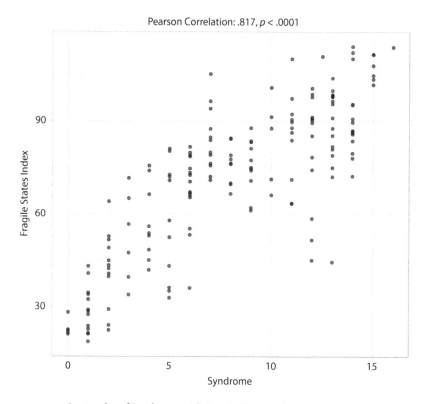

Pearson Correlation: .817, $p < .0001$

FIGURE 7.1.1 Scatterplot of Syndrome with Fragile States Index

States Index scores, and the only two variables achieving significance are the Syndrome and Percent Urban Population. See appendix III, table AIII.7.1.1, for full results. The coefficients of these two variables are opposite, that is, the higher the Syndrome score, the more fragile the state, but the higher the Urbanization percentage, the less fragile the state. The effect size for the Syndrome, however, is more than twice that of Urban Population. The bivariate correlation reveals a strong association between the Syndrome and State Fragility, with a very strong correlation of .817 ($p < .0001$) and a fairly tight clustering shown in the scatterplot in figure 7.1.1.

Because the Syndrome is significant in the general linear regression model, we also ran a logistic regression model (using a binary version of the response variable). The cutoff was determined by the mean, and "worse outcome" is defined as worse than average. Details of the cutoff are included in appendix IV. The Syndrome, Urbanization, and Religious Fractionalization are the only variables that are significant in predicting the logits or predicted probabilities of a more fragile state. We specifically find that for every one unit increase in the Syndrome, the odds increase by 113 percent, or alternatively, there is a 2.13 times greater risk, that the country will experience greater fragility, after holding all other control variables constant.

We wanted to perform a robustness check on the modeling of the Fragile States Index, by adding in GDP per capita (log transformed purchasing power parity, PPP) to the model, and then as a secondary check to swap out Urbanization Rate with GDP per capita (log transformed, PPP), and see how Syndrome fares under those circumstances. That is, is wealth a more important predictor of state fragility than the Syndrome? When GDP per capita is added to the model, it renders Urbanization insignificant. Even so, the Syndrome remains significant and its effect size (.419) is larger than that of GDP per capita (.302). We also tried exchanging Urbanization with GDP per capita, and the results were very similar: the Syndrome remained significant and its effect size (.448) remained slightly larger than that of GDP per capita (.432). We find that noteworthy: whether or not women are disempowered at the household level is more important in explaining state fragility than the nation's level of wealth.

We also used our Lack of Security, Stability, and Legitimacy factor as an ancillary analysis for the Fragile States Index. The analysis showed a remarkably strong .605 adjusted R-squared, indicating that the specified model explained at least 60.5 percent of the variability of this factor. Consistent with the results for Fragile States Index, the Syndrome is a significant predictor of the stability, peacefulness, and legitimacy of a nation. The only two variables in the model for this factor that are significant are the Syndrome and Number of Land Neighbors, but the effect size for Syndrome is almost four times larger than that of land neighbors. The coefficient for the Syndrome variable is positive, meaning that the higher the Syndrome score, the more unstable, the less peaceful, and the less legitimate the state. The coefficient for land neighbors is also positive, which means that having more neighbors predisposes a state to lower levels of stability.

We also used the Global Peace Index in an ancillary analysis for the Fragile States Index and, again, we found that Syndrome is a significant predictor of nation-state peacefulness, and in the hypothesized direction with high-Syndrome nations experiencing lower levels of peace. The analysis yielded a moderate adjusted R-squared value of .365. The other significant predictor of peacefulness was the Number of Land Neighbors. The more land neighbors a country had, the lower the level of peacefulness for the country.

1.2 Government System and Effectiveness Factor

(This factor combines several variables: World Bank Government Effectiveness, Functioning of Government, Democratic Political Culture Index, Political System Type, and Equal Protection Index. Lower scores are considered worse.)

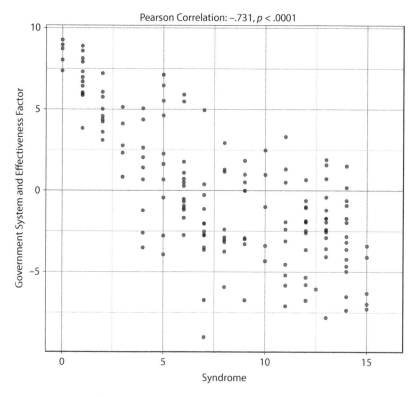

FIGURE 7.1.2 Scatterplot of Syndrome with Government System and Effectiveness Factor

The adjusted R-squared for this model is a strong .565, indicating that the specified model explained at least 56.5 percent of the variability of the Government System and Effectiveness factor. See appendix III, table AIII.7.1.2, for full results. Interestingly, the only significant variable in the model is the Syndrome, and the coefficient is negative, which means that the higher the Syndrome score, the lower the score on this factor. The effect size of the Syndrome is .280, much larger than the effect sizes of any other variable in the model. The bivariate correlation bears out this very strong relationship ($r = -.731, p < .0001$), as does the bivariate scatterplot shown in figure 7.1.2. High Syndrome scores are strongly associated with a lack of democracy and a lack of governmental effectiveness. This large N analysis corroborates our theoretical framework and suggests that the horizon for democracy and for effective governance is constrained by the presence of the Syndrome as the first political order of the society.

Because the Syndrome is significant in the general linear regression model, we also ran a logistic regression model (using a binary version of the response variable). The Syndrome and Religious Fractionalization are the only variables that are significant in predicting the logits or predicted probabilities of more autocratic government systems and lower levels of government effectiveness. We specifically find that for every one unit increase in the Syndrome, the odds increase by 253 percent, or alternatively, the risk is 3.53 times higher that the country will experience a more autocratic governmental system and a lower level of government effectiveness, after holding all other control variables constant.

We examined the World Bank's Government Effectiveness scale as well as a Regime Type variable as ancillary analyses for the Government System and Effectiveness factor. The first ancillary analyses showed that the model had a strong adjusted R-squared of .612 with Syndrome, Urbanization, and Religious Fractionalization as the three best predictors of government effectiveness. The negative coefficient for the Syndrome shows that higher Syndrome scores are associated with significantly lower levels of government effectiveness. The second ancillary analyses showed that the model had an adjusted R-squared of .314 for Regime Type with the Syndrome as the only significant predictor. As signified by its negative coefficient, the higher the Syndrome score, the more autocratic the nation's regime type. Whether or not women are subordinated has significant influence on regime type and regime effectiveness.

1.3 World Bank Corruption

(Lower scores are considered worse.)

The adjusted R-squared is a strong .563, indicating that the specified model explained at least 56.3 percent of the variability of corruption, and three independent variables are statistically significant: Never Colonized, the Syndrome, and Percent Urban Population. See appendix III, table AIII.7.1.3. Although never having been colonized and having a higher percent of urban population are associated with lower levels of corruption, the Syndrome is associated with significantly higher levels of corruption. Note that the effect size for the Syndrome is the largest of the model, which is consistent with our hypotheses. The bivariate correlation is a moderately strong −.684 ($p < .0001$), and the scatterplot in figure 7.1.3 shows a distinctive negative slope. Corruption at the household level by means of Syndrome practices does indeed appear to be associated with corruption in the larger polity, as predicted by our theoretical framework.

Because the Syndrome is significant in the general linear regression model, we also ran a logistic regression model (using a binary version of the response variable). The Syndrome, Urbanization, and Land Neighbors are the only variables that are significant in predicting the logits or predicted probabilities of a country experiencing high levels of corruption. We specifically find that for every one unit increase in the Syndrome, the odds increase by 23 percent, or alternatively, the risk is 1.23 times greater that the country will experience high levels of corruption, after holding all other control variables constant.

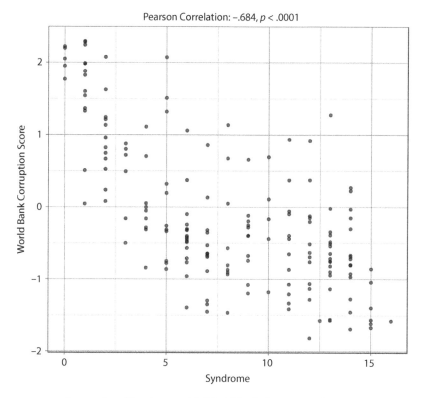

Pearson Correlation: −.684, p < .0001

FIGURE 7.1.3 Scatterplot of Syndrome with World Bank Corruption Score

1.4 World Bank Rule of Law
(Lower scores are considered worse.)

The adjusted R-squared is a strong .561, indicating that the specified model explained at least 56.1 percent of the variability in degree of rule of law, and three variables achieve significance: the Syndrome, Percent Urban Population, and Religious Fractionalization. See appendix III, table AIII.7.1.4, for full results. Religious Fractionalization and Percent Urban Population have positive coefficients, meaning they are associated with better rule of law. The Syndrome's coefficient is negative, however, which means the higher the Syndrome score, the more diminished the rule of law. The effect size for the Syndrome is the highest of the three significant variables, and the bivariate correlation is a moderately strong −.694 ($p < .0001$), with a distinctive negative slope as shown in the scatterplot in figure 7.1.4. Again, we consider this a very significant finding from a theoretical standpoint: a lack of rule of law at the household level for women is strongly and significantly associated with lack of rule of law at the level of the polity.

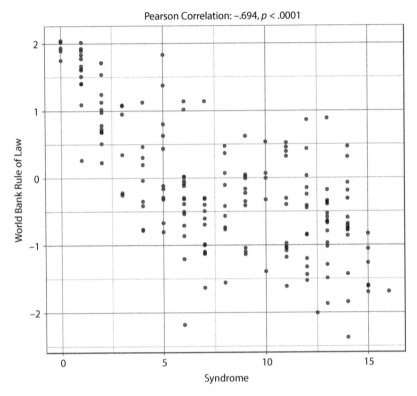

FIGURE 7.1.4 Scatterplot of Syndrome with World Bank Rule of Law Score

Because the Syndrome is significant in the general linear regression model, we also ran a logistic regression model (using a binary version of the response variable). The Syndrome, Urbanization, and Religious Fractionalization are the only variables that are significant in predicting the logits or predicted probabilities of a country experiencing a diminished rule of law. We specifically find that for every one unit increase in the Syndrome, the odds increase by 22 percent, or alternatively, the risk is 1.22 times that the country will experience a diminished rule of law, after holding all other control variables constant.

We used Private Property Rights in an ancillary analysis for the Rule of Law model and the ancillary analysis showed a strong adjusted R-squared of .513, indicating that the specified model explained at least 51.3 percent of the variability of the private property rights, and the four variables that achieve significance are Colonial Heritage Status, the Syndrome, Percent Urban Population/Urbanization, and Number of Land Neighbors. The effect size for the Syndrome is slightly larger than any of the other significant variables. The coefficients indicate that both countries that were never colonized and those with greater Urbanization are associated with greater property rights; higher scores on both the Syndrome and the Number of Land Neighbors are associated with significantly lower levels of property rights.

1.5 Lack of Freedom Factor

(This factor combines two variables: Press Freedom Index 2017 and Freedom House Index Political Rights 2016. Higher scores are considered worse.)

The adjusted R-squared is a strong .415, indicating that the specified model explained at least 41.5 percent of the variability of the Lack of Freedom factor, and the only variable in the model that was significant was the Syndrome. The coefficient for the Syndrome was positive, which means that the worse the Syndrome score, the worse the situation of political rights and press freedom in a nation. See appendix III, table AIII.7.1.5, for full results. The bivariate correlation with Syndrome was a moderately strong .625 ($p < .0001$), but the scatterplot in figure 7.1.5 shows quite a bit of "scatter" for middle-range Syndrome countries. So, for example, some of the countries in the central part

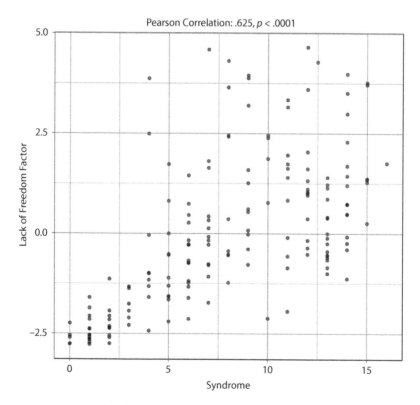

FIGURE 7.1.5 Scatterplot of Syndrome with Lack of Freedom Factor

of the graph, falling in the middle on the Syndrome scale but scoring high on this factor indicating lack of freedom, include North Korea, Cuba, and Belarus. Interestingly, these are former communist countries where the Syndrome was nominally ameliorated, at least in formal law, but nevertheless these countries still lack these political freedoms.

Because the Syndrome is significant in the general linear regression model, we also ran a logistic regression model (using a binary version of the response variable). The Syndrome is the only variable that is significant in predicting the logits or predicted probabilities of low levels of press freedom and political rights. We specifically find that for every one unit increase in the Syndrome, the odds increase by 49 percent, or alternatively, the risk is 1.49 times greater that the country will experience low levels of press freedom and political rights, after holding all other control variables constant.

Note that we used Civil Liberties and Freedom House's Index of Political Rights as ancillary variables for the Lack of Freedom Factor. The results of the former ancillary analysis also showed a strong adjusted R-squared of .459, indicating that the specified model explained at least 45.9 percent of the variability of the Civil Liberties, and the only significant variable in the model was also the Syndrome, with a noteworthy effect size. The coefficient for the Syndrome was negative, which means that higher Syndrome scores are associated with significantly lower levels of civil liberties.

The second ancillary analysis also showed a strong adjusted R-squared value of .426 and, consistent with the previous findings, the Syndrome is the only significant predictor of the political rights a country bestows on its citizens: the higher the Syndrome score, the lower the level of political rights for a country's citizens, on average.

1.6 Freedom to Establish Religion
(Lower scores are considered worse.)

The adjusted R-squared is a moderate .245, indicating that the specified model explained at least 24.5 percent of the variability of the freedom to establish religion, and three variables in the model were significant: the Syndrome, Percent Arable Land, and Ethnic Fractionalization. See appendix III, table AIII.7.1.6, for full results. Both Percent Arable Land and Ethnic Fractionalization have positive coefficients, meaning the higher the Percent of Arable Land and the higher the Ethnic Fractionalization, the more likely it is that the nation offered the freedom to establish religion. The coefficient for the Syndrome is negative, indicating that countries with higher Syndrome scores are on average less likely to offer the freedom to establish religion. The effect sizes for the three variables are essentially the same. The bivariate correlation with Syndrome is a weak −.380, though the scatterplot in figure 7.1.6 reveals that the

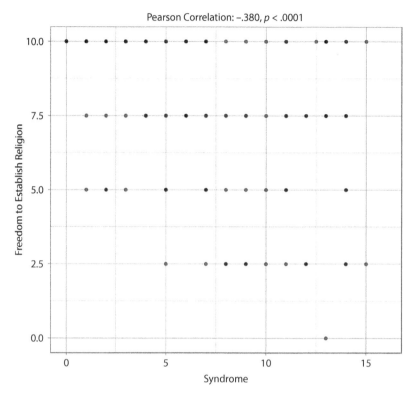

FIGURE 7.1.6 Scatterplot of Syndrome with Freedom to Establish Religion

nations with the worst levels of freedom of religion also have higher Syndrome scores. The country in the lowest right-hand corner of the graph, with a high Syndrome score and very low Freedom to Establish Religion (the only one in the lowest category), is the United Arab Emirates.

Because the Syndrome is significant in the general linear regression model, we also ran a logistic regression model (using a binary version of the response variable). The Syndrome, Terrain, and Ethnic Fractionalization are the only variables that are significant in predicting the logits or predicted probabilities of a country having less freedom to establish religion. We specifically find that for every one unit increase in the Syndrome, the odds increase by 26 percent, or alternatively, the risk is 1.26 times greater that the country experiences less freedom to establish religion, after holding all other control variables constant.

We used our Freedom of Religion and Deliberative Component factor in an ancillary analysis, and we obtained an adjusted R-squared of .276 in the ancillary analysis. The only significant predictor of this factor is the Number of Land Neighbors.

1.7 Percent of Seats in Parliament Held by Women
(Lower scores are considered worse.)

The adjusted R-squared is a weak .116, indicating that the specified model explained only 11.6 percent of the variability of the percentage of parliament seats held by women, and the only significant variable in the model was the Syndrome. See appendix III, table AIII.7.1.7, for full results. This suggests that the percent of seats in parliament held by women may have very little to do with personal empowerment of women at the household level (as Hudson's acquaintance who was an Afghan minister of parliament noted in the introduction). The coefficient was negative, which means the higher the Syndrome score, the lower the percentage of women in parliament. The bivariate correlation was a weak $-.322$ ($p < .0001$), with quite a bit of spread across the distribution, as shown in the scatterplot in figure 7.1.7. The outlier in the top middle of the plot is Rwanda, where the situation of women is still not very good, despite excellent levels of female representation in parliament, which we term the Rwanda Paradox.[39]

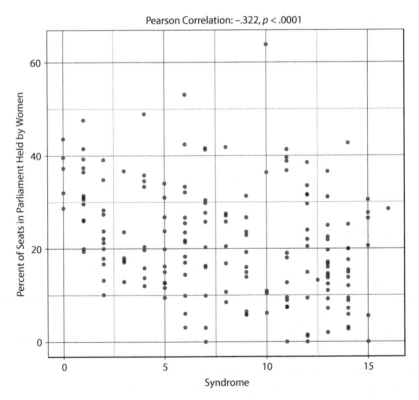

FIGURE 7.1.7 Scatterplot of Syndrome with Percent of Seats in Parliament Held by Women

Because the Syndrome is significant in the general linear regression model, we also ran a logistic regression model (using a binary version of the response variable). Because the model does not meet the validity requirements, we do not report the results.

We also used Government Participation of Women in an ancillary analysis for Percent of Seats in Parliament held by Women. The WomanStats scale of the participation of women in government looks not only at seats in parliament, but also at women in top posts in the executive branch. The adjusted R-squared is a moderate .221, indicating that the specified model explained at least 22.1 percent of the variability of the government participation by women, again showing that government participation by women is not necessarily associated with personal empowerment of women in households. The two variables of significance in the model are the Syndrome and Muslim Civilization, each of which have a positive coefficient because higher scores on this Government Participation scale indicate worse representation of women in these government positions. The effect size for the Syndrome was almost twice that of Muslim Civilization.

Concluding Discussion for the Political Stability and Governance Dimension

For our Political Stability and Governance dimension empirical probe, we ran sixteen separate GLM analyses. Of those sixteen models, the Syndrome was significant in fifteen, was the *only* significant variable in six of those fifteen, and was the significant variable with the largest effect size in another eight of the analyses. Also noteworthy is that the control variables of Huntington civilization, Terrain, and Ethnic Fractionalization appear not to be overly determinative for this dimension, in contrast to a greater showing for Urbanization, Number of Land Neighbors, Religious Fractionalization, and Colonial Heritage Status.

Across the sixteen models, the findings are quite robust and consistent: the single best determinant of Political Stability overall was the Syndrome. If you wished to understand the political stability of a nation, including measures of state fragility, quality of governance, type of governance, and freedom of religion and corruption, you would derive greater explanatory power by looking at the subordination of women at the household level through the components of the Syndrome than any of the other variables examined in the model, including ethno-religious fractionalization, urbanization, colonial history, civilization, terrain, and geographic borders.

Importantly, the horizon of possibility for democracy is significantly constrained by the presence of the Syndrome, and autocracy, corruption, and lack of rule of law at the household level are strongly and significantly associated with the Syndrome at the level of the polity. That finding contradicts those of other researchers who fail to find a significant relationship between women's empowerment and democracy, perhaps because these scholars did not use any variables in our Syndrome index that measure that empowerment at the household level.[40] Our theoretical framework anticipated these relationships, and large N analysis has corroborated it.

Dimension 2. Security and Conflict

Our hypothesis is that, *ceteris paribus*, we expect societies with a higher Syndrome score to experience higher rates of conflict and higher rates of national and societal insecurity. We took a broad approach to this Security and Conflict dimension, looking at measures of terrorism, crime, grievance, military expenditures, internal and external conflicts, trafficking, and even a measure of women's mobility in public spaces.

Analyses for the Security and Conflict Dimension

We begin our empirical analysis of this dimension by looking at our Violence and Stability Factor derived from factor analysis, on which loaded nine indicators. These indicators are: States of Concern to the International Community, which measures state compliance to international norms in terms of use of force, international political norms, and international economic norms; Group Grievance, a subcomponent of the Fragile States Index, which assesses the extent of cleavages between groups in society and focuses on divisions based on social or political characteristics especially those related to access to resources and services; the Political Terror Scale, which measures a country's levels of violence and terror for a specific year; the Trafficking of Women scale, which ranks states as to laws governing trafficking of women and the degree of state compliance to that law; Intensity of Internal Conflicts, which ranks states in terms of the severity of conflict within the state; Violent Demonstrations, which ranks the frequency of violent demonstrations within a state; Political Terror, a subcomponent of the Global Peace Index, which measures a country's levels of political terror and violence for a given year; Women's Mobility scale, which assesses the ability of a woman to be in and to move within public spaces; and Neighboring Country Relations, a subcomponent of the Global Peace Index, which measures relations with neighboring countries on a scale from peaceful to very aggressive.

We identified six variables for ancillary analyses for the Violence and Instability factor. The first ancillary analysis used our Absence of Violent Terrorism and Freedom of Domestic Movement factor, on which loaded two indicators: Political Stability and Absence of Violence/Terrorism from the World Bank, which gauges the political instability and politically motivated violence for a given state, and Freedom of Domestic Movement, which measures the ability to move freely in a country from severely restricted to unrestricted movement. The second ancillary analysis used the World Bank's Political Stability and Absence of Violence/Terrorism in isolation, apart from the larger factor. The third and fourth ancillary analyses used Trafficking of Women and the Political Terror Scale (both are indicators within our Violence and Instability factor, which we analyzed separately to probe more deeply into these phenomena).

Second, we look at the Societal Violence Scale, which provides data on the extent of violence within a given country in terms of scope, severity, and numbers affected.

Third, we utilize the Military Expenditures and Weapons Importation factor, on which loaded three indicators, in the main analysis. The first indicator is Military Expenditure as a percentage of GDP. This variable uses the North Atlantic Treaty Organization's definition, which includes all expenditures labeled military, including capital expenditures, peacekeeping, personnel, pensions, social services, and maintenance figured as a percentage of a nation's GDP. The second indicator, Military Expenditures, a subcomponent of the Global Peace Index, also measures military expenditures defined as the outlays of governments to meet costs of national armed forces, as a percentage of GDP. The third indicator in this factor, Weapons Imports, another subcomponent of the Global Peace Index, measures major conventional weapons imported for a period of time, calculated per capita, for a given country. We use Access to Weapons in an ancillary analysis. Yet another subcomponent of the Global Peace Index, this measures the ease of access to small arms and light weapons within the nation.

Fourth, we look at Monopoly on the Use of Force, which measures the central government's control over weapons of force and whether that control extends to all regions of the country or is challenged by nongovernmental groups.

Fifth, we use the Global Terrorism Index, an oft-used and inclusive source that scales the impact of terrorism, including fatalities, incidents, injuries, and property damage in our main analysis. We use our Terrorism Incidents and Internal Conflict factor in the first ancillary analysis. Three indicators load on this factor: Incidents of Terrorism in a given year, a subcomponent of the Global Terrorism Index, which gives the total number of actual terrorist attacks in a given year; Internal Conflicts Fought, which measures the number and duration of a country's internal conflicts; and the Global Terrorism Index. The second ancillary analysis used the variable Terrorism Impact, which combines terrorism injury, fatality, and property damage data. The third ancillary analysis uses the Terrorism Injury and Violent Conflict factor. Four indicators loaded on this factor: Terrorism Injuries, which scales the number injured by terrorism in a year; Terrorism Fatalities, which scales the number killed through terrorism in a given year by country; and Intensity of Violent Conflicts, which assesses the intensity of conflicts experienced by the nation-state, which are then ranked from no conflict to severe crisis; and the Overall Index of Disappearance, Conflict, and Terrorism, which includes variables such as violent conflicts, internally organized conflicts, politically motivated disappearances, battle-related deaths, and impact of armed conflict in personal freedoms. The fourth ancillary analysis uses Deaths from Internal Conflict, which is a subcomponent of the Global Peace Index.

Sixth, we examine the Perceptions of Criminality, which utilizes assessments of levels of perceived criminality in a given country, in the main analysis. We use three variables for ancillary analysis. The first is our Homicide and Violent Crime factor, on which loaded three indicators: Homicide Rates, a subcomponent of the Social Progress Index (using data from the United Nations Office on Drugs and Crime), which measures the number of homicides per one hundred thousand people; Homicide, a subcomponent of the Global Peace Index, which measures the total number of deliberate inflictions of death (penal code offences) per one hundred thousand people; and Violent Crime, which assesses whether violent crime poses significant problems for government or business. The second ancillary analysis uses Homicide, a subcomponent of the Human Freedom Index, which examines rates of intentional homicide for one hundred thousand people and then scales the data. The third ancillary analysis uses Incarceration Rate, which measures the prison population per one hundred thousand people.

Last, we look at two external conflict indicators: Deaths from External Conflict, a subcomponent of the Global Peace Index, which measures the number of deaths from conflicts external to the country analyzed, in a main analysis; and External Conflicts Fought, which measures the number and duration of conflicts outside its own territory, which a country is involved in, in an ancillary analysis.

Model Results

We ran twenty general linear model analyses under the Security and Conflict dimension; seven of these were used in the main analysis and the other thirteen were used as ancillary analyses. We found that the Syndrome was significant in fourteen of these twenty models. The six models for which the Syndrome was not significant include the following dependent variables: (1) Homicide and Violent Crime factor, (2) Homicide (Human Freedom Index, HFI), (3) Deaths from Internal Conflicts, (4) Deaths from External Conflicts, (5) External Conflicts Fought, and (6) Incarceration Rates. It is interesting that most of these aspects of the dimension are related to crime and external conflict. Table 7.2 summarizes the GLM results of the analyses for the Security and Conflict dimension. We discuss the outcome variables in descending order of the R-squared values of the explanatory model, which values are indicators of the usefulness and explanatory power of the model.

We elaborate on the GLM results for the seven dependent variables used in the main analysis, noting ancillary analysis results associated with each of the seven.

Dependent Variable	Adjusted R-squared (N)	Independent Variables (significant at .001 in descending order of effect size)
1. Violence and Instability Factor • States of Concern to the International Community • Group Grievance • Political Terror Scale • Trafficking of Women • Intensity of Internal Conflicts • Violence Demonstrations • Political Terror • Women's Mobility • Relations with Neighboring Countries	.642 (145)	Syndrome Number of Land Neighbors
Absence of Violent Terrorism and Freedom of Domestic Movement Factor • *Political Stability and Absence of Violence/Terrorism* • *Freedom of Domestic Movement*	*.525 (157)*	*Syndrome* *Number of Land Neighbors* .
Political Stability and Absence of Violence/Terrorism	*.547 (176)*	*Syndrome* *Number of Land Neighbors*
Trafficking of Women	*.454 (174)*	*Syndrome*
Political Terror Scale	*.425 (163)*	*Syndrome* *Number of Land Neighbors*
2. Societal Violence Scale	.377 (174)	Syndrome Number of Land Neighbors
3. Military Expenditures and Weapons Importation Factor • Military Expenditure as Percentage of GDP • Military Expenditures • Weapons Imports	.318 (152)	Urbanization Syndrome
Access to Weapons	*.383 (163)*	*Syndrome*

(continued)

TABLE 7.2 *(continued)*

Dependent Variable	Adjusted R-squared (N)	Independent Variables (significant at .001 in descending order of effect size)
4. Monopoly on the Use of Force	.234 (128)	Syndrome
5. Global Terrorism Index	.239 (163)	Syndrome Number of Land Neighbors
Terrorism Incidents and Internal Conflict Factor • *Incidents of Terrorism in a Given Year* • *Internal Conflicts Fought* • *Global Terrorism Index*	*.220 (163)*	*Syndrome*
Terrorism Impact	*.213 (163)*	*Syndrome* *Number of Land Neighbors*
Terrorism Injury and Violent Conflict Factor • *Terrorism Injuries* • *Terrorism Fatalities* • *Intensity of Violent Conflicts* • *Overall Index of Disappearance, Conflict, and Terrorism*	*.137 (156)*	*Syndrome*
Deaths from Internal Conflict	*.135 (163)*	*None*
6. Perceptions of Criminality	.188 (163)	Syndrome
Homicide and Violent Crime Factor • *Homicide Rates* • *Homicide from Global Peace Index* • *Violent Crime*	*.180 (154)*	*Syndrome*
Homicide from Human Freedom Index	*.110 (156)*	*None*
Incarceration Rate	*.047 (163)*	*None*
7. External Conflicts Fought	.044 (163)	None
Deaths from External Conflict	*.011 (163)*	*None*

Note: Ancillary analyses are in italics. GDP, gross domestic product.

2.1 Violence and Instability Factor

(This factor combines several variables, including the States of Concern Scale, Group Grievance, Political Terrorism Scale, Trafficking, Internal Conflict, Violent Demonstrations, Political Terror, Women's Mobility, and Neighboring Country Relations. Higher scores are considered worse.)

The adjusted R-squared is a remarkably strong .642, indicating that the specified model explained at least 64.2 percent of the variability of the several different measures of violence, instability, and insecurity. See appendix III, table AIII.7.2.1, for full results. Only two variables emerged as significant: the Syndrome and Number of Land Neighbors. Both variables are positively related to this factor; that is, the higher the Syndrome score or the greater the number of land neighbors, the higher the level of instability and insecurity. The effect for the Syndrome is the largest in the model, more than three times that of Land Neighbors. The bivariate relationship between the Syndrome and this factor is very strong at .773 ($p < .0001$), and the scatterplot in figure 7.2.1 demonstrates this well. The Syndrome is strongly and significantly associated with greater violence and instability for the nation-state.

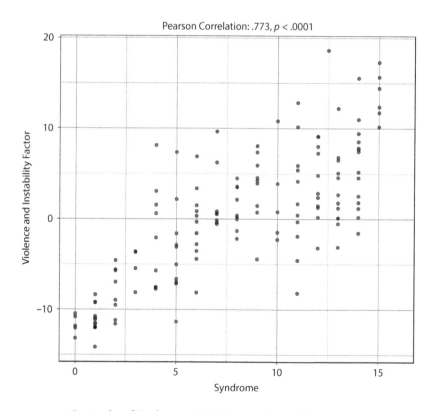

FIGURE 7.2.1 Scatterplot of Syndrome with Violence and Instability Factor

Because the Syndrome is significant in the general linear regression model, we also ran a logistic regression model (using a binary version of the response variable). The Syndrome and Number of Land Neighbors are the only variables that are significant in predicting the logits or predicted probabilities of higher levels of violence and instability. We specifically find that for every one unit increase in the Syndrome, the odds increase by 47 percent, or alternatively, the risk is 1.47 times greater that the country experiences higher levels of violence and instability, after holding all other control variables constant.

We used four other variables in ancillary analyses as a check for the Violence and Instability factor. The first is our Absence of Violent Terrorism and Freedom of Movement factor. The adjusted R-squared for this model is a strong .525, indicating that the specified model explained at least 52.5 percent of the variability of this factor, and very much like the previous factor examined, only the Syndrome and Number of Land Neighbors were significant. This time, however, both variables are negatively associated with this factor, which means the higher the Syndrome score and the greater the Number of Land Neighbors, the lower the level of freedom of domestic movement and the more unstable, violent, and subject to terrorism is the nation-state. The effect size for the Syndrome is the strongest in the model.

The second ancillary analysis used Political Stability and Absence of Violence/Terrorism. The results showed a strong adjusted R-squared value of .547, indicating that our specified model explained at least 54.7 percent of the variability in the Political Stability and Absence of Violence/Terrorism of the countries in our study. The same two variables were significant: Syndrome and Number of Land Neighbors, with directionality as predicted. High Syndrome scores are associated with a lack of political stability and the presence of violence and terrorism.

The third ancillary analysis used Trafficking of Women. The results showed a strong adjusted R-squared value of .454, indicating that the specified model explained at least 45.4 percent of the variability of the Trafficking of Women scores, and only one variable emerges as significant: the Syndrome. The coefficient is positive, which means the higher the Syndrome score, the higher the levels of trafficking of women.

The fourth ancillary analysis used the Political Terror Scale, which yielded a strong adjusted R-squared value of .425, indicating that the specified model explained at least 42.5 percent of the variability of the Political Terror Scale scores, and two variables are significant: the Syndrome and Number of Land Neighbors, with the effect size of the former larger than that of the latter. Both variables have positive coefficients, which means the higher the Syndrome score or the greater the Number of Land Neighbors, the higher the score on the Political Terror Scale.

2.2 Societal Violence Scale

(Higher scores are considered worse.)

The adjusted R-squared is a moderate .377, indicating that the specified model explained at least 37.7 percent of the variability of the Societal Violence Scales scores, and only two variables were significant: the Syndrome and Number of Land Neighbors, with the effect size of the former being almost twice that of the latter. See appendix III, table AIII.7.2.2. The coefficients for these variables are both positive, which means the higher the Syndrome score or the greater the Number of Land Neighbors, the higher the level of societal violence. The bivariate correlation between the Syndrome and the Societal Violence Scale is moderately strong at .529 ($p < .0001$), and the scatterplot in figure 7.2.2 shows the distinctive trapezoidal shape we have come to recognize. The two outlier countries identified on the scatterplot with relatively high Syndrome scores but fairly low societal violence levels include Vanuatu and Brunei, two very small states.

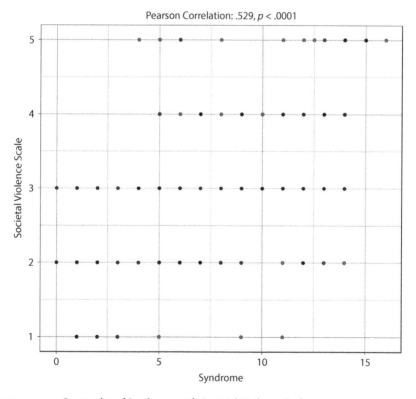

FIGURE 7.2.2 Scatterplot of Syndrome with Societal Violence Scale

Because the Syndrome is significant in the general linear regression model, we also ran a logistic regression model (using a binary version of the response variable). The Syndrome and Ethnic Fractionalization are the only variables that are significant in predicting the logits or predicted probabilities of a country scoring poorly on the Societal Violence Scale. We specifically find that for every one unit increase in the Syndrome, the odds increase by 26 percent, or alternatively, the risk is 1.26 times greater that the country scores poorly on the Societal Violence Scale, after holding all other control variables constant.

2.3 Military Expenditure and Weapons Importation Factor
(This factor combines three variables: Military Expenditure as Percentage of GDP, Military Expenditure, and Weapons Importation. Higher scores are considered worse.)

The adjusted R-squared is a moderate .318, indicating that the specified model explained at least 31.8 percent of the variability of this factor, and only two variables emerge as significant; the Syndrome and Urbanization. See appendix III, table AIII.7.2.3, for full results. Both have positive coefficients, which means the higher the Syndrome score or the higher the rate of Urbanization, the higher military expenditures and weapons imports. The finding for urbanization is somewhat intuitive, but the finding for the Syndrome is thought-provoking, especially because the effect sizes are fairly similar. The bivariate correlation between the Syndrome and this factor is weak at only .250, however, and it is not significant at the $p < .001$ level. The scatterplot in figure 7.2.3 reveals a considerable spread on the dependent variable across the Syndrome scores. Some countries with high expenditures and imports and also high Syndrome scores include Oman and Saudi Arabia. Israel, scoring a 6 on the Syndrome, has noticeably higher expenditures and imports than other nations at that same Syndrome level. (The United States has such a large GDP that its outsize military expenditures do not appear as a very high percentage of GDP.) Australia, scoring a 0 on the Syndrome, has a middle-range score on this outcome measure.

Because the Syndrome is significant in the general linear regression model, we also ran a logistic regression model (using a binary version of the response variable). Because the model does not meet the validity requirements, we do not report the results.

We also used Access to Weapons in an ancillary analysis for our Military Expenditures and Weapons Importation factor. The results show a moderately strong adjusted R-squared value of .383, indicating that the specified model explained at least 38.3 percent of the variability of access to weapons. The only significant variable in the GLM analysis is the Syndrome. Although Syndrome's effect size is quite small, the coefficient value is in the predicted direction. We find that countries with higher Syndrome scores have higher levels of access to weapons.

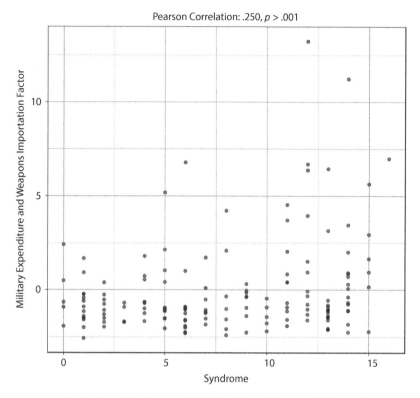

FIGURE 7.2.3 Scatterplot of Syndrome with Military Expenditures and Weapons Importation Factor

2.4 Monopoly on the Use of Force

(Lower scores are considered worse, meaning that other forces or even a "deep state" compromise the state's monopoly on the use of force.)

The adjusted R-squared is a moderate .234, indicating that the specified model explained at least 23.4 percent of the variability of monopoly on the use of force, and only one variable emerges as significant, the Syndrome, with a moderate effect size and a negative coefficient (meaning that the higher the Syndrome score, the worse the situation concerning the government's use of force). See appendix III, table AIII.7.2.4, for full results. The bivariate correlation is a moderately strong $-.513$ ($p < .001$), with the scatterplot in figure 7.2.4 showing a clearly empty lower-left quadrant. At Syndrome scale point 7, Haiti has a very low monopoly on the use of force, and Somalia, with Syndrome scale point 14, has the worst overall score on this outcome variable.

Because the Syndrome is significant in the general linear regression model, we also ran a logistic regression model (using a binary version of the response variable). Because the model does not meet the validity requirements, we do not report the results.

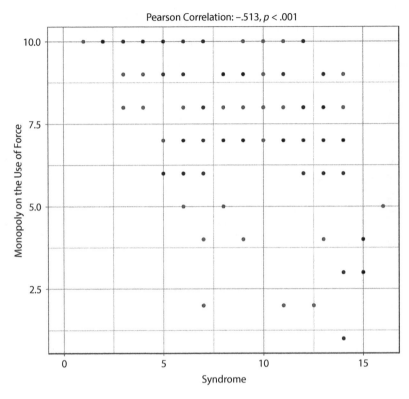

FIGURE 7.2.4 Scatterplot of Syndrome with Monopoly on the Use of Force

2.5 Global Terrorism Index
(Higher scores are considered worse.)

We obtained a moderate adjusted R-squared value of .239, indicating that the specified model explained at least 23.9 percent of the variability of the Global Terrorism Index scores, and two variables emerge as significant: the Syndrome and Number of Land Neighbors. Both coefficients are positive, meaning the higher the Syndrome score and the greater the number of land neighbors, the higher the Global Terrorism score. The effect size for Syndrome is somewhat larger than that for land neighbors. See appendix III, table AIII.7.2.5. The bivariate correlation with the Syndrome is a weak .321 ($p < .001$), and the scatterplot in figure 7.2.5 shows that the nations with the worst scores on the Global Terrorism Index are all high-Syndrome countries, such as Iraq, Nigeria, Afghanistan, Pakistan, and Syria. At a low Syndrome score of 4, Ukraine has a high terror score, but we feel this is associated with that nation's external conflict with Russia.

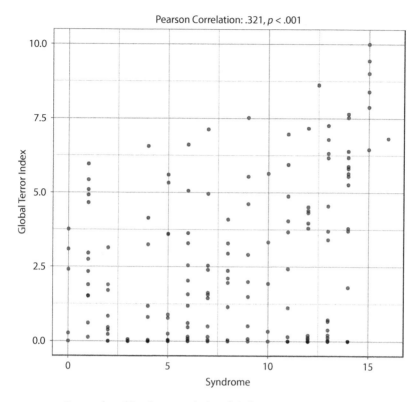

FIGURE 7.2.5 Scatterplot of Syndrome with the Global Terrorism Index

Because the Syndrome is significant in the general linear regression model, we also ran a logistic regression model (using a binary version of the response variable). Because the model does not meet the validity requirements, we do not report the results.

We used four variables in ancillary analyses as checks for the Global Terrorism Index model results. The first is Terrorism Incidents and Internal Conflict factor, which consists of Incidents of Terrorism in a given year, Internal Conflicts Fought, and the Global Terrorism Index. The adjusted R-squared for this factor is a moderate .220, indicating that the specified model explained at least 22 percent of the variability of this factor, a fairly low percentage. We note, however, that the Syndrome is the only significant variable, even though the effect size is small. The coefficient is in the expected positive direction, which means that the higher the Syndrome score, the higher the incidence of terrorism and number of internal conflicts fought.

The second variable used in ancillary analysis is Terrorism Impact. The adjusted R-squared for the GLM analysis for this dependent variable is a moderate .213, indicating that the specified model explained at least 21.3 percent of the variability of the terrorism impact ratings. The two variables that are significant are the Syndrome and the Number of Land Neighbors, each with modest effect sizes. Both coefficients are positive, meaning that the higher the Syndrome score or Number of Land Neighbors, the greater the impact of terrorism on the nation-state.

The third variable used in the analysis was the Terrorism Injury and Violent Conflict factor which combines several variables: Terrorism Injuries, Terrorism Fatalities, Intensity of Violent Conflict, and the Overall Index of Disappearance, Conflict, and Terrorism Score. The adjusted R-squared for this analysis is a weak .137, indicating that the specified model explained only at least 13.7 percent of the variability of this factor. It is noteworthy that the only significant variable in the model is the Syndrome, with the predicted negative association—that is, the higher the Syndrome score, the more affected by terrorism and internal conflict the nation, although the effect size is modest.

The fourth variable used in ancillary analysis is Deaths from Internal Conflict. The GLM results yielded a very low R-squared value of .135, and none of the independent variables in the model was significant. Given the otherwise strong relationship between the Syndrome and internal conflict, it is possible that the scale of death in any such conflict may be more dependent on internal circumstances and the nature of the adversarial groups.

2.6 Perceptions of Criminality
(Higher scores are considered worse.)

The adjusted R-squared for this variable is a weak .188, indicating that the specified model explained only at least 18.8 percent of the variability of perceptions of criminality, and the only significant variable is the Syndrome, with a modest effect size. See appendix III, table AIII.7.2.6, for full results. The coefficient is positive, which means the higher the Syndrome score, the greater the perception of criminality within the society. The bivariate association with the Syndrome is shown in the scatterplot in figure 7.2.6.

Because the Syndrome is significant in the general linear regression model, we also ran a logistic regression model (using a binary version of the response variable). Because the model does not meet the validity requirements, we do not report the results.

We used our Homicide and Violent Crime factor, as well as Homicide from the Human Freedom Index, and Incarceration Rate as ancillary analyses for this analysis. The first had a weak adjusted R-squared value of .180, indicating that the specified model explained at least 18.0 percent of the variability of the Homicide and Violent Crime factor. The Syndrome is not a significant predictor of this factor. The ancillary analyses for Homicide from the Human Freedom Index and Incarceration rate also had very low R-squared values

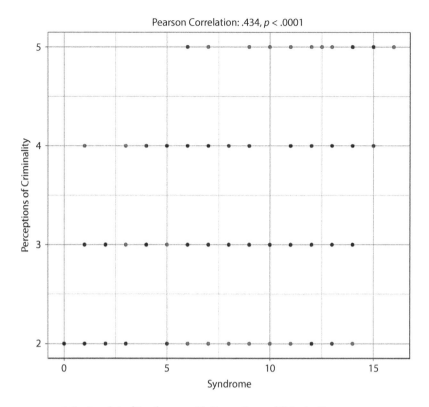

FIGURE 7.2.6 Scatterplot of Syndrome with Perceptions of Criminality

(.110 and .047, respectively) with no significant independent variables in the models, so we do not report the results. Further investigation of this relationship is warranted, particularly given the extant literature surveyed in chapter 5 that does find an association. Crime rate variables are usually uneven in their accuracy and consistency across nations, so these low correlations may reflect those underlying data issues.

2.7 External Conflicts
(Higher scores are considered worse.)

We used two indicators of external conflicts, but the model was a poor fit for the data. The first indicator is the External Conflicts Fought scale, obtained from the Global Peace Index. It had a very low R-squared value of .044 with no significant independent variable.

The second indicator is Deaths from External Conflict, which is also a component of the Global Peace Index. The GLM results for this model yielded a low R-squared value of .011 with no significant independent variable. Because this variable cannot distinguish whether a nation is involved in an external conflict as an aggressor or as a victim, while our theoretical framework speaks primarily to aggression, this relationship will need to be probed further with more suitable variables.

Concluding Discussion for the Security and Conflict Dimension

We ran twenty analyses on numerous variables related to several aspects of the Security and Conflict dimension, such as internal conflict and violent instability, external conflict, criminal behavior, military expenditures/weapons imports/ access to weapons, and terrorism. In five of these analyses, the Syndrome did not prove significant: more specifically, we found no relationship between the Syndrome and external conflict and found very little relationship between the Syndrome and criminal behavior (with the exception of the variable of Perception of Criminality). This might be an important caveat to the broader "women and peace" thesis, which suggests that as levels of gender equality rise, a nation experiences greater levels of peace and security. We note, however, that the external conflict variables used in the analysis do not capture whether the nation was the aggressor or the victim in the conflict. Further testing on the scope conditions of the relationship between the Syndrome and external conflict is needed, particularly in light of the literature reviewed in chapter 4 that does show a relationship. Furthermore, crime rate data are very uneven in quality, so again we would want to probe the relationship between the Syndrome and crime with additional variables before reaching any conclusions on the relationship.

In relation to the remaining fifteen analyses, using variables indicating internal conflict and terrorism, the Syndrome emerged as a persistently significant explanatory variable across fourteen of the fifteen models. In seven of these fifteen models, the Syndrome was the only significant variable in the model, and in seven others, it was the significant variable with the largest effect size.

Although the adjusted R-squared values ranged across the spectrum from weak to strong, and likewise for the effect sizes for the Syndrome when significant, the consistency of the findings across the model runs is noteworthy. Countries with higher Syndrome scores experience significantly greater levels of internal conflict, violent instability, and terrorism, and they are much more interested in acquiring, accessing, and importing weapons. Also noteworthy is the lack of importance of most of the other control variables, with the exception of Number of Land Neighbors.

Dimension 3. Economic Performance

We hypothesize that across a variety of measurements, nations high on the Syndrome scale should experience lower economic performance. Because we look at the character of the economic system in our Rentierism dimension, indicators related to rentierism are not examined in this discussion of the Economic Performance dimension.

Analyses for the Economic Performance Dimension

We first looked at Food Security, which measures access to sufficient and nutritious food that meets dietary standards. This index measures affordability, quality, and availability of food.

Second, we examine our Reliance on Agriculture and Lack of Prosperity factor. As the name indicates, two indicators loaded on this factor: Agriculture Value Added as Percentage of GDP and the Prosperity Index. The first indicator measures the net output of the entire agriculture sector, which includes forestry, hunting, and fishing as well as cultivation of crops and livestock production. The Prosperity Index investigates the general conditions required for prosperity, such as economic quality, business, environment, governance, security, natural environment, and health. We also separated these two variables and ran each separately as ancillary analyses.

Third, we used GDP per capita PPP (log transformed), a standard measure of income that uses a nation's GDP for a year divided by the total population converted to international dollars and using PPP rates.

Fourth, we examined Poverty and Economic Decline. This index utilizes a number of variables, such as per capita income, GNP, unemployment, inflation, and debt to discern patterns of economic decline.

Fifth, we used our Wealth Infrastructure and Economic Freedom factor as our main analysis. Eight indicators loaded on this factor: (1) The HFI (Cato Institute) Economic Freedom Index, which presents a sweeping measure of human freedom, which it defines as the absence of coercive constraints, using seventy-nine indicators of personal and economic freedom. (2) The Index of Economic Freedom (Heritage Institute), which measures economic freedom for a country based on quantitative and qualitative factors under the headings of judicial effectiveness, government size (including spending and tax burden), regulatory efficiency, and open markets. (3) GDP per capita PPP (also analyzed separately above), which is a nation's gross domestic product using PPP rates. (4) Property Rights, which measures the extent to which laws protect private property rights and how these laws are enforced. (5) Quality of Electrical Supply, which measures the electrical supply in terms of reliability and lack of voltage fluctuations. (6) Mobile Telephone Subscriptions, which gives the number of mobile cellular telephone subscriptions per one hundred inhabitants of a given country. (7) Internet Users, which measures the number of individuals with access to the Internet for a given country. (8) Availability of

Affordable Housing, which presents survey answers to queries of satisfaction of good affordable available housing in respondent's area. For an ancillary analysis, we used GDP Annual Growth Percentage, which measures the percent by which GDP grows or declines in a given year.

Sixth, we used the Global Competitiveness Index in a main analysis. This index addresses institutions and infrastructure that support competitiveness, human capital, markets, and capability for innovation. We used two variables in ancillary analyses: Final Consumption (log transformed), which adds the sums of expenditures by private consumption and general government consumption; and High-Technology Exports, which gives the percentage of manufactured exports in sectors with high research and development input and includes aerospace, pharmaceuticals, scientific instruments, and computer and communications technology.

Seventh, we used our Economic Inequality factor on which loaded two variables: the Gini Index and the Uneven Economic Development Index. The Gini Index is the most commonly used measurement of inequality. The Uneven Economic Development Index separates inequality within the economy from the economy's actual performance. It notes structural inequality based on identity or class indicators and also measures opportunities for economic mobility within a given society.

Eighth, we used Female Labor Force Participation, which measures the percent of women in the total labor force.

Ninth, we used Government Expenditures as Percentage of GDP, which calculates general government spending as a share of GDP and indicates the size of government and the viability of a given state economy. It has a secondary use, which is to indicate a country's approach to delivering public goods and services and providing social protection. For an ancillary analysis, we used Government Debt to GDP, which examines the ability of a country to make future payment on its debt given present economic data. Last, we examined in another ancillary analysis the variable Unemployment Rate, which calculates the percent of the total labor force that is unemployed but actively seeking employment.

Model Results
We ran sixteen general linear model analyses under Economic Performance and found that the Syndrome was significant in ten of those models. The six models for which the Syndrome was not significant include the following: (1) High-Technology Exports, (2) Final Consumption (log transformed), (3) Government Expenditure as Percentage of GDP, (4) Unemployment rate, (5) GDP Annual Growth Percentage, and (6) Government Debt to GDP Ratio. These results are summarized in table 7.3.

TABLE 7.3 Summary of GLM Results for the Economic Performance Dimension
Ordered by Descending Adjusted R-squared Values

Dependent Variable	Adjusted R-squared (N)	Independent Variables (significant at .001 by descending order of effect size)
1. Food Security Index	.809 (113)	Syndrome Urbanization
2. Reliance on Agriculture and Lack of Prosperity Factor • Agriculture Value Added as Percentage of GDP • Prosperity Index	.740 (146)	Syndrome Urbanization
Prosperity Index	*.746 (146)*	*Syndrome Urbanization*
Agriculture, Forestry, and Fishing Value Added as Percentage of GDP	*.535 (168)*	*Syndrome Urbanization*
3. GDP per Capita PPP (log transformed)	.695 (170)	Syndrome Urbanization Muslim Civilization
4. Poverty and Economic Decline	.612 (171)	Urbanization Syndrome
5. Wealth Infrastructure and Economic Freedom Factor • Human Freedom Index (HFI) Economic Freedom Index 2016 • Economic Freedom Index 2017 • GDP per Capita PPP (log transformed) • Property Rights • Quality of Electricity Supply • Mobile Telephone Subscriptions • Internet Users • Availability of Affordable Housing	.600 (138)	Syndrome Urbanization
GDP Annual Growth Percentage	*.034 (163)*	*None*

(continued)

TABLE 7.3 *(continued)*

Dependent Variable	Adjusted R-squared (N)	Independent Variables (significant at .001 by descending order of effect size)
6. Global Competitiveness Index Rankings	.564 (137)	Syndrome Urbanization
Final Consumption (log transformed)	*.444 (174)*	*Urbanization Number of Land Neighbors*
High Technology Exports	*.156 (155)*	*None*
7. Economic Inequality Factor • Gini • Uneven Economic Development Indicator	.482 (139)	Syndrome
8. Female Labor Force Participation	.471 (174)	Syndrome Urbanization Muslim Civilization Religious Fractionalization
9. Government Expenditure as Percentage of GDP	.095 (168)	None
Government Debt to GDP	*.056 (168)*	*None*
10. Unemployment Rate	.013 (174)	None

Note: The italicized variables and factors are used in ancillary analyses. GDP, gross domestic product; PPP, purchasing power parity.

3.1 Food Security Index
(Lower scores are considered worse.)

The adjusted R-squared is a remarkably strong .809, indicating that the specified model explained, impressively, at least 80.9 percent of the variability of food security. Only two variables reached significance: the Syndrome and Urbanization. See appendix III, table AIII.7.3.1, for full results. Although the effect size of Urbanization is much larger than that of the Syndrome, their effects are in the opposite direction. Higher rates of Urbanization are associated with higher levels of Food Security; higher scores on the Syndrome are associated with significantly lower levels of Food Security. The bivariate correlation (−.750, $p < .0001$) is very strong, and again the scatterplot in

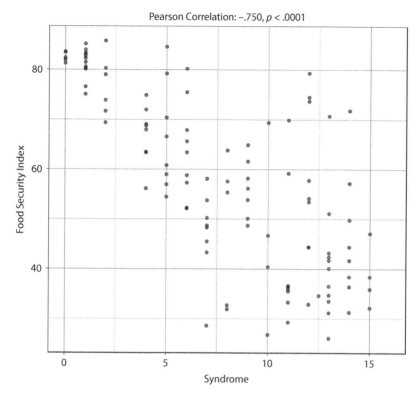

FIGURE 7.3.1 Scatterplot of Syndrome with the Food Security Index

figure 7.3.1 shows the characteristic pattern of an empty lower-left quadrant and considerable spread in the right half of the graph, although most scores anchor the negative association.

Because the Syndrome is significant in the general linear regression model, we also ran a logistic regression model (using a binary version of the response variable). Because the model does not meet the validity requirements, we do not report the results.

3.2 Reliance on Agriculture and Lack of Prosperity Factor
(This factor combines several variables: Agriculture Value Added as Percentage of GDP and Prosperity Index. Higher scores are considered worse.)

The adjusted R-squared is a remarkably strong .740, indicating that the specified model explained at least 74 percent of the variability of this factor. For this factor, combining indicators of agriculture value added and prosperity index, once again only two variables reach significance—the Syndrome and

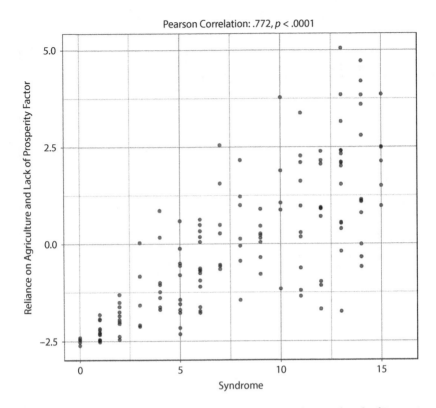

FIGURE 7.3.2 Scatterplot of Syndrome with Reliance on Agriculture and Lack of Prosperity Factor

Urbanization—and the larger effect size of the two is for the Syndrome, at .325. See appendix III, table AIII.7.3.2, for full results. The very strong bivariate correlation in the scatterplot in figure 7.3.2 (correlation = .772, p < .0001) shows a strong positive relationship between the Syndrome and reliance on agriculture and lack of prosperity.

Because the Syndrome is significant in the general linear regression model, we also ran a logistic regression model (using a binary version of the response variable). The Syndrome and Urbanization are the only variables that are significant in predicting the logits or predicted probabilities of higher levels of reliance on agriculture and lack of prosperity. We specifically find that for every one unit increase in the Syndrome, the odds increase by 49 percent, or alternatively, this risk is 1.49 times greater that the country experiences higher levels of reliance on agriculture and lack of economic prosperity, after holding all other control variables constant.

We run two ancillary analyses, the Prosperity Index as well as Agriculture, Forestry, and Fishing Value Added as Percentage of GDP. The former had a high adjusted R-squared of .746 and the latter had an adjusted R-squared of .535.

Both had the same significant independent variables as the overall factor, which were the Syndrome and Urbanization. Higher values of the Syndrome were associated with significantly lower levels of prosperity and higher levels of agriculture/forestry/fishing as percent of GDP.

3.3 GDP per Capita PPP 2017

(Log transformed; lower scores are considered worse.)

The adjusted R-squared is a remarkably strong .695, indicating that the specified model explained at least 69.5 percent of the variability of GDP per capita PPP. Three variables reach significance: Muslim-Majority Countries, the Syndrome, and Urbanization. See appendix III, table AIII.7.3.3, for full results. Although Muslim-majority nations and urbanized nations have higher GDP per capita, countries with high Syndrome scores have significantly lower GDP per capita. (Because several Muslim-majority nations are also arguably rentier states, look to the Rentierism dimension for further analysis.) Although the effect size for Urbanization is almost twice that of Syndrome, the Syndrome's effect size is more than twice that of Muslim-majority nations. We can see in the moderately strong bivariate correlation in the scatterplot in figure 7.3.3

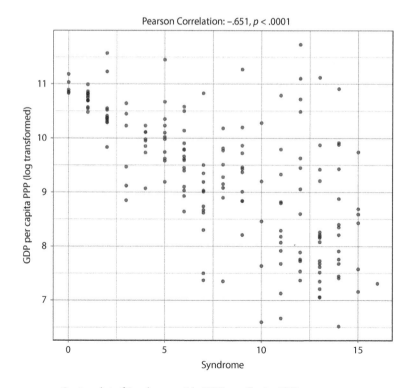

FIGURE 7.3.3 Scatterplot of Syndrome with GDP per Capita PPP 2017

($r = -.651$, $p < .0001$) the same large and empty lower-left quadrant, whereas the right half of the graph, although anchoring the negative correlation, sees greater spread.

Because the Syndrome is significant in the general linear regression model, we also ran a logistic regression model (using a binary version of the response variable). The Syndrome, Urbanization, and Muslim Civilization are the only variables that are significant in predicting the logits or predicted probabilities of higher GDP per capita PPP. We specifically find that for every one unit increase in the Syndrome, the odds increase by 31 percent, or alternatively, the risk is 1.31 times greater that the country experiences a lower GDP PPP, after holding all other control variables constant.

Indeed, because GDP per capita PPP (log transformed) and urbanization are correlated (with a strong bivariate correlation of .749 ($p < .0001$)[41], which does make sense because manufactured goods have favorable terms of trade compared with commodities, it might be interesting to see the results of the same multivariate model but excluding urbanization as one of the explanatory variables. When that model is analyzed, the R-squared is diminished to .528, but the effect size of the Syndrome more than doubles, becoming the most predictive variable in the model compared with the other three significant variables (Muslim-Majority Nations and now also Never Colonized Status and Terrain (indicated by percentage of arable land)). The effect size for the Syndrome is now more than triple that of the next largest effect size variable. We also ran the logistic regression model also excluding Urbanization (using a binary version of the response variable) and find that for every one unit increase in the Syndrome, the odds increase by 50 percent, or alternatively, the risk is 1.5 times greater that the country experiences lower GDP per capita, after holding all other control variables (except Urbanization) constant.

3.4 Poverty and Economic Decline
(Higher scores are considered worse.)

The adjusted R-squared is a remarkably strong .612, indicating that the specified model explained at least 61.2 percent of the variability of poverty and economic decline, with only two out of the eight variables appearing significant: the Syndrome and Urbanization. See appendix III, table AIII.7.3.4, for full results. Although Urbanization's effect size is slightly larger than the Syndrome, they are fairly close. Additionally, we find that the coefficient for the Syndrome is positive, indicating that countries with higher Syndrome scores have higher levels of poverty and economic decline on average. In the bivariate correlation between the Syndrome and Poverty and Economic Decline, we find a clear, positive, moderately strong relationship, with a correlation value of .650 ($p < .0001$). The scatterplot in figure 7.3.4 shows this relationship.

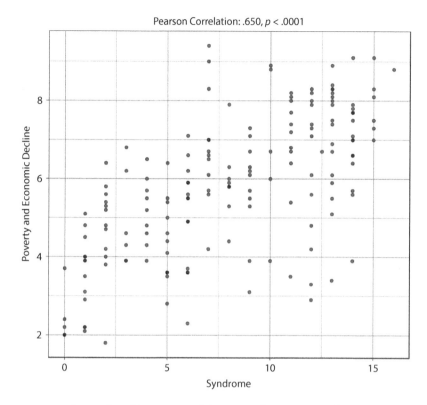

FIGURE 7.3.4 Scatterplot of Syndrome with Poverty and Economic Decline

Because the Syndrome is significant in the general linear regression model, we also ran a logistic regression model (using a binary version of the response variable). The Syndrome, Urbanization, and Muslim Civilization are the only variables that are significant in predicting the logits or predicted probabilities of higher levels of poverty and economic decline. We specifically find that for every one unit increase in the Syndrome, the odds increase by 40 percent, or alternatively, the risk is 1.4 times greater that the country experiences higher levels of poverty and economic decline, after holding all other control variables constant.

3.5 Wealth Infrastructure and Economic Freedom Factor

(This factor combines several variables: HFI Economic Freedom Index 2016, Economic Freedom Index 2017, GDP PPP (log transformed), Property Rights, Quality of Electricity Supply, Mobile Telephone Subscriptions, Internet Users, and Availability of Affordable Housing. Lower scores are considered worse.)

The adjusted R-squared is a remarkably strong .600, indicating that the specified model explained at least 60 percent of the variability of this factor. The only two variables significantly associated with measures of economic freedom, property rights, and electricity and Internet access were Urbanization and the Syndrome. High-Syndrome countries had significantly worse scores than low-Syndrome countries, and the effect size for the Syndrome is actually somewhat greater than that for Urbanization. See appendix III, table AIII.7.3.5, for full results. In the scatterplot in figure 7.3.5 for the moderately strong bivariate correlation between this factor and the Syndrome ($r = -.657$, $p < .0001$), we see a marked negative slope to the line, with virtually no countries in the lower-left quadrant of the graph. Some of the countries that appear relatively high in their wealth infrastructure and economic freedom given their high Syndrome values include, predictably, the United Arab Emirates, Qatar, and Bahrain.

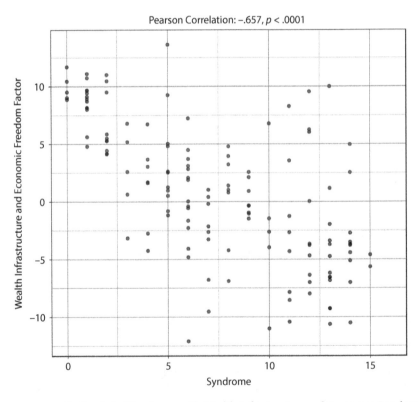

FIGURE 7.3.5 Scatterplot of Syndrome with Wealth Infrastructure and Economic Freedom Factor

Because the Syndrome is significant in the general linear regression model, we also ran a logistic regression model (using a binary version of the response variable). The Syndrome, Urbanization, and Muslim Civilization are the only variables that are significant in predicting the logits or predicted probabilities of lower levels of Wealth Infrastructure and Economic Freedom. We specifically find that for every one unit increase in the Syndrome, the odds increase by 55 percent, or alternatively, the risk is 1.55 times greater that the country experiences lower levels of Wealth Infrastructure and Economic Freedom, after holding all other control variables constant.

An ancillary analysis was run using GDP annual growth percentage. The adjusted R-squared value was a very low .034 with no significant independent variable appearing.

3.6 Global Competitiveness Index Rankings
(Higher scores are considered worse.)

The adjusted R-squared is a strong .564, indicating that the specified model explained at least 56.4 percent of the variability of the Global Competitiveness Index rankings. The only two significant variables in the model are, once again, the Syndrome and Urbanization. See appendix III, table AIII.7.3.6, for full results. Higher Urbanization is associated with higher economic competitiveness, and higher Syndrome scores are associated with lower economic competitiveness (because higher scores are worse in the ranking system for the index). The scatterplot in figure 7.3.6 shows a fairly diffuse, moderately strong bivariate relationship ($r = .607$, $p < .0001$), but with a noticeable positive trend.

Because the Syndrome is significant in the general linear regression model, we also ran a logistic regression model (using a binary version of the response variable). The Syndrome and Urbanization are the only variables that are significant in predicting the logits or predicted probabilities of worse Global Competitiveness Index rankings. We specifically find that for every one unit increase in the Syndrome, the odds increase by 26 percent, or alternatively, the risk is 1.26 times greater that the country ranks worse on the Global Competitiveness Index, after holding all other control variables constant.

We used two ancillary variables in this main analysis of Global Competitiveness Index. Final consumption (log transformed) had an adjusted R-squared of .444 with Urbanization and Land Neighbors as the only significant predictors of Global Competitiveness Index. High-technology exports had an R-squared value of .156 and no significant predictors. Because the Syndrome is not significant in these findings, we do not report the GLM results.

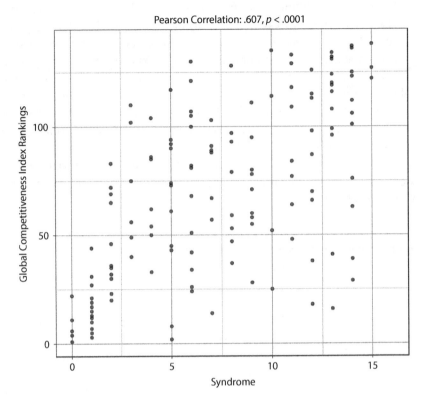

FIGURE 7.3.6 Scatterplot of Syndrome with Global Competitiveness Index

3.7 Economic Inequality Factor

(This factor combines two variables: the Gini Index and Uneven Economic Development. Higher scores are considered worse.)

The adjusted R-squared is a strong .482, indicating that the specified model explained at least 48.2 percent of the variability of this factor. The only variable that is significant in this model is the Syndrome. See appendix III, table AIII.7.3.7, for full results. We find a positive coefficient, indicating that on average as the Syndrome score increases (worsens), so too does a country's economic inequality. This is consistent with our hypotheses (i.e., that a tolerance for inequality originates in the first political order). The scatterplot in figure 7.3.7 shows the clear and moderately strong positive relationship between the Syndrome and economic inequality (r = .616, p < .0001).

Because the Syndrome is significant in the general linear regression model, we also ran a logistic regression model (using a binary version of the response variable). Because the model does not meet the validity requirements, we do not report the results.

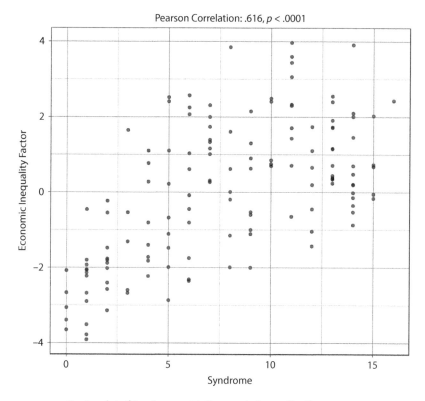

FIGURE 7.3.7 Scatterplot of Syndrome with Economic Inequality Factor

3.8 Female Labor Force Participation
(Lower scores are considered worse.)

The adjusted R-squared is a strong .471, indicating that the specified model explained at least 47.1 percent of the variability of Female Labor Force Participation, and the variables that reached significance include Muslim majority, the Syndrome, Urbanization, and Religious Fractionalization. See appendix III, table AIII.7.3.8, for full results. Muslim-majority nations and nations with high Syndrome scores have significantly lower female labor force participation; countries with higher levels of Religious Fractionalization also experience lower female labor force participation. The effect size for the Syndrome, however, dwarfs that of the other significant variables. This is explored in the bivariate scatterplot in figure 7.3.8, in which we can see a large empty lower-left quadrant (moderately strong correlation of $-.414, p < .0001$). On the right-hand side of the graph, however, we see no empty quadrant at all, suggesting that high-Syndrome countries range from very high to very low female labor force participation. This suggests that those viewing female labor

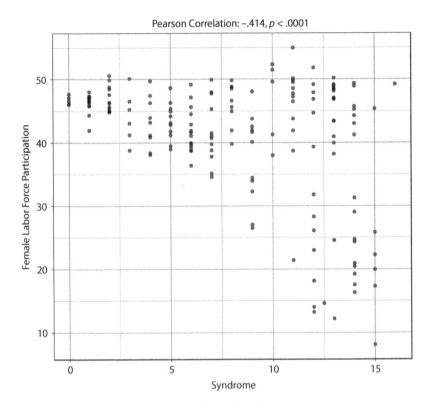

FIGURE 7.3.8 Scatterplot of Syndrome with Female Labor Force Participation

force participation as critical to women's empowerment may need to rethink that proposition.

Because the Syndrome is significant in the general linear regression model, we also ran a logistic regression model (using a binary version of the response variable). Because the model does not meet the validity requirements, we do not report the results.

3.9 Government Expenditure as Percentage of GDP and Unemployment Rate

(Lower scores are considered worse for government expenditure; higher scores are considered worse for the unemployment rate.)

Because the GLM results for these two analyses in the economic performance dimension had very low adjusted R-squared values (.095 and .013, respectively) and the Syndrome was not significant in either analysis, we do not report the details of the analyses. There is a small set of wealthy nations in cultures that highly subordinate women, which may explain the negative results for the first variable. Furthermore, unemployment rates, like many rate variables, are often inconsistent and unreliable across nations. We would want to inquire further about this relationship before making any conclusions.

Concluding Discussion for the Economic Performance Dimension

Overall, we see that in ten of the sixteen analyses conducted on indicators of Economic Performance, the Syndrome showed significance—in one of the models, Economic Inequality, it was the only significant variable, and in another eight, it held the largest effect size in the model. We find the Syndrome to be highly useful in explaining a set of variables representing Wealth Infrastructure and Economic Freedom, a set of variables representing Reliance on Agriculture and Lack of Prosperity, and a set of variables representing Poverty and Economic Decline. It was the only significant variable in the model explaining Income Inequality, which is highly noteworthy given our theoretical framework, and it was also a significant variable in models of Female Labor Force Participation and Global Competitiveness. Also important, Food Security was strongly determined by Syndrome score, with nations scoring high (worse) on the Syndrome having the lowest levels of food security. The analysis for GDP (PPP) is also worth considering. Many have suggested that poor countries treat women worse, but is it possible that nations that treat women worse wind up poorer? The only control variable that added to the explanatory power of the models was Urbanization, and to a lesser degree, Civilization. In sum, countries with high Syndrome scores are simply less wealthy, more economically unequal, less competitive, less food secure, and less economically secure than nations with low Syndrome scores.

Dimension 4. Economic Rentierism

We hypothesize that countries with higher Syndrome scores will be associated with rent-based economies because the first rents are typically exacted from women. We also hypothesize that the ability of the state to concentrate assets in the hands of the government through an economy that foregrounds extraction rather than production may reflect characteristics associated with the Syndrome. In addition, the "resource curse" has been identified as being associated with higher levels of gender inequality.[42] The variables that exist to tap into this concept are highly imperfect measures; we identify fuel, ore, tourism, and aid rents as possible sources of state control of rents. There is no good overall measure of rentierism, and we hope others will be able to probe this relationship with better tools than currently available.

Analyses for the Rentierism Dimension

We examine the six different variables in the rentierism dimension separately, so a factor analysis is not performed for these variables. The main outcome variable used is Total Natural Resources Rents as Percentage of GDP: Rentier states may derive a large part of national revenues from extraction and sale of resources rather than by production of goods and provision of services in country. Rentier economies are generally not highly diversified, although some states, like Russia, while well diversified, receive a large share of the state budget from the oil and gas sector. These states may have policies of very low or no taxation of citizens and pay for state services from rent profits. This has the potential to concentrate power in the hands of state elites. We then analyze the other five variables beginning with Ores and Metals Exports and Fuel Experts. These two variables account for a large percentage of some states' economies and small sectors of others. They measure the extent of rents for these resources as the foundation of a state's economy. Natural Resource Depletion measures the loss of a given resource, such as minerals, fishing, and fossil fuels. The variables Aid per Capita GDP and Tourism as a Percentage of GDP present alternative sectors of a state's economy in which rentierism may be present. Whether by currency transfers for tourism or by grants of funds from bilateral and multilateral organizations, state income comes from outside sources, not local production. These two variables may have a moderate impact on a given economy, but generally they help ameliorate economic challenges rather than supply a large share of the state budget.

Model Results

We ran six general linear models under Economic Rentierism and found that the Syndrome was significant in only one of those models. The five models for which the Syndrome was not significant include (1) Ores and Metals Exports, (2) Fuel Exports, (3) Natural Resource Depletion, (4) Aid per Capita GDP, and (5) Tourism as a Percentage of GDP. Table 7.4 summarizes the results of these GLM analyses.

We elaborate on the one model for which the Syndrome was significant.

4.1 Natural Resources as a Percentage of GDP

(Higher scores are considered worse.)

The adjusted R-squared is a moderate .303, indicating that the specified model explained at least 30.3 percent of the variability of natural resources as a percentage of GDP, demonstrating moderate explanatory power for the model. See appendix III, table AIII.7.4.1, for full results. Only one variable was

TABLE 7.4 Summary of GLM Results for the Rentierism Dimension in Descending Order of R-squared Values

Dependent Variable	Adjusted R-squared (N)	Independent Variables (significant at .001 by descending order of effect size)
Natural Resources as Percentage of GDP	.303 (173)	Syndrome
Fuel Exports	.250 (158)	Urbanization
Natural Resource Depletion	.243 (164)	Terrain
Tourism as a Percentage of GDP	.158 (160)	Number of Land Neighbors
Ores and Metals Exports	.061 (159)	None
Aid per Capita GDP	.024 (130)	None

Note: GDP, gross domestic product.

significant in the model (the Syndrome), although the effect size is modest. The bivariate correlation was a moderately strong .496, significant at the $p \leq .001$ level. The scatterplot in figure 7.4.1 shows that those with highest levels of natural resources as a percentage of GDP all tend to have high Syndrome scores. The upper-left quadrant of the scatterplot is empty.

Because the Syndrome is significant in the general linear regression model, we also ran a logistic regression model (using a binary version of the response variable). The Syndrome, Terrain, and Ethnic Fractionalization are the only variables that are significant in predicting the logits or predicted probabilities of higher levels of natural resources rents as a percentage of GDP. We specifically find that for every one unit increase in the Syndrome, the odds increase by 18 percent, or alternatively, the risk is 1.18 times greater that the country experiences higher levels of natural resources rents as a percentage of GDP, after holding all other control variables constant. Although the ancillary analyses show no significant results, it is noteworthy that the most comprehensive variable among the outcome indicators is that used in the main analysis and that model did demonstrate the Syndrome's significance.

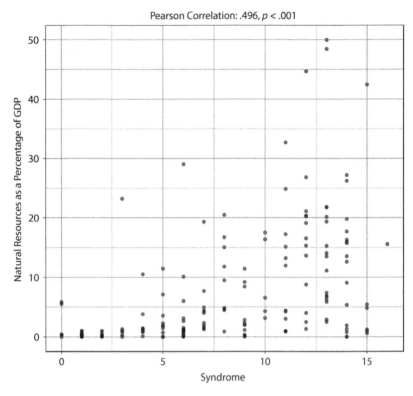

FIGURE 7.4.1 Scatterplot of Syndrome with Natural Resources as a Percentage of GDP

Concluding Discussion for the Rentierism Dimension

We were interested in exploring measures of the Rentierism dimension because the structures of state economic productivity may be related to its social structures. Our empirical analysis demonstrates that existing measures of the state's ability to extract resource-based rents are not well explained by any of the variables in the overall model tested. Only the more comprehensive variable of Natural Resources as a Percentage of GDP showed any significant correlation to the Syndrome, with the bivariate scatterplot showing that a higher percentage of these rents are significantly associated with higher Syndrome scores. In multivariate modeling, the effect size was modest; however, the Syndrome emerged as the only significant variable. The control variables Urbanization, Terrain, and Number of Land Neighbors help explain some of the ancillary rentierism outcome variables. This putative relationship between the Syndrome and rentierism deserves greater study, using better, more comprehensive indicators of rentierism once these are developed. The existing variables examine only subsets of sources of rents, which makes straightforward testing of our hypothesis difficult.

Dimension 5. Health and Well-Being

We hypothesize that nations with higher Syndrome scores will have lower levels of health and life expectancy for women, men, and children, including vulnerability to various illnesses; lower levels of spending on health; less prenatal care; higher birth rates; higher rates of habits detrimental to health; less access to clean water and sanitary facilities; undernourishment, greater hunger, and less adequate diet; and greater prevalence of female genital mutilation.

Analyses for the Health and Well-Being Dimension

We present ten separate analyses for the Health and Well-Being dimension. The first analysis includes five variables. We first examine the Healthcare Access Factor, on which three variables loaded: Access to Improved Sanitation Facilities measures the percent of the population with improved methods of sanitation. Percent of Births Attended by Skilled Staff measures the percentage of deliveries that trained personnel supervise during pregnancy, labor, and the postpartum period. This includes the training to conduct deliveries on their own and care for newborns. The third variable that loaded on this factor, Life Expectancy, measures the average number of years that a newborn, male or female, could live given death rates that apply both to their year of birth and their given locale. We also include two variables for ancillary analysis: The Sustainable Society Index combines a number of variables related to human well-being, including nutrition, improved water, sanitation, education, life expectancy, gender equality, income distribution, rates of population growth, and good governance. The final variable, Percent of Pregnant Women Receiving Prenatal Care, measures the percentage of women attended at least once by trained health workers because of her pregnancy.

The second analysis looks at national health expenditures. The main analysis variable is Health Expenditure Per Capita, which is a state's total health expenditure per capita figured in PPP. The ancillary variable, Health Expenditure as a Percentage of GDP, includes the sum of public and private health expenditures (e.g., insurance, government funds, external borrowings and grants) calculated against a state's GDP. It includes a large range of health services, preventive and curative, family planning activities, nutrition activities, and emergency aid.

The third analysis utilizes the Preventable Death factor as its primary analysis and applies seven variables as ancillary analyses. Four variables loaded on this factor: Lifetime Risk of Maternal Death assesses the risk of a reproductive-age woman dying from a cause related to childbearing. Infant Mortality Rate gives the number of children dying before reaching one year of age, per one thousand live births in a given year and locale. Births per One Thousand Women Ages

Fifteen to Nineteen is also called the adolescent fertility rate; it calculates the births (per one thousand) by women in that age group. The final variable that loaded on this factor is Difference Between Female and Male Life Expectancy, which measures the difference between male and female life expectancy rates for a given locale. The first ancillary variable examined is Life Expectancy at Birth for Females, which gives the number of years a female newborn could live given both the age-specific death rates for the year of her birth and her locale. Maternal Mortality Rate measures a woman's risk of death while pregnant or giving birth from any cause related to her pregnancy or childbearing, calculated per one hundred thousand live births. Deaths Due to Diarrhea of Children Under Five measures the percent of children under five years old whose deaths are due to diarrhea. The Percent of Children Under Five Who Are Stunted measures the percentage of children under five years old whose height is significantly below international standards. The Percent of Children Under Five Who Are Underweight measures the percentage of children under age five years old whose weight is significantly below international standards. Prevalence of Wasting—Percent of Children Under Five gives the percentage of children whose weight for their height is significantly below international standards. The seventh ancillary variable is Percent of Children Ages Twelve to Twenty-Three Months Immunized Against Measles. This measures the percentage of children ages twelve to twenty-three months who received at least one dose of the measles vaccination.

The fourth analysis has one variable, Total Alcohol Consumption Per Capita, which estimates the total amount of alcohol by liter consumed over a calendar year figured per capita for the population over fifteen years of age.

The fifth analysis measures three variables concerned with HIV/AIDS. The main variable analyzed is Prevalence of HIV Among Women Ages Fifteen and Over, which is women's share of population age fifteen years old and over infected with HIV, meaning that it is the percentage of women out of the total HIV population. The first ancillary analysis uses Population Between Fifteen and Forty-Nine with HIV, measures the percentage of people ages fifteen to forty-nine years old who are infected with HIV. The second ancillary analysis uses Percentage of Adults Ages Fifteen and Forty-Nine with HIV/ AIDS, measures the percentage of adults who are fifteen and forty-nine years old living with HIV/AIDS.

The sixth analysis looks at variables associated with hunger, malnutrition, and illness. We use the Global Hunger Index, which measures hunger, undernourishment, child wasting and stunting, and child mortality, in our main analysis. We use two variables in ancillary analyses. The first ancillary analysis uses our Malnutrition and Illness factor on which two indicators load: Percent of Population That Is Undernourished, which measures the percent who consume below the minimum level of dietary energy consumption continually, and Incidence of Tuberculosis per One Hundred Thousand People, which measures the estimated number of new and relapse cases of tuberculosis for one hundred thousand persons in a given year. The second ancillary analysis uses Average Dietary Energy Supply Adequacy, which assesses the adequacy of calorie intake by calculating the percentage of the Average Dietary Energy Requirement needed for dietary adequacy.

The seventh analysis has one variable, Female Genital Cutting/Mutilation, which is defined by the practice of scratching, cutting, circumcising, or stitching the external genitalia of a girl or woman. This ranges from mild forms to severe forms, such as infibulation. Type and prevalence of the practice are both examined in this variable.

The eighth analysis also has one variable, Access to Improved Water Sources, which measures the percentage of the rural population with piped water to a house or yard, or with access to a public tap, well, protected spring, or other protected water source.

The ninth analysis has one variable, Cigarette Consumption, which measures the number of cigarettes, whether machine rolled or consumer rolled, smoked per year for population over fifteen years old, figured per capita.

The tenth analysis uses the Open Defecation factor, on which load two variables: Percent of Total Population Using Open Defecation measures the percentage of population whose sanitary practices are open defecation, and Percent of Population Using Open Defecation in Urban Areas measures the percentage of population in urban areas whose sanitary practices are open defecation.

Model Results

We ran twenty-four general linear model analyses under Health and Well-Being and found that the Syndrome was significant in seventeen of those twenty-four models. The seven models for which the Syndrome was not significant include (1) Open Defecation factor, (2) Percent of Children Ages Twelve to Twenty-Three Months Immunized Against Measles, (3) Access to Improved Water, (4) Average Dietary Energy Supply Adequacy, (5) Cigarette Consumption, (6) Percent of Population Between Fifteen and Forty-Nine with HIV, and (7) Percentage of Adults Ages Fifteen and Forty-Nine with HIV/AIDS. Table 7.5 summarizes the results of the GLM analyses.

5.1 Healthcare Access Factor

(This factor combines three variables: Access to Improved Sanitation Facilities, Percentage of Births Attended by Skilled Staff, and Life Expectancy. Lower scores are considered worse.)

TABLE 7.5 Summary of GLM Results for the Health and Well-Being Dimension in Descending Order of R-squared Values

Dependent Variables	Adjusted R-squared (N)	Independent Variables (significant at .001 by descending order of effect size)
1. Healthcare Access Factor • Access to Improved Sanitary Facilities • Percentage Birth Attended by Skilled Staff • Life Expectancy	.702 (159)	Syndrome Urbanization Muslim Civilization Ethnic Fractionalization
Sustainable Society Index Human Well-Being	*.715 (154)*	*Syndrome* *Ethnic Fractionalization* *Muslim Civilization*
Percentage of Pregnant Women Receiving Prenatal Care	*.332 (144)*	*Syndrome* *Urbanization*
2. Health Expenditure per Capita	.616 (168)	Syndrome Urbanization Colonial Heritage Status
Health Expenditure as Percentage of GDP	*.254 (169)*	*Colonial Heritage Status* *Syndrome*
3. Preventable Death Factor • Risk of Maternal Death • Infant Mortality Rate • Births per One Thousand Women Ages Fifteen to Nineteen • Difference in Life Expectancy Between Men and Women	.594 (172)	Syndrome Urbanization Ethnic Fractionalization
Life Expectancy at Birth for Females	*.746 (173)*	*Syndrome* *Urbanization* *Muslim Civilization* *Ethnic Fractionalization*
Maternal Mortality Rate	*.699 (175)*	*Urbanization* *Syndrome* *Muslim Civilization* *Ethnic Fractionalization*
Deaths Due to Diarrhea of Children Under Five	*.628 (171)*	*Urbanization* *Syndrome* *Ethnic Fractionalization*
Percentage Under Five Who Are Stunted	*.550 (117)*	*Urbanization* *Syndrome*

TABLE 7.5 *(continued)*

Percentage Under Five Who Are Underweight	*.516 (116)*	*Urbanization Syndrome*
Prevalence of Wasting—Percentage Under Five	*.359 (116)*	*Urbanization Syndrome*
Percentage Children Ages Twelve to Twenty-Three Months Immunized Against Measles	*.209 (173)*	*None*
4. Total Alcohol Consumption per Capita	.535 (171)	Syndrome Religious Fractionalization Terrain
5. Prevalence of HIV Among Women Ages Fifteen and Over	.525 (131)	Muslim Civilization Syndrome
Percentage of Population Between Fifteen and Forty-Nine with HIV	*.243 (131)*	*Religious Fractionalization Western Civilization*
Percentage of Adults Ages Fifteen and Forty-Nine with HIV/AIDS	*.243 (130)*	*Religious Fractionalization Western Civilization*
6. Global Hunger Index	.577 (118)	Urbanization Syndrome
Malnutrition and Illness Factor • *Percentage of Population Undernourished* • *Incidence of Tuberculosis per 100,000 People*	*.432 (159)*	*Urbanization Syndrome Muslim and Western Civilizations*
Average Dietary Energy Supply Adequacy	*.309 (162)*	*Urbanization*
7. Female Genital Cutting/ Mutilation (FGM)	.297 (176)	Syndrome Colonial Heritage Status Ethnic Fractionalization
8. Access to Improved Water	.436 (171)	Urbanization Ethnic Fractionalization
9. Cigarette Consumption	.379 (171)	None
10. Open Defecation Factor • Percentage of Total Population Using Open Defecation • Percentage of Population Using Open Defecation in Urban Areas	.295 (171)	None

Note: Ancillary analysis in italics. GDP, gross domestic product.

The adjusted R-squared is a remarkably strong .702, indicating that the specified model explained at least 70.2 percent of the variability of this factor. Four variables proved significant: the Syndrome, Urbanization, Muslim Civilization, and Ethnic Fractionalization. See appendix III, table AIII.7.5.1, for full results. The coefficients for the Syndrome and Ethnic Fractionalization are negative, showing that the higher (worse) these two variables, the poorer the government's ability to provide basic services to their citizens. Urbanization and Muslim Civilization were both positive meaning that the higher their score, the better health and sanitation services provided and accessed on a national basis, which also was associated with improved life expectancy. The Syndrome showed the largest effect size (.267) followed by Urbanization at .212, and Muslim Civilization at .147. Ethnic Fractionalization showed the smallest effect size out of the significant variables (.094). The bivariate correlation between Syndrome and Healthcare Access Factor is negative and very strong ($r = -.707$, $p < .0001$) as the scatterplot in figure 7.5.1 illustrates. The outliers in the lower portion of the upper-left quadrant include Mongolia, which ranks

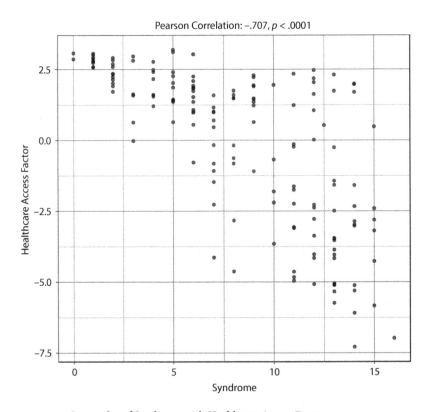

FIGURE 7.5.1 Scatterplot of Syndrome with Healthcare Access Factorv

as a 3 for the Syndrome and −.02 in Healthcare Access; Haiti, which ranks as a 7 for the Syndrome and −4.14 in Healthcare Access; and Madagascar, which ranks as an 8 for the Syndrome and −4.63 in Healthcare Access.

Because the Syndrome is significant in the general linear regression model, we also ran a logistic regression model (using a binary version of the response variable). The Syndrome and Urbanization are the only variables that are significant in predicting the logits or predicted probabilities of lower healthcare access for its citizens. We specifically find that for every one unit increase in the Syndrome, the odds increase by 48 percent, or alternatively, the risk is 1.48 times greater that the country experiences lower healthcare and sanitation access for its citizens, which also is associated with lower life expectancy, after accounting for the other control variables.

We used the Human Well-Being component of the Sustainable Society Index in an ancillary analysis and found a high adjusted R-squared value of .715 with Syndrome, Ethnic Fractionalization, and Muslim Civilization as the three most significant predictors of this outcome variable. Another ancillary variable used was Percentage of Pregnant Women Receiving Prenatal Care. The adjusted R-squared value was a comparatively lower .332, but the Syndrome and Urbanization were still significant predictors.

5.2 Health Expenditure per Capita

(Lower scores are considered worse.)

The adjusted R-squared is a remarkably strong .616, indicating that the specified model explained at least 61.6 percent of the variability of health expenditure per capita. Three variables are significant: Colonial Status/Never Colonized, the Syndrome, and Urbanization. See appendix III, table AIII.7.5.2, for full results. The effect size for the Syndrome was the highest, although it was only slightly higher than the effect size for Urbanization. Colonial Heritage Status/Never Colonized and Urbanization have positive coefficients that show that countries that were not colonized as well as urbanized countries have higher health expenditures per capita. The Syndrome's negative coefficient shows that the higher the Syndrome score, the less countries spend on health care per capita, even controlling for all the other variables in the model. The bivariate correlation between Health Expenditure per Capita and the Syndrome is likewise significant and moderately strong, a negative ($r = −.667$, $p < .0001$). The scatterplot in figure 7.5.2 demonstrates a strong negative bivariate correlation with countries high on the Syndrome spending less on health. Outliers in the upper-left quadrant include the United States, which ranks 1 on Syndrome and a high $9,536 on health expenditures per capita. In the middle of the plot outliers are Japan and Singapore, which both rank as 5 on the Syndrome and spend $4,405 and $3,681, respectively, on Health Expenditure. We also find a few outliers in

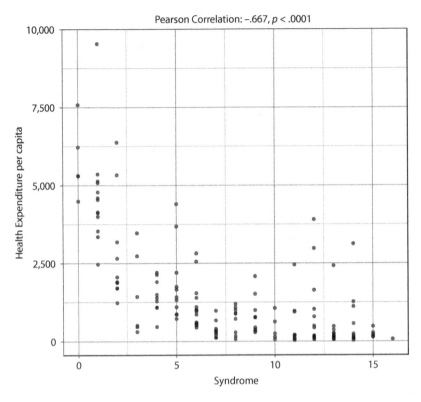

FIGURE 7.5.2 Scatterplot of Syndrome with Health Expenditure per Capita

the lower-left quadrant: Qatar and Kuwait, both with Syndrome scores of 12; the United Arab Emirates, with a Syndrome score of 13; and Saudi Arabia, with a Syndrome score of 14.

Because the Syndrome is significant in the general linear regression model, we also ran a logistic regression model (using a binary version of the response variable). The Syndrome, Urbanization, and Religious Fractionalization are the only variables that are significant in predicting the logits or predicted probabilities of lower health expenditure per capita. We specifically find that for every one unit increase in the Syndrome, the odds increase by 70 percent, or alternatively, the risk is 1.7 times greater that the country experiences lower health expenditure per capita, after accounting for the other control variables.

We used Health Expenditure as a Percentage of GDP in an ancillary analysis but obtained a much lower adjusted R-squared value of .254. However, the Syndrome was still significant, as was Colonial Heritage Status.

5.3 Preventable Death Factor

(This factor combines four variables: Risk of Maternal Death, Infant Mortality Rate, Births per One Thousand Women Ages Fifteen to Nineteen, and Difference in Life Expectancy Between Men and Women. Higher scores are considered worse.)

The adjusted R-squared is a strong .594, indicating that the specified model explained at least 59.4 percent of the variability of this factor. Three variables are significant in this model: The Syndrome, Urbanization, and Ethnic Fractionalization. See appendix III, table AIII.7.5.3, for full results. The coefficient for the Syndrome is positive, which means that higher Syndrome countries score worse on this factor. The Ethnic Fractionalization coefficient is also positive, which means that countries that score higher in Ethnic Fractionalization score worse on this factor. The coefficient for the Urbanization variable is negative, which means that countries that are more urbanized score better on the Preventable Death factor. The effect size for Urbanization (.104) and Ethnic Fractionalization (.092) are similar, but both are smaller than that of the Syndrome (.200). The bivariate correlation between the Syndrome and the Preventable Death factor bears out this moderately strong correlation ($r = .696$, $p = .0001$) as does the scatterplot in figure 7.5.3. High Syndrome scores are associated with the

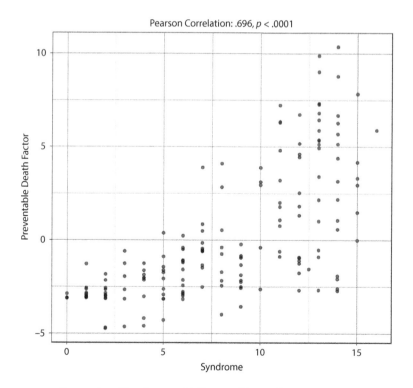

FIGURE 7.5.3 Scatterplot of Syndrome with Preventable Death Factor

variables combined in this Preventable Death factor: a higher risk of maternal death spread over the woman's lifetime, higher mortality rates for children under five years of age, higher number of births for women ages fifteen to nineteen years old, and higher discrepancies in life expectancy between men and women. These correlations show that health for women and children is severely compromised in Syndrome countries.

Because the Syndrome is significant in the general linear regression model, we also ran a logistic regression model (using a binary version of the response variable). The Syndrome and Urbanization are the only variables that are significant in predicting the logits or predicted probabilities of high instances of preventable death. We specifically find that for every one unit increase in the Syndrome, the odds increase by 84 percent, or alternatively, the risk is 1.84 times greater that the country experiences high instances of preventable death, after accounting for the other control variables.

We used seven ancillary variables (see table 7.5) in a GLM analysis and the adjusted R-squared values ranged from .209 to .746. The Syndrome is significant in six of these ancillary analyses, including female life expectancy, maternal mortality, infant mortality, and various measures of stunting, wasting, and malnutrition in children. The only outcome variable that is not significant is percentage of children ages twelve to twenty-three months immunized against measles; this variable has also the lowest adjusted R-squared. Overall, many important health variables concerning women and children are best explained by the Syndrome.

5.4 Total Alcohol Consumption per Capita

(Higher scores are considered worse.)

The adjusted R-squared is a strong .535, indicating that the specified model explained at least 53.5 percent of the variability of total alcohol consumption per capita. Three variables are significant: the Syndrome (effect size .292), Percent of Arable Terrain (.082), and Religious Fractionalization (.086). See appendix III, table AIII.7.5.4, for full results. The coefficient for the Syndrome is negative, which means that countries that rank higher on the Syndrome consume less alcohol per capita. The other two variables are positive, which means that countries that rank high on percent of Arable Terrain and Religious Fractionalization have higher rates of alcohol consumption per capita. The bivariate correlation between the Syndrome and Alcohol Consumption is moderately strong and negative ($-.655$, $p < .0001$). The bivariate scatterplot in figure 7.5.4 also illustrates this relationship in its downward slope. Our original hypothesis was that societies with strong male kin networks may correlate with higher alcohol consumption. Research on health issues link higher alcohol consumption with increased incidence of (male)

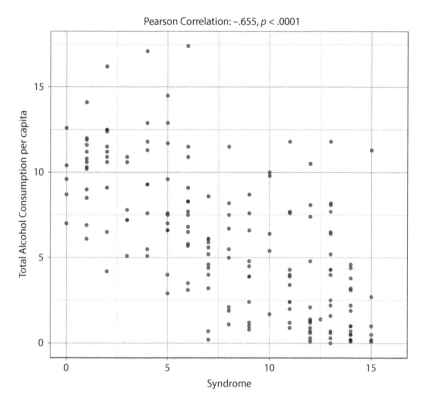

FIGURE 7.5.4 Scatterplot of Syndrome with Total Alcohol Consumption per Capita

suicide and illness. These data do not support our hypothesis, and countries that score higher on the Syndrome have lower rates of alcohol consumption per capita. Many high-Syndrome countries are Muslim-majority nations and have lower availability of alcohol for consumption for religious reasons. The country on the far right ranking 15 on the Syndrome and in the middle rank on alcohol consumption is Nigeria. The country with the highest alcohol consumption is Moldova, the second-highest country is Belarus. Both rank low in Syndrome but high in Alcohol Consumption.

Because the Syndrome is significant in the general linear regression model, we also ran a logistic regression model (using a binary version of the response variable). The Syndrome is the only variable that is significant in predicting the logits or predicted probabilities of higher levels of total alcohol consumption. We specifically find that for every one unit increase in the Syndrome, the odds decrease by 37 percent that the country experiences high levels of total alcohol consumption per capita, after accounting for the other control variables.

5.5 Prevalence of HIV Among Women Ages Fifteen and Over
(Higher scores are considered worse.)

The adjusted R-squared is a strong .525, indicating that the specified model explained at least 52.5 percent of the variability of prevalence of HIV among women. Two variables are significant: Muslim Civilization (CIV = 2) with an effect size of .176 and the Syndrome with an only slightly smaller effect size of .163. See appendix III, table AIII.7.5.5, for full results. The coefficient for Muslim Civilization is negative, which means that the prevalence of HIV among women over fifteen years of age is lower in Muslim-majority countries. The coefficient for the Syndrome is positive, which means that there is a higher prevalence of HIV among women age fifteen and over in higher-Syndrome-scoring countries. The bivariate correlation between the Syndrome and Prevalence of HIV Among Women Age Fifteen and Over is a moderately strong .553 ($p < .0001$). This is demonstrated in the upward slant of the scatterplot in figure 7.5.5.

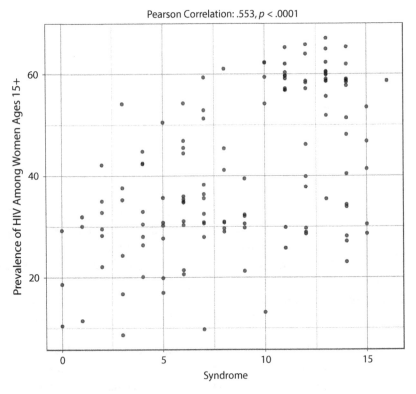

FIGURE 7.5.5 Scatterplot of Syndrome with Prevalence of HIV Among Women Ages Fifteen and Over

Because the Syndrome is significant in the general linear regression model, we also ran a logistic regression model (using a binary version of the response variable). The Syndrome is the only variable that is significant in predicting the logits or predicted probabilities of higher prevalence of HIV among women age fifteen and over. We specifically find that for every one unit increase in the Syndrome, the odds increase by 58 percent, or alternatively, the risk is 1.58 times greater that the country experiences higher prevalence of HIV among women ages fifteen and over, after holding all other control variables constant.

We use Percentage of Population Between Fifteen and Forty-Nine with HIV and Percentage of Adults Ages Fifteen to Forty-Nine with HIV/AIDS as ancillary variables. The adjusted values for these two ancillary analyses are .243 and .245, respectively. Because the Syndrome was not significant in either analysis, we do not report the results. These findings illustrate the need to use more than one variable measuring HIV burden so that a more nuanced picture of the relationship with the Syndrome can be observed.

5.6 Global Hunger Index

(Higher scores are considered worse.)

The adjusted R-squared is a strong .577, indicating that the specified model explained at least 57.7 percent of the variability of Global Hunger Index scores. The two variables that prove significant are the Syndrome (effect size .213) and Urbanization (effect size .294). See appendix III, table AIII.7.5.6, for full results. The coefficient for the Syndrome is positive and for Urbanization is negative. This means that levels of hunger are higher on average in Syndrome countries and lower in urbanized countries. The bivariate correlation between the Syndrome and the Global Hunger Index is a moderately strong .682 ($p < .0001$). The bivariate scatterplot in figure 7.5.6 demonstrates this relationship, showing an upward curve. We identify some of the outliers in the upper middle portion of the scatterplot: Haiti (Syndrome = 7) and Madagascar (Syndrome = 8). We also find that the Central African Republic and Chad, both with high Syndrome scores of 14, achieve the two highest (worst) values for the Global Hunger Index.

Because the Syndrome is significant in the general linear regression model, we also ran a logistic regression model (using a binary version of the response variable). The Syndrome and Urbanization are the only variables that are significant in predicting the logits or predicted probabilities of worse scores on the Global Hunger Index. We specifically find that for every one unit increase in the Syndrome, the odds increase by 80 percent, or alternatively, the risk is 1.8 times greater that the country experiences worse scores on the Global Hunger Index, after holding all other control variables constant.

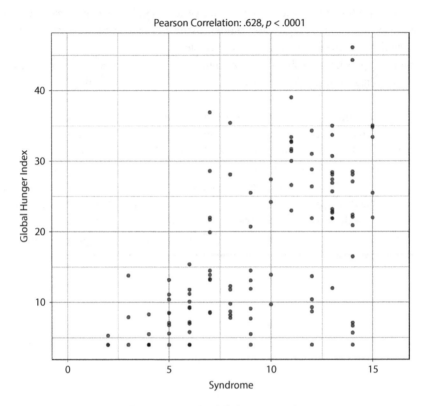

FIGURE 7.5.6 Scatterplot of Syndrome with Global Hunger Index

We use our Malnutrition and Illness factor and Average Dietary Energy Supply Adequacy as ancillary variables and their adjusted R-squared values are .432 and .309 respectively. The Syndrome is a significant predictor of the former, but not of the latter. We question the results of the latter test, given the results we have seen with the Global Hunger Index, as well as the Food Security Index analyzed in a previous dimension. Overall, the Syndrome appears highly determinative of food insecurity, hunger, and malnutrition within nations.

5.7 Female Genital Cutting/Mutilation

(Higher scores are considered worse.)

The adjusted R-squared is a moderate .297, indicating that the specified model explained at least 29.7 percent of the variability of female genital cutting/mutilation. Three variables are significant in this model: Colonial Heritage Status /Never Colonized, the Syndrome, and Ethnic Fractionalization.

The Syndrome has a higher effect size (.113) than does Colonial Heritage Status/Never Colonized (.088) or Ethnic Fractionalization (.082). See appendix III, table AIII.7.5.7, for full results. The bivariate correlation between the Syndrome and female genital cutting/mutilation (FGM) is moderately strong ($r = .439$, $p < .0001$). The coefficients for all three variables are positive, which shows that the higher scores on each correlate with higher use of FGM.

The positive Colonial Heritage Status/Never Colonized coefficient proves significant largely because FGM is not randomly distributed over countries as it is a civilization-specific practice. Most never-colonized nations are rated 1 on the FGM scale (i.e., the practice is rare or found in small enclaves of minority populations that practice FGM). Of the countries ranked 1, FGM is confined to enclaves. When we ran an ANOVA to test this relationship, the relationship between Colonial Heritage Status/Never Colonized with FGM was not significant.

The scatterplot in Figure 7.5.7 tells the story that only high-Syndrome countries rank higher (i.e., 2, 3, and 4) on the FGM scale. Low-Syndrome

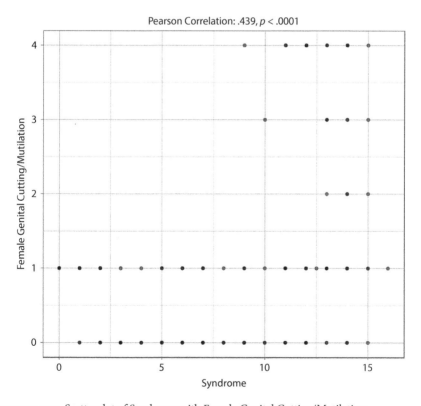

FIGURE 7.5.7 Scatterplot of Syndrome with Female Genital Cutting/Mutilation

countries have no or rare prevalence of FGM. The blank upper-left quadrant on the scatterplot shows that the prevalence of FGM for countries that rank low on the Syndrome is essentially nonexistent or very rare (<11 percent) for prevalence of FGM, whereas countries with higher Syndrome scores show significant prevalence of FGM.

Because the Syndrome is significant in the general linear regression model, we also ran a logistic regression model (using a binary version of the response variable). The Syndrome and Ethnic Fractionalization are the only variables that are significant in predicting the logits or predicted probabilities of FGM occurring (more than rarely). We specifically find that for every one unit increase in the Syndrome, the odds increase by 76 percent, or alternatively, the risk is 1.76 times greater that FGM occurs in a country, after holding all other control variables constant.

5.8 Access to Improved Water
(Lower scores are considered worse.)

We ran a GLM analysis for access to improved water and find a moderate adjusted R-squared value of .436. Because the Syndrome is not a significant predictor, we do not report the results.

5.9 Cigarette Consumption
(Higher scores are considered worse.)

The GLM analysis for cigarette consumption shows a low adjusted R-squared value of .379. Because the Syndrome is not a significant predictor, we do not report the results.

5.10 Open Defecation Factor
(This factor includes Percent Population Using Open Defecation and also Percent Population Using Open Defecation in Urban Areas. Higher scores are considered worse.)

This factor has an even lower adjusted R-squared (.295) than cigarette consumption. Because the Syndrome was not significant, we do not report the results.

Concluding Discussion for the Health and Well-Being Dimension
For our Health and Well-Being dimension's empirical analysis, we ran twenty-four GLM analyses of health and well-being using twenty single dependent variables and four extracted factors. Syndrome was significant in

three of the four factors, and for fourteen of the twenty single variables, for a total of seventeen of the twenty-four models run. The Syndrome had the largest effect size in eight of the models, showing strong predictive power not only for variables directly related to women's health, such as female life expectancy, maternal mortality, FGM, and prevalence of HIV among women, but also child-related health indices, such as percent under age five who are stunted, wasted, or underweight, as well as population-wide indicators of hunger, illness, mortality, and levels of government investment in healthcare expenditures. Also noteworthy in explaining some of the national health outcome variables were the control variables of Urbanization, Civilization, Ethnic Fractionalization, and Colonial Heritage Status. The Syndrome, however, was by far the most consistently determinative explanatory variable. To understand issues of national health and nutrition, we need to look at Syndrome-encoding practices within the country. The subordination of women at the household level clearly undermines national health and nutrition outcomes. Our theoretical framework anticipated this relationship and our large N analysis corroborated it.

Dimension 6. Demographic Security

We hypothesize that nations manifesting a strong patrilineal/fraternal culture as measured by the Syndrome Index tend to have higher levels of demographic insecurity, to wit, higher fertility rates, lower contraceptive prevalence, higher unmet need for contraception, a larger youth bulge, and greater demographic pressures.

Analyses for the Demographic Security Dimension

We performed five main analyses for the Demographic Security dimension. First, we look at Mother's Mean Age at First Birth, which provides data on early pregnancies before the age of eighteen, which adversely affect women's health and future opportunities as well as raises fertility rates overall. For an ancillary analysis, we utilize Fertility Rates Ages Fifteen to Nineteen. High numbers of births among this age cohort often correlate with the practice of child marriage.

The second analysis consists of one variable, Demographic Pressure, which measures the impact of population size upon the state. On one hand, a growing population may produce pressures related to food supply, access to safe water, and the ability to provide needed infrastructure. On the other hand, insufficient population growth in various sectors of the population may lead to insufficient economic growth to support social security and pensions for aging citizens.

The third analysis consists of one variable, Total Fertility, which gives the number of children that a woman would give birth to if she were to live to the end of her childbearing years and her childbearing falls in line with the fertility rates of a specified year. Generally, it is the total number of births for a woman in her lifetime.[43]

The fourth analysis consisted of two variables measuring contraceptive use. Contraceptive Prevalence, our main variable, measures use of any contraceptive for women ages fifteen to forty-nine. The ancillary analysis used the variable Unmet Need for Contraception, which measures the percentage of women of reproductive age, married or in a union, who say they want to stop or delay childbearing, but who are not currently using any method of contraception.

The fifth analysis looks at the Youth Risk Factor (which is not a factor in the sense we have been using that term, but rather the name given this variable by its creators). This variable looks at the size of the seventeen- to twenty-six-year-old age cohort in ratio to the size of a country's total labor force. High values of this variable signify a large youth bulge, which has been associated with higher levels of internal instability and violence.

Model Results

We ran seven general linear model analyses under Demographic Security and found that the Syndrome was significant in five of those seven models. The two models for which the Syndrome was not significant include (1) Fertility Rates for Females Ages Fifteen to Nineteen and (2) Unmet Need for Contraception. Note, however, that variables similar in conceptualization, such as Mother's Age at First Birth and Contraceptive Prevalence, are significantly associated with the Syndrome. Table 7.6 summarizes the results of the GLM analyses.

6.1 Mother's Mean Age at First Birth

(Lower scores are considered worse.)

The adjusted R-squared is a remarkably strong .712, indicating that the specified model explained at least 71.2 percent of the variability of mother's mean age at first birth. The Syndrome was the only significant predictor of this dependent variable, with the Syndrome having an effect size that was much larger than any other variable. See appendix III, table AIII.7.6.1, for full results. There is a significant negative correlation between the Syndrome and mother's mean age at first birth (beta = −.436): the higher the Syndrome score for a country, the lower the mother's age at first birth. This is confirmed by the scatterplot in figure 7.6.1 in which we find a very strong linear relationship between mean age of first birth and the Syndrome ($r = -.818$, $p < .001$). We find a few countries that buck this

TABLE 7.6 Summary of GLM Results for the Demographic Security Dimension in Descending Order of R-squared Values

Dependent Variables	Adjusted R-squared (N)	Independent Variables (significant at .001 by descending order of effect size)
1. Mother's Mean Age at First Birth	.712 (123)	Syndrome
Fertility Rates Ages Fifteen to Nineteen	*.486 (174)*	*Urbanization*
		Ethnic Fractionalization
2. Demographic Pressure	.707 (172)	Syndrome
		Urbanization
3. Total Fertility Rate	.602 (175)	Syndrome
		Urbanization
		Ethnic Fractionalization
4. Contraceptive Prevalence	.491 (135)	Syndrome
		Ethnic Fractionalization
Unmet Need for Contraception	*.304 (116)*	*None*
5. Youth Risk Factor	.479 (166)	Syndrome

Note: Ancillary analysis in italics.

trend, including Jamaica and Mongolia, with Syndrome values of 3, which both have surprisingly low mean age at first birth, and Jordan (Syndrome = 14), which has surprisingly high mean age at first birth.

Because the Syndrome is significant in the general linear regression model, we also ran a logistic regression model (using a binary version of the response variable). The Syndrome is the only variable that is significant in predicting the logits or predicted probabilities of lower average age of first birth for the mother. We specifically find that for every one unit increase in the Syndrome, the odds increase by 62 percent, or alternatively, the risk is 1.62 times greater that the country experiences a lower average age of first birth for the mother, after holding all other control variables constant.

We use fertility rates for ages fifteen to nineteen as a variable in an ancillary analysis, and the GLM analysis show a moderately strong adjusted R-squared value of .486. Because the Syndrome is not a significant predictor, we do not report the results. The contrast in the findings of the main and ancillary analysis are interesting and bear further scrutiny.

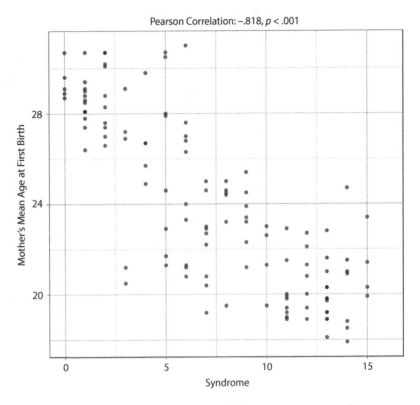

Pearson Correlation: −.818, *p* < .001

FIGURE 7.6.1 Scatterplot of Syndrome with Mother's Mean Age at First Birth

6.2 Demographic Pressure
(Higher scores are considered worse.)

The Fund for Peace's Demographic Pressure variable is defined as pressures on the population, such as disease and natural disasters, which make it difficult for the government to protect its citizens or if the government demonstrates a lack of capacity or will to do so. It combines measures related to natural disasters, disease, environment, pollution, food scarcity, malnutrition, water scarcity, population growth, youth bulge, and mortality. Higher scores mean higher demographic pressure.

We regressed Demographic Pressure on our eight independent variables and found that the adjusted R-squared is a remarkably strong .707, indicating that at least 70 percent of the variability in demographic pressure can be explained by our model. The only two significant predictors in the model are the Syndrome and percent Urbanization, with the Syndrome having an effect size almost twice as large as percent Urbanization. See appendix III, table AIII.7.6.2, for full results. These findings support our claim that nations that manifest a strong patrilineal culture as measured by the Syndrome Index tend to experience

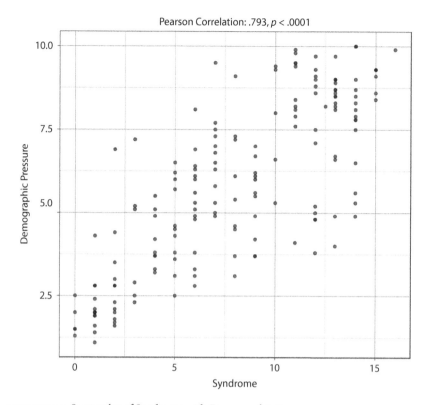

FIGURE 7.6.2 Scatterplot of Syndrome with Demographic Pressure

higher demographic pressures. The bivariate scatterplot in figure 7.6.2 further amplifies this finding: a very strong linear correlation exists between the Syndrome and Demographic pressure ($r = .793$, $p < .0001$). We find that the Bahamas and Cape Verde have surprisingly high demographic pressure given their low Syndrome scores (2 and 3, respectively). Some of the countries with the highest Syndrome scores and the highest Demographic Pressure scores include Somalia, South Sudan, and Malawi. On the other end of the plot, countries with both the lowest Syndrome scores and lowest Demographic Pressure scores include Australia and Finland.

Because the Syndrome is significant in the general linear regression model, we also ran a logistic regression model (using a binary version of the response variable). The Syndrome and Urbanization are the only variables that are significant in predicting the logits or predicted probabilities of higher levels of demographic pressure. We specifically find that for every one unit increase in the Syndrome, the odds increase by 39 percent, or alternatively, the risk is 1.39 times greater that the country experiences higher levels of demographic pressure, after holding all other control variables constant.

6.3 Total Fertility Rate

(Higher scores are considered worse.)

The adjusted R-squared is a remarkably strong .602, indicating that the specified model explained at least 60.2 percent of the variability in total fertility rates. Three of the eight independent variables had significant explanatory power: the Syndrome, Percent Urbanization, and degree of Ethnic Fractionalization, in descending order of effect size. See appendix III, table AIII.7.6.3, for full results. The effect size of the Syndrome is twice that of either of the other two variables. The subordination of women at the household level, as represented by the Syndrome score, is critical in predicting total fertility rates, more so than Urbanization and Ethnic Fractionalization. These findings support our hypothesis that nations with strong patrilineal cultures as measured by the Syndrome Index tend to have higher fertility rates, after controlling for the effects of our control variables. The scatterplot in figure 7.6.3 confirms this finding when Syndrome is regressed alone against fertility rate: the correlation coefficient is very strong ($r = .714, p < .001$).

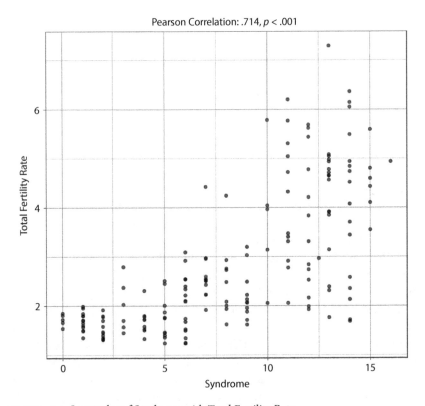

FIGURE 7.6.3 Scatterplot of Syndrome with Total Fertility Rate

We find the significance of Ethnic Fractionalization understandable; as demographer Richard Cincotta notes, "the more a state politically, economically, and socially marginalizes an ethnic group, the more likely that group is to grow demographically."[44]

Because the Syndrome is significant in the general linear regression model, we also ran a logistic regression model (using a binary version of the response variable). The Syndrome, Urbanization, and Ethnic Fractionalization are the only variables that are significant in predicting the logits or predicted probabilities of higher total fertility rates. We specifically find that for every one unit increase in the Syndrome, the odds increase by 92 percent, or alternatively, the risk is 1.92 times greater that the country experiences higher total fertility rates, after holding all other control variables constant.

6.4 Contraceptive Prevalence

(Lower scores are considered worse.)

The adjusted R-squared is a strong .491, indicating that at least 49.1 percent of the variability in the prevalence of contraceptive use can be explained by the specified model and only two of the independent variables had significant explanatory powers: the Syndrome and Ethnic Fractionalization. See appendix III, table AIII.7.6.4, for full results. The Syndrome had a slightly higher effect size, .195 versus .102. This finding shows that women in nations with higher Syndrome scores have a harder time accessing contraceptive methods (beta estimate $= -2.542$, $p < .0001$) after controlling for the effects of the other covariates. Similarly, women in highly ethnically fractionalized societies face similar problems in accessing contraception. The results for the Syndrome are supported by the bivariate scatterplot in figure 7.6.4, which shows a moderately strong negative linear correlation ($r = -.636$, $p < .0001$) between Syndrome and Contraceptive Prevalence.

Because the Syndrome is significant in the general linear regression model, we also ran a logistic regression model (using a binary version of the response variable). The Syndrome is the only variable that is significant in predicting the logits or predicted probabilities of lower percentages of women ages fifteen to forty-nine who are practicing, or whose sexual partners are practicing, any form of contraception (less than 49.42 percent). We specifically find that for every one unit increase in the Syndrome, the odds increase by 32 percent, or alternatively, the risk is 1.32 times greater that the country experiences lower contraceptive prevalence, after holding all other control variables constant.

We used Unmet Need for Contraception as an ancillary variable and the GLM analysis yielded an adjusted R-squared value of .304. Because the Syndrome was not a significant predictor, we do not report the results. It is possible that contraceptive prevalence is more tightly related to subordinative

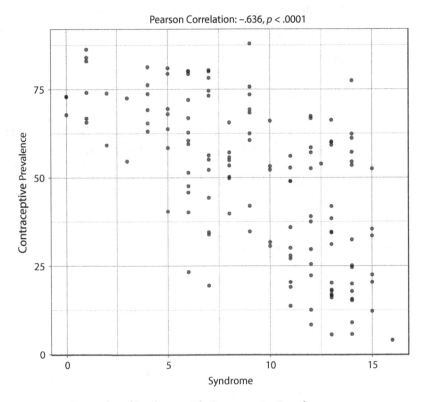

Pearson Correlation: –.636, $p < .0001$

FIGURE 7.6.4 Scatterplot of Syndrome with Contraceptive Prevalence

mechanisms than the operationalization of unmet need, for which responses may vary as a result of cultural norms.

6.5 Youth Risk Factor

(Higher scores are considered worse.)

The Youth Risk Factor includes variables that measure the stress that large youth cohorts exert within a given country, defined as the ratio of the seventeen- to twenty-six-year-old age cohort to the size of the laborforce. High values of this factor signify a large youth bulge, which has been associated with higher levels of internal instability and violence.[45]

The adjusted R-squared is a strong .479, indicating that the specified model explained at least 47.9 percent of the variability of the Youth Risk Factor or youth bulge. Of the eight independent variables, only one had significant explanatory power: the Syndrome. See appendix III, table AIII.7.6.5, for full results. The Syndrome's effect size was much larger than any of the other variables.

This finding shows that Syndrome is a good predictor of youth bulge after controlling for the effects of the other covariates. The coefficient for the Syndrome is positive, meaning the higher the Syndrome score, the greater the score on the youth risk factor or bigger youth bulge.

The scatterplot in figure 7.6.5 supports this finding when only Syndrome is compared against Youth Risk Factor, which measures the size of the youth bulge. We can see that there is a moderately strong positive and significant linear correlation ($r = .699$, $p < .001$) between these two variables: higher Syndrome scores are associated with a higher youth bulge, on average. The countries with a Syndrome score of 3 that appear to be outliers in the scatterplot are Jamaica, Cape Verde, and Mongolia, with surprisingly high youth risk factor levels given their low Syndrome score. Some of the countries with both the highest Syndrome and the highest youth risk factor levels include Syria, Jordan, Iraq, and Yemen.

Because the Syndrome is significant in the general linear regression model, we also ran a logistic regression model (using a binary version of the response variable). The Syndrome and Religious Fractionalization are the only variables

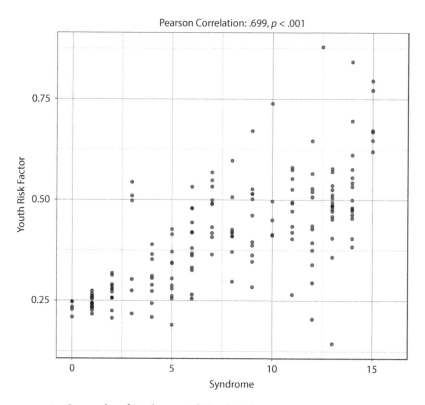

FIGURE 7.6.5 Scatterplot of Syndrome with Youth Risk Factor

that are significant in predicting the logits or predicted probabilities of higher ratio of the number of seventeen- to twenty-six-year-olds to the size of the country's total labor force. We specifically find that for every one unit increase in the Syndrome, the odds increase by 68 percent, or alternatively, the risk is 1.68 times greater that the country experiences a higher youth risk factor, after holding all other control variables constant.

Concluding Discussion for the Demographic Security Dimension

The Patrilineal/Fraternal Syndrome was a highly significant predictor of five of the seven demographic variables we analyzed, after controlling for the effects of our covariates of interest. The Syndrome also had the highest overall explanatory power as measured by effect size in these five runs. Only the control variables of Urbanization and Ethnic Fractionalization somewhat contributed to the explanatory power of the models for these national outcome variables. These findings support our hypothesis that nations manifesting a strong patrilineal culture as measured by the Syndrome Index tend to have higher fertility rates, have lower contraceptive prevalence, have a lower age at first birth for mothers, possess a larger youth bulge, and experience greater demographic pressures. Demographic insecurity is clearly related to the Patrilineal/Fraternal Syndrome as a security provision mechanism, with its low levels of women's empowerment at the household level.

Dimension 7. Education of the Population

We hypothesize that countries with higher Syndrome scores will experience lower levels of literacy and education, both as a whole and specifically among women and girls. We also predict that high-Syndrome countries will have larger discrepancies in the education and literacy between men and women.

Analyses for the Education Dimension

The first analysis uses the variable, Average Years of Schooling, which uses the average numbers of years of education received by people age twenty-five and older as our main analysis. We also analyze two ancillary variables: the Gender Parity Index for Secondary School, which calculates the ratio of girls to boys enrolled at the secondary level in public and private schools, and the Gender Parity Index for Primary School, which does the same for primary school.

The second analysis uses one variable, Access to Basic Knowledge, a Social Progress Index subcomponent, which measures adult literacy rate, primary school enrollment, secondary school enrollment, gender parity in secondary enrollment, and access to quality education.

The third analysis has one variable, Access to Information and Communications, which measures mobile phone subscriptions, internet users, access to online governance, and access to independent media for a given country.

The fourth analysis utilizes Overall Literacy Rate of Males and Females, defined as the percent of total population age fifteen and above that can read and write a simple statement (generally numeracy is required as well) as the main analytical variable. We add one ancillary analysis, which uses our Male-Female Literacy and Education Difference Factor on which load two variables: Discrepancy in Educational Attainment Between Females and Males measures and scales the difference between male and female education level reached, and Male-Female Difference in Literacy Rates measures the difference in percent of male and female literacy rates (age twenty-five and older).

The fifth, sixth, and seventh analyses all use one variable apiece. The fifth analysis looks at the Female Literacy Rate Ages Fifteen to Twenty-Four, which is the percentage of women ages fifteen to twenty-four who can read and write simple statements and do simple arithmetic. The sixth analysis examines Survival Rate to Last Year of Primary School for Females, which measures children enrolled in first grade who eventually reach the last grade by percent. Survival figures often are quite different from enrollment figures, and so this is an important variable to include. The seventh analysis examines Government Expenditures per Student Secondary as Percentage of GDP per Capita, which gives the average general government expenditures per student in a given level of education, here secondary, as a percent of GDP per capita.

Model Results

We ran ten general linear model analyses under Education of the Population and found that the Syndrome was significant in six of those ten models. The four models for which the Syndrome was not significant include (1) the Male-Female Literacy Ratio and Discrepancy in Educational Attainment Factor, (2) the Gender Parity Index for Primary School, (3) the Gender Parity Index for Secondary School, and (4) Government Expenditures per Student Secondary as Percentage of GDP per Capita. Table 7.7 summarizes the results of these analyses.

7.1 Average Years of Schooling

(Lower scores are considered worse.)

The adjusted R-squared is a remarkably strong .676, indicating that the specified model explained at least 67.6 percent of the variability of average years of schooling. We find that Civilization (Muslim), Patrilineal/Fraternal Syndrome, Urbanization, and Religious Fractionalization are all significant variables in this model. See appendix III, table AIII.7.7.1, for full results. We further note that the Syndrome has by far the largest effect size—more than

TABLE 7.7 Summary of GLM Results for the Education Dimension in Descending Order of R-squared Values

Dependent Variables	Adjusted R-squared (N)	Independent Variables (significant at .001 by descending order of effect size)
1. Average Years of Schooling	.676 (172)	Syndrome Urbanization Religious Fractionalization Muslim Civilization
Gender Parity Index for Secondary School	*.238 (163)*	*None*
Gender Parity Index for Primary School	*.110 (169)*	*None*
2. Access to Basic Knowledge	.608 (158)	Syndrome Muslim Civilization Urbanization
3. Access to Information and Communications	.569 (168)	Urbanization Syndrome
4. Overall Literacy Rate	.555 (148)	Syndrome Urbanization Ethnic Fractionalization

Male–Female Literacy and Education Difference Factor
  • *Discrepancy in Educational Attainment Between Females and Males*
  • *Male–Female Difference in Literacy Rates*
	.064 (124)	*None*

5. Female Literacy Rate Ages Fifteen to Twenty-Four	.495 (126)	Syndrome Urbanization Ethnic Fractionalization
6. Survival Rate to Last Year of Primary School for Females	.485 (150)	Muslim Civilization Urbanization Syndrome
7. Government Expenditures per Student Secondary as Percentage of GDP per Capita	.042 (129)	None

Note: Ancillary analysis in italics. GDP, gross domestic product.

twice as large as any of the other significant variables. The sign of the Syndrome coefficient is in the predicted direction (negative, meaning the lower (better) the Syndrome score, the higher the average years of schooling for men and women ages twenty-five and older). It appears that the strongest determinant of average years of schooling is the Patrilineal/Fraternal Syndrome, which corroborates our hypothesis.

We further note that the direction of the coefficient for Urbanization is positive, which indicates that as the level of urbanization increases, a country's average years of schooling improves. We find that the direction of the coefficient for Religious Fractionalization is positive, which indicates that as the fractionalization increases, a country's average years of schooling also increases. We also find that the coefficient for Muslim civilizations is positive, which indicates that predominantly Muslim countries experience higher average years of schooling.

In further analysis, we note the bivariate correlation between the Syndrome and the Average Years of Schooling is a very strong $-.754$ ($p < .0001$), with the scatterplot in figure 7.7.1 showing this relationship. All of the lowest scores for

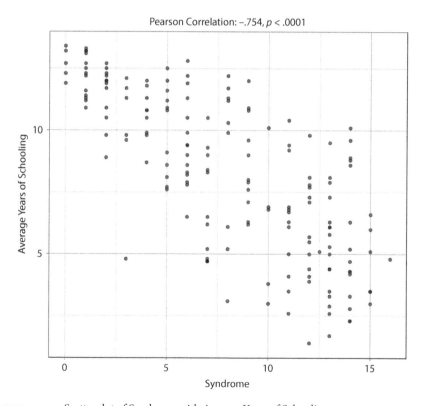

FIGURE 7.7.1 Scatterplot of Syndrome with Average Years of Schooling

this variable are found in the countries with the highest Syndrome scores and in the vast majority of medium-lower scores (with the exception of Cape Verde, which can be found in the lower-left quadrant, with a Syndrome Score of 3 and only 4.8 average years of schooling). Countries with the lowest (best) Syndrome scores attain the highest levels of average years of schooling.

Because the Syndrome is significant in the general linear regression model, we also ran a logistic regression model (using a binary version of the response variable). The Syndrome, Urbanization, and Religious Fractionalization are the only variables that are significant in predicting the logits or predicted probabilities of average years of schooling being less than or only to the completion of primary education. We specifically find that for every one unit increase in the Syndrome, the odds increase by 57 percent, or alternatively, the risk is 1.57 times greater that the country experiences average years of schooling less than or only to the completion of primary education, after holding all other control variables constant.

We use two variables in ancillary analyses: Gender Parity Index for secondary school and Gender Parity Index for primary school. The former had a low adjusted R-squared value of .238, whereas the latter had an even lower R-squared value of .110. Because the Syndrome was not significant in either of these analyses, we do not report the details of the analyses. Parity has increased dramatically over the past two decades, and so this result is not unexpected.

7.2 Access to Basic Knowledge
(Lower scores are considered worse.)

The adjusted R-squared is a remarkably strong .608, indicating that the specified model explained at least 60.8 percent of the variability of access to basic knowledge. We find that Civilization (Muslim), Patrilineal/Fraternal Syndrome, and Urbanization are all significant variables in this model. See appendix III, table AIII.7.7.2, for full results. We further note that Syndrome has the largest effect size—more than twice as large as Muslim Civilizations or Urbanization, which also appear as significant in that model run. The sign of the Syndrome coefficient is in the predicted direction (negative, meaning the lower (better) the Syndrome score the higher the access to basic knowledge). This variable is an index that considers adult literacy rates, primary school enrollment, lower secondary school enrollment, upper secondary school enrollment, and gender parity in secondary enrollment. When a country has a worse Syndrome score, a country's score for the combination of these knowledge assets worsens. It appears that the strongest determinant of access to basic knowledge in a society is the Patrilineal/Fraternal Syndrome, which corroborates our hypothesis.

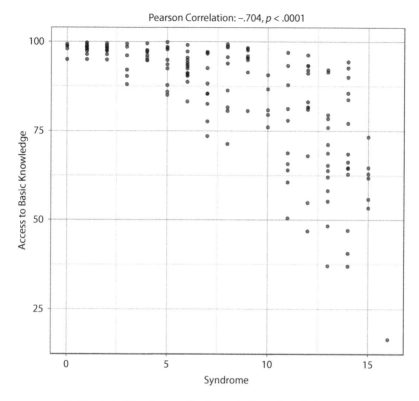

FIGURE 7.7.2 Scatterplot of Syndrome with Access to Basic Knowledge

We further note that the direction of the coefficient for Urbanization is positive, which indicates that as the level of urbanization increases, a country's access to basic knowledge score improves. We also find that the coefficient for Muslim civilizations is positive, which indicates that predominantly Muslim countries experience greater access to basic knowledge than the comparison group.

In further analysis, we note the bivariate correlation between the Syndrome and the Access to Basic Knowledge variable is a very strong −.704 ($p < .0001$), with the bivariate scatterplot in figure 7.7.2 showing the relationship. Although higher scores can be found at every different level of Syndrome, all of the lowest scores for this variable are found in the countries with the highest Syndrome scores. This indicates that, although higher scores for access to basic knowledge can occur at any level, lower scores are essentially eliminated when countries have lower levels of Syndrome practices. We additionally note that the country that experiences the lowest level of access to basic knowledge is also the country that experiences the worst Syndrome score (16), South Sudan.

Because the Syndrome is significant in the general linear regression model, we also ran a logistic regression model (using a binary version of the response variable). The Syndrome, Urbanization, and Muslim Civilization are the only variables that are significant in predicting the logits or predicted probabilities of lower access to basic knowledge. We specifically find that for every one unit increase in the Syndrome, the odds increase by 66 percent, or alternatively, the risk is 1.66 times greater that the country experiences lower access to basic knowledge, after holding all other control variables constant.

7.3 Access to Information and Communications
(Lower scores are considered worse.)

This variable is an index that considers mobile telephone subscriptions, internet users, and the Press Freedom Index. The adjusted R-squared is a strong .569, indicating that the specified model explained at least 56.9 percent of the variability of access to information and communication. We find that Patrilineal/Fraternal Syndrome and Urbanization are the only significant variables in this model. See appendix III, table AIII.7.7.3, for full results. We note that Syndrome does not have the largest effect size for this variable, but that the effect size of Urbanization is only slightly larger than Syndrome. The coefficient for Urbanization indicates that as the level of urbanization increases, the access to information and communication also increases on average. The sign of the Syndrome coefficient is also in the predicted direction (negative, meaning the lower/better the Syndrome score, the higher the access to information and communication).

In further analysis, we note the bivariate correlation between the Syndrome and the Access to Information and Communication variable is a moderately strong −.674 ($p < .0001$), with the scatterplot in figure 7.7.3 showing the relationship. With the exception of one outlier in the lower-left quadrant (Cuba with a Syndrome score of 4), lower scores of access are not found for countries with lower (better) Syndrome levels. Additionally, the highest access scores attained are found for countries with better Syndrome scores.

Because the Syndrome is significant in the general linear regression model, we also ran a logistic regression model (using a binary version of the response variable). The Syndrome and Urbanization are the only variables that are significant in predicting the logits or predicted probabilities of lower access to information and communications. We specifically find that for every one unit increase in the Syndrome, the odds increase by 28 percent, or alternatively, the risk is 1.28 times greater that the country experiences lower access to information and communications, after holding all other control variables constant.

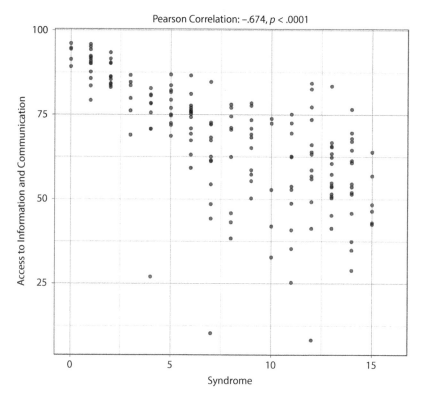

FIGURE 7.7.3 Scatterplot of Syndrome with Access to Information and Communication

7.4 Overall Literacy Rate for the Fifteen and Over Population
(Lower scores are considered worse.)

The adjusted R-squared is a strong .555, indicating that the specified model explained at least 55.5 percent of the variability of overall literacy rates. We find that Patrilineal/Fraternal Syndrome, Urbanization, and Ethnic Fractionalization are all significant variables in this model. See appendix III, table AIII.7.7.4, for full results. We note that the Syndrome has the largest effect size in this model, more than twice as large as Ethnic Fractionalization and almost twice as large as Urbanization. The sign of the Syndrome coefficient is in the predicted direction (negative, meaning the worse the Syndrome score, the lower the overall literacy of men and women in a country). It appears that the strongest determinant of the overall literacy in the adult population is the Patrilineal/Fraternal Syndrome, which corroborates our hypothesis.

We additionally note that coefficients indicate that countries with higher levels of urbanization have higher overall literacy rates on average, and countries

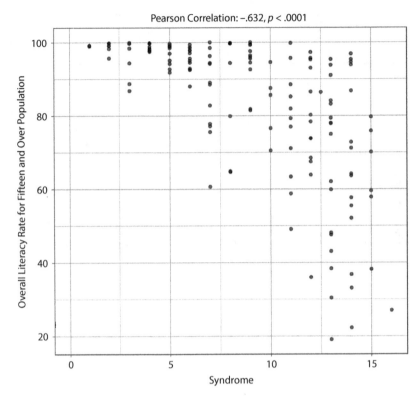

FIGURE 7.7.4 Scatterplot of Syndrome with Overall Literacy Rate for Fifteen and Over Population

with higher levels of ethnic fractionalization have lower levels of literacy rates on average. In further analysis, we note the bivariate correlation between the Syndrome and the overall literacy of men and women variable is a moderately strong $-.632$ ($p < .0001$), with the scatterplot in figure 7.7.4 showing the relationship. We find an empty lower-left quadrant in the scatterplot, indicating that lower overall literacy rates are only found in countries with higher Syndrome scores.

Because the Syndrome is significant in the general linear regression model, we also ran a logistic regression model (using a binary version of the response variable). The Syndrome is the only variable that is significant in predicting the logits or predicted probabilities of an overall literacy rate below (or equal to) 95 percent. We specifically find that for every one unit increase in the Syndrome, the odds increase by 45 percent, or alternatively, the risk is 1.45 times greater that the country's overall literacy rate is below 95 percent, after accounting for the other control variables.

We examined discrepancy in educational attainment between men and women and male/female differences in literacy rates as ancillary analyses. The GLM analyses yielded a very low adjusted R-squared value of .064. Because the Syndrome was not significant, we do not report the results. As mentioned previously, discrepancies in male/female education have decreased sharply over the past twenty years through global efforts such as the Millennium Development Goals, so this is not an entirely unexpected finding.

7.5 Female Literacy Rate Ages Fifteen to Twenty-Four
(Lower scores are considered worse.)

The adjusted R-squared is a strong .495, indicating that the specified model explained at least 49.5 percent of the variability of female literacy rates. We find that the Patrilineal/Fraternal Syndrome, Urbanization, and Ethnic Fractionalization are all significant variables in this model. See appendix III, table AIII.7.7.5, for full results. Although the effect size of Syndrome is fairly small (.162), it has the largest effect size in this model. The sign of the Syndrome coefficient is in the predicted direction (negative, meaning the worse the Syndrome score, the lower the literacy rates for females ages fifteen to twenty-four). It appears that the strongest determinant of this variable is the Patrilineal/Fraternal Syndrome, which corroborates our hypothesis.

We further note that the direction of the coefficient for Urbanization is positive, which indicates that as the level of urbanization increases, a country's literacy rates for girls ages fifteen to twenty-four also increases. We find that the direction of the coefficient for Ethnic Fractionalization is negative, which indicates that as the ethnic fractionalization in a country increases, the country's literacy rates for girls in this age group decreases as well.

In further analysis, we note the bivariate correlation between the Syndrome and the female literacy rate variable is a moderately strong −.617 ($p < .0001$), with the scatterplot in figure 7.7.5 showing the relationship. Although higher scores can be found at every different level of Syndrome, all of the worst scores for this variable are found in the countries with the highest (worst) Syndrome scores.

Because the Syndrome is significant in the general linear regression model, we also ran a logistic regression model (using a binary version of the response variable). The Syndrome and Urbanization are the only variables that are significant in predicting the logits or predicted probabilities of literacy rates for females below (or equal to) 95 percent. We specifically find that for every one unit increase in the Syndrome, the odds increase by 126 percent, or alternatively, the risk is 2.26 times greater that the country's literacy rates for females ages fifteen to twenty-four is below 95 percent, after holding all other control variables constant.

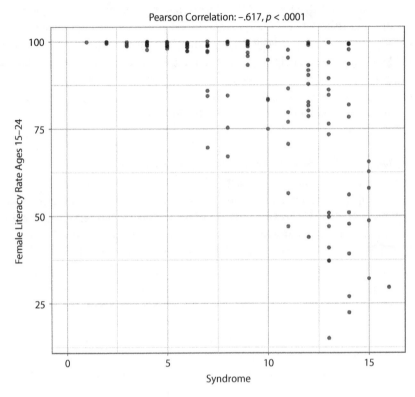

FIGURE 7.7.5 Scatterplot of Syndrome with Female Literacy Rate Ages Fifteen to Twenty-Four

7.6 Survival Rate to the Last Year of Primary School for Females
(Lower scores are considered worse.)

The adjusted R-squared is a strong .485, indicating that the specified model explained at least 48.5 percent of the variability of girls' survival rate to final year of primary school. The only significant variables in this model are Muslim Civilization, the Syndrome, and Urbanization. See appendix III, table AIII.7.7.6, for full results. Although Muslim Civilization appears the strongest determinant of this variable, its effect size is only slightly larger than both the Syndrome and Urbanization. We find that the coefficient for Muslim Civilization is positive, which indicates that predominantly Muslim countries experience higher survival rates of girls to the last year of primary school than the comparison group of African civilization countries. The sign of the coefficient for Urbanization is positive, meaning the higher the percentage of people living in urban areas in a country, the higher survival rates of girls to the last year of primary school. The Syndrome's negative coefficient indicates that countries with higher Syndrome scores will have lower survival rates to the last year of primary school for females, which is consistent with our hypothesis.

The bivariate correlation between the Syndrome and Survival Rates is a moderately strong −.551 ($p < .0001$), and the bivariate scatterplot in figure 7.7.6 shows a generally negative trend. We note that the countries with higher Syndrome scores in the scatterplot experience much higher variation in survival rates. We find the lower-left quadrant is completely empty, indicating that countries that have lower Syndrome scores have the highest survival rates for females to the end of primary school. We do note that Nicaragua and Madagascar, with moderate Syndrome scores (7 and 8, respectively), experience lower survival rates than would be expected given their scores.

Because the Syndrome is significant in the general linear regression model, we also ran a logistic regression model (using a binary version of the response variable). The Syndrome and Urbanization are the only variables that are significant in predicting the logits or predicted probabilities of lower percentage

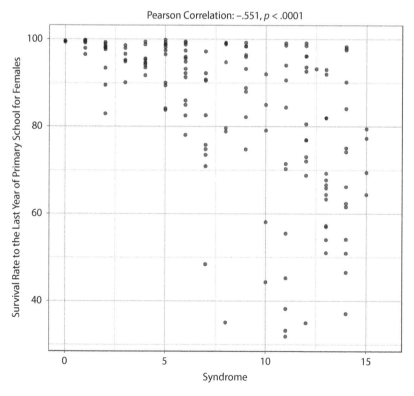

FIGURE 7.7.6 Scatterplot of Syndrome with Survival Rate to Last Year of Primary School for Females

of girls who survive to the last year of primary school (less than 90 percent). We specifically find that for every one unit increase in the Syndrome, the odds increase by 31 percent, or alternatively, the risk is 1.31 times greater that the country experiences lower percentages of girls who survive to the last year of primary school, after holding all other control variables constant.

7.7 Government Expenditures per Student in Secondary School as Percentage of GDP per Capita
(Lower scores are considered worse.)

The GLM analysis yielded a very low adjusted R-squared value of .042. Because the Syndrome was not significant, we do not report the results. This finding is largely due to the presence of a small set of wealthy countries with high educational expenditures that nevertheless subordinate women.

Concluding Discussion for the Education Dimension
Although the Patrilineal/Fraternal Syndrome is not significantly related to all of the variables in this Education dimension, it is a significant predictor variable in six out of the ten analyses performed. In four of these six, it is the most significant determinant of the dependent variable in terms of effect size. The outcome variables for which the Syndrome had the largest effect size were as follows:

- Average Years of Schooling (for men and women age twenty-five and over)
- Access to Basic Knowledge and Communication
- Female Literacy Rate Ages Fifteen to Twenty-Four
- Overall Literacy Rate for Fifteen and Over of Population

These are noteworthy results. A wide variety of education and literacy indicators appear to be significantly determined by the degree to which the Patrilineal/Fraternal Syndrome is encoded within the behavior of the society. The results for Female Literacy Rates indicate that the Syndrome is a significant determinant of girls' literacy. The results for both Average Years of Schooling and Access to Basic Knowledge, measures of the education access and experience of both men and women, indicate that the Syndrome significantly affects overall access to knowledge in a society. Although countries with worse Syndrome scores do not always have poor levels of education and literacy or low government expenditures on education, we find that the absence of the Syndrome essentially eliminates poor education and literacy levels. The control variables that aid the explanatory power of the models for national outcomes in education include Urbanization, which is as consistently significant as the Syndrome, and for certain other outcomes, Civilization and Ethnic Fractionalization matter as well.

Dimension 8. Social Progress

We hypothesize that Syndrome countries will suffer in comparison with non-Syndrome countries in a number of areas that can be roughly summed up as pertaining to a variety of aspects of social progress. In this dimension, we include access to electricity, which is critical for household functions and children's school homework and thus links to education as well as women's work. We include indicators that touch on human happiness and unhappiness, including the Happiness Index and suicide rates. We look at state respect for diversity in tolerance for immigrants and religious tolerance. The provision of social safety nets and pensions indicates a state's protection of disabled and aged citizens.

The Social Progress dimension also analyzes the relationship of the Syndrome countries to respected international gender indicators and includes five gender equality indexes as well as a state's formal commitment to the Convention on the Elimination of All Forms of Discrimination Against Women (CEDAW). We hypothesize that countries that rank high on the Syndrome will also rank low on these scales for women's status. Finally, we examine the relation of Syndrome countries and the best international model of human well-being, the United Nations Human Development Index (HDI), and we hypothesize that Syndrome countries will rank lower.

Analyses for the Social Progress Dimension

We performed nine main analyses on the Social Progress dimension and seven ancillary analyses. In our first analysis, we examine a key variable for our study, the HDI. This widely used and respected index, created by United Nations Development Program (UNDP), measures human development through three variables: life expectancy, education, and per capita income.

The second analysis examines one variable, the Gender Inequality Index (GII), which measures gender inequalities in human development (reproductive health, maternal mortality, and early marriage), empowerment (legislative seats held and education levels), and economic status (labor force participation). The GII was also created by UNDP in conjunction with the Human Development Report and uses the same overall template as the HDI. Therefore, we include these two variables sequentially in our Social Progress dimension results section. (Additional gender variables can be found later in this same dimension.) We used the GII in chapter 3 to validate the Syndrome index, but here we perform a multivariate analysis to probe this relationship more deeply.

The third analysis examines two variables. Our main analysis is the Happiness Index, which ranks countries on a package of factors that respondents to Gallup World Poll surveys consider necessary for a best possible life. Respondents name income, healthy life expectancy, social support, freedom, trust, and generosity. For an ancillary analysis, we use Female Suicide Rates, the reported number of suicides among women in a given country per one hundred thousand population.

The main variable for the fourth analysis is the Percentage of Pension-able-Age Persons Receiving Social Security or Pensions defined as the percent of beneficiaries covered by old-age pensions. Social Safety nets, used in ancillary analysis, measures the services provided by state or other institutions, such as welfare, unemployment benefits, universal health care, free education, and workers compensation, that cushion individuals from falling into poverty. As noted in the beginning of this analysis, we see this variable as a key contextual variable, but we were unable to include it as part of the model because of N-size considerations. Here, we probe our proposition that nations with low pension rates will rank high on the Syndrome, as the elderly rely on sons for financial support because the state is incapable of providing that support. In chapter 9, we single out the relationship between sex ratios and pension provision.

The fifth analysis focuses on one variable, Access to Electricity Percent of Population, which measures the percent of population with access to electricity. In the contemporary era, it is difficult to make social progress without access to this form of power.

The sixth analysis uses the Hofstede Individualism Score as a main analysis. Legal frameworks in liberal democracies benefit the rights of individuals (contract societies) as opposed to loyalty and dependence on groups (status societies). This variable contrasts individualism and collectivism as a characteristic of national culture. As noted in part I, the Syndrome is the most dominant expression of collectivism across time and history. We include it in the Social Progress dimension because the quest for human development is impaired to the extent that the individual is not recognized as the primary unit of society.

The seventh analysis examines the well-known Gender Gap Index (GGI), which measures gender disparities in terms of health, education, economy, and politics. As with the GII, we used the GGI in chapter 3 to validate the Syndrome index, but here we are able to delve more deeply through multivariate analysis.

The eighth analysis uses Discrimination and Violence Among Minorities for its major analysis. This subcomponent of the Social Progress Index, measures discrimination and violence against ethnic, sectarian, religious, and communal groups by state. We use two variables in ancillary analyses: Religious Tolerance, a subcomponent of the Social Progress Index that compiles measures of thirteen types of religious hostility by private individuals, organizations, or groups in society including religion-related armed conflict or terrorism, mob or sectarian violence, harassment over attire for religious reasons, or other religion-related intimidation or abuse; and Tolerance for Immigrants, also a subcomponent of the Social Progress Index which presents the percentage of respondents answering yes to the question on a Gallup World Poll, "Is the city or area where you live a good place or not a good place to live for immigrants from other countries?"

The ninth analysis returns to more specifically gender-related issues, and uses Legal Declaration of Gender Equality in the main analysis. This variable measures the extent of a country's codification of gender equality in law, whether in the constitution or through legislation. We utilize three variables for ancillary analysis: Formal Commitment to CEDAW, which ranks the degree to which a country has committed to meet the goals of the Convention; Government Framework for Gender Equality, which measures and scales the degree to which a country enacts feminist goals into policy on three dimensions (i.e., legal declaration of gender equality, presence of a gender equality action plan, and commitment to international goals as expressed in CEDAW); and we also look separately at Presence of National Gender Equality Action Plan, which indicates whether country has a comprehensive and current national gender equality action plan.

Model Results

We ran sixteen general linear model analyses under Social Progress and found that the Syndrome was significant in twelve of those models. The four models for which the Syndrome was not significant include (1) Female Suicide Rates, (2) Tolerance for Immigrants, (3) Formal Commitment to CEDAW, and (4) Presence of National Gender Equality Action Plan. The last two findings are interesting for they suggest that formal government commitment to gender equality may not translate into meaningfully greater levels of women's empowerment at the household level. Table 7.8 summarizes the results of the GLM analysis.

8.1 Human Development Index (HDI)

(Lower scores are worse.)

The adjusted R-squared is a remarkably strong .788, indicating that the specified model explained at least 78.8 percent of the variability of the HDI scores. Four variables proved significant: Muslim Civilization (effect size .111), Syndrome (effect size .347), Urbanization (.385), and Ethnic Fractionalization (.090). See appendix III, table AIII.7.8.1, for full results. The effect sizes of the Syndrome and Urbanization are more than three times larger than that of Ethnic Fractionalization or Muslim Civilization.

The Syndrome effect size is slightly less than Urbanization. The coefficients of Urbanization and Muslim Civilization are positive, which means that countries with higher urbanization and those with predominantly Muslim civilizations will score higher on the HDI. The coefficients for the Syndrome and Ethnic Fractionalization are negative, which means that countries that rank high (worse) on those two indexes will rank low on the HDI. The bivariate correlation between the Syndrome and the HDI is significant and very strong ($r = -.764, p < .0001$). The scatterplot in figure 7.8.1 illustrates this relationship as it forms a steep negative curve. Some of the countries with high HDI scores in

TABLE 7.8 Summary of GLM Results for the Social Progress Dimension in Descending Order of R-squared Values

Dependent Variable	Adjusted R-squared (N)	Independent Variables (significant at .001 by descending order of effect size)
1. Human Development Index	.788 (172)	Urbanization Syndrome Muslim Civilization Ethnic Fractionalization
2. Gender Inequality Index	.718 (155)	Syndrome Urbanization Ethnic Fractionalization
3. Happiness Index	.643 (157)	Syndrome Urbanization Muslim Civilization
Female Suicide Rates (World Health Organization)	*.097 (173)*	*None*
4. Percentage of Pensionable-Age Persons Receiving Social Security or Pensions	.533 (159)	Syndrome
Social Safety Nets	*.509 (128)*	*Urbanization Syndrome*
5. Percent of Population with Access to Electricity	.495 (175)	Urbanization Syndrome Muslim Civilization
6. Hofstede Individualism Score	.471 (101)	Syndrome
7. Gender Gap Index	.445 (144)	Syndrome
8. Discrimination and Violence Against Minorities	.399 (160)	Number of Land Neighbors Syndrome
Religious Tolerance	*.324 (160)*	*Number of Land Neighbors Syndrome Colonial Heritage Status*
Tolerance for Immigrants	*.089 (152)*	*None*
9. Legal Declaration of Gender Equality	.384 (176)	Syndrome
Government Framework for Gender Equality	*.251 (176)*	*Syndrome*
Formal Commitment to CEDAW	*.125 (176)*	*Muslim Civilization*
Presence of National Gender Equality Action Plan	*.044 (176)*	*None*

Note: Ancillary analyses in italics.

addition to the highly ranked Western European countries, found in the upper-right quadrant, include wealthy Gulf states, such as United Arab Emirates, Qatar, and Saudi Arabia. The HDI is highly respected as a model of social well-being and for measuring a country's level of development as its component indices go beyond economic growth or income alone. The components of the index include life expectancy, knowledge (which includes education), and gross national income. That the Syndrome has such a strong negative correlation validates our overall hypothesis that the Syndrome represents a set of practices that compromise the well-being of men, women, and children—not just women.

Because the Syndrome is significant in the general linear regression model, we also ran a logistic regression model (using a binary version of the response variable). The Syndrome and Urbanization are the only variables that are significant in predicting the logits or predicted probabilities of worse scores on the HDI. We specifically find that for every one unit increase in the Syndrome, the odds increase by 66 percent, or alternatively, the risk is 1.66 times greater that the country experiences lower scores on the HDI, after holding all other control variables constant.

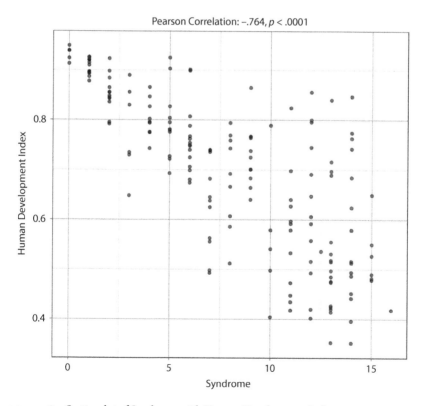

FIGURE 7.8.1 Scatterplot of Syndrome with Human Development Index

8.2 Gender Inequality Index
(Higher scores are considered worse.)

The adjusted R-squared is a remarkably strong .718, indicating that the specified model explained at least 71.8 percent of the variability of the GII scores. Three variables reach significance: Syndrome with an effect size of .392, Urbanization with an effect size of .123, and Ethnic Fractionalization with an effect size of .078. We note that the effect size of the Syndrome is three and a half times larger than that of Urbanization. See appendix III, table AIII.7.8.2, for full results. The coefficient of Syndrome is positive, which means that Syndrome countries are more likely to rank high on the GII. The Urbanization coefficient is negative, which means that more urbanized countries are less likely to rank high on the GII. There is a very strong correlation between Syndrome and GII ($r = .800$, $p < .0001$). The scatterplot in figure 7.8.2 shows a strong upward pattern that substantiates the correlation between the two factors. The strong relationship between Syndrome and this index mirrors the strong correlation between Syndrome and the HDI (see figure 7.8.1).

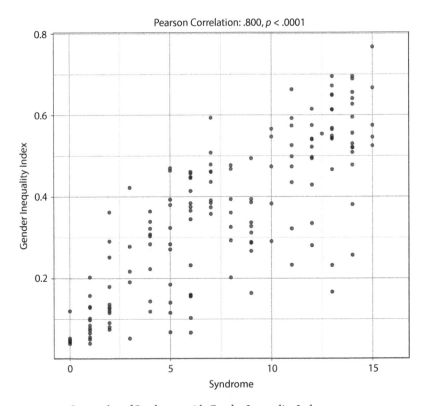

FIGURE 7.8.2 Scatterplot of Syndrome with Gender Inequality Index

Because the Syndrome is significant in the general linear regression model, we also ran a logistic regression model (using a binary version of the response variable). The Syndrome and Muslim Civilization are the only variables that are significant in predicting the logits or predicted probabilities of worse scores on the GII. We specifically find that for every one unit increase in the Syndrome, the odds increase by 81 percent, or alternatively, the risk is 1.81 times greater that the country scores worse on the GII, after holding all other control variables constant.

8.3 Happiness Index

(Lower scores are considered worse.)

The adjusted R-squared is a strong .643, indicating that the specified model explained at least 64.3 percent of the variability of the Happiness Index scores. Three variables prove significant: Muslim Civilization (effect size .080), the Syndrome (.242), and Urbanization (.222). See appendix III, table AIII.7.8.3, for full results. The effect size of Syndrome is a little larger than Urbanization, and both are around three times the effect size of Muslim Civilization. The coefficients for Muslim Civilization and Urbanization are positive, which means that these countries rank higher on the Happiness Index. The Syndrome's coefficient is negative, which means that countries high on Syndrome rank significantly lower on the Happiness Index.

The bivariate correlation is significant and moderately strong at $-.662$ ($p < .0001$). The scatterplot in figure 7.8.3 illustrates this relationship with a strong negative pattern showing that countries higher on Syndrome have citizens who are less happy. We note that in the lower-right quadrant, we find both Muslim and non-Muslim countries: Syria and Afghanistan are majority Muslim countries, but Togo, Burundi, and Benin are not majority Muslim.

Because the Syndrome is significant in the general linear regression model, we also ran a logistic regression model (using a binary version of the response variable). The Syndrome and Urbanization are the only variables that are significant in predicting the logits or predicted probabilities of worse scores on the Happiness Index. We specifically find that for every one unit increase in the Syndrome, the odds increase by 45 percent, or alternatively, the risk is 1.45 times greater that the country scores worse on the Happiness Index, after holding all other control variables constant. That is noteworthy: all, and not just women, are significantly less happy when the first sexual political order is based on subordination, coercion, and exploitation of women—including men.

We use the World Health Organization's female suicide rates as an ancillary variable and the GLM analysis yields a very low adjusted R-squared value of .097 with no significant independent variables. In our experience, we have found that the existing data on female suicide rates are patently not reliable,

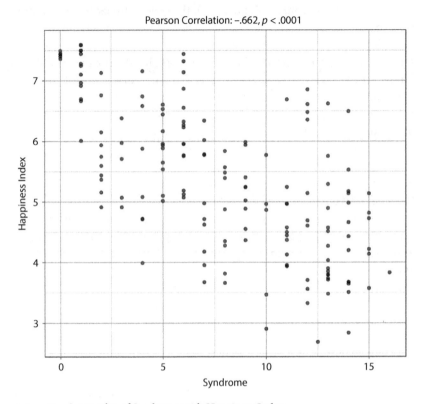

FIGURE 7.8.3 Scatterplot of Syndrome with Happiness Index

and so this is not an unexpected finding. In the future, we hope to create a scale to overcome some of the data deficiencies for female suicide, as this is an important relationship to examine.

8.4 Percentage of Pensionable-Age Persons Receiving Social Security or Pensions

(Lower scores are considered worse.)

The adjusted R-squared is a strong .533, indicating that the specified model explained at least 53.3 percent of the variability of the percentage of pensionable aged persons receiving social security or pensions. One variable, Syndrome, achieves significance with an effect size of .330. See appendix III, table AIII.7.8.4, for full results. Its coefficient is negative, which means that Syndrome countries are far less likely to provide retirement-age individuals with social security or pensions, which corroborates our hypotheses. The bivariate correlation is a very strong at $-.718$ ($p < .0001$). The scatterplot in figure 7.8.4 shows

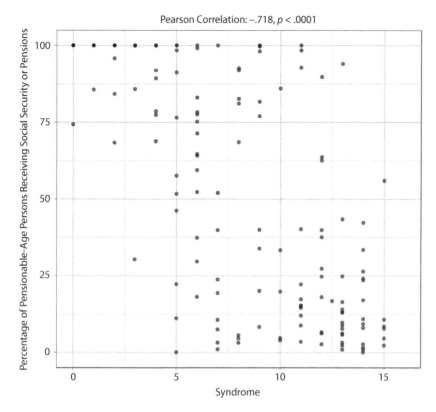

Pearson Correlation: −.718, p < .0001

FIGURE 7.8.4 Scatterplot of Syndrome with Percentage of Pensionable-Age Persons Receiving Social Security or Pensions

a downward slope. The distribution is complicated by a number of outliers for mid- and high-Syndrome scores. A number of Syndrome countries (e.g., Central Asia) were part of the former Union of Soviet Socialist Republics. These countries have a history of strong government involvement in care for elderly. Most other high-Syndrome countries expect kinship units to care for their elderly. Sons, in particular, are traditionally assigned the duty of caring for their parents in need or old age. As we have seen in previous chapters, the expectation that sons care for their parents is also a factor in son preference as well as in higher birth rates as families desire sons to guarantee their security in their old age. In the upper-left quadrant, we have Norway, Iceland, New Zealand, and Australia, which all are low on the Syndrome and high on those of retirement-age people receiving social security or pensions. In the upper-right quadrant, we have Lesotho, which is high on Syndrome and high on those of retirement age receiving social security or pensions. In the lower-right quadrant, we find Afghanistan, Yemen, Lebanon, and Chad, which are high on the Syndrome and low on those of retirement-age people receiving social security or pensions.

Because the Syndrome is significant in the general linear regression model, we also ran a logistic regression model (using a binary version of the response variable). The Syndrome is the only variable that is significant in predicting the logits or predicted probabilities of lower percentages of pensionable-age people receiving social security or pensions. We specifically find that for every one unit increase in the Syndrome, the odds increase by 86 percent, or alternatively, the risk is 1.86 times greater that the country experiences lower percentages of pensionable-age persons receiving social security or pensions, after holding all other control variables constant. This corroborates our proposition that nations without pension schemes are, in effect, prodding their citizens to rely on the Patrilineal/Fraternal Syndrome. It may also be the case that when the Syndrome is strong, nations see no need to provide pensions. Given the totality of our findings, that is a short-sighted conclusion.

We use Social Safety Nets as an ancillary variable and the GLM analysis results in a high adjusted R-squared value of .509, for which the Syndrome is a significant predictor of this outcome variable, along with Urbanization, both in the expected direction.

8.5 Percent of Population with Access to Electricity
(Lower scores are considered worse.)

The adjusted R-squared is a strong .495, indicating that the specified model explained at least 49.5 percent of the variability of access to electricity. Three indicators are significant: Muslim Civilization (effect size .088), Syndrome (.099), and Urbanization (.152). See appendix III, table AIII.7.8.5, for full results. The coefficients for Muslim Civilization and Urbanization are positive, which means that majority Muslim countries and countries that are more urbanized have greater access to electricity on a per capita basis. The populations of Syndrome countries have less access to electricity on a per capita basis. The bivariate correlation is a moderately strong −.569 ($p < .0001$). As the scatterplot in figure 7.8.5 shows, the relationship between electricity per capita and the Syndrome is uneven. Although some Syndrome countries have excellent access to electricity, a number of countries have less access. Some countries rank medium on Syndrome, but have little access to electricity. Not unexpectedly, countries in the upper-left quadrant, which are low on the Syndrome but high on access to electricity, include Switzerland, the United States, and Spain. In the upper-right quadrant, countries that are high on the Syndrome and also high on access to electricity, include Iraq, Pakistan, Saudi Arabia, and Iran. Countries in the lower-right quadrant, which are high on the Syndrome and low on access to electricity, include South Sudan, Chad, Central African Republic, and Liberia.

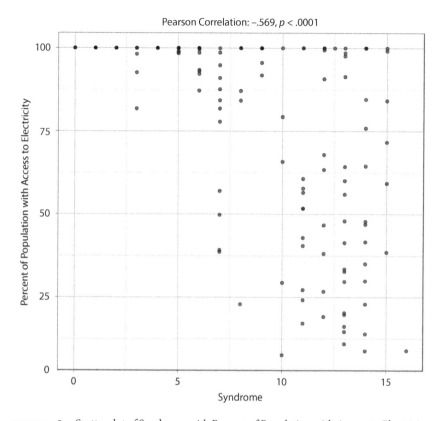

FIGURE 7.8.5 Scatterplot of Syndrome with Percent of Population with Access to Electricity

Because the Syndrome is significant in the general linear regression model, we also ran a logistic regression model (using a binary version of the response variable). The Syndrome, Urbanization, and Muslim Civilization are the only variables that are significant in predicting the logits or predicted probabilities of lower percentages of the population with access to electricity (less than 93.3 percent). We specifically find that for every one unit increase in the Syndrome, the odds increase by 35 percent, or alternatively, the risk is 1.35 times greater that the country experiences lower access to electricity, after holding all other control variables constant.

8.6 Hofstede Individualism Score
(Higher scores are associated with more individualistic cultures.)
The adjusted R-squared is a strong .471, indicating that the specified model explained at least 47.1 percent of the variability of the Hofstede Individualism Scores. The only significant predictor variable was the Syndrome, with

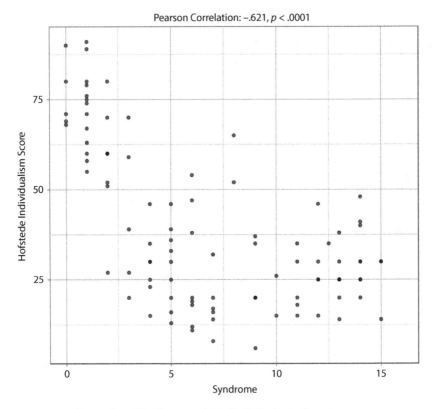

FIGURE 7.8.6 Scatterplot of Syndrome with Hofstede Individualism Score

a negative coefficient, which means the higher the Syndrome score, the less individualistic the culture. See appendix III, table AIII.7.8.6, for full results. This certainly makes sense in that the Syndrome imposes, shall we say, a lack of individualism particularly on all women, and the clan network also embeds men less as individuals and more as lineage representatives. The correlation with the Syndrome is a moderately strong −.621 ($p < .0001$), and the scatterplot in figure 7.8.6 shows the bivariate relationship between the Syndrome and individualism.

Because the Syndrome is significant in the general linear regression model, we also ran a logistic regression model (using a binary version of the response variable). The Syndrome is the only variable that is significant in predicting the logits or predicted probabilities of a country experiencing worse Hofstede Individualism Scores. We specifically find that for every one unit increase in the Syndrome, the odds increase by 35 percent, or alternatively, the risk is 1.35 times greater that the country scores lower on the Hofstede Individualism measure, after holding all other control variables constant.

8.7 Gender Gap Index

(Lower scores are considered worse.)

The adjusted R-squared is a strong .445, indicating that the specified model explained at least 44.5 percent of the variability of GGI scores. The only variable that is significant in this model is the Syndrome, with an effect size of .318. See appendix III, table AIII.7.8.7, for full results. The variable's coefficient is negative, which means that Syndrome countries rank worse on the GGI, which, in turn, means that Syndrome countries have larger gaps between men's and women's achievement as measured on subindices of Health and Survival, Educational Attainment, Economic Participation and Opportunity, and Political Empowerment. The bivariate correlation is a moderately strong −.670 ($p < .0001$). The scatterplot in figure 7.8.7 shows that high-Syndrome countries are slightly more likely to have more significant gender gaps. We identify some of the outliers in the plot. The country with the lowest (worst) score on the

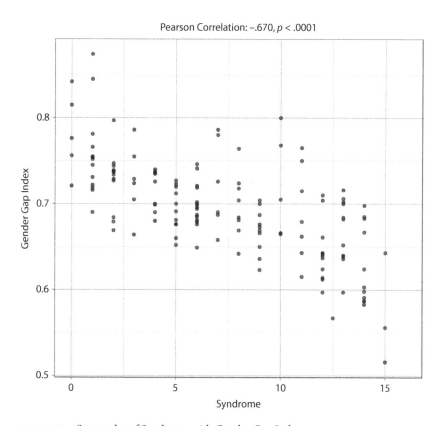

FIGURE 7.8.7 Scatterplot of Syndrome with Gender Gap Index

GGI is Yemen, with a Syndrome score of 15. Additionally, the three countries with the highest (best) scores on the GGI include Iceland, Finland, and Norway.

Because the Syndrome is significant in the general linear regression model, we also ran a logistic regression model (using a binary version of the response variable). The Syndrome is the only variable that is significant in predicting the logits or predicted probabilities of worse scores on the GGI. We specifically find that for every one unit increase in the Syndrome, the odds increase by 55 percent, or alternatively, the risk is 1.55 times greater that the country will score worse on the GGI, after holding all other control variables constant.

8.8 Discrimination and Violence Against Minorities
(Higher scores are considered worse.)

The adjusted R-squared is a moderate .399, indicating that the specified model explained at least 39.9 percent of the variability of discrimination and violence against minorities. Two variables prove significant: Syndrome and Number of Land Neighbors. The effect sizes are .097 and .141, respectively. See appendix III, table AIII.7.8.8, for full results. The coefficients for both are positive, which means that discrimination and violence against minorities increases the higher on the Syndrome scale a country ranks and the more land neighbors a country has. Thus, given more potentially competitive or even hostile neighbors on a state's border, a state tends to discriminate, often violently, against outsiders in country. The bivariate correlation is a moderately strong .545 ($p < .0001$). The scatterplot in figure 7.8.8 bears out the bivariate relationship between the Syndrome and discrimination and violence against minorities in a positive trend. The three low-Syndrome and low–Discrimination and Violence Against Minorities countries in the lower-left quadrant are Sweden, Finland, and Iceland. These data support our claim that high-Syndrome countries are associated with harsher attitudes and policies toward citizens outside the majority national groups.

Because the Syndrome is significant in the general linear regression model, we also ran a logistic regression model (using a binary version of the response variable). Although the model does meet the validity requirements, the Syndrome is not significant in this model ($p = .03$), and we do not report the results.

We use two variables in ancillary analyses to supplement the Discrimination and Violence Against Minorities analysis. We find a comparable adjusted R-squared value of .324 for Religious Tolerance, with Number of Land Neighbors, the Syndrome and Colonial Heritage Status as significant independent variables with the expected directionality (e.g., the higher/worse the Syndrome, the lower the level of religious tolerance). The second ancillary variable used, Tolerance for Immigrants, had a low adjusted R-squared value of .089 and the GLM analyses showed no significant predictors. Given that two of the variables

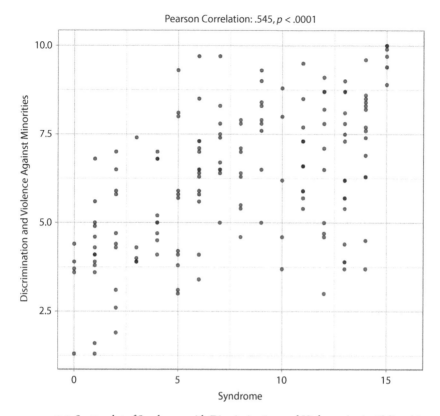

FIGURE 7.8.8 Scatterplot of Syndrome with Discrimination and Violence Against Minorities

in this cluster support our hypothesis, we are unclear why the third would not; there may be issues of operationalization at work in this last result. For this reason, we attempt to run multiple related indices, given the vagaries of operationalization, so that we may triangulate the results.

8.9 Legal Declaration of Gender Equality
(Higher scores are considered worse.)

The adjusted R-squared is a moderate .384, indicating that the specified model explained at least 38.4 percent of the variability of this scale on Legal Declaration of Gender Equality. One variable, the Syndrome, achieves significance with an effect size of .270. See appendix III, table AIII.7.8.9, for full results. The coefficient is positive, which means that Syndrome countries are more likely to sign on to the United Nations Legal Declaration of Gender Equality. This variable looks at the extent to which states codify gender equality in law,

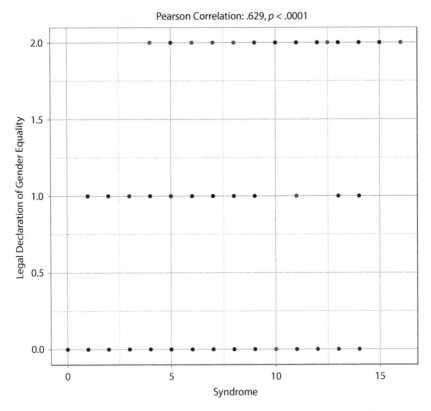

FIGURE 7.8.9 Scatterplot of Syndrome with Legal Declaration of Gender Equality

whether in its constitution or through legislation. This declaration is scaled in three levels, with higher scores showing less legal commitment to gender equality. Level 2 reflects no meaningful legal declaration for the country. Level 1 countries have nondiscrimination legislation only or customary law prioritized. Level 0 countries have enacted constitutional or comprehensive legal frameworks for gender equality. The scatterplot in figure 7.8.9 shows how countries are distributed along these three levels, and the relationship is significant (ANOVA $F = 67.41$, $p < .0001$). Generally speaking, high-Syndrome countries have no or little constitutional language or legislation committed to gender equality. Level 2 also denotes the countries where customary or personal laws are valid sources of law even if they violate legal provisions of nondiscrimination or equality. It is important to note that high-Syndrome countries scoring at level 0 or 1 on this outcome measure are not likely to fully implement their legal and constitutional commitments to gender equality, even if they have made such commitments. For example, countries in the lower-left quadrant, which are low on the Syndrome and have legal guarantees for gender equality, include Switzerland and the United Kingdom. In the lower-right quadrant, the countries include Somalia and the Solomon Islands, which are high on the Syndrome and also have legal guarantees for gender equality. Because of their Syndrome scores, we are more suspicious that Somalia and the Solomon Islands may not be implementing these guarantees than we are of Switzerland and the United Kingdom.

Because the Syndrome is significant in the general linear regression model, we also ran a logistic regression model (using a binary version of the response variable). The Syndrome is the only variable that is significant in predicting the logits or predicted probabilities of no gender equality or nondiscrimination clause in the constitution or legislation. We specifically find that for every one unit increase in the Syndrome, the odds increase by 69 percent, or alternatively, the risk is 1.69 times greater that the country does not have a gender equality or nondiscrimination clause in either its constitution or any legislation, after holding all other control variables constant.

We use three variables in ancillary analyses. The GLM analysis for Government Framework for Gender Equality has an adjusted R-squared value of .254, with the Syndrome as the only significant independent variable, and with the expected directionality. This finding is consistent with the results of the main analysis. The Formal Commitment to CEDAW variable has an adjusted R-squared value of .125, and the Syndrome is not a significant independent variable in the GLM analysis. Similar results are obtained for Presence of National Gender Equality Action Plan, which has a much lower adjusted R-squared value of .044. These are noteworthy negative results, indicating that ratifying CEDAW and having a national gender equality action plan may not necessarily correlate with the actual empowerment of women, but that having a formal declaration of the legal equality of women, or a government framework for gender equality, may indicate greater state commitment. Even so, the adjusted R-squared values are moderate for these variables.

Concluding Discussion for the Social Progress Dimension

Of the sixteen dependent variables measuring Social Progress examined here, the Syndrome proved significant for twelve. For five of the twelve dependent variables or factors for which the Syndrome was significant in multivariate modeling, it was the only variable demonstrating significance, and in another two models, it was the variable with the largest effect size. Other control variables that helped the explanatory power of the models included Urbanization, Ethnic Fractionalization, Civilization, and Number of Land Neighbors. Yet the Syndrome is far more consistent in its explanatory effects than these other variables.

Each of these social progress outcomes provides valuable information for our argument. Two areas prove particularly important. Development experts constructed the HDI to provide a more comprehensive measure of state development. By measuring life expectancy, educational attainment, and gross national income, the concept of development becomes multidimensional and provides a more accurate depiction of the condition of a state than is possible by measuring only GDP. The bivariate correlation between the Syndrome and HDI is extremely strong, and thus the Syndrome becomes an excellent predictor of negative outcomes regarding human development. We note that our empirical analysis includes data on the Syndrome's relation to each of the three major areas measured by HDI and refer readers to our other dimensions for results on the Syndrome's relation to health and life expectancy, educational attainment, and economic performance. Also noteworthy was the strong association between high Syndrome score and generalized societal levels of unhappiness. The subordination of women does not lead to a happy society for anyone, even men.

The second area that deserves attention is the poor correlation between variables that concern gender: Formal Commitment to CEDAW showed no correlation to Syndrome, Presence of National Gender Equality Action Plan showed no correlation to Syndrome, Legal Declaration of Gender Equality showed a significant but low correlation to Syndrome, Government Framework for Gender Equality showed a moderately low correlation to Syndrome, GGI showed a moderately low correlation to Syndrome, and GII showed a moderately high correlation to Syndrome.

One would expect that Syndrome as a negative measure of women's well-being would correlate significantly with all of these six variables. The results, however, are diverse. The lack of correlation between Syndrome and Formal Commitment to CEDAW and Presence of National Gender Equality Action Plan suggests that states may sign on to international accords like CEDAW, or adopt international standards such as the National Gender Equality Plan without following through on reforms that would improve women's well-being at the household level. In the case of CEDAW, states may either ignore the international standards, not have resources to commit to policy changes, or join only for face value. The relatively low correlation between Legal Declaration of Gender Equality and Government Frameworks for Gender Equality may reflect more rhetoric than real state effort and achievement.

The GGI and the GII show respectable correlations with our multivariate model, and in the case of the latter, a strong correlation. We already knew the bivariate associations from chapter 3, for which we used these variables to help validate the Syndrome index, but we wanted to see a fuller picture through multivariate analysis. We suggest that those two indexes capture *effects* of the Syndrome in their index compositions. Many of the commonly used variables to indicate women's well-being are, in our judgment, secondary factors that are visible and easily measured, such as education rates, health and life expectancy, labor force participation, and women's participation in government. Our theoretical framework holds that the Syndrome focuses on the practices embedded in informal social organizations that subsequently give rise to these more visible indicators of women's status.

Another item of interest is the robust relationship between subordinating women and not providing pensions. The subordination of women, in a sense, substitutes for pension provision through the Syndrome's components, including patrilocal marriage and lesser property and inheritance rights for women.

Last, the subordination of women is associated with significantly higher rates of discrimination against and violence toward minorities, which corroborates not only our theoretical framework but also the findings of scholars such as Elin Bjarnegard and Erik Melander. Hating "the other" has its roots in the character of male-female relations within the society.

Dimension 9. Environmental Protection

We hypothesize that countries with worse Syndrome scores will experience lower air quality, lower levels of environmental protection, and higher risks from environmental factors. We predict that societies that subordinate and exploit women also subordinate and exploit Mother Earth.

Analyses for the Environmental Protection Dimension

We perform four main analyses in the Environmental Protection dimension. The first looks at the Water and Environmental Well-Being factor, on which four indicators loaded in factor analysis. These four variables include Water and Sanitation, a subcomponent of the Environment Performance Index, which evaluates quality of sanitation and drinking water; the Environmental Performance Index itself, which is a respected measure giving an overall sense of a country's performance on environmental issues, which includes health impacts, air quality, water and sanitation, water resources, agriculture, biodiversity and climate, and energy; Wastewater Treatment gauges the percentage of produced wastewater treated by centralized treatment facilities; and Foundations of Well-Being combines indicators of the country's access to basic knowledge, access to information and communications, health and wellness, and environmental quality. We then conduct two ancillary analyses using the Environmental Performance Index separately and also Air Quality, which measures air quality by assessing household fuel use and minute atmospheric particulate matter (PM2.5).

The second analysis uses the Air Pollution Factor as the main analysis. Two indicators loaded on this factor: Household Indoor Air Pollution Attributable Deaths, which measures deaths that can be attributed to illnesses linked to household air pollution, and Greenhouse Gases, which measures emissions of carbon dioxide, methane, nitrous oxide, hydrofluorocarbons, perfluorocarbons, and sulfur hexafluoride. The ancillary analysis performed used Outdoor Air Pollution Attributable Deaths, which measures the rate of deaths resulting from emissions from households, industry, and vehicles per one hundred thousand people.

The third analysis is the Biodiversity and Pest regulation factor. Two indicators load on this factor, including Biodiversity and Habitat, which measures the percentage of naturally occurring community of flora and fauna in protected areas against the communities naturally occurring nationally, and Pesticide Regulation, a subcomponent of the Environmental Performance Index, which measures whether countries allow, restrict, or ban twelve toxic chemical pollutants used in agriculture, industry, and household products.

The fourth analysis has one variable, the Global Climate Risk Index, which assesses the impact of weather-related events (e.g., floods, hurricanes, heat waves) on nation-states.

Model Results

We ran seven general linear model analyses under Environmental Protection and found that the Syndrome was significant in six of those seven models. The model for which the Syndrome is not significant is the one that involves the Global Climate Risk Index. Table 7.9 summarizes the results of the GLM analyses

9.1 Water and Environmental Well-Being Factor

(This factor combines several variables: Water and Sanitation, Environmental Performance Index, Wastewater Treatment, and Foundations of Well-Being. Lower scores are considered worse.)

The adjusted R-squared is a remarkably strong .808, indicating that the specified model impressively explained at least 80.8 percent of the variability of this factor. We find that Colonial Heritage Status, Patrilineal/Fraternal Syndrome, Urbanization, and Ethnic Fractionalization are all significant variables in this model. See appendix III, table AIII.7.9.1, for full results. We note that Syndrome does not have the largest effect size for this model, but that the effect size of Urbanization is only slightly larger than Syndrome, and that Syndrome's effect size is more than three times as large as the other two significant variables.

Dependent Variables	Adjusted R-squared (N)	Independent Variables (significant at .001 by descending order of effect size)
1. Water and Environmental Well-Being Factor • Water and Sanitation • Environmental Performance Index • Wastewater Treatment • Foundations of Well-Being	.808 (149)	Urbanization Syndrome Ethnic Fractionalization Colonial Heritage Status
Environmental Performance Index	*.639 (171)*	*Syndrome* *Urbanization*
Air Quality	*.411 (172)*	*Syndrome* *Terrain* *Urbanization*
2. Air Pollution Factor • Household Indoor Air Pollution Attributable Deaths • Greenhouse Gases Emissions	.587 (156)	Urbanization Syndrome
Outdoor Air Pollution Attributable Deaths	*.383 (160)*	*Syndrome* *Number of Land Neighbors*
3. Biodiversity and Pest Regulation Factor • Biodiversity • Pest Regulations	.207 (160)	Syndrome
4. Global Climate Risk Index	.022 (172)	None

Note: Ancillary analyses in italics.

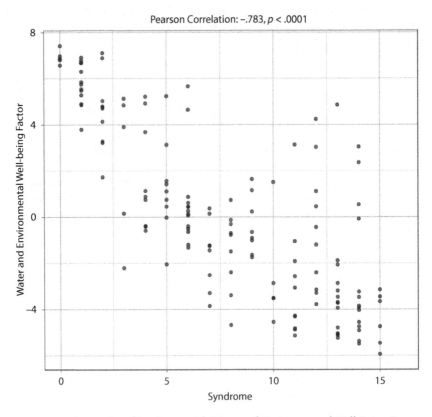

FIGURE 7.9.1 Scatterplot of Syndrome with Water and Environmental Well-Being Factor

We would expect that a country's level of urbanization would be the best predictor of water and environmental well-being, but we are surprised to find that the Syndrome is significant even when controlling for Urbanization and that its effect size is only slightly smaller than that variable. This is a noteworthy result to find that while we might expect only urbanization to affect water and environmental well-being, the Syndrome has a significant and almost as large of an impact. The sign of the Syndrome coefficient is in the predicted direction (negative, meaning the higher/worse the Syndrome score, the worse the water and environmental well-being).

We additionally find that countries that have never been colonized have better water and environmental well-being scores. We also find that countries with higher levels of Ethnic Fractionalization have lower levels of water and environmental well-being, suggesting that the more a country is fractionalized, the less it will focus on treating and sanitizing its water and their environmental well-being, on average.

In further analysis, we note the correlation between the Syndrome and the Water and Environmental Well-Being is a very strong $-.783$ ($p < .0001$), as shown in the scatterplot in figure 7.9.1. The lowest scores for Water and Environmental Well-Being are found only for countries with worse Syndrome scores. Additionally, although some outliers with higher scores appear in the upper-right quadrant, we find that only countries with the best Syndrome scores achieve the highest levels of Water and Environmental Well-Being. The six outliers in the upper-right quadrant include the United Arab Emirates, Qatar, Bahrain, Kuwait, Lebanon, and Saudi Arabia. The outlier in the lower-left quadrant is Mongolia, with a Syndrome score of 3 and a Water and Environmental Well-Being score of -2.2.

Because the Syndrome is significant in the general linear regression model, we also ran a logistic regression model (using a binary version of the response variable). The Syndrome and Urbanization are the only variables that are significant in predicting the logits or predicted probabilities of worse water and environmental well-being. We specifically find that for every one unit increase in the Syndrome, the odds increase by 55 percent, or alternatively, the risk is 1.55 times greater that the country experiences worse water and environmental well-being, after holding all other control variables constant.

We performed two ancillary analyses using the Environmental Performance Index by itself and also Air Quality. The GLM analyses yield high adjusted R-squared values of .639 and .411, respectively, and the Syndrome is a significant predictor of both outcome variables.

9.2 Air Pollution Factor (Without Outlier)

(This factor combines two variables: Household Indoor Air Pollution Attributable Deaths and Greenhouse Gases; higher scores are considered worse.) We identified an extreme outlier in the data, the Central African Republic (score of 13.07), and thus we present the model with that one outlier removed.

The adjusted R-squared is a strong .587, indicating that the specified model explained at least 58.7 percent of the variability of this factor without the outlier, which was much higher than the adjusted R-squared with the outlier. We find that Patrilineal/Fraternal Syndrome and Urbanization are both significant in this model. See appendix III, table AIII.7.9.2, for full results. We note that the Syndrome has a smaller effect size compared with Urbanization in this model. We are again impressed that the Syndrome is significantly associated with air quality even when controlling for a country's level of urbanization. We find that the sign of the Syndrome coefficient is in the predicted direction (positive, meaning the worse the Syndrome score, the worse the air pollution).

We further note that the direction of the coefficient for Urbanization is negative, which indicates that as the level of urbanization increases, a country's air

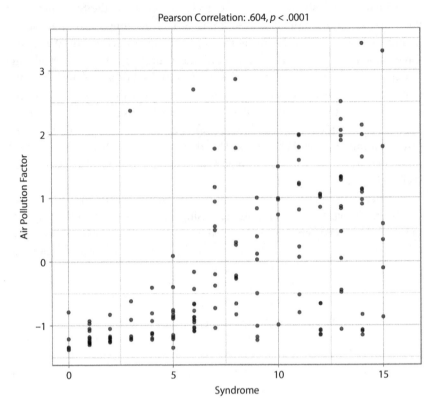

FIGURE 7.9.2 Scatterplot of Syndrome with Air Pollution Factor

pollution decreases on average. This finding is counterintuitive, but it may indicate diminished use of wood-burning stoves in more urbanized environments.

In further analysis, we note the correlation between the Syndrome and the Air Pollution Factor (when the outlier is removed) is a moderately strong .604 ($p < .0001$) as shown in the scatterplot in figure 7.9.2. The slope in the scatterplot is not very steep, but we do find that only countries with the worst Syndrome scores have the highest (worst) values for the Air Pollution Factor.

Because the Syndrome is significant in the general linear regression model, we also ran a logistic regression model (using a binary version of the response variable). The Syndrome and Urbanization are the only variables that are significant in predicting the logits or predicted probabilities of higher levels of air pollution. We specifically find that for every one unit increase in the Syndrome, the odds increase by 39 percent, or alternatively, the risk is 1.39 times greater that the country experiences higher levels of air pollution, after holding all other control variables constant.

We use Outdoor Air Pollution Attributable Deaths as an ancillary variable and the analysis yields an adjusted R-squared value of .383. The Syndrome is also a significant predictor for this outcome variable.

9.3 Biodiversity and Pest Regulation Factor

(This factor combines two variables: Biodiversity and Pesticide Regulation. Lower scores are considered worse.)

The adjusted R-squared is a moderate .207, indicating that the specified model explained at least 20.7 percent of the variability of this factor. We find that Patrilineal/Fraternal Syndrome is the only significant variable in this model, and has the largest effect size. See appendix III, table AIII.7.9.3, for full results. The sign of the Syndrome coefficient is in the predicted direction (negative, meaning the worst the Syndrome score, the lower the pest regulation and biodiversity in a country), corroborating our hypothesis.

In further analysis, we note the moderately strong correlation between the Syndrome and the Biodiversity and Pest Regulation factor ($r = -.482, p < .0001$) as shown in the scatterplot in figure 7.9.3. We find that the worst scores for

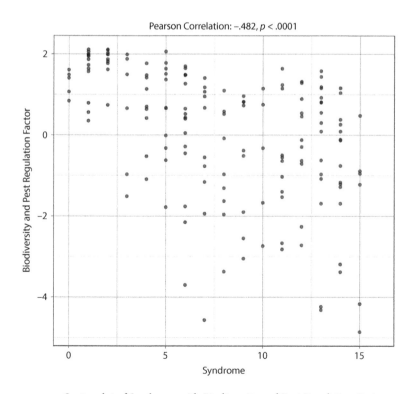

FIGURE 7.9.3 Scatterplot of Syndrome with Biodiversity and Pest Regulation Factor

the factor are found only in countries with worse (higher) Syndrome scores. Additionally, we find that only countries with the best Syndrome scores achieve the highest levels of biodiversity and pest regulation. Because the Syndrome is significant in the general linear regression model, we also ran a logistic regression model (using a binary version of the response variable). Because the model does not meet the validity requirements, we do not report the results.

9.4 Global Climate Risk Index
(Higher scores are considered worse.)

The GLM results for this variable yielded a very low adjusted R-squared value of .022 with no significant terms so we do not report the results. Climate risk may be due to factors whose origins lie outside of the nation-state's control.

Concluding Discussion for the Environmental Protection Dimension

The Patrilineal/Fraternal Syndrome is a significant predictor variable in six of the seven analyses performed (this tally includes the subanalysis of the Air Pollution Factor without the one outlier). In four of those six analyses, the Syndrome is either the only significant determinant of the dependent variable or it has the largest effect size. In the other two models, we find that Urbanization has the strongest effect size, which is expected for environmental indicators. We find, however, that even in these two analyses, the Syndrome's effect size is only slightly smaller than Urbanization. The outcome variables for which the Syndrome was the only significant predictor or had the largest effect size included the following:

- Biodiversity and Pest Regulation factor
- Outdoor Air Pollution Attributable Deaths
- Air Quality

The outcome variables for which Syndrome was significant, and its effect size was only slightly smaller than Urbanization included the following:

- Water and Environmental Well-Being Factor
- Air Pollution Factor (Without Outlier)

These are noteworthy results. A wide variety of environmental indicators appear to be significantly determined by the degree to which the Patrilineal/Fraternal Syndrome is encoded within the behavior of the society. These results are especially interesting because Syndrome is still significant when Urbanization, which we might expect to better explain environmental factors, is controlled for. These results are consistent with our hypothesis—that is, that countries that care more for their women take better care of their environment. The concern for those who Manne calls "the givers"—women—appears to extend to another female-coded "giver," Mother Earth.[46]

Overall Conclusion

These results raise several interesting points. First and foremost, the Syndrome matters, and it matters greatly—the Syndrome emerges as a consistent and useful predictor of national outcome measures. The Syndrome was significant in 87 out of the 122 general linear model analyses run (71.3 percent). More specifically, the Syndrome is significant for fifteen out of sixteen (93.8 percent) Political Stability and Governance analyses, fifteen out of twenty (75 percent) Security and Conflict analyses, ten out of sixteen (62.5 percent) Economic Performance analyses, one out of six (16.7 percent) Economic Rentierism analyses, seventeen out of twenty-four (70.8 percent) Health and Well-Being analyses, five out of seven (71.4 percent) Demographic Security analyses, six out of ten (60 percent) Education analyses, twelve out of sixteen (75 percent) Social Progress analyses, and six out of seven (85.7 percent) Environmental Protection analyses. Typically, in these models, the Syndrome also displayed the largest or second-largest effect size.

Furthermore, the odds ratios calculated from these analyses are well worth considering, and we present a summary table (table 7.10) of those analyses for which the Syndrome was significant in multivariate modeling and for which the model conditions for logistic regression were met.

These numbers are illuminating. If a collective chooses a first, sexual political order based on the subordination of women to build up male-bonded kin networks as its preferred security provision mechanism, it will face a wide range of increasing probabilities of poor outcomes. For example, if women are subordinated through the Syndrome's components, the collective will face 80 percent higher odds for hunger for every step up the Syndrome scale it goes, 66 percent increased odds for underweight children for every step, 41 percent increased odds for autocracy for every step, 50 percent increased odds for lower GDP for every step, 113 percent increased odds for state fragility for every step, 57 percent increased odds of political violence and terrorism for every step, 55 percent increased odds for poorer environmental quality for every step, 92 percent increased risk for high fertility for every step, 45 percent increased risk of national unhappiness for every step, and 253 percent increased odds of poor government effectiveness for every step. It is almost as if in choosing male-bonded kin networks as a security provision mechanism with its accompanying subordination of women, a collective chooses to curse itself.

TABLE 7.10 Syndrome Odds Ratio and Percentage for Performing Poorly from the Logistic Regression Results for Each Variable for Which the Syndrome Was Significant in the GLM Analysis

Dimension	Variable/Factor	Syndrome Odds Ratio (_ times higher risk of performing poorly for each unit increase in the Syndrome, holding all other control variables constant)	Percentage Increase (_% increase in the odds of performing poorly for each unit increase in the Syndrome, holding all other control variables constant)
Political Stability and Governance	Government System and Effectiveness Factor	3.53** the risk of performing poorly on this measure for each 1 point increase in Syndrome score	253% the odds of performing poorly on this measure for each 1 point increase in Syndrome score
	Security, Stability, and Legitimacy Factor	1.43**	43%
	Lack of Freedom Factor	1.49**	49%
	Civil Liberties	1.56**	56%
	Regime Types (risk for autocracy)	1.41**	41%
	Freedom to Establish Religion	1.26*	26%
	Private Property Rights	1.46**	46%
	Fragile States Index	2.13**	113%
	World Bank Corruption	1.23*	23%
	World Bank Rule of Law	1.22*	22%
	Percent of Seats in Parliament Held by Women	Syndrome is significantly related, but model assumptions for logistic regression not met, so odds cannot be calculated. (MANM)	Syndrome is significantly related, but model assumptions for logistic regression not met, so the percentage increase in odds cannot be calculated. (MANM)
	Government Participation of Women	MANM	MANM

TABLE 7.10 (*continued*)

Security and Conflict	Violence and Instability Factor	1.46**	46%
	Political Stability and Absence of Violence/ Terrorism and Freedom of Domestic Movement Factor	1.57**	57%
	Terrorism Injury and Violent Conflict Factor	1.38**	38%
	Terrorism Incidents and Internal Conflict Factor	1.28*	28%
	Societal Violence Scale	1.26*	26%
	Disappearances	1.35**	35%
	Political Terror Scale	1.42**	42%
	Trafficking of Women	1.41**	41%
	Military Expenditures and Weapons Importation Factor	MANM	MANM
	Access to Weapons	MANM	MANM
	Perceptions of Criminality	MANM	MANM
	Monopoly on the Use of Force	MANM	MANM
	Terrorism Impact	MANM	MANM
	Global Terror Index	MANM	MANM
Economic Performance	Wealth Infrastructure and Economic Freedom Factor	1.55**	55%
	Reliance on Agriculture and Lack of Prosperity Factor	1.49**	49%
	Poverty and Economic Decline	1.40**	40%
	Global Competitiveness Index Rankings	1.26*	26%
	GDP per Capita PPP (log transformed)	1.31*	31%
	GDP per Capita PPP (log transformed) (Without Urbanization)	1.50**	50%
	Economic Inequality Factor	MANM	MANM
	Female Labor Force Participation	MANM	MANM
	Food Security	MANM	MANM

(*continued*)

TABLE 7.10 (*continued*)

Dimension	Variable/Factor	Syndrome Odds Ratio (_ times higher <u>risk of performing poorly</u> for each unit increase in the Syndrome, holding all other control variables constant)	Percentage Increase (_% increase in the <u>odds of performing poorly</u> for each unit increase in the Syndrome, holding all other control variables constant)
Economic Rentierism	Natural Resources as Percentage of GDP	1.18*	18%
Health and Well-Being	Preventable Death Factor	1.83**	83%
	Health Care Access Factor	1.48**	48%
	Illness and Mortality Factor	1.29**	29%
	Deaths Due to Diarrhea of Children Under Five	1.49**	49%
	Maternal Mortality Rate	1.48**	48%
	Health Expenditure per Capita	1.70**	70%
	Health Expenditure as Percentage of GDP	1.22*	22%
	Percentage of Pregnant Women Receiving Prenatal Care	1.35*	35%
	Total Alcohol Consumption per Capita	0.63**	37% (less likely to have high alcohol consumption)
	Sustainable Society Index Human Well-Being	1.81**	81%
	Percentage Under Five Who Are Stunted	1.49**	49%
	Prevalence of Wasting—Percentage Under Five	1.35*	35%
	Percentage Under 5 Who Are Underweight	1.66**	66%
	Prevalence of HIV Among Women Ages Fifteen and Over	1.58**	58%
	Global Hunger Index	1.80**	80%
	Life Expectancy at Birth for Females	1.48**	48%
	Female Genital Cutting/ Mutilation	1.76**	76%

TABLE 7.10 (*continued*)

Demographic Security	Youth Risk Factor	1.68**	68%
	Total Fertility Rate	1.92**	92%
	Demographic Pressure	1.39**	39%
	Mother's Mean Age at First Birth	1.62**	62%
	Contraceptive Prevalence	1.32**	32%
Education of the Population	Survival Rate to the Last Year of Primary School	1.31**	31%
	Average Years of Schooling	1.57**	57%
	Access to Basic Knowledge	1.66**	66%
	Access to Information and Communications	1.28*	28%
	Female Literacy Rate Ages Fifteen to Twenty-Four	2.26**	126%
	Overall Literacy Males and Females	1.45**	45%
Social Progress	Human Development Index	1.66**	66%
	Social Safety Nets	1.40**	40%
	Percentage of Pensionable-Age Persons Receiving Social Security or Pensions	1.86**	86%
	Discrimination and Violence Against Minorities	1.16	16%
	Religious Tolerance	1.16	16%
	Happiness Index	1.45**	45%
	Percent of Population with Access to Electricity	1.35**	35%
	Legal Declaration of Gender Equality	1.69**	69%
	Hofstede Individualism	1.35*	35%
	Gender Gap Index	1.55**	55%
	Gender Inequality Index	1.81**	81%
	Government Framework for Gender Equality	MANM	MANM
	Discrimination and Violence Against Minorities	Significant in multivariate modeling, but not logistic regression	Significant in multivariate modeling, but not logistic regression
	Religious Tolerance	Significant in multivariate modeling, but not logistic regression	Significant in multivariate modeling, but not logistic regression

(*continued*)

TABLE 7.10 (*continued*)

Dimension	Variable/Factor	Syndrome Odds Ratio (_ times higher risk of performing poorly for each unit increase in the Syndrome, holding all other control variables constant)	Percentage Increase (_% increase in the odds of performing poorly for each unit increase in the Syndrome, holding all other control variables constant)
Environmental Protection	Water and Environmental Well-Being factor	1.55*	55%
	Air Pollution Factor (Without Outlier)	1.39*	39%
	Outdoor Air Pollution Attributable Deaths	1.42**	42%
	Air Quality	1.39**	39%
	Biodiversity and Pest Regulation factor	MANM	MANM

**Syndrome is significant at 0.001

*Syndrome is significant at 0.01

Note: MANM, model assumptions were not met. Some variables did not meet the model assumptions, which means that there is significant relationship in multivariate modeling, but because the model assumptions of logistic regression were not met, no odds or risk could be computed. GDP, gross domestic product; PPP, purchasing power parity.

The findings are so strong that we wonder why these multidimensional linkages between poor national outcomes and women's subordination at the household level are not square one in both policy and scholarly conversations about national and international security. The Syndrome is the natural starting point for understanding outstanding differences in national stability, resilience, security, health, wealth, and well-being. As McDermott puts it, "If these findings were about something not related to women, chances are that they would be treated as revolutionary in international relations theory; indeed, the effects are much stronger than those supporting the notion of the democratic peace that has spawned an entire cottage industry of inquiry. I leave it to the reader to ponder why powerful effects regarding the treatment of women on the health and security of states do not receive such extensive attention."[47] That is a question well worth pondering, indeed.

Second, it is important to consider which control variables were significantly related to the outcome measures in addition to the Syndrome. Of the models for which the Syndrome was significant, Urbanization was the next most significant predictor followed by Ethnic Fractionalization, Number of Land Neighbors, and Muslim Civilization. The only variable that was never significant in these models was Hindu/Sinic/Buddhist Civilization, and Western Civilization was only significant in one model. As noted in part I, civilizational identity is not the engine of these poor results; it is the subordination of women at the household level that should draw our attention, instead. These findings tell us that Urbanization is clearly one important path to the amelioration of at least some components of the Syndrome, such as patrilocal marriage, whereas Ethnic Fractionalization and Number of Land Neighbors may represent societal stressors that synergize with and exacerbate the effects of Syndrome practices that subordinate women to their male-bonded kin/identity networks.

Third, it is also significant that the variability in outcome measures for high-Syndrome-scoring countries is much larger than for low-Syndrome-scoring countries. Sociologist Christine Bose has found a similar phenomenon, noting large variation for outcomes such as maternal mortality, adolescent fertility rates, female labor force participation, secondary education, and literacy ratios among societies that rank lower on measures of women's empowerment.[48] The megaphone pattern of some of our scatterplots indicates that low-Syndrome countries have consistent "good" outcomes as measured by the security of the state and well-being of its citizens and environment. In contrast, high-Syndrome countries have a comparatively wide range of results, with most of these countries tending toward "bad" outcomes for the state, the people, and the environment.

Why this variation? Although a low Syndrome score appears to be "protective" of national outcomes, high-Syndrome countries operate without such protection. Even so, the potential for worse outcomes among high-Syndrome-encoding nations might be mitigated by a country's wealth and natural resources. For example, a number of oil-rich countries in the Middle East have high Syndrome scores, but they also have some excellent outcomes in areas such as literacy and maternal mortality, and these excellent outcomes have been made possible by their remarkably high level of wealth. Should those extraordinary factors fade, however, we would expect a regression toward more typical (i.e., worse) high-Syndrome-score national outcomes. We identified the countries in our sample that had better-than-expected national outcomes given their relatively high Syndrome scores (see appendix V for details). These included Bahrain, Jordan, Kuwait, Malaysia, Oman, Qatar, Saudi Arabia, and the United Arab Emirates, but also, interestingly, Botswana. In future work, we would like to explore how a country like Botswana achieved such unusual national outcomes given its relatively high Syndrome score of 11. Social psychologist Khandis Blake suggests, for example, that Botswana has an unusually high rate of male labor migration and, as a result, there is less opportunity for patrilocality and many households are, perforce, female-headed households.[49] This deserves more in-depth investigation.

Our results show that when there is strong emphasis placed on the subordination of women at the household level via the Patrilineal/Fraternal Syndrome's components due to reliance on male-bonded kin groups or clans for security, that societal choice is strongly associated with instability and insecurity, environmental degradation, low levels of well-being and prosperity for its citizens, poor governance and autocracy, and many other negative outcomes at the state level in aggregate statistical testing. Deepening that associational analysis, in previous chapters we have traced the causal mechanisms linking these variables, providing a clearer understanding of why these negative national outcomes obtain. But perhaps even more important, our results suggest that disruption of the Syndrome's mechanisms might provide a path to greater stability and security for nations and the international system.

Is such change possible? Has it ever successfully happened before, and what have been the results? Have such attempts ever failed before, and if so, why did they fail? And what lessons for today might we derive? In part III, we turn to these important questions.

PART III

CHANGE

CHAPTER 8

CHANGE

Historical Successes and Failures

To understand the fate of families, and that of kingdoms as well, it will no longer do to exclude the female portion of humankind.

—Mary Hartman

When we step back and examine the consequences of relying on a patrilineal/fraternal system for security provision, we cannot help but notice the dysfunctionality created by that choice. Malcolm Potts and Thomas Hayden put it best:

Warfare, terrorism, and their attendant horrors are based on just this sort of inherited predisposition for team aggression which, whatever its origins, has become a horribly costly and counterproductive behavior in the modern world . . . The original survival advantage enjoyed by individual males with a predisposition for team aggression has long since been replaced by a major, verging on suicidal, disadvantage for our species as a whole . . . To a very large extent . . . *the natural tendencies of men are not consistent with the survival and well-being of their sexual partners, their children, and future generations to come.* [emphasis added][1]

But all is not set in stone. Though we outline the Patrilineal/Fraternal Syndrome as a self-reinforcing phenomenon, and though 120 of the 176 nations in our dataset encode the Syndrome to a greater or lesser degree, it is also true that 56 other societies have rejected many of the Syndrome's component parts. In other words, across the world's countries, there is a true spectrum of greater or lesser expression of the Syndrome.

The enabling factor that catalyzes the Syndrome—sexual dimorphism in upper-body strength enabling physical coercion of almost every woman by almost every man—likely will remain unchanged. This suggests that even in societies in which women have many rights, levels of domestic violence and intimate partner violence may continue to be relatively high. For example, Sweden, which is seen as a bastion of gender equality in the West, has one of the highest rates of domestic violence in Europe.[2] Violence against women is endemic in our own country, the United States. Yet by no stretch of the imagination could one claim that either Sweden or the United States is a patrilineal culture today, although fraternal mind-sets may still be present. This suggests there will always be a reservoir from which the Syndrome might well resurge in any society, and that reservoir is violence against women.[3] Vigilance, even in Post-Syndrome societies, therefore is warranted.

In this chapter, we focus primarily on those 120 nations in which the Syndrome remains encoded to a greater or lesser degree. When a society has relied for so long on the patrilineal/fraternal order for its security, how can it transition beyond such reliance? We know it is possible to build societies that are not founded on patrilineality for, as noted, 56 nation-states have arguably moved beyond that security provision mechanism. As Richard Wrangham and Dale Peterson note,

> Patriarchy is not inevitable, . . . Patriarchy emerged not as a direct mapping of genes onto behavior, but out of the particular strategies that men [and women] invent for achieving their emotional goals. And the strategies are highly flexible, as every different culture shows . . . People have long known such things intuitively and so have built civilizations with laws and justice, diplomacy and mediation, ideally keeping always a step ahead of the old demonic principles.[4]

Even before the rise of the modern state, rulers faced with the task of uniting a patchwork of clans have tried, some successfully but all too briefly, to overcome the resulting violent instability. Genghis Khan was one such ruler. Plagued by conflicts among the lineages that had sworn loyalty to him, he attempted to develop a new form of fraternal alliance, one based not on blood, but on loyalty to him as a ruler. Anthropologist Jack Weatherford describes how, by assigning warriors into non-kin groups of ten, Genghis Khan created the building blocks to unify men under a non-kin-related organizing principle.

They were ordered to live and fight together as loyally as brothers; in the ultimate affirmation of kinship, no one of them could ever leave the other behind in battle as a captive . . . By forcing them into new units that no man could desert or change, under penalty of death, he broke the power of the old-system lineages, clans, tribes, and ethnic identities. . . . In the new organization, all people belonged to the same bone [clan]. . . . All of his followers were now one united people.[5]

Likewise, near the beginning of the sixth century BCE, Cleisthenes abolished the clans and assigned everyone to ten units of ten to create the Athenian city-state, which is why he is called "the father of Athenian democracy." Similarly, Muhammad organized his new religion of Islam along a hierarchy of faith and ethical actions rather than kinship, an initiative that the highly tribal Arabs quickly undermined within the next generation.[6] It is remarkable that even at these early time points in human history, the destabilizing tendencies of male-bonded extended kin groups not only were recognized by leaders but also were the subject of innovative and even radical policy initiatives to offset these tendencies. Given that the culture of these time periods was steeped in the Patrilineal/Fraternal Syndrome, such efforts lasted only as long as their charismatic leaders did, before relapsing into the status quo ante.

A key question for those who see a linkage between the sexual political order and the societal political order, then, is to suggest *how* societies manage to more or less permanently cast aside the Syndrome and its shackles. It would appear that stable, secure states are those that have somehow broken the power of agnatic lineages, relying on other sources for the provision of security. Clans can support a state if it is in their interest to do so, as we have seen, but that state will still tend toward instability and insecurity. Furthermore, insecurity can also increase the power of clans, such as in the context of an enemy invasion or endemic economic shortages in which kin network mobilization can be swift. A two-way street of causality exists here, as with most social phenomena, between reliance on male-bonded extended kin networks as a security provision mechanism and instability/insecurity. Nevertheless, breaking the power of the clans is clearly associated with increased levels of security and stability, as our empirical analysis and the historical record show, and thus is to be sought. But how is this done?

Scholars studying clans have traditionally explored pathways that emphasize the rule of law, a more equitable distribution of wealth, a robust market economy that obviates the need for special access networks, and a commitment to affiliation above clan levels, such as that which might be provided by a religious community (e.g., the *umma*).[7] For example, Kathleen Collins suggests that "a growing market economy and dispersed wealth will more likely prevent the centralization of wealth under authoritarian leaders and their clan and patronage networks, thereby transforming clan politics and stabilizing these regimes."[8] This analysis, however, begs the questions of how to move from point A to point B. After all, powerful clans in control of the state apparatus will not be able to create the conditions Collins specifies nor are they predisposed to do so. Collins herself admits that "clan politics becomes self-reinforcing; it is a vicious cycle difficult to end."[9] Mark Weiner, too, contrasts "status" societies (in which the position in the kin network determines one's fate) and "contract societies" (in which the individual stands solo under rule of law), and asks the pivotal questions, "How do societies move from Status to Contract? How do peoples governed by the rule of the clan transform into nations guided by the liberal rule of law? How can reformers within clan societies build states that treat individuals as worthy in themselves, as citizens, rather than as members of their kin groups, as cousins?"[10]

Weiner considers it a puzzle how "the 'progressive' societies of the world had been set on their course from Status to Contract through an internal force," and wonders whether "an important social choice [had been] made in the ancient past, or a unique accident of history."[11]

Our research may be of assistance. Our findings suggest that one important key to this puzzle is the degree of female subordination in marriage through the components of the Patrilineal/Fraternal Syndrome. As David Jacobson asserts, "The focal point is women's status and sexuality. We will elicit much through the lens of gender, not just about women as such, but about attitudes towards civic tolerance and governance more broadly."[12] We agree. It is female subordination at the household level—brought about by such mechanisms as early marriage for girls, prevalent polygyny, patrilocality, patrilineal monopoly of household assets, and endogamy—that reproduces the exclusivity neces-sary to perpetuate male-bonded extended kin network influence and salience within a society.

If so, might one pathway to diluting the dysfunctional influence of agnatic clans then be to ameliorate female subordination in marriage? Two vastly different historical tales can be told: one hopeful, and one far less hopeful. We start with the hopeful tale first, by highlighting the work of several scholars, including Jack Goody, John Hajnal, Mary Hartman, Francis Fukuyama, and others, who have all examined the successful divergence of northwestern Europe from the Syndrome pattern.

The Anomalous Path Taken in Northwestern Europe

Northwestern Europe was arguably the first region to successfully suppress its powerful agnatic lineages. Jack Goody points primarily to changes in marriage and inheritance law consolidated during the time of Pope Gregory I in the early seventh century with catalyzing real change, commenting, "Europe began to differ substantially from Asia and from the surrounding Mediterranean when it adopted Christianity with its very specific selection of new norms . . . The effects of these specific norms and general pressures ran against the strategies of heirship that Eurasian families had used to continue their lines and to prolong the association between kin and property which preserved their hierarchical status."[13]

Roman society, within which Christianity emerged during this era, embraced many elements of the Syndrome, including close kin marriage and other practices. But by the time of Pope Gregory at the end of the sixth century CE, a revolution in marriage law took place, in which close kin marriage, levirate marriage of kin widows, forced marriage, polygyny, divorce, concubinage, inheritance by illegitimate children, disinheritance of widows, bans on remarriage of widows, and even adoption all were forbidden in an astounding historical first. These changes had been in the making for some time, but they solidified under Pope Gregory. For example, as far back as 460 CE, Saint Albin was excommunicating those who married cousins, a common practice in countries encoding the Patrilineal/Fraternal Syndrome. Goody explains the rationale behind this stringent punishment:

> Close kinship marriages can be seen as consolidating the wider relationships between kin, especially within kin groups. The church was concerned to weaken these wider ties, whether of clanship or of kinship, lest they threaten its increasing control of the population and its power to acquire bequests from them. Marrying cousins and other kin can do both of these, for it can keep family and property firmly together rather than dispersing ties and goods more widely.[14]

By the time of Charlemagne at the end of the eighth century CE, close kin marriage merited not only excommunication but also confiscation of property—that is, bringing about the very opposite of the reason for endogamy's existence.[15]

Note that the practices being banned in this historical time period are at the heart of Patrilineal/Fraternal Syndrome: close kin marriage, levirate marriage of kin widows, forced marriage, polygyny, asymmetrical rights to divorce, concubinage, inheritance by illegitimate children, disinheritance of widows, bans on widow remarriage outside the dead husband's kin group, and adoption were all strategies undertaken to benefit the patriline and agnatic kin above all else. The prohibition of these practices thus constituted stunning changes that proved profoundly significant for Europe's path. Just consider that by the mid-twelfth century, women no longer had to obtain parental consent to marry.[16] The Church was openly attempting to prise marriage away from kin hands;

Goody notes that the Church "turned marriage into a private affair, 'voluntary and not forced.' The nuclear family was stressed . . . [which contributed] to the emergence of a Western type of individualism and privatization of social relations parallel to what the Church was advocating."[17] The prohibition of polygyny may have been especially critical. Potts and Hayden goes so far as to say, "For all the wrong ideas and destructive traditions of medieval Christianity, its theologians did at least outlaw polygamy. And this has had profound and positive effects. Indeed, without the Christian teaching on monogamy, Western civilization might not have emerged in its current form."[18] Given polygyny's devastating effects on stability, human capital investment, and economic performance, this was a critical move.

The totality of these changes in northwestern Europe from the sixth to thirteenth centuries went far beyond polygyny, however. As economist Avner Greif notes, "The actions of the church caused the nuclear family—consisting of a husband and wife, children, and sometimes a handful of close relatives—to dominate Europe by the late medieval period. The medieval church instituted marriage laws and practices that undermined kinship groups," leading to the rise of corporations such as guilds and fraternities to provide the social safety nets "that were alternatives to those provided by kinship groups, enabl[ing] individuals to take risks and make other economic decisions without interference by members of such groups."[19]

Greif highlights the role of such "corporations" in preparing the ground for the rise of democracy in Western Europe (as well as Europe's global economic ascendancy), in "foster[ing] the beliefs and norms that justify and support self-governance, the rule of law, the legitimacy of majority rule, respect for minority rights, individualism, and trust among non-kin."[20] Weiner concurs, noting, "Among the pagan Anglo-Saxons, as among all stateless peoples, law was inseparable from the customs and the interests of the extended family group of the tribe. Christianity introduced a universal set of norms by which rulers were meant to abide—what today we know as the rule of law [which also] made it possible to imagine a common public."[21] We would assert that the prior undermining of kinship structures—and women's place in those structures—deserves as much or more attention than corporations. After all, the first "non-kin" that men must learn to live and cooperate with in a patrilineal society are typically their wives.

The dynamics of this change must be understood more fully. Goody poses the natural question: "Why should the Christian Church institute a whole set of new patterns of behavior in the sphere of kinship and marriage, when these ran contrary to the customs of the inhabitants they had come to convert, contrary to the Roman heritage upon which they drew, and contrary to the teaching of their sacred texts?"[22]

Goody's answer is that the crux was the disposition of inheritances. The early Church forbade the kin of a widow's husband from marrying her;

forbade adoption of a son or the taking of another wife (through divorce[23] or polygyny) in case a first wife produced no male heir; and forbade bastards from inheriting at all. By Goody's calculations, this would leave up to 40 percent of families in early European society with no immediate male heirs. Why would the Church want that to happen? Goody explains, "If [the Church] inhibited the possibilities of a family retaining its property, then they would also facilitate its alienation . . . one of the most profound changes that accompanied the introduction of Christianity [into Europe] was the enormous shift of property from private ownership to the hand of the Church."[24] Furthermore, the Church fiercely defended the right of a widow to inherit her husband's estate—rather than his agnatic kin. Goody comments, "The encouragement of out-marriage in a system that allocated property to women, especially as heiresses, would promote the dispersal of estates and weaken the corporations of kin based upon them . . . their freedom as testators and controllers of their own property was, like continued widowhood and spinsterhood, clearly in the Church's interest."[25]

In other words, the Church strengthened the hand and voice of women within families by opposing certain elements of marriage and inheritance law that disfavored women in patrilineal societies, undermining patrilineal control of both property and women. Goody notes, "The Church's insistence on consent and affection, as well as on the freedom of the testament, meant taking a stand against the power of the heads of households in matters of marriage . . . indeed, against male supremacy, for it asserted the equality of the sexes in concluding the marriage pact."[26] This undercut the power of the old *lignages des freres*, and Francis Fukuyama suggests that only two to three generations passed before a significant weakening of kinship could be felt in Western Europe after various tribes, such as the Anglo-Saxon, German, Norse, and Magyar tribes, converted to Christianity.[27] He notes that Pope Gregory I gave explicit instructions to Augustine about needed changes in marriage and inheritance law before he sent Augustine to convert the pagan king Ethelbert of Britain. Consider that by medieval times, a woman could "inherit and transmit property, as well as bloodlines, and her property could not be stripped from her and taken over by her husband or his kin."[28] For example, when Eleanor of Aquitaine divorced Louis VII of France, she took her territory with her.

Furthermore, Stephanie Coontz notes that old, gendered norms of impunity for men and lack of impunity for women were worn down by women's property and inheritance rights. So, for example, a husband was more likely to put up with adultery by an heiress wife; after all, if she chose to, say, leave him and join a nunnery, not only might her property leave with her, but the Church would probably not allow the husband to remarry to produce a legitimate heir. Women gained the ability to "checkmate" the ambition of men. Indeed, Coontz notes the "queen" in chess, which originally had been the "vizier" in Persia, the game's country of origin, was modeled on these powerful medieval European queens.[29]

Goody opines, "Women became the spearheads in the transformation of domestic structures that Christianity brought about, even if it was the male clerics who in the end benefited most."[30] Remembering that by the mid-twelfth century (except for the elites) in northwestern Europe "women were freed from the necessity of seeking parental consent [in marriage]," Goody concludes that this allowed for greater equality between husband and wife, along with mate choice based on love and not lineage.[31] This was devastating enough, but from the perspective of the patriline, the Church created even more trouble when it insisted that husband and wife be judged by the same standards, such as with regard to adultery, which meant that complete impunity for men would no longer be automatic. Greater equality, greater access to property by women, greater love, and less male impunity created a truly revolutionary mix, to be sure, and, for all intents and purposes, it was mandated by God![32]

Auxiliary customs, such as the introduction of legal wills overseen by ecclesiastical courts and making the estates of bastards open to confiscation by the Church, were also intended to ensure alienability. As Goody puts it, "It does not seem accidental that the Church appears to have condemned the very practices that would have deprived it of property."[33] The Church justified this accumulation of land and wealth by its missions to support the poor and the celibate, but it is noteworthy that over time, the Church became the largest landowner in Europe, holding one-third to one-half of the land in various European countries, including England, France, and what we now know as Germany.

What was unique in the case of historical northwestern Europe, then, was the claim of a divine mandate that superseded all earthly mandates, even those of the government and tribe: "The religion [of western Europe] preached a doctrine of universal equality that ran counter to the hierarchy of an honor-based tribal society."[34] No matter that the Church used this doctrine to change marriage and inheritance law out of economic and political self-interest. In empowering women against their agnatic kin, Fukuyama argues that the Church established the rule of law in Europe in the form of a divine law that was "higher than the will of the current government and that limit[ed] the scope of that government's legislative acts."[35] And, of course, "the growth of the power and legitimacy of European states came to be inseparable from the emergence of the rule of law."[36]

In a very real sense, then, as Fukuyama explains, "Individualism in the family is the foundation of all other individualism."[37] Fukuyama extends his analysis to explain why China does not have the rule of law, and why Russia is experiencing democratic reversals: these societies are still organized on the principle of agnatic lineages.[38] It also suggests that these "veneered" societies—modern states veneered over a social order based on agnatic lineages—will struggle to maintain economic prosperity. Fukuyama adds, "The absence of a strong rule of law is indeed one of the principal reasons why poor countries can't achieve higher rates of growth."[39]

Demographer John Hajnal suggests that an additional factor that led to such a marked divergence from Syndrome characteristics was the unprecedented rise in the age of marriage of women in medieval Europe.[40] Indeed, Hajnal asserts that this anomalous late-marriage system "presumably arose only once in human history,"[41] and he suggests that developments in the older Roman law concerning property ownership in the Dark Ages may have catalyzed the anomaly by incentivizing farmers to keep daughters unmarried later than usual in order to claim larger land holdings based on the size of the household.[42] But once a custom of later marriage among the nonelite arose, a virtuous cycle began that tended to perpetuate the custom and further undercut the various components of the Syndrome.

For example, later marriage for women meant that women and men were age peers in their mid-twenties, and Hajnal notes, "The emotional content of marriage, the relation between the couple and other relatives, the methods of choosing or allocating marriage partners—all this and many other things cannot be the same in a society where a bride is usually a girl of 16 and one in which she is typically a woman of 24."[43] Goody also agrees with Hajnal's analysis, although again his emphasis is on women's property rights rather than their age of marriage, asserting that "the fact that women are heirs to significant property affects the whole nature of the conjugal relationship, leading it in a monogamous direction. With this individualizing form of marriage is associated the concept of "love" . . . [whereas] in polygynous societies, 'love,' in the sense of a preference of one above another, is a dangerous thing."[44] Goody also paints a relevant contrast between the character of monogamous versus polygynous societies. He quotes Eileen Krige as noting, "Polygyny, reinforced by the seg-regation of the sexes in everyday life and interests, renders the personal bond between husband and wife much less intimate . . . Men are unwilling to spend much time in the company of women."[45] That means that something quite deep has changed when men and women assume more equal status within marriage, and the first political order begins to be transformed.

Mary Hartman takes the analyses of Hajnal and Goody one step further, suggesting that as the character of male–female relations changed—that is, as the character of *marriage* changed—the character of the political order, and even the economic order, could not help but change as well.[46] Goody also sees the logic here: "the late marriage age of women, combined with the necessity of accumulating property for their marriage, may have been a significant factor in both the supply and the demand for goods in the early stage of industrialization in western Europe."[47]

In this historically unusual context, this older-age-at-marriage, neolocal (and non-polygynous) marital relationship becomes one of significantly mitigated male structural control over women. In speaking of Holland in the sixteenth and seventeenth centuries, Jacobson notes,

[The Dutch] were known for having the most vigorous economy of the time, essentially capitalist in nature. Travelers from elsewhere in Europe were struck by the participation of women in public and economic life—at least compared to customs in their own countries . . . Women moved about freely and could be seen feasting in taverns . . . Women were also practiced in matters of money. As one Italian visitor, Lodovico Guicciardini commented in 1567, "The women in this country . . . not only go to and forth in town to manage their own affairs, but they travel from town to town through the country, without any company to speak of, and without anybody commenting upon it . . [They] occupy themselves also in buying and selling, and are industrious in affairs that properly belong to men, and that with such an eagerness and skillfulness that in many places, as in Holland and Zeeland, men leave it to women to do everything" . . . By the second half of the seventeenth century, women in the Netherlands were accepted into the same intellectual and cultural circles as men in an unprecedented way.[48]

The Netherlands was not a complete anomaly, either. Fukuyama notes that "Englishwomen had the right to hold and dispose of property freely and sell it to individuals outside the family from a point not long after the Norman Conquest in 1066. Indeed, from at least the thirteenth century, they could not only own land and chattels, they could sue and be sued, and make wills and contracts without permission of a male guardian."[49] Historian Charlotte Stanford has also found that women were active in the building trades in England as far back as the time of Henry VIII, becoming respectable and prosperous businesswomen in their own right—and apparently paid on a par with their male compatriots.[50] Types of employment for these businesswomen included as ironworkers, lime burners, purveyors of wood and other raw materials, and cart and boat haulers.

The development of this pattern and its increasing prevalence indicated that the power of agnatic clans had been mortally weakened. Hartman's work indicates how, at the household level, this took place:

Within households, men came to depend less on their own male blood relatives and more on their wives for livelihood and support, whereas outside households they came increasingly to rely on unrelated men rather than on kin networks. Women, for their part, emerged as more active if not equal partners with their husbands in decision-making within households and also within their local communities. . . . Husbands requiring responsible partners were obliged, however reluctantly, to abandon the image of the irrational and unruly female, and to refashion women's image more closely to their own. . . . the whole society was becoming less, not more, patriarchal, starting at the basic level of the household . . . the unity of kin and property that for thousands of years had been the central focus of most men's worlds began to dissolve.[51]

Notice how pivotal women's rights in marriage are to that old "unity of kin and property," for the kin meant here are, of course, *male* kin. When marriage rights no longer favor men to the degree they once did, that unity—and the economic and political power of the patriline it defines—is seriously diminished. Hartman contends that it was the breaking of this unity of male kin and property that eventually propelled northwestern Europe into capitalism, as the old economy of clan rents was destroyed. Fukuyama concurs: "Capitalism was the consequence rather than the cause of a change in social relationship and custom"[52] and avers that the rise of neolocal marriage by the thirteenth century made it "harder to carry on blood feuds, because the circle of vengeance kept getting smaller."[53] Economist Avner Greif agrees that capitalism arose only as neolocal marriage increased, noting that "the decline of kinship groups in medieval Europe and . . . the resulting nuclear family structure, along with other factors, led to corporations. European economic growth . . . was based on an unprecedented institutional complex of corporations and nuclear families, which still characterizes the West."[54] James Foreman-Peck and Peng Zhou highlight the human capital accumulation that could occur over the generations as later marriage became a norm, given that later marriage is strongly associated with a higher level of literacy.[55] A woman who was literate would become a mother who was capable of greater human capital investment in her children, and this was an indispensable prerequisite of the Industrial Revolution.

Furthermore, neolocal marriage, according to Coontz, offered a template of companionate cooperation across recognized difference:

In cities, as in the countryside, marriage was often a business partnership with far-reaching economic implications . . . In many areas of northwestern Europe, a merchant's wife became her husband's partner in economic activities. She might keep the books for the family business or help out in the shop, act as an agent for her husband in his absence, and carry on her husband's trade after his death. . . . The married couple was thus more prominent in Western Europe than in societies where each partner's first allegiance remained to his or her own kinship group and extended family.[56]

Needless to say, a wife in such a marriage would have far greater bargaining power than in a patrilocal marriage.

Furthermore, given the Church's stricture on endogamy, marrying outside the kin group was found both among the nobility and also the lower classes, leading to a more open social group.[57] This type of marriage, much less tied to the agnatic kin group, diluted kin group resources available to the neolocal couple, requiring a greater emphasis on savings and capital formation.

But capitalism and economic growth are not the only consequences of undermining the subordination of female interests, especially in marriage. Hartman feels that the development of democracy is also directly traceable to the anomalous late-marriage pattern of northwestern Europe. She argues that state power structures are grounded in household power structures—when the latter changes, the former will, too. Hartman describes how marriages in northwestern Europe gradually evolved as "joint enterprises" between husband and wife, in which both parties had to work and save, and thus postponed marriage until there were sufficient resources. These types of marriages, according to Hartman, encouraged individual self-reliance "long before individualism itself became an abstract social and political ideal."[58] This new nature of marriage was to have major ramifications, not just in the social sphere, but also the political sphere:

> A sense of equality of rights was further promoted by such arrangements long before notions of egalitarianism became the popular coin of political movements. These later marriages, forged now through consent by the adult principals, offered themselves as implicit models to the sensibilities of political and religious reformers grappling with questions of authority. Experience in families, which were miniature contract societies unique to northwestern Europe, offers a plausible explanation for popular receptivity to the suggestion that the state itself rests upon a prior and breakable contract with all its members. And if this is so, the influence of family organization on the ways people were coming to conceive and shape the world at large can hardly be exaggerated. The lingering mystery about the origins of a movement of equal rights and individual freedom can be explained. Contrary to notions that these were imported items, it appears that they, along with charity, began at home.[59]

In a sense, Hartman argues that the companionate marriages of the system in which husband and wife were age peers, with neolocal marriage and property rights for wives (and no polygyny), were a training ground for participatory democracy, for she asserts that there are critical "links between household and state power structures."[60] Such marriages radically undermined the power of patrilineal clans and thus enhanced the stability and resilience of these societies. To live domestic parity day in and day out, year after year, in the small collective of the household allowed the majority of individuals in society to appreciate the virtues of voluntary association in larger collectives, including the state.

As Hartman puts it, "More important than [class and religious divisions] for the appearance of equality as a popular political ideal was the shared domestic governance most people had experienced from the Middle Ages."[61] The voluntary nature of late marriage (as opposed to child marriage) was critical to this new social ideal of voluntary association. She explains:

> That ordinary persons ultimately came to perceive the state itself as an entity whose origins and authority rested upon a voluntary compact—one that might be subject to renegotiation or even termination—begins to make more sense within that framework. . . . Everywhere a common denominator was the experience of men and women in partnership households that promoted participatory governance and raised new questions about the legitimate bases of authority inside and outside those households.[62]

In other words, Hartman argues that democracy could not have arrived in northwestern Europe when it did unless the nature of marriage had previously changed and generations of children had been socialized within such households to value participatory government.

Men in northwestern Europe did not start out by applying norms of egalitarian treatment to women, and they would have thought such an idea preposterous or even radical and dangerous. Hartman notes, "Political equality for all, including women, admittedly emerges as a conscious ideal only in the later stages of this new story; but the running theme from the early medieval era is the unpremeditated undercutting of patriarchal power. Men who continued to be the acknowledged senior partner in households were sooner ready to admit formal ideals of equality in their relations with other men than with women, but that is no news."[63]

Far more important, Hartman notes, is that "before equality was widely touted in [the] public realm, there was grounding in daily experience to make that abstraction meaningful and to encourage its application to political rhetoric and action. [Furthermore], the children born into these households were raised on their mother's milk of egalitarianism simply by being socialized in such anomalous families."[64] Just as the Syndrome "is not a prior 'given' of some sort, but rather a constantly reenacted social process,"[65] the birth and socialization of a new type of citizen primed for egalitarian beliefs and practices was being continually reenacted in these nonelite households and thus became self-perpetuating.

Hartman's conclusion is straightforward: "Women's late ages at marriage were nothing less than a necessary precondition for the most critical developments we associate with the era—major religious upheaval, new systems of political authority, and transformed structures of livelihood . . . the stronger currents of change in this period continued to flow from households to the wider society rather than from the wider society back to households."[66]

Indeed, Hartman contends that any society can reap the same rewards if it adopts this different structuring of male–female relationships—there is no "Western genius," she avers:

> One irony here is that long-range planning, risk-taking, personal responsibility, and independence have yet to be recognized as mass behaviors generated by the demands of life in distinctive sorts of households—in other words, as normative conduct required of everyone in late-marriage, weak-family settings. To the contrary, these features have been held up as evidence of a peculiar European genius, a mistaken view that has bolstered many a chauvinist case for the superiority of Western civilization. Since maintaining unstable households, let alone enhancing their assets, quite literally depended upon these qualities, it is hardly surprising that they turned up with some regularity in the humblest households, and in the behavior of women as well as men.[67]

The great key, then, to the breaking of the power of agnatic clans in Europe was to break, at least to a significant degree, the power of men to control women's marriage choices to favor the men's patrilines. The elimination of polygyny, cousin marriage, and forced marriage, in concert with the increasing age of marriage for women and the diminution of patrilocality, proved to be some of the most effective stratagems used against patrilineal power in historical northwestern Europe. Although the Church certainly precipitated many of these changes, Goody notes that the salutary effects of these Church strategies for women were purely "unintentional,"[68] but nonetheless highly effective. Fukuyama adds,

> The relatively high status of women in western Europe was an accidental by-product of the church's self-interest. The church made it difficult for a widow to remarry within the family group so she had to own the property herself. And the women's right to own property spelled the death knell for agnatic lineages by undermining the principle of unilineal descent. These changes had a correspondingly devastating impact on tribal organization throughout western Europe.[69]

Table 8.1 contrasts the two structurations according to Hartman's analysis, which look very much like our own characterization of the Syndrome components.

With Fukuyama, we believe "change in the family" was *the* "facilitative condition for modernization to happen in the first place."[70] Thinking of this proposition in terms of our research, a critical marker that such a transition is possible is clearly an improved situation for women in marriage. Where women's marriage choices are not controlled by men pursuing their agnatic clan's interests, where women's rights within marriage begin to parallel those of men's under

TABLE 8.1 Mary Hartman's Characterization of Traditional and Aberrant Marriage Patterns

Traditional Marriage Pattern	Aberrant Marriage Pattern (arose first among nonelites in northwest Europe)
Gender segregation, seclusion of women	Women not segregated, not secluded; men's and women's lives do not look as different as in traditional marriage
Household is main unit of production, and extended kin are main collaborators	Voluntary associations may be main unit of production, and nonkin and wives may be partners
Hierarchical marriage with honor/shame revolving around women's chastity	Companionate marriage leading to nuclear households
Unity of male kin and land/livestock; cousin marriage to facilitate; little to no property or inheritance rights for women	Breaks link between male kin and land—fortunes are not tied to the land. Women have real property and inheritance rights and are economic agents; no need for cousin marriage
Arranged, universal, patrilocal marriage	Nonarranged, nonuniversal, neolocal marriage
Bride married at puberty (twelve to thirteen years old); grooms in their mid-twenties or even older	Brides married in early to mid-twenties; grooms married in mid-twenties
Female infanticide and neglect; mother–son relationship is the strongest in the family	No female infanticide; mother–daughter relationships blossom
Brideprice/dowry	Reciprocal exchange, usually token, as both brides and grooms bring their own economic assets into the marriage
Eldest son or youngest son stays on the land and serves as parents' eldercare	Daughters may be default eldercare providers
Domestic violence and double standard of marital fidelity	Lower rates of domestic violence and at least a rhetorical stand against double standards of marital fidelity
Polygyny	No polygyny
High fertility	Lower fertility
Hartman's Assessment of Effects: • Lack of innovation/economically stagnant • Accustomed to political hierarchy and inegalitarianism • Lack of sense of personal responsibility for men; male impunity, resulting in no real rule of law • Nonmobile (will not leave land or livestock)	Hartman's Assessment of Effects: • Creative, innovative • Embrace egalitarian ideals in all associations, including the form of state governance • Sense of personal responsibility for men; lower level of male impunity, leading to a more viable rule of law • Mobile

Source: Adapted from Mary Hartman, The Household and the Making of History: A Subversive View of the Western Past (Cambridge: Cambridge University Press, 2004).

the law, and where violence against women by male kin is de-normalized by the state, a tipping point has been reached: *patrilineal governance cannot be perpetuated where women enjoy this status.* Those with the least power under patrilineal clan governance—women—ironically possess the key to the system's entire dismantlement.[71] To lift the curse of insecurity and instability on the nation-state, the nation-state must lift the curse on its women.

When patrilineal governance cannot be perpetuated, a new form of governance can arise. Goody describes this change in the European context in this way, "In general, kin networks seem to have shrunk by the end of the Middle Ages. Central governments now looked after law and order, so that wider kin groups like armed factions tended to become things of the past."[72] Notice Goody is implying that the security provision mechanism of the society has now permanently shifted away from male-bonded extended kin networks to central governments.

Jacobson expresses the same sentiment:

> The idea of a woman imbued with rights, self-determination, and economic freedom is a remarkable global revolution. At base this is a freedom that is expressed through the body. . . . We are well aware of the war and conflict that have ensued from capitalist and democratic revolutions, but we have yet to comprehend in any coherent or systemic way the ripple effects of the unbinding of the woman through the literal and figurative freeing of her body.[73]

The freeing of women is nothing less than the freeing of all mankind from the Syndrome and its pernicious effects. To treat the first "Other" as oneself, fully deserving of respect, voice, and bodily integrity, is arguably the key microfoundation of civility and self-government within a society. Jacobson adds that empathy for the situation of women "is shadowed by a growing empathy for humans more broadly."[74]

The story of historical northwestern Europe instructs us in the most effective strategies to break the reliance on male-bonded extended kin networks as the society's security provision mechanism. What we understand from the analysis of these scholars is that, first and foremost, if Syndrome-style marriage and inheritance practices remain unchanged, the power of these male-bonded networks will remain—no matter whether phenomena such as female literacy, female labor force participation, female representation in government, and other such indicators of women's empowerment are all high.

Other Paths, Other Outcomes

Instructive in this regard are the widely divergent paths taken by Roman Catholic lands and the Byzantine Empire, where what was later characterized as the

Eastern Orthodox Church held ecclesiastical authority. Noting the difference between the Roman Catholic Church's "assault on extended kinship" through changing marriage and inheritance laws versus the lack of any such effort in the Byzantine Empire, Fukuyama opines, "As a result, tightly knit kin communities survived in most lands ruled by Byzantium."[75] The contrast between Byzantium and northwestern Europe is noteworthy: apparently the lesson to be learned is that one cannot veneer rule of law over a society based on male-bonded extended kin networks or patrilineal clans and expect real improvements in societal stability and resilience. Fukuyama elaborates this point:

> Early social organization in China, India, and the Middle East was based on agnatic lineages; the state was created to overcome the limitations imposed by tribal-level societies. In each case, state builders had to figure out how to make individuals loyal to the state rather than to their local kin group. Institutions based on territory and centralized legal authority had to be layered on top of strongly segmentary societies. In *none* of these cases did the top-down state-building effort succeed in abolishing kinship as a basis for local social organizations . . . Europe was very different from these other societies insofar as exit from tribalism was not imposed by rulers from the top down but came about on a social level through rules mandated by the Catholic Church. In Europe alone, state-level institutions did not have to be built on top of tribally organized ones.[76]

The case of Byzantium was mirrored in that of the Soviet Union, which tried to enforce the equality of women in its Central Asian republics by an open attack on the Patrilineal/Fraternal Syndrome in those societies. The Soviets proceeded straightforwardly through outright prohibition of underage marriage, polygyny, and brideprice as well as promulgation of equality in right to divorce and in property rights for women. This was a fascinating social experiment—could the power bases of clans be destroyed by an out-and-out frontal attack by outsiders on the Syndrome mechanisms of female subordination? The Soviets' purpose in this was clear: as Adrienne Edgar notes, "The campaign to emancipate women was in many ways an extension of the campaign to undermine [clan] kinship structures."[77] Rather than centuries of chipping away at the straightjacket of the Syndrome, for the first time in history, a head-on, comprehensive assault on the Syndrome was launched.

The reader will not be surprised to learn that this attempt failed spectacularly, despite Soviet success in increasing levels of women's education, women's labor force participation, and women's political representation. This is important to note: it is perfectly possible to subordinate women at the household level through the Syndrome mechanisms, despite high female education rates, labor force participation, and even parliamentary representation.[78] As we have seen, the real action is the struggle over the mechanisms of subordination at the household level, and it is there that resistance will be fiercest.

The result of Soviet efforts to loosen the Syndrome mechanisms was predictable—the efforts met with stiff resistance and were eventually abandoned. Edgar tells us,

> Of all the activities of the Soviet regime, measures designed to emancipate women and "modernize" [Central Asian] family life aroused the most passion and controversy. Party officials reported that peasants who were passive throughout the conference proceedings, dozing through discussions of village soviet elections and land reform "came alive exactly as if shot from a cannon as soon as the women question came up."[79]

Edgar's recounting of the Soviet attempt to quash brideprice (*galling*) and underage marriage for girls in Turkmenistan is illustrative. Soviets rightly saw that brideprice was a cause of instability; as Edgar notes, "it prevented poor men from marrying, facilitated polygamy among the rich; and perpetuated child marriage by encouraging poor fathers to 'sell' their young daughters for a profit."[80] Yet the abolition of brideprice would become the centerpiece of the conflict between Turkmen and the Soviets:[81]

> Turkmen peasants said bluntly that they regarded bridewealth as compensation for the expense of raising a daughter, who would contribute nothing to her own family's future growth.
>
> As one peasant in Leninsk province defiantly said[,] "If the authorities want to ban *galling*, then let them prepare a place for girls [to live], and we'll send them there from the day of their birth."
>
> [Another said,] "If we have to give them away without *galling*, then our wives will kill their daughters at birth."
>
> [There] were also objections to raising the marriage age for girls to sixteen. As one Turkmen peasant commented, "The authorities want to raise the marriage age for girls to sixteen, but will they give parents the means to support them?"
>
> Poor peasants . . . saw the marriage of a daughter as an opportunity for a financial windfall. As one ethnographer noted, "Every poor man who has daughters looks on them as a unique source of income."
>
> [Another peasant said,] "I have not fed my daughter for nothing, and won't sell her for less than 500 rubles."
>
> [Party officials were of the same mind, saying] "If we don't pay bridewealth, all of us party members are condemned to a bachelor's life. They won't give a single girl to us. We can't practice abduction of girls, since that will cause us to lose our authority among the peasant masses."[82]

As a result of the backlash, the Soviets reversed their position on *galling*, acknowledging the payments would simply be made in secret even if the practices were banned. Thus, despite a serious Soviet effort to punish transgressors with prison time and hard labor, brideprice went underground but remained universal even among party members. Births and marriages went unregistered so that underage marriage and polygyny could not be detected, the threat of intermarriage caused some clan groups to flee the USSR entirely, and the uproar over female divorce rights was so extreme that the Soviets backtracked and judges were instructed to turn down requests from women for divorce. Consider the case of Turkmenistan: because only married men had a right by custom to shares of land and water, it was unthinkable for women to have the right to divorce. Edgar quotes the Turkmen saying: "A husband's death is a wife's divorce." By the early 1930s, the Soviets realized that they were alienating the precise constituency—peasant clans*men*—whose support they needed for governance, and for the most part, they dropped their efforts to liberate Central Asian women.[83] Eurasian expert Gregory Massell reports that local judges in Soviet Central Asia not only would not grant divorces to women, they would not punish perpetrators of domestic violence—or even of honor killings.[84] (Political scientist Sophia Wilson suggests that legacy has continued in the post-Soviet era.[85])

Furthermore, the few legal improvements for married women originated by the Soviets that do remain, including the legal ban on polygyny, are now under active assault in several Central Asian states. In her study of post–Soviet era Uzbekistan, Central Asian expert Elizabeth Constantine notes the age of marriage for girls has fallen, enrollment of girls in schools has decreased, and unemployment rates for women have increased.[86] Indeed, as Edgar writes,

> Because the Soviet state was a multiethnic, universalizing socialist state centered in Moscow, female emancipation and nationalism in Central Asia came to be seen as opposed to each other, instead of forming mutually supportive components of modernity. For many Central Asians, as for many colonized Arabs, women and the family became a sphere that needed to be protected from "foreign" interference, while Islamic and customary marriage and family practices came to be valued as crucial components of "national" identity.[87]

Many commentators noticed the swift withdrawal of women from public life just as soon as these nations became independent of the Soviet Union in the 1990s. This phenomenon was driven not only by nationalism but also by the disappearance of strong institutions along with the emergence of civil conflict and high unemployment rates. With the demise of the Soviet Union, the ancient security provision mechanism of the Syndrome resurged with a vengeance.[88]

It was not only the Soviet Union that tried a frontal assault on the Syndrome. China under Mao also tried to hit the clans hard. Monica Das Gupta describes the first efforts:

A radical effort to destroy lineages was made in Mao's China, to remove their potential for challenging local government. Genealogies and ancestral halls were destroyed, and ancestor worship rituals banned, along with the assembling of large clans or lineages. This was a sea change from the pre-modern effort to promote these practices to administer the country and unify it politically and culturally. Lineage control was replaced with commune control, and the old system of lineages regulating their members was replaced by direct intervention by local cadres in citizens' personal lives. Local cadres were expected to mediate in family disputes, raise consciousness of how women are oppressed in households, address issues like husbands drinking too much, make sure that women participated in the community's political life and resolve familial disputes about caring for old parents.[89]

Similar to the Soviet experience, even while noting that legal reforms have been "powerful tools for disseminating new ideas about gender equality . . . represent[ing] an ideological sea-change,"[90] Das Gupta also notes that after laws were passed in China giving equal inheritance to women, setting minimum marriage ages for girls, and allowing women to divorce,

These laws met deep-seated and violent resistance in China, and resulted in an estimated 70,000 to 80,000 suicides and murders of women between 1950 and 1953. Widespread peasant opposition threatened social and political instability, and the state backed off from implementing these controversial aspects of the law. Further efforts to protect divorced women's rights were made in the 1980 New Marriage Law, and the 1985 Inheritance Law sought to counter gender discrimination in inheritance. In reality, land in China is allocated on the basis of village residence, and residence continues with few exceptions to be determined patrilineally. In the allocation of village land, a daughter's share is deleted on her marriage and a new share is granted for her in her husband's village.[91]

Male-bonded extended kin networks began to make a comeback in China as subsequent Chinese leaders moved back toward household responsibility, rather than communal governance. When the "iron rice bowl," the name for early China's job security and social benefits guarantee, disappeared, male-bonded extended kin networks again became salient. Political scientist Jie Fan and coauthors note:

With the establishment of people's communes in the second half of the 1950s, the traditional clan connections were supposed to be destroyed. With the disbanding of the communes and the return to family economic activities in the 1980s, individuals could not rely on fictitious collectives, but had to rely on family or clan bonds. . . . The weakening of political control has led to a revival of traditional structures (kinship relations, secret societies, clans) that locally have even started to organize themselves politically. All over China there are reports on the new power of clans and on violent and bloody clan fights concerning forests, irrigation, building lots, and borderlines of fields and lanes. In regions where clans dominate the villages, they have frequently taken over local power.[92]

This resurgence predictably encouraged other practices associated with the Syndrome. The one-child policy, for example, was the primary force catalyzing sex-selective abortion and female infanticide after 1978. As business journalist Geoffrey Murray notes,

While the revival of clans began in the early 1980s, they have become larger and much better organized recently. Rural cadres complain that clan activities have siphoned off badly needed funds for agriculture and education. The security departments cited villages in Hunan as having clan units so powerful they had refused to pay taxes or implement family planning measures. At the same time, since only males can join clans, their revival has fuelled families' desires for male children in rural areas.[93]

Given the cautionary tales of Byzantium, the Soviet Union, and China, how is it possible that northwestern Europe was able to sustain a different path? States in northwestern Europe became powerful and prosperous in part because the Church laid the groundwork by asserting a supercessionary religious law that unintentionally empowered women, which in turn broke up agnatic allegiances. This is remarkable, because usually, "religion and kinship are closely connected in tribal societies,"[94] and as noted earlier in this volume, Katherine Young reminds us that "when a religion has a predominantly ethnic base . . . any threat to the family is also a fundamental threat to the religion."[95] In patrilineal clan societies, "God" typically supports the patriline. In contrast, in historical northwestern Europe, "God" *opposed* the patriline (although God did not oppose patriarchy[96]). The success of the Catholic Church instructs us that rule of law starts with real property rights for individuals, which begins with real property rights for *women*—not for their male kin who already hold those rights as part of the patriline. Real property rights for women, in turn, are based on personal status rights for women in marriage, reflected in such indicators as the average age of first marriage for women, the prevalence of patrilocal marriage, inheritance and property rights for women, and the degree to which family law favors male interests.

South Korea's Dismantlement of Patrilineality

In 1990, only five nations had abnormal birth sex ratios favoring male births (see chapter 3); by 2015, however, that number had increased to nineteen countries, which included Christian nations (Armenia), Muslim nations (Azerbaijan), and Confucian/Buddhist societies (Vietnam). In the past seventy years, only one country has moved in the opposite direction, that is, from an abnormal birth sex ratio to a normal birth sex ratio: South Korea. Although South Korea is arguably the most Christian nation in East Asia, barring the Philippines, we believe that it was not religion in the first place that ameliorated the abnormal birth sex ratio there. Das Gupta explains, "South Korea sought to maintain an authoritarian government and traditional gender hierarchies for a long time, but these broke down eventually under strong pressure from civil society . . . modern ideas of individualism, freedom and equality gradually swept away Confucian morality in South Korea."[97] In other words, change came from a concerted effort by the government and civil society actors to dismantle the legal framework encoding patrilineality. That effort is worth examining in some detail, drawing on the work of Andrea Den Boer and Valerie Hudson.[98]

By 1990, South Korea's sex ratio at birth had climbed from a normal ratio just ten years earlier to 116.5 (Korean Statistical Information Service).[99] By 2007, the birth sex ratio was back down to 106.2, well within the normal range. Recent fertility surveys demonstrate that the respondents' desired sex ratio for off-spring has also shifted from a consistently masculine sex ratio (more than one hundred boys per one hundred girls) before 2003 to a feminine sex ratio of 86 in 2012.[100] One South Korean woman with three sons summed up the *volte-face* in this manner: "When I tell people I have three sons and no daughter, they say they are sorry for my misfortune . . . Within a generation, I have turned from the luckiest woman possible to a pitiful mother."[101] Indeed, the change arguably came within *less* than a generation, despite conventional wisdom suggesting such swift social change would be unlikely. How was South Korea able to be so effective in reverting its birth sex ratio, despite the fact that scholars opine South Korea had one of the highest levels of son preference of any human society? After all, as the demographer Daniel Goodkind stated in 1999, "South Korea is well noted for having the strongest son preference in the world."[102]

In a nutshell, the South Korean government, especially its courts, attacked patrilineality at its roots, stripping men of privilege in inheritance, control of assets and children, and even ability to create lineage. Indeed, the South Korean government might be viewed as following in the footsteps of the Catholic Church during Middle Ages. The South Korean case echoes the European one in suggesting that interference in the reproduction of agnatic kin exclusivity by improving the legal situation of women in marriage, particularly if not imposed by perceived "outsiders," has great potential to subvert patrilineality.

Throughout the late 1980s, women's rights nongovernmental organizations (NGOs) were receiving training and support through sessions sponsored by the International Women's Rights Action Watch and the United Nations Development Fund for Women, which enabled them to more effectively challenge issues of gender inequality in the state. The women's rights movement focused its attention on the patrilineal institution of the family register and family law.[103] South Korea's family law revolved around its traditional patrilineal clans and their interests. Women were not considered full members with equal rights in their birth clan, and upon marriage, they were removed from their birth family's clan register yet were not considered members of their husband's clan. Furthermore, the husband could determine unilaterally where the married couple would live, ensuring patrilocality could be practiced. In a sense, then, women were "homeless." As is typical in patrilineal societies, resources were kept fairly strictly within the male line. Early attempts of activists to pressure the government to change family laws were met with extreme opposition—the patriarchal practices of the "head of family" register system called the *hoju* were designed to strengthen family bonds as well as link families to state rule, thus attempts to revise the law were viewed as an attack on state order and state nationalism.[104]

Although women had been granted their first rights of inheritance in 1977, the laws were still fairly unequal in nature. Daughters received only 25 percent of the inheritance that their brothers received, fathers had complete child custody rights in divorce, and division of assets after divorce was highly unequal favoring men. Following state ratification of the Convention on the Elimination of all Forms of Discrimination Against Women (CEDAW) in 1984, global actors supported local NGOs and women's activists in applying pressure to the government to revise family law.[105] Concluding observations from CEDAW, the United Nations Commission on Human Rights and the Committee overseeing the Economic, Social, and Cultural Rights Convention all expressed concerns regarding South Korea's Family Law, urging the state to bring its family law in line with principles of gender equality.[106] In 1989 (and effected beginning in 1991), the first wave of revision to family law began, stemming from lawsuits invoking the Korean Constitution's provision in Article 36(1) that states, "Marriage and family life shall be entered into and sustained on the basis of individual dignity and equality of the sexes, and the State shall do everything in its power to achieve that goal."[107]

The 1991 revisions brought significant changes: the new law asserted that a married couple's domicile had to be decided jointly; it provided that the wife's name would be entered into her husband's family register and his name could be entered into her family's register if he so chose; paternal right to child custody was no longer automatic; and the inheritance shares of daughters and sons would be equal. Although the 1991 revisions struck at the taproot of patrilineality, it is also true that it took several years for people, especially in rural areas, to become aware that the law had changed.[108] Nevertheless, the government continued to revise family law. In 1998, courts for the first time ruled that a child could acquire South Korean nationality through its maternal line. Previously, only the paternal line could bestow citizenship rights.[109]

The most significant changes to the laws upholding patrilineality, however, came at the turn of the century. The Citizens for the Abolition of the Head-of-Family System, an alliance of more than 130 civic groups organized in 2000 by feminist activist Kwang-soon Ko-Eun, campaigned throughout the state to garner support for their demands for revising family law.[110] In 2003, the government revised laws permitting women to head households, and the number of female-headed households began to slowly increase.[111] Interestingly, the majority of married women in a 2003 study, when asked why sons were necessary, replied that sons were needed for psychological satisfaction and family happiness. Only a minority indicated that sons were necessary for main-taining the family line or for retirement or economic reasons.[112] These responses suggest that the patrilineal and material benefits previously associated with sons had declined greatly by 2003—a year that corresponded with a drop in the sex ratio at birth to 108.7. For the first time, this decrease was not followed by a subsequent rise, as seen previously, but rather was followed by a continuous decline until the sex ratio reached normal ratios in 2007.

The civic alliance then brought a law suit against the state claiming that the revised family law was still unconstitutional. In 2005, the unfavorable headship system was eliminated, meaning that women are no longer legally subordinate to the male family head.[113] The Constitutional Court in South Korea declared that the *hoju* system was unconstitutional because it violated the constitutional right to gender equality. In its place would be a new system of family registra-tion, in which every family member would now have his or her own individual record book. In addition, children could use their mother's surname if both parents agreed, and take the surname of a stepfather even without agreement of the biological father. Children of unmarried mothers would be permitted to have their mother's surname. Stepchildren and adopted children would now have full legal and inheritance rights. The right to unilaterally dispose of prop-erty within marriage was eliminated, and the equal right of both spouses to the marital home was asserted. Additionally, in 2005, the government enacted a Framework Act on Healthy Families, which stipulated that the government would promote an equitable family culture.[114]

These changes marked the beginning of other legal gains for women that identified a married woman as a distinct, equal, and autonomous individual. Law enforcement related to domestic violence has been enhanced, for example, followed by a decrease in domestic violence-related arrests.[115] In 2009, a court ruling found marital rape unconstitutional, establishing a precedent in the absence of explicit criminalization by prosecuting cases.[116] A law specifically criminalizing marital rape was later passed in 2013. Although there is room for additional progress, South Korea has continued to march toward the legal protection of women within marriage, severely undercutting patrilineality in the process.

As patrilineality was significantly undermined, so, too, was patrilocal marriage, along with the expectation that one's sons would provide old-age support. Attitudes toward the responsibilities of sons to provide financial and emotional care for elderly parents have been changing rapidly, as the role traditionally held by sons is replaced by the state and by the elderly. This change has been accompanied by a shift from the multigenerational household to the nuclear household. In 1980, 80 percent of the elderly lived with one of their children, but this number has decreased significantly over the years.[117] In 1990, 49.6 percent of those age sixty-five years old and over were living in households with more than three generations, dropping to 30.8 percent in 2000.[118] In rural areas, where multigenerational households were once common, a 2012 survey recorded that only 20.9 percent of the elderly population lived with their offspring.[119] Of particular importance to this discussion of patrilocality is the fact that the number of parents living with the eldest son has declined dramatically. According to a 2014 nationwide Social Survey, 50.2 percent of elderly parents are now supporting themselves, and only 10.1 percent are supported by the eldest son (compared with 46.3 percent self-support and 22.7 percent eldest son support in 2002).[120]

Urbanization has contributed to rapidly changing attitudes toward caring for elderly parents, both from the perspective of the children and from the parents. As Woojin Chung and Monica Das Gupta note, the fact that South Korea is now predominantly urban (80 percent) has undermined traditional patrilineal and patrilocal practices.[121] Daughters no longer move to a patrilocal residence after marriage, and they are just as likely as sons to live near their parents and contribute to their economic support, thus weakening the pattern of eldest sons caring for their parents and reducing the gap between the value of daughters and sons. Urban assets are also transferred more easily to both sons and daughters than rural land, which further affects the valuation of daughters. Urban life also makes it possible for the elderly to work longer and save for their retirement through pensions.[122]

Another interesting factor in the South Korean case is what has *not* changed in terms of gendered expectations. More specifically, sociologist Sung Yong Lee notes that the marriage cost for a groom's family is still three times that incurred by the bride's family, because the groom's family is supposed to procure housing for the new couple as part of the brideprice.[123] This is clearly a legacy of patrilocal marriage, but the patrilineal social structure that made such a large investment rational has crumbled. Indeed, Lee argues that the normalization of South Korea's sex ratios did not come about because the value of daughters has increased in that nation. Rather, he argues that it is explicitly the value of *sons* that has *decreased* so dramatically in the course of a very few years. It is now the case that although parents can no longer expect a son to provide for them in their old age, at the same time, they are currently still required by custom to expend much more money to ensure a son's place in life.[124]

What the South Korean government accomplished, then, was not only the elevation of the status of daughters but also a lowering of the value and privilege assigned to sons. By eliminating all male privilege in inheritance, in lineage formation, and in control of assets—and enforcing this elimination in a nation that is increasingly urban and therefore not as dependent on land—the value of sons has decreased. Furthermore, due to one of the sole remaining legacies of patrilocality (i.e., the patrilineal custom that the groom's family is responsible for finding housing for a new couple), it is now sons and not daughters who are the children upon whom parents lose their money. Furthermore, because daughters and sons now inherit equally, sons are no longer expected to provide for parents in old age to a greater degree than daughters. Many sons now walk away from the intergenerational contract their parents had been counting on. The South Korean government's provision of old age insurance, even though still somewhat unreliable, has lessened reliance on patrilineal groups for individual security.

We stress that these changes in patrilineal laws and practices could not have been accomplished without the pressure applied by civil society actors in South Korea—women's groups, for example, were instrumental in bringing about changes in discriminatory family laws and practices in the state. Their efforts were supported by pressure applied from the international women's rights regime, particularly CEDAW. Urbanization played an important role as well—the reduced focus on rural land assets and the shift from multigenerational to nuclear households facilitated by urban living have both further diminished the importance of patrilineal practices. South Korea is also smaller, both in territory and population, than other countries we have examined in this chapter, such as China, perhaps making policy change easier to disseminate and enforce.

Summary

After reviewing the work of Goody, Hajnal, Hartman, Das Gupta, Fukuyama, and others, along with the various cases studies presented in this chapter, we come to the conclusion that improvement in conventional measures of women's empowerment, such as increased female educational attainment, or women's greater labor force participation, or greater representation of women in national legislatures are *simply not enough* to create lasting divergence from the Syndrome and its negative ramification for political and economic order. Yes, all of these have important positive effects, but the Syndrome can coexist with comparatively good performance on all of these measures. The contemporary examples of Saudi Arabia in the first instance (education) and China in the second instance (labor force participation) and Rwanda in the third (political participation) make that proposition plain.

What appears more important in creating a more stable and resilient political and economic order is the structure of marriage, with its accompanying property rights. For example, what the Catholic Church did starting in the seventh century by asserting its authority to declare what was a legitimate marriage and what was not, Goody argues, was to reduce the "molecule of kinship to its constituent atoms, the individual, whose consent—to marriage, to alienation, and to many other activities—could not be challenged by recalcitrant or powerful relatives."[125] For the first time, a woman could be such an individual in marriage. The same could be said about developments in South Korea almost thirteen hundred years later. The consequences for the patrilineal clans were devastating—and the consequences for political and economic order, not to mention the situation of women, were salutary.

Elder provision schemes, such as pensions, are extremely important in the equation of change, but, of course, these are derivative of women's property rights in marriage. In cases in which women are "disinherited" through lack of property rights, the state will not feel it necessary to offer old age insurance schemes, and care of the elderly will predictably devolve to sons, fueling son preference and restarting patrilineality and its attendant lamentable effects on society. The South Korean case shows how women's property rights plus social insurance can turn that situation around. As Avraham Ebenstein notes about South Korea, "the data available implicate the large scale social insurance program in South Korea [as having] led to a normalization of the sex ratio at birth. As predicted, the groups targeted in the pension expansion experienced a large decline in the sex ratio at birth . . . the 'missing girls' phenomenon can be properly framed as a problem of missing social insurance."[126] Provide the insurance and the property rights, and the girls no longer go missing.

Change Is Possible

Although the interlocking components of the Syndrome sometimes seem like an almost inescapable straitjacket, that is not an entirely accurate view. In this chapter, we have seen how both historically and in the present day, certain societies have ceased (for the most part) encoding the Patrilineal/Fraternal

Syndrome. At the same time, we have also seen how other explicit attempts to undermine the Syndrome failed miserably. Furthermore, we see remarkable stasis in many Syndrome-encoding societies worldwide, in which the components of the Syndrome have remained virtually untouched to the present day.

Change is possible, then, but one cannot assume its inevitability. The security provision mechanism of male-bonded extended kin networks is not an irrational choice, but it is a foolish one. There is a better way. Sociologist Theodore Kemper put it this way,

> The human potential is to stand evolution on its head. Not the "survival of the fittest," but making all fit to survive is the program of the most advanced societies. This evolutionary capability is not genetic in origin, but is due rather to culture and social organization and to the expression of the power of the weak (in the form of politics) and the conscience of the strong (in the form of normative ethics).[127]

The final chapter of the book, to which we now turn, takes up Kemper's challenge. What is necessary in post-Syndrome countries (Syndrome scale points 0–5) to prevent regression? How can progress already underway in Transition countries (scale points 6–9) be shored up and further encouraged? And, most difficult to contemplate, how can change in Syndrome-encoding countries (scale points 10–16) be catalyzed?

CHAPTER 9

CONCLUSION

Contemporary Applications

What will the writing of history be like, when that umbrella of dominance is removed and definition is shared equally by men and women? Will we devalue the past, overthrow the categories, supplant order with chaos? No—we will simply step out under the free sky ... Men are not the center of the world, but men and women are, [and this] consciousness can also liberate men from the unwanted and undesired consequences of the system of male dominance.

—Gerda Lerner

In 1996, biologist William Rice reported on an experiment in which he engineered female fruit flies to be genetically static and allowed male fruit flies to continue to evolve. In less than fifty generations, male fruit flies evolved in what Rice has termed a "sexually antagonistic" manner, resulting in "hyper-male" fruit flies that caused physical damage to the female fruit flies through their sexual behavior, significantly increasing female mortality rates.[1] This behavior did not benefit the male flies in any other way than mating success, and higher rates of female injury and mortality meant that offspring viability was far lower, canceling out any natural selection advantage. Ecological biologist Patricia Adair Gowaty calls Rice's endeavor "the most important experiment of the twentieth century."[2] Her rationale for this assessment is her conclusion that "when experimental manipulation allows one sex to dominate completely the interests of the other sex, there is catastrophe."[3] When female fruit flies are not so dominated, as in other experiments conducted by Rice,[4] one sees lower variance in male mating success, lower female mortality, and higher offspring viability. In other words, argues Gowaty, the whole world is better for fruit flies when male dominance is checked.

We suggest that Gowaty's conclusion applies not only to fruit flies but also to humankind.[5] This book has traversed a lot of ground in attempting to lay out a fairly comprehensive theoretical framework linking the situation, status, and security of women in their households to broader phenomena of governance, stability, and national security within the larger society. We have outlined a syndrome of female subordination and devaluation that feeds off itself in an ourobouros-like fashion and that produces societies that are unstable, insecure, poorly governed, corrupt, and prone to conflict. We have subjected that theoretical framework to extensive empirical testing and process-tracing. Figure 9.1 reminds the reader of those linkages.

What is the way forward, then, for the 120 societies that still encode the Syndrome to a greater or lesser degree? As demonstrated in the previous chapter, education, economic participation, and even political representation are not enough to dismantle the Syndrome. What has mattered, historically, are meaningful changes to the structuration of marriage and family law and changes in property rights for women (as examined in chapter 8).

How, then, to effect such changes? The theoretical framework of this volume suggests one clear answer: disrupt and dismantle the components of the Syndrome. We have good reason to believe, from both case studies and our large N results, that dismantling the Syndrome profoundly undercuts the dominance of extended male kin networks. These findings suggest it may be difficult to construct a more stable or more secure or even more democratic society in a context where households are profoundly inegalitarian between the sexes. Scholars have noted that "the tribe is based upon the legitimation of inequality by ideology."[6] Perhaps that legitimation finds its foundational expression in the subordination of women in marriage; if so, meaningful change cannot obtain without change at that foundation. Those with the least power under the system of agnatic clans—women—may ironically possess the key to dismantling the entire system. If true, then in a meaningful sense, the situation of women at the household level, especially in marriage, is an important determinant of state security, stability. and governance. As such, it deserves recognition and consideration by scholars and professionals in the fields of international relations, political science, and security studies.

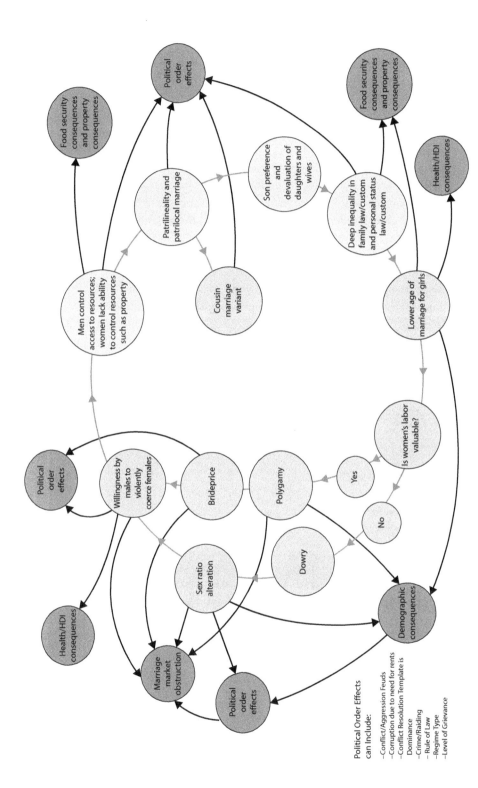

Political Order Effects
can Include:

-Conflict/Aggression Feuds
-Corruption due to need for rents
-Conflict Resolution Template is
  Dominance
- Crime/Raiding
- Rule of Law
– Regime Type
-Level of Grievance

FIGURE 9.1 The Relationship Between the Components of the Patrilineal/Fraternal Syndrome and Nation-State-Level Outcomes

Post-Syndrome, Transition, and Syndrome Societies

As we contemplate disruption of the Syndrome's components, we recognize that contemporary societies are arrayed along a spectrum. Countries at Syndrome scale points 0–5 have largely left the Syndrome behind, although the reservoir of domestic coercion is ever present, and legacy inequities in family, personal status, and property rights law may continue to color facts on the ground. At the opposite end of the spectrum, countries at Syndrome scale points 10–16 are still encoding virtually all of the subordinative components of patrilineality and fraternity. In the middle are Transition countries at scale points 6–9—that is, in these societies, many of the Syndrome's components have been disrupted, but others are fairly intact. Such societies may go either way, as we have seen: the transition may be in the direction of leaving the Syndrome behind, or if there is sufficient stress and exigency, the society may quickly regress to a fuller instantiation of the Syndrome, as we saw happen in post-Soviet Central Asia.[7]

It is worth considering which countries we code as being in transition. Table 9.1 lists them by Syndrome scale point. These Transition nations are from virtually every continent, including Europe, and we also see a wide variety of regime types represented, from democracies to autocracies to totalitarian states. Furthermore, each one of these nations has its own set of particular Syndrome components that have been retained. For example, while Albania struggles with child marriage, China is not facing this challenge. Belize does

TABLE 9.1 Transition Countries

Syndrome Scale Score	Countries
6	Belize, Bolivia, Bosnia-Herzegovina, Brazil, El Salvador, Israel, Kosovo, Macedonia, Mexico, Moldova, Montenegro, Panama, South Korea, Suriname, Thailand, Venezuela
7	Burma/Myanmar, Cambodia, Comoros, Ecuador, Fiji, Guyana, Haiti, Honduras, Nicaragua, North Korea, Peru, Philippines, Taiwan
8	Armenia, Azerbaijan, Bhutan, Georgia, Kazakhstan, Laos, Madagascar, South Africa, Turkmenistan
9	Albania, Brunei, China, Guatemala, Kyrgyzstan, Maldives, Sri Lanka, Tunisia, Turkey, Uzbekistan, Vietnam

not have brideprice, whereas Kyrgyzstan does. Thus, any recommendations for Transition countries must be based on a comprehensive understanding of which Syndrome components persist.

In a way, rather than the old categorization schemes of viewing the nations of the world in economic or political terms as first world, second world, and third world, or of Global North and Global South, we suggest that the most important way to categorize nations is according to their level of encoding of the Syndrome: Post-Syndrome, Transition, and Syndrome nations. We suggest these categorizations will offer more information on political and economic challenges than the traditional distinctions. For example, what will be appropriate ways forward for one set of nations likely will not be applicable to others: efforts at democratization are far more likely to be successful in Transition countries where the subordination of women at the household level has been somewhat abated than these efforts could possibly be in countries that fully encode the Syndrome where there has been no ground-level experience with any type of democracy within the home.

These distinctions are borne out in empirical analysis. Consider how well or how poorly each of these different categories of nations performs on the wide variety of national outcome measures examined in chapter 7. Table 9.2 was constructed by taking the dichotomous versions of the dependent variables created for our logistic regression analysis in chapter 7 (also see appendix IV) and evaluating how often Post-Syndrome, Transition, and Syndrome countries fell into the "good" or "worse" category for each of the dependent variables where the Syndrome was significant in the general linear model. Specifically, we first determined for each national outcome where each nation would fall using the logistic regression cut-points, that is, if the nation was above the cut point or below (and noting whether above the cut point was "good" or "worse" for a given outcome variable). We then examined the results for each subset of nations. So, for each outcome variable, we would ask what percentage of the subset of Post-Syndrome nations were found in the "good" range and

TABLE 9.2 Comparison of Good and Worse Outcomes for Post-Syndrome, Transition, and Syndrome Countries

	Post-Syndrome Countries	Transition Countries	Syndrome Countries
Good Outcome	84.68%	55.64%	30.12%
Worse Outcome	15.32%	44.36%	69.88%

what percentage in the "worse" range, with the sum of these two percentages by definition equalling 100 percent. These calculations yielded a set of percentages, which we then averaged across all the outcome variables to provide the mean percentage of Post-Syndrome nations in the "good" range for all national outcomes and the mean percentage in the "worse" range. Again, the sum of these two percentages always equals 100 percent. Then the same procedure was followed for the subset of Transition countries, and then again for the subset of Syndrome countries. This gives us, if you will, an average "profile" of how each group of nations fares across an array of national outcomes.

We find from table 9.2 that Post-Syndrome countries experience a much higher percentage of good outcomes on measures of national, governmental, economic, human, and environmental security than worse outcomes on average (85 percent good outcomes to 15 percent worse), that Transition countries experience fairly balanced instances of each (56 percent good to 44 percent worse), and that high Syndrome-encoding countries fall in the worse category for the dichotomous variables more often than good (30 percent good to 70 percent worse). We performed a two-way analysis of variance (ANOVA) test to evaluate whether a significant difference exists between the average proportions of good and worse outcomes for the three different Syndrome levels. The test was significant at the .001 level ($F = 175.5$) and a follow-up Tukey multiple comparisons of means test showed that each pair-wise difference was significant (Post-Syndrome versus Transition, Post-Syndrome versus Syndrome, Transition versus Syndrome).

Table 9.2 shows fairly definitively that the distinctions we are making (Post-Syndrome, Transition, Syndrome) reveal a large and significant difference in national outcomes. Even dismantling some but not all of the Syndrome components, as we see in Transition countries, vastly improves outcomes for a nation. Any movement toward the dismantling of the Syndrome, then, is worthwhile, for such efforts are associated with significant improvements in a nation's security, stability, prosperity, health, demographic security, governance, and many other important outcomes. In essence, these efforts are changing that first sexual political order and are the most revolutionary of all possible reforms.

There are some countries that do not follow the general pattern indicated by the average percentages in table 9.2. For example, Russia is the only Post-Syndrome country that fell in the "worse" outcomes category more often than the "good," but the difference was slight (51 percent bad and 49 percent good). Nine of the high-Syndrome countries (scores 10–16) experience an unexpectedly higher percentage of "good" outcomes (see appendix V); most of these are oil-rich Gulf states whose wealth can provide better outcomes in areas such as health care and literacy. We also note that some Transition countries more closely follow the outcome pattern of Post-Syndrome countries (e.g., Albania,

Brunei, Israel, Moldova, Montenegro, Panama, South Korea, and Taiwan), whereas other Transition countries appear to follow more the pattern of high-Syndrome countries (Burma/Myanmar, Cambodia, Haiti, and Laos).

Table 9.2 makes it apparent that nation-states desiring improved outcomes should also desire to cease practices that disempower half the population, women, at the household level. Indeed, empowerment of women at the household level may be the precondition for desired outcomes, such as meaningful democracy, rule of law, and national security and stability. The critical question, then, is by what means the Syndrome may be effectively dismantled.

In the discussion that follows, we first address the issue of whether it is appropriate to speak of disrupting the Syndrome. Then, we explore thoughts about how to effectively disrupt Syndrome components in Transition and more fully Syndrome-encoding countries. We follow that with a discussion of the unique challenges facing Post-Syndrome societies.

Cultural Imperialism?

The theme of this book is that the disempowerment and subordination of women at the household level has far-reaching negative effects on societal stability, security, prosperity, health, and resilience. We performed an empirical analysis on a set of 176 countries, representing every continent, region, religion, and race as well as a wide variety of ethnic identities. This research tells us something very important—the subordination of women is not an idiosyncratic cultural or religious or regional phenomenon. Rather, it is a universal political order—a first *sexual* political order—that exists prior to and molds what we perceive to be cultural and religious differences between countries and regions.

Thus, to suggest that the goal of disrupting and dismantling the Syndrome's components is somehow a form of Western imperialism simply does not compute. The true clash of civilizations is not West versus East, or North versus South: the true clash is subordination of women versus nonsubordination of women as the first political order upon which a civilization is built. That clash is occurring within nations just as much as it is between nations. In a sense, it is a great test given to each and every people—to choose security, stability, prosperity, health, and resilience or to choose the sequelae of male dominance that offer the opposite. As David Jacobson puts it, in terms of national outcomes, "gender is the hinge."[8]

Thus, it is entirely possible to imagine, say, a culturally Muslim society that has largely dismantled the Syndrome's components. Certainly nongovernmental organizations (NGOs), such as Musawah and Sisters in Islam, work for just that goal, particularly in terms of making marriage more equitable for women in the Islamic faith community. Rose McDermott and Jonathan Cowden suggest in their analysis of polygyny, which might well be applied to all of the Syndrome components, that we must

> recognize the historical and economic forces that engendered this reality and work to transform it within the context of a universal responsibility to mitigate injustice and prevent harm and injury to all humans, while respecting genuine cultural preferences that do not impinge on basic human rights. . . . Only when these structures no longer present an opportunity for such men to benefit from their dominance of women will women's emancipation no longer present a fundamental threat to these cultures.[9]

Removing such opportunities will therefore be key.

Navigating this path is a task that cannot be performed by outsiders; it must come from within. As we learned in chapter 8, external efforts to force change are doomed to failure. Those outside the culture can be cheerleaders and provide assistance when requested, but the effort must come from the society. As Mark Weiner suggests, "for a society to overcome the rule of the clan, it must forge, and it must maintain, a common identity that rises above the particular clan groups of which it is composed. The existence of a public identity enables the state to protect its citizens not as members of corporate groups but rather as individuals."[10] Furthermore, this identity must be developed from within the culture; as we have seen with the case of the Soviet Union, foreign imposition of Syndrome dismantlement is a cause for deep resentment. Adrienne Edgar notes about the Turkmenistan case:

> In its policy towards women, the Soviet Union resembled Kemal Ataturk's Turkey, which pursued gender reform as part of a modernizing project, more than it resembles the French and British empires. Yet Turkey was able to successfully reform personal status laws and promote unveiling precisely because these changes in women's status were associated with strengthening the modern nation-state and not with colonial coercion. Because the Soviet regime carried the taint of alien rule, communist authorities were unable to persuade most Turkmen that the emancipation of women was essential to their future as a nation.[11]

Even though members of the society must find their own path to dismantling the Syndrome, it is also true that the path away from the Syndrome is not likely to be linear, but rather will often involve both progress and regress in tandem. This is to be expected. Furthermore, societies or regimes may choose a path of dismantlement that may have significant negative consequences, and which therefore may be justifiably criticized by the international community. For example, one guiding principle in this regard might be that an attack on the Patrilineal/Fraternal Syndrome that simultaneously undermines the security of women is not likely to reap a good harvest. An excellent example is that of China's one-child policy. The policy was created ostensibly to reduce births, yes, but another purpose of the policy was arguably to break the power of the agnatic lineages by severely restricting their size. The effects on women of this policy were anything but empowering (see chapter 5). That China has been forced to abandon the one-child policy because of its effects on national security and prosperity suggests the wisdom of adhering to this principle. Likewise, other morally ambiguous approaches, such as Italy's programs to forcibly remove children from Mafioso homes to curb the power of those male-bonded networks, should undergo a similar searching evaluation.[12] Troublingly, a Danish version of such a program targets immigrant children for removal from their families.[13]

Recognizing that efforts to dismantle the Syndrome must always originate from within that society, whether or not assistance is provided from external sources, what might change agents wish to consider as they attempt to move forward?

Disrupting the Syndrome at Its Weakest Points

We assert that the Syndrome has weak points, and that this weakness can be usefully exploited. Where can policymakers attempt the most effective first undercuts in Syndrome-encoding countries and in Transition countries? Figure 9.2 opens this discussion: the arrows indicate points at which we believe the Syndrome is currently most vulnerable.

Opportunities for Direct Action

Child Marriage
The first area of weakness in the Syndrome is child marriage. The appalling consequences of child marriage are apparent for all to see, and international public opinion has swayed decisively to the side of ending child marriage, including statements made against child marriage by the G-8 and the United Nations Secretary General in 2012, as well as by the United Nations Commission on the Status of Women in 2013. The Elders, a group of respected elder statesmen and stateswomen, have launched the "Girls Not Brides" initiative. Even more impressively, since the turn of this century, fifty-two countries have increased their marriage age to eighteen years old or higher[14], and an additional eight countries have endeavored to close loopholes in their marriage laws that permit under-eighteen-year-olds to marry despite the fact that the stipulated

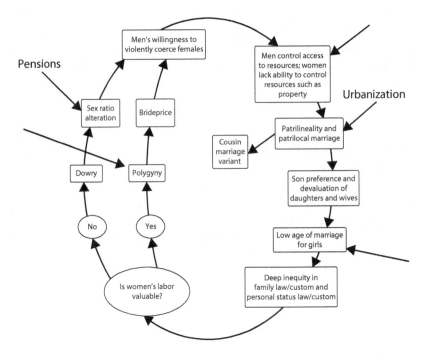

FIGURE 9.2 The Weakest Components of the Syndrome (indicated by the arrows)

age of marriage is eighteen.[15] Some nations, such as Norway, refuse to recognize child marriages even if they were contracted in countries where the marriage was deemed legal. International agreements, such as the African Charter on the Rights and Welfare of the Child and the South Asian Initiative to End Violence Against Children (SAIEVAC), among others, have encouraged regional neighbors to stand united against the practice, and eliminating child marriage is a target of Sustainable Development Goals (SDG Target 5.3). Enforcement lags behind, sometimes egregiously so, and crisis threatens reversal in several areas, such as Syria and Yemen, but nevertheless this tally shows real global progress.

One shining example of change comes from Malawi, which has a high rate of child marriage. In 2015, Senior Chief Inkosi Kachindamoto annulled more than 850 child marriages performed under customary law, just weeks after the passage of Malawi's new marriage law in 2015 raising the minimum age of marriage without parental consent to eighteen. In addition, the chief "suspended village heads that had consented to child marriages" until they annulled those unions. She also stopped the practice of "sexual cleansing," which sometimes is practiced on girls before marriage in which they are, in essence, raped by a stranger to give them sexual experience.[16]

Post-Syndrome countries have an opportunity to assist this effort. For example, the United States under the Obama administration joined the international campaign against child marriage, with the State Department including child marriage in its annual Human Rights Reports, and also in 2013, the U.S. Agency for International Development (USAID) announced an ongoing new initiative entitled "Ending Child Marriage and Meeting the Needs of Married Children."[17] Ambassador Catherine Russell, the former head of the State Department's Office of Global Women's Issues, explained in September 2016 that "child marriage is addressed in three interagency policies. That includes the first-ever U.S. strategy on adolescent girls, which Secretary Kerry launched earlier this year . . . and we are proud that three other agencies—USAID, the Peace Corps, and the Millennium Challenge Corporation—as well as PEPFAR are part of this effort."[18] (Note that since Ambassador Russell's departure, no new ambassador for Global Women's Issues has been appointed at the time of this writing, and the State Department has reportedly been told to "trim" its section on women in the human rights reports.[19] In light of our book's analysis, this de-prioritization is a grievous mistake.)

As highlighted in part II, child marriage is a pivotal issue. It links with many of our dependent variables, especially those concerning health, and we have noted the work of John Hajnal and Mary Hartman in tracing the entire character of marriage—and by extension, the larger society—to whether early or later marriage is the norm. Something very, very deep changes when girls are no longer married at (or even before) puberty, as Hartman and Hajnal pointed out in their discussion of the divergent path of northwestern Europe (see chapter 8).

Polygyny

Polygyny is another Syndrome component that is vast in its import for the society and that is more susceptible to direct challenge than many of the other components. First, as research by McDermott and colleagues[20] show in their survey of six countries where the practice is legal, "the majority of *both* men and women see little to no benefit from the practice and, in fact, are harmed by it."[21] Indeed, McDermott and her colleagues found less than 50 percent support among men for the practice in their survey. The harm, then, is not only to women. Most men in society will face a far more difficult marriage market as a result of the polygynous aspirations of the subset of elite men, and they are quite aware of this fact. In reality, it is only elite men, or aspirants to such status, who support the practice; this is a point of weakness in the Syndrome.

Furthermore, McDermott and her colleagues found that women are far less supportive of polygyny than men in societies where the practice exists. In their experimental survey design, men (although generally unsupportive of polygyny) were twice as likely to approve of polygyny as women in almost all the countries included in the study. That suggests that if attempts to ban child marriage are successful, then later age of marriage for girls and a resultant lower age gap between spouses can be expected to curb the prevalence of polygyny, for these developments would support greater female influence on nuptiality.[22] As McDermott notes, "As polygyny increases, the age of marriage for women declines, often well into childhood," which implies that as prohibitions on child marriage are enforced, polygyny should decline as well.[23]

Furthermore, to the extent that women's political rights lead to increasing influence on the content of law, an increase in women's political influence should lead to attempts to curtail or even ban the practice. As we have seen, such political influence may not necessarily derive from an increase in formal representation in government bodies; nongovernmental activism may in fact be more important. Muslim women in India, for example, were recently successful in getting the national government to ban the so-called triple talaq manner of divorce by men, are also now pushing for a complete ban on polygyny.[24] Similar attempts have been made by women's groups in countries such as Uganda,[25] Nigeria,[26] Namibia,[27] and others. These groups may have male allies, as well. In Nigeria, the (male) Emir of Kano, Sanusi Lamido Sanusi, who has proposed such a ban, has gone on record as saying, "Those of us in the [mainly Muslim] north have all seen the economic consequences of men who are not capable of maintaining one wife, marrying four. They end up producing 20 children, not educating them, leaving them on the streets, and they end up as thugs and terrorists."[28]

This suggests a second reason why polygyny may be vulnerable to direct action: men themselves are capable of seeing both the familial harms and the larger societal harms that derive from the practice. As the emir notes, children are significantly worse off under polygyny than under monogamy. Fathers cannot afford to support the number of children sired, and inheritances must be split many times over. When the inheritance is land, conflict is often the result.[29] For example, in Nigeria, Justice Modupe Onyeabo of the Lagos State High Court tells the story of a chief who had nine wives and thirty-six children, with a substantial estate. Thirty years later, his children still have yet to inherit because of litigation among the siblings. Said the justice, "The man might have enjoyed a nice family life with many children, but that legacy is now completely destroyed . . . Perhaps the most prominent factor that causes disharmony in families is polygamy."[30]

Justice Onyeabo goes on to note that the harms of polygyny are widely acknowledged in Nigerian society, giving a Yoruba saying that,

"It is only one wife that brings pleasure, when there are two wives, they become rivals; when they are three, they destroy the wine; when they increase to four, they laugh one another to scorn; when they are five, they accuse one of them of monopolising the husband's property; when they are six, they become wicked people; and when they are seven, they become witches." So you see the society itself knows that polygamy has a negative effect on family cohesion.[31]

In other words, men realize that polygyny is simply not a "fitness enhancing strategy," for additional wives bring "diminishing marginal returns."[32] At some point in society's development, the quality of the children a man produces will matter more to his reputation than the quantity produced, and monogamy concentrates a father's attention, care, and wealth in a way that maximizes that quality. As we have seen in the remarks of the emir of Kano, men may also begin to realize the larger social problems deriving from the practice of polygyny and seek to curb those. Summarized by *The Economist*, "Polygamous societies are bloodier, more likely to invade their neighbours and more prone to collapse than others are. The taking of multiple wives is a feature of life in all of the 20 most unstable countries on the Fragile States Index compiled by the Fund for Peace."[33] Indeed, political economist Seung-Yun Oh and colleagues[34] suggest hopefully that polygynous societies may notice that monogamous societies outcompete them both economically and militarily, and as a result, may seek to emulate their norms.

Furthermore, an international human rights framework to ban polygyny exists—for example, in 2000 the United Nations Human Rights Committee, commenting on the International Covenant on Civil and Political Rights, stated, "It should also be noted that equality of treatment with regard to the right to marry implies that polygamy is incompatible with this principle. Polygamy violates the dignity of women. It is an inadmissible discrimination against women. Consequently, it should be definitely abolished wherever it continues to exist."[35] The Convention on the Rights of the Child can similarly be read to ban practices injurious to the girl child, and this would include polygynous unions involving girls under eighteen.[36] The Convention on the Elimination of all Forms of Discrimination Against Women's (CEDAW's) General Recommendation No. 21, dated 1994, states,

> Polygamous marriage contravenes a woman's right to equality with men, and can have such serious emotional and financial consequences for her and her dependents that such marriages ought to be discouraged and prohibited. The Committee notes with concern that some States parties, whose constitutions guarantee equal rights, permit polygamous marriage in accordance with personal or customary law. This violates the constitutional rights of women, and breaches the provisions of article 5 (a) of the Convention.[37]

Most heartening, in 2011 the Canadian courts declared that polygyny is inherently harmful, regardless of why or how it is practiced or who is practicing it (see chapter 3). This ruling also becomes a body of precedent from which international law can draw. A key takeaway from the ruling is that "the harms associated with the practice are endemic; they are inherent. This conclusion is critical because it supports the view that the harms found in polygynous societies are not simply the product of individual misconduct; they arise inevitably out of the practice."[38] Ample grounds exist under international law to legally challenge the practice of polygyny, and we applaud groups such as Equality Now that work toward that end.[39]

Furthermore, we especially praise the work of religious figures who question polygamy. Recently, for example, Egypt's top cleric, the Grand Imam of Al-Azhar in Cairo, Sheikh Ahmed al-Tayeb, commented on Egyptian state television that polygamy "is often an injustice to women and children," also stating that "women represent half of society. If we don't care for them it's liking walking on one foot only."[40] His statements set off a firestorm of controversy but were welcomed by many who see that hurting women through practices such as polygyny hurts everyone in society.

Property Rights for Women

Polygyny and child marriage are tightly wound up with women's property rights—that is, both practices severely undercut those rights, and when they are curbed, women's property rights significantly improve. Polygyny and child marriage are also intertwined with patrilocal marriage, which significantly undermines women's property rights as well. Even so, the legal case for equality in property rights between men and women is, if anything, even easier to make under current international and even national law than it is for child marriage and polygyny. As the global economic system has become more completely capitalist in nature following the end of the Cold War, the right of an individual to hold property and make contracts in their own name has been upheld across every continent. Thus, it is almost always the case that the formal law of the land upholds the property rights of all individuals, including women. International law also supports such rights for both men and women, the foundational case in point being the International Covenant on Economic, Social, and Cultural Rights which explicitly states that the economic rights it enumerates belong to women as well as men.[41] Rather, the problem stems from cultural practices that constrain the application of the law—practices such as patrilocal marriage, polygyny, and child marriage. As we have seen, the Syndrome does not countenance female control over valuable resources, for that would dilute the power of the male-bonded extended kin networks.

The maps featured in figures 9.3 and 9.4 are instructive in this regard. The first (figure 9.3) shows cross-national variation in formal, legal property rights for women, including inheritance rights. In contrast, when we scale

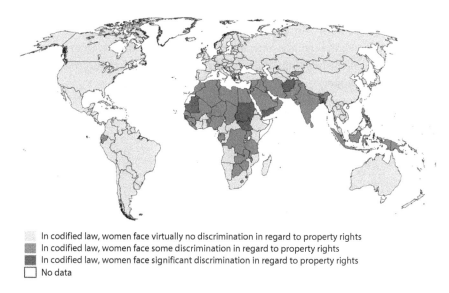

In codified law, women face virtually no discrimination in regard to property rights
In codified law, women face some discrimination in regard to property rights
In codified law, women face significant discrimination in regard to property rights
No data

FIGURE 9.3 Property Rights for Women in Law, scaled 2017

In practice, women face virtually no discrimination in regard to property rights
In practice, women face some discrimination in regard to property rights
In practice, women face significant discrimination in regard to property rights
No data

FIGURE 9.4 Property Rights for Women in Practice, scaled 2017

women's property rights *in practice*, a different—and far worse—picture emerges (figure 9.4). The stark contrast in these two maps suggests to us that government efforts to enforce the rights women already have under formal law are critically important in the dismantling of the Syndrome. We have seen just how pivotal a role women's property rights played in the historical transition away from the Patrilineal/Fraternal Syndrome (chapter 8), especially in northwestern Europe. These rights can play a similar role in other areas of the world today.

The challenges, however, are stiff. Transparency International's recent report "Women, Land, and Corruption"[42] lists several:

- Women are regularly disadvantaged by not being made aware of their rights to own property and land.
- Women are often excluded from negotiations on land deals and community discussions with investors on potential land sales. They are less likely to receive their fair share of compensation for land acquired by external parties.
- Even when women are involved in land deals, they rarely see financial benefits, as men are usually in charge of household income.
- Engagement with traditional leaders over land is often challenging for women.
- In countries where legislation supports women's claims to land rights, law enforcement is often weak and women's claims are undermined by practice and custom, which men can manipulate for their own gain.
- As competition for land increases, women's land rights are weakened. Even in cases where there is support for women's rights and gender equality, many people reject the idea of women inheriting land.
- Women are vulnerable to sexual extortion as a form of corruption and are often forced to trade sexual favors for land deals.
- Women and men often perceive the land they use as jeopardized by the interests of external investors and traditional leaders and that they lack a say in decisions about that land.
- Even when land sales create new jobs for local populations, women lose out as employment opportunities tend to favor men disproportionally.

There are already numerous efforts by governments, intergovernmental organizations, and NGOs—often working together—to ensure women's property rights. For example, the World Bank sponsors land title projects in forty-eight countries, including Ethiopia, Kosovo, Honduras, and Vietnam. One explicit goal of the initiative is to increase the percentage of women with title to land. Government buy-in is critical; for example, in Ethiopia and Bolivia, the law was changed to accord women joint rights in all marital property.[43]

USAID also initiated a program to increase title to land for women in Afghanistan. Experts note that although equal property rights for women are guaranteed under the 2004 Afghan Constitution, land rights are almost always adjudicated under tribal law, which disfavors women. Even in the case where a woman has a small share of inheritance of land, tribal law "pressures a woman to relinquish her share of an inheritance to her brothers in order to ensure her social protection in case of divorce; demonstrate family loyalty; and avoid discrimination and shame at the hands of her community."[44] USAID administered the Land Reform in Afghanistan (LARA) program from 2011 to 2014 to try and increase access to land by women, centering on Jalalabad. This program established a Women's Land Rights Task Force of Afghan nationals to advise USAID and also sponsored public awareness campaigns to increase citizens' understanding of women's inheritance rights to land. Unfortunately, we could not find any data about whether these efforts resulted in greater titling for women.[45]

NGOs such as Landesa and Habitat for Humanity are active in developing innovative programs to support women's property rights; for example, teaching women how to apply for title certificates from the government.[46] Legal guidance and access to trained paralegals who can assist women in pursuing their legal rights are imperative. The African Union recently undertook a continental Land Policy Initiative establishing codes of conduct for governments and investors mandating the consent of small landholders, and the need to safeguard women's rights to land is highlighted therein.[47] Such efforts to bolster women's property rights are a crucial dimension of Syndrome dismantlement, ones that can be openly undertaken under formal national law in almost every country.

Disrupting the Context in Which the Syndrome Operates

The Syndrome persists because it *appears* functional as a security provision mechanism. As we have seen, it is anything but functional if we look at the larger picture. Part of the reason for that appearance is the context in which the Syndrome operates. Change the context, and the apparent functionality of the Syndrome can effectively be called into question. We offer several examples here.

Urbanization

Urbanization is a global trend that undermines the perceived usefulness of the Syndrome. It is far more difficult, for example, to maintain patrilocal marriage customs in a highly urbanized environment; neolocal marriage is much more prevalent in such circumstances because of differences in the average size and cost of land holdings and living space, among other things. Neolocal marriage may also loosen other forms of patrilineal control, such as polygyny. Furthermore, an urbanized environment may provide women greater opportunities to increase their intrahousehold bargaining status, such as offering greater assurance of property rights and greater access to education and formal employment. Finally, in a densely populated urbanized environment, personal success may no longer be so strongly linked to fertility, and relatives become less invested in each other's reproductive success. Rather, other forms of success begin to substitute for genetic success, weakening male-bonded kin networks.[48] Our results bear this out: as the empirical results presented in chapter 7 show, after the Syndrome, urbanization was a significant variable in many of our regression models. Supporting this proposition is that, in general, the more a nation's economy is based on agricultural production, the higher the Syndrome score. (The bivariate correlation between percent of gross domestic product derived from Agriculture and the Syndrome is .559, significant at the .001 level.)

Pensions

Urban dwellers are far more likely to have access to pension systems. As we have seen, one reason why the Patrilineal/Fraternal Syndrome appears functional to many is that without the dependable support of economically productive offspring, elderly parents might well starve. Because men have far greater access to resources in Syndrome-encoding societies and are considered "true" family because sons stay while daughters marry exogamously, families privilege the birth of sons. Such son preference can, under certain circumstances, translate into the culling of girls from the birth population through female infanticide or sex-selective abortion.

The most reliable way to undermine such son preference is to provide alternatives to sons for elder support. If daughters are given the opportunity to become economically productive, they often are favored as caregivers over sons by elderly parents. For example, in China, one popular saying is "having a daughter is like having a warm jacket in wintertime [i.e., old age]." Parents recognize that even though in a social sense their son is responsible for their care in old age, such care is likely to be more financial and perhaps less personal than it might be with a daughter. But finances count, and so son preference endures. Increasing the economic opportunities of daughters may undercut that calculation.

But the same result can be achieved by providing a social security scheme for elderly parents. As we saw in chapter 8, the creation of a pension scheme may actually engender a recalculation of the costs and benefits of having a son. A son may come to be seen as more of an economic liability in some cases, as was seen in the case study of South Korea. We ran a bivariate correlation between the WomanStats scale of Son Preference/Sex Ratio and a dependent variable used in the empirical analysis in chapter 8, Percent Pensionable Persons Receiving a Pension. The correlation was $-.268$, significant at the $p <.001$ level, meaning the lower the percent of the population receiving a pension, the higher the level of son preference and the greater the alteration of sex ratios. In our opinion, there is no faster route to diminishing son preference than dependable pension provision.

Other Forms of Contextual Tinkering

Although urbanization and pensions are key contextual variables auguring against the persistence of the Syndrome, other forms of contextual change can be helpful as well. First, we have noted in other work[49] that government intervention to cap brideprice and wedding costs can be useful in preventing the dramatic and often rapid rise in those costs. Because such inflationary bubbles can be destabilizing given their propensity to completely upend the marriage market, the enforcement of caps can be seen as shoring up societal stability. Several countries, including Saudi Arabia, have undertaken just such measures, as discussed in chapter 5.

Second, as we have seen, there is often a large gap between formal law and on-the-ground practice where women are concerned. Given that interpretation and enforcement of the law are the purview of the judicial system, including the police, and given that the judicial system in nearly every country is predominantly male, this is another possible arena for contextual change. Although countries have made strides to ensure that the legislative and executive branches of government see increasing representation of women, that has not been the case where the judicial system is concerned. Yet that branch of government is arguably of greatest importance to women. How the law is interpreted and how the law is (or is not) enforced are critical in terms of meaningful dismantlement of the Syndrome's components. To give but one striking example, Rule 96 of the International Criminal Tribunal for the Former Yugoslavia, which was the first ever legal prohibition of rape in war and set the parameters of the International Criminal Court, was passed only because of the insistence of the female judges, Gabrielle MacDonald and Elizabeth Odio.[50] Efforts to increase the representation of women as judges, lawyers, and police officers will go a long way toward improving the empowerment of women at the household level.

Other contextual factors that could facilitate Syndrome component dismantlement include increasing human capital investment in women, such as through greater educational opportunities, greater representation in government, greater investment in women's health and reproductive planning, greater access to capital such as through microloan programs, and greater overall economic autonomy. Despite the fact that one of the themes of this volume is that improved levels of education/labor-force participation/government representation for women and girls are insufficient to undermine the Syndrome's components, these are still important goals. It is true that we can find the Syndrome encoded in countries in which we find virtual parity in education, low maternal mortality, high female labor force participation, and/or high representation of women in the national legislature. We have called this the "Rwanda Paradox," after the nation with the highest percentage of women in the legislature anywhere in the world but which is still a Syndrome-encoding country with a comparatively high score of 10. Nevertheless, we absolutely concur that investments in women's potential are important adjunct strategies facilitating the transition to a Post-Syndrome state by altering the context in which the Syndrome operates.

Preventing Resurgence of the Syndrome in Post-Syndrome and Transition Countries

Post-Syndrome and Transition countries, as we have seen, are not immune from regression, and may begin to reintroduce components of the Syndrome that previously had been dismantled or disrupted. In the twenty-first century, we have seen birth sex ratios become abnormal in some countries where they had long been normal; we have seen efforts to relegalize polygyny where it has been illegal for decades or even up to a century; we have even seen the age of marriage for girls begin to fall in some countries after having risen for quite a while. Thus, it is important to consider how Post-Syndrome countries can guard against such regression when crisis or exigency may start to prod society along that path.

Two primary reservoirs allow for swift regression toward the Syndrome in ostensibly Post-Syndrome countries in times of crisis: high levels of domestic violence and lingering echoes of inequity in family and personal status laws. The first, as we have seen, is the original training ground for the Syndrome, and the second provides justification for differential treatment of women under the law.

We cannot overstate how the normalization and acceptance of domestic violence undermines the stability and security of the nation-state. The Syndrome could never come into existence absent this foundation. Such violence is literally a boot camp in the use and functionality of terror. Yet domestic violence rates are quite high even in Post-Syndrome countries, such as the United States.

Recently, however, the blinders obscuring our vision of how vital attention to domestic violence really is have begun to lift. For example, the link between perpetration of domestic violence and mass killings has been increasingly noted in the press. For example, the *Washington Post* states, "mass shootings in the United States are carried out, overwhelmingly, by men with a history of domestic violence. 54 percent of mass shootings in the United States involve a former or current partner or a family member being killed."[51] But this figure seriously understates the case, because it does not include male shooters who had only injured or harmed and not killed partners or family members. For example, Nikolas Cruz, the Parkland, Florida, shooter, had not killed family members or partners before going on his rampage or during it, but he had been physically abusive to both his mother and his girlfriend. Ditto for Tamerlan Tsarnaev, Omar Mateen, Esteban Santiago, Robert Lewis Dear, John Houser, and so on. Pamela Shifman and Shalamishah Tillet point out that "a felony domestic violence conviction is the single greatest predictor of future violent crime among men," and they rightfully suggest, "Until women are safe in the home, none of us will be safe outside the home."[52]

We would add to their statement that until domestic violence is treated as the perpetration of terrorism that it is, societies will not be immune to regression toward the Syndrome. What would the world be like if perpetrators of domestic violence were charged under criminal statutes against *terrorism* and punished accordingly? What if the State Department not only penned a Trafficking in Persons Report each year, but a Domestic Terrorism Report each year? (Unfortunately, the United States would be a Tier 3 country in its own report.) Former UK chief crown prosecutor Nazir Afzal has argued that men with histories of domestic violence should be monitored as being at risk for terrorism, noting that the Westminster Bridge, Manchester Arena, London Bridge, and Finsbury Park attacks in the United Kingdom were all carried out by men with a history of domestic abuse.[53] Elevating this issue to central importance would not be an overreaction; it would finally be the appropriate reaction.[54]

Likewise, echoes of women's differential treatment under the law may justify inequality between men and women and potentially facilitate regression if circumstances seem threatening. Gender wage gaps, gendered laws on retirement age, and gendered laws on night work or other types of work may seem unremarkable or trivial, but they express in legal terms that a woman and a man are not equal. Of course, equal does not mean "same," and we believe there is room for laws that acknowledge pertinent differences between the sexes.[55] However, when the law in Russia forbids a woman from being a ship's captain, but not from working as a sailor on that same boat, or when men are required to retire at sixty-five in Poland, but women are required to retire at sixty, what we are seeing are echoes of an older Syndrome-based view of women that can facilitate and justify regression. Post-Syndrome and Transition societies should be vigilant in rooting out these legacy legal differences that reify inequity between men and women, while still being mindful of pertinent sex differences in cases in which such would help better define equity.

Last, Post-Syndrome societies should be watchful in situations in which there is mass immigration from countries more fully encoding the Syndrome. Even though the components of the Syndrome are no doubt illegal in Post-Syndrome destination countries, if significant numbers of those emigrating from Syndrome countries to Post-Syndrome countries practice these components *sub rosa*, such reintroduction will jeopardize the gains made in eliminating the untoward consequences of these components as documented in this book. As Jacobson notes, "Surprisingly, the gender dimension [of immigration] and its implications for social and national integration have been, until recently at least, largely ignored. One still reads major contemporary studies on national integration of immigrant groups in which the gender issue is barely addressed,"[56] and Mark Weiner elaborates:

> The challenges Europe faces today with its Muslim immigrants will be seen in time to arise less from religious differences than from differences in family structure—differences between the nuclear family and the extended lineage group—and from the generally skeptical attitude toward government immigrants learned under the rule of the clan. It is not Islam but rather the social and psychological importance of extended kinship that typically hinders assimilation into liberal society.[57]

Jacobson and Weiner are telling us something very important. Although no individual should be prevented from immigrating because of the Syndrome score of his or her society, special care must be taken to ensure that migrants from high-Syndrome-scoring country are prepared to abandon Syndrome components. Some nation-states have already recognized this potential problem. Countries such as Norway and Australia, for example, have proactively developed orientation courses for new immigrants that make it clear that Syndrome components, such as polygyny, underage marriage, domestic violence, and other practices such as public harassment of women and forced marriage are strictly forbidden and carry substantial penalties. Both male and female immigrants are taught that women have the same rights as men, and how women can access police enforcement of their rights.[58] Australia now implements a "values test" for immigrants applying for citizenship that explicitly asks questions such as "Can you strike your spouse?" "Does Australia's principle of freedom of religion mean that in some situations it is permissible to force your children to marry?" "Under what circumstances is it appropriate to prohibit girls from education?"[59] In other countries, such as Belgium, NGOs have attempted to inform immigrants about cultural differences in communicating with members of the opposite sex.[60] This all seems eminently sensible, as do efforts by nations such as Canada to protect its nation's normal sex ratios by refusing admittance to unaccompanied male asylum seekers, who otherwise often make up the bulk of initial waves of immigration.[61]

Polygyny is a special problem; various countries have struggled with existing polygynous marriages among migrants. France, for example, insists on "de-cohabitation," and polygamous families can apply for only one-year residence permits instead of the normal ten-year residence permits until de-cohabitation is chosen. In contrast, the United Kingdom recognizes polygamous marriages if they took place in a country where the practice is legal, although only one spouse is allowed to settle in the United Kingdom as a spouse. Additional spouses may arrive under other immigration categories, though they are allowed to request family support from the state. Conversely, Australia refuses to acknowledge the validity of polygamous marriages even if they were contracted in a state where the practice is legal. The diversity of approaches adopted by Post-Syndrome countries with regard to polygyny is quite striking.[62] On the basis of our own evidence, as well as the extensive work of McDermott,[63] allowing polygyny to enter through the back door is a foolish thing for a Post-Syndrome nation to countenance. Nations should be wary of allowing wives to be "imported" from home countries, which practice unfortunately tends to ensure that children continue to be born into Syndrome-encoding households even though their fathers may be second-, third-, or even fourth-generation migrants. Complicating matters further, these migrant brides are often underage.[64]

Religious law enclaves have been viewed as a way to bridge the gap for migrants from Syndrome-encoding countries. Nations such as the United Kingdom, however, have worked hard to ensure that enclaves of Syndrome-encoding religious law operate under severe constraint within the society, for inequity in family and personal status law is a key component of the Syndrome's straitjacket. So, for example in the United Kingdom, all religious courts and tribunals must subordinate themselves to British law under the Arbitration Act of 1996. Jack Straw, justice minister in 2008, stated the principle in these terms with regard to Islamic religious courts: "There is nothing whatsoever in English law that prevents people abiding by Shariah principles if they wish to, provided they do not come into conflict with English law," adding that British law "would always remain supreme" and that "regardless of religious belief, we are all equal before the law."[65] The "*niqab* laws" spreading through Europe seem an attempt to signal this stance; Jacobson comments, "Absent face cover, the individual has a new accountability. . . . This changes the character of public space . . . she is in a position of self-presentation and thus negotiation."[66] Jacobson's view suggests that in civil society seeing a woman's face in public is an integral element in society's ability to ensure both her humanity and her security.

Although there is nothing inherently harmful about immigration, it is the harm inherent in the Syndrome's components, including the potential for altered sex ratios, that a Post-Syndrome society should avoid when developing its immigration policy and determining its stance toward religious law enclaves.[67]

Building a Post-Syndrome Society

Of supreme importance when we speak of the context in which the Syndrome operates is the relationship between the state and the male-bonded extended kin networks of the Patrilineal/Fraternal Syndrome. It goes without saying that governments that rely on such networks to maintain their rule will be in no position to make any meaningful headway on Syndrome disruption. In fact, the price of the clans' support is often a strictly hands-off approach to issues of women's rights in family and personal status law, as we saw in the case of Soviet Central Asia. Creating a context in which the state is not beholden to these male-bonded extended kin networks is clearly the key trick—how is that to be achieved?

We spoke of attenuating the power of the clans by dismantling the Syndrome's components, which is a necessary condition; that is, you cannot attenuate the power of male-bonded extended kin networks unless you undermine their ability to recreate themselves from generation to generation. It is also true that component dismantlement takes concerted effort over time. Are there complementary strategies that can aid that process, aside from those we have already discussed such as greater investment in women's potential and pension schemes? In the next section, we turn to the dynamics of societal change in security provision mechanism.

Changing a Society's Security Provision Mechanism

We argue that it is time for a variety of stakeholders—government leaders, religious leaders, men, women—to consider more fully the costs of choosing the Patrilineal/Fraternal Syndrome as the security provision mechanism for the nation-state. Any discussion of the Syndrome must also entail a simultaneous consideration of the costs of women's subordination at the household level, which undergirds the Syndrome. It is time for societies to ask: Does the Syndrome and its attendant subordinative practices really provide security, stability, prosperity, health, and so forth? We hope this book has set the groundwork for such a consideration by asserting that the answer to that question is a resounding *no*.

If "no" is indeed the answer, the compromise of these goods caused by the Faustian bargain that Syndrome-encoding societies have made with male-bonded extended kin networks should be reconsidered, for the price of that bargain for all of us, male and female alike, is simply too high. Let's look anew at the bargain struck by states, religions, men, and women.

The State's Faustian Bargain

Unless the territory involved is quite small and ethnically homogeneous, governance by a central authority is typically quite challenging in Syndrome-encoding societies. Segmentary lineages, which also capture ethnic and religious differences, are often fiercely independent and unwilling to be governed by outsiders. As we have seen, states often strike a bargain with these male-bonded extended kin networks—pay tribute, come to the government's aid if it is threatened, do not rebel, and you will be left alone. This bargain barely masks the fact that the government is in reality at the mercy of these kin networks.

Mounira Charrad examines the efforts of three states—Morocco, Tunisia, and Iraq—to handle the clans.[68] Morocco pronounced its clans "subclans" of the state, with the Moroccan king's descent from the Prophet Muhammad as the sweetener making this effort to subordinate them palatable. If obedient, these subclans became the hand of the king in far-flung regions. The Tunisian state, by contrast according to Charrad, tried to eradicate and marginalize the clans. Iraq vacillated between the two positions depending on the strength of the state at the time.[69]

Charrad feels that Tunisia was the most successful of the three states and that Morocco's success came only later as it began to emulate the Tunisian approach. Iraq's vacillation meant the clans always retained the upper hand, and Charrad attributes Iraq's current instability to this path. As a result, the Syndrome components and their unfortunate sequelae are on prominent display in that country.

Charrad also asserts that Tunisia was successful in marginalizing clan power because it was the first to undermine the Syndrome's components through reform of personal status law in 1956. This reform, says Charrad, "attempted to undercut kin-based patriarchy and the authority of patriarchs over members of a kin group. The family law reform not only departed from the model of the family associated with kin groupings, but in fact steered individuals away from the extended kin group by fostering individual rights and nuclear families."[70] This attempt was backed up by creating a formal judiciary that was intended to take the place of traditional justice systems based on patriarchal clan law. It took Morocco much longer—until 2004—to reform its personal status law, and in like fashion, Charrad believes this reform strengthened the hand of the state in relation to the tribes. Both of these countries are bastions of relative stability in a region awash in violence.

If we take Charrad's lesson to heart, we would conclude that ruling "through" clans is not a sustainable approach. As the state finds its feet, so to speak, it must destroy the clans' replication strategy, and that means empowering women at the household level. Ironically, centralized states are strengthened when women are strengthened within their households.

That means the typical state strategy of ignoring what male kin groups do to women to "keep the peace" within the nation will produce exactly the opposite result. "Appeasing" such groups by offering to reintroduce or turn a blind eye to previously banned practices such as polygyny is utterly foolish. (Are you listening, Vladimir Putin? Putin has countenanced the de facto reintroduction of polygyny to Russian lands such as Chechnya.)[71] These tactics will only make the clans stronger, not weaker. The smart state will look for every feasible opportunity to meaningfully empower women at the household level, even if those opportunities come over a protracted period of time, as was the case in Morocco. We urge starting with the weakest links in the ouroboros, as explicated in the last section, such as child marriage, polygyny, and women's property rights in marriage, and moving outward from there in an inexorable fashion.

This analysis also suggests a conundrum that we call the "Dictator's Paradox." In Syndrome-encoding societies, it may be long-term dictators, not democrats, who are the most effective champions of women's empowerment at the household level. Both new dictators and democrats must pander to the desires of the existing male-bonded kin networks due to their relative weakness within the political system. Long-term dictators, less vulnerable to public opinion, often are the only actors capable and willing to move in support of meaningful change for women. We have all heard of the old Vulcan saying, "Only Nixon could go to China," but it is also true that "Only Qaddafi could ban polygyny," and "Only Mubarak could reform Egypt's divorce law," and "Only Bourguiba could so drastically change Tunisia's personal status law." (One cannot help but wonder whether long-term dictators have noticed that the women around them have been more loyal and trustworthy than the men who surround them.)

Long-term dictators, then, may be the critical bridge to segue from a full Syndrome-encoding society to a Transitional one. As Richard Cincotta puts it, what is required is "a leader modeled after Tunisia's late Habib Bourguiba: an in-your-face advocate for women's rights and women's participation in a secular society."[72]

Indeed, a long-term dictator may be able to undermine Syndrome components by controlling honor-based systems, and may do so much more effectively than other types of leaders. As psychologist Andrzej Nowak and colleagues find in their simulation experiments, only two types of social systems are effective against aggressive out-groups: honor-based systems, such as we describe encoding Syndrome, and rational interest systems, which we describe as Post-Syndrome societies. In the absence of consolidated state power, honor-based systems may be the only sheriff in town. The authors conclude, "Western rational and interest-based strategies are exported—often unsuccessfully—to contexts of weak institutional authority in which reputation and honor-based strategies have been critical for survival. This research shows that unless changes are made to strengthen institutions in such contexts, rational and interest-based strategies will fail."[73] At a minimum, such strengthening of societal institutions would include a functional judiciary and a representative legislature.

This suggests a role for a transitional leader strong enough within an honor-based context to begin to dismantle the Syndrome in their society. This in turn might lay the groundwork for the establishment of a state-based security provision mechanism encoding at least a rudimentary rule of law establishing a foundation for trust within the society. Such leaders are also perhaps better equipped to handle the inevitable backlash that will come from both elite and low-status men who will lose entitlements and privileges in relation to women in the process. At the same time, we must remember that long-term dictators often originally began their reign by subordinating women to gain crucial male allegiance.[74] For example, in Algeria after the war for independence, part of the bargain the newly independent authoritarian government made and kept with its male citizens was that the regime would control political life, and the men could control the women in their family. As one Algerian feminist commented about this pact, "Give men power over women and they ask for nothing else."[75] It may be only after several decades that the dictator feels secure enough to tinker with that allegiance bargain, if at all. Is it possible that support of long-term dictators *who are actively improving the situation of women at the household level* is a rational foreign policy if long-term national and international stability and security are the goals?[76]

This also suggests something that in Valerie Hudson and Patricia Leidl's book *The Hillary Doctrine* was called "The Steinem Rule."[77] Supporting Syndrome-encoding subnational actors in contests of power seems an untenable policy for Post-Syndrome countries, given all that we have explored in this volume. These actors are certainly not going to stabilize their country. We call this the Steinem Rule because of a story Gloria Steinem told Hudson in 2013, which we share again here.

Steinem remembers attending a briefing of women's organizations in a State Department auditorium toward the end of the Carter administration. Although the subject was an upcoming UN women's conference and Afghanistan wasn't mentioned, the Soviets had rolled into Kabul that very same day in December 1979. Newspapers were full of articles about the *mujahadee*n and their declaration of war against their own Soviet-supported government. Their leaders gave three reasons for why they wanted to drive the Soviets out: girls were being allowed to go to school; girls and women could no longer be married off without their consent; and women were being invited to political meetings.

During the discussion that followed the meeting, Steinem stood up and posed an obvious question: *Given what the mujahadeen themselves had said that day, wasn't the United States supporting the wrong side?* Steinem remembers the question falling into that particular hush reserved for the ridiculous. She doesn't remember the exact answer, but the State Department made it clear that the United States opposed anything that the Soviets supported—the spokesman made no mention that the United States was arming violent, antidemocratic, misogynist religious extremists.

It was clear that matters of war and peace were about Realpolitik and oil pipelines—and not about honoring the human rights of the more peaceful female half of the human race. And so it happened that the *mujahadeen* waged their brutal war with weapons supplied by the United States and, of course, Saudi Arabia—the birthplace of the doctrinaire interpretation of Islam known as *wahabism*. Together, they gave birth to the Taliban, al-Qaeda, and other affiliated terror networks that now reach far beyond the borders of Afghanistan. Steinem says she has never stopped regretting that she didn't chain herself to the seats of that State Department auditorium in public protest.[78] We urge Post-Syndrome nations to seriously consider the defects of ideological foreign policy prescriptions in comparison to the greater long-term benefits of aligning their foreign policy with the Steinem Rule.[79] Serious inquiry about attitudes toward women's subordination held by subnational contestants for power must be part of any decision to support such groups.

Finally, states must avoid the fate of Iraq, which Charrad notes vacillated between undercutting and upholding clan power. When exigencies arise, the temptation to fall back on male-bonded extended kin networks to meet the threat may be intense—and that fallback usually entails selling out the rights of women. Such a temptation must be resisted; the society will be far better able to handle its challenges and threats with women as full, equal partners rather than oppressed second-class citizens. Selling out or disempowering women in the face of exigency weakens the nation-state, making it significantly less resilient, as our empirical analysis shows.

We freely admit that desperate leaders, typically autocratic ones at that, are not going to think about what is good for the long-term when their grip on power is at stake. In other work, we have suggested that this points to a possible role for the international community.[80] We envision a different form of the Responsibility to Protect (R2P) framework—an R2PW (Responsibility to Protect Women), if you will. An R2PW principle would apply the Steinem Rule at the level of the international system and its organizations, such as the United Nations. Support from the international community for a nation-state in times of crisis would be contingent on meaningful attention by that nation-state to the security of women and women's rights. The international community must make plain that regimes that throw women under the bus, so to speak, in times of exigency will be criticized and punished, perhaps through instruments such as economic sanctions, instead of supported.

Religion's Deal with the Devil

From one perspective, the critical issue behind the need for a security provision mechanism is that of trust. This is a gendered problem. Under the Syndrome, men can "trust" women because men can harm or even kill women and those women care about, especially their children. But how can a man trust another man, a being who could potentially harm or kill *him*? The creation of patrilines and fraternal networks is the traditional answer to this male conundrum. Blood ties, whether biological or fictive, have typically formed the basis for trust between men throughout most of human history.

Other forces have posed alternatives to kinship as the basis of trust, however. In the twentieth century, for example, we saw the rise of communist regimes that asserted class as the foundation of trust (e.g., the proletariat) and of fascist regimes that posited race as that foundation. Personalist regimes have stoked allegiance to a particular individual or family as a source for societal trust, such as we have seen in North Korea. All of these alternatives have sought to eradicate kinship-based networks, perceiving them (rightly) as a threat to their power. The fate of these alternatives has always been dismal. They simply have not provided a viable foundation for ongoing trust between men in the absence of the type of rule of law found only in Post-Syndrome societies.

Another force has repeatedly shown its viability in this regard, and that is religion. Whether we speak of a concept such as "the body of Christ," or "the *umma*," most religions suggest we are or may all become kin to one another under God. This transcendent view of kinship thus becomes a potentially strong foundation of trust, at least within a religion's membership. At its peak, religion may even make claims of universal kinship that extend beyond formal membership.

Furthermore, people tend to care what God thinks of them (as we read in chapter 8). When the Roman Catholic Church banned polygyny and cousin marriage under Pope Gregory, for example, there were plenty of complaints and even some noncompliance by elites. Over time, however, the spiritual, social, and temporal penalties for mocking God (and the Pope) proved to be too much and the ban was accepted as normative.

The potential for religion to provide an alternative to the patrilineal/fraternal security provision mechanism would thus appear to be significant. Yet, what we have seen throughout human history (with some important exceptions outlined in chapter 8) is religion by and large upholding the subordination of women, particularly at the household level. In doing so, religion serves as an accomplice in fomenting instability, insecurity, poverty, and other dysfunctional outcomes within society, including its membership.

We could write an entire book about how it is possible that the very force that views itself as providing the greatest possible good for humankind has so betrayed that cause by justifying the subordination of women. Truly, religion can never play the role it envisions playing until and unless it becomes a force for empowering women as equals under God to men.

All too often religion justifies the very components of the Syndrome we have detailed in this volume as being ordained by God. As David Barash puts it, it's almost as if God is seen as the archetypal alpha male harem master, who would without a doubt vigorously endorse the Syndrome.[81] From the standpoint of our empirical analysis, that could only be so if God desires the misery, rather than the happiness, of humankind. This thought defies reason.

Perhaps the problem is that the divine will has been almost exclusively interpreted and translated by men. In that case, efforts to include women in authoritative religious interpretation would be salutary. In the modern era, these efforts are many, and all are to be applauded. For example, with regard to Islam, organizations such as Musawah and Sisters in Islam have been effective in bringing women's voices to bear on the interpretation of the Quran, and by extension, legal reformation of marriage and personal status law. For example, Sisters in Islam, based in Malaysia, is a strong force advocating for the minimum age of marriage for girls to be raised to eighteen, and members of that organization feel that stance is completely in harmony with Islamic teachings. Their explication of why they contend that Aisha was not nine years old, but rather nineteen, when married to the Prophet Muhammad is based on a careful textual and historical analysis and makes for fascinating reading.[82]

The organization Musawah (which means "equality" in Arabic) is also active in this space, as journalist Carla Power describes:

> From Cambridge to Cairo to Jakarta, women are going back to Islam's classical texts and questioning the way men have read them for centuries. In the Middle East, activists are contesting outdated family laws based on Islamic jurisprudence, which give men the power in marriages, divorces, and custody issues. In Europe and the United States, women are chipping away at the customs that have had a chilling effect on women praying in mosques or holding leadership positions. This winter, the first women-only mosque opened in Los Angeles.[83]

Islam is not the only religious tradition that has seen this type of exegetical effort by women to redefine basic terms. For example, in one Christian denomination, female scholars have concluded that the phrase *m'shl bet* has been mistranslated in the King James version of Genesis. While in the Garden of

Eden, God purportedly says to Eve, "and he [Adam] shall rule over thee." According to their interpretation, the Hebrew phrase *m'shl bet* should instead be translated as "rule with." That is, God intended Adam to rule *with* Eve, not *over* Eve. If the scriptural texts indicate that God did not subordinate Eve to Adam, then Eve must not have done something terrible by initiating the Fall, but rather did something wise and courageous in partaking of the fruit of the tree of knowledge of good and evil. The whole world changes when women are invited to interpret the words of God alongside men.

Could religion help humankind avoid the ouroboros-like Syndrome as a security provision mechanism? Yes, it has that potential, but only if it preaches that God's will is that the equal worth of men and women be acknowledged by all, and that God's ideal form of the relationship between men and women is an equal partnership bearing no mark of coercion, subordination, or exploitation. For it is *that* God, and that God alone, who can credibly be said to desire the happiness of humankind.

Waking Men, Waking Women

The Syndrome can persist only if individuals, both men and women, either acquiesce to or embrace it in their personal lives. We have seen the straitjacket-like character of the Syndrome's grip and can understand why it is hard to leave the ouroboros behind. From the male point of view, that "leaving behind" would entail leaving behind a sense of personal security among one's brothers as well as all the "rents" to be enjoyed through the subordination of women.

But there is a larger vision to be seen. We agree with gender and development scholar Deniz Kandiyoti, who asserts that "the subjugation of women ultimately mutilates and distorts the male psyche."[84] This mutilation may begin even from the earliest days of a male child's life by witnessing his father's domination of his mother, the woman who gave him life and nourished him from her own body. Furthermore, the general subjugation of women also means men have to live in societies that, generally speaking, are violent, dysfunctional, insecure, unstable, and poor. Thus, men are mutilated both within and without the household, as they are immersed in the society-wide domination of women. Surely, at some point, men will eschew what is being done to them? Gerda Lerner puts this hope eloquently,

> The system of patriarchy is a historic construct; it has a beginning; it will have an end. Its time seems to have nearly run its course—it no longer serves the needs of men or women and in its inextricable linkage to militarism, hierarchy, and racism it threatens the very existence of life on earth. . . . As long as both men and women regard the subordination of half the human race to the other as "natural," it is impossible to envision a society in which differences do not connote either dominance or subordination.[85]

If men were able to see the harm to *them* in women's subordination, might things change? Could men "awake" and realize that a better, richer, more personally satisfying, more peaceful, and more secure world is in fact available to them if only they let go of the thistle of domination over women? We have met many such men in our lives, though we recognize that even in the United States, ostensibly a Post-Syndrome country, they are relatively few in number.

One organization that shares this vision of waking men to a better way of life is Promundo.[86] Indeed, if we could provide a nomination to the Nobel Committee for its Peace Prize, our top choice would probably be Promundo.[87] Their programs are found across every continent, including North America. Promundo explores the linkages between norms of masculinity and propensity for violence, and puts this understanding to work in developing innovative programs that allow men to escape what Promundo calls the "mask of masculinity" and what we call the Syndrome.

The most effective programs, they have found, are male groups formed with the purpose of deconstructing through dialogue what it means to be a man. Trust formed in male peer groups facilitates sincere change. Sometimes Promundo's initiatives are brash, and refreshing in their brashness. For example, noting how in Kinshasa, Democratic Republic of the Congo, young men would form gangs to provide the fraternity they craved, Promundo began to create young men's clubs to fight violence. One of their greatest contributions is the inauguration of the IMAGES (International Men and Gender Equality Survey) cross-national survey, which has been implemented in almost forty countries with more than sixty thousand interviews. The topics covered in this survey include men's experiences in childhood and in relationships, division of power in households and attitudes related to parenting, perceptions of the gender norms, awareness of gender-sensitive legislation, and attitudes on gender-based violence. Survey findings are then used to plan programs to address harmful attitudes that prevent men from living in peace with women. One such program created by Promundo helped men in the Democratic Republic of the Congo (DRC) rekindle their love for wives who had been raped during the civil war.

This approach of men deciding for themselves among supportive male peers that the path of subordinating women does not end well for them or for women or for the children they create together is hugely important. As we have noted, however, it is also critical that the government take seriously—and punish seriously—crimes such as domestic violence. Until men are able to experience for themselves that the use of gender-based violence is *not functional* for them (e.g., it results in lengthy jail time and onerous fines and social opprobrium), the generalized subordination of women will persist. This suggests that the traditional male entitlement to impunity for crimes such as domestic violence must end for the society to move beyond the Syndrome. In this respect, developments such as the #MeToo movement have been most heartening.

Because nothing will change until men change, women will continue to find themselves caught in the straitjacket of the Syndrome. They are entrapped by it, and they may over time come to embrace it and use that embrace to police other women. This is truly tragic, for in a sense, the Syndrome socializes women to be their own worst enemies.

Nowhere is this more poignantly observed than in the weakening of the conjugal bond in relation to the maternal bond in Syndrome-encoding societies, which is often fiercely enforced by women themselves. McDermott expresses it well:

> As long as the bond between husband and wife is weak relative to the bond between mother and son, then violence against women will promulgate at higher rates. Of course, patrilocality exacerbates this effect, because under such conditions, a woman's safety from other men can be assured only by the loyalty of her son's protection, since she no longer has access to her father or brothers for safety and succor. All these processes sit on a fundamental foundation of male coalitionary psychology that privileges group cohesion over dyadic engagement, contrary to female psychology, which tends to privilege pair bonds.[88]

McDermott does not accept this as a hopeless problem, however. She notes that both the mother and the father of a child "want to raise their children successfully, on average. This is the place where rational and emotional interest can coalesce and intervene to encourage parents to join in reducing the intergenerational transmission of the kind of gender-based violence that compromised the prospects for peace in the future for all of us."[89]

If McDermott is right, and we believe she is, then it is the possibility of real love between husband and wife, despite being differentiated due to sex, that is the seed of the dismantling of the Syndrome within the household and for the generation born within it. But in most Syndrome-encoding societies, that love's greatest foe is often the man's own mother—who is a woman. If this is true, what hope is there? This conundrum reveals that women must "wake" to the idea that there might be a better way to live, just as men must. At a minimum, that waking would involve a greater sense of female solidarity than the Syndrome usually permits.

The lack of female solidarity is easy to explain. In a Syndrome-encoding society, the scarcest resource in society for women is sincere male concern. In a system in which women have been rendered economically prostrate compared with men, and in which violent coercion of women is unremarkable, women will compete intensely for provision and protection by a man who is capable of and willing to provide both. It is ironic that some men in the modern day, such as those in the so-called incel (involuntary celibates) movement, view the propensity of women to choose such powerful men as unfair or hypocritical. Historically speaking, it was men who purposefully created and reinforced this female predisposition for their (male) benefit. Women cannot effectively resist male domination if they are incapable of cooperating together to do so. Consider this commentary by Stephanie Coontz:

> Even in the late 20th century, a study of upper-class Hindu men and women found that most men were loath to develop close ties with their wives because time spent together as a couple undermined the intense bonds between men as fathers and sons and brothers. The women maximized their limited influence in the family not by seeking to deepen their relation with their husbands but by trying to maintain the allegiance of their sons; this they did by undercutting each son's attachment to his wife. A woman in a classical patriarchal society can wield formidable power within the family, even over her own husband, but only by maneuvering within the family's reproductive system. In doing that, rather than by resisting male dominance within marriage or seeking closer ties with her husband, she ends up strengthening the patriarchal family. In such societies, women are likely to fear ideologies and movements that undermine family hierarchies, even if they elevate women's individual autonomy. Any such disruption would be a threat to the protections they need when young and the power they gain when old.[90]

Furthermore, being a mother of sons can cause women to prefer a tighter policing of women. For example, Khandis Blake and her coauthors have found in a study of attitudes in Tunisia that mothers of sons are far more likely to support the veiling of women and to wear veils themselves than mothers of daughters.[91] Blake and colleagues hypothesize that the reproductive interests of these mothers are now intertwined with that of their sons, and so they feel that such policing of young women favors their interests as well as those of their sons.

Are women capable of seeing this trap and refusing to fall prey to it? The role of older women is key as both enablers of female resistance and as role models for younger women in so doing. Consider how bonobo females, our primate cousins, accomplish this by forming alliances with females who are not kin:

> Adult females responded to a broad range of male provocations—unwanted sexual overtures, food disputes, pushing, kicking, vocal threats, persistent pestiness—by forming coalitions of two or more females, who would then jointly take on their male tormentors . . . coalitions arose when a senior female would step in and take the side of a younger peer caught up in an escalating conflict with a resident male. . . . Female bonobos can reject suitors without fearing for their lives. Infanticide is common among chimpanzees, but unheard-of among bonobos.[92]

What would it take for human females to adopt this allied approach to male domination attempts? Perhaps we see a foreshadowing of that possibility in the recent #MeToo movement.

Efforts to help both men and women see and comprehend the precise nature of the trap inherent in the Patrilineal/Fraternal Syndrome can lead to more effective resistance against its strictures. It is also important, however, that a society provide the normative and legal framework necessary to preclude and prevent any functionality of the Syndrome for men—or for women tempted to acquiesce or collude.

Sundry Implications

In this section, we connect a variety of implications from this work.

First, path dependencies matter. Research has shown that the earlier a society begins to shift its norms, the sooner results will be seen—whether this shift is made either toward or away from the Syndrome. For example, James Fenske demonstrates that areas in French West Africa that experienced earlier missionary teaching against polygyny today have lower rates of this practice.[93] Conversely, one male Iranian dissident, during the abortive Green Revolution of 2009, donned the *rusari*, or mandatory head scarf worn by women, perceptively noting, "We Iranian men are late doing this. If we did this when *rusari* was forced on those among our sisters who did not wish to wear it 30 years ago, we would have perhaps not been here today."[94] If you start earlier in undermining Syndrome components, you will have a far easier time dismantling it than if you start later.

A second implication is that the principle of freedom must respect the limits set by the principle of equality between men and women. If those limits based on sexuate equality are not respected and women are once again subjugated, one's political freedoms will eventually and inevitably disappear. Again, we feel this is part of the symbolic import behind the wave of "*niqab* laws" we have seen passed in Europe; these laws symbolize that sexuate and political freedoms are linked and that both will be defended by the society. Our empirical results have shown that political autocracy and the subordination of women prop each other up. Carole Pateman expresses it this way:

> If political relations are to lose all resemblance to slavery, free women and men must willingly agree to uphold the social conditions of their autonomy. That is to say, they must agree to uphold *limits*. Freedom requires order and order requires limits. In modern civil society individual freedom is unconstrained— and order is maintained through mastery and obedience. If men's mastery is to be replaced by a real partnership of women and men, individual freedom must be limited by the structure of social relations in which freedom inheres.[95]

That insight leads to a third implication: attempts to move toward electoral democracy (including attempting to "export" it) while skipping the step of breaking the power of the male-bonded networks by dismantling the Syndrome components that ensure women's disempowerment at the household level, are not going to work. In fact, the "democrats" that emerge under such conditions are not only not likely to be interested in the empowerment of women; they are much more likely to be representative of the agnatic networks that ardently desire to keep women subordinated. Journalists Nellie Peyton and Lamin Jahateh point to the example of Gambia, where when the long-ruling autocrat fell and democratic elections were held, Gambians felt democracy meant they had the freedom to return to their old practices of female genital mutilation and child marriage, which had been banned under the autocrat.[96] Empowering women at the household level can set the stage for meaningful democracy, but veneering procedural democracy over a society organized around women's disempowerment may actually worsen the situation of both women and the nation-state. That type of government will reify hostility between male-bonded networks and also will permit the forces most devoted to women's subordination to have an authoritative voice in government. Those forces include not only fundamentalists but also low-status males who feel they must keep women down to keep their own heads up.[97] And when such low-status males rebel, elite males are often all too ready to throw them the bone of increased subordination of women.

In other words, sincere democratization efforts will be best focused on Transition countries, and not to those fully encoding Syndrome countries. In a way, the best method of determining the timing of such efforts will be to gauge the situation of women with regard to the components of the Syndrome. If the Syndrome score is high, the country may not be ready to become meaningfully democratic. We feel India, often touted as "the world's largest democracy," is an example. But are governments tracking those indicators of women's situation when making foreign policy plans about democratization efforts? No, they are not.

This leads to a fourth implication, which we will cast in U.S. terms as we are Americans. If the United States is not tracking the situation of women, especially at the household level, how can it expect to have an effective foreign policy? More specifically,

- How will it accurately anticipate instability in other countries if it is unaware of linkages related to Syndrome components, such as brideprice and polygyny?
- How will it decide which subnational actors are most likely to bring stability in the long term, if it is not guided by the Steinem Rule?
- How will it avoid the trap of peace negotiations in which the rights of women are bargained away to make "peace" between warlords, if it does not

understand the linkage between sustainable peace and the empowerment of women?

- How will it track which of its own citizens are the greatest internal threat, if domestic violence is not taken more seriously?
- How will it rationally approach immigration policy, if it does not comprehend that the true clash of civilizations is not about religion or ethnicity but about the subordination of women?
- How will it know that ending child marriage worldwide would do more for world peace than almost any other investment?
- How will it understand that tolerating enclaves of family and personal status law that subordinate women will destabilize its society?
- How will it know when exporting democracy makes sense, and when it doesn't?

One day, we predict, the idea that foreign policy and national security policy could ignore the situation of women will be seen as laughably naïve.[98]

If that is true of governments, it is equally true of social science fields such as international relations, political science, and security studies. McDermott and colleagues understate the case when they say: "Different patterns of marriage allocate resources to men, women, and children in different ways . . . it is important to provide a better and more systematic understanding of the relationship between microlevel practices in powerful and ubiquitous family institutions such as marriage with macrolevel outcomes such as conflict and development."[99] Scholarly inquiry in these fields is severely handicapped by the neglect of this relationship. We dream of the day when no introductory-level course examining issues of war and peace could be considered complete without an examination of the first political order between men and women.

A final implication is that catastrophe, whatever its form, is likely to lead to greater subordination of women. International efforts to ameliorate all forms of catastrophe—drought, famine, natural disasters, war, and even a political vacuum—are eminently worthwhile. These efforts have the potential to stem the swift slide back to the Syndrome by fearful men who would otherwise seek security among their "brothers."

Concluding Thoughts: The Stakes

We began this book by noting that the many august tomes written on the development of political order never even mention the sexual political order and its effect on political order at all. Yet, as noted by Jacobson, "The idea of a woman imbued with rights, self-determination, and economic freedom is a remarkable global revolution."[100] Factors such as inequity in family law, early age of marriage for women, prevalence of polygyny, marriage market obstruction, and the like, are virtually never examined by these scholars for they are not viewed as being relevant to the political order or to national security. After publication of this book and its research findings, we hope that stance will no longer be seen as tenable, either theoretically or empirically. That crucial conversation Hudson had with the female Afghan member of parliament more than a decade ago was truly a journey from blindness to sight. Our purpose in this volume was to take our readers along with us on that path as well.

We hope our research will suggest a way forward, past the misery produced by the Syndrome. After all, that first political order need not be viewed as set in stone; Fukuyama notes that many human institutions "exist not because they are efficient or well adapted to their environment, but simply because they crowded out other alternatives at an early stage of development."[101] We agree with this view. Perhaps Malcolm Potts and Thomas Hayden say it best: "Peace needs strong allies in order to persist, and the ally that has been most consistently overlooked is the one that make up slightly [under] half of the human race—women."[102]

It is time to take off the blinders and see the world in realistic terms, for the stakes are enormous for men, women, children, nation-states, the international system, and the world. Simply put, there can be no peace on earth until there is peace between men and women. The time has come to slay that old serpent, that old ouroboros, and for men and women to build together a new first political order in its stead. That new order of equal partnership is the sturdy foundation of all good, all peace, all security, all freedom—and all hope.

APPENDIX I

SYNDROME SCORES FOR 176 COUNTRIES

Method of Calculating the Syndrome Scale Scores

We created the Patrilineal/Fraternal Syndrome scale (table AI.1) using the following variables (note that the scale date is not the date of the data; all of these scales should be assumed to have examined data for the five-year period from 2010 to 2015):

- Prevalence and Legality of Polygyny (2016), The WomanStats Project, ordinal (0–4), higher scores are worse
- Inequitable Family Law and Practice Favoring Males (2016), The WomanStats Project, ordinal (0–4), higher scores are worse
- Bride Price/Dowry/Wedding Costs (2017), The WomanStats Project, ordinal (0–10); higher scores are worse
- Women's Property Rights in Law and Practice (2016), The WomanStats Project, ordinal (0–4), higher scores are worse
- Prevalence and Legality of Cousin Marriage (2016), The WomanStats Project, ordinal (0–3), higher scores are worse
- Age of Marriage for Girls in Law and Practice (2016), The WomanStats Project, ordinal (0–4), higher scores are worse
- Legal Exoneration for Rapists Offering to Marry Victims (2016), The WomanStats Project, ordinal (0–1), higher scores are worse
- Son Preference and Sex Ratios (2015), The WomanStats Project, ordinal (0–4), higher scores are worse

- Prevalence of Patrilocal Marriage (2016), The WomanStats Project, ordinal (0–2), higher scores are worse
- Overall Level of Violence Against Women (2014), The WomanStats Project, ordinal (0–4), higher scores are worse
- Societal Sanction for Femicide (2016), The WomanStats Project, ordinal (0–2), higher scores are worse

TABLE AI.1 Syndrome Scale Scores Scaled in 2017 for the Time Period from 2010 to 2015

Country	Syndrome Scale Scores 2017
Afghanistan	15
Albania	9
Algeria	12
Angola	11
Argentina	4
Armenia	8
Australia	0
Austria	1
Azerbaijan	8
Bahamas	2
Bahrain	11
Bangladesh	14
Barbados	2
Belarus	4
Belgium	1
Belize	6
Benin	13
Bhutan	8
Bolivia	6
Bosnia-Herzegovina	6
Botswana	11
Brazil	6
Brunei	9
Bulgaria	4
Burkina Faso	12
Burma/Myanmar	7
Burundi	10

Country	Syndrome Scale Scores 2017
Cambodia	7
Cameroon	13
Canada	1
Cape Verde	3
Central African Republic*	14
Chad	14
Chile	4
China	9
Colombia	5
Comoros	7
Congo	11
Costa Rica	4
Cote D'Ivoire	13
Croatia	5
Cuba	4
Cyprus	2
Czech Republic	1
Democratic Republic of the Congo	11
Denmark	1
Djibouti	11
Dominican Republic	5
East Timor	12
Ecuador	7
Egypt	12
El Salvador	6
Equatorial Guinea	12
Eritrea	12
Estonia	2
Ethiopia	11
Fiji	7
Finland	1
France	1
Gabon	13
Gambia	14
Georgia	8

(continued)

Country	Syndrome Scale Scores 2017
Germany	1
Ghana	10
Greece	4
Guatemala	9
Guinea	13
Guinea-Bissau	13
Guyana	7
Haiti	7
Honduras	7
Hungary	2
Iceland	1
India	14
Indonesia	13
Iran	14
Iraq	15
Ireland	2
Israel	6
Italy	1
Jamaica	3
Japan	5
Jordan	14
Kazakhstan	8
Kenya	13
Kosovo	6
Kuwait	12
Kyrgyzstan	9
Laos	8
Latvia	3
Lebanon	14
Lesotho	13
Liberia	13
Libya*	13
Lithuania	2
Luxembourg	2
Macedonia	6

Country	Syndrome Scale Scores 2017
Madagascar	8
Malawi	13
Malaysia	10
Maldives	9
Mali	14
Malta	3
Mauritania	14
Mauritius	5
Mexico	6
Moldova	6
Mongolia	3
Montenegro	6
Morocco	12
Mozambique	11
Namibia	11
Nepal	12
Netherlands	0
New Zealand	1
Nicaragua	7
Niger	13
Nigeria	15
North Korea	7
Norway	0
Oman	12
Pakistan	15
Palestine	14
Panama	6
Papua New Guinea	14
Paraguay	5
Peru	7
Philippines	7
Poland	2
Portugal	2
Qatar	12
Romania	4

(continued)

Country	Syndrome Scale Scores 2017
Russia	5
Rwanda	10
Saudi Arabia	14
Senegal	14
Serbia	5
Sierra Leone	13
Singapore	5
Slovakia	2
Slovenia	3
Solomon Islands	13
Somalia	14
South Africa	8
South Korea	6
South Sudan	16
Spain	2
Sri Lanka	9
Sudan	15
Suriname	6
Swaziland	10
Sweden	0
Switzerland	0
Syria*	13
Taiwan	7
Tajikistan	11
Tanzania	13
Thailand	6
Togo	14
Trinidad and Tobago	5
Tunisia	9
Turkey	9
Turkmenistan	8
Uganda	12
Ukraine	4
United Arab Emirates	13
United Kingdom	1

TABLE AI.1   *(continued)*

Country	Syndrome Scale Scores 2017
United States	1
Uruguay	5
Uzbekistan	9
Vanuatu*	11
Venezuela	6
Vietnam	9
Yemen	15
Zambia	11
Zimbabwe	12

*Countries with imputations. Four countries among the 176 analyzed were missing one subscale score in the 2017 scaling used in our present statistical analysis, and their values were imputed to keep the national score comparable to the rest of the nations. These nations are Central African Republic, Libya, Syria, and Vanuatu. The final result of Syria's imputation was actually 12.5, which was rounded up to 13 for input into the database to allow mapping in chapter 3 to be possible.

The initial exploratory factor analysis (EFA) results of these eleven indicator variables extracted two factors using principal axis factoring and promax oblique rotation methods in the SPSS Statistics 24 software package. These two factors had a Kaiser-Meyer-Olkin sampling adequacy measure of .897, which is in the good range for a sample size of 176 countries.[1] We used multiple imputation in R on two subcomponent scores for two countries. The pattern matrix showed some substantial cross-loadings between these two factors. The pattern matrix contains the factor loadings, and if the loadings for two factors are similar for a given variable, this indicates that the variable is measuring the same construct or factor. The correlation between these two factors was also highly significant with $r = .666$. These results corroborate the theoretical framework's assertion that these mechanisms of control of females at the household level interlock as the Syndrome. These substantial cross-loadings and correlation between the two extracted factors justify our decision to combine the eleven components into one index (table AI.1).

We also implemented a confirmatory factor analysis (CFA) as a more robust evaluation into whether a one-dimensional scale could adequately represent the eleven subcomponents of the Syndrome. Because each of the eleven variables included in the CFA are ordinal, we use an unweighted least squares estimation technique for the analysis. In the CFA, we test whether the one-factor

TABLE AI.2 Exploratory Factor Analysis Pattern Matrix for the Eleven Syndrome Component Variables

Pattern Matrix	Factor	
	1	2
Polygyny 2016	.993	
Inequitable Family Law 2016	.919	
BridePrice Dowry 2017	.814	
Property Rights Combined 2016	.807	
Cousin Marriage 2016	.668	
Age Of Marriage Combined 2015	.596	
Rape Exemption 2016	.314	
Son Preference 2015		.890
Patrilocality 2016	.365	.480
Physical Security Of Women 2014	.458	.346
Honor Killing 2016	.427	.287

model fits our data sufficiently well using four model diagnostics: adjusted goodness of fit (AGFI), the normed-fit index (NFI), the standardized root mean square residual (SRMR), and the average value explained (AVE). The AGFI should be greater than or equal to 0.90, the NFI greater than or equal to 0.95, the SRMR less than or equal to 0.08, and the AVE greater than or equal to 0.5. We find that all of our measures of model fit for the one factor model meet these criteria (AGFI = 0.99, NFI = 0.99, SRMR = 0.05, AVE = 0.50). We also calculate the root mean square error of approximation (RMSEA) for this one factor model and find that it again indicates that a single scale is a good fit for the data (RMSEA = 0.00). All p-values for the coefficient estimates corresponding with the eleven subcomponents are significant in the CFA (at alpha ≤ 0.001), indicating that all of the variables are significantly related to the single factor. Overall, we find sufficient evidence to conclude that a single scale to represent these eleven subcomponents is a sufficient fit for the data and significantly describes the variation in the individual variables.

We call this overall index the Patrilineal/Fraternal Syndrome scale. On the basis of this theoretical framework, we used the following algorithm to create the Syndrome scale from the eleven subcomponent scales. Values of this index range from 0 to 16, with higher scores indicating that more of the subcomponents of the Syndrome are present. Based on the EFA, CFA, and the Cronbach alpha's reliability estimate of .898 for these eleven indicator variables (which is in the very good range for internal consistency), we conclude this index is a valid and reliable indicator of the patrilineal/fraternal security provision mechanism as defined in this paper.

- Use Inequitable Family Law/Practice as the base for the index.[2]
- Add Patrilocality score to the index.
- If Brideprice/Dowry is present (score of 6 or above), add 1 to the index.
- If Prevalence and Legality of Polygyny is 3 or 4, add 1 to the index.
- If Age of Marriage Combined Law and Practice scale is 3 or 4, add 1 to the index.
- If Cousin Marriage is 3, add 1 to the index.
- If Women's Property Rights Combined Law and Practice scale is 3 or 4, add 1 to the index.
- If Son Preference and Sex Ratio Scale is 2, add 1 to the index; if it is 3 or 4, add 2 to the index.
- If Violence Against Women (Physical Security of Women scale) is 3 or 4, add 1 to the index.
- If Societal Sanction for Women's Murder/Femicide (Murder-Scale-1) is 2, add 1 to the index.
- If Exemption to Rape Law is present (1), add 1 to the index.

APPENDIX II

COLONIAL HERITAGE STATUS SCORES

Operationalization: A dichotomous measure, with 0 for countries that were not colonized and 1 for countries that had been colonized. This measure looks at the period 1700–2017 and assigns a score of 1 to any country that was colonized not only during war but also in peacetime for at least ten consecutive years. This criterion includes having been colonized by the Union of Soviet Socialist Republics (USSR) in addition to traditional colonizing powers. We define "colonized" as having occurred when a country has sent in and stationed its troops to effect fairly direct control over a country.

Note: Yemen is coded as a 0 because the northern part of the country had never been colonized (with the exception of one section of the highlands by the Ottomans), whereas the port of Aden was colonized by the British. As Yemen had only been partially colonized, we chose to give it a score of 0.

Country	Colonial Heritage Status Score Colonized according to our operational definition? (0 = No, 1 = Yes)	Colonial History
Afghanistan	1	Britain, independence in 1919; USSR, independence in 1989
Albania	1	Ottoman Empire; Italy; Germany, independence in 1943
Algeria	1	France, independence in 1962
Angola	1	Portugal, independence in 1975
Argentina	1	Spain, independence in 1816
Armenia	1	Iran; Imperial Russia; Ottoman Empire, brief independence in 1918; USSR, independence in 1991
Australia	1	Britain, independence in 1901
Austria	0	Not colonized
Azerbaijan	1	Russia, independence in 1918; USSR, independence in 1991
Bahamas	1	Britain, independence in 1973
Bahrain	1	Britain, independence in 1971
Bangladesh	1	Britain, independence in 1971
Barbados	1	Britain, independence in 1966
Belarus	1	USSR, independence in 1991
Belgium	1	Austria; then France, independence in 1830
Belize	1	Britain and Guatemala, independence in 1981
Benin	1	France, independence in 1960
Bhutan	1	Britain, independence in 1947
Bolivia	1	Spain, independence in 1825
Bosnia-Herzegovina	1	Ottoman Empire, Austro-Hungarian Empire, independence from Yugoslavia in 1992
Botswana	1	Britain, independence in 1966

Brazil	1	Portugal, independence in 1822
Brunei	1	Britain, independence in 1984
Bulgaria	1	Ottoman Empire, independence in 1908; USSR, independence in 1990
Burkina Faso	1	France, independence in 1960
Burma/ Myanmar	1	Britain, independence in 1948
Burundi	1	Belgium, independence in 1962
Cambodia	1	France, independence in 1953
Cameroon	1	France, independence in 1960; Britain, independence in 1972
Canada	1	Britain, independence in 1867
Cape Verde	1	Portugal, independence in 1975
Central African Republic	1	France, independence in 1960
Chad	1	France, independence in 1960; Libya, independence in 1990
Chile	1	Spain, independence in 1818
China	1	Several colonial powers; republic in 1912
Colombia	1	Spain, independence in 1810
Comoros	1	France, independence in 1975
Congo	1	France, independence in 1960
Costa Rica	1	Spain, independence in 1821
Cote D'Ivoire	1	France, independence in 1960
Croatia	1	Austro-Hungarian Empire, independence in 1918; then part of Yugoslavia until 1991
Cuba	1	Spain, independence in 1898
Cyprus	1	Britain, independence in 1960
Czech Republic	1	Austro-Hungarian Empire, independence in 1918; Soviet occupation as Czechoslovakia
Democratic Republic of the Congo	1	Belgium, independence in 1960
Denmark	0	Not colonized

(continued)

Country	Colonial Heritage Status Score Colonized according to our operational definition? (0 = No, 1 = Yes)	Colonial History
Djibouti	1	France, independence in 1977
Dominican Republic	1	Spain; independence in 1865
East Timor	1	Portugal, independence in 1974; Indonesia, independence in 2002
Ecuador	1	Spain, independence in 1822
Egypt	1	Ottoman Empire; Britain, independence in 1952
El Salvador	1	Spain, independence in 1821; Central American Federation, independence in 1839
Equatorial Guinea	1	Spain, independence in 1968
Eritrea	1	Italy; Britain; Ethiopia, independence in 1993
Estonia	1	Denmark; Sweden; Germany; Russia, independence in 1918; USSR, independence in 1991
Ethiopia	0	Not colonized
Fiji	1	Britain, independence in 1970
Finland	1	Sweden; Russia, independence in 1917
France	0	Not colonized
Gabon	1	France, independence in 1960
Gambia, The	1	Britain, independence in 1965
Georgia	1	USSR, independence in 1991
Germany	0	Not colonized; short-term Allied occupation after World War II
Ghana	1	Britain, independence in 1957
Greece	1	Ottoman Empire, independence in 1830
Guatemala	1	Spain, independence in 1821
Guinea	1	France, independence in 1958
Guinea-Bissau	1	Portugal, independence in 1974

Guyana	1	Netherlands; Britain, independence in 1966
Haiti	1	France, independence in 1804
Honduras	1	Spain, independence in 1821
Hungary	1	USSR, independence in 1989
Iceland	1	Denmark, independence in 1918
India	1	Britain, independence in 1947
Indonesia	1	The Netherlands, independence in 1949
Iran	0	Not colonized
Iraq	1	League of Nations mandate nation under Britain, independence in 1932
Ireland	1	Britain, independence in 1921
Israel	0	Not colonized
Italy	0	Not colonized
Jamaica	1	Britain, independence in 1962
Japan	0	Not colonized; short-term Allied occupation after World War II
Jordan	1	Mandate nation under Britain, independence in 1946
Kazakhstan	1	Russian Empire; USSR, independence in 1990
Kenya	1	Britain, independence in 1963
Kosovo	1	Serbia, independence in 2008
Kuwait	1	Britain, independence in 1961
Kyrgyzstan	1	USSR, independence in 1991
Laos	1	Thailand; France, independence in 1953
Latvia	1	USSR, independence in 1991
Lebanon	1	Mandate nation under France, independence in 1943
Lesotho	1	Britain, independence in 1966
Liberia	0	Not colonized
Libya	1	Italy, independence in 1951
Lithuania	1	USSR, independence in 1990
Luxembourg	1	The Netherlands, independence in 1839
Macedonia	1	Yugoslavia, independence in 1991

(continued)

Country	Colonial Heritage Status Score Colonized according to our operational definition? (0 = No, 1 = Yes)	Colonial History
Madagascar	1	France, independence in 1960
Malawi	1	Britain, independence in 1964
Malaysia	1	Britain, independence in 1957
Maldives	1	Britain, independence in 1965
Mali	1	France, independence in 1960
Malta	1	Britain, independence in 1964
Mauritania	1	France, independence in 1960
Mauritius	1	France; Britain, independence in 1960
Mexico	1	Spain, independence in 1821
Moldova	1	USSR, independence in 1990
Mongolia	1	USSR; China, independence in 1911
Montenegro	1	Turkey; then a kingdom; then part of Yugoslavia, independence in 2006
Morocco	1	France, independence in 1956
Mozambique	1	Portugal, independence in 1975
Namibia	1	Germany; South Africa, independence in 1990
Nepal	0	Not colonized
Netherlands	0	France, independence in 1830
New Zealand	1	Britain, independence in 1907
Nicaragua	1	Spain, independence in 1821
Niger	1	France, independence in 1960
Nigeria	1	Britain, independence in 1960
North Korea	1	Japan, independence in 1945
Norway	1	Denmark, independence in 1814
Oman	1	De facto British colonization; independence came gradually in mid-20th century
Pakistan	1	Britain, independence in 1947

Palestine	1	Britain; Israel, independence in 1988
Panama	1	Spain, independence in 1821; Colombia, independence in 1903
Papua New Guinea	1	Germany; Britain; Australia, independence in 1975
Paraguay	1	Spain, independence in 1811
Peru	1	Spain, independence in 1821
Philippines	1	Spain; United States, independence in 1946
Poland	1	Russia; Prussia; Austria; USSR, independence in 1990
Portugal	0	Not colonized
Qatar	1	Britain, independence in 1971
Romania	1	Ottoman Empire, independence in 1877; USSR, independence in 1989
Russia	0	Not colonized
Rwanda	1	Belgium, independence in 1962
Saudi Arabia	0	Not colonized
Senegal	1	France, independence in 1960
Serbia	1	Ottoman Empire; former Yugoslavia, independence in 1992
Sierra Leone	1	Britain, independence in 1961
Singapore	1	Britain, independence in 1965
Slovakia	1	Hungary; Czechoslovakia; USSR, independence in 1989
Slovenia	1	Hungary; Austria; Yugoslavia, independence in 1991
Solomon Islands	1	Britain, independence in 1978
Somalia	1	Britain, independence in 1960
South Africa	1	Netherlands; Britain, independence in 1910
South Korea	1	Japan, independence in 1945
South Sudan	1	Egypt, Britain; Sudan, independence in 2011
Spain	0	Not colonized
Sri Lanka	1	Netherlands; Britain, independence in 1948
Sudan	1	Britain; Egypt, independence in 1956

(continued)

Country	Colonial Heritage Status Score Colonized according to our operational definition? (0 = No, 1 = Yes)	Colonial History
Suriname	1	Netherlands, independence in 1975
Swaziland	1	Britain, independence in 1968
Sweden	0	Not colonized
Switzerland	0	Not colonized
Syria	1	Turkey; France, independence in 1946
Taiwan	1	China; Japan, de facto independence in 1945
Tajikistan	1	Russia; USSR, independence in 1991
Tanzania	1	Britain, independence in 1964
Thailand	0	Not colonized
Togo	1	France, independence in 1960
Trinidad and Tobago	1	Spain; Britain, independence in 1962
Tunisia	1	France, independence in 1956
Turkey	0	Not colonized
Turkmenistan	1	Russia; USSR, independence in 1991
Uganda	1	Britain, independence in 1962
Ukraine	1	Russia; USSR, independence in 1991
United Arab Emirates	1	Britain, independence in 1971
United Kingdom	0	Not colonized
United States	1	Britain, independence in 1783
Uruguay	1	Spain; Brazil, independence in 1828
Uzbekistan	1	Russia; USSR, independence in 1991
Vanuatu	1	Britain; France, independence in 1980
Venezuela	1	Spain; Colombia, independence in 1845

Vietnam	1	France, independence in 1954
Yemen	0	North Yemen's highlands; Ottoman Turks, independence in 1918; South Yemen: Britain, independence in 1967 (0 because only partially colonized)
Zambia	1	Britain, independence in 1964
Zimbabwe	1	Britain, independence in 1965

*Scaled by Donna Lee Bowen and Valerie M. Hudson in 2017, using multiple online sources, the foremost of which was Wikipedia.

APPENDIX III

TESTING THE EFFECTS

Methods and Extended Results

C hapter 7 assesses the relationship between national outcomes and Syndrome status through regression analyses, including general linear model (GLM) and logistic regression. Our method was to comprehensively survey outcome variables related to each of the nine dimensions in which the Syndrome plays out: Political Stability and Governance, Security and Conflict, Economic Performance, Economic Rentierism, Health and Well-Being, Demographic Security, Education of the Population, Social Progress, and Environmental Protection. Once these dimensions were compiled, we examined whether the N size for each variable would allow us to roughly match that of our dataset of 176 nations; if the N size was below 140, we searched for a similarly conceptualized alternative variable with a higher N size or, in some special cases, ran an ancillary analysis. If more than a handful of variables were identified as pertinent to a given dimension, we also attempted to reduce that number through factor analysis, reserving variables that did not load highly on the identified factors for separate analysis. Before including variables in the factor analysis, we eliminated certain dependent variables that were highly correlated (i.e., $r > .90$) with other variables in the same dimension. When several dependent variables loaded highly on a given factor, we combined the country-level Z-scores on the component variables (keeping directionality consistent across the variables) to provide a score for that factor for each nation before running our multivariate models.

In presenting the results, we first identify the specific variables we examined for each dimension, noting in endnotes which variables were of potential interest but had to be excluded for reasons of N size or overly high intercorrelations with other variables in the same dimension. If a factor analysis was used to reduce the number of variables in the dimension, those factor analysis results are presented next, and variables reserved for separate analysis are also noted. All of our factor analysis used the principal axis factoring and promax oblique rotation methods. All of the results had a Kaiser-Meyer-Olkin sampling adequacy measures in the good range (greater than .800) and explained at least 50% of the common variance.

After this presentation, the results of the multivariate modeling are displayed and discussed for each dimension. Because of space considerations, we identified certain variables in each dimension as used for "primary analysis," and others as used for "ancillary analysis." The full table of results and scatterplots are presented for each primary analysis; the tables and scatterplots for all ancillary variables can be found on the WomanStats Project website (http://womanstats.org/fpo.html) along with the full replication data sheet for all analyses. If the GLM analysis for a dependent variable found the Syndrome significant, we performed these follow-up analyses: (1) calculated a bivariate correlation between the Syndrome and the quantitative dependent variable and generated a scatterplot for these two variables or performed an ANOVA test between the Syndrome and categorical or ordinal dependent variables with less than five levels and presented a jittered scatterplot, and (2) where model assumptions are met, we also performed a logistic regression analysis to evaluate the effect of a one unit increase in Syndrome score on a country's likelihood to be in the "worse outcome" category for the dependent variable in question.

To perform these follow-up logistic regression analyses, the method required dichotomization of each of these dependent variables for which the Syndrome is significant. We split the values for these variables into a 0 or 1, where for every variable, 0 indicates a good outcome and 1 indicates a worse outcome. We chose a split for each variable by examining histograms, means, and standard deviations to determine which range of scores would indicate a "worse outcome." For most quantitative variables, we use the mean as the cutoff and "worse outcome" is defined as worse than average. For a few variables, we look at a natural split in the histogram of the data; most of these splits occurred around the mean value. For ordinal variables, we use the upper values of the worse outcomes for cutoff points. The details of the justifications for the cutoff points for each logistic regression variable are presented in appendix IV. We report the logistic results at the $\alpha \leq .01$ level because the purpose in these logistic analyses was to report on risk levels, as a follow-up on significant multivariate modeling results at the more stringent α value of .001. The logistic regression model is as follows:

$Y_i = \beta_0 + \beta_1$ Syndrome $+ \beta_2$ Urbanization $+ \beta_3$ Type of Civilization
    $+ \beta_4$ Colonial Heritage Status $+ \beta_5$ Percent Arable Land
    $+ \beta_6$ Number of Unique Land Neighbors $+ \beta_7$ Aggregated Ethnic Fractionalization
    $+ \beta_8$ Religious Fractionalization $+ \varepsilon_i$

where Y_i is the logit for worse outcomes (e.g., target group has a worse level of violence and instability). We checked for model validity for the logistic regression models and used results which satisfied the following conditions: (1) a significant Omnibus test of model coefficients, which indicates that the variables in the model collectively influence the logits, (2) a nonsignificant Hosmer and Lemeshow test, which indicates a good fit, and (3) a Nagelkerke R-squared of .30 or higher.

A note on GLM multivariate modeling issues is also in order. The possible effects of both multicollinearity and model dependency were of concern to us. As noted previously, we avoided control variables with intercorrelations higher than .70, and we also examined variance inflation factors (VIFs) when running our multivariate models. To guard against model dependency, we sought to limit the number of control variables to avoid what Christopher Achen has called "garbage can" multivariate models,[1] where, as Phil Schrodt picturesquely describes, "even minor changes in model specification can lead to coefficient estimates that bounce around like a box full of gerbils on methamphetamines."[2] We also probed for robustness in model specification by swapping out theoretically related variables, such as examining for certain models whether results changed if we substituted, say, gross domestic product (GDP) per capita in place of urbanization. In addition, we examined consistency of statistical significance and magnitude of effect size across the numerous dependent variables in these nine broad dimensions of outcomes so that idiosyncratic operationalizations could not be used to cherry-pick results. Although no statistical analysis can ever completely avoid the uncertainty inherent in multivariate modeling, we feel these measures offered some tangible mitigation.

We systematize the categorization of both the adjusted R-squared values and the Pearson correlation (r) values. The adjusted R-squared categorization is as follows: below .2 is considered weak, .2 to .4 is considered moderate, .4 to .6 is considered strong, and .6 and above is considered remarkably strong. The Pearson correlation (r) categorization is as follows: 0 to .4 is considered weak, .4 to .7 is considered moderately strong, and .7 to 1 is considered very strong (note that all of these values are the absolute values for the correlations). We also included the effect sizes for each independent variable in the GLM analysis, using partial eta-squared values from SPSS Statistics 24.

Results and Analysis by Dimension

Dimension 1. Political Stability and Governance

Variables in the Political Stability and Governance Dimension
The variables that are most commonly used in the international relations field and that the authors deemed to be the most valid measures of political stability and governance are listed in alphabetical order. (Some potential variables of interest had to be excluded because of low N size or correlation less than .9 with the variables in this list.[3]) The list provides the variable name; the source from which the variable was obtained; whether the measure is nominal, ordinal, or continuous and the range where applicable; which directionality the variable takes; the N size for the variable; and whether any transformations were used:

1. Civil Liberties (2015), Economist Intelligence Unit (Accessed from the Quality of Government Institute), ordinal (0–10), lower scores are worse, N = 165
2. Deliberative Component Index (2017), V-Dem Annual Report Version 7.1, continuous scale (min = .021, max = .989), lower scores are worse, N = 169
3. Democratic Political Culture Index (2015), Economist Intelligence Unit (Accessed from the Quality of Government Institute), ordinal (0–10), lower scores are worse, N = 165
4. Equal Protection Index (2017), V-Dem Annual Report Version 7.1, continuous scale (min = .042, max = .976), lower scores are worse, N = 169
5. Fragile States Index (2016), The Fund for Peace, continuous scale (min = 18.8, max = 114.0), higher scores are worse, N = 172
6. Freedom House Index Political Rights (2016), Freedom House, ordinal (1–7), higher scores are worse (1 = most free and 7 = least free), N = 176
7. Freedom of Religion (2016), Social Progress Index, ordinal (1–4), lower scores are worse, N = 171
8. Freedom to Establish Religion (2014), Human Freedom Index, ordinal (0–10), lower scores are worse, N = 133 (The N size is too low to include in exploratory factor analysis (EFA), so this outcome variable was analyzed separately.)
9. Functioning of Government (2015), Economist Intelligence Unit, Index of Democracy (Accessed from the Quality of Government Institute), ordinal (0–10), lower scores are worse, N = 165
10. Global Peace Index (2017), Vision of Humanity, continuous scale (min = 1.11, max = 3.81), higher scores are worse, N = 163
11. Government Participation of Women (2016), The WomanStats Project, ordinal (0–4), higher scores are worse, N = 176 seats in parliament and also cabinet positions held by women
12. Percent of Seats in Parliament Held by Women (2016), World Bank, percent, lower scores are worse, N = 172

13. Political Instability (2017), Vision of Humanity, ordinal (1–5), higher scores are worse, N = 162
14. Political System Type (2013), Freedom Rising (subcomponent of the World Values Survey) (Accessed from the Quality of Government Institute), ordinal (0–1), lower scores are worse (0 = unbound autocracy, 1 = effective democracy), N = 170
15. Press Freedom Index (2016), Reporters without Borders World Press Freedom Index (Accessed from the Quality of Government Institute), ordinal (0–100), higher scores are worse (0 = total press freedom, 100 = no press freedom), N = 170
16. Private Property Rights (2016), Social Progress Index, ordinal (0–100), lower scores are worse, N = 170
17. Regime Types (2013), Freedom Rising (subcomponent of the World Values Survey) (Accessed from the Quality of Government Institute), ordinal (1–4), lower scores are worse (1 = pure autocracy, 4 = minimal democracy), N = 168
18. Security Apparatus (2016), subcomponent of the Fragile States Index, continuous scale (min = 1.3, max = 10.0), higher scores are worse indicating that Security Apparatus lacks a monopoly on the use of force or is used malevolently, N = 171
19. State Legitimacy (2016), subcomponent of the Fragile States Index, continuous scale (min = .50, max = 9.90), higher scores are worse, N = 171
20. World Bank Corruption (2015), World Bank, continuous scale (min = −1.81, max = 2.30), lower scores are worse, N = 176
21. World Bank Government Effectiveness (2015), World Bank, continuous scale (min = −2.26, max = 2.21), lower scores are worse, N = 176
22. World Bank Rule of Law (2015), World Bank, continuous scale (min = −2.37, max = 2.04), lower scores are worse, N = 176

We wanted to reduce the number of variables examined through factor analysis to find variables that loaded highly on the same factor and thus could be analyzed together. In this manner, we identified four factors and three variables that did not load sufficiently high on either one of these factors.

The EFA extracted the following four factors below, discussed in the order they were extracted, and the z-scores of the variables in each factor were added to create the score for the factor, after checking for consistency in their directionality:

1. **Government System and Effectiveness Factor** (higher scores are considered better, N = 158): This factor consists of these five variables with loadings ranging from .447 to 1.121: (1) World Bank Government Effectiveness 2015, (2) Functioning of Government 2017, (3) Democratic Political Culture Index, (4) Political System Type, and (5) Equal Protection Index.

   2.   Lack of Security, Stability, and Legitimacy Factor (higher scores are considered worse on these variables, N = 158): This factor consists of these four variables with loadings ranging from −.951 to −.775: (1) Security Apparatus, (2) Political Instability, (3) State (Il)Legitimacy, and (4) Global Peace Index.
   3.   Lack of Freedom Factor (higher scores are considered worse, N = 170): This factor consists of these two variables with loadings ranging from −.839 to −.668: (1) Press Freedom Index 2017 and (2) Freedom House Index of Political Rights 2016.
   4.   Freedom of Religion and Deliberative Component Factor (higher scores are considered better, N = 164): This factor consists of these two variables with loadings ranging from .615 to .812: (1) Freedom of Religion and (2) Deliberative Component Index.

Model Specifications

The model for each of these dependent variables or factors takes the following form in each case:

$$\text{Dependent variable or factor}_i = \text{Syndrome} + \text{Civilization}$$
$$+ \text{Colonial Heritage Status} + \text{Urbanization} + \text{Terrain}$$
$$+ \text{Number of Land Neighbors}$$
$$+ \text{Religious Fractionalization}$$
$$+ \text{Aggregated Ethnic Fractionalization} + \varepsilon_i$$

We used a GLM procedure to investigate the statistical significance and explanatory power of these eight independent variables for each outcome variable or factor in this dimension. We hypothesized that, after controlling for the influence of the other seven control variables, the Patrilineal/Fraternal Syndrome will be a significant predictor of these three factors and four dependent variables for the nations in our study. Significance is defined as $p \leq .001$, a stringent standard for significance in social science research.

GLM Results for Variables Used in the Main Analysis of the Political Stability and Governance Dimension

1.1.   Fragile States Index (higher scores are considered worse, N = 172): The results are as follows:

TABLE AIII.7.1.1 General Linear Model Results for Fragile States Index (Adjusted R-squared = .744)

Independent/ Control Variable	Parameter Estimate	Standard Error	p-value	Effect Size
Intercept	57.153	6.303	.000	.357
Colonial Heritage Status = 0 (Never Colonized)	−3.867	3.059	.208	.011
Colonial Heritage Status = 1 (Ever Colonized)	0			
CIV = 1 (West/Orthodox/Latin)	2.591	2.704	.340	.006
CIV = 2 (Muslim)	−4.406	3.165	.166	.013
CIV = 4 (Hindu/Sinic/Buddhist)	5.109	3.900	.192	.011
CIV = 5 (Africa)	0			
Syndrome 2017	3.433	.331	.000*	.422
Urbanization 2015	−.315	.053	.000*	.194
Number of Land Neighbors	1.019	.406	.013	.041
Terrain 2014	.066	.074	.372	.005
Religious Fractionalization 2003	−10.562	4.503	.020	.036
Ethnic Fractionalization 2003	8.064	4.837	.098	.018

*significant at .001

1.2.   Government System and Effectiveness Factor (lower scores are considered worse, N = 158): Recall that this factor combines several variables (World Bank Government Effectiveness, Functioning of Government, Democratic Political Culture Index, Political System Type, and Equal Protection Index), the results are as follows:

TABLE AIII.7.1.2 General Linear Model Results for Government System and Effectiveness Factor (Adjusted R-squared = .565)

Independent/ Control Variable	Parameter Estimate	Standard Error	*p*-value	Effect Size
Intercept	2.950	1.468	.047	.028
Colonial Heritage Status = 0 (Never Colonized)	1.782	.709	.013	.044
Colonial Status = 1 (Ever Colonized)	0			
CIV = 1 (West/Orthodox/Latin)	−.846	.634	.185	.013
CIV = 2 (Muslim)	−.541	.750	.471	.004
CIV = 4 (Hindu/Sinic/Buddhist)	−1.314	.894	.144	.015
CIV = 5 (Africa)	0			
Syndrome 2017	−.566	.077	.000*	.280
Urbanization 2015	.035	.013	.006	.053
Number of Land Neighbors	−.260	.096	.008	.050
Terrain 2014	.003	.017	.850	.000
Religious Fractionalization 2003	2.025	1.068	.060	.025
Ethnic Fractionalization 2003	−.227	1.130	.841	.000

*significant at .001

1.3.   World Bank Corruption 2015 (Lower scores are considered worse, N = 176): The results are as follows:

TABLE AIII.7.1.3 General Linear Model Results for World Bank Corruption 2015 (Adjusted R-squared = .563)

Independent/ Control Variable	Parameter Estimate	Standard Error	*p*-value	Effect Size
Intercept	.372	.343	.281	.008
Colonial Heritage Status = 0 (Never Colonized)	.543	.167	.001*	.066
Colonial Heritage Status = 1 (Ever Colonized)	0			
CIV = 1 (West/Orthodox/Latin)	−.297	.147	.045	.027
CIV = 2 (Muslim)	−.154	.173	.375	.005
CIV = 4 (Hindu/Sinic/Buddhist)	−.402	.213	.061	.023
CIV = 5 (Africa)	0			
Syndrome 2017	−.106	.018	.000*	.191
Urbanization 2015	.013	.003	.000*	.115
Number of Land Neighbors	−.069	.022	.002	.062
Terrain 2014	−.004	.004	.314	.007
Religious Fractionalization 2003	.549	.244	.026	.033
Ethnic Fractionalization 2003	−.360	.257	.164	.013

*significant at .001

1.4. World Bank Rule of Law 2015 (Lower scores are considered worse, N = 176): The results are as follows:

TABLE AIII.7.1.4 General Linear Model Results for World Bank Rule of Law 2015 (Adjusted R-squared = .561)

Independent/ Control Variable	Parameter Estimate	Standard Error	p-value	Effect Size
Intercept	.173	.341	.612	.002
Colonial Heritage Status = 0 (Never Colonized)	.523	.166	.002	.062
Colonial Heritage Status = 1 (Ever Colonized)	0			
CIV = 1 (West/Orthodox/Latin)	−.187	.146	.203	.011
CIV = 2 (Muslim)	.033	.172	.850	.000
CIV = 4 (Hindu/Sinic/Buddhist)	−.364	.212	.088	.019
CIV = 5 (Africa)	0			
Syndrome 2017	−.104	.018	.000*	.186
Urbanization 2015	.011	.003	.000*	.096
Number of Land Neighbors	−.059	.022	.008	.046
Terrain 2014	.000	.004	.935	.000
Religious Fractionalization 2003	.832	.243	.001*	.073
Ethnic Fractionalization 2003	−.495	.256	.055	.024

*significant at .001

1.5. Lack of Freedom Factor (higher scores are considered worse, N = 170): Recall that this factor combines two variables (Press Freedom Index 2017 and Freedom House Index Political Rights 2016), the results are as follows:

TABLE AIII.7.1.5 General Linear Model Results for Lack of Freedom Factor (Adjusted R-squared = .415)

Independent/ Control Variable	Parameter Estimate	Standard Error	*p*-value	Effect Size
Intercept	−1.761	.734	.018	.038
Colonial Heritage Status = 0 (Never Colonized)	−.522	.353	.142	.015
Colonial Heritage Status = 1 (Ever Colonized)	0			
CIV = 1 (West/Orthodox/Latin)	.386	.313	.220	.010
CIV = 2 (Muslim)	1.022	.366	.006	.051
CIV = 4 (Hindu/Sinic/Buddhist)	1.071	.451	.019	.037
CIV = 5 (Africa)	0			
Syndrome 2017	.231	.038	.000*	.199
Urbanization 2015	−.005	.006	.449	.004
Number of Land Neighbors	.128	.047	.008	.048
Terrain 2014	−.008	.009	.365	.006
Religious Fractionalization 2003	−.560	.524	.286	.008
Ethnic Fractionalization 2003	−.759	.560	.177	.012

*significant at .001

1.6.   Freedom to Establish Religion (lower scores are considered worse, N = 133): The results of the GLM analysis are given in the table below:

TABLE AIII.7.1.6 General Linear Model Results for Freedom to Establish Religion (Adjusted R-squared = .245)

Independent/ Control Variable	Parameter Estimate	Standard Error	p-value	Effect Size
Intercept	6.323	1.570	.000	.123
Colonial Heritage Status = 0 (Never Colonized)	−.145	.627	.818	.000
Colonial Heritage Status = 1 (Ever Colonized)	0			
CIV = 1 (West/Orthodox/Latin)	−.094	.610	.878	.000
CIV = 2 (Muslim)	−1.320	.721	.070	.028
CIV = 4 (Hindu/Sinic/Buddhist)	.913	.900	.312	.009
CIV = 5 (Africa)	0			
Syndrome 2017	−.259	.075	.001*	.092
Urbanization 2015	.012	.013	.381	.007
Number of Land Neighbors	−.049	.089	.582	.003
Terrain 2014	.060	.017	.001*	.092
Religious Fractionalization 2003	.113	1.024	.913	.000
Ethnic Fractionalization 2003	3.749	1.145	.001*	.085

*significant at .001

1.7.   Percent of Seats in Parliament Held by Women (lower scores are considered worse, N = 172): The results are as follows:

TABLE AIII.7.1.7 General Linear Model Results for Percent of Seats in Parliament Held by Women (Adjusted R-squared = .116)

Independent/ Control Variable	Parameter Estimate	Standard Error	p-value	Effect Size
Intercept	35.160	5.841	.000	.197
Colonial Heritage Status = 0 (Never Colonized)	3.357	2.844	.240	.009
Colonial Heritage Status = 1 (Ever Colonized)	0			
CIV = 1 (West/Orthodox/Latin)	−2.278	2.510	.366	.006
CIV = 2 (Muslim)	−3.955	2.944	.181	.012
CIV = 4 (Hindu/Sinic/Buddhist)	−3.006	3.627	.409	.005
CIV = 5 (Africa)	0			
Syndrome 2017	−1.214	.304	.000*	.097
Urbanization 2015	−.058	.049	.234	.010
Number of Land Neighbors	.344	.375	.360	.006
Terrain 2014	.000	.068	.998	.000
Religious Fractionalization 2003	−6.281	4.168	.134	.015
Ethnic Fractionalization 2003	5.270	4.377	.230	.010

*significant at .001

Dimension 2. Security and Conflict

Variables in the Security and Conflict Dimension

The variables that are most commonly used in the international relations field and that the authors deemed as the most valid measures of national security and conflict are listed in alphabetical order. (Some potential variables of interest had to be excluded because of low N size or correlation greater than or equal to .9 with the variables in this list.[4]) The list provides the variable name; the source from which the variable was obtained; whether the measure is nominal, ordinal, or continuous and the range, where applicable; which directionality the variable takes; the N size for the variable; and whether any transformations were used:

1. Access to Weapons (2017), Vision of Humanity's Global Peace Index, scale from 1–5, higher scores are worse, N = 163

2. Deaths from External Conflicts (2017), Vision of Humanity's Global Peace Index, scale from 1–5, higher scores are worse, N = 163

3. Deaths from Internal Conflict (2017), Vision of Humanity's Global Peace Index, scale from 1–5, higher scores are worse, N = 163

4. Disappearances (2014), Human Freedom Index, scale from 0–10, lower scores are worse, N = 157

5. External Conflicts Fought (2017), Vision of Humanity's Global Peace Index, scale from 1–5, higher scores are worse, N = 163

6. Freedom of Domestic Movement (2014), Human Freedom Index, scale from 0–10, lower scores are worse, N = 157

7. Global Terrorism Index (2017), Vision of Humanity's Global Terrorism Index, scale from 0–10, higher scores are worse, N = 163

8. Group Grievance (2014), Fund for Peace's Fragile State Index (Accessed from the Quality of Government Institute), scale from 1–10, higher scores are worse, N = 171

9. Homicide Rate (2016), Social Progress Index, rate of deaths per 100,000 population, higher scores are worse, N = 160

10. Homicide (2014), Human Freedom Index, scale from 0–10, lower scores are worse, N = 156

11. Homicide (2017), Vision of Humanity's Global Peace Index, rates per 100,000 population scaled 1–5, higher scores are worse, N = 163

12. Incarceration Rate (2017), Vision of Humanity's Global Peace Index, rates per 100,000 population scaled 1–5, higher scores are worse, N = 163

13. Incidents of Terrorism in a Given Year (2017), Vision of Humanity's Global Terrorism Index, number of terrorism incidents in a year, higher scores are worse, N = 163

14. Intensity of Internal Conflicts (2017), Vision of Humanity's Global Peace Index, scale from 1–5, higher scores are worse, N = 163

15. Intensity of Violent Conflict (2014), Human Freedom Index, scale from 0–10, lower scores are worse, N = 157

16. Internal Conflicts Fought (2017), Vision of Humanity's Global Peace Index, scale from 1–5, higher scores are worse, N = 163

17. Military Expenditures as Percentage of GDP (2016, or most recent without searching earlier than 2007), World Bank, percent, higher scores are worse, N = 158

18. Military Expenditures (2017), Vision of Humanity's Global Peace Index, scale from 1–5, higher scores are worse, N = 163

19. Monopoly on the use of force (2016), Bertelsmann Stiftung's Transformation Index (Accessed from the Quality of Government Institute), scale from 1–10, lower scores are worse, N = 128 (This variable was excluded from the factor analysis because its sample size was too small [<140], but it was analyzed separately.)

20. Neighboring Country Relations (2017), Vision of Humanity's Global Peace Index, scale from 1–5, higher scores are worse, N = 163

21. Overall index of Disappearance, Conflict, and Terrorism Score (2014), Human Freedom Index, scale from 0–10, lower scores are worse, N = 157

22. Perceptions of Criminality (2017), Vision of Humanity's Global Peace Index, rates per 100,000 population scaled 1–5, higher scores are worse, N = 163

23. Political Stability and Absence of Violence/Terrorism (2016), World Bank, scale from −2.5 to 2.5 (actual range is −2.91 to +1.53), lower scores are worse, N = 176

24. Political Terror Scale (2016), Political Terror Scale (this is terror inflicted by the state, such as torture and extrajudicial killings), scale from 1–5, higher scores are worse, N = 175

25. Political Terror (2017), Vision of Humanity's Global Peace Index, scale from 1–5, higher scores are worse, N = 163

26. Societal Violence Scale (2014, or 2013 if 2014 value was unavailable), Political Terror Scale, scale from 1–5, higher scores are worse, N = 174

27. States of Concern to the International Community Scale (2011), SOCIC Scale, scale from 0–4, higher scores are worse, N = 157

28. Terrorism Fatalities (2014), Human Freedom Index, scale from 0–10, lower scores are worse, N = 157

29. Terrorism Impact (2017), Vision of Humanity's Global Peace Index, ordinal scale from 1–5, higher scores are worse, N = 163 (This variable was excluded from the factor analysis because it was too highly correlated with the Global Terrorism Index variable [>.9], but it was analyzed separately.)

30. Terrorism Injuries (2014), Human Freedom Index, scale from 0–10, lower scores are worse, N = 156

31. Trafficking in Women (2015), The WomanStats Project, scale from 0–4, higher scores are worse, N = 174

32. Violent Crime (2017), Vision of Humanity's Global Peace Index, scale from 1–5, higher scores are worse, N = 163

33. Violent Demonstrations (2017), Vision of Humanity's Global Peace Index, scale from 1–5, higher scores are worse, N = 163

34. Weapons Imports (2017), Vision of Humanity, scale from 1–5, rates, higher scores are worse, N = 163

35. Women's Mobility (2017), The WomanStats Project, scale from 0–4, higher scores are worse, N = 173

To reduce the number of variables, we ran a factor analysis to find variables loading highly on the same factors and thus could be analyzed together. In this manner, we identified six factors, and the z-scores of the variables in each factor were added to create the score for each factor, after checking for consistency in direction (or multiplied by –1 to maintain consistency):

1.   **Violence and Instability Factor** (higher scores are considered worse, N = 145): This factor consists of these nine variables with loadings ranging from .607 to 1.018: (1) States of Concern, (2) Group Grievance, (3) Political Terror Scale, (4) Trafficking of Women, (5) Intensity of Internal Conflicts, (6) Violence Demonstrations, (7) Political Terror, (8) Women's Mobility, and (9) Relations with Neighboring Countries.

2.   **Absence of Violent Terrorism and Freedom of Domestic Movement Factor** (lower scores are considered worse, N = 157): This factor consists of these two variables with loadings ranging from –.817 to –.529: (1) Political Stability and Absence of Violence/Terrorism and (2) Freedom of Domestic Movement.

3.   **Terrorism Injury and Violent Conflict Factor** (lower scores are considered worse, N = 156): This factor consists of these four variables with loadings ranging from –.977 to –.607: (1) Terrorism Injuries, (2) Terrorism Fatalities, (3) Intensity of Violent Conflicts, and (4) Overall Index of Disappearance, Conflict, and Terrorism.

4.   **Homicide and Violent Crime Factor** (higher scores are considered worse, N = 154): This factor consists of these three variables with loadings ranging from .615 to .943: (1) Homicide Rates (SPI), (2) Homicide (GPI), and (3) Violent Crime.

5.   **Terrorism Incidents and Internal Conflict Factor** (higher scores are considered worse, N = 163): This factor consists of these three variables with loadings ranging from .517 to .831: (1) Incidents of Terrorism in a Given Year, (2) Internal Conflicts Fought, and (3) Global Terrorism Index.

6.   **Military Expenditure and Weapons Importation Factor** (higher scores are considered worse, N = 152): This factor consists of these three variables with loadings ranging from .727 to .923: (1) Military Expenditure as a Percentage of GDP, (2) Military Expenditures (GPI), and (3) Weapons Imports.

Model specification

The model for each dependent variable or factor takes the same form in each case:

Dependent variable or factor$_i$ = Syndrome + Civilization
+ Colonial Heritage Status + Urbanization + Terrain
+ Number of Land Neighbors + Religious Fractionalization
+ Aggregated Ethnic Fractionalization + ε_i

We used GLM to investigate the statistical significance and explanatory power of these eight independent variables. We hypothesized that, after controlling for the influence of the other seven control variables, the Patrilineal/ Fraternal Syndrome will still be a significant predictor of these dependent variables and factors for the nations in our study.

GLM Results for the Security and Conflict Dimension

2.1. Violence and Instability Factor (higher scores are considered worse, N = 145): Recall that this factor combines several variables (States of Concern Scale, Group Grievance, Political Terrorism Scale, Trafficking, Internal Conflict, Violent Demonstrations, Political Terror, Women's Mobility, and Neighboring Country Relations); the results obtained are as follows:

TABLE AIII.7.2.1 General Linear Model Results for Violence and Instability Factor (Adjusted R-squared = .642)

Independent/ Control Variable	Parameter Estimate	Standard Error	*p*-value	Effect Size
Intercept	−10.720	2.428	.000	.134
Colonial Heritage Status = 0 (Never Colonized)	−.656	1.130	.562	.003
Colonial Heritage Status = 1 (Ever Colonized)	0			
CIV = 1 (West/Orthodox/Latin)	2.528	1.019	.014	.047
CIV = 2 (Muslim)	3.061	1.198	.012	.049
CIV = 4 (Hindu/Sinic/Buddhist)	4.210	1.440	.004	.064
CIV = 5 (Africa)	0			

(continued)

TABLE AIII.7.2.1   *(continued)*

Independent/ Control Variable	Parameter Estimate	Standard Error	*p*-value	Effect Size
Syndrome 2017	1.013	.127	.000*	.334
Urbanization 2015	−.031	.020	.132	.018
Number of Land Neighbors	.581	.152	.000*	.104
Terrain 2014	.039	.026	.147	.017
Religious Fractionalization 2003	−4.205	1.733	.017	.045
Ethnic Fractionalization 2003	2.461	1.913	.201	.013

2.2. Societal Violence Scale (higher scores are considered worse, N = 174): The results are as follows:

TABLE AIII.7.2.2 General Linear Model Results for Societal Violence Scale (Adjusted R-squared = .377)

Independent/ Control Variable	Parameter Estimate	Standard Error	*p*-value	Effect Size
Intercept	1.664	.443	.000	.087
Colonial Heritage Status = 0 (Never Colonized)	.294	.216	.175	.012
Colonial Heritage Status = 1 (Ever Colonized)	0			
CIV = 1 (West/Orthodox/Latin)	.258	.190	.177	.012
CIV = 2 (Muslim)	−.153	.223	.494	.003
CIV = 4 (Hindu/Sinic/Buddhist)	.293	.275	.288	.008
CIV = 5 (Africa)	0			
Syndrome 2017	.114	.023	.000*	.140
Urbanization 2015	−.005	.004	.172	.013
Number of Land Neighbors	.100	.028	.001*	.076
Terrain 2014	.012	.005	.018	.037
Religious Fractionalization 2003	−.344	.318	.281	.008
Ethnic Fractionalization 2003	.572	.332	.088	.020

*significant at .001

2.3.   Military Expenditure and Weapons Importation Factor (higher scores are considered worse, N = 152): Recall that this factor combines three variables (Military Expenditure as a Percentage of GDP, Military Expenditure, and Weapons Importation); the results are as follows:

TABLE AIII.7.2.3 General Linear Model Results for Military Expenditure and Weapons Importation Factor (Adjusted R-squared = .318)

Independent/ Control Variable	Parameter Estimate	Standard Error	p-value	Effect Size
Intercept	−4.277	1.147	.000	.097
Colonial Heritage Status = 0 (Never Colonized)	.101	.517	.845	.000
Colonial Heritage Status = 1 (Ever Colonized)	0			
CIV = 1 (West/Orthodox/Latin)	.224	.474	.638	.002
CIV = 2 (Muslim)	1.271	.563	.026	.038
CIV = 4 (Hindu/Sinic/Buddhist)	.406	.697	.561	.003
CIV = 5 (Africa)	0			
Syndrome 2017	.258	.057	.000*	.135
Urbanization 2015	.048	.009	.000*	.173
Number of Land Neighbors	.044	.071	.534	.003
Terrain 2014	−.030	.013	.021	.040
Religious Fractionalization 2003	.518	.801	.519	.003
Ethnic Fractionalization 2003	−2.088	.850	.015	.044

*significant at .001

2.4.   Monopoly on the Use of Force (lower scores are considered worse meaning that other forces or even a "deep state" compromise the state's monopoly on the use of force, N = 128): The results are as follows:

TABLE AIII.7.2.4 General Linear Model Results for Monopoly on the Use of Force (Adjusted R-squared = .234)

Independent/ Control Variable	Parameter Estimate	Standard Error	p-value	Effect Size
Intercept	9.558	1.266	.000	.348
Colonial Heritage Status = 0 (Never Colonized)	.265	.751	.725	.001
Colonial Heritage Status = 1 (Ever Colonized)	0			
CIV = 1 (West/Orthodox/Latin)	−.584	.519	.263	.012
CIV = 2 (Muslim)	.548	.563	.333	.009
CIV = 4 (Hindu/Sinic/Buddhist)	−.357	.694	.608	.002
CIV = 5 (Africa)	0			
Syndrome 2017	−.291	.064	.000*	.164
Urbanization 2015	.008	.010	.447	.005
Number of Land Neighbors	−.059	.078	.452	.005
Terrain 2014	−.002	.014	.863	.000
Religious Fractionalization 2003	2.154	.896	.018	.051
Ethnic Fractionalization 2003	−.859	.911	.348	.008

*significant at .001

2.5. Global Terrorism Index (higher scores are considered worse, N = 163): The results are as follows:

TABLE AIII.7.2.5 General Linear Model Results for the Global Terror Index (Adjusted R-squared = .239)

Independent/Control Variable	Parameter Estimate	Standard Error	p-value	Effect Size
Intercept	−2.759	1.261	.030	.034
Colonial Heritage Status = 0 (Never Colonized)	1.558	.576	.008	.050
Colonial Heritage Status = 1 (Ever Colonized)	0			
CIV = 1 (West/Orthodox/Latin)	.969	.530	.069	.024
CIV = 2 (Muslim)	.826	.616	.182	.013
CIV = 4 (Hindu/Sinic/Buddhist)	1.244	.748	.099	.020
CIV = 5 (Africa)	0			
Syndrome 2017	.246	.063	.000*	.099
Urbanization 2015	.013	.010	.200	.012
Number of Land Neighbors	.290	.079	.000*	.089
Terrain 2014	.025	.014	.082	.022
Religious Fractionalization 2003	.189	.894	.833	.000
Ethnic Fractionalization 2003	.224	.934	.811	.000

*significant at .001

2.6. Perceptions of Criminality (higher scores are considered worse, N = 163): The results are as follows:

TABLE AIII.7.2.6 General Linear Model Results for Perceptions of Criminality (Adjusted R-squared = .188)

Independent/ Control Variable	Parameter Estimate	Standard Error	p-value	Effect Size
Intercept	2.200	.456	.000	.144
Colonial Heritage Status = 0 (Never Colonized)	−.258	.208	.218	.011
Colonial Heritage Status = 1 (Ever Colonized)	0			
CIV = 1 (West/Orthodox/Latin)	.229	.192	.233	.010
CIV = 2 (Muslim)	−.169	.223	.449	.004
CIV = 4 (Hindu/Sinic/Buddhist)	.157	.271	.564	.002
CIV = 5 (Africa)	0			
Syndrome 2017	.086	.023	.000*	.092
Urbanization 2015	−1.163E−6	.004	1.000	.000
Number of Land Neighbors	.068	.029	.018	.040
Terrain 2014	.004	.005	.417	.005
Religious Fractionalization 2003	−.146	.323	.653	.001
Ethnic Fractionalization 2003	.165	.338	.626	.002

*significant at .001

Dimension 3. Economic Performance

Variables in the Economic Performance Dimension
The variables that are most commonly used in social science research and that the authors deemed as the most valid measures of economic performance are listed in alphabetical order. (Some potential variables of interest had to be excluded because of low N size or correlation >.9 with the variables in this list.[5]) The list provides the variable name; provides the variable; the source from which the variable was obtained; whether the measure is nominal, ordinal,

continuous and the range, where applicable; which directionality the variable takes; the N size for the variable; and whether any transformations were used:

1. Agriculture, Forestry, and Fishing Value Added as Percentage of GDP (2016, or most recent without searching earlier than 2007), World Bank, percent, higher scores are worse, N = 168

2. Availability of Affordable Housing (2016), Social Progress Index, percentage (0–1) of respondents answering satisfied to the question, "In your city or area where you live, are you satisfied or dissatisfied with the availability of good, affordable housing?" lower scores are worse, N = 153

3. Economic Freedom Index (2017), Economic Freedom Index, ordinal (0–100), lower scores are worse, N = 169

4. GDP Annual Growth Percentage (2016), World Bank (Accessed from Knoema), percent (negative if GDP decreased), lower scores are worse, N = 163

5. GDP per Capita PPP (2017), International Monetary Fund's World Economic Outlook Database (Accessed from Knoema), GDP per capita based on purchasing power parity in current prices, lower scores are worse, N = 170 (This variable was log transformed in the analysis.)

6. Gini (2016, or most recent without searching earlier than 2007), World Bank, indicates the degree of economic inequality in the society, ordinal (0–100), higher scores are worse (0 = perfect equality, 100 = perfect inequality), N = 143

7. Global Competitiveness Index Rankings (2016), World Economic Forum's Global Competitiveness Report (Accessed from Knoema), ranking (1 = best), higher scores are worse, N = 137 (the N size was too low to include in the EFA, but a separate analysis was done for this variable)

8. Government Debt to GDP (2013–2018), Trading Economics, percent, higher scores are worse, N = 168

9. Government Expenditures as Percentage of GDP (2016 or most recent without searching earlier than 2007), World Bank, percent, lower scores are worse, N = 168

10. Female Labor Force (2016, or most recent without searching earlier than 2007), World Bank, percent of total labor force, lower scores are worse, N = 174

11. Final Consumption (2016), National Accounts Main Aggregates Database (Accessed from Knoema), U.S. dollars, lower scores are worse, N = 174 (This variable was log transformed in the analysis.)

12. Food Security (2016), Global Food Security Index, scale (min = 26.1, max = 85.8), lower scores are worse, N = 113 (the N size was too low to include in the EFA, but a separate analysis was done for this variable)

13. Human Freedom Index (HFI) Economic Freedom (2016), Cato Institute, ordinal (0–10), lower scores are worse, N = 157

14. High-Technology Exports (2016, or most recent without searching earlier than 2007), World Bank, percent of manufactured exports, lower scores are worse, N = 155

15. Internet Users (2016), Social Progress Index, percent of population, lower scores are worse, N = 160

16. Mobile Telephone Subscriptions (2016), Social Progress Index, number per 100 inhabitants, lower scores are worse, N = 160

17. Poverty and Economic Decline (2016), Fragile States Index from the Failed States Index published by the Fund for Peace (Accessed from the Quality of Government Institute), scale (min = 1.8, max = 9.4), higher scores are worse, N = 171

18. Property Rights (2017), Heritage Foundation's Index of Economic Freedom (Accessed from the Quality of Government Institute), ordinal (0–100), lower scores are worse, N = 169

19. Prosperity Index (2016), Legatum Institute (Accessed from Knoema), rankings (1 = best), higher scores are worse, N = 148

20. Quality of Electricity Supply (2016), Social Progress Index, ordinal (1–7), average response to the question: "In your country, how would you assess the reliability of the electricity supply (lack of interruptions and lack of voltage fluctuations)?" lower scores are worse (1 = not reliable at all, 7 = extremely reliable), N = 144

21. Unemployment Rate (2016), World Bank, percent of the total labor force, higher scores are worse, N = 174

22. Uneven Economic Development (2016), Fragile States Index from the Failed States Index published by the Fund for Peace (Accessed from the Quality of Government Institute), scale (min = 1.3, max = 9.5), higher scores are worse, N = 171

We wanted to reduce the number of variables examined through factor analysis to find those variables that loaded highly on the same factors and thus could be analyzed together. One of the variables in this dimension, GDP per capita PPP (log transformed), was both included in the EFA and analyzed separately because we wanted to directly observe the effects of the Syndrome on countries' GDP per capita.

The factor analysis yielded three distinct loading patterns,[6] and the z-scores of the variables in each factor were added to create the score for each factor, after checking for consistency in direction (or multiplied by −1 to maintain consistency):

1. **Wealth Infrastructure and Economic Freedom Factor** (lower scores are considered worse, N = 138): This factor consists of these eight variables with loadings ranging from .316 to 1.220: (1) Economic Freedom Index, (2) HFI Economic Freedom, (3) GDP per Capita PPP (log transformed), (4) Property

Rights, (5) Quality of Electricity Supply, (6) Mobile Telephone Subscriptions, (7) Internet Users, and (8) Availability of Affordable Housing.

2.   Reliance on Agriculture and Lack of Prosperity Factor (higher scores are considered worse, N = 146): This factor consists of these two variables with loadings ranging from −.742 to −.681: (1) Agriculture Value Added as Percentage of GDP and (2) Prosperity Index.

3.   Economic Inequality Factor (higher scores are considered worse, N = 139): This factor consists of these two variables with loadings ranging from .635 to .967: (1) Gini and (2) Uneven Economic Development.

Model Specification

The model for each dependent variable or factor takes the same form in each case:

Dependent variable or factor = Syndrome + Civilization
                              + Colonial Heritage Status + Urbanization + Terrain
                              + Number of Land Neighbors
                              + Religious Fractionalization
                              + Aggregated Ethnic Fractionalization + ε_i

We used a GLM procedure to investigate the statistical significance and explanatory power of these eight independent variables. We hypothesized that, after controlling for the influence of the other seven control variables, the Patrilineal/Fraternal Syndrome will still be a significant predictor of these dependent variables and factors for the nations in our study.

GLM Results for the Economic Performance Dimension

3.1. **Food Security Index** (lower scores are considered worse, N = 113): The results are as follows:

TABLE AIII.7.3.1 General Linear Model Results for Food Security (Adjusted R-squared = .809)

Independent/ Control Variable	Parameter Estimate	Standard Error	p-value	Effect Size
Intercept	44.999	5.315	.000	.425
Colonial Heritage Status = 0 (Never Colonized)	6.341	2.167	.004	.081
Colonial Heritage Status = 1 (Ever Colonized)	0			
CIV = 1 (West/Orthodox/Latin)	−.914	2.125	.668	.002
CIV = 2 (Muslim)	3.842	2.455	.121	.025
CIV = 4 (Hindu/Sinic/Buddhist)	.778	3.097	.802	.001
CIV = 5 (Africa)	0			
Syndrome 2017	−1.334	.286	.000*	.183
Urbanization 2015	.406	.044	.000*	.465
Number of Land Neighbors	.027	.294	.927	.000
Terrain 2014	−.072	.057	.209	.016
Religious Fractionalization 2003	4.933	3.486	.160	.020
Ethnic Fractionalization 2003	−8.437	4.132	.044	.041

*significant at .001

3.2.   Reliance on Agriculture and Lack of Prosperity Factor (higher scores are considered worse, N = 146): Recall that this factor combines several variables (Agriculture Value Added as Percentage of GDP and Prosperity Index), the results are as follows:

TABLE AIII.7.3.2 General Linear Model Results for Reliance on Agriculture and Lack of Prosperity Factor (Adjusted R-squared = .740)

Independent/ Control Variable	Parameter Estimate	Standard Error	p-value	Effect Size
Intercept	−.543	.554	.328	.008
Colonial Heritage Status = 0 (Never Colonized)	−.049	.236	.837	.000
Colonial Heritage Status = 1 (Ever Colonized)	0			
CIV = 1 (West/Orthodox/Latin)	.195	.228	.392	.006
CIV = 2 (Muslim)	−.297	.263	.261	.010
CIV = 4 (Hindu/Sinic/Buddhist)	.235	.322	.466	.004
CIV = 5 (Africa)	0			
Syndrome 2017	.215	.027	.000*	.325
Urbanization 2015	−.031	.004	.000*	.279
Number of Land Neighbors	.053	.034	.120	.019
Terrain 2014	.010	.006	.090	.022
Religious Fractionalization 2003	−.351	.373	.349	.007
Ethnic Fractionalization 2003	.924	.399	.022	.040

*significant at .001

3.3. GDP per Capita PPP 2017 (log transformed) (lower scores are considered worse, N = 170): The results are as follows:

TABLE AIII.7.3.3 General Linear Model Results for GDP per capita PPP 2017 (log transformed) (Adjusted R-squared = .695)

Independent/ Control Variable	Parameter Estimate	Standard Error	p-value	Effect Size
Intercept	8.793	.343	.000	.820
Colonial Heritage Status = 0 (Never Colonized)	.102	.166	.541	.003
Colonial Heritage Status = 1 (Ever Colonized)	0			
CIV = 1 (West/Orthodox/Latin)	.010	.146	.946	.000
CIV = 2 (Muslim)	.608	.174	.001*	.078
CIV = 4 (Hindu/Sinic/Buddhist)	−.055	.216	.799	.000
CIV = 5 (Africa)	0			
Syndrome 2017	−.099	.018	.000*	.178
Urbanization 2015	.026	.003	.000*	.363
Number of Land Neighbors	.002	.022	.935	.000
Terrain 2014	−.011	.004	.007	.050
Religious Fractionalization 2003	.439	.245	.075	.022
Ethnic Fractionalization 2003	−.768	.261	.004	.056

*significant at .001

3.4.   Poverty and Economic Decline (higher scores are considered worse, N = 171): The results are as follows:

TABLE AIII.7.3.4 General Linear Model Results for Poverty and Economic Decline (Adjusted R-squared = .612)

Independent/ Control Variable	Parameter Estimate	Standard Error	p-value	Effect Size
Intercept	6.718	.571	.000	.485
Colonial Heritage Status = 0 (Never Colonized)	−.302	.282	.286	.008
Colonial Heritage Status = 1 (Ever Colonized)	0			
CIV = 1 (West/Orthodox/Latin)	.033	.245	.894	.000
CIV = 2 (Muslim)	−.868	.286	.003	.059
CIV = 4 (Hindu/Sinic/Buddhist)	.006	.352	.985	.000
CIV = 5 (Africa)	0			
Syndrome 2017	.185	.030	.000*	.206
Urbanization 2015	−.036	.005	.000*	.274
Number of Land Neighbors	−.028	.037	.453	.004
Terrain 2014	.010	.007	.125	.016
Religious Fractionalization 2003	−.646	.407	.114	.017
Ethnic Fractionalization 2003	.080	.437	.855	.000

*significant at .001

3.5.   Wealth Infrastructure and Economic Freedom Factor (lower scores are considered worse, N = 138): Recall that this factor combines several variables (HFI Economic Freedom Index 2016, Economic Freedom Index 2017, GDP per Capita PPP (log transformed), Property Rights, Quality of Electricity Supply, Mobile Telephone Subscriptions, Internet Users, and Availability of Affordable Housing), the results are as follows:

TABLE AIII.7.3.5 General Linear Model Results for Wealth Infrastructure and Economic Freedom Factor (Adjusted R-squared = .600)

Independent/ Control Variable	Parameter Estimate	Standard Error	p-value	Effect Size
Intercept	.466	2.283	.838	.000
Colonial Heritage Status = 0 (Never Colonized)	1.341	.981	.174	.015
Colonial Heritage Status = 1 (Ever Colonized)	0			
CIV = 1 (West/Orthodox/Latin)	−.810	.937	.389	.006
CIV = 2 (Muslim)	2.157	1.107	.054	.030
CIV = 4 (Hindu/Sinic/Buddhist)	−.688	1.273	.590	.002
CIV = 5 (Africa)	0			
Syndrome 2017	−.636	.117	.000*	.197
Urbanization 2015	.095	.019	.000*	.173
Number of Land Neighbors	−.222	.139	.113	.021
Terrain 2014	−.029	.026	.268	.010
Religious Fractionalization 2003	3.651	1.569	.022	.043
Ethnic Fractionalization 2003	−2.504	1.656	.133	.019

*significant at .001

3.6.   Global Competitiveness Index (higher scores are considered worse, N = 137): The results are as follows:

TABLE AIII.7.3.6 General Linear Model Results for Global Competitiveness Index Rankings (Adjusted R-squared = .564)

Independent/ Control Variable	Parameter Estimate	Standard Error	p-value	Effect Size
Intercept	88.301	15.827	.000	.209
Colonial Heritage Status = 0 (Never Colonized)	−16.980	6.720	.013	.051
Colonial Heritage Status = 1 (Ever Colonized)	0			
CIV = 1 (West/Orthodox/Latin)	3.811	6.547	.562	.003
CIV = 2 (Muslim)	−19.346	7.630	.013	.052
CIV = 4 (Hindu/Sinic/Buddhist)	1.268	8.858	.886	.000
CIV = 5 (Africa)	0			
Syndrome 2017	3.656	.787	.000*	.154
Urbanization 2015	−.623	.129	.000*	.164
Number of Land Neighbors	−.449	.931	.631	.002
Terrain 2014	.058	.172	.735	.001
Religious Fractionalization 2003	−24.777	10.609	.021	.044
Ethnic Fractionalization 2003	20.166	11.676	.087	.025

3.7.   Economic Inequality Factor (higher scores are considered worse, N = 139): Recall that this factor combines two variables (Gini and Uneven Economic Development), the results are as follows:

TABLE AIII.7.3.7 General Linear Model Results for Economic Inequality Factor (Adjusted R-squared = .482)

Independent/ Control Variable	Parameter Estimate	Standard Error	p-value	Effect Size
Intercept	.183	.836	.827	.000
Colonial Heritage Status = 0 (Never Colonized)	−.561	.366	.128	.020
Colonial Heritage Status = 1 (Ever Colonized)	0			
CIV = 1 (West/Orthodox/Latin)	−.560	.320	.083	.026
CIV = 2 (Muslim)	−1.019	.414	.015	.050
CIV = 4 (Hindu/Sinic/Buddhist)	−.841	.488	.088	.025
CIV = 5 (Africa)	0			
Syndrome 2017	.158	.042	.000*	.110
Urbanization 2015	−.014	.008	.068	.028
Number of Land Neighbors	.021	.048	.670	.002
Terrain 2014	−.024	.009	.006	.063
Religious Fractionalization 2003	.108	.579	.852	.000
Ethnic Fractionalization 2003	.811	.578	.163	.017

*significant at .001

3.8.   Female Labor Force Participation (lower scores are considered worse, N = 174): The results are as follows:

TABLE AIII.7.3.8 General Linear Model Results for Female Labor Force Participation (Adjusted R-squared = .471)

Independent/ Control Variable	Parameter Estimate	Standard Error	p-value	Effect Size
Intercept	54.977	3.445	.000	.631
Colonial Heritage Status = 0 (Never Colonized)	.867	1.677	.606	.002
Colonial Heritage Status = 1 (Ever Colonized)	0			
CIV = 1 (West/Orthodox/Latin)	−2.726	1.476	.067	.022
CIV = 2 (Muslim)	−6.977	1.736	.000*	.098
CIV = 4 (Hindu/Sinic/Buddhist)	−.378	2.139	.860	.000
CIV = 5 (Africa)	0			
Syndrome 2017	−1.219	.179	.000*	.237
Urbanization 2015	−.142	.029	.000*	.140
Number of Land Neighbors	.239	.221	.281	.008
Terrain 2014	.039	.040	.336	.006
Religious Fractionalization 2003	7.939	2.452	.001*	.066
Ethnic Fractionalization 2003	4.477	2.581	.085	.020

*significant at .001

Dimension 4. Economic Rentierism Dimension

Variables in the Economic Rentierism Dimension

The variables that are most commonly used in social science research and that the authors deemed as the most valid measures of rentierism are listed in alphabetical order. (Some potential variables of interest had to be excluded because of low N size or correlation >.9 with the variables in this list.[7]) The list provides the variable; the source from which the variable was obtained; whether the measure is nominal, ordinal, or continuous and the range, where applicable; which directionality the variable takes; the N size for the variable; and whether any transformations were used:

1. Aid per Capita GDP (2016, or most recent without searching earlier than 2007), World Bank, U.S. dollars, higher scores are worse, N = 130
2. Fuel Exports (2016, or most recent without searching earlier than 2007), World Bank, percent of merchandise exports, higher scores are worse, N = 158
3. Natural Resource Depletion (2014), United Nations Development Program Human Development Reports, as percent of gross national income (GNI), higher scores are worse, N = 164
4. Ores and Metals Exports (2016, or most recent without searching earlier than 2007), World Bank, percent of merchandise exports, higher scores are worse, N = 159
5. Total Natural Resources Rents as Percentage of GDP (2016, or most recent without searching earlier than 2007), World Bank, percent, higher scores are worse, N = 173
6. Tourism as a Percentage of GDP (2017), World Travel and Tourism Council (Accessed from Knoema), percent, higher scores are worse, N = 160

Model Specification

The model for each dependent variable or factor takes the same form in each case:

$$
\begin{aligned}
\text{Dependent variable or factor}_i = {} & \text{Syndrome} + \text{Civilization} \\
& + \text{Colonial Heritage Status} + \text{Urbanization} \\
& + \text{Terrain} + \text{Number of Land Neighbors} \\
& + \text{Religious Fractionalization} \\
& + \text{Aggregated Ethnic Fractionalization} + \varepsilon_i
\end{aligned}
$$

We used a GLM procedure to investigate the statistical significance and explanatory power of these six independent variables. We hypothesized that, after controlling for the influence of the other seven control variables, the Patrilineal/Fraternal Syndrome will still be a significant predictor of these dependent variables for the nations in our study.

GLM Results for Variables Used in Primary Analyses for the Economic Rentierism Dimension

4.1.   Natural Resources as Percentage of GDP (higher scores are considered worse, N = 173): The results are as follows:

TABLE AIII.7.4.1 General Linear Model Results for Natural Resources as a Percentage of GDP (Adjusted R-squared = .303)

Independent/ Control Variable	Parameter Estimate	Standard Error	p-value	Effect Size
Intercept	−7.327	4.194	.083	.020
Colonial Heritage Status = 0 (Never Colonized)	.959	2.042	.639	.001
Colonial Heritage Status = 1 (Ever Colonized)	0			
CIV = 1 (West/Orthodox/Latin)	1.575	1.792	.381	.005
CIV = 2 (Muslim)	2.916	2.125	.172	.013
CIV = 4 (Hindu/Sinic/Buddhist)	.950	2.661	.721	.001
CIV = 5 (Africa)	0			
Syndrome 2017	.887	.218	.000*	.101
Urbanization 2015	.042	.035	.235	.010
Number of Land Neighbors	.253	.269	.349	.006
Terrain 2014	−.120	.049	.015	.039
Religious Fractionalization 2003	2.835	2.984	.344	.006
Ethnic Fractionalization 2003	7.373	3.171	.021	.035

*significant at .001

Dimension 5. Health and Well-Being Dimension

Variables in the Health and Well-Being Dimension

The variables that are most commonly used in social science research and that the authors deemed as the most valid measures of health and well-being of a nation are listed in alphabetical order. (Some variables were excluded because of N size reasons, their data were not recent enough, or because their bivariate correlation with another variable in this dimension exceeded .90.[8]) The list provides the variable name; the variable; the source from which the variable was obtained; whether the measure is nominal, ordinal, or continuous and the range, where applicable; which directionality the variable takes; the N size for the variable; and whether any transformations were used:

1. Access to Improved Sanitary Facilities (2016), Social Progress Index, percent, lower scores are worse, N = 172
2. Access to Improved Water Sources (2016), Social Progress Index, percent of the rural population, lower scores are worse, N = 171
3. Average Dietary Energy Supply Adequacy (2014–2016), Food and Agriculture Organization of the United Nations, percent (three-year average), lower scores are worse, N = 162
4. Births per One Thousand Women Ages Fifteen to Nineteen (2016), World Bank, rate per 1,000, higher scores are worse, N = 174
5. Cigarette Consumption, number of cigarettes smoked per person per year ages fifteen and over, (2016), The Tobacco Atlas, higher scores are worse, N = 171
6. Deaths Due to Diarrhea of Children Under Five (2010), Global Health Observatory (Accessed from Knoema), percent, higher scores are worse, N = 171
7. Difference Between Female and Male Life Expectancy (2015), The WomanStats Project, ordinal (0–2), higher scores are worse, N = 173
8. Female Genital Cutting/Mutilation (2015), The WomanStats Project, ordinal (0–4), higher scores are worse, N = 176
9. Global Hunger Index (2016), Global Hunger Index, scale (min = 4, max = 46.1), higher scores are worse, N = 118 (This variable was excluded from the EFA because its sample size was too low, but it was analyzed separately.)
10. Health Expenditure as Percentage of GDP (2015), World Health Organization, percent, lower scores are worse, N = 169
11. Health Expenditure Per Capita (2015), World Health Organization (Accessed from Wikipedia), U.S. dollars, lower scores are worse, N = 168
12. Incidence of Tuberculosis per 100,000 People (2016), World Bank, rate per 100,000, higher scores are worse, N = 174
13. Infant Mortality Rate (2016), World Bank, rate per 1,000 live births, higher scores are worse, N = 174
14. Life Expectancy at Birth for Females (2015), World Health Organization, years, lower scores are worse, N = 173
15. Life Expectancy (2015), World Health Organization, years, lower scores are worse, N = 173
16. Lifetime Risk of Maternal Death (2015), World Bank, percent, higher scores are worse, N = 174

17. Maternal Mortality Rate (2015), The WomanStats Project, ordinal (0–4), higher scores are worse, N = 173

18. Percentage of Adults Ages Fifteen to Forty-Nine with HIV/AIDS (2016), CIA *World Factbook*, percent, higher scores are worse, N = 130

19. Prevalence of HIV Among Women Ages Fifteen and Over (2016), World Bank, percent ("Women's share of population ages fifteen and over living with HIV (%)," meaning that this is the percentage, out of the total HIV population, of women), higher scores are worse, N = 131 (This variable was excluded from the EFA because its sample size was too low, but it was analyzed separately.)

20. Prevalence of Wasting—Percentage Under Five (2015, or most recent without searching earlier than 2007), World Bank, percent, higher scores are worse, N = 116 (This variable was excluded from the EFA because its sample size was too low, but it was analyzed separately.)

21. Sustainable Society Index Human Well-Being (2016), Sustainable Society Index, continuous scale (min = 3.1; max = 9.0), higher scores are worse, N = 154.

22. Total Alcohol Consumption per Capita (2015), World Bank, liters of pure alcohol per capita, higher scores are worse, N = 171

23. Percent Births Attended by Skilled Staff (2017, or most recent without searching earlier than 2007), World Bank, percent; lower scores are worse, N = 162

24. Percent Children Ages Twelve to Twenty-Three Months Immunized Against Measles (2016), World Bank, percent, lower scores are worse, N = 173

25. Percent of Population Between Fifteen and Forty-Nine with HIV (2016), World Bank, percent, higher scores are worse, N = 131 (This variable was excluded from the EFA because its sample size was too low, but it was analyzed separately.)

26. Percent of Population that is Undernourished (2015), World Bank, percent, higher scores are worse, N = 159

27. Percent Population Using Open Defecation in Urban Areas (2015), World Health Organization/United Nations Children's Fund, percent, higher scores are worse, N = 171 (If this value was missing and Percentage of Total Population Using Open Defecation variable's value was 0, we used a 0.)

28. Percent of Pregnant Women Receiving Prenatal Care (2017, or most recent without searching earlier than 2007), World Bank, percent, lower scores are worse, N = 144

29. Percent Total Population Using Open Defecation (2015), World Health Organization/United Nations Children's Fund, percent, higher scores are worse, N = 174

30. Percent Under Five Who Are Stunted (2015, or most recent without searching earlier than 2007), World Bank, percent, higher scores are worse, N = 117

(This variable was excluded from the EFA because its sample size was too low, but it was analyzed separately.)

31. Percent Under Five Who Are Underweight (2015, or most recent without searching earlier than 2007), World Bank, percent, higher scores are worse $N = 116$ (This variable was excluded from the EFA because its sample size was too low, but it was analyzed separately.)

We wanted to reduce the number of variables examined through factor analysis to find variables that clustered highly on the same factors and thus could be analyzed together. In this manner and through theoretical considerations, we identified four factors, with twenty variables requiring individual modeling, for a total of twenty-four outcome variables. The z-scores of the variables in each factor were added to create the score for each factor, after checking for consistency in direction (or multiplied by −1 to maintain consistency):

1. **Preventable Death Factor** (higher scores are considered worse, $N = 172$): This factor consists of these four variables with loadings ranging from .737 to 1.063: (1) Lifetime Risk of Maternal Death, (2) Infant Mortality Rate, (3) Births per One Thousand Women Ages Fifteen to Nineteen, and (4) Difference Between Female and Male Life Expectancy.

2. **Open Defecation Factor** (higher scores are considered worse, $N = 171$): This factor consists of these two variables with loadings ranging from .845 to .920: (1) Percentage of Total Population Using Open Defecation and (2) Percentage of Population Using Open Defecation in Urban Areas.

3. **Healthcare Access Factor** (lower scores are considered worse, $N = 159$): This factor consists of these three variables with loadings ranging from −.826 to −.648: (1) Access to Improved Sanitary Facilities, (2) Percentage of Birth Attended by Skilled Staff, and (3) Life Expectancy.

4. **Malnutrition and Illness Factor** (higher scores are considered worse, $N = 159$): This factor consists of these two variables with loadings ranging from −.923 to −.533: (1) Percentage of Population That Is Undernourished and (2) Incidence of Tuberculosis per 100,000 People.

Model Specification

The model for each dependent variable or factor takes the same form in each case:

Dependent variable or factor$_i$ = Syndrome + Civilization
$$+ \text{Colonial Heritage Status} + \text{Urbanization}$$
$$+ \text{Terrain} + \text{Number of Land Neighbors}$$
$$+ \text{Religious Fractionalization}$$
$$+ \text{Aggregated Ethnic Fractionalization} + \varepsilon_i$$

We used a GLM procedure to investigate the statistical significance and explanatory power of these eight independent variables. We hypothesized that, after controlling for the influence of the other seven control variables, the Patrilineal/Fraternal Syndrome will still be a significant predictor of these dependent variables and factors for the nations in our study.

GLM Results for the Health and Well-Being Dimension

5.1. Healthcare Access factor (lower scores are considered worse, N = 159): Recall that this factor combines three variables (Access to Improved Sanitary Facilities, Percentage of Birth Attended by Skilled Staff, and Life Expectancy), the results are as follows:

TABLE AIII.7.5.1 General Linear Model Results for Healthcare Access Factor (Adjusted R-squared = .702)

Independent/ Control Variable	Parameter Estimate	Standard Error	p-value	Effect Size
Intercept	.589	.774	.448	.004
Colonial Heritage Status = 0 (Never Colonized)	−.444	.425	.299	.008
Colonial Heritage Status = 1 (Ever Colonized)	0			
CIV = 1 (West/Orthodox/Latin)	.636	.329	.055	.027
CIV = 2 (Muslim)	1.891	.392	.000*	.147
CIV = 4 (Hindu/Sinic/Buddhist)	1.465	.477	.003	.065
CIV = 5 (Africa)	0			
Syndrome 2017	−.297	.042	.000*	.267
Urbanization 2015	.040	.007	.000*	.212
Number of Land Neighbors	.024	.050	.628	.002
Terrain 2014	−.015	.009	.107	.019
Religious Fractionalization 2003	−.201	.573	.726	.001
Ethnic Fractionalization 2003	−2.273	.608	.000*	.094

*significant at .001

5.2.   Health Expenditure per Capita (lower scores are considered worse, N = 168): The results are as follows:

TABLE AIII.7.5.2 General Linear Model Results for Health Expenditure per Capita (Adjusted R-squared = .616)

Independent/ Control Variable	Parameter Estimate	Standard Error	p-value	Effect Size
Intercept	898.993	550.601	.105	.018
Colonial Heritage Status = 0 (Never Colonized)	1233.852	265.153	.000*	.131
Colonial Heritage Status = 1 (Ever Colonized)	0			
CIV = 1 (West/Orthodox/Latin)	−131.194	233.721	.575	.002
CIV = 2 (Muslim)	354.210	277.603	.204	.011
CIV = 4 (Hindu/Sinic/Buddhist)	−408.168	345.440	.239	.010
CIV = 5 (Africa)	0			
Syndrome 2017	−171.859	28.565	.000*	.201
Urbanization 2015	26.679	4.585	.000*	.190
Number of Land Neighbors	−45.079	34.966	.199	.011
Terrain 2014	−4.178	6.349	.512	.003
Religious Fractionalization 2003	1114.804	395.845	.006	.052
Ethnic Fractionalization 2003	−298.892	416.299	.474	.004

*significant at .001

5.3.   **Preventable Death Factor** (higher scores are considered worse, N = 172): Recall that this factor combines four variables (Risk of Maternal Death, Infant Mortality Rate, Births per One Thousand Women Ages Fifteen to Nineteen, Difference in Life Expectancy Between Men and Women), the results are as follows:

TABLE AIII.7.5.3 General Linear Model for Preventable Death Factor (Adjusted R-squared = .594)

Independent/ Control Variable	Parameter Estimate	Standard Error	p-value	Effect Size
Intercept	−1.076	1.146	.349	.006
Colonial Heritage Status = 0 (Never Colonized)	.463	.556	.406	.005
Colonial Heritage Status = 1 (Ever Colonized)	0			
CIV = 1 (West/Orthodox/Latin)	−.598	.491	.225	.010
CIV = 2 (Muslim)	−1.752	.575	.003	.059
CIV = 4 (Hindu/Sinic/Buddhist)	−1.118	.709	.117	.017
CIV = 5 (Africa)	0			
Syndrome 2017	.366	.060	.000*	.200
Urbanization 2015	−.040	.010	.000*	.104
Number of Land Neighbors	−.091	.074	.218	.010
Terrain 2014	.002	.013	.893	.000
Religious Fractionalization 2003	−.120	.818	.884	.000
Ethnic Fractionalization 2003	3.394	.879	.000*	.092

*significant at .001

5.4. Total Alcohol Consumption per Capita (higher scores are considered worse, N = 171): The results are as follows:

TABLE AIII.7.5.4 General Linear Model Results for Total Alcohol Consumption per Capita (Adjusted R-squared = .535)

Independent/ Control Variable	Parameter Estimate	Standard Error	p-value	Effect Size
Intercept	6.957	1.438	.000	.137
Colonial Heritage Status = 0 (Never Colonized)	−.499	.695	.474	.003
Colonial Heritage Status = 1 (Ever Colonized)	0			
CIV = 1 (West/Orthodox/Latin)	−.503	.621	.420	.004
CIV = 2 (Muslim)	−1.314	.721	.071	.022
CIV = 4 (Hindu/Sinic/Buddhist)	−.360	.891	.687	.001
CIV = 5 (Africa)	0			
Syndrome 2017	−.587	.075	.000*	.292
Urbanization 2015	.007	.012	.573	.002
Number of Land Neighbors	.282	.092	.002	.060
Terrain 2014	.060	.017	.000*	.082
Religious Fractionalization 2003	3.796	1.015	.000*	.086
Ethnic Fractionalization 2003	.923	1.071	.390	.005

*significant at .001

5.5.   Prevalence of HIV Among Women Ages Fifteen and Over (higher scores are considered worse, N = 131): The results are as follows:

TABLE AIII.7.5.5 General Linear Model Results for Prevalence of HIV Among Women Age Fifteen and Over (Adjusted R-squared = .525)

Independent/ Control Variable	Parameter Estimate	Standard Error	p-value	Effect Size
Intercept	29.178	6.185	.000	.168
Colonial Heritage Status = 0 (Never Colonized)	−.257	3.450	.941	.000
Colonial Heritage Status = 1 (Ever Colonized)	0			
CIV = 1 (West/Orthodox/Latin)	−5.899	2.617	.026	.044
CIV = 2 (Muslim)	−14.630	3.015	.000*	.176
CIV = 4 (Hindu/Sinic/Buddhist)	−7.974	4.070	.053	.034
CIV = 5 (Africa)	0			
Syndrome 2017	1.599	.345	.000*	.163
Urbanization 2015	−.109	.052	.040	.038
Number of Land Neighbors	.269	.485	.580	.003
Terrain 2014	.053	.073	.472	.005
Religious Fractionalization 2003	7.906	4.526	.083	.027
Ethnic Fractionalization 2003	9.711	5.031	.056	.033

*significant at .001

5.6.   Global Hunger Index (higher scores are considered worse, N = 118): The results are as follows:

TABLE AIII.7.5.6 General Linear Model Results for Global Hunger Index (Adjusted R-squared = .577)

Independent/ Control Variable	Parameter Estimate	Standard Error	p-value	Effect Size
Intercept	18.402	4.530	.000	.142
Colonial Heritage Status = 0 (Never Colonized)	−1.983	2.811	.482	.005
Colonial Heritage Status = 1 (Ever Colonized)	0			
CIV = 1 (West/Orthodox/Latin)	−1.426	1.829	.437	.006
CIV = 2 (Muslim)	−3.649	2.098	.085	.029
CIV = 4 (Hindu/Sinic/Buddhist)	−1.072	2.815	.704	.001
CIV = 5 (Africa)	0			
Syndrome 2017	1.227	.236	.000*	.213
Urbanization 2015	−.244	.038	.000*	.294
Number of Land Neighbors	−.056	.292	.847	.000
Terrain 2014	−.028	.051	.582	.003
Religious Fractionalization 2003	−1.295	3.348	.700	.001
Ethnic Fractionalization 2003	6.297	3.400	.067	.033

*significant at .001

5.7.   Female Genital Cutting/Mutilation (FGM) (higher scores are considered worse, N = 176): The results are as follows:

TABLE AIII.7.5.7 General Linear Model Results for Female Genital Cutting/
Mutilation (Adjusted R-squared = .297)

Independent/ Control Variable	Parameter Estimate	Standard Error	p-value	Effect Size
Intercept	−.877	.518	.092	.019
Colonial Heritage Status = 0 (Never Colonized)	.953	.252	.000*	.088
Colonial Heritage Status = 1 (Ever Colonized)	0			
CIV = 1 (West/Orthodox/Latin)	.179	.222	.422	.004
CIV = 2 (Muslim)	−.166	.261	.526	.003
CIV = 4 (Hindu/Sinic/Buddhist)	−.459	.321	.155	.014
CIV = 5 (Africa)	0			
Syndrome 2017	.118	.027	.000*	.113
Urbanization 2015	.006	.004	.153	.014
Number of Land Neighbors	−.039	.033	.239	.009
Terrain 2014	.000	.006	.978	.000
Religious Fractionalization 2003	−.390	.369	.291	.007
Ethnic Fractionalization 2003	1.418	.388	.000*	.082

*significant at .001

Dimension 6. Demographic Security

Variables in the Demographic Security Dimension
The variables that are most commonly used in social science research and that the authors deemed as the most valid measures of demographic security are listed in alphabetical order. (Some potential variables of interest had to be excluded because of low N size or correlation >.9 with the variables in this list.[9]) The list provides the variable name; the source from which the variable was obtained; whether the measure is nominal, ordinal, or continuous and the range, where applicable; which directionality the variable takes; the N size for the variable; and whether any transformations were used:

1. Contraceptive Prevalence (2016, or most recent without searching earlier than 2007), World Bank, percentage of women ages fifteen to forty-nine, lower scores are worse, N = 135
2. Demographic Pressures (2017), Fund for Peace Fragile States Index, ordinal scale (min = 1.1, max = 10.0), higher scores are worse, N = 172
3. Fertility Rates Ages Fifteen to Nineteen (2010–2015), United Nations Development Program World Population Prospects, births per 1,000 women, higher scores are worse, N = 174
4. Mother's Mean Age at First Birth (2006–2016), CIA *World Factbook*, continuous (age), lower scores are worse, N = 123
5. Total Fertility (2015), World Bank, births per woman "the number of children that would be born to a woman if she were to live to the end of her childbearing years and bear children in accordance with age-specific fertility rates of the specified year," higher scores are worse, N = 175
6. Unmet Need for Contraception (2016, or most recent without searching earlier than 2007), World Bank, percentage of married women ages fifteen to forty-nine, higher scores are worse, N = 116
7. Youth Risk Factor (2013)[10], ratio of the number of seventeen- to twenty-six-year-olds to the size of a country's total labor force, higher scores are worse, N = 166

Model Specification
The following model was used for each dependent variable:

Dependent variable or factor$_i$ = Syndrome + Civilization + Colonial Heritage Status
$$+ \text{Urbanization} + \text{Terrain}$$
$$+ \text{Number of Land Neighbors}$$
$$+ \text{Religious Fractionalization}$$
$$+ \text{Aggregated Ethnic Fractionalization} + \varepsilon_i$$

We used GLM to investigate the statistical significance and explanatory power of each of these eight independent variables. We hypothesized that, after controlling for the influence of the other control variables, the Patrilineal/Fraternal Syndrome will still be a significant predictor of these demographic dependent variables for the nations in our study.

GLM Results for the Demographic Security Dimension

6.1.   Mother's Mean Age at First Birth (lower scores are considered worse, N = 123): The results are as follows:

TABLE AIII.7.6.1 General Linear Model Results for Mother's Mean Age at First Birth (Adjusted R-squared = .712)

Independent/ Control Variable	Parameter Estimate	Standard Error	p-value	Effect Size
Intercept	24.794	1.335	.000	.772
Colonial Heritage Status = 0 (Never Colonized)	.919	.565	.107	.025
Colonial Heritage Status = 1 (Ever Colonized)	0			
CIV = 1 (West/Orthodox/Latin)	.324	.523	.537	.004
CIV = 2 (Muslim)	.487	.657	.460	.005
CIV = 4 (Hindu/Sinic/Buddhist)	.780	.765	.310	.010
CIV = 5 (Africa)	0			
Syndrome 2017	−.436	.074	.000*	.254
Urbanization 2015	.040	.013	.002	.090
Number of Land Neighbors	.002	.092	.986	.000
Terrain 2014	.016	.014	.266	.012
Religious Fractionalization 2003	.944	.952	.324	.010
Ethnic Fractionalization 2003	−2.471	1.038	.019	.053

*significant at .001

6.2.   Demographic Pressure (higher scores are considered worse, N = 172): The results are as follows:

TABLE AIII.7.6.2 General Linear Model Results for Demographic Pressure (Adjusted R-squared = .707)

Independent/ Control Variable	Parameter Estimate	Standard Error	p-value	Effect Size
Intercept	5.241	.691	.000	.280
Colonial Heritage Status = 0 (Never Colonized)	.195	.336	.562	.002
Colonial Heritage Status = 1 (Ever Colonized)	0			
CIV = 1 (West/Orthodox/Latin)	−.392	.297	.189	.012
CIV = 2 (Muslim)	−1.042	.347	.003	.057
CIV = 4 (Hindu/Sinic/Buddhist)	−.091	.428	.833	.000
CIV = 5 (Africa)	0			
Syndrome 2017	.331	.036	.000*	.360
Urbanization 2015	−.034	.006	.000*	.190
Number of Land Neighbors	.005	.045	.914	.000
Terrain 2014	−.003	.008	.693	.001
Religious Fractionalization 2003	−.195	.494	.694	.001
Ethnic Fractionalization 2003	.918	.531	.086	.020

*significant at .001

6.3. Total Fertility Rate (higher scores are considered worse, N = 175): The results are as follows:

TABLE AIII.7.6.3 General Linear Model Results for Total Fertility Rate (Adjusted R-squared = .602)

Independent/ Control Variable	Parameter Estimate	Standard Error	*p*-value	Effect Size
Intercept	2.408	.449	.000	.162
Colonial Heritage Status = 0 (Never Colonized)	.111	.219	.613	.002
Colonial Heritage Status = 1 (Ever Colonized)	0			
CIV = 1 (West/Orthodox/Latin)	−.247	.192	.202	.011
CIV = 2 (Muslim)	−.720	.226	.002	.064
CIV = 4 (Hindu/Sinic/Buddhist)	−.571	.279	.042	.027
CIV = 5 (Africa)	0			
Syndrome 2017	.144	.023	.000*	.203
Urbanization 2015	−.016	.004	.000*	.105
Number of Land Neighbors	.009	.029	.759	.001
Terrain 2014	−.002	.005	.751	.001
Religious Fractionalization 2003	−.275	.320	.391	.005
Ethnic Fractionalization 2003	1.280	.336	.000*	.089

*significant at .001

6.4.   Contraceptive Prevalence (lower scores are considered worse, N = 135): The results are as follows:

TABLE AIII.7.6.4 General Linear Model Results for Contraceptive Prevalence (Adjusted R-squared = .491)

Independent/ Control Variable	Parameter Estimate	Standard Error	p-value	Effect Size
Intercept	69.109	9.193	.000	.337
Colonial Heritage Status = 0 (Never Colonized)	−5.154	4.484	.253	.012
Colonial Heritage Status = 1 (Ever Colonized)	0			
CIV = 1 (West/Orthodox/Latin)	2.164	3.792	.569	.003
CIV = 2 (Muslim)	6.450	4.436	.149	.019
CIV = 4 (Hindu/Sinic/Buddhist)	12.692	5.635	.026	.044
CIV = 5 (Africa)	0			
Syndrome 2017	−2.542	.489	.000*	.195
Urbanization 2015	.155	.079	.051	.034
Number of Land Neighbors	1.297	.563	.023	.046
Terrain 2014	.061	.104	.562	.003
Religious Fractionalization 2003	−3.576	6.405	.578	.003
Ethnic Fractionalization 2003	−22.455	6.314	.001*	.102

*significant at .001

6.5.   Youth Risk Factor (higher scores are considered worse, N = 166): The results are as follows:

TABLE AIII.7.6.5 General Linear Model Results for Youth Risk Factor (Adjusted R-squared = .479)

Independent/Control Variable	Parameter Estimate	Standard Error	p-value	Effect Size
Intercept	.355	.052	.000	.241
Colonial Heritage Status = 0 (Never Colonized)	−.031	.025	.219	.010
Colonial Heritage Status = 1 (Ever Colonized)	0			
CIV = 1 (West/Orthodox/Latin)	−.010	.022	.670	.001
CIV = 2 (Muslim)	−.044	.026	.095	.019
CIV = 4 (Hindu/Sinic/Buddhist)	−.025	.033	.443	.004
CIV = 5 (Africa)	0			
Syndrome 2017	.020	.003	.000*	.270
Urbanization 2015	−.001	.000	.203	.011
Number of Land Neighbors	.001	.003	.789	.000
Terrain 2014	.000	.001	.579	.002
Religious Fractionalization 2003	−.093	.037	.014	.041
Ethnic Fractionalization 2003	−.009	.040	.829	.000

*significant at .001

Dimension 7. Education of the Population

Variables in the Education of the Population Dimension

The following list provides the variable; the source from which the variable was obtained; whether the measure is nominal, ordinal, or continuous and the range, where applicable; which directionality the variable takes; the N size for the variable; and whether any transformations were used. (Five variables were excluded because their bivariate correlation with another variable in this dimension exceeded .90, and another variable was excluded because its measure was too close conceptually to other variables.[11]):

1. Access to Basic Knowledge (2016), Social Progress Index, ordinal (0–100), lower scores are worse, N = 158
2. Access to Information and Communications (2016), Social Progress Index, ordinal (0–100), lower scores are worse, N = 168
3. Average Years of Schooling (2015), United Nations Development Program Human Development Reports, years, lower scores are worse, N = 172
4. Discrepancy in Educational Attainment Between Males and Females (2015), The WomanStats Project, ordinal (0–4), higher scores are worse, N = 175
5. Female Literacy Rate Ages Fifteen to Twenty-Four (2016, or most recent without searching earlier than 2007), World Bank, percentage of women ages fifteen to twenty-four years old "who can both read and write with understanding a short simple statement about their everyday life," lower scores are worse, N = 126
6. Gender Parity Index for Primary School (2017, or most recent without searching earlier than 2007), World Bank, ratio of girls to boys enrolled at primary level in public and private schools, lower scores are worse, N = 169
7. Gender Parity Index for Secondary School (2017, or most recent without searching earlier than 2007), World Bank, ratio of girls to boys enrolled at secondary level in public and private schools, lower scores are worse, N = 163
8. Government Expenditures per Student Secondary as Percentage of GDP per Capita (2017, or most recent without searching earlier than 2007), World Bank, percent, lower scores are worse, N = 129[12]
9. Male Female Difference in Literacy Rates (2016, or most recent without searching earlier than 2007), World Bank (this value was calculated from the World Bank's Female Literacy and Male Literacy Rates), difference in percent between males and females, higher scores are worse, N = 124
10. Overall Literacy Rate Between Males and Females (2009–2016), CIA *World Factbook*, percentage of total population ages fifteen and over that can read and write, lower scores are worse, N = 148

11. Survival Rate to the Last Year of Primary School for Females (2016, or most recent without searching earlier than 2007), World Bank, percent of cohort, lower scores are worse, N = 150

We wanted to reduce the number of variables examined through factor analysis to find variables that loaded highly on the same factors and thus could be analyzed together. The factor analysis extracted only one factor, however, so all variables in this dimension were analyzed separately, except for two variables, which we combined because they are conceptually similar: Discrepancy in Educational Attainment Between Males and Females and Male-Female Difference in Literacy Rates. After checking for consistency in direction, the z-score for these variables were added to create the score to form the Male–Female Literacy and Education Difference factor (N = 124) (lower scores are considered better).

Model Specification

The model for each dependent variable or factor takes the same form in each case:

Dependent variable or factor$_i$ = Syndrome + Civilization
+ Colonial Heritage Status + Urbanization + Terrain
+ Number of Land Neighbors
+ Religious Fractionalization
+ Aggregated Ethnic Fractionalization + ε_i

We used a GLM procedure to investigate the statistical significance and explanatory power of these eight independent variables. We hypothesized that, after controlling for the influence of the other seven control variables, the Patrilineal/Fraternal Syndrome will still be a significant predictor of these dependent variables for the nations in our study.

GLM Results for the Education of the Population Dimension

7.1.   Average Years of Schooling (lower scores are considered worse, N = 172): The results are as follows:

TABLE AIII.7.7.1 General Linear Model Results for Average Years of Schooling (Adjusted R-squared = .676)

Independent/ Control Variable	Parameter Estimate	Standard Error	p-value	Effect Size
Intercept	7.755	.923	.000	.325
Colonial Heritage Status = 0 (Never Colonized)	−.219	.449	.627	.002
Colonial Heritage Status = 1 (Ever Colonized)	0			
CIV = 1 (West/Orthodox/Latin)	.568	.394	.152	.014
CIV = 2 (Muslim)	1.855	.466	.000*	.097
CIV = 4 (Hindu/Sinic/Buddhist)	.839	.585	.154	.014
CIV = 5 (Africa)	0			
Syndrome 2017	−.414	.048	.000*	.336
Urbanization 2015	.041	.008	.000*	.162
Number of Land Neighbors	.061	.059	.303	.007
Terrain 2014	−.008	.011	.453	.004
Religious Fractionalization 2003	2.977	.663	.000*	.121
Ethnic Fractionalization 2003	−1.482	.701	.036	.029

*significant at .001

7.2.   Access to Basic Knowledge (lower scores are considered worse, N = 158): The results are as follows:

TABLE AIII.7.7.2 General Linear Model Results for Access to Basic Knowledge (Adjusted R-squared = .608)

Independent/ Control Variable	Parameter Estimate	Standard Error	p-value	Effect Size
Intercept	88.623	5.020	.000	.696
Colonial Heritage Status = 0 (Never Colonized)	−3.055	2.344	.195	.012
Colonial Heritage Status = 1 (Ever Colonized)	0			
CIV = 1 (West/Orthodox/Latin)	3.208	2.129	.134	.016
CIV = 2 (Muslim)	9.935	2.549	.000*	.100
CIV = 4 (Hindu/Sinic/Buddhist)	7.178	2.991	.018	.041
CIV = 5 (Africa)	0			
Syndrome 2017	−1.638	.261	.000*	.225
Urbanization 2015	.167	.044	.000*	.097
Number of Land Neighbors	.311	.322	.335	.007
Terrain 2014	.004	.058	.945	.000
Religious Fractionalization 2003	1.230	3.540	.729	.001
Ethnic Fractionalization 2003	−11.860	3.774	.002	.068

*significant at .001

7.3.   Access to Information and Communications (lower scores are considered worse, N = 168): The results are as follows:

TABLE AIII.7.7.3 General Linear Model Results for Access to Information and Communications (Adjusted R-squared = .569)

Independent/ Control Variable	Parameter Estimate	Standard Error	p-value	Effect Size
Intercept	66.288	5.768	.000	.477
Colonial Heritage Status = 0 (Never Colonized)	1.960	2.799	.485	.003
Colonial Heritage Status = 1 (Ever Colonized)	0			
CIV = 1 (West/Orthodox/Latin)	−2.292	2.471	.355	.006
CIV = 2 (Muslim)	.421	2.914	.885	.000
CIV = 4 (Hindu/Sinic/Buddhist)	−5.482	3.645	.135	.015
CIV = 5 (Africa)	0			
Syndrome 2017	−1.774	.302	.000*	.192
Urbanization 2015	.294	.049	.000*	.202
Number of Land Neighbors	−.337	.373	.367	.006
Terrain 2014	−.024	.068	.728	.001
Religious Fractionalization 2003	7.631	4.149	.068	.023
Ethnic Fractionalization 2003	−4.658	4.421	.294	.008

*significant at .001

7.4.   Overall Literacy Rate for Fifteen and Over of Population (CIA World Factbook) (lower scores are considered worse, N = 148): The results are as follows:

TABLE AIII.7.7.4 General Linear Model Results for Overall Literacy Rate for Fifteen and Over of Population (Adjusted R-squared = .555)

Independent/ Control Variable	Parameter Estimate	Standard Error	p-value	Effect Size
Intercept	91.149	6.948	.000	.583
Colonial Heritage Status = 0 (Never Colonized)	−4.994	4.046	.219	.012
Colonial Heritage Status = 1 (Ever Colonized)	0			
CIV = 1 (West/Orthodox/Latin)	3.304	3.095	.288	.009
CIV = 2 (Muslim)	11.146	3.460	.002	.078
CIV = 4 (Hindu/Sinic/Buddhist)	7.261	4.409	.102	.022
CIV = 5 (Africa)	0			
Syndrome 2017	−2.230	.383	.000*	.216
Urbanization 2015	.256	.059	.000*	.133
Number of Land Neighbors	−.030	.468	.949	.000
Terrain 2014	−.118	.083	.156	.016
Religious Fractionalization 2003	11.173	5.504	.045	.032
Ethnic Fractionalization 2003	−19.402	5.495	.001*	.092

*significant at .001

7.5.   Female Literacy Rate Ages Fifteen to Twenty-Four (lower scores are considered worse, N = 126): The results are as follows:

TABLE AIII.7.7.5 General Linear Model Results for Female Literacy Rate Ages Fifteen to Twenty-Four (Adjusted R-squared = .495)

Independent/ Control Variable	Parameter Estimate	Standard Error	*p*-value	Effect Size
Intercept	97.287	8.952	.000	.532
Colonial Heritage Status = 0 (Never Colonized)	−4.936	5.003	.326	.009
Colonial Heritage Status = 1 (Ever Colonized)	0			
CIV = 1 (West/Orthodox/Latin)	−1.182	3.887	.762	.001
CIV = 2 (Muslim)	6.994	4.330	.109	.024
CIV = 4 (Hindu/Sinic/Buddhist)	5.527	5.316	.301	.010
CIV = 5 (Africa)	0			
Syndrome 2017	−2.228	.496	.000*	.162
Urbanization 2015	.278	.078	.001*	.108
Number of Land Neighbors	−.197	.592	.740	.001
Terrain 2014	−.009	.108	.936	.000
Religious Fractionalization 2003	10.204	6.911	.143	.021
Ethnic Fractionalization 2003	−23.518	6.967	.001*	.099

*significant at .001

7.6.   Survival Rate to the Last Year of Primary School for Females (lower scores are considered worse, N = 150): The results are as follows:

TABLE AIII.7.7.6 General Linear Model Results for Survival Rate to the Last Year of Primary School for Females (Adjusted R-squared = .485)

Parameter	Parameter Estimate	Standard Error	p-value	Partial Eta Squared
Intercept	82.516	6.997	.000	.523
Colonial Heritage Status = 0 (Never Colonized)	−3.931	3.637	.282	.009
Colonial Heritage Status = 1 (Ever Colonized)	0			
CIV = 1 (West/Orthodox/Latin)	7.100	3.078	.023	.040
CIV = 2 (Muslim)	13.412	3.451	.000*	.106
CIV = 4 (Hindu/Sinic/Buddhist)	5.932	4.257	.166	.015
CIV = 5 (Africa)	0			
Syndrome 2017	−1.408	.383	.000*	.096
Urbanization 2015	.229	.059	.000*	.105
Number of Land Neighbors	.085	.507	.867	.000
Terrain 2014	−.086	.079	.275	.009
Religious Fractionalization 2003	1.400	5.176	.787	.001
Ethnic Fractionalization 2003	−12.915	5.468	.020	.042

*significant at .001

Dimension 8. Social Progress

Variables in the Social Progress Dimension
The variables that are most commonly used in social science research and that the authors deemed as the most valid measures of social progress are listed in alphabetical order. (Some variables were excluded because of N size reasons, for theoretical reasons, or because their bivariate correlation with another variable in this dimension exceeded .90.[13]) The list provides the variable name; the source from which the variable was obtained; whether the measure is nominal, ordinal, or continuous and the range, where applicable; which directionality the variable takes; the N size for the variable; and whether any transformations were used:

1. Percent of Population with Access to Electricity (2016), World Bank, percent, lower scores are worse, N = 175
2. Discrimination and Violence Against Minorities (2016), Social Progress Index, ordinal (0–10), higher scores are worse, N = 160
3. Female Suicide Rates (2015), World Health Organization, rates per 100,000 female population, higher scores are worse, N = 173
4. Formal Commitment to the Convention on the Elimination of All Forms of Discrimination Against Women (2015), The WomanStats Project, ordinal (0–3), higher scores are worse, N = 176
5. Gender Gap Index (2016), World Economic Forum, ordinal (0–1), lower scores are worse (0 = inequality, 1 = equality), N = 144
6. Gender Inequality Index (2015), United Nations Development Program, scale (min = .040, max = .767), higher scores are worse, N = 155
7. Government Framework for Gender Equality (2015), The WomanStats Project, ordinal (0–7), higher scores are worse, N = 176
8. Happiness Index (2015), World Happiness Report (Accessed from the Quality of Government Institute), ordinal (0–10), lower scores are worse, N = 157
9. Hofstede Individualism Score (2018), Geert-Hofstede, ordinal (0–100), higher scores are for countries that are more individualistic, N = 101
10. Human Development Index (2015), United Nations Development Program Human Development Reports, scale (min = .352, max = .949), lower scores are worse, N = 172
11. Legal Declaration of Gender Equality (2015), The WomanStats Project, ordinal (0–2), higher scores are worse, N = 176
12. Percentage of Pensionable-Age Persons receiving Social Security or Pensions (2005–2016), percent, lower scores are worse, N = 159
13. Presence of National Gender Equality Action Plan (2015), The WomanStats Project, ordinal (0–2), higher scores are worse, N = 176

14. Religious Tolerance (2016), Social Progress Index, ordinal (1–4), lower scores are worse, N = 160
15. Social Safety Nets (2016), Bertelsmann Stiftung's Transformation Index (Accessed from the Quality of Government Institute), scale (1–10), lower scores are worse (1 = Social Safety Nets do not exist, 10 = Social Safety Nets are comprehensive), N = 128
16. Tolerance for Immigrants (2016), Social Progress Index, percent (0–1) of respondents answering yes to the question, "Is the city or area where you live a good place or not a good place to live for immigrants from other countries?" lower scores are worse, N = 152

We wanted to reduce the number of variables examined through factor analysis to find variables that loaded highly on the same factors and thus could be analyzed together. The factor analysis would not load, however, because the matrix was positive definite. We therefore chose to analyze all of the sixteen variables separately.

Model Specification

The model for each dependent variable or factor takes the same form in each case:

$$
\begin{aligned}
\text{Dependent variable or factor}_i = {} & \text{Syndrome} + \text{Civilization} + \text{Colonial Heritage Status} \\
& + \text{Urbanization} + \text{Terrain} \\
& + \text{Number of Land Neighbors} \\
& + \text{Religious Fractionalization} \\
& + \text{Aggregated Ethnic Fractionalization} + \varepsilon_i
\end{aligned}
$$

We used a GLM procedure to investigate the statistical significance and explanatory power of these eight independent variables. We hypothesized that, after controlling for the influence of the other seven control variables, the Patrilineal/Fraternal Syndrome will still be a significant predictor of these dependent variables for the nations in our study.

GLM Results for the Social Progress Dimension

8.1. Human Development Index (lower scores are considered worse, N = 172): The results are as follows:

TABLE AIII.7.8.1 General Linear Model Results for Human Development Index (Adjusted R-squared = .788)

Independent/ Control Variable	Parameter Estimate	Standard Error	p-value	Effect Size
Intercept	.658	.037	.000	.680
Colonial Heritage Status = 0 (Never Colonized)	.016	.018	.390	.005
Colonial Heritage Status = 1 (Ever Colonized)	0			
CIV = 1 (West/Orthodox/Latin)	.019	.016	.228	.010
CIV = 2 (Muslim)	.081	.019	.000*	.111
CIV = 4 (Hindu/Sinic/Buddhist)	.037	.024	.122	.016
CIV = 5 (Africa)	0			
Syndrome 2017	−.017	.002	.000*	.347
Urbanization 2015	.003	.000	.000*	.385
Number of Land Neighbors	.001	.002	.697	.001
Terrain 2014	−.001	.000	.064	.023
Religious Fractionalization 2003	.063	.027	.020	.036
Ethnic Fractionalization 2003	−.108	.028	.000*	.090

*significant at .001

8.2. Gender Inequality Index (higher scores are considered worse, N = 155): The results are as follows:

TABLE AIII.7.8.2 General Linear Model Results for Gender Inequality Index (Adjusted R-squared = .718)

Independent/ Control Variable	Parameter Estimate	Standard Error	p-value	Effect Size
Intercept	.256	.057	.000	.131
Colonial Heritage Status = 0 (Never Colonized)	−.033	.025	.191	.013
Colonial Heritage Status = 1 (Ever Colonized)	0			
CIV = 1 (West/Orthodox/Latin)	.016	.024	.501	.003
CIV = 2 (Muslim)	−.047	.028	.089	.021
CIV = 4 (Hindu/Sinic/Buddhist)	−.014	.034	.686	.001
CIV = 5 (Africa)	0			
Syndrome 2017	.026	.003	.000*	.392
Urbanization 2015	−.002	.000	.000*	.123
Number of Land Neighbors	−.005	.003	.167	.014
Terrain 2014	3.160E−5	.001	.959	.000
Religious Fractionalization 2003	−.048	.039	.223	.011
Ethnic Fractionalization 2003	.140	.041	.001*	.078

*significant at .001

8.3. **Happiness Index** (lower scores are considered worse, N = 157): The results are as follows:

TABLE AIII.7.8.3 General Linear Model Results for Happiness Index (Adjusted R-squared = .643)

Independent/ Control Variable	Parameter Estimate	Standard Error	p-value	Effect Size
Intercept	5.102	.400	.000	.545
Colonial Heritage Status = 0 (Never Colonized)	.267	.183	.147	.015
Colonial Heritage Status = 1 (Ever Colonized)	0			
CIV = 1 (West/Orthodox/Latin)	.220	.171	.201	.012
CIV = 2 (Muslim)	.667	.194	.001*	.080
CIV = 4 (Hindu/Sinic/Buddhist)	.471	.241	.052	.027
CIV = 5 (Africa)	0			
Syndrome 2017	−.137	.021	.000*	.242
Urbanization 2015	.021	.003	.000*	.222
Number of Land Neighbors	−.028	.026	.287	.008
Terrain 2014	−.013	.005	.008	.050
Religious Fractionalization 2003	.003	.282	.993	.000
Ethnic Fractionalization 2003	.196	.305	.523	.003

*significant at .001

8.4.   Percentage of Pensionable-Age Persons Receiving Social Security or Pensions (lower scores are considered worse, N = 159): The results are as follows:

TABLE AIII.7.8.4 General Linear Model Results for Percentage of Pensionable-Age Persons Receiving Social Security to Pensions (Adjusted R-squared = .533)

Independent/ Control Variable	Parameter Estimate	Standard Error	p-value	Effect Size
Intercept	94.528	14.779	.000	.231
Colonial Heritage Status = 0 (Never Colonized)	2.893	6.998	.680	.001
Colonial Heritage Status = 1 (Ever Colonized)	0			
CIV = 1 (West/Orthodox/Latin)	−.458	6.062	.940	.000
CIV = 2 (Muslim)	7.830	7.273	.284	.008
CIV = 4 (Hindu/Sinic/Buddhist)	−4.739	9.030	.601	.002
CIV = 5 (Africa)	0			
Syndrome 2017	−6.028	.737	.000*	.330
Urbanization 2015	.058	.120	.627	.002
Number of Land Neighbors	2.232	.902	.015	.043
Terrain 2014	−.132	.163	.422	.005
Religious Fractionalization 2003	6.060	10.228	.554	.003
Ethnic Fractionalization 2003	−15.671	10.861	.151	.015

*significant at .001

8.5. Percent of Population with Access to Electricity (lower scores are considered worse, N = 175): The results are as follows:

TABLE AIII.7.8.5 General Linear Model Results for Percent of Population with Access to Electricity (Adjusted R-squared = .495)

Independent/ Control Variable	Parameter Estimate	Standard Error	p-value	Effect Size
Intercept	73.579	10.328	.000	.254
Colonial Heritage Status = 0 (Never Colonized)	−4.114	5.028	.415	.004
Colonial Heritage Status = 1 (Ever Colonized)	0			
CIV = 1 (West/Orthodox/Latin)	8.390	4.425	.060	.024
CIV = 2 (Muslim)	19.746	5.205	.000*	.088
CIV = 4 (Hindu/Sinic/Buddhist)	10.635	6.413	.099	.018
CIV = 5 (Africa)	0			
Syndrome 2017	−2.177	.538	.000*	.099
Urbanization 2015	.445	.086	.000*	.152
Number of Land Neighbors	.375	.663	.572	.002
Terrain 2014	−.050	.120	.675	.001
Religious Fractionalization 2003	−8.234	7.353	.265	.008
Ethnic Fractionalization 2003	−14.498	7.738	.063	.023

*significant at .001

8.6.   Hofstede Individualism Score (higher scores are associated with more individualistic cultures, N = 101): The results are as follows:

TABLE AIII.7.8.6 General Linear Model Results for Hofstede Individualism Score (Adjusted R-squared = .471)

Independent/ Control Variable	Parameter Estimate	Standard Error	p-value	Effect Size
Intercept	25.475	12.371	.043	.048
Colonial Heritage Status = 0 (Never Colonized)	9.902	4.472	.030	.055
Colonial Heritage Status = 1 (Ever Colonized)	0			
CIV = 1 (West/Orthodox/Latin)	−3.087	4.870	.528	.005
CIV = 2 (Muslim)	−4.199	5.662	.460	.006
CIV = 4 (Hindu/Sinic/Buddhist)	−10.578	6.572	.111	.030
CIV = 5 (Africa)	0			
Syndrome 2017	−2.131	.530	.000*	.160
Urbanization 2015	.261	.098	.009	.077
Number of Land Neighbors	−.293	.646	.652	.002
Terrain 2014	.283	.132	.036	.051
Religious Fractionalization 2003	17.710	7.442	.020	.062
Ethnic Fractionalization 2003	2.960	8.877	.740	.001

*significant at .001

8.7.   Gender Gap Index (lower scores are considered worse, N = 144): The results are as follows:

TABLE AIII.7.8.7 General Linear Model Results for Gender Gap Index (Adjusted R-squared = .445)

Independent/ Control Variable	Parameter Estimate	Standard Error	p-value	Effect Size
Intercept	.799	.025	.000	.894
Colonial Heritage Status = 0 (Never Colonized)	−.004	.011	.683	.001
Colonial Heritage Status = 1 (Ever Colonized)	0			
CIV = 1 (West/Orthodox/Latin)	−.013	.010	.214	.012
CIV = 2 (Muslim)	−.015	.012	.220	.012
CIV = 4 (Hindu/Sinic/Buddhist)	.000	.014	.991	.000
CIV = 5 (Africa)	0			
Syndrome 2017	−.010	.001	.000*	.318
Urbanization 2015	.000	.000	.038	.034
Number of Land Neighbors	−.001	.002	.709	.001
Terrain 2014	.000	.000	.985	.000
Religious Fractionalization 2003	.004	.017	.802	.001
Ethnic Fractionalization 2003	.010	.018	.600	.002

*significant at .001

8.8.   Discrimination and Violence Against Minorities (higher scores are considered worse, N = 160): The results are as follows:

TABLE AIII.7.8.8 General Linear Model Results for Discrimination and Violence Against Minorities (Adjusted R-squared = .399)

Independent/ Control Variable	Parameter Estimate	Standard Error	*p*-value	Effect Size
Intercept	4.767	.806	.000	.200
Colonial Heritage Status = 0 (Never Colonized)	.222	.384	.565	.002
Colonial Heritage Status = 1 (Ever Colonized)	0			
CIV = 1 (West/Orthodox/Latin)	.265	.341	.437	.004
CIV = 2 (Muslim)	.365	.408	.372	.006
CIV = 4 (Hindu/Sinic/Buddhist)	.762	.500	.130	.016
CIV = 5 (Africa)	0			
Syndrome 2017	.162	.042	.000*	.097
Urbanization 2015	−.018	.007	.010	.047
Number of Land Neighbors	.249	.052	.000*	.141
Terrain 2014	.007	.009	.460	.004
Religious Fractionalization 2003	−.862	.577	.138	.016
Ethnic Fractionalization 2003	.488	.620	.432	.004

*significant at .001

8.9.   Legal Declaration of Gender Equality (higher scores are considered worse, N = 176): The results are as follows:

TABLE AIII.7.8.9 General Linear Model Results for Legal Declaration of Gender Equality (Adjusted R-squared = .384)

Independent/ Control Variable	Parameter Estimate	Standard Error	p-value	Effect Size
Intercept	−.480	.348	.169	.013
Colonial Heritage Status = 0 (Never Colonized)	.147	.169	.388	.005
Colonial Heritage Status = 1 (Ever Colonized)	0			
CIV = 1 (West/Orthodox/Latin)	−.185	.149	.216	.010
CIV = 2 (Muslim)	−.154	.175	.381	.005
CIV = 4 (Hindu/Sinic/Buddhist)	−.286	.216	.187	.012
CIV = 5 (Africa)	0			
Syndrome 2017	.134	.018	.000*	.270
Urbanization 2015	.006	.003	.052	.025
Number of Land Neighbors	−.001	.022	.964	.000
Terrain 2014	.000	.004	.922	.000
Religious Fractionalization 2003	.635	.247	.011	.042
Ethnic Fractionalization 2003	−.206	.260	.431	.004

*significant at .001

Dimension 9. Environmental Protection Dimension

Variables in the Environmental Protection Dimension

The variables that are most commonly used in social science research and that the authors deemed as the most valid measures of environmental protection are listed in alphabetical order. (One variable was excluded because its bivariate correlation with another variable in this dimension exceeded .90.[14]) The list provides the variable name; the source from which the variable was obtained;

whether the measure is nominal, ordinal, or continuous and the range, where applicable; which directionality the variable takes; the N size for the variable; and whether any transformations were used:

1. Air Quality (2014), Environmental Performance Index (Accessed from the Quality of Government Institute), scale (min = 13.83, max = 100), lower scores are worse, N = 172

2. Biodiversity and Habitat (2016), Social Progress Index, ordinal (0–100), lower scores are worse (0 = no protection, 100 = high protection), N = 160

3. Environmental Performance Index (2014), Environmental Performance Index (Accessed from the Quality of Government Institute), scale (min = 15.47, max = 87.67), lower scores are worse, N = 171

4. Foundations of Well-Being (2016), Social Progress Index; this variable combines indicators of the country's Access to Basic Knowledge, Access to Information and Communications, Health and Wellness, and Environmental Quality, ordinal (0–100), lower scores are worse, N = 152

5. Global Climate Risk Index (2014), German Watch, continuous scale (min = 8.17, max = 117.67), higher scores are worse, N = 172

6. Greenhouse Gases (2016), Social Progress Index, "emissions of carbon dioxide (CO_2), methane (CH_4), nitrous oxide (N_2O), hydrofluorocarbons (HFCs), perfluorocarbons (PFCs), and sulfur hexafluoride (SF_6) expressed in CO_2 equivalents," higher scores are worse, N = 157

7. Household Indoor Air Pollution Attributable Deaths (2016), Social Progress Index, rate of deaths resulting from household air pollution per 100,000 people, higher scores are worse, N = 160

8. Outdoor Air Pollution Attributable Deaths (2016), Social Progress Index, rate of deaths "resulting from emissions from industrial activity, households, and cars and trucks" per 100,000 people, higher scores are worse, N = 160

9. Pesticide Regulation (2016), Environmental Performance Index (Accessed from the Quality of Government Institute), scale (min = 0, max = 96), lower scores are worse, N = 173

10. Wastewater Treatment (2016), Social Progress Index, percentage of wastewater that is treated, lower scores are worse, N = 156

11. Water and Sanitation (2014), Environmental Performance Index (Accessed from the Quality of Government Institute), scale (min = 1.29, max = 100), lower scores are worse, N = 173

We wanted to reduce the number of variables examined through factor analysis to find variables that loaded highly on the same factors and thus could be analyzed together. In this manner, we identified three factors and three variables requiring individual modeling, for a total of six outcome variables. The three variables to be examined separately because they did not load sufficiently highly on the other factors are as follows:

- Outdoor Air Pollution Attributable Deaths
- Global Climate Risk Index
- Air Quality

The EFA results utilizing principal axis factoring yielded three distinct loading patterns, and the z-scores of the variables in each factor were added to create the score for each factor, after checking for consistency in direction (or multiplied by −1 to maintain consistency):

1.   **Water and Environmental Well-Being Factor** (higher scores are considered better, N = 149): This factor consists of these four variables with loadings ranging from .737 to 1.099: (1) Water and Sanitation, (2) Environmental Performance Index, (3) Wastewater Treatment, and (4) Foundations of Well-Being.

2.   **Air Pollution Factor** (lower scores are considered better, N = 157): This factor consists of these two variables with loadings ranging from −.799 to −.284: (1) Household Indoor Air Pollution Attributable Deaths and (2) Greenhouse Gases Emissions.

3.   **Biodiversity and Pest Regulation Factor** (higher scores are considered better, N = 160): This factor consists of these two variables with loadings ranging from .449 to .624: (1) Biodiversity and (2) Pest Regulation.

Model Specification
The model for each dependent variable or factor takes the same form in each case:

Dependent variable or factor$_i$ = Syndrome + Civilization
              + Colonial Heritage Status + Urbanization + Terrain
              + Number of Land Neighbors
              + Religious Fractionalization
              + Aggregated Ethnic Fractionalization + ε_i

We used a GLM procedure to investigate the statistical significance and explanatory power of these eight independent variables. We hypothesized that, after controlling for the influence of the other seven control variables, the Patrilineal/Fraternal Syndrome will still be a significant predictor of these dependent variables and factors for the nations in our study.

GLM Results for the Environmental Protection Dimension

9.1. Water and Environmental Well-Being factor (lower scores are considered worse, N = 149): Recall that this factor combines several variables (Water and Sanitation, Environmental Performance Index, Wastewater Treatment, and Foundations of Well-Being), the results are as follows:

TABLE AIII.7.9.1 General Linear Model Results for Water and Environmental Well-Being Factor (Adjusted R-squared = .808)

Independent/ Control Variable	Parameter Estimate	Standard Error	p-value	Effect Size
Intercept	−1.171	.951	.220	.012
Colonial Heritage Status = 0 (Never Colonized)	1.407	.414	.001*	.081
Colonial Heritage Status = 1 (Ever Colonized)	0			
CIV = 1 (West/Orthodox/Latin)	−.073	.390	.851	.000
CIV = 2 (Muslim)	.857	.461	.066	.026
CIV = 4 (Hindu/Sinic/Buddhist)	.248	.567	.662	.001
CIV = 5 (Africa)	0			
Syndrome 2017	−.360	.047	.000*	.312
Urbanization 2015	.075	.008	.000*	.406
Number of Land Neighbors	−.043	.058	.460	.004
Terrain 2014	−.002	.010	.879	.000
Religious Fractionalization 2003	1.576	.656	.018	.043
Ethnic Fractionalization 2003	−2.579	.687	.000*	.098

*significant at .001

9.2. Air Pollution Factor (Without Outlier) (higher scores are considered worse, N = 156): Recall that this factor combines two variables (Household Indoor Air Pollution Attributable Deaths and Greenhouse Gases). We determined that the insignificant results for the entire Air Pollution factor were largely because of an extreme outlier in the model, Central African Republic (13.07). To evaluate this, we removed this outlier from the model and reran the analysis. The results are found below.

TABLE AIII.7.9.2 General Linear Model Results for Air Pollution Factor (Without Outlier) (Adjusted R-squared = .587)

Independent/ Control Variable	Parameter Estimate	Standard Error	p-value	Effect Size
Intercept	.699	.418	.097	.020
Colonial Heritage Status = 0 (Never Colonized)	.148	.196	.451	.004
Colonial Heritage Status = 1 (Ever Colonized)	0			
CIV = 1 (West/Orthodox/Latin)	.042	.177	.814	.000
CIV = 2 (Muslim)	−.374	.209	.076	.023
CIV = 4 (Hindu/Sinic/Buddhist)	−.305	.257	.237	.010
CIV = 5 (Africa)	0			
Syndrome 2017	.080	.021	.000*	.092
Urbanization 2015	−.027	.003	.000*	.303
Number of Land Neighbors	−.028	.027	.287	.008
Terrain 2014	3.426E−5	.005	.994	.000
Religious Fractionalization 2003	−.242	.298	.418	.005
Ethnic Fractionalization 2003	.983	.316	.002	.066

*significant at .001

9.3. **Biodiversity and Pest Regulation Factor** (lower scores are considered worse, N = 160): Recall that this factor combines two variables (Biodiversity and Pesticide Regulation), the results are as follows:

TABLE AIII.7.9.3 General Linear Model Results for Biodiversity and Pest Regulation Factor (Adjusted R-squared = .207)

Independent/ Control Variable	Parameter Estimate	Standard Error	p-value	Effect Size
Intercept	.290	.759	.703	.001
Colonial Heritage Status = 0 (Never Colonized)	−.002	.362	.995	.000
Colonial Heritage Status = 1 (Ever Colonized)	0			
CIV = 1 (West/Orthodox/Latin)	−.129	.321	.689	.001
CIV = 2 (Muslim)	.113	.384	.770	.001
CIV = 4 (Hindu/Sinic/Buddhist)	.363	.472	.443	.004
CIV = 5 (Africa)	0			
Syndrome 2017	−.205	.039	.000*	.163
Urbanization 2015	.005	.006	.391	.005
Number of Land Neighbors	.054	.049	.268	.009
Terrain 2014	.006	.009	.469	.004
Religious Fractionalization 2003	.268	.544	.623	.002
Ethnic Fractionalization 2003	1.401	.584	.018	.040

*significant at .001

APPENDIX IV

DICHOTOMIZATION CUTPOINTS FOR LOGISTIC REGRESSION ANALYSIS

To perform logistic regression to analyze the effect of a one unit increase in the Syndrome on a country's likelihood to be in the "worse outcomes" category for each significant variable, we dichotomized each of the variables in this appendix to define "worse outcomes" (see chapter 7). This appendix specifies the split between better and worse outcomes that we chose for each variable and justifies the selection. For continuous variables, the number at which the variable was split indicates that that number and below would be marked as different from all values above that number. If the variable's directional meaning is that higher scores are worse, then the lower numbers are assigned 0 and the higher numbers are assigned 1 for the logistic regression. Alternatively, if the variable's directional meaning is that lower scores are worse, then the lower numbers are assigned 1 and the higher numbers are assigned 0 for purposes of the logistic regression.

Our general rules of thumb for demarcating "better" from "worse" outcomes are as follows: (1) if a continuous variable's histogram showed two clear separate distributions, then we split between those; (2) if a continuous variable's histogram was extremely skewed and one or two adjacent bins had the highest peaks, then we created a split to ensure that those bins were grouped together; (3) if a continuous variable did not have a clear split in its histogram, then we split at the mean; (4) ordinal variables with an even number of scale points were split in half; and (5) ordinal variables with an uneven number of scale points were split with one extra scale point in the "0" group so that the "worse" outcome category was smaller than the "better" outcome category. Rare exceptions to these rules are discussed, when applicable.

Dimension 1. Political Stability

1.1 Fragile States Index: Split at 70.45, approximately at the mean.
   - Security, Stability, and Legitimacy Factor: Split at 1.67, natural split in the histogram.

1.2 Government System and Effectiveness Factor: Split at 2.171, mean + ½ standard deviation. We added half a standard deviation to the mean because this would make the worse outcome higher than just above average which is a stricter criterion.
   - Regime Types: Split 1–3 and 4. This split is different from our rule, but we chose this for theoretical reasons, namely, that values 1–3 are all different levels of autocracy and 4 is the only scale point that indicates that there is some sort of democracy.

1.3 World Bank Corruption: Split at −0.13, approximately at the mean.

1.4 World Bank Rule of Law: Split at −0.13, approximately at the mean.
   - Private Property Rights: Split at 41.38, approximately at the mean.

1.5 Lack of Freedom Factor: Split at 0, approximately at the mean.
   - Civil Liberties: Split at 6.67, natural split in the histogram.

1.6 Freedom to Establish Religion: Split between 5 and 7.5. This is a factor variable with possible values of 0, 2.5, 5, 7.5, and 10. The general rule is that a factor variable with an uneven number of scale points are split with one extra in the "0" group. But here only one observation has the lowest value (0), so the split was made so that 0, 2.5, 5 = 1, and 7.5, 10 = 0.

1.7 Percent of Seats in Parliament Held by Women: Split at 21.56, approximately at the mean.
   - Government Participation of Women: Split 0–2 ("better") and 3–4 ("worse").

Dimension 2. Security and Conflict

2.1 Violence and Instability Factor: Split at 3.794, mean + ½ standard deviation. We added half a standard deviation to the mean. This would make the worse outcome higher than just above average which is a stricter criterion.
   - Political Stability and Absence of Violence/Terrorism and Freedom of Domestic Movement Factor: Split at −1.5, natural split in the histogram.
   - Trafficking of Women: Split 0–2 and 3–4.
   - Political Terror Scale: Split 1–3 and 4–5.

2.2 Societal Violence Scale: Split 1–3 and 4–5.

2.3 Military Expenditure and Weapons Importation Factor: Split at 0, natural split in the histogram.
   - Access to Weapons: Split 1–3 and 4–5.

2.4 Monopoly on the Use of Force: Split 1–5 and 6–10.
2.5 Global Terrorism Index: Split at 0.67. We note that the bin in the leftmost side of the histogram has the highest frequency and we used the upper limit of the bin as the cutoff.
   - Terrorism Injury and Violent Conflict Factor: Split at 0, both natural split in the histogram and also approximately the mean.
   - Terrorism Incidents and Internal Conflict Factor: Split at 0, both natural split in the histogram and also approximately the mean.
   - Terrorism Impact: Split at 1.25.
   We note that the bin in the leftmost side of the histogram has the highest frequency and we used the upper limit of the bin as the cutoff.
   - Overall Index of Disappearances: Split 0–5 and 10. The three possible scale points are 0, 5, and 10.
2.6 Perceptions of Criminality: Split 2–3 and 4–5.

Dimension 3. Economic Performance

3.1 Food Security: Split at 57.92, approximately at the mean.
3.2 Reliance on Agriculture and Lack of Prosperity Factor: Split at 0, approximately at the mean.
3.3 GDP per Capital PPP 2017 (log transformed): Split at 9.32, approximately at the mean.
3.4 Poverty and Economic Decline: Split at 5.78, approximately at the mean.
3.5 Wealth Infrastructure and Economic Freedom Factor: Split at 0.88, approximately at the mean.
3.6 Global Competitiveness Index: Split at 70, approximately at the mean.
3.7 Economic Inequality Factor: Split at 0, approximately at the mean.
3.8 Female Labor Force Participation: Split at 36.7, natural split in the histogram.

Dimension 4. Economic Rentierism

4.1 Natural Resources as Percentage of GDP: Split at 3.33. Note that the highest bar in the histogram stood on its own.

Dimension 5. Health and Well-Being

5.1 Healthcare Access Factor: Split at 0, approximately the mean.
   - Percent of Pregnant Women Receiving Prenatal Care: Split at 90, approximately the mean.
   - Sustainable Society Index Human Well-Being: Split at 7, close to the mean.

5.2 Health Expenditure per Capita: Split at 1,333.
      We note that the two bins in the leftmost side of the histogram had the highest
      frequencies so we grouped these bins together.
      - Health Expenditure as Percentage of GDP: Split at 5.83 due to a natural split
         in the histogram.
5.3 Preventable Death Factor: Split at 0, approximately the mean.
      - Illness and Mortality Factor: Split at 0, approximately the mean.
      - Life Expectancy at Birth for Females: Split at 73.7, approximately at
         the mean.
      - Maternal Mortality Rate: Split 0–2 and 3–4.
      - Deaths Due to Diarrhea of Children Under Five: Split at 2.
      We note that the two bins in the leftmost side of the histogram had the highest
      frequencies so we grouped these bins together.
5.4 Total Alcohol Consumption per Capita: Split at 6, approximately the mean.
5.5 Prevalence of HIV Among Women Ages Fifteen and Over: Split at 45 due to
      a natural split in the histogram.
5.6 Global Hunger Index: Split at 17.13, approximately at the mean.
5.7 Female Genital Cutting/Mutilation (FGM): Split 0–1 and 2–4. This split is
      different from our rule, but we chose this for theoretical reasons, namely,
      that 0–1 scores indicate that FGM rarely or never occurs, which we defined
      as the only acceptable "good" score for this variable.
      Other variables:
      - Percent Under Five Who are Stunted: Split at 20, due to a natural split in the
         bimodal histogram. The mean is 24.40 and the median is 23.90, so the split
         is lower than these values.
      - Prevalence of Wasting Percentage Under Five: Split at 5, due to a natural
         split in the histogram. The mean is 6.26 and the median is 4.90, so the split is
         between these two values. There are two "distributions" in the histogram—
         one more evenly distributed and one right-skewed distribution.
      - Percent Under Five Who Are Underweight: Split at 10, due to a natural split
         in the histogram. The mean is 12.57 and the median is 11.10, so the split is
         lower than both these two. There were two right-skewed "distributions" in
         the histogram.

Dimension 6. Demographic Security

6.1 Mother's Mean Age at First Birth: Split at 23.95, mean.
6.2 Demographic Pressure: Split at 5.82, mean.
6.3 Total Fertility Rate: Split at 3.67, due to a natural split in the histogram. The
      mean is 2.82 and the median is 2.34, so the split is higher than both of these
      values. This histogram is also bimodal, but also right-skewed, and the sec-
      ond peak is much lower than the first.

6.4 Contraceptive Prevalence: Split at 49.42, mean.

6.5 Youth Risk Factor: Split at 0.35, due to a natural split in the bimodal histogram. The mean is .412 and the median is .415, so the split is lower than either of these values.

Dimension 7. Education of the Population

7.1 Average Years of Schooling: Split at 8, close to the mean. We did not choose the precise mean because we wanted years of school through the completion of primary school to be grouped together.

7.2 Access to Basic Knowledge: Split at 90. We used the natural split in the histogram.

7.3 Access to Information and Communications: Split at 60, due to a natural split in the histogram.

7.4 Overall Literacy for Fifteen and Over of Population: Split at 95. We used the natural split in the histogram.

7.5 Female Literacy Rate Ages Fifteen to Twenty-Four: Split at 95. We used the natural split in the histogram.

7.6 Survival Rate to the Last Year of Primary School for Females: Split at 90. We used the natural split in the histogram.

Dimension 8. Social Progress

8.1 Human Development Index: Split at 0.7, approximately the mean.

8.2 Gender Inequality Index: Split at 0.4, approximately the mean.

8.3 Happiness Index: Split at 5.67, due to a natural split in the bimodal histogram. The mean is 5.36 and the median is 5.24, and the split is a little above these two values.

8.4 Percentage of Pensionable-Age Persons Receiving Social Security or Pensions: Split at 79.9. This split is different from our rule, but we chose this for theoretical reasons, namely, that we did not consider the value for this variable to be "good" unless 80 percent or more of pensionable-age persons were receiving their benefits.
  - Social Safety Nets: Split 0–5 and 6–10.

8.5 Percent of Population with Access to Electricity: Split at 93.3. We note that the bin on the right side of the histogram has the highest frequency and we used the lower limit of the bin as the cutoff.

8.6 Hofstede Individualism Score : Split at 39, approximately at the mean.

8.7 Gender Gap Index: Split at 0.7, approximately the mean.

8.8 Discrimination and Violence Against Minorities: Split at 5.5, due to a natural split in histogram.

- Religious Tolerance: Split 1–3 and 4. This split is different from our rule, but we chose this because more than 60 countries scaled at a 4, so the typical split, 1-2 versus 3-4, would have produced uneven sample sizes in each of the two groups.
8.9 Legal Declaration of Gender Equality: Split 0–1 and 2.
  - Government Framework for Gender Equality: Split 0–2 and 3–7. This was partially chosen because there are many scale points in this distribution. We considered using the continuous variable rule and then found a clear split in distributions in the histogram (this is where we split the variable). The split is close to the mean. The mean is 2.43 and the median is 2.00, so the mean is right in between the split.

Dimension 9. Environmental Protection

9.1 Water and Environmental Well-Being Factor: Split at 2, due to a natural split in the histogram.
9.2 Air Pollution Factor (Without Outlier): Split at −0.10, approximately at the mean.
9.3 Biodiversity and Pest Regulation Factor: Split at 0, approximately at the mean.
9.4 Global Climate Risk Index
  - Outdoor Air Pollution Attributable Deaths: Split at 40, approximately at the mean.
  - Air Quality: Split at 87, mean + ½ standard deviation. We added half a standard deviation to the mean. This would make the worse outcome higher than just above average which is a stricter criterion.

APPENDIX V

HIGH-SYNDROME-ENCODING NATIONS WITH UNEXPECTEDLY GOOD NATIONAL OUTCOMES

TABLE AV.1 Variables That Each High-Syndrome-Encoding Country Performed Well On That Most Higher Syndrome Countries Performed Poorly On

Country	Variables for which the country performed well and for which between 50% and 80% of higher Syndrome countries performed poorly	Variables for which the country performed well and for which 80% or more of higher Syndrome countries performed poorly
Bahrain	Access to Weapons	World Bank Corruption
	Societal Violence Scale	World Bank Rule of Law
	Wealth Infrastructure and Economic Freedom Factor	Food Security
	Reliance on Agriculture and Lack of Prosperity Factor	Water and Environmental Well-Being Factor
	Poverty and Economic Decline	Youth Risk Factor
	Global Competitiveness Index	Demographic Pressure
	GDP (log transformed)	Average Years of Schooling
	Air Pollution Factor	Overall Literacy Rate Age Fifteen and Over of Population
	Outdoor Air Pollution Attributable Deaths	Deaths Due to Diarrhea of Children Under Five
	Total Fertility	Health Expenditure per Capita

(continued)

Country	Variables for which the country performed well and for which between 50% and 80% of higher Syndrome countries performed poorly	Variables for which the country performed well and for which 80% or more of higher Syndrome countries performed poorly
	Survival Rate to the Last Year of Primary School for Females	Life Expectancy at Birth for Females
	Access to Basic Knowledge	Human Development Index
	Access to Information and Communications	Happiness Index
	Female Literacy Rate Ages Fifteen to Twenty-Four	Gender Inequality Index
	Preventable Death Factor	
	Healthcare Access Factor	
	Maternal Mortality Rate	
	Prevalence of HIV Among Women Ages Fifteen and Over	
	Social Safety Nets	
	Access to Electricity, Percentage of Population	
Botswana	Security, Stability, and Legitimacy Factor	Government System and Effectiveness
	Lack of Freedom Factor	Civil Liberties
	Violence and Instability Factor	World Bank Corruption
	Access to Weapons	World Bank Rule of Law
	Societal Violence Scale	Food Security
	Perceptions of Crime	Air Quality
	Terrorism Impact	Average Years of Schooling
	Global Terrorism Index	Percentage of Pensionable-Age Persons Receiving Social Security or Pensions
	Wealth Infrastructure and Economic Freedom Factor	
	Reliance on Agriculture and Lack of Prosperity Factor	
	Global Competitiveness Index Rankings	
	GDP (log transformed)	
	Natural Resources as Percentage of GDP	
	Air Pollution Factor	

	Outdoor Air Pollution Attributable Deaths	
	Total Fertility	
	Contraceptive Prevalence	
	Survival Rate to the Last Year of Primary School for Females	
	Access to Information and Communications	
	Health Expenditure as Percentage of GDP	
	Social Safety Nets	
	Discrimination and Violence Against Minorities	
	Religious Tolerance	
	Gender Gap Index	
Jordan	Security, Stability, and Legitimacy Factor	World Bank Corruption
	Violence and Instability	World Bank Rule of Law
	Access to Weapons	Mother's Mean Age at First Birth
	Societal Violence Scale	Average Years of Schooling
	Wealth Infrastructure and Economic Freedom Factor	Overall Literacy Rate Age Fifteen and Over of Population
	Reliance on Agriculture and Lack of Prosperity Factor	Percentage Under 5 Who Are Stunted
	Economic Inequality Factor	Percentage Under 5 Who Are Underweight
	Global Competitiveness Index Rankings	Life Expectancy at Birth for Females
	GDP (log transformed)	Human Development Index
	Natural Resources as Percentage of GDP	
	Air Pollution Factor	
	Outdoor Air Pollution Attributable Deaths	
	Total Fertility	
	Contraceptive Prevalence	
	Survival Rate to the Last Year of Primary School for Females	
	Access to Basic Knowledge	
	Access to Information and Communications	

(continued)

Country	Variables for which the country performed well and for which between 50% and 80% of higher Syndrome countries performed poorly	Variables for which the country performed well and for which 80% or more of higher Syndrome countries performed poorly
	Female Literacy Rate Ages Fifteen to Twenty-Four	
	Preventable Death Factor	
	Healthcare Access Factor	
	Illness and Mortality Factor	
	Maternal Mortality Rates	
	Health Expenditure as Percentage of GDP	
	Prevalence of Wasting— Percentage Under Five	
	Prevalence of HIV Among Women Ages Fifteen and Over	
	Global Hunger Index	
	Access to Electricity	
Kuwait	Security, Stability, and Legitimacy Factor	World Bank Rule of Law
	Violence and Instability Factor	Food Security
	Access to Weapons	Water and Environmental Well-Being Factor
	Societal Violence Scale	Youth Risk Factor
	Perceptions of Criminality	Demographic Pressure
	Wealth Infrastructure and Economic Freedom Factor	Overall Literacy Rate Age Fifteen and Over of Population
	Reliance on Agriculture and Lack of Prosperity Factor	Deaths Due to Diarrhea of Children Under Five
	Poverty and Economic Decline	Health Expenditure per Capita
	Global Competitiveness Index Rankings	Percentage Under Five Who Are Stunted
	GDP (log transformed)	Percentage Under Five Who Are Underweight
	Air Pollution Factor	Life Expectancy at Birth for Females
	Biodiversity and Pest Regulation Factor	Human Development Index
	Total Fertility	Happiness Index
	Survival Rate to the Last Year of Primary School for Females	Gender Inequality Index

	Access to Basic Knowledge	
	Access to Information and Communications	
	Female Literacy Rate Ages Fifteen to Twenty-Four	
	Preventable Death Factor	
	Healthcare Access Factor	
	Illness and Mortality Factor	
	Maternal Mortality Rates	
	Prevalence of Wasting—Percentage Under Five	
	Prevalence of HIV Among Women Ages Fifteen and Over	
	Global Hunger Index	
	Social Safety Nets	
	Discrimination and Violence Against Minorities	
	Access to Electricity, Percentage of Population	
Malaysia	Security, Stability, and Legitimacy Factor	Government System and Effectiveness Factor
	Violence and Instability Factor	World Bank Corruption
	Access to Weapons	World Bank Rule of Law
	Societal Violence Scale	Food Security
	Perceptions of Criminality	Air Quality
	Wealth Infrastructure and Economic Freedom Factor	Demographic Pressure
	Reliance on Agriculture and Lack of Prosperity Factor	Average Years of Schooling
	Poverty and Economic Decline	Deaths Due to Diarrhea of Children Under Five
	Global Competitiveness Index Rankings	Life Expectancy at Birth for Females
	GDP (log transformed)	Human Development Index
	Air Pollution Factor	Happiness Index
	Biodiversity and Pest Regulation Factor	Gender Inequality Index
	Total Fertility	
	Contraceptive Prevalence	
	Survival Rate to the Last Year of Primary School for Females	

(continued)

Country	Variables for which the country performed well and for which between 50% and 80% of higher Syndrome countries performed poorly	Variables for which the country performed well and for which 80% or more of higher Syndrome countries performed poorly
	Access to Basic Knowledge	
	Access to Information and Communications	
	Female Literacy Rate Ages Fifteen to Twenty-Four	
	Preventable Death Factor	
	Healthcare Access Factor	
	Illness and Mortality Factor	
	Maternal Mortality Rates	
	Prevalence of HIV Among Women Ages Fifteen and Over	
	Global Hunger Index	
	Social Safety Nets	
	Access to Electricity, Percentage of Population	
Oman	Security, Stability, and Legitimacy Factor	World Bank Corruption
	Violence and Instability Factor	World Bank Rule of Law
	Societal Violence Scale	Food Security
	Perceptions of Criminality	Air Quality
	Terrorism Impact	Demographic Pressure
	Global Terrorism Index	Average Years of Schooling
	Wealth Infrastructure and Economic Freedom Factor	Deaths Due to Diarrhea of Children Under Five
	Reliance on Agriculture and Lack of Prosperity Factor	Health Expenditure per Capita
	Poverty and Economic Decline	Percentage Under Five Who Are Stunted
	Global Competitiveness Index Rankings	Percentage Under Five Who Are Underweight
	GDP (log transformed)	Life Expectancy at Birth for Females
	Air Pollution Factor	Human Development Index
	Total Fertility	Happiness Index
	Survival Rate to the Last Year of Primary School for Females	Gender Inequality Index
	Access to Basic Knowledge	

	Access to Information and Communications	
	Female Literacy Rate Ages Fifteen to Twenty-Four	
	Preventable Death Factor	
	Healthcare Access Factor	
	Illness and Mortality Factor	
	Maternal Mortality Rates	
	Global Hunger Index	
	Social Safety Nets	
	Discrimination and Violence Against Minorities	
	Religious Tolerance	
	Access to Electricity, Percentage of Population	
Qatar	Security, Stability, and Legitimacy Factor	World Bank Corruption
	Access to Weapons	World Bank Rule of Law
	Societal Violence Scale	Food Security
	Perceptions of Criminality	Water and Environmental Well-Being Factor
	Terrorism Impact	Youth Risk Factor
	Global Terrorism Index	Demographic Pressure
	Wealth Infrastructure and Economic Freedom Factor	Average Years of Schooling
	Reliance on Agriculture and Lack of Prosperity Factor	Overall Literacy Rates Ages Fifteen and Over of Population
	Poverty and Economic Decline	Deaths Due to Diarrhea of Children Under Five
	Global Competitiveness Index Rankings	Health Expenditure per Capita
	GDP (log transformed)	Life Expectancy at Birth for Females
	Air Pollution Factor	Human Development Index
	Outdoor Air Pollution Attributable Deaths	Happiness Index
	Total Fertility	
	Survival Rate to the Last Year of Primary School for Females	
	Access to Basic Knowledge	
	Access to Information and Communications	
	Female Literacy Rates	

(*continued*)

Country	Variables for which the country performed well and for which between 50% and 80% of higher Syndrome countries performed poorly	Variables for which the country performed well and for which 80% or more of higher Syndrome countries performed poorly
	Preventable Death Factor	
	Healthcare Access Factor	
	Maternal Mortality Rate	
	Prevalence of HIV Among Women Ages Fifteen and Over	
	Social Safety Nets	
	Discrimination and Violence Against Minorities	
	Religious Tolerance	
	Access to Electricity, Percentage of Population	
Saudi Arabia	Access to Weapons	World Bank Corruption
	Societal Violence Scale	World Bank Rule of Law
	Perceptions of Criminality	Food Security
	Wealth Infrastructure and Economic Freedom Factor	Water and Environmental Well-Being Factor
	Reliance on Agriculture and Lack of Prosperity Factor	Demographic Pressure
	Poverty and Economic Decline	Average Years of Schooling
	Global Competitiveness Index Rankings	Deaths Due to Diarrhea of Children Under Five
	GDP (log transformed)	Health Expenditure per Capita
	Air Pollution Factor	Life Expectancy at Birth for Females
	Biodiversity and Pest Regulation Factor	Human Development Index
	Total Fertility	Happiness Index
	Access to Basic Knowledge	Gender Inequality Index
	Access to Information and Communications	
	Female Literacy Rate Ages Fifteen to Twenty-Four	
	Preventable Death Factor	
	Healthcare Access Factor	
	Illness and Mortality Factor	
	Maternal Mortality Rate	
	Health Expenditure as Percentage of GDP	

	Prevalence of HIV Among Women Ages Fifteen and Over	
	Global Hunger Index	
	Social Safety Nets	
	Access to Electricity Percentage of Population	
United Arab Emirates	Security, Stability, and Legitimacy Factor	World Bank Corruption
	Women in Parliament	World Bank Rule of Law
	Violence and Instability Factor	Food Security
	Access to Weapons	Water and Environmental Well-Being Factor
	Societal Violence Scale	Youth Risk Factor
	Perceptions of Criminality	Demographic Pressure
	Terrorism Impact	Average Years of Schooling
	Global Terrorism Index	Deaths Due to Diarrhea of Children Under Five
	Wealth Infrastructure and Economic Freedom Factor	Health Expenditure per Capita
	Reliance on Agriculture and Lack of Prosperity Factor	Sustainable Society Index Human Well-Being
	Poverty and Economic Decline	Life Expectancy at Birth for Females
	Global Competitiveness Index Rankings	Human Development Index
	GDP (log transformed)	Happiness Index
	Air Pollution Factor	Gender Inequality Index
	Biodiversity and Pest Regulation Factor	
	Total Fertility	
	Survival Rate to the Last Year of Primary School for Females	
	Access to Information and Communications	
	Preventable Death Factor	
	Healthcare Access Factor	
	Illness and Mortality Factor	
	Maternal Mortality Rate	
	Social Safety Nets	
	Discrimination and Violence Against Minorities	
	Access to Electricity, Percentage of Population	

NOTES

Introduction

1. Yuval Noah Harari, *Sapiens: A Brief History of Humankind* (New York: Harper Perennial, 2018), 144.
2. Henry Maine, *Ancient Law: Its Connection with the Early History of Society and Its Relation to Modern Ideas* (Tucson: University of Arizona Press, 1986).
3. Maine, *Ancient Law*.
4. The replication dataset for this book's empirical analysis, as well as other material relevant to that analysis, can be found at http://womanstats.org/fpo.html.
5. The original meaning of the ouroboros as used symbolically in cemeteries is to remind a mourner of the eternities, presumably a consoling thought. Given our use of the ouroboros as a metaphor for the Patrilineal/Fraternal Syndrome, we view the grief of the figure as a reaction to the ouroboros-like, and thus seemingly never-ending, nature of that Syndrome.

1. The First Political Order Is the Sexual Political Order

1. Francis Fukuyama, *The Origins of Political Order* (New York: Farrar, Straus, and Giroux, 2011); Douglass North, John Wallis, and Barry Weingast, *Violence and Social Orders* (2009; repr., Cambridge: Cambridge University Press, 2013); Service Elman, *Origins of the State and Civilization* (New York: Norton, 1975); Friedrich Engels, *The Origins of Family, Private Property, and the State*, Vol. 3, *Karl Marx and Frederick Engels: Selected Works in Three Volumes* (Hottingen-Zurich, 1884), https://www.marxists.org/archive /marx/works/download/pdf/origin_family.pdf; Daron Acemoglu and James Robinson, *Why Nations Fail: The Origins of Power, Prosperity, and Poverty* (New York: Crown, 2013); Anthony D. Smith, *The Ethnic Origins of Nations* (New York: Wiley-Blackwell, 1991);

Howard Sherman, *How Society Makes Itself: The Evolution of Political and Economic Institutions* (New York: M. E. Sharpe, 2005); Azar Gat, *Nations: The Long History and Deep Roots of Ethnicity and Nationalism* (Cambridge: Cambridge University Press, 2013); Peter Turchin, *War and Peace and War: The Rise and Fall of Empires* (New York: Plume, 2007); Walter Scheidel, *The Great Leveler: Violence and the History of Inequality from the Stone Age to the Twenty-First Century* (Princeton, NJ: Princeton University Press, 2017).

2. Engels's *The Origins of Family* is an exception, of course, and William Tucker's *Marriage and Civilization* is a nonacademic attempt. William Tucker, *Marriage and Civilization* (New York: Regnery, 2014). We might even cite the classic 1976 anthropological study by William T. Divale and Marvin Harris, which examines the relationship between warfare and treatment of women. William T. Divale and Marvin Harris, "Population, Warfare and the Male Supremacist Complex," *American Anthropologist* 78 (1976): 521–538.

3. Sylviane Agacinski, *The Parity of the Sexes* (New York: Columbia University Press, 2001). Of course, artificial reproduction techniques, such as turning adult cells into pluripotent stem cells, are in the offing. Nevertheless, in a sense, even adult cells are of "mixed" heritage and always will be no matter what technologies are introduced.

4. Karen Offen, *European Feminisms: A Political History 1700–1950* (Stanford, CA: Stanford University Press, 2000), 14.

5. Yuval Noah Harari, *Sapiens: A Brief History of Humankind* (New York: Harper Perennial, 2018), 144.

6. Patricia Adair Gowaty, ed., *Feminism and Evolutionary Biology: Boundaries, Intersections, and Frontiers* (New York: Springer, 1997), 32; Patricia Adair Gowaty, "Evolutionary Biology and Feminism," *Human Nature* 3 (1992): 219.

7. Gowaty, "Evolutionary Biology and Feminism," 227.

8. Kate Manne, *Down Girl: The Logic of Misogyny* (Oxford: Oxford University Press, 2018), 111.

9. Gerda Lerner, *The Creation of Patriarchy* (New York: Oxford University Press, 1986), 99.

10. Richard Alexander et al., "Sexual Dimorphisms and Breeding Systems in Pinnipeds, Ungulates, Primates, and Humans," in *Evolutionary Biology and Human Behavior*, ed. Napoleon A. Chagnon and Wiliam Irons (North Scituate, MA: Duxbury Press, 1979), 77.

11. Sylviane Agacinski, *The Parity of the Sexes*, ix, 63.

12. Agacinski, *The Parity of the Sexes*, xxxiv.

13. Theodore Kemper, *Social Structure and Testosterone: Explorations of the Socio-Bio-Social Chain* (New Brunswick, NJ: Rutgers University Press, 1990), 11, 52.

14. Michel Foucault, *Power/Knowledge* (New York: Vintage, 1980), 103.

15. Peggy Reeves Sanday, *Fraternity Gang Rape: Sex, Brotherhood, and Privilege on Campus* (1990; repr., New York: New York University Press, 2007), 89.

16. Sanday, *Female Power and Male Dominance*.

17. Agacinski, *The Parity of the Sexes*, viii, 24.

18. Offen, *European Feminisms*, 36.

19. There are quite a few others, of course; see, for example, Joan Wallach Scott, "Gender: A Useful Category of Historical Analysis," *American Historical Review* 91, no. 5 (1986): 1053–1075; Valentine Moghadam, *Gender and National Identity* (New York: Zed Books, 1996), and Nira Yuval-Davis, *Gender and Nation* (New York: Sage, 1997). The works of several, such as historian Mary Hartman, will be discussed later in this volume.

20. John Stuart Mill, *The Subjection of Women* (1861; repr., Lexington, KY: , 2013), 5. Page references are to the 2013 edition.

21. Mill, *The Subjection of Women*, 5.

22. Mill, *The Subjection of Women*, 14.
23. Engels, *The Origins of Family*, 31.
24. Engels, *The Origins of Family*, 34.
25. Engels, *The Origins of Family*, 35.
26. Engels, *The Origins of Family*, 34–35.
27. Engels, *The Origins of Family*, 35, 39.
28. Engels, *The Origins of Family*, 81, 95.
29. Of course, totalitarian political regimes are *always* interested in the family as either a complement to their efforts to remake society or as a possibly subversive entity. Wilhelm Reich, in *The Mass Psychology of Fascism*, states, "It is the family that is the factory in which the state's structure and ideology are molded." Wilhelm Reich, *The Mass Psychology of Fascism*, 3rd ed. (New York: Farrar, Straus and Giroux, 1980).
30. Carole Pateman, *The Sexual Contract* (Stanford, CA: Stanford University Press, 1988), 7.
31. Pateman, *The Sexual Contract*, 99.
32. Lerner, *The Creation of Patriarchy*, 9.
33. This is Lerner's argument, which is worth citing in full:

> [For slavery] to become institutionalized, people had to be able to form a mental concept of the possibility that such dominance could actually work. The "invention of slavery" consisted in the idea that one group of persons can be marked off as an out-group, branded enslaveable, forced into labor and subordination—and that this stigma of enslaveability combined with the reality of their status would make them accept it as a fact . . . . The crucial invention, over and above that of brutalizing another human being and forcing him or her to labor against their will, is the possibility of designating the group to be dominated as *entirely different* from the group exerting dominance. . . . [M]en must have known that such a designation would indeed work. We know that mental constructs usually derive from some model in reality and consist of a new ordering of past experience. That experience which was available to men prior to the invention of slavery, was the subordination of the women of their own group. The oppression of women antedates slavery and makes it possible. Out of [an unequal division of labor] kinship structured social relations in such a way that women were exchanged in marriage and men had certain rights in women, which women did not have in men. Women's sexuality and reproductive potential became a commodity to be exchanged or acquired for the service of families; thus women were thought of as a group with less autonomy than men. . . . While men "belonged in" a household or lineage, women "belonged to" males who had acquired rights in them. In most societies women are more vulnerable to becoming marginal than are men. Once deprived of the protection of male kin, through death, separation, or by no longer being wanted as a sexual partner, women become marginal. At the very beginning of state formation and the establishment of hierarchies and classes, *men must have observed this greater vulnerability in women and learned from it that difference can be used to separate and divide one group of humans from another* . . . [There arises] the concept, in the dominant as well as in the dominated, that permanent powerlessness on the one side and total power on the other are acceptable conditions of social interaction. . . . [T]he process of enslavement was at first developed and perfected upon female war captives; that it was reinforced by already known practices of marital exchange and concubinage. . . . [E]xperience would show the captors that women would endure enslavement and adapt to it in the hope of

saving their children and eventually improving their lot. Most historians dealing with the subject of slavery have noted the fact that the majority of those first enslaved were women. . . . Physical terror and coercion, which were an essential ingredient in the process of turning free persons into slaves, took, for women, the form of rape. Women were subdued physically by rape; once impregnated, they might become psychologically attached to their masters. From this derived the institutionalization of concubinage, which became the social instrument for integrating captive women into the households of their captors, thus assuring their captors not only their loyal services but those of their offspring. . . . By experimenting with the enslavement of women and children, men learned to understand that all human beings have the potential for tolerating enslavement, and they developed the techniques and forms of enslavement which would enable them to make of their absolute dominance a social institution. [emphasis added]. Lerner, *The Creation of Patriarchy*, 77–78, 80, 87.

34. Pateman, *The Sexual Contract*, 3.
35. Pateman, *The Sexual Contract*, 95, 109. Pateman asks, "Where is the story of the true origin of political right? In the stories of political origins, sex-right is incorporated into father-right, and this nicely obscures the fact that the necessary beginning is missing. All the stories lack a political book of genesis. . . . Sex-right must necessarily precede paternal right; but does the origin of political right lie in a rape?" Although most people believe father-right came into existence when men learned about the concept of paternity, Pateman goes on to say:

    Psychoanalyst Gregory Zilboorg said, "Mother-right was overthrown when, one day [a man] became sufficiently conscious and sure of his strength to overpower the women, to rape her." Zilboorg argues that the original deed was prompted purely by "the need to possess and master." The subjugation of women provided the example required to enable men to extend their possession and mastery beyond their immediate needs. Economic mastery quickly followed sexual mastery.

    Pateman continues, "Even if the story of the primal scene is written to incorporate a woman of unlimited, unbridled sexual appetite, so that she 'tempts' the man, the act could not occur at her behest if the man (the father) is to have dominion. His will must prevail. The original deed is *his* deed, and the passionate woman must be subject to his will if his order is to prevail." She notes, "The story of the sexual contract explains why a signature, or even a speech act, is insufficient for a valid marriage. The act that is required, the act that seals the contract, is (significantly) called the *sex act*. Not until a husband has exercised his conjugal right is the marriage contract complete." Pateman, *The Sexual Contract*, 104, 107, 149.
36. Pateman, *The Sexual Contract*, 102.
37. Pateman, *The Sexual Contract*, 6.
38. Pateman, *The Sexual Contract*, 25.
39. Pateman, *The Sexual Contract*, 107.
40. Pateman, *The Sexual Contract*, 115.
41. Pateman, *The Sexual Contract*, 149.
42. Pateman, *The Sexual Contract*, 29.
43. Pateman, *The Sexual Contract*, 124.
44. Pateman, *The Sexual Contract*, 53.

45. Pateman, *The Sexual Contract*, 57.
46. Pateman, *The Sexual Contract*, 61.
47. Lerner, *The Creation of Patriarchy*, 64.
48. Lerner, *The Creation of Patriarchy*, 66.
49. Pateman, *The Sexual Contract*, 176.
50. Pateman, *The Sexual Contract*, 177.
51. Lerner, *The Creation of Patriarchy*, 208, 215.
52. Manne, *Down Girl*.

2. The Oldest Security Provision Mechanism

1. Kate Manne, *Down Girl: The Logic of Misogyny* (Oxford: Oxford University Press, 2018).
2. Manne, *Down Girl*.
3. See Handwerk, "An Ancient, Brutal Massacre May Be the Earliest Evidence of War," *The Smithsonian Magazine*, January 20, 2016, https://www.smithsonianmag.com /science-nature/ancient-brutal-massacre-may-be-earliest-evidence-war-180957884/; and also Charles Q. Choi, "Ancient Human Sacrifice Victims Faced Slavery Before Death," *LiveScience*, June 16, 2017, https://www.livescience.com/59513-ancient-china-human -sacrifice-revealed.html.
4. Richard Wrangham and Dale Peterson, *Demonic Males: Apes and the Origins of Human Violence* (New York: Mariner Books, 1996).
5. Tian Chen Zeng, Alan Aw, and Marcus Feldman, "Cultural Hitchiking and Competition Between Patrilineal Kin Groups Explain the Post-Neolithic Y-Chromosome Bottleneck," *Nature Communications*, May 25, 2018, https://www.nature.com/articles /s41467-018-04375-6.
6. Inigo Olalde et al. "The Genomic History of the Iberian Peninsula Over the Past 8000 Years," *Science* 363, no. 6432 (2019): 1230–1234, http://science.sciencemag.org /content/363/6432/1230.
7. Mark S. Weiner, *The Rule of the Clan: What an Ancient Form of Social Organization Reveals About the Future of Individual Freedom* (New York: Farrar, Straus and Giroux, 2013), 46–47, 58.
8. Weiner, *The Rule of the Clan*, 86, 204–205. Although cohesive, Lois Beck explains, "Tribes were not static entities, however, but were historically and situationally dynamic." Lois Beck, "Tribes and the State 19th and 20th Century Iran," in *Tribes and State Formation in the Middle East*, ed. Philip Khoury and Joseph Kostiner (Berkeley: University of California Press, 1990), 190. As Flagg Miller explains, rather than being "conceptually stable over time," these affiliations are instead "on-going objects of affiliation" that are "rearticulated" encounter by encounter. Furthermore, "fictive kinship" through the enactment of ritual can be as strong a force as blood kinship. Although we use the term "clan" to explicate our thesis and explain our data, we recognize that we are reducing a great deal of diversity and nuance into a more simplified concept—an analytic—for the purposes of operationalization and empirical testing. Flagg Miller, *The Moral Resonance of Arab Media: Audiocassette Poetry and Culture in Yemen* (Cambridge, MA: Harvard Middle East Monograph Series, 2007), 189.
9. Kathleen Collins notes,

Because there is much conceptual confusion in the literature, I will briefly address what the clan is not (but is sometimes confused with): clientelism, patronage, corruption, blat, mafias, regions, ethnic groups, nations, or tribes. In contrast to the clan, clientelism (often used inter changeably with "patron-client relations") is an informal institution involving the exchange of goods/services through an asymmetric, dyadic tie between patron and client, based not on ascription or affection but on need. It is explicitly tied to a political/economic inequality that trades political support for public goods; consequently, the relationship dissolves when its economic basis disappears. Corruption is an informal, illegal practice that involves exchanging money to obtain a public good/decision for private use. Similarly, *blat* refers to obtaining goods through weak, transient ties. None of these necessarily involves a network or identity, much less kinship. These are informal institutions, not organizations. Like clans, mafias are informal organizations with identities. Although some clans exhibit criminal behavior, a mafia is by definition a criminal organization and is not necessarily based on kinship bonds. Regions are sometimes assumed to have an identity, but in fact, regions are amalgamations of other characteristics. . . . Clans, by contrast, are subethnic groups, within which greater particularism is key and therefore less likely to foster broad ethnonational movements or nation-state identities. Conceptually, the tribe is most closely related to the clan; historically, tribes were larger conglomerations of interrelated clans claiming to be of the same patrilineal descent line. This belief in common descent, mythical or actual, was the source of norms, values, and symbols of kin ship and tribal loyalty. Conglomerations of clans compose a tribe. Tribal groupings form confederations and in some cases ethnic groups (for example, Arabs, Kurds, or Turkmen).

She adds, "Although often regionally based, since localism helps maintain ties, clans depend upon the genealogical relationship, which endures with migration." Kathleen Collins, "The Logic of Clan Politics: Evidence from the Central Asian Trajectories," *World Politics* 56, no. 2 (2004): 233, 174.

10. Collins, "The Logic of Clan Politics," 231.
11. For example, Richard Tapper asserts,

Tribe and state are best thought of as two opposed modes of thought or models of organization that form a single system. As a basis for identity, political allegiance, and behavior, tribe gives primacy to ties of kinship and patrilineal descent, whereas state insists on the loyalty of all persons to a central authority, whatever their relation to each other. Tribe stresses personal, moral, and ascriptive factors in status; state is impersonal and recognizes contract, transaction, and achievement. The tribal mode is socially homogeneous, egalitarian, and segmentary; the state is heterogeneous, stratified, and hierarchical. Tribe is within the individual; state is external.

Richard Tapper, "Anthropologists, Historians, and Tribespeople on Tribe and State Formation in the Middle East," in *Tribes and States Formation in the Middle East*, ed. Philip S. Khoury and Joseph Kostiner (Los Angeles: University of California Press, 1990), 68.

12. Steven C. Caton, "Anthropological Theories of Tribe and State Formation in the Middle East: Ideology and the Semiotics of Power," in *Tribes and States Formation in the Middle East*, ed. Philip S. Khoury and Joseph Kostiner (Los Angeles: University of

California Press, 1990), 102. Speaking of Iran, Beck explains how tribes and the state experience both cooperation and conflict in their unending relationship in that country:

> First, tribal politics fulfilled necessary functions for the state and became part of the state apparatus. They were instruments of state administration. State rulers depended on tribal leaders for local administration and control and for collecting revenue and assembling levies. Second, tribal polities and the state were in opposition. State rulers, aiming at centralization and control and threatened by the political autonomy and military prowess of tribal polities, attempted to eliminate this threat. Some tribal polities were successful in resisting such efforts, often by becoming more centralized themselves or by dissolving the structures that state rulers perceived to be threatening. Third, tribal leaders competed, sometimes successfully, against existing state rulers for state hegemony. . . . Fourth, tribal polities were fragmented and therefore hard to organize and administer from outside. For lack of military and financial means, and because of territorial distance and the frequent inaccessibility of tribal groups, state rulers were unable or unwilling to exert control or influence over them. Tribal leaders relied predominantly on local sources of legitimacy, power, and authority. Fifth, foreign powers intervened in Iran and substituted their influence for that of the state. The state, weak and decentralized, had little impact on tribal polities, whereas foreign powers, often professing to act on behalf of the state, exploited tribal polities in their own struggles and for their own interests. The presence of foreign powers served to impede the emergence of new, more powerful state rulers who might have threatened tribal autonomy. (Beck, "Tribes and the State," 214.)

13. Caton, "Anthropological Theories," 191.
14. Tapper, "Anthropologists, Historians," 48–73. Patricia Crone has a more nuanced view, with which we agree, feeling that tribes and states are not sequential stages but "alternative answers to the problem of security." Patricia Crone, "The Tribe and the State," in *States in History*, ed. John A. Hall (Oxford: Basil Blackwell, 1986), 48–77. Tapper echoes this when he says that both clan and state are "guides for practical action in crises and disputes." Tapper, "Anthropologists, Historians," 69.
15. Kathleen Collins, *Clan Politics and Regime Transition in Central Asia* (Cambridge: Cambridge University Press, 2006), 331.
16. Edward Schatz, *Modern Clan Politics* (Seattle: University of Washington Press, 2004), 165.
17. Bassam Tibi, "The Simultaneity of the Unsimultaneous: Old Tribes and Imposed Nation-State in the Modern Middle East," in *Tribes and States Formation in the Middle East*, ed. Philip S. Khoury and Joseph Kostiner (Los Angeles: University of California Press, 1990), 148.
18. Schatz, *Modern Clan Politics*, xix.
19. Weiner, *The Rule of the Clan*, 29.
20. Patrimonialism refers to a type of governance system in which the traditional domination seen in a patriarchal system is expanded to a larger scale and rule is filtered through a specialized bureaucratic administration, as in historical monarchies. See Reinhard Bendix, *Max Weber: An Intellectual Portrait* (New York: Simon and Schuster, 1961), 330–384; and James Bill and Robert Springborg, *Politics in the Middle East*, 5th ed. (New York: Pearson, 2000), 112–130; also Mounira M. Charrad, "Central and Local Patrimonialism: State-Building in Kin-Based Societies," *The Annals of the American Academy of Political and Social Science* 636, no. 1 (July 2011): 49–68.

21. Collins, "The Logic of Clan Politics," 233.
22. As Lucretia Mott put it, "The world has never yet seen a truly great and virtuous nation, because in the degradation of women, the very fountains of life are poisoned at their source." Lucretia Mott, AZ Quote, http://www.azquotes.com/quote/546799.
23. Weiner, *The Rule of the Clan*, 39.
24. Manne, *Down Girl.*
25. Carole Pateman, *The Sexual Contract* (Stanford, CA: Stanford University Press, 1988).
26. Miles Melander Dawson, *The Ethics of Confucius* (1915), 140, reproduced online http://www.sacred-texts.com/cfu/eoc/eoc09.htm.
27. David P. Barash, *Out of Eden: The Surprising Consequences of Polygamy* (Oxford: Oxford University Press, 2016), 151.
28. Kristen R. Monroe, ed., *The Evils of Polygyny: Rose McDermott* (Ithaca, NY: Cornell University, 2018), 98.
29. Thomas Barfield, *Afghanistan: A Cultural and Political History* (Princeton, NJ: Princeton University Press, 2010), 20.
30. Mounira M. Charrad, *States and Women's Rights: The Making of Postcolonial Tunisia, Algeria, and Morocco* (Berkeley: University of California Press, 2001), 53.
31. Schatz, *Modern Clan Politics*, 128.
32. Beck, "Tribes and the State," 194.
33. Collins, "The Logic of Clan Politics," 232
34. Charrad, *States and Women's Rights*, 5.
35. Schatz, *Modern Clan Politics*, 13.
36. Gerda Lerner, *The Creation of Patriarchy* (New York: Oxford University Press, 1986), 24–25, 47.
37. Schatz, *Modern Clan Politics*, xxiv, xxii, 95.
38. Schatz, *Modern Clan Politics*, xx, 13.
39. Schatz, *Modern Clan Politics*, xx.
40. Azar Gat, *War in Human Civilization* (Oxford: Oxford University Press, 2006), 77.
41. Barash, *Out of Eden*, 7.
42. Barbara Smuts, "The Evolutionary Origins of Patriarchy," *Human Nature* 6, no. 1 (1995): 1–32.
43. This is not to say that females are essentially peace-loving. They are not. Theodore D. Kemper states, "Across the spectrum of the social sciences, the results show that females are not essentially pacific, retiring, unaggressive, lacking in motives and psychological need for power and dominance. While successful ideological socialization may persuade many women that this is true of themselves, it is not biologically true." Theodore D. Kemper, *Social Structure and Testosterone: Explorations of the Socio-Bio-Social Chain* (New Brunswick, NJ: Rutgers University Press, 1990), 149.
44. Patricia Adair Gowaty, ed., *Feminism and Evolutionary Biology: Boundaries, Intersections, and Frontiers* (New York: Springer, 1997), 378. Interestingly, Gowaty's own research demonstrates that in contrast to the typical "coy" behavior of female animals in a typical group setting, when males and females have been reared separately (and thus females have never witnessed male-on-female violence), females do not exhibit "coyness" or choosiness when introduced to males, suggesting that they had not yet learned to fear male aggression. Patricia Adair Gowaty, "Sexual Natures: How Feminism Changed Evolutionary Biology," *Signs: Journal of Women in Culture and Society* 28, no. 3 (2003): 901–921. Why do we feel like weeping when reading this?
45. Gethin Chamberlain, "South Sudan's Battle for Cattle Is Forcing Schoolgirls to Become Teenage Brides." *The Guardian*, June 8, 2017, https://www.theguardian.com/global-development/2017/jun/08/south-sudan-battle-for-cattle-is-forcing-schoolgirls-to-become-teenage-brides.

46. Jean Dreze and Reetika Khera, "Crime, Gender, and Society in India: Insights from Homicide Data." *Population and Development Review* 26, no. 2 (June 2000): 346.

47. Wrangham and Peterson, *Demonic Males*, 125.

48. Gat, *War in Human Civilization*, 79.

49. Barash, *Out of Eden*, 9, 27.

50. Wrangham and Peterson, *Demonic Males*, 159.

51. Barbara Smuts, "Male Aggression Against Women: An Evolutionary Perspective," *Human Nature* 3, no. 1 (1992): 6.

52. Malcolm Potts and Thomas Hayden, *Sex and War* (Dallas, TX: Benbella Books, 2008), 101.

53. Wrangham and Peterson, *Demonic Males*, 146. The echo of this survivalist choice may be found in rituals handed down from ancient times. For example, among the Hamar of southern Ethiopia, "women willingly submit themselves to be whipped during the ceremony of Ukuli Bula. It indicates their courage and capacity to love, and is a form of insurance policy. Should they fall on hard times in later life, they will look to the boys who whipped them to request help." Dave Burke, "The Women Who Beg to Be Whipped," *Daily Mail*, May 11, 2017, http://www.dailymail.co.uk/news/article-4494904 /The-women-whipped-LOVE.html. The legacy can also be found in norms; for example, an Old Russian proverb reportedly is echoed in other cultures (such as among the Aborigines in Australia), that "If he beats you, it means he loves you." Daria Litvinova, "If He Beats You, It Means He Loves You," *Moscow Times*, August 5, 2016, https://www .themoscowtimes.com/2016/08/05/if-he-beats-you-it-means-he-loves-you-a54866.

54. Smuts, "Male Aggression Against Women: An Evolutionary Perspective."

55. Smuts, "Male Aggression Against Women: An Evolutionary Perspective," 26.

56. Francis Fukuyama, *The Great Disruption: Human Nature and the Reconstitution of Social Order* (New York: Free Press, 1999), 217. See also Manne, *Down Girl*.

57. Manne, *Down Girl*, 117, 301.

58. Manne, *Down Girl*, 113.

59. Maria Mies, "Social Origins of the Sexual Division of Labor;" in *Women: The Last Colony*, ed. Maria Mies, Veronika Bennholdt-Thomsen, and Claudia Von Werlhof (London: Zed Books, 1988), 67–95; Alberto Alesina, Paola Giuliano, and Nathan Nunn, "On the Origins of Gender Roles: Women and the Plough," *Quarterly Journal of Economics* 128, no. 2 (2013): 469–530; Jeanet Bentzen, Nicolai Kaarsen, and Asger Wingender, "Irrigation and Autocracy," *Journal of the European Economics Association* (June 29, 2016), https://onlinelibrary.wiley.com/doi/abs/10.1111/jeea.12173.

60. Smuts, "The Evolutionary Origins of Patriarchy." Brigid Grund argues this subjugation predated agriculture; her argument is that while the *atlatl* allowed all, including women, to hunt, the development of the bow and arrow made men's greater upper-body strength a tremendous asset that eventually resulted in the exclusion of women from the role of hunting. Brigid Grund, "Behavioral Ecology, Technology, and the Organization of Labor: How a Shift from Spear Thrower to Self Bow Exacerbates Social Disparities," *American Anthropologist* 119, no. 1 (2017):104–119, https://anthrosource.onlinelibrary .wiley.com/doi/pdf/10.1111/aman.12820.

61. Barbara Diane Miller, "The Anthropology of Sex and Gender Hierarchies," in *Sex and Gender Hierarchies*, ed. Barbara D. Miller (Cambridge: Cambridge University Press, 1993), 22.

62. Peggy Reeves Sanday, *Female Power and Male Dominance: On the Origins of Sexual Inequality* (Cambridge: Cambridge University Press, 1981), 46.

63. Robin Morgan, *The Demon Lover* (New York: Washington Square Press, 2001), 21.

64. Potts and Hayden, *Sex and War*, 60.

65. John Archer, "Testosterone and Human Aggression: An Evaluation of the Challenge Hypothesis." *Neuroscience and Biobehavioral Reviews* 30, no. 3 (2006): 319–345. Andrzej Nowak et al. add that the purpose of honor is to signal that force will be used even when the one using force is weaker than those he uses it against; a kind of porcupine strategy for deterrent purposes. An excellent example of this is the *Chechenskaya bratva*, or "Chechen brotherhood," who are known as fierce, brutal purveyors of violence-for-hire in post-Soviet lands. Andrzej Nowak et al., "The Evolutionary Basis of Honor Cultures," *Psychological Science* (2015): 1–13.

   Mark Galeotti quotes one as saying, "you don't mess with the Chechens. If you challenge them, even if they know they will lose, they will fight, and they'll summon their brothers and their cousins and their uncles and keep fighting. Even if they are going to lose, they'll fight just to bring you down, too. They are maniacs." Notice the confluence of the extended male-bonded kin group and the strong deterrent signal produced. Mark Galeotti, "The Making of a Chechen Hitman," *Foreign Policy*, May 24, 2018, https://foreignpolicy.com/2018/05/24/the-making-of-a-chechen-hitman/.

66. David Jacobson, *Of Virgins and Martyrs: Women and Sexuality in Global Conflict* (Baltimore, MD: Johns Hopkins University Press, 2013), 60. Patricio Asfura-Heim notes that in Arab culture, male honor is *sharaf*, and revolves around pride, dignity, and respect, and the avoidance of shame, disgrace, and humiliation. But male honor also involves *'ird*, which is held by their male relatives but is determined by the chastity of females' sexual behavior. Patricio Asfura-Heim, "Tribal Customary Law and Legal Pluralism in al Anbar, Iraq," in *Customary Justice and the Rule of Law in War-Torn Societies*, ed. Deborah H. Isser (Washington, DC: United States Institute of Peace Press, 2011), 248.

67. Stephen Rosen, *War and Human Nature* (Princeton, NJ: Princeton University Press, 2005), 87–88.

68. Dominic Johnson and Bradley Thayer, "The Evolution of Offensive Realism," *Politics and the Life Sciences* 35, no. 1 (March 2016): 1–26.

69. Smuts, "The Evolutionary Origins of Patriarchy," 13; Smuts, "Male Aggression Against Women," 15.

70. Furthermore, as Smuts notes, "men may use their alliances with other men to prevent actions that may benefit the women, but at a cost to the men." Smuts, "Male Aggression Against Women," 19.

71. Potts and Hayden, *Sex and War*, 50. But Julia Adams rightly notes, "The evidence weighs on the side of [kinsmen] having generally (not always) acted in the interests of their lineage . . . which might easily have involved sacrificing the interests of particular family members, no matter how closely genetically related they might have been." Julia Adams, "Politics, Patriarchy and Frontiers of Historical Sociological Explanation," *Political Power and Social Theory* 19 (2008): 292.

72. Ivan Ermakoff, "Patrimonial Rise and Decline: The Strange Case of the Familial State," *Political Power and Social Theory* 19 (2008): 258.

73. Jonathan Gottschall, *The Rape of Troy: Evolution, Violence, and the World of Homer* (Cambridge: Cambridge University Press, 2008), 134.

74. Markel Palmstierna et al., "Family Counts: Deciding When to Murder Among the Icelandic Vikings," *Evolution and Human Behavior* 38, no. 2 (2017): 175–180, http://dx.doi.org/10.1016/j.evolhumbehav.2016.09.001.

75. Wrangham and Peterson, *Demonic Males*, 24, 25. It is not coincidental that alt-rightists have, in the modern day, extolled the virtues of what they call the "Mannerbund." Although their rhetoric is vile and their aims worse, these reactionaries recognize the power of the fraternity as a historical security provision mechanism—and so they want

to bring it back to nations that have largely left it behind. Hear what one of the Manner-bund's fans, alt-rightist Mark Yuray, has to say in his essay "Mannerbund 101":

> The source of civilization is not the family, the market, the electoral process, or the scientific committee of "experts." The source of civilization is the *Männerbund*, hereafter rendered in English as the Mannerbund. The Mannerbund is the source of property rights and sexual morality, as well as the vehicle through which effective group action is performed. For our purposes, we will define a Mannerbund as a group of men organized in an organic hierarchy that springs from the male competitive instinct. The Mannerbund forms quickly and naturally between men in any group because it is predicated on the male competitive instinct. Men, far from being epicene, atomized "individuals" with strictly "rational" tastes and preferences, have an easily roused and conspicuous instinct towards competition and—more importantly—hierarchy realized through competition. In other words, the natural and default state of men among men is hierarchy, because hierarchy is the end-product of competition, and men instinctively compete with each other. . . . The Ur-form of the Mannerbund is undoubtedly the gang or team of men who act cohesively to defend and expand a perimeter, and the essential facets of civilized masculinity are undoubtedly derived from the behaviors necessary to defend and expand a perimeter in a team of men—courage, honor, discipline, strength, and so forth. When thinking about contemporary Mannerbunds, the "perimeter" may be more metaphorical than physical, but the principles and mechanisms of cooperation remain the same. . . . The most basic working socio-political arrangement between humans is the Mannerbund. The only unit smaller than the Mannerbund is the man—not the individual, but the man. It could be argued that the family (specifically the nuclear family) is a more basic socio-political unit than the Mannerbund, but this approach is incorrect. To paraphrase Mencius Moldbug, hominids need government and politics because hominids are social and violent. To clarify Moldbug, hominids need government and politics because *male* hominids are social and violent. A man's woman and children are extensions of the man and dependent on the man's capacity for violence on their behalf, i.e. on their man's capacity to defend them physically from other men. Women and children are social but their capacity for violence—physical, but also psychological—is negligible compared to that of men's, and for this reason they are *de facto* property, not political agents themselves. The Mannerbund, not the family, is the basic working socio-political unit. A solid and dependable Mannerbund is a necessity for every man. No man is an island, they say, and a man without a local Mannerbund is going have deeply limited capacities when it comes to securing his property and legacy. Individualistic proponents of neomasculinity are missing the point already: no man is more "alpha" than a Mannerbund. Without a Mannerbund, a man cannot control his women, he cannot ensure his immobile property's security in the case of state failure (deliberate or not), and without security of his women or property, he cannot secure the futures of his children. . . . Great risks lead to great rewards and great wealth, and they can only be effectively undertaken by groups of men oathbound to each other, implicitly or explicitly. Effective large-scale cooperation and action must be undertaken by Mannerbunds. Great civilizations require great Mannerbunds to found and lead them.

Mark Yuray, "Mannerbund 101," *Social Matter*, February 23, 2016, https://www.socialmatter.net/2016/02/23/mannerbund-101/.

76. Wrangham and Peterson, *Demonic Males*, 231.

77. Weiner, *The Rule of the Clan*, 59. The Arab Human Development Report of 2004 expresses it eloquently in this fashion:

> In Arab custom, the agnate is the principle of cohesion within the tribe. The agnate . . . is based on *al-taraf* (paternity, filiation) and *al-janib* (fraternity, relationship to the paternal uncle). [These are] the closest of his paternal male kin who are capable of fighting, providing reinforcement, conquering, and defending. A man is surrounded and protected by (and also responsible towards) a preceding generation (the father), a succeeding generation (the sons), and a coexisting generation (brothers and paternal male cousins).

United Nations Development Programme, Regional Bureau for Arab States, *Arab Human Development Report 2004: Towards Freedom in the Arab World* (New York: United Nations Development Programme, 2005), 163.

78. Indeed, Potts and Hayden assert, "Young men [have an inherited predisposition] to display intense loyalty and love for one another, and to dehumanize and attack their neighbors for the simple reason that they *are* neighbors, and so occupy an adjacent territory." Potts and Hayden, *Sex and War*, 111, 252. They go on to quote Johannes Hasselbroeck, who was the Nazi commandant of Gross Rosen concentration camp in the Netherlands: "Even the ties of love between a man and a woman are not stronger than that same friendship there was among us [the male Nazis at the camp]. This friendship was all. It gave us strength, and held us together in a covenant of blood. It was worth living for; it was worth dying for. This was what gave us the physical strength and courage to do what others dare not do because they were too weak." This type of fraternal love is a veritable fountain of bloody destruction and brutality.

79. Weiner notes, "By the rule of the clan I mean the anti-liberal social and legal structures that tend to grow in the absence of state authority or when the state is weak, for instance of petty criminal gangs, the Mafia, and international crime organizations— groups that look a great deal like clans and in many respects act like them." Weiner, *The Rule of the Clan*, 9. On a related note, Nowak et al. use simulation research to show that honor societies such as we have described wither and fade away when institutions capable of reliably enforcing codes of conduct appear, for then institutions are able to constrain aggressive agents more effectively than what they call "honor agents," or what we are calling male extended kin groups. We would suggest this is the case because male extended kin groups are usually able to contain, but not to eliminate, aggressors. (Indeed, these groups may sometimes *be* the aggressors.) Nowak et al. find, "Without the presence of the honor agents, only the aggressive agents survived when the effectiveness of authorities was weak. When the effectiveness of authorities was relatively higher, the aggressive agents are eliminated, and only interest and rational agents remained. In sum, in conditions of low institutional authority, honor agents were critical to stopping the aggressive agents from proliferating." Nowak et al., "The Evolutionary Basis of Honor Cultures," 7. This is an interesting perspective on why male-bonded kin groups are "selected for" in human groups—*they are absolutely "better than nothing" in the face of aggression by outgroups.*

80. Fukuyama, *The Great Disruption*, 83.

81. Luke Glowacki et al., "Formation of Raiding Parties for Intergroup Violence Is Mediated by Social Network Structure," *Proceedings of the National Academy of Sciences* 113, no. 43 (2016): 12114–12119, www.pnas.org/cgi/doi/10.1073/pnas.1610961113.

82. Brooke Adams, "Teen Age Girl Talks of FLDS Wedding," *Salt Lake Tribune*, April 5, 2006, http://www.rickross.com/reference/polygamy/polygamy432.html.

83. Dominic Johnson and Bradley Thayer, "The Evolution of Offensive Realism," *Politics and the Life Sciences* 35, no. 1 (March 2016): 7. Manson et al. note a similar theme for both humans and chimpanzees: "long-term social bonds facilitate the formation of cooperatively attacking subgroups, and variation in subgroup size reduces the cost of damaging aggression to attackers with sufficient numerical superiority." Joseph H. Manson et al., "Intergroup Aggression in Chimpanzees and Humans" [and Comments and Replies] by Author(s)," *Current Anthropology* 32, no. 4 (August–October 1991): 371.

84. Manne, *Down Girl*.

85. Potts and Hayden, *Sex and War*, 49.

86. Marvin Harris, "The Evolution of Human Gender Hierarchies," in *Sex and Gender Hierarchies*, ed. Barbara D. Miller (Cambridge: Cambridge University Press, 1993), 67.

87. Dominic Johnson et al., "Overconfidence in Wargames: Experimental Evidence on Expectations, Aggression, Gender, and Testosterone," *Proceedings of the Royal Society B* (June 20, 2006): 2513–2520; Coren Apicella et al., "Testosterone and Financial Risk Performance," *Evolution and Human Behavior* 29, no. 6 (208): 384–390, https://www.ehbonline.org/article/S1090-5138(08)00067-6/abstract; Coren Apicella, Justin Carre, and Anna Dreber, "Testosterone and Financial Risk Taking: A Review," *Adaptive Human Behavior and Physiology* 1, no. 3 (2015): 358–385; S. N. Geniole, M. A. Busseri, and C. M. McCormick, "Testosterone Dynamics and Psychopathic Personality Traits Independently Predict Antagonistic Behavior Towards the Perceived Loser of a Competitive Interaction," *Hormones and Behavior* 64 (2013): 790–798; Allan Mazur and Alan Booth, "Testosterone and Dominance in Men," *Behavioral and Brain Science* 21, no. 3 (June 1998): 353–397; Margo Wilson and Martin Daly, "Competitiveness, Risk Taking, and Violence: The Young Male Syndrome," *Ethology and Sociobiology* 6, no. 1 (1985): 59–73; J. M. Carré, S. K. Putnam, and C. M. McCormick, "Testosterone Responses to Competition Predict Future Aggressive Behaviour at a Cost to Reward in Men," *Psychoneuroendocrinology* 343 (2009): 561–570.

88. Stephen Rosen, *War and Human Nature* (Princeton, NJ: Princeton University Press, 2005), 74.

89. Johnson and Thayer, "The Evolution of Offensive Realism," 9.

90. John D. Wagner, Mark V. Flinn, and Barry G. England, "Hormonal Response to Competition Among Male Coalitions," *Evolution and Human Behavior* 23, no. 6 (November 2002): 437–442.

91. Rose McDermott, Anthony C. Lopez, and Peter K. Hatemi, "'Blunt Not the Heat, Enrage It': The Psychology of Revenge and Deterrence," *Texas National Security Review*, October 24, 2017, https://tnsr.org/2017/10/blunt-not-heart-enrage-psychology-revenge-deterrence/.

92. Johnson and Thayer, "The Evolution of Offensive Realism," 8–9.

93. Michael Kasumovic and Jeffrey Kuznekoff, "Insights into Sexism: Male Status and Performance Moderates Female-Directed Hostile and Amicable Behavior," *PLOS One* 10, no. 9 (2015): e0138399.

94. Kasumovic and Kuznekoff, "Insights into Sexism." See also Manne, *Down Girl*.

95. James L. Boone, "Noble Family Structure and Expansionist Warfare in the Late Middle Ages: A Socioecological Approach," in *Rethinking Human Adaptation: Biological and Cultural Models*, ed. Rada Dyson-Hudson and Michael A. Little (Boulder, CO: Westview, 1983), 85.

96. William T. Divale and Marvin Harris, "Population, Warfare, and the Male Supremacist Complex," *American Anthropologist* 78 (1976): 521.

97. Divale and Harris, "Population, Warfare," 523.
98. Martin Sikora et al., "Ancient Genomes Show Social and Reproductive Behavior of Early Upper Paleolithic Foragers," *Science*, October 5, 2017, doi:10.1126/science.aao1807, http://science.sciencemag.org/content/early/2017/10/04/science.aao1807.
99. Patrilineal societies have endogamous predispositions because under endogamy no clan wealth need be alienated from the group in the form of brideprice.
100. Steph Yin, "In South Asian Social Castes, a Living Lab for Genetic Disease," *New York Times*, July 17, 2017, https://www.nytimes.com/2017/07/17/health/india-south-asia-castes-genetics-diseases.html. Of course, serious sex ratio imbalances can force exogamy—consider the rape of the Sabine women. Some, including Engels, have suggested capture marriage customs derive as a legacy from historical experiences with sex ratio problems. Friedrich Engels, *The Origins of Family, Private Property, and the State*, 1884, Marxist Internet Archive, proofed and corrected 2010, https://www.marxists.org/archive/marx/works/download/pdf/origin_family.pdf.
101. Furthermore, there are ancillary benefits to such exogamy, such as the extension of kinship to additional males through marriage ties. As Weiner notes, "segmentary lineage systems and similarly-organized tribal societies derive their strength from the principle of exogamy. Lineage members, that is, are required to marry outside their core lineage group. As a practical matter, the rule of exogamy forges complex links between lineage groups and the bodies of land they inhabit." Weiner, *The Rule of the Clan*, 59. For this very reason, invaders often insist on marriages to the daughters of powerful kin groups in the lands they invade, whether we speak of the time of the Mughals in India or that of ISIS in Iraq. These kin groups in turn may resist, and force may be used on both sides. Some have even suggested female infanticide first arose in India due to the absolute refusal of native kin groups to give their daughters in marriage to the invading Mughals. A. J. O'Brien, "Female Infanticide in the Punjab," *Folklore* 19, no. 3 (1908): 261–275.
102. Divale and Harris, "Population, Warfare," 521. We can see the importance of postmarital residence in several historical examples. For example, Andrey Korotayev argues that matrilocality may develop in contexts where women's greater contribution to subsistence is recognized; however, he also asserts that matrilocality is usually undermined by the emergence of nonsororal polygyny under these conditions as males begin to understand that additional wives mean additional production. Andrey Korotayev, "Form of Marriage, Sexual Division of Labor, and Postmarital Residence in Cross-Cultural Perspective: A Reconsideration," *Journal of Anthropological Research* 59, no. 1 (2003): 69–89. As another example, Mark Dyble and colleagues note a strong relationship between sexual egalitarianism and degree of within-group relatedness; that is, they found that in more egalitarian cultures, there is a reduced level of within-group relatedness, which they attribute to reduced exogamy of women (that is, marriages might be patrilocal, matrilocal, or neolocal, thereby undermining the otherwise strictly patrilineal-fraternal nature of the kin group). Mark Dyble et al., "Sex Equality Can Explain the Unique Social Structure of Hunter-Gatherer Bands," *Science* 348, no. 6236 (2015): 796–798. Even so, the more powerful a kin group, the more likely it would continue to practice a class-based endogamy revolving around patrilocal marriage; as Coontz explains:

> With the growth of inequality in society, the definition of an acceptable marriage narrowed. Wealthy kin groups refused to marry with poorer ones and disavowed any children born to couples whose marriage they hadn't authorized. This shift

constituted a revolution in marriage that was to shape people's lives for thousands of years. Whereas marriage had once been a way of expanding the number of cooperating groups, it now became a way for powerful kin groups to accumulate both people and property.

As we have seen, sexual inequality and economic inequality (and all other types of inequality) go hand in hand. Stephanie Coontz, *Marriage, A History* (New York: Penguin Books, 2005), 45.

103. Weiner, *The Rule of the Clan*, 59.
104. Tanika Chakraborty and Sukkoo Kim, "Kinship Institutions and Sex Ratios in India," *Demography* 47, no. 4 (November 2010): 1008.
105. Corina Knipper et al., "Female Exogamy and Gene Pool Diversification at the Transition from the Final Neolithic to the Early Bronze Age in Central Europe," *Proceedings of the National Academy of Sciences of the United States of America* (2017): 1–6.
106. Engels, *The Origins of Family*, 87.
107. Thomas Barfield, *Afghanistan: A Cultural and Political History* (Princeton, NJ: Princeton University Press, 2010), 22; Dale Eickelman, *The Middle East and Central Asia: An Anthropological Approach* (Upper Saddle River, NJ: Prentice Hall, 2002), 75; William Lancaster, *The Rwala Bedouin Today* (Prospect Heights, IL: Waveland Press, 1997), 36–42. Furthermore, even in matrilineal societies, power often devolves to brothers who are the sons of the same mother. That is, power is still held by males in the groups. Lerner notes, "There is not a single society known where women-as-a-group have decision-making power *over* men or where they define the rules of sexual conduct or control marriage exchanges." Lerner, *The Creation of Patriarchy*, 30. In Kerala, for example, in which matrilineal culture was once ascendant, it was the mother's brother (or *Karnavan*) who had final say in all matters. Among the matrilineal Mosuo of China, the same can be said. Siobhan Mattison, "Economic Impacts of Tourism and Erosion of the Visiting System Among the Mosuo of Lugu Lake," *Asia Pacific Journal of Anthropology* 11, no. 2 (2010): 159–176. One difference, however, is that there may be a slight daughter preference among matrilineal cultures. Siobhan Mattison et al., "Offspring Sex Preferences Among Patrilineal and Matrilineal Mosuo in Southwest China Revealed by Differences in Parity Progression," *Royal Society Open Science* 3, no. 9 (2016): 160526, http://dx.doi.org/10.1098/rsos.160526.
108. Weiner, *The Rule of the Clan*, 57.
109. Francis Fukuyama, *The Origins of Political Order* (New York: Farrar, Straus, and Giroux, 2011), 233. A special pathos is associated with the role of the ruler's widow. As Coontz notes, "Conquerors routinely married the widow of an ousted king to strengthen their claims to the crown. If a conqueror died, his son and heir would reaffirm his claim by marrying his stepmother." Coontz, *Marriage, A History*, 91.
110. Henry Maine, *Ancient Law: Its Connection with the Early History of Society and its Relation to Modern Ideas* (Tucson: University of Arizona Press, 1986), 143.
111. Jack Goody and Stanley J. Tambiah, *Bridewealth and Dowry*, Cambridge Papers in Social Anthropology (Cambridge: Cambridge University Press, 1974), 28.
112. Adrienne Edgar, *Tribal Nation (The Making of Soviet Turkmenistan.* Princeton, NJ: Princeton University Press, 2004), 222.
113. Monica Das Gupta, "Family Systems, Political Systems, and Asia's 'Missing Girls': The Construction of Son Preference and Its Unraveling" (World Bank, Washington, DC, December 2009), 5.
114. Anne Campbell, "Sex Differences in Direct Aggression: What Are the Psychological Mediators?" *Aggression and Violent Behavior* 11, no. 3 (2006): 237–264.

115. Smuts, "Male Aggression Against Women," 8. Very different social systems can emerge in cases where female networks are in place. Rebecca Hannagan supports the theory of the cooperative-forming female, arguing that women made a significant contribution toward the development of cooperative groups in hunter-gatherer societies. Women, she argues, may have been supportive of cooperative behavior to protect their offspring. Pregnant women, in particular, stood to benefit from food sharing in times of scarcity. "Maintaining certainty in their position in the lunch line, so to speak, is of greater concern to females than males due to the fundamental trade-off between somatic effort and reproductive effort." Female hunter-gatherers are believed to have cooperated among one another for gathering, hunting, and child-rearing, but Hannagan argues that their role as facilitators may have extended to the males and the group as a whole: "In foraging societies women are as likely as men to curb the deviant behavior of 'upstarts'—those who attempt to disrupt the social balance by violating group norms." Rebecca J. Hannagan, "Gendered Political Behavior," *Sex Roles* 59: 465–475, at 469. The sexual freedom and independence of females, Campbell argues, changed with the onset of agriculture ten thousand years ago when women began to be confined to smaller spaces of home and land, and men, who became the suppliers of food and other resources, were able to exercise greater control over women and achieve parental certainty. Anne Campbell, "Sex Differences in Direct Aggression: What Are the Psychological Mediators?" *Aggression and Violent Behavior* 11, no. 3 (2006): 237–264. Although male dominance hierarchies may have become entrenched at this time, other scholars believe male aggression and patriarchal practices to have been dominant strategies used in sexual selection even during hunter-gatherer periods of human history. Smuts, "The Evolutionary Origins of Patriarchy."
116. Divale and Harris, "Population, Warfare."
117. Divale and Harris, "Population, Warfare," 526–527.
118. Avraham Ebenstein, "Patrilocality and Missing Women," Hebrew University of Jerusalem, April 2014, 8–9, http://in.bgu.ac.il/en/humsos/Econ/Documents/seminars/October%2030-2014.pdf. The type of agriculture practiced may also be relevant. For example, Alesina et al. have suggested that descendants of those who practiced plough agriculture before industrialization have more persistently unequal gender norms than descendants of those who practiced hoe agriculture, because plough agriculture places a value on superior upper-body body strength. Alesina et al., "On the Origins of Gender Roles."
119. Peggy Reeves Sanday, *Fraternity Gang Rape: Sex, Brotherhood, and Privilege on Campus* (1990; repr. New York: New York University Press, 2007), 35–36.
120. Sanday, *Female Power and Male Dominance*, 205.
121. Charles Lindholm, *Generosity and Jealousy: The Swat Pukhtun of Northern Pakistan* (New York: Columbia University Press, 1982), 148–149.
122. Valerie M. Hudson and Andrea Den Boer, *Bare Branches: The Security Implications of Asia's Surplus Male Population* (Cambridge, MA: MIT Press, 2004); Valerie M. Hudson and Andrea Den Boer, "When a Boy's Life Is Worth More Than His Sister's," *Foreign Policy*, July 30, 2015, http://foreignpolicy.com/2015/07/30/when-a-boys-life-is-worth-more-than-his-sisters-sex-ratio/.
123. Priya Nanda et al., *Study on Masculinity, Intimate Partner Violence and Son Preference in India* (New Delhi: International Center for Research on Women, 2014).
124. Jack Goody, *The Development of Marriage and Family in Europe* (Cambridge: Cambridge University Press, 1983), 12–13.
125. Rebecca Solnit, *The Mother of All Questions* (Chicago: Haymarket Books, 2017). As Carrie Chapman Catt famously put it in 1902,

The world taught woman nothing skillful and then said her work was valueless. It permitted her no opinions and then said she did not know how to think. It forbade her to speak in public, and said the sex had no orators. It denied her the schools, and said the sex had no genius. It robbed her of every vestige of responsibility, and then called her weak. It taught her that every pleasure must come as a favor from men, and when to gain it she decked herself in paint and fine feathers, as she had been taught to do, it called her vain.

126. Goody, *The Development of Marriage and Family*, 11.
127. Divale and Harris, "Population, Warfare," 523. Do not confuse these terms with "dower," which refers to assets given directly to a bride by either the groom or the bride's father. However, to make matters even more confusing, dower is typically found in societies where one may also find either brideprice or dowry.
128. Goody and Tambiah, *Bridewealth and Dowry*, 11.
129. Laura Betzig notes that

in the simplest societies, like the !Kung in Botswana or the Yanomamo in Venezuela, the strongest men typically kept up to ten women; in medium-sized societies that organized above the local level, like the Samoans and other Polynesians, men at the top kept up to a hundred women; and in the biggest societies, including the "pristine" societies in Mesopotamia and Egypt, India and China, Aztec Mexico and Inca Peru, and in many empires that came later, powerful men kept hundreds, or thousands, or even tens of thousands of women—along with one, two, or three at most legitimate wives; lesser men kept progressively fewer women.

Laura Betzig, "Roman Polygyny," *Ethology and Sociology* 13, (1992): 310.
130. Goody and Tambiah, *Bridewealth and Dowry*, 64.
131. Goody and Tambiah, *Bridewealth and Dowry*, 52.
132. Joseph H. Manson et al., "Intergroup Aggression in Chimpanzees and Humans" [and Comments and Replies] Author(s)," *Current Anthropology* 32, no. 4 (August–October 1991): 387.
133. John Stuart Mill, *The Subjection of Women* (1861; repr. Lexington, KY: [publisher unknown], 2013), 58.
134. Valerie M. Hudson and Patricia Leidl, *The Hillary Doctrine: How Sex Came to Matter in American Foreign Policy* (New York: Columbia University Press, 2015). The following discussion follows Hudson and Leidl, *The Hillary Doctrine*, 88–89.
135. Ann Jones, *War Is Not Over When It's Over: Women Speak Out from the Ruins of War* (New York: Metropolitan Books, 2010).
136. Sanday, *Fraternity Gang Rape*.
137. Jones, *War Is Not Over When It's Over*, 27, 37, 38, 76, 78.
138. John Mearsheimer, *The Tragedy of Great Power Politics* (New York: Norton, 2003).

3. Assessing the Patrilineal/Fraternal Syndrome Today

1. Mark S. Weiner, *The Rule of the Clan: What an Ancient Form of Social Organization Reveals About the Future of Individual Freedom* (New York: Farrar, Straus and Giroux, 2013), 47.
2. Indeed, even in many matrilineal societies, the real power unit may be "sons of the same mother." In that case, many of the same Syndrome components will be seen even in such a nonpatrilineal context, because that fraternal alliance system is still present.

3. Weiner, *The Rule of the Clan*, 8.
4. Weiner, *The Rule of the Clan*, 8.
5. Weiner, *The Rule of the Clan*, 9, 29.
6. United Nations Development Program, Regional Bureau for Arab States, *Arab Human Development Report 2004: Towards Freedom in the Arab World* (New York: United Nations Development Program, 2005), 146.
7. Andrea Den Boer and Valerie M. Hudson Hudson, "Patrilineality, Son Preference, and Sex Selection in South Korea and Vietnam," *Population and Development Review* 43, no. 1 (2017): 119–147.
8. Lindsay Benstead, "Why Quotas Are Needed to Achieve, Gender Equality," in *Women and Gender in Middle East Politics*, The Project on Middle East Political Science (May 10, 2016b): 55–57.
9. Allison Brysk, *The Struggle for Freedom from Fear: Contesting Violence Against Women at the Frontiers of Globalization* (New York: Oxford University Press, 2018).
10. David Jacobson, *Of Virgins and Martyrs: Women and Sexuality in Global Conflict* (Baltimore, MD: Johns Hopkins University Press, 2013).
11. Weiner, *The Rule of the Clan*.
12. Sociologist David Jacobson developed the Tribal Patriarchy Index using the following formula:

    > Jacobson's Tribal Patriarchy Index = Corruption Perception Index + 0. 5 × (Ethno – Linguistic Fractionalization Index) + 0. 5 × (Indigenous Population as a Percentage of × Total PopulationData + 2 × (World Economic Forum's Gender Gap Data) + Group Grievance Data.

    Notice that corruption is a component of Jacobson's index, whereas it is an outcome variable in our theoretical framework. Notice also the heavy weight given to the Global Gender Gap component, which seems in line with our own approach. However, the Global Gender Gap measure does not include marriage customs or violence against women. Instead, it examines women's participation in the labor force and the government, the educational attainment of women relative to men, sex ratio, and women's life expectancy. As mentioned previously in the text, we believe these variables, with the exception of the sex ratio, are epiphenomenal to the subordination of women's interests to men's interests in marriage and men's corresponding use of physical coercion of women. It is female subordination in marriage, specifically, that allows male-bonded kin groups to reproduce in exclusive fashion. We believe our index will correlate fairly strongly with Jacobson's, but at the same time captures the most theoretically pertinent bases of patrilineal/fraternal strength. Legal scholar Mark Weiner's book does not contain his scale; Weiner was gracious enough to send us his scale by personal communication. Weiner rated 160 countries according to the prevalence of clan rule, concentrating on the salience of consanguineous relations; government functions; education levels and the extent of personal freedom for women; and tendencies toward intergroup violence, although political instability per se did not factor into the rankings. With regard to the concept of personal freedom for women, Weiner examines "the ability to own and devise property, the ability to enter the workforce and to have a professional career, the ease of divorce, the extent of allowed sexual freedom, the extent to which female family roles restrict their life opportunities, and the relative strength of socio-cultural pressures to conform to mainstream expectations regarding a woman's proper role." Weiner, email to authors, February 22, 2014. As with Jacobson's scaling, there are some similarities between the Syndrome scale and Weiner's rankings, particularly in the areas of cousin marriage, property rights, and divorce. Nevertheless, like Jacobson, Weiner includes nongender-related dimensions in determining the degree of clan governance and excludes other important gendered variables, such as patrilocality. Because Weiner is not working from a dataset as much as from impressions regarding women's status, his rankings are thus not replicable. See Jacobson, *Of Virgins and Martyrs*, and Weiner, *The Rule of the Clan*.

13. Jacobson, *Of Virgins and Martyrs*, 2.
14. Jacobson, *Of Virgins and Martyrs*.
15. Jacobson, *Of Virgins and Martyrs*.
16. Some of the material in this subsection is adapted from Valerie M. Hudson and Hilary Matfess, "In Plain Sight: The Neglected Linkage Between Brideprice, Raiding, and Rebellion," *International Security* 42, no. 1 (Summer 2017): 7–40.
17. Quanbao Jiang and Jesus Sanchez-Barricarte, "Brideprice in China: The Obstacle to 'Bare Branches' Seeking Marriage," *The History of the Family* 17, no. 1 (2012): 2–15.
18. David Barash, *Out of Eden: The Surprising Consequences of Polygamy* (Oxford: Oxford University Press, 2016), 95. As noted previously, there is also "dower," which is the practice of the bride herself receiving assets from either the groom or her own father. Dower is typically found in societies where either brideprice or dowry are also present.
19. Jack Goody and Stanley J. Tambiah, *Bridewealth and Dowry*, Cambridge Papers in Social Anthropology (Cambridge: Cambridge University Press, 1974), 51.
20. Alice Schlegel and Rohn Eloul, "Marriage Transactions: Labor, Property, Status." *American Anthropologist* 90, no. 2 (1988): 290–309.
21. Andrew E. Barnes, *Making Headway: The Introduction of Western Civilization in Colonial Northern Nigeria* (Rochester, NY: University Rochester Press, 2009).
22. Robert Seidensticker, "Christianity Becomes an African Religion, Islam Overtakes Christianity, and Other Upcoming Changes." *Patheos*, May 11, 2015, http://www.patheos.com/blogs/crossexamined/2015/05/christianity-becomes-an-african-religion-islam-overtakes-christianityand-other-upcoming-changes.
23. India, and countries surrounding India, may wind up with a mixture of dowry and brideprice. Thus, for example, even though in Islam a brideprice is typically paid, there may be a dowry exchange as well among Muslims in India and Pakistan. Shaikh Azizur Rahman, "'We Decide to Take a Stand': Why Some Indian Families are Returning Dowries." *The Guardian*, June 5, 2017, https://www.theguardian.com/global-development/2017/jun/05/take-a-stand-indian-families-returning-dowries-dahez-roko-abhiyan-campaign. The Brideprice/Dowry scaling rubric would code these mixed countries as having higher scores because of the presence of dowry. In other words, please note that brideprice may be present as well in countries having those higher scores.
24. "Human Rights Study Links Payment of Bride Price to Abuse of Women," *IRIN News*, May 16 2006, http://www.irinnews.org/report/59032/tanzania-study-links-payment-bride-price-abusewomen.
25. Efia Akese, "Reduce Dowry and Let's Marry," *The Mirror* (Ghana), September 12–18, 2014, https://www.graphic.com.gh/lifestyle/relationships/reduce-dowry-and-let-s-marry.html
26. Susan Rees et al. "Associations Between Brideprice Obligations and Women's Anger, Symptoms of Mental Distress, Poverty, Spouse and Family Conflict, and Preoccupations with Injustice in Conflict-Affected Timor-Leste," *British Medical Journal-Global Health*, May 26, 2016, http://gh.bmj.com/content/1/1/e000025.info; and Susan Rees et al., "Associations Between Brideprice Stress and Intimate Partner Violence Amongst

Pregnant Women in Timor-Leste," *Globalization and Health* 13, no. 66 (2017), https://doi.org/10.1186/s12992-017-0291-z.

27. "Human Rights Study Links Payment." Also, as a note, indeed, Uganda made the news when its Supreme Court ruled in 2015 that brideprices were not subject to refund if the couple split up. Unfortunately, the practice of brideprice itself was not ruled as unconstitutional. "Uganda Brideprice Refund Outlawed by Top Judges," BBC, August 6, 2015, http://www.bbc.com/news/world-africa-33800840.

28. Akese, "Reduce Dowry and Let's Marry."

29. Marc Ellison, "Tales of a Child Bride: 'My Father Sold Me for 12 Cows,'" *Al Jazeera*, July 12, 2016. https://www.aljazeera.com/indepth/features/2016/07/tales-child-bride-father-sold-12-cows-160711100933281.html.

30. Schlegel and Eloul, "Marriage Transactions."

31. Goody and Tambiah, *Bridewealth and Dowry*, 50.

32. Goody and Tambiah, *Bridewealth and Dowry*, 52.

33. John L. McCreery, "Women's Property Rights and Dowry in China and South Asia." *Ethnology* 15, no. 2 (1976): 173.

34. P. N. Mari Bhat and Shiva S. Halli, "Demography of Brideprice and Dowry: Causes and Consequences of the Indian Marriage Squeeze," *Population Studies* 53, no. 2 (1999): 130.

35. Bhat and Halli, "Demography of Brideprice," 130.

36. Fazal Muzhary, "The Bride Price: The Afghan Tradition of Paying for Wives," *Afghanistan Analysts Network*, October 25, 2016, https://www.afghanistan-analysts.org/the-bride-price-the-afghan-tradition-of-paying-for-wives/.

37. Joseph Goldstein, "At Afghan Weddings, His Side, Her Side, and 600 Strangers," *New York Times*, April 18, 2015, https://www.nytimes.com/2015/04/19/world/asia/at-afghan-weddings-his-side-her-side-and-600-strangers.html.

38. Valentine Moghadam also notes,

> By the way, in Iran the exorbitant "*mehrieh*" seems to have originated with young women and their families, as a sort of financial protection and social insurance in the face of highly discriminatory laws (and easy divorce for men) as well as gender bias in the labor market. (Before the revolution, it was becoming unfashionable.) Rising *mehrieh* has been accompanied by both increasing female educational attainment and fertility rates that are now at replacement level.

Personal communication with Valentine Moghadam, August 2, 2017.

39. Farangis Najibullah and Mahmudjon Rahmatzoda, "Not Austere Enough: Tajik Authorities Seize Wedding Feast," *RadioFreeEurope*, September 19, 2017, https://www.rferl.org/a/tajikistan-wedding-feast-confiscated/28745090.html.

40. Hudson and Matfess, "In Plain Sight."

41. Farea Al-Muslimi, "The Social Politics of Weddings in Yemen," *Al-Monitor*, November 20, 2013, http://www.al-monitor.com/pulse/originals/2013/11/yemen-weddings-politics-social-discrimination.html?utm_source=&utm_medium=email&utm_campaign=8603.

42. Monica Das Gupta, "Family Systems, Political Systems, and Asia's 'Missing Girls': The Construction of Son Preference and Its Unraveling" (World Bank, Washington, DC, December 2009), 11.

43. Goody and Tambiah, *Bridewealth and Dowry*, 18

44. Goody and Tambiah, *Bridewealth and Dowry*, 10.

45. Goody and Tambiah, *Bridewealth and Dowry*, 5.

46. "Big Money for Niger's Child Brides," *BBC*, May 30, 2014. https://ru-clip.com/video/bFCM4Jo4ToE/big-money-for-niger-s-child-brides-bbc-news.html.

47. Jiang and Sanchez-Barricarte, "Brideprice in China."

48. Nasser Al-Sakkaf, "Hard Times Drive Down Price of Marriage in War-Torn Taiz," *Middle East Eye*, January 26, 2016, http://www.middleeasteye.net/news/hard-times-drive-down-price-marriage-war-torn-taiz-1067666593.

49. "Brideprices in China Have Shot Up, Bending the Country's Society and Economy Out of Shape," *The Economist*, January 16, 2018. https://twitter.com/theeconomist/status/953388324835741701.

50. Goody and Tambiah, *Bridewealth and Dowry*, 10.

51. Siwan Anderson, "The Economics of Dowry and Brideprice," *Journal of Economic Perspectives* 21, no. 4 (Fall 2007): 151–174.

52. Rose McDermott and Jonathan Cowden, "Polygyny and Violence Against Women," *Emory Law Journal* 64 (2015): 1772.

53. Majd Al-Waheidi, "Gaza Dating Site Matches Widows to Men Seeing Second (or Third) Wife," *New York Times*, June 4, 2017, https://www.nytimes.com/2017/06/04/world/middleeast/gaza-palestinians-hamas-wesal-polygamy.html.

54. Goody and Tambiah, *Bridewealth and Dowry*, 64.

55. Jacobson notes that Osama bin Laden would urge his lieutenants to marry sisters, to tamp down incipient rivalries through the creation of a blood tie between the rivals. Marriage can establish horizontal bonds of fraternal alliance, which is why ISIS and al-Qaeda (AQ) strategically attempt to marry within groups whose support they would like to claim, such as among Sunnis in Iraq. See Jacobson, *Of Virgins and Martyrs*, 122. David Kilcullen writes of the Anbar uprising against al-Qaeda in Iraq (AQI) that

> one key difference is marriage custom, the tribes only giving their women within the tribe or (on rare occasions to cement a bond or resolve a grievance, as part of a process known as *sulha*) to other tribes or clans in their confederation (*qabila*). Marrying women to strangers, let alone foreigners, is just not done. AQ, with their hyper-reductionist version of "Islam" stripped of cultural content, discounted the tribes' view as ignorant, stupid and sinful. This led to violence, as these things do: AQI killed a sheikh over his refusal to give daughters of his tribe to them in marriage, which created a revenge obligation (*tha'r*) on his people, who attacked AQI. The terrorists retaliated with immense brutality, killing the children of a prominent sheikh in a particularly gruesome manner, witnesses told us. This was the last straw, they said, and the tribes rose up. Neighboring clans joined the fight, which escalated as AQI (who had generally worn out their welcome through high-handedness) tried to crush the revolt through more atrocities. Soon the uprising took off, spreading along kinship lines through Anbar and into neighboring provinces.

David Kilcullen, "Anatomy of a Tribal Revolt," *Small Wars Journal*, 2007, http://smallwarsjournal.com/blog/anatomy-of-a-tribal-revolt. (As a footnote to a footnote, Ahram asserts these foreign fighters were each given a $10,000 brideprice by AQI.) Ariel I. Ahram, "Sexual Violence and the Making of ISIS," *Survival* 57, no. 3 (2015): 57–78.

56. Thomas Barfield, "Tribe and State Relations: The Inner Asian Perspective," in *Tribes and State Formation in the Middle East*, ed. Philip Khoury and Joseph Kostiner (Berkeley: University of California Press, 1990), 163.

57. Madawi Al-Rasheed and Loulouwa Al-Rasheed. "The Politics of Encapsulation: Saudi Policy Towards Tribal and Religious Opposition," *Middle Eastern Studies* 32, no. 1 (1996): 96–119. As a note, even in societies without polygyny, marriage may be viewed

first and foremost as a means of cementing male fraternal alliances. Vladimir Putin, for example, purportedly helps arrange marriages between the sons and daughters of the men he wishes to retain as allies, and apparently can also insist on strategic divorces, as well. Elizabeth Piper, "Putin's Daughter and Russia's Second-Generation Elite," *Japan Times*, November 12, 2015, https://www.japantimes.co.jp/news/2015/11/12/world/putins-daughter-russias-second-generation-elite/#.WvB9IiOZNZo. In societies encoding the Syndrome more explicitly, such as Yemen, marriage *is* politics. Al-Muslimi notes, "Marriage in Yemen is also an unofficial means for political and tribal alliances. The intermarriage between the offspring of Gen. Ali Mohsen—presidential adviser for defense and security and the leader of the Southern Movement—and former al-Qaeda figure Tariq al-Fadhli affected the latter's political affiliation, and he became a leader in the General People's Congress Party, which used to be in power." Al-Muslimi, "The Social Politics of Weddings."

58. Goody and Tambiah, *Bridewealth and Dowry*, 13.
59. Goody and Tambiah, *Bridewealth and Dowry*, 13.
60. Kristen R. Monroe, ed., *The Evils of Polygyny: Rose McDermott* (Ithaca, NY: Cornell University, 2018).
61. Richard D. Alexander, "Evolution, Culture, and Human Behavior: Some General Considerations," in *Natural Selection and Social Behavior*, ed. Richard D. Alexander and Donald W Tinkle (Chiron Press, New York, 1981), 509–520.
62. McDermott and Cowden "Polygyny and Violence Against Women," 1767.
63. Satoshi Kanazawa, "Evolutionary Psychological Foundations of Civil Wars," *Journal of Politics* 71, no. 1 (January 2009): 25–34.
64. Supreme Court of British Columbia, "Reference Re: Section 293 of the Criminal Code of Canada, 2011 BCSC 1588 (CanLII) (2011), https://www.canlii.org/en/bc/bcsc/doc/2011/2011bcsc1588/2011bcsc1588.html#.
65. Barash, *Out of Eden*, 97.
66. McDermott and Cowden, "Polygyny and Violence Against Women," 1767–1814.
67. Barash, *Out of Eden*, 103.
68. Supreme Court of British Columbia, "Reference Re: Section 293," para 499.
69. Joseph Henrich, Robert Boyd, and Peter J. Richerson, "The Puzzle of Monogamous Marriage," *Philosophical Transactions of the Royal Society* 367 (2012): 666.
70. Barash, *Out of Eden*, 88–90.
71. Jesse Hyde, "Inside 'The Order,' One Mormon Cult's Secret Empire," *Rolling Stone*, June 15, 2011, https://www.rollingstone.com/culture/news/inside-the-order-one-mormon-cults-secret-empire-20110615.
72. "Judge Tosses Convicted British Columbia Polygamists' Constitutional Challenge," CBC News, March 9, 2018, http://www.cbc.ca/news/canada/british-columbia/polygamy-conviction-bc-winston-blackmore-james-oler-1.4569158.
73. Some of these effects are mediated by the socioeconomic status of the family, and thus what we are presenting here are generalizations. For example, Goody and Tambiah quote Nur Yalman as saying,

    Rich and poor families do not act in the same way. . . . The most important difference between them concerned the position of women, with regard both to their inheritances and to the freedom of choice they were allowed. The rich, however, actively controlled the property rights of the daughters and used this as a tool in the arrangement of marriage. In contrast, labourers did not control the property rights of daughters and all siblings shared alike. There was no emphasis of unilineal descent along them . . . [among the poor] it was largely a matter of indifference exactly where the young couple chose to live.

Goody and Tambiah, *Bridewealth and Dowry*, 132. Anthropologists have noted that in poor families girls may actually be treated better than sons, especially in hypergynous cultures where very poor young men may not be able to marry. Lee Cronk, "Low Socio-economic Status and Female-Biased Parental Investment: The Mukogodo Example," *American Anthropologist* 91, no. 2 (June 1989): 414–429, https://anthrosource .onlinelibrary.wiley.com/doi/abs/10.1525/aa.1989.91.2.02a00090.

74. Louise Grogan, "Patrilocality and Human Capital Formation: Evidence from Central Asia," *Economics of Transition* 15, no. 4 (2007): 685–705.

75. Avraham Ebenstein, "Patrilocality and Missing Women," Hebrew University of Jerusalem, April 2014, 9, http://in.bgu.ac.il/en/humsos/Econ/Documents/seminars/October %2030-2014.pdf.

76. Grogan, "Patrilocality and Human Capital Formation."

77. *China from the Inside, Episode 2: Women of the Country*," transcript, PBS, 2007, http:// www.pbs.org/kqed/chinainside/pdf/pbschina-ep2.pdf.

78. Grogan, "Patrilocality and Human Capital Formation," 1167.

79. Grogan, "Patrilocality and Human Capital Formation," 1167.

80. Afghan Women's Writing Project ("Nasima"), "The Herat Maternity Clinic," July 11, 2014, http://awwproject.org/2014/07/the-herat-maternity-clinic/.

81. Das Gupta, "Family Systems, Political Systems," 2.

82. One sees underinvestment in daughters whether brideprice or dowry is the custom. Even though sons' marriages cost more in brideprice societies, you still see almost universal preference for and preferential treatment of sons because the basic kin unit is still the corporation of related males. It may be that, as Das Gupta asserts, "the costs of raising a girl were resented as encroaching on the sons' inheritance." Das Gupta, "Family Systems, Political Systems," 6. One hypothesis we have not yet tested is that in dowry societies, one sees frank culling of girls, but in brideprice societies, one sees neglect and underinvestment rather than outright culling, for these girls will one day fetch a brideprice and hence offer more value to the natal family.

83. Ebenstein, "Patrilocality and Missing Women," 3.

84. Ebenstein, "Patrilocality and Missing Women."

85. Ebenstein, "Patrilocality and Missing Women," 7, 21–23.

86. Ebenstein, "Patrilocality and Missing Women," 23.

87. Geraldine Duthe et al., "High Sex Ratios at Birth in the Caucasus: Modern Technology to Satisfy Old Desires," *Population and Development Review* 38, no. 3 (2012): 487–501.

88. Andrea Den Boer, "Son Preference, Sex Ratios, and Security in the South Caucasus" (unpublished paper, May 2017).

89. Das Gupta, "Family Systems, Political Systems," 10.

90. Andrew M. Francis, "Sex Ratios and the Red Dragon: Using the Chinese Communist Revolution to Explore the Effect of the Sex Ratio on Women and Children in Taiwan," *Journal of Population Economics* 24, no. 3 (2011): 815.

91. Narjis Rizvi, Kauser S. Khan, and Babar T. Shaikh, "Gender: Shaping Personality, Lives, and Health of Women in Pakistan," *BMC Women's Health* 14, no. 53 (2014): https://doi .org/10.1186/1472-6874-14-53."

92. Francis, "Sex Ratios and the Red Dragon."

93. He Linlin, Yang Hai, and Lan Tianming, "Deeper Investigation: How Difficult Is It for Rural Men to Get Married?" *China Youth Daily*, February 25, 2016.

94. He et al., "Deeper Investigation."

95. He et al., "Deeper Investigation."

96. Valerie M. Hudson and Andrea Den Boer, "When a Boy's Life Is Worth More Than His Sister's," *Foreign Policy*, July 30, 2015, http://foreignpolicy.com/2015/07/30/when-a-boys-life-is-worth-more-than-his-sisters-sex-ratio/.

97. Robert Ferguson, "Health Minister 'Deeply Disturbed' by Report of 'Son Preference' Sex-Selective Abortions," *The Star*, April 12, 2016, https://www.thestar.com/news/queenspark/2016/04/12/health-minister-deeply-disturbed-by-report-son-preference-linked-to-sex-selective-abortions.html.

98. Valerie M. Hudson, "Europe's Man Problem," *Politico*, January 5, 2016, http://www.politico.com/magazine/story/2016/01/europe-refugees-migrant-crisis-men-213500.

99. John T. Dalton and Tin Cheuk Leung, "Why Is Polygyny More Prevalent in Western Africa? An African Slave Trade Perspective," *Economic Development and Cultural Change* 62, no. 4 (July 2014): 599–632.

100. Gerda Lerner, *The Creation of Patriarchy* (New York: Oxford University Press, 1986), 251 (note 8). See also Valerie M. Hudson and Andrea Den Boer, *Bare Branches: The Security Implications of Asia's Surplus Male Population* (Cambridge, MA: MIT Press, 2004).

101. Christophe Guilmoto, "Sex-Ratio Imbalance in Asia: Trends, Consequences, and Policy Responses," United Nations Population Fund, 2007, https://www.unfpa.org/sites/default/files/resource-pdf/regional_analysis.pdf.

102. Rachel Vogelstein, *Ending Child Marriage: How Elevating the Status of Girls Advances U.S. Foreign Policy Objectives* (New York: Council on Foreign Relations, May 14, 2013), 1.

103. United Nations Population Fund, "Motherhood in Childhood: Facing the Challenge of Adolescent Pregnancy," UNFPA State of World Population 2013, https://www.unfpa.org/sites/default/files/pub-pdf/EN-SWOP2013-final.pdf.

104. Save the Children, *Too Young to Wed, The Growing Problem of Child Marriages Among Syrian Refugees in Jordan*, 2014, https://www.savethechildren.org.uk/sites/default/files/images/Too_Young_to_Wed.pdf.

105. Nour Youssef, "Two Paths for Yemen's War-Scarred Children Combat, or Marriage," *New York Times*, October 9, 2017, https://www.nytimes.com/2017/10/09/world/middleeast/yemen-war-children.html; Sara Malm, "Girls as Young as Three Are Being Married Off in Yemen as Starving Families Try to Ensure They Have One Less Mouth to Feed and Use Dowry Payments to Buy Themselves Food," *Daily Mail*, March 4, 2019, https://www.dailymail.co.uk/news/article-6768425/Girls-young-THREE-married-Yemen-Oxfam-claims.html. Youssef notes that boys are being forced into becoming soldiers, because families need the small salary the boys receive for their service.

106. Personal Communication with Louisa Chiang, October 24, 2016.

107. He et al., "Deeper Investigation."

108. Nadia Zahel, "Beaten and Tortured for 24 Years to Pay for Her Father's Mistake," *Huffington Post*, 2017, https://testkitchen.huffingtonpost.com/saharspeaks/#nadiazahel/.

109. Vogelstein, *Ending Child Marriage*, 1.

110. Fae Bidgoli, "Iran, Yemen and the Plague of Forced Marriages: Millions of Girls Are Made to Become Child Brides," *New York Daily News*, November 28, 2010, http://www.nydailynews.com/opinion/iran-yemen-plague-forced-marriages-millions-girls-made-child-brides-article-1.456314.

111. United Nations Children's Fund, "Early Marriage: A Harmful Traditional Practice," UNICEF, 2005, http://www.unicef.org/ publications/files/Early Marriage 12.lo.pdf.

112. Vogelstein, *Ending Child Marriage*, 18.

113. Quentin Wodon, "Child Marriage, Family Law, and Religion," *Review of Faith and International Affairs* 13, no. 3 (2015): https://www.tandfonline.com/doi/full/10.1080/15570274.2015.1075761.

114. Note that it is not just child marriage that is the issue, but also initiation of girl children into a sexual relationship based on asymmetrical power. In Latin America, for example, older "boyfriends" may establish sexual relationships with girls as young as twelve or thirteen, usually deserting them once they get pregnant. In the United States, the Centers for Disease Control and Prevention (CDC) reports that girls are having a first sexual experience at an equally early age and that in a large majority of cases the girl has been coerced into having sex. CDC, "Sexual Violence: Risk and Protective Factors," https://www.cdc.gov/violenceprevention/sexualviolence/riskprotectivefactors.html.

115. Stephanie Sinclair, "Interview/Documenting Child Marriage for Over a Decade—And Still Going," *National Geographic*, September 14, 2015, https://www.national geographic.com/photography/proof/2015/09/14/documenting-child-marriage -for-over-a-decade-and-still-going/.

116. Alexia Sabbe et al., "Determinants of Child and Forced Marriage in Morocco: The Sulaliyyates Movement," in *Women and Gender in Middle East Politics*, The Project on Middle East Political Science (May 10, 2016): 50, https://pomeps.org/wp-content /uploads/2016/05/POMEPS_Studies_19_Gender_Web.pdf.

117. In Latin America, note that cohabitation with a young girl may take place in the absence of formal marriage, as well. Prensa Latina, "Child Marriage, Growing Phenomenon in Latin America and the Caribbean," April 9, 2018, http://www.plenglish.com/index .php?o=rn&id=26907&SEO=child-marriage-growing-phenomenon-in-latin -america-and-the-caribbean. Also, forms of child prostitution take cover under the term "marriage." For example, in Egypt there is a form of marriage called *zawaj al-misyar*, or summer marriage, in which wealthy businessmen (many from Saudi Arabia) travel to Egypt to marry a girl for a few months, paying a "brideprice" to her family to do so. One report notes Egyptian girls that have been thus sold by their families as many as sixty times by the time they turn eighteen—they are married only for a few days or weeks. International Center for Missing and Exploited Children. "Child Marriage in the Middle East and North Africa," white paper, 2013, https://www.icmec.org/wp-content /uploads/2015/10/Child_Marriage_in_the_MENA_Region.pdf. Under Egyptian law, children of these unions are not considered Egyptian, and thus such children may be left stateless.

118. Sabbe, "Determinants of Child and Forced Marriage."

119. Vogelstein, *Ending Child Marriage*, 12.

120. Another form of endogamy is the marriage of sisters to create a fraternal bond between unrelated men. As noted previously, Jacobson observes that Osama bin Laden would urge his lieutenants to marry sisters, to tamp down incipient rivalries through the creation of a blood tie between the rivals. Jacobson, *Of Virgins and Martyrs*, 122.

121. Goody and Tambiah, *Bridewealth and Dowry*, 23; see also Bernard Chapais, *Primeval Kinship* (Cambridge, MA: Harvard University Press, 2010).

122. Chapais, *Primeval Kinship*.

123. "Consanguineous Marriage: Keeping It All in the Family," *The Economist*, February 25, 2016, http://www.economist.com/news/middle-east-and-africa/21693632-marriage -between-close-relatives-much-too-common-keeping-it-family.

124. Sue Reid, "The Tragic Truth About Cousin Marriages," *Daily Mail*, July 6, 2018, http://www.dailymail.co.uk/news/article-5927581/The-tragic-truth-cousin-marriages.html.

125. Bernard Strauss, "Genetic Counseling for Thalassemia in the Islamic Republic of Iran," *Perspectives in Biology and Medicine* 52, no. 3 (Summer 2009): 364–76.

126. Ghazi Tadmouri et al., "Consanguinity and Reproductive Health Among Arabs," *Reproductive Health* 6, no. 17 (October 2009): http://www.reproductive-health-journal.com/content/6/1/17.

127. Abdul Al Lily, *The Bro Code of Saudi Culture* (San Bernardino, CA: Al Lily, 2016), 25.

128. Al Lily, *The Bro Code of Saudi Culture*, 25–26. The family may also feel the bride may be treated better if she marries within her agnatic line; at other times, the demand she marry her cousin may result in violence if she refuses, even though she is kin to her bridegroom.

129. Hanan G. Jacoby and Ghazala Mansuri, "Watta Satta: Bride Exchange and Women's Welfare in Rural Pakistan" (World Bank Development Research working paper no. 4126, World Bank, Washington DC, 2007).

130. Al-Muslimi, "The Social Politics of Weddings in Yemen."

131. Akbar Ahmed, *The Thistle and the Drone: How America's War on Terror Became a Global War on Tribal Islam* (Washington, DC: Brookings Institution, 2013).

132. Goody and Tambiah, *Bridewealth and Dowry*, 19.

133. Goody and Tambiah, *Bridewealth and Dowry*, 11.

134. Tanika Chakraborty and Sukkoo Kim, "Kinship Institutions and Sex Ratios in India," *Demography* 47, no. 4 (November 2010): 993.

135. Alberto Alesina, Benedetta Brioschi, and Eliana La Ferrara, "Violence Against Women: A Cross-Cultural Analysis for Africa" (NBER working paper no. 21901, National Bureau of Economic Research, Cambridge, MA, January 2016), 21.

136. Lerner, *The Creation of Patriarchy*, 46–47.

137. Pippa Norris and Ronald Inglehart, "The True Clash of Civilizations," *Foreign Policy* 135 (March-April 2003): 66.

138. Norris and Inglehart, "The True Clash of Civilizations," 64–65.

139. This discussion is adapted from Valerie M. Hudson, Donna Lee Bowen, and Perpetua Lynne Nielsen "What Is the Relationship Between Inequity in Family Law and Violence Against Women? Approaching the Issue of Legal Enclaves," *Politics and Gender* 7, no. 4 (Winter 2012): 453–492.

140. Weiner, *The Rule of the Clan*, 12.

141. Donna Lee Bowen, Valerie M. Hudson, and Perpetua Lynne Nielsen, "State Fragility and Structural Gender Inequality in Family Law: An Empirical Investigation," *Laws* 4, no. 4 (2015): 654–672.

142. Lerner, *The Creation of Patriarchy*, 106. For example, Lerner notes that the Code of Hammurabi says,

> "The father shall give his daughter who has been ravished as a spouse to her ravisher." The rapist must pay brideprice to the father whether or not the father gives him his daughter as a wife. If she is given to the rapist as a wife, the rapist can never divorce her. The Code of Hammurabi also says that men can punish their wives by violence, including tearing out their breasts, cutting off nose or ears, whipping her, plucking out her hair; "There is no liability therefore." If a man hits and kills someone's daughter, the punishment is the death of the daughter of the man who struck the blow; the same if a man causes another man's wife to miscarry—his wife will be treated the same. A man who kills a pregnant woman will be killed.

> Lerner, *The Creation of Patriarchy*, 116, 119.

143. Lerner, *The Creation of Patriarchy*, 266, note 28.
144. Al Lily, *The Bro Code of Saudi Culture*, 38.
145. Some scholars believe that intense control of females by males only arose after agriculture and animal husbandry developed. See, for example, Maria Mies, "Social Origins of the Sexual Division of Labor," in *Women: The Last Colony*, ed. Maria Mies, Veronika Bennholdt-Thomsen, and Claudia Von Werlhof (London: Zed Books, 1988), 67–95. Other scholars, such as Richard Wrangham and Dale Peterson, believe such control stretched unbroken from prehistoric times. Richard Wrangham and Dale Peterson, *Demonic Males: Apes and the Origins of Human Violence* (New York: Mariner Books, 1996).
146. Mala Htun and Laurel Weldon, "Sex Equality in Family Law: Historical Legacies, Feminist Activism, and Religious Power in 70 Countries" (World Development Report 2012, Gender Equality and Development, World Bank, 2011), http://siteresources.worldbank .org/INTWDR2012/Resources/7778105-1299699968583/7786210-1322671773271/Htun -Weldon-family-law-paper-april-11.pdf.
147. This discussion is adapted from Hudson et al., "What Is the Relationship."
148. Annie Gowan, "An Indian Teen Was Raped by Her Father. Village Elders Had Her Whipped," *Washington Post*, May 9, 2016, https://www.washingtonpost.com/world /asia_pacific/an-indian-teenager-was-raped-by-her-father-village-elders-had-her -whipped/2016/05/09/f6d6c840-c531-11e5-8965-0607e0e265ce_story.html.
149. Gowan, "An Indian Teen Was Raped."
150. It may also trump religious law. Goody notes that the Catholic Church promulgated a family law code that was obligatory for both men and women. Even so, he notes,

> The *jus occidendi* (law of homicide) in *jus commune* (common law) was an unequal affair, applying to women's adultery but not to men's, as was its extension to other killings for the sake of honor . . . it ran quite against the law of the church which insisted that husband and wife must be judged by the same standards. . . . [T]he notion of an honourable killing allowed to men and not women, continued in Italian law until 1981, linking female sexuality to largely male family honour.

> Jack Goody, *The European Family* (New York: Wiley-Blackwell, 2000), 67.
151. "Forced Marriages in Council of Europe Member States: A Comparative Study of Legislation and Political Initiatives," Council of Europe, October 3, 2005, 22, https:// eige.europa.eu/resources/CDEG(2005)1_en.pdf .
152. Bob Stritof and Sheri Stritof, "Marriage Laws in the US by Age—U.S. Teen Marriage License Laws," The Spruce, June 27, 2019, http://marriage.about.com/cs/teenmarriage /a/teenus_5.htm.
153. Brooke Adams, "Teen Age Girl Talks of FLDS Wedding," *Salt Lake Tribune*, April 5, 2006, http://www.rickross.com/reference/polygamy/polygamy432.html.
154. Suad Joseph, "Political Familism in Lebanon," *Annals of the American Academy of Political and Social Science* 636, no. 1 (2011): 159; Deniz Kandiyoti, "Bargaining with Patriarchy," *Gender and Society* 2, no. 3 (1988): 274–290.
155. Thaier Al-Sudani. "Iraq: Islamist MPs Propose a Change in the Personal Status Law That Would Allow Child Marriages," *Al Monitor*, November 17, 2017, https://www.al-monitor .com/pulse/originals/2017/11/iraq-personal-status-law-child-marriage.html?utm _campaign=20171117&utm_source=sailthru&utm_medium=email&utm_term =Daily%20Newsletter.
156. Human Rights Watch, "Unequal and Unprotected: Women's Rights Under Lebanese Personal Status Laws," 2015, https://www.hrw.org/report/2015/01/19/unequal-and -unprotected/womens-rights-under-lebanese-personal-status-laws.

157. Human Rights Watch, "Unequal and Unprotected," 357.

158. Ann Elizabeth Mayer, "Reform of Personal Status Laws in North Africa: A Problem of Islamic or Mediterranean Laws?" *Middle East Journal* 49, no. 3 (1995): 432–446.

159. Htun and Weldon, "Sex Equality in Family Law."

160. Htun and Weldon operationalize a family law index (0–13) examining issues of minimum age of marriage, consent in marriage, name, marital property, divorce, custody, and inheritance, but there was only an N of 70. They found that being a current or former communist country was associated with a significant increase in family law equity, whereas former colonies of Britain saw significant decreases. Having an established state religion was strongly associated with great inequity in family law for women, while having an autonomous women's movement was significantly associated with increases in equity for women. Htun and Weldon. "Sex Equality in Family Law."
    With reference to their finding about Britain, Adrienne Edgar notes:

    In British-ruled Egypt and Palestine and French-ruled North Africa and Syria in the interwar period, the discourse of female oppression was primarily aimed at justifying European rule, rather than bringing about real change in women's lives. This was evident in colonial policies on veiling and seclusion, as well as in British and French policies on Islamic and customary personal status law—the codes that regulated marriage and family life among Muslims and that were roundly condemned by Europeans for their presumed degradation of women. While British and French colonizers imposed European-style criminal and commercial legal codes on their Muslim subjects, they refrained from changing indigenous family law.

    Adrienne Edgar, "Bolshevism, Patriarchy, and the Nation: The Soviet 'Emancipation' of Muslim Women in Pan-Islamic Perspective," *Slavic Review* 65, no. 2(2006): 257.

161. Rawi Abdelal et al., "Identity as a Variable," *Perspectives on Politics* 4 no. 4 (2006): 695–711.

162. Sophia Wilson, "Human Rights and Law Enforcement in the Post-Soviet World: Or How and Why Judges and Police Bend the Law," lecture, Brigham Young University, Provo, UT, November 12, 2010.

163. Aisuluu Kamchybekova, Project Component Coordinator, Promotion of Women to Civil Service and Politics, United Nations Development Program, interview date August 25, 2009, interviewed by Carl Brinton, Original Language English, recorded in the WomanStats Database.

164. Becky Schulthies, personal communication with author Bowen, 2009.

165. For example, a Muslim woman in India seeking a divorce must appeal to an Islamic religious court, whereas a Hindu woman in the same position would petition a government court, and the outcome for each of these women may differ dramatically as a result. U.S. Department of State, "India: International Religious Freedom Report," 2007, http://www.state.gov/g/drl/rls/irf/2007/90228.htm. As we go to press, "triple talaq" for Muslim women has been officially deemed unconstitutional in India.

166. Although legal pluralism assumes homogeneity within the community, with Muslim groups, this can produce controversy. Personal status law differs not only by whether one is Sunni, Shi`a, or Ibadi, but also by schools of law—that is, Maliki, Hanifi, Shafi`i, or Hanbali.

167. United Nations, "Declaration on the Rights of Persons Belonging to National or Ethnic, Religious and Linguistic Minorities," A/RES/47/135, 1992, http://www.un.org/documents/ga/res/47/a47r135.htm.

168. David S. Pearl, "Islamic Family Law and Its Reception by the Courts in England," Islamic Legal Studies Program, Harvard Law School, Occasional Publications 1, 2000, http://www.law.harvard.edu/programs/ilsp/publications/pearl.pdf.
169. United Nations Economic and Social Council, "Civil and Political Rights, Including the Question of Religious Intolerance," E/CN.4/2002/73/Add.2, April 24, 2009, point 3:5, http://www.wunrn.com/un_study/english.pdf.
170. Susanne H. Rudolph and Lloyd Rudolph, "Living with Difference in India," *Political Quarterly* 71, (Supplement 1 2000): 20–38.
171. Katherine Young, "Introduction," in *Today's Woman in World Religions*, ed. Arvind Sharma (New York: State University of New York Press, 1994), 35.
172. Pascale Fournier, "The Reception of Muslim Family Law in Western Liberal States," paper written for the Canadian Council of Muslim Women, September 30, 2004, http://www.ccmw.com/documents/Pascalepaper.pdf.
173. Jytte Klausen, *The Islamic Challenge: Politics and Religion in Western Europe* (Oxford: Oxford University Press, 2005), 194.
174. This is no doubt the reason that ECOSOC has opined, "With regard to women's rights in the light of religion, beliefs and traditions, universality must be clearly understood; it is not the expression of the ideological or cultural domination of one group of States over the rest of the world." ECOSOC, "Civil and Political Rights, Including the Question of Religious Intolerance," point 33:11.
175. Klausen, *The Islamic Challenge*, 194–195.
176. Robin Fretwell Wilson quoted in Adam Liptak, "When God and the Law Don't Square," *New York Times*, February 17, 2008, 3. As a note, states, such as Canada, which value multiculturalism have experimented with arbitration courts for religious minorities. Ontario's Arbitration Act sets up a separate area for resolution of family issues outside of the traditional court system. Arbitration as experienced in Ontario may be deemed as positive in that it allows individuals to resolve issues tied to religion that may not be decided by the judicial system, as one judge puts it, "issues that 'bind the conscience' as opposed to matters of 'enforceable civil law.' " However, certain cases, such as divorce, show that arbitration councils may be less successful in guaranteeing women's rights than the rights of minority communities. Natasha Bakht, "Family Arbitration Using Sharia Law: Examining Ontario's Arbitration Act and Its Impact on Women," *Muslim World Journal of Human Rights* 1, no. 7 (2004): 1, 11.
177. Hudson et al., "What Is the Relationship," and Bowen et al., "State Fragility."
178. Center for Reproductive Rights, *Legal Grounds: Reproductive and Sexual Rights in African Commonwealth Courts* (New York: Center for Reproductive Rights, 2005).
179. Htun and Weldon, "Sex Equality in Family Law."
180. Francis Fukuyama, *The Origins of Political Order* (New York: Farrar, Straus, and Giroux, 2011), 233.
181. In this regard, Al Lily's observation about Saudi Arabia is quite interesting: according to Al Lily, a Saudi family tree "normally includes only male members. Family pictures include only male family members." Al Lily, *The Bro Code of Saudi Culture*, 39.
182. Goody and Tambiah, *Bridewealth and Dowry*, 31.
183. Tina Rosenberg, "Letting (Some of) India's Women Own Land," *New York Times*, March 22, 2016. https://opinionator.blogs.nytimes.com/2016/03/22/letting-some-of-indias-women-own-land/.
184. "Consanguineous Marriage: Keeping It All in the Family."
185. Das Gupta, "Family Systems, Political Systems," 6.
186. Rosenberg, "Letting (Some of) India's Women Own Land."

187. Astrid Zweynert, "Misinterpreting Islamic Law Robs Muslim Women of Land: Experts," *Reuters*, March 1, 2018, https://www.reuters.com/article/us-women-landrights-inheritance/misinterpreting-islamic-law-robs-muslim-women-of-land-experts-idUSKCN1GD56W.
188. Rosenberg, "Letting (Some of) India's Women Own Land."
189. Landesa, "Women's Land Rights," Resources: Infographics, December 21, 2015, https://www.landesa.org/resources/womens-land-rights-and-the-sustainable-development-goals/.
190. Siwan Anderson, "Legal Origins and Female HIV," *American Economic Review* 108 no. 6 (2018): 1407–1439.
191. Renee Giovarelli, Beatrice Wamalwa, and Leslie Hannay, "Land Tenure, Property Rights, and Gender," USAID, August 16, 2013, https://www.land-links.org/issue-brief/land-tenure-property-rights-and-gender/.
192. "Equal Inheritance Rights: Next Battle for Morocco's Women," *North Africa Post*, March 23, 2018, http://northafricapost.com/22834-equal-inheritance-rights-next-battle-moroccos-women.html; and Tarek Amara, "Tunisian Women March for Equal Inheritance Rights," *Reuters*, March 10, 2018, https://www.reuters.com/article/us-tunisia-women/tunisian-women-march-for-equal-inheritance-rights-idUSKCN1GM0OT.
193. Goody and Tambiah, *Bridewealth and Dowry*, 134.
194. Goody and Tambiah, *Bridewealth and Dowry*, 37.
195. Goody observes, "In polygynous societies, 'love,' in the sense of a preference of one above another, is often a dangerous thing." Goody and Tambiah, *Bridewealth and Dowry*, 37.
196. Hilde Jakobsen, "How Violence Constitutes Order: Consent, Coercion, and Censure in Tanzania," *Violence Against Women* 24, no. 1 (2018): 47.
197. Jakobsen, "How Violence Constitutes Order," 53.
198. Jakobsen, "How Violence Constitutes Order," 54.
199. Jakobsen, "How Violence Constitutes Order," 58.
200. Jakobsen, "How Violence Constitutes Order," 60.
201. Jakobsen, "How Violence Constitutes Order," 61.
202. Peggy Reeves Sanday, *Female Power and Male Dominance: On the Origins of Sexual Inequality* (Cambridge: Cambridge University Press, 1981); Peggy Reeves Sanday, *Women at the Center: Life in a Modern Matriarchy* (Ithaca, NY: Cornell University Press, 2003). For example, Sanday states,

> Abusive behavior toward women is not necessary to male development. Viewed cross-culturally, it can be demonstrated that many societies are free of sexual assault while others are rape-prone. Social ideologies, not human nature, prepare men to abuse women. . . . It is interesting to note that my informants in West Sumatra were as adamant about the role of culture in establishing a rape-free society as comparable informants in the US were adamant about the role of biology in establishing a rape-prone society.

> She also states,

> A sexist mentality cannot be explained in terms of universal unconscious processes in men. In many societies, demeaning women and negating the feminine in boys are not evident in the larger social ideology, nor are they strategies for male bonding. . . . [For example], silencing the feminine is not necessary for becoming a proud and independent male in Minangkabau society. Indeed, the main feature that defines adult male and female behavior is expressed in terms of "good deeds and kindheartedness." . . . [Men] do not kill vulnerability

in themselves by flexing their muscles vis-à-vis women. There is no theory of the mother-child bond as being oppressive to masculine development. There is no symbol system by which males define their gender identity as the antithesis of the feminine. For the Minangkabau the dominant social image is not the exclusively male social group, but the family of mother and children and the bond among siblings. Not surprisingly, the Minangkabau do not exhibit the sexual abuse and aggression seen in societies where the fraternal patriarchy is synonymous with the public domain.

Peggy Reeves Sanday, *Fraternity Gang Rape: Sex, Brotherhood, and Privilege on Campus* (1990; repr. New York: New York University Press, 2007), 183, 192.
In more recent times, however, things may have changed for the Minangkabau. Hussin notes, "The matriarchal laws of the *Minangkabau* of West Sumatra began to be replaced by more patriarchal *adat temenggong*, and British interpretations of Islamic law from India came to be accepted legal practice for some areas of Malay religion and custom: marriage and divorce, for example." Iza Hussin, "The Pursuit of the Perak Regalia: Islam, Law and the Politics of Authority in the Colonial State," *Law and Social Inquiry* 32, no. 3 (2007): 759–788.

203. Enrique Gracia and Juan Merlo, "Intimate Partner Violence Against Women and the Nordic Paradox," *Social Science and Medicine* 157 (2016): 27–30. DOI: 10.1016/j.socscimed.2016.03.040.

204. Brysk, *The Struggle for Freedom from Fear.*

205. Ellen Wulfhorst, "Violence Is the Biggest Challenge Facing Women," *Thomson Reuters*, March 6, 2017. http://news.trust.org/item/20170306050632-czatd/.

206. Deepa Narayan, "India's Abuse of Women Is the Biggest Human Rights Violation on Earth," *The Guardian*, April 27, 2018, https://www.theguardian.com/commentisfree/2018/apr/27/india-abuse-women-human-rights-rape-girls.

207. Shima Baradaran, "Eyinyani and Rape Among the Xhosa in South Africa" (honors thesis, Department of Sociology, Brigham Young University, Provo, UT, February 2001), 5.

208. Baradaran, "Eyinyani and Rape Among the Xhosa," 13.

209. Baradaran, "Eyinyani and Rape Among the Xhosa," 16.

210. Baradaran, "Eyinyani and Rape Among the Xhosa," 30.

211. Sanday, *Fraternity Gang Rape*, 18.

212. Sanday, *Fraternity Gang Rape*, 8–9.

213. Sam Polk, "How Wall Street Bro Talk Keeps Women Down," *New York Times*, July 7, 2016, https://www.nytimes.com/2016/07/10/opinion/sunday/how-wall-street-bro-talk-keeps-women-down.html.

214. Sanday, *Fraternity Gang Rape*, 151.

215. Theodore D. Kemper, *Social Structure and Testosterone: Explorations of the Socio-Bio-Social Chain* (New Brunswick, NJ: Rutgers University Press, 1990). Interestingly, Kemper suggests that the chronic subjugation and abuse of women lead to an altered and seriously suboptimal uterine environment for the sons and daughters who are born to them. It is interesting to think that Mother Nature might be responding in this physiological way to the encoding of the Patrilineal/Fraternal Syndrome by a society.

216. Kemper, *Social Structure and Testosterone*, 109.

217. Sanday, *Fraternity Gang Rape*, 133.

218. Ariel Ahram, "Sexual Violence, Competitive State Building, and the Islamic State in Syria and Iraq" (unpublished manuscript, 2015).

219. Soraya Chemaly, "If You Don't Take Women's Harassment Seriously You Don't Want to Understand the Problem," *HuffPost* (blog), January 27, 2016, https://www .huffingtonpost.com/soraya-chemaly/if-you-dont-take-womens-harassment -seriously-you-dont-want-to-understand-the-problem_b_9082952.html?utm_source =Alert-blogger&utm_medium=email&utm_campaign=Email%2BNotifications.

220. "Morocco OKs Law Against Violence on Women, Wives Excluded," ANSAMed, February 15, 2018, http://www.ansamed.info/ansamed/en/news/sections/politics/2018 /02/15/morocco-oks-law-against-violence-on-women-wives-excluded_8114f746-2c38 -41ec-a783-60388b1d031a.html.

221. Rizvi et al., "Gender: Shaping Personality."

222. Rizvi et al., "Gender: Shaping Personality."

223. Associated Press, "One Indian Woman Killed Every Hour Over Dowry," *Al Jazeera*, September 3, 2013, https://www.aljazeera.com/news/asia/2013/09/201393134051503366 .html.

224. Jill Schnoebelen, "Witchcraft Allegations, Refugee Protection, and Human Rights: A Review of the Evidence" (UNHCR research paper no. 169, United Nations High Commissioner for Refugees, January 2009), http://www.unhcr.org/afr/4981ca712.pdf.

225. Rachel Jewkes et al., "Prevalence of and Factors Associated with Non-Partner Rape Perpetration: Findings from the UN Multi-Country Cross-Sectional Study on Men and Violence in Asia and the Pacific," *The Lancet* 1, no. 4 (October 2013): e208–e218; and Chris Niles, "UNICEF Strives to Help Papua New Guinea Break Cycle of Violence," UNICEF, August 14, 2008, https://www.unicef.org/infobycountry/papuang_45211.html.

226. Margo Wilson, Martin Daly, and Joanna Scheib, "Femicide: An Evolutionary Psychological Perspective," in *Feminism and Evolutionary Biology: Boundaries, Intersections, and Frontiers*, ed. Patricia Adair Gowaty (New York: Chapman and Hall, 1997), 431–465.

227. Al Lily, *The Bro Code of Saudi Culture*, 126.

228. Melissa Paredes, personal communication with Valerie Hudson, January 12, 2007.

229. Court of Criminal Appeals of the State of Texas, Nos. 1460–01, 1461–01, April 3, 2002, https://caselaw.findlaw.com/tx-court-of-criminal-appeals/1000114.html.

230. Lulu Morris, "Witch Hunting in Papua New Guinea," *National Geographic*, April 12, 2017, http://www.nationalgeographic.com.au/people/witch-hunting-in-papua-new-guinea .aspx.

231. Rana Husseini, "Honor Killings," PBS.org. http://www.pbs.org/speaktruthtopower/rana .html.

232. U.S. Department of State "Country Report on Human Rights: Rwanda," 2007, https:// www.state.gov/j/drl/rls/hrrpt/2007/100499.htm.

233. Agence France Presse, "Algeria Passes Law Banning Violence Against Women," *Al Arabiya*, March 6, 2015, http://english.alarabiya.net/en/News/africa/2015/03/06/Algeria -passes-law-banning-violence-against-women.html.

234. World Health Organization, "Violence Against Women," November 29, 2017, http:// www.who.int/en/news-room/fact-sheets/detail/violence-against-women.

235. Yuval Harari, *Sapiens: A Brief History of Humankind* (New York: Harper Perennial, 2018), 145.

236. Jacobson, *Of Virgins and Martyrs*, 34–35. Ahram notes that the idea that women's bodies belong to the patriline means that war between fraternal groups can be, in a very real sense, "fought" on the battleground of women's bodies. He writes, "Sexual violence, then, offers a means to replace the old order and build the (quasi) familial ties and masculine identities that form the core of the nascent state. . . . Sexual stratification is closely related ethno-sectarian hierarchy." Thus, Ahram views the egregious sexual violence

undertaken by ISIS (such as enslavement of Yazidi women) as an attempt to build state hegemony, noting that "sexual violence rends the pre-existing fabric of family life while tightening the binding strictures of the nascent familial state. The control of sexuality, then, stands as the material and symbolic fulcrum on which the structure of statehood itself is hoisted—or demolished." Ahram, "Sexual Violence and the Making of ISIS."
237. LRW-SCALE-9, WomanStats, 2015 scaling.
238. Aida Alami, "A Loophole for Rapists Is Eliminated in Morocco," *New York Times*, January 23, 2014, https://www.nytimes.com/2014/01/24/world/africa/after-debate -moroccan-government-amends-rape-law.html.
239. Samantha Raphelson, "Countries Around the World Move to Repeal 'Marry Your Rapist' Laws," NPR, August 9, 2017, https://www.npr.org/2017/08/09/542468265/countries-around -the-world-move-to-repeal-marry-your-rapist-laws.
240. United Nations Human Rights Council, " 'I Lost My Dignity': Sexual and Gender-Based Violence in the Syrian Arab Republic," A/HRC/37/CRP.3, March 8, 2018, http://www .ohchr.org/Documents/HRBodies/HRCouncil/CoISyria/A-HRC-37-CRP-3.pdf.

4. The Effects of the Syndrome, Part One: Governance and National Security

1. Scott Weiner, "Rethinking Patriarchy and Kinship in Arab Gulf States," in *Women and Gender in Middle East Politics*, The Project on Middle East Political Science, (2016): 13, https://pomeps.org/wp-content/uploads/2016/05/POMEPS_Studies_19_Gender_Web .pdf.
2. Mark S. Weiner, *The Rule of the Clan: What an Ancient Form of Social Organization Reveals About the Future of Individual Freedom* (New York: Farrar, Straus and Giroux, 2013), 35.
3. Weiner, *The Rule of the Clan*, 61–62.
4. Edward Schatz, *Modern Clan Politics* (Seattle: University of Washington Press, 2004), 111.
5. Jerry Mitchell, "Most Dangerous Time for Battered Women? When They Leave," *Clarion-Ledger*, January 28, 2017, http://www.clarionledger.com/story/news/2017/01/28 /most-dangerous-time-for-battered-women-is-when-they-leave-jerry-mitchell /96955552/.
6. Clare Castillejo, "Gender Inequality and State Fragility in the Sahel" (FRIDE policy brief no. 204, *Fundación para las Relaciones Internacionales y el Diálogo Exterior*, June 2015), 1.
7. Patricia Gowaty, ed., *Feminism and Evolutionary Biology*, 112.
8. Malcolm Potts and Thomas Hayden, *Sex and War* (Dallas, TX: Benbella Books, 2008), 96.
9. Charles S. Maier, "Peace and Security for the 1990s" (unpublished paper for the MacArthur Fellowship Program, Social Science Research Council, Washington, DC, June 12, 1990); Joseph J. Romm, *Defining National Security: The Nonmilitary Aspects*, Pew Project on America's Task in a Changed World, Pew Project Series, (Washington, DC: Council on Foreign Relations, 1993), 5.
10. This discussion is adapted from Valerie M. Hudson, Donna Lee Bowen, and Perpetua Lynne Nielsen, "Clan Governance and State Stability: The Relationship Between Female Subordination and Political Order." *American Political Science Review* 109, no. 3 (August 2015): 535–555.

11. Ashraf Ghani, Michael Carnahan, and Clare Lockhart, "Stability, State Building and Development Assistance: An Outside Perspective," The Princeton Project on National Security, 2006, https://www.princeton.edu/ppns/papers/ghani.pdf.
12. International Monetary Fund, "Security, Stability Measures Needed to Fix Fragile States," IMF Survey Interview, March 29, 2013, http://www.imf.org/external/pubs/ft/survey/so/2013/int032913a.
13. Barry Buzan, "What Is National Security in the Age of Globalisation?" Utenriks departementet, 2007, http://www.regjeringen.no/nb/dep/ud/kampanjer/refleks/innspill/sikkerhet/buzan.html?id=493187.
14. Ira Lapidus, "Tribes and State Formation in Islamic History," in *Tribes and States Formation in the Middle East*, ed. Philip S. Khoury and Joseph Kostiner (Los Angeles: University of California Press, 1990), 28.
15. Kathleen Collins, "The Logic of Clan Politics: Evidence from the Central Asian Trajectories," *World Politics* 56, no. 2 (2004): 244–245; Kathleen Collins, "The Political Role of Clans in Central Asia," *Comparative Politics* 35, no. 2 (2003): 187. Observing the case of Kyrgyzstan, Collins notes,

    clans have to a large degree subverted or replaced the formal institutions that link state and society. The presidential and parliamentary electoral results and the widespread failure of parties to gain power are particularly interesting in this respect. In Kyrgyzstan, where the first set of post-Soviet elections was considered free and fair, and where the legal and actual conditions of party competition were open and competitive, the results show that it is not election-rigging or corruption as such that undermines the most basic process of democracy, but the practice of clan-based voting.

    Kathleen Collins, "Clans, Pacts, and Politics in Central Asia," *Journal of Democracy* 13, no. 3 (2002): 143.
16. Collins, "The Logic of Clan Politics," 244–245; Collins, "The Political Role of Clans," 187.
17. Richard Tapper, "Anthropologists, Historians, and Tribespeople on Tribe and State Formation in the Middle East," in *Tribes and States Formation in the Middle East*, ed. Philip S. Khoury and Joseph Kostiner (Los Angeles: University of California Press, 1990), 51–52.
18. Elin Bjarnegard, Karen Brouneus, and Erik Melander, "Honor and Political Violence: Micro-Level Findings from a Survey in Thailand," *Journal of Peace Research* 546, no. 6 (2017): 748–761; Elin Bjarnegard and Erik Melander, "Pacific Men: How the Feminist Gap Explains Hostility," *The Pacific Review* 30, no. 4 (2017): 478–493; Victor Asal et al., "Gender Ideologies and Forms of Contentious Mobilization in the Middle East," *Journal of Peace Research* 50, no. 3 (2013): 305–318; Victor Asal , Marcus Schulzke, and Amy Pate, "Why Do Some Organizations Kill While Others Do Not: An Examination of Middle Eastern Organizations," *Foreign Policy Analysis* 13, no. 4 (October 2017): 811–831.
19. Peggy Reeves Sanday, *Fraternity Gang Rape: Sex, Brotherhood, and Privilege on Campus* (1990; repr. New York: New York University Press, 2007), 7–8. Such fraternal ties can also be created among non-kin: "Working closely with a small band of men of roughly the same age seems to spark deep impressions of kinship, even when the men around you are not in fact your blood relatives." Potts and Hayden, *Sex and War*, 79. This is the principle militaries use to create combat teams.
20. Valerie M. Hudson et al., *Sex and World Peace* (New York: Columbia University Press, 2012).

21. Gerald R. Patterson, "A Comparison of Models for Interstate War and for Individual Violence," *Perspectives on Psychological Science* 3, no. 3 (2008): 203–223.

22. Theodore Kemper, *Social Structure and Testosterone: Explorations of the Socio-Bio-Social Chain* (New Brunswick, NJ: Rutgers University Press, 1990), 21.

23. Priya Nanda et al., *Study on Masculinity, Intimate Partner Violence and Son Preference in India* (New Delhi: International Center for Research on Women, 2014), 447.

24. Charles L. Whitfield et al., "Violent Childhood Experiences and the Risk of Intimate Partner Violence in Adults," *Journal of Interpersonal Violence* 18, no. 2 (2003): 166–185.

25. Chandra Johnson, "How a Stable Home Life Can Help Prevent Mass Violence," *Deseret News*, August 5, 2016, https://www.deseretnews.com/article/865659350/How-a-stable -home-life-can-help-prevent-mass-violence.html.

26. Kristen R. Monroe, ed., *The Evils of Polygyny: Rose McDermott* (Ithaca, NY: Cornell University, 2018), 31.

27. Max Margan, "I'll Slit Your Throat and Put a Bullet to Your Brain," *Daily Mail Australia*, January 29, 2017, http://www.dailymail.co.uk/news/article-4169084/Boy-abused-mother -thought-normal.html.

28. Dara Kay Cohen, *Rape During Civil War* (Ithaca, NY: Cornell University Press, 2016), 40.

29. Kari Hill and Harvey Langholtz, "Rehabilitation Programs for African Child Soldiers," *Peace Review* 15, no. 3(2003): 280.

30. Comment on nytimes.com by theodora30 on June 11, 2013, at 5:06 am following the article http://www.nytimes.com/2013/06/11/opinion/bruni-sexisms-puzzling-stamina .html?src=rechp.

31. Potts and Hayden, *Sex and War*, 191.

32. Bjarnegard and Melander, "Pacific Men."

33. Sulome Anderson, "Women Brutalized by ISIS," *Foreign Policy*, October 11, 2016, http:// foreignpolicy.com/2016/10/11/women-survive-they-do-not-live-isis-islam-yazidi/.

34. Richard Wrangham and Dale Peterson, *Demonic Males: Apes and the Origins of Human Violence*. New York: Mariner Books, 1996), 233.

35. Aaron Sell et al., "Formidability and the Logic of Human Anger," *Proceedings of the National Academy of Sciences of the United States of America* 106, no. 35 (Sep. 1, 2009): 15073–15078.

36. Dominic Johnson et al., "Overconfidence in Wargames: Experimental Evidence on Expectations, Aggression, Gender, and Testosterone," *Proceedings of the Royal Society B* (June 20, 2006): 2513–2520.

37. Bjarnegard et al., "Honor and Political Violence"; Anna Velitchkova, "World Culture, Uncoupling, Institutional Logics, and Recoupling: Practices and Self-identification as Institutional Microfoundations of Political Violence," *Sociological Forum* 30, no. 3 (2015): 698–720.

38. Bjarnegard et al., "Honor and Political Violence," 749.

39. Sebastian Maisel, "The Resurgent Tribal Agenda in Saudi Arabia" (issue paper no. 5, The Arab Gulf States Institute in Washington, 2015), 8.

40. Sanday, *Fraternity Gang Rape*, 48.

41. Marvin Harris, "The Evolution of Human Gender Hierarchies," in *Sex and Gender Hierarchies*, ed. Barbara D. Miller (Cambridge: Cambridge University Press, 1993), 62–64.

42. Potts and Hayden, *Sex and War*, 60, 267.

43. William T. Divale and Marvin Harris, "Population, Warfare, and the Male Supremacist Complex," *American Anthropologist* 78 (1976): 521–538.

44. Dan Reiter, "The Positivist Study of Gender and International Relations," *Journal of Conflict Resolution* 59, no. 7 (2015): 1301–1326.

45. Monty G. Marshall and Donna Ramsey, "Gender Empowerment and the Willingness of States to Use Force" (unpublished research paper, Center for Systemic Peace, 1999), http://www.members.aol.com/CSPmgm/.

46. Mary Caprioli, "Gendered Conflict," *Journal of Peace Research* 37, (2000): 51–68; Mary Caprioli, "Gender Equality and State Aggression: The Impact of Domestic Gender Equality on State First Use of Force," *International Interactions* 29, no. 3 (2003): 195–214; Mary Caprioli, "Democracy and Human Rights Versus Women's Security: A Contradiction?" *Security Dialogue: Special Issue Gender and Security* 35, no. 4 (2004): 411–428.

47. Mary Caprioli and Mark A. Boyer, "Gender, Violence, and International Crisis," *Journal of Conflict Resolution* 45, (2001): 503–518.

48. Patrick M. Regan and Aida Paskeviciute, "Women's Access to Politics and Peaceful States," *Journal of Peace Research* 40, (2003): 287–302.

49. Mary Caprioli and Peter F. Trumbore, "Human Rights Rogues in Interstate Disputes, 1980–2001," *Journal of Peace Research* 43, no. 2 (2006): 131–148; David Sobek, M. Rodwan Abouharb, and Christopher G. Ingram, "The Human Rights Peace: How the Respect for Human Rights at Home Leads to Peace Abroad," *Journal of Politics* 68, no. 3 (2006): 519–529.

50. Caprioli and Trumbore, "Human Rights Rogues"; Erik Melander, "Gender Equality and Interstate Armed Conflict," *International Studies Quarterly* 49, no. 4 (2005): 695–714.

51. Cameron Harris and Daniel James Milton, "Is Standing for Women a Stand Against Terrorism? Exploring the Connection Between Women's Rights and Terrorism," *Journal of Human Rights* 15, no. 1 (2016): 60–78.

52. Victor Asal et al., "Gender Ideologies."

53. Mary Caprioli et al., "The WomanStats Project Database: Advancing an Empirical Research Agenda," *Journal of Peace Research* 46, no. 6 (November 2009): 1–13.

54. Erik Melander, "The Masculine Peace," in *Debating the East Asian Peace*, ed. Elin Bjarnegard and Joakim Kreutz (Copenhagen: NIAS Press, 2017), 208–209.

55. Reed Wood and Mark Ramirez, "Exploring the Microfoundations of the Gender Equality Peace Hypothesis," *International Studies Review* 20, no. 3 (2018): 345–367. In their conclusion, Wood and Ramirez note: "This finding uncovers a potentially important mechanism by which gender equality may lead states to consider alternative means to conflict. It is through the changing beliefs of men regarding gender equality that we might observe an overall reduction in state-level conflict given that men among the masses often support men in control of government and military organizations."

56. Anthony Lopez, Rose McDermott, and Michael Petersen, "States in Mind: Evolution, Coalitional Psychology, and International Politics," *International Security* 36, no. 2 (Fall 2011): 79. Richard Cincotta concludes that a broader definition of demographically at-risk states would acknowledge that the youthful age structure of a politically organized minority is a significant risk factor for intrastate conflict. See Richard Cincotta, "Minority Youth Bulges and the Future of Intrastate Conflict," *New Security Beat*, October 13, 2011, https://www.newsecuritybeat.org/2011/10/minority-youth-bulges-and-the-future-of-intrastate-conflict/, 9.

57. Lopez et al., "States in Mind," 81–82.

58. Divale and Harris, "Population, Warfare"; see also Azar Gat, *War in Human Civilization* (Oxford: Oxford University Press, 2006).

59. Richard D. Alexander et al., "Sexual Dimorphisms and Breeding Systems in Pinnipeds, Ungulates, Primates, and Humans," in *Evolutionary Biology and Human Behavior*, ed. Napoleon A. Chagnon and Wiliam Irons (North Scituate, MA: Duxbury Press, 1979), 423, 432–433.

60. Harris, "The Evolution of Human Gender Hierarchies"; Satoshi Kanazawa, "Evolutionary Psychological Foundations of Civil Wars," *Journal of Politics* 71, no. 1 (January 2009): 25–34; Kristian Gleditsch et al., "Polygyny or Misogyny? Reexamining the 'First Law on Intergroup Conflict,'" *Journal of Politics* 73, no. 1 (January 2011): 265–270.

61. Kanazawa, "Evolutionary Psychological Foundations of Civil Wars," 32.

62. James L. Boone, "Noble Family Structure and Expansionist Warfare in the Late Middle Ages: A Socioecological Approach," in *Rethinking Human Adaptation: Biological and Cultural Models*, ed. Rada Dyson-Hudson and Michael A. Little (Boulder, CO: Westview, 1983), 79–96.

63. Jillian Keenan, "The Blood Cries Out," *Foreign Policy*, March 27, 2015, http://foreignpolicy .com/2015/03/27/the-blood-cries-out-burundi-land-conflict.

64. Azar Gat, "So Why Do People Fight? Evolutionary Theory and the Causes of War," *European Journal of International Relations* 15, no. 4 (December 2009): 586.

65. Wrangham and Peterson, *Demonic Males*, 165, 167, 168, 231, 233.

66. Wrangham and Peterson, *Demonic Males*, 233.

67. Potts and Hayden, *Sex and War*, 96.

68. Gat, "So Why Do People Fight?" 591.

69. Stephen Rosen, *War and Human Nature* (Princeton, NJ: Princeton University Press, 2005), 89–90, 95.

70. Rosen, *War and Human Nature*, 96.

71. Dominic Johnson and Bradley Thayer, "The Evolution of Offensive Realism," *Politics and the Life Sciences* 35, no. 1 (March 2016): 14.

72. Rose McDermott, personal communication, July 2017.

73. Potts and Hayden, *Sex and War*, 25–26, 197, 301.

74. John Stuart Mill, *The Subjection of Women* (1861; repr. Lexington, KY: [publisher unknown], 2013), 7.

75. Mill, *The Subjection of Women*, 23, 31.

76. Marilyn Waring, *Counting for Nothing: What Men Value and What Women Are Worth* (Toronto: University of Toronto Press, 1999), xiv.

77. Helen Moffett, "Sexual Violence, Civil Society and the New Constitution," in *Women's Activism in South Africa: Working Across Divides*, ed. Hannah Evelyn Britton, Jennifer Natalie Fish, and Sheila Meintjes (Scottsville, South Africa University of KwaZulu-Natal Press, 2007), 172.

78. Nellie Peyton and Lamin Jahateh, "Gambia: Resurgence of FGM and Child Marriage, Formerly Banned, But Returning with New Political Leadership," *Thomson Reuters Foundation*, January 23, 2018. http://news.trust.org/item/20180123090036-m8b8o/.

79. Steven C. Caton, "Anthropological Theories of Tribe and State Formation in the Middle East: Ideology and the Semiotics of Power," in *Tribes and States Formation in the Middle East*, ed. Philip S. Khoury and Joseph Kostiner (Los Angeles: University of California Press, 1990), 82.

80. M. Steven Fish, "Islam and Authoritarianism," *World Politics* 55, no. 1 (2002): 30.

81. Gerda Lerner, *The Creation of Patriarchy* (New York: Oxford University Press, 1986), 140.

82. Ariel I. Ahram, "Sexual and Ethnic Violence and the Making of ISIS," *Survival* 57, no. 3 (2015): 57–78.

83. Julia Adams, "The Rule of the Father: Patriarchy and Patrimonialism in Early Modern Europe," in *Max Weber's Economy and Society: A Critical Companion*, ed. C. Camic, P. S. Gorski and D. M. Trubek (Stanford, CA: Stanford University Press, 2005), 5, http://sociology .yale.edu/sites/default/files/adams_rulefather.pdf. Page citations are from the pdf.

84. Quoted in Adams, "The Rule of the Father: Patriarchy and Patrimonialism in Early Modern Europe," 5.
85. Barbara Smuts, "Male Aggression Against Women: An Evolutionary Perspective," *Human Nature* 3, no. 1 (1992): 1–44.
86. Barbara Smuts, "The Evolutionary Origins of Patriarchy," *Human Nature* 6, no. 1 (1995): 18.
87. N. Pound, Martin Daly, and Margo Wilson, "There's No Contest: Human Sex Differences Are Sexually Selected," *Behavioral and Brain Sciences* 32, no. 3/4 (2009): 286–287.
88. Francis Fukuyama, *The Origins of Political Order* (New York: Farrar, Straus, and Giroux, 2011), 256.
89. David Hart, "Clan, Lineage and the Feud in a Rifian Tribe [Aith Waryaghar, Morocco]," in *Peoples and Cultures of the Middle East*, ed. Louise Sweet (Garden City, NY: Natural History Press, 1970), 74.
90. David Jacobson, *Of Virgins and Martyrs: Women and Sexuality in Global Conflict* (Baltimore, MD: Johns Hopkins University Press, 2013), 60.
91. Monica Das Gupta tells the same tale about Korea:

    The process of Korea's Confucianization has been studied closely. During the Choson dynasty (1392–1910), a process of rigorous social engineering was carried out, borrowing heavily from readings of the Chinese texts. The existing bilateral family system was replaced with a rigidly patrilineal system, abolishing girls' rights to parental property and the possibility of couples living with either the man's or the woman's family. Ancestor worship was strenuously promoted, to strengthen corporate bonds within the lineage and to the rulers. A Department of Rites refined the details of this patriarchal authoritarian regime, and fought relentlessly over centuries against the survival of traces of the old bilateral system of kinship. Social organization was tied together by a threefold mechanism: the domestic sphere, represented by the wife, was subordinated to the public sphere, represented by the father and son, they in turn were the sovereign's subjects.

    Monica Das Gupta, "Family Systems, Political Systems, and Asia's 'Missing Girls': The Construction of Son Preference and Its Unraveling" (World Bank, Washington, DC, December 2009), 10.
92. Das Gupta, "Family Systems, Political Systems," 6–7.
93. Jack Goody and Stanley J. Tambiah, *Bridewealth and Dowry*, Cambridge Papers in Social Anthropology (Cambridge: Cambridge University Press, 1974), 146.
94. Robert Wright, *The Moral Animal* (New York: Vintage, 1995), 98.
95. Laura Betzig, *Despotism and Differential Reproduction: A Darwinian View of History* (New York: Aldine de Gruyter, 1986).
96. Fish, "Islam and Authoritarianism," 31.
97. Collins, "The Logic of Clan Politics," 226, 244–245.
98. Kathleen Collins, *Clan Politics and Regime Transition in Central Asia* (Cambridge: Cambridge University Press, 2006), 243.
99. Schatz, *Modern Clan Politics*, 8.
100. Scott Shane and Jo Becker, "A New Libya, with 'Very Little Time Left,'" *New York Times*, February 27, 2016, https://www.nytimes.com/2016/02/28/us/politics/libya-isis-hillary-clinton.html.
101. Jack Goody, *The Development of Marriage and Family in Europe* (Cambridge: Cambridge University Press, 1983), 16.
102. Elissa Braunstein, "The Feminist Political Economy of the Rent-Seeking Society: An Investigation of Gender Inequality and Economic Growth," *Journal of Economic Issues* 42, no. 4, December 2008): 967.

103. Kate Manne, *Down Girl: The Logic of Misogyny* (Oxford: Oxford University Press, 2018).

104. Goody, *The Development of Marriage and Family in Europe*.

105. James M. Warner and D. A. Campbell, "Supply Response in an Agrarian Economy with Nonsymmetric Gender Relations," *World Development* 28, no. 7 (2000): 1330. It may be argued the first rents are those produced by Mother Nature in the form of food and water, which sustain the lives of human beings.

106. Maria Mies, "Social Origins of the Sexual Division of Labor," in *Women: The Last Colony*, ed. Maria Mies, Veronika Bennholdt-Thomsen, and Claudia Von Werlhof (London: Zed Books, 1988), 67–95.

107. Joseph Manson et al., "Intergroup Aggression in Chimpanzees and Humans," *Current Anthropology* 32, no. 4 (1991): 369–390, p. 374. They add that "where crucial material resources are alienable the accumulation of wealth will be associated with polygyny" (374).

108. William Tucker, *Marriage and Civilization* (New York: Regnery, 2014), 170.

109. Thomas Barfield, "Tribe and State Relations: The Inner Asian Perspective," in *Tribes and State Formation in the Middle East*, ed. Philip Khoury and Joseph Kostiner (Berkeley: University of California Press, 1990), 153–184.

110. Barfield, "Tribe and State Relations," 171.

111. Collins, "The Logic of Clan Politics," 233.

112. Schatz, *Modern Clan Politics*.

113. J. E. Peterson, "Tribes and Politics in Eastern Arabia," *Middle East Journal* 31, no. 3 (Summer 1977): 306.

114. David Kirkpatrick, "Saudi Crown Prince's Mass Purge Upends a Longstanding System," *New York Times*, November 5, 2017, https://www.nytimes.com/2017/11/05/world /middleeast/saudi-crown-prince-purge.html.

115. Tapper, "Anthropologists, Historians," 58.

116. Joseph Kostiner, "Transforming Dualities: Tribe and State Formation in Saudi Arabia," in *Tribes and States Formation in the Middle East*, ed. Philip S. Khoury and Joseph Kostiner (Los Angeles: University of California Press, 1990), 230. Joseph Kostiner comments about Saudi Arabia,

> Patron-client networks drew on tribal cooperation and familiarity for political support and for help in coping with the administration. In their ultimate form such networks created a large clientele dependent on the royal family. In Aziz al-Azmeh's words, "The Saudi polity tributarises other clan groups, no longer nomadic, and ties them . . . to the redistribution of Saudi wealth; for plunder is substituted by subsidy and the privilege of citizenship, such as the legal sponsorship of foreign business (*kafala*) is akin in many ways to the exaction of protection money (*khuwwa*). Thus tribalism becomes ascendant, not merely a *modus vivendi* or an additional structure of society." (Kostiner, "Transforming Dualities," 245.)

117. Collins, *Clan Politics and Regime Transition in Central Asia*, 233.

118. Schatz, *Modern Clan Politics*, 8.

119. Schatz, *Modern Clan Politics*, 97.

120. You-Ming Liou and Paul Musgrave, "Oil, Autocratic Survival, and the Gendered Resource Curse: When Inefficient Policy Is Politically Expedient," *International Studies Quarterly* 60, no. 3 (2016): 440–456.

121. Valentine Moghadam notes that other countries have oil rents but do not subordinate women—such as Norway—but these countries had significantly dismantled the components of the Syndrome before they began to extract these resources. Moghadam, personal communication, July 18, 2016.

122. Lerner, *The Creation of Patriarchy*, 216.
123. Collins, "The Logic of Clan Politics," 260.
124. Braunstein, "The Feminist Political Economy," 969.
125. Braunstein, "The Feminist Political Economy," 974.
126. Sri Mulyani Indrawati, "Discriminating Against Women Keeps Countries Poorer," *World Bank Voices* (blog), September 10, 2015, http://blogs.worldbank.org/voices /discriminating-against-women-keeps-countries-poorer?CID=ECR_TT_worldbank _EN_EXT&utm_content=bufferfb296&utm_medium=social&utm_source=facebook .com&utm_campaign=buffer.
127. Christopher Butler, Tali Gluch, and Neil J. Mitchell, "Security Forces and Sexual Violence," *Journal of Peace Research* 44, no. 6 (2007): 678.
128. Weiner, *The Rule of the Clan*, 81. Sometimes government positions are "marked" as belonging to particular lineages (such as we see in some Gulf states today). Indeed, in the past, this parceling out of government positions along family lines might even be codified. Adams gives an example from European history:

> For example, the Contracts of Correspondence in the eighteenth-century Netherlands—which could, without too much of a stretch, be termed a cartel of fifty-some cities—formalized the distribution of city offices in written succession rules, laying out systems by which all eligible elite families would take turns getting mayoralties, East Indies Company directorships, and other top corporate privileges. The contracts regulated the membership in and control over corporate bodies, which were the conditions for capital accumulation, political power, and family honor. The settlements, which were ratified by the Stadholder and States-General, protected specific families' stake in an office and guaranteed that regent families' collective office genealogies would continue unbroken. They also tightened the political vise on each family head accordingly, so that he could do nothing without the permission of his fellows. (Adams, "The Rule of the Father: Patriarchy and Patrimonialism in Early Modern Europe, 249.")

129. Collins, "The Logic of Clan Politics," 249.
130. Collins, "The Logic of Clan Politics," 245, 249.
131. Collins, *Clan Politics and Regime Transition*, 349, 350.
132. Collins, *Clan Politics and Regime Transition*, 340.
133. Samuel Mondays Atuobi, "Corruption and State Instability in West Africa: An Examination of Policy Options" (occasional paper, Kofi Annan International Peacekeeping Training Center, December 2007), 2, http://reliefweb.int/sites/reliefweb.int/files /resources/9BD8A1F729CEB5B8C125746C0049D740-kaiptc-dec2007.pdf.
134. Michela Wrong, *It's Our Turn to Eat: The Story of a Kenyan Whistle-Blower* (New York: Harper Perennial, 2010).
135. Goody and Tambiah, *Bridewealth and Dowry*, 166.
136. Collins, *Clan Politics and Regime Transition*, 339.
137. Francis Fukuyama, *The Great Disruption: Human Nature and the Reconstitution of Social Order* (New York: Free Press, 1999), 241.
138. Douglass North, John Wallis, and Barry Weingast, *Violence and Social Orders* (2009; repr. Cambridge: Cambridge University Press, 2013), xii.
139. North et al., *Violence and Social Orders*, 18.
140. Ernest Gellner, "Tribalism and the State in the Middle East," in *Tribes and States Formation in the Middle East*, ed. Philip S. Khoury and Joseph Kostiner (Los Angeles: University of California Press, 1990), 116.

141. Weiner, *The Rule of the Clan*, 81.
142. Jamil Anderlini, "China: Blueprint for Reform Targets Corruption," *Financial Times*, November 26, 2013, http://www.ft.com/intl/cms/s/0/d4bd3de0-4fb6-11e3-b06e-00144 feabdc0.html#axzz2lnTmx4fF.
143. Kostiner, "Transforming Dualities," 240.
144. David Skidmore, "Understanding Chinese President's Xi's Anti-Corruption Campaign," *The Conversation*, October 27, 2017, https://theconversation.com/understanding-chinese -president-xis-anti-corruption-campaign-86396; see also David Kirkpatrick, "Saudi Arabia Arrests 11 Princes," *New York Times*, November 4, 2017, https://www.nytimes .com/2017/11/04/world/middleeast/saudi-arabia-waleed-bin-talal.html.
145. Collins, *Clan Politics and Regime Transition*, 339.
146. Nadwa al-Dawsari, "Tribal Governance and Stability in Yemen" (The Carnegie Papers, Middle East, Carnegie Endowment for International Peace, Washington, DC, April 2012), 4, http://carnegieendowment.org/files/yemen_tribal_governance.pdf.
147. Weiner, *The Rule of the Clan*, 78. Although phrased a bit obscurely, Dresch's observation is also worth reflection: "If tribes somehow lead to states, then states lead as often to tribes." Paul Dresch, "Imams and Tribes: The Writing and Acting of History in Upper Yemen," in *Tribes and States Formation in the Middle East*, edited by Philip S. Khoury and Joseph Kostiner, 253 (Los Angeles: University of California Press, 1990).
148. Collins, "Clans, Pacts, and Politics in Central Asia," 5.
149. Fukuyama, *The Great Disruption*, 201–202.
150. United Nations Development Program, Regional Bureau for Arab States, *Arab Human Development Report 2004: Towards Freedom in the Arab World* (New York: United Nations Development Program, 2005), 145.
151. Ivan Ermakoff, "Patrimony and Collective Capacity: An Analytical Outline," *Annals of the American Academy of Political and Social Science* 636, no. 1 (2011): 182.
152. Weiner, *The Rule of the Clan*, 104.
153. Collins, "The Logic of Clan Politics," and Collins, *Clan Politics and Regime Transition*.
154. Sarah Chayes, *Thieves of State* (New York: Norton, 2016), 6, 7, 69, 75, 77.
155. Chayes, *Thieves of State*, 62, 67.
156. Chayes, *Thieves of State*, 148.
157. Chayes, *Thieves of State*, 71, 77, 88.
158. Chayes, *Thieves of State*, 96.
159. Chayes, *Thieves of State*, 86.
160. Christopher Schwartz and Alisher Khamidov, "Kyrgyzstan: Corrupt, Anarchic—and Stable?" *The Diplomat*, August 16, 2016, https://thediplomat.com/2016/08/kyrgyzstan -corrupt-anarchic-and-stable/?utm_source=Active+Subscribers&utm_campaign =152b4b5b10-MR_08182016&utm_medium=email&utm_term=0_35c49cbd51 -152b4b5b10-64183517.
161. Bassam Tibi, "The Simultaneity of the Unsimultaneous: Old Tribes and Imposed Nation-State in the Modern Middle East," in *Tribes and States Formation in the Middle East*, ed. Philip S. Khoury and Joseph Kostiner (Los Angeles: University of California Press, 1990), 115. Lisa Blaydes and Eric Chaney discuss the role of the *mamluks*—alien elite military slaves—in the emergence of a strong bureaucracy in Islamic lands. These mamluks were forbidden from marrying local women, to prevent their cooptation by the clans. Unfortunately, in several cases, they became a praetorian guard that overthrew the ruler and established their own sultanate. Lisa Blaydes and Eric Chaney, "The Feudal Revolution and Europe's Rise: Political Divergence of the Christian West and the Muslim World Before 1500 CE," *American Political Science Review* 107, no. 1

(February 2013): doi:10.1017/S0003055412000561. Fukuyama suggests that the creation of the mamluk social category solved a consistent problem for larger states at this pre-modern period of time:

> Early social organization in China, India, and the Middle East was based on agnatic lineages. . . . In each case, state builders had to figure out how to make individuals loyal to the state rather than to their local kin group. Institutions based on territory and centralized legal authority had to be layered on top of strong segmentary societies. The most extreme response to this problem was that of the Arabs and Ottomans, who literally kidnapped children and raised them in artificial households so they would be loyal to the state and not to their kin. (Fukuyama, *The Origins of Political Order*).

One could argue that another extreme example was the imposed celibacy of the Catholic Church on its priests, which prevented these men from having any heirs at all, and thus was designed to focus the mind on the good of the Church rather than personal benefit. Church bureaucracy in this sense may have been the first truly professional, modern bureaucracy.

162. Fukuyama, *The Great Disruption*, 17.
163. Jacobson, *Of Virgins and Martyrs*, 61.
164. Schatz, *Modern Clan Politics*, xix.
165. Hudson et al., *Sex and World Peace*.
166. North et al., *Violence and Social Orders*, 63.
167. Weiner, *The Rule of the Clan*, 9.
168. Patricio Asfura-Heim, "Tribal Customary Law and Legal Pluralism in al Anbar, Iraq," in *Customary Justice and the Rule of Law in War-Torn Societies*, ed. Deborah H. Isser (Washington, DC: United States Institute of Peace Press, 2011), 247.
169. Weiner, *The Rule of the Clan*, 97.
170. Weiner, *The Rule of the Clan*.
171. Laura Betzig, "Despotism and Differential Reproduction: A Cross-Cultural Correlation of Conflict Asymmetry, Hierarchy, and Degree of Polygyny," *Ethology and Sociobiology* 3 (1982): 213–214.
172. Fukuyama, *The Great Disruption*, 37. Indeed, Fukuyama is of the opinion that rule of law cannot emerge unless a transcendent vision of universal kinship—rooted in a belief in deity—is present. According to Fukuyama, it was China's lack of transcendent religion that resulted in its being the only major civilization that did not develop rule of law.
173. Weiner, *The Rule of the Clan*, 124.
174. Weiner, *The Rule of the Clan*, 37.
175. North et al., *Violence and Social Orders*, 173.
176. Obaid Ali, "'You Must Have a Gun to Stay Alive': Ghor, A Province with Three Governments," *Afghanistan Analysts Network*, August 4, 2013, http://www.afghanistan-analysts.org/you-must-have-a-gun-to-stay-alive-ghor-a-province-with-three-governments.
177. Jacobson, *Of Virgins and Martyrs*, 113–114.
178. Jacobson, *Of Virgins and Martyrs*, 114.
179. Gellner, "Tribalism and the State," and Akbar Ahmed, *The Thistle and the Drone: How America's War on Terror Became a Global War on Tribal Islam* (Washington, DC: Brookings Institution, 2013).
180. Weiner, *The Rule of the Clan*, 36, 38.
181. Caton, "Anthropological Theories," and Noah Coburn, *Bazaar Politics: Power and Pottery in an Afghan Market Town* (Stanford, CA: Stanford University Press, 2011), 5.
182. Tapper, "Anthropologists, Historians," 91.

183. Asfura-Heim, "Tribal Customary Law," 244–245.
184. Ahmed, *The Thistle and the Drone*.
185. Andrew Vonasch et al., "Death Before Dishonor: Incurring Costs to Protect Moral Reputation," *Social Psychological and Personality Science*, July 21, 2017, http://journals .sagepub.com/doi/pdf/10.1177/1948550617720271.
186. Tapper "Anthropologists, Historians," 94.
187. Collins, "The Political Role of Clans," 187.
188. Schatz, *Modern Clan Politics*, 9.
189. Schatz, *Modern Clan Politics*, 36.
190. Weiner notes that King Alfred of England introduced the crime of disturbing the "King's Peace" to do just this. Would-be fighters had to ride to the king and notify him before beginning a fight, and fighting within the King's hall was prohibited. Eventually, "the requirement that peace be kept in the King's personal residence eventually grew into the principle that there ought to be peace over the King's entire realm—the King's peace, which the King had the responsibility to maintain." Weiner, *The Rule of the Clan*, 146.
191. Allan Dafoe and Devin Caughey find that U.S. presidents who were Southerners raised in a culture of rigid male honor were far more likely to go to war for reputational reasons than those not raised in that culture. Honor becomes operationalized as resolve to act, and thus what is important is that reputation for resolve is bolstered through such forceful action. They note that in practice this means, "any issue, no matter how trivial, can become a test of resolve." Allan Dafoe and Devin Caughey, "Honor and War: Southern US Presidents and the Effects of Concern for Reputation," *World Politics* 68, no. 2 (April 2016): 348. See also Barbara Walter, *Reputation and Civil War: Why Separatist Conflicts Are So Violent*. (Cambridge: Cambridge University Press, 2009).
192. Bjarnegard et al., "Honor and Political Violence."
193. Ahram, "Sexual and Ethnic Violence and the Construction of the Islamic State."
194. Divale and Harris, "Population, Warfare," 532.
195. Mounira M. Charrad, "Central and Local Patrimonialism: State-Building in Kin-Based Societies," *Annals of the American Academy of Political and Social Science* 636, no. 1 (July 2011): 49–68; see also Ahmed, *The Thistle and the Drone*.
196. Ahmed, *The Thistle and the Drone*.
197. Goody and Tambiah, *Bridewealth and Dowry*, 146. See also Tim Krieger and Laura Renner, "A Cautionary Tale on Polygyny, Conflict, and Gender Inequality," (University of Freiburg discussion paper 2018–02, Wilfried-Guth-Stiftungsprofessor fur Ordnungs- und Wettbewerbspolitik, April 2018).
198. Goody and Tambiah, *Bridewealth and Dowry*, 147.
199. Peggy Reeves Sanday, *Female Power and Male Dominance: On the Origins of Sexual Inequality* (Cambridge: Cambridge University Press, 1981), 47.
200. Jonathan Gottschall, *The Rape of Troy: Evolution, Violence, and the World of Homer* (Cambridge: Cambridge University Press, 2008), 4.
201. Ben Raffield and Mark Collard, "Male-Biased Operational Sex Ratios and the Viking Phenomenon: An Evolutionary Anthropological Perspective on Late Iron Age Scandinavian Raiding," *Evolution and Human Behavior* 38, no. 3 (2016): 315–324.
202. Divale and Harris, "Population, Warfare," 526. In another interesting observation, Tanika Chakraborty and Sukkoo Kim, in their study of regional, caste, and tribal variation in Indian sex ratios, note that both dowry-practicing groups as well as brideprice-practicing groups (such as tribes) in India both had abnormal sex ratios. Tanika Chakraborty and Sukkoo Kim, "Kinship Institutions and Sex Ratios in India," *Demography* 47, no. 4 (November 2010): 997. This suggests that the mechanism matters less than the overall aim of subordinating women.

203. Schatz, *Modern Clan Politics*, 46.
204. United Nations Development Program, *Arab Human Development Report 2004*, 166.
205. Katy Migiro, "More Child Marriage in Drought-Hit Ethiopia with Risk of 'Full-Blown' Disaster," *Thomson Reuters News*, December 11, 2015, http://news.trust.org//item /20151211164911-qtgz4/?source=dpMostPopular.
206. Girls Not Brides, "Syrian Arab Republic," http://www.girlsnotbrides.org/child-marriage /syrian-arab-republic/.
207. Sanday, *Female Power and Male Dominance*, 136.
208. Sanday, *Female Power and Male Dominance*, 146–147.
209. Sanday, *Female Power and Male Dominance*, 158, 201.
210. Sheila Meintjes, Anu Pillay, and Meredeth Turshen, "There Is No Aftermath for Women," in *The Aftermath: Women in Post-Conflict Transformation*, ed. Sheila Meintjes, Anu Pullay, and Meredeth Turshen (New York: Zed Books 2001), 13.
211. Rina Chandran, "Hunger, Child Marriage, Prostitution: India Drought Hurts Women, Low-Caste Dalits More," *Thomson Reuters*, May 23, 2016, http://news.trust.org/item /20160523133537-m9pde/.
212. Chandran, "Hunger, Child Marriage, Prostitution."
213. Peggy Reeves Sanday, "The Socio-Cultural Context of Rape: A Cross-Cultural Study," *Journal of Social Issues* 37, no. 4 (1981): 25.

5. The Tremors Caused by Obstructed Marriage Markets: A Closer Look

1. Patrick Cockburn, "Iraq Crisis: As ISIS Terror Spreads, Its Fighters Look for Wives," *The Independent*, June 21, 2014, https://www.independent.co.uk/news/world/middle -east/iraq-crisis-as-the-sunni-terror-spreads-its-fighters-look-for-wives-9554231 .html?origin=internalSearch.
2. Hajer Naili, "Iraq Women's Shelter Responds to Growing Crisis," *Women's E-News*, June 19, 2014, https://womensenews.org/2014/06/iraq-womens-shelter-responds-growing -crisis/.
3. Laura Betzig, "Despotism and Differential Reproduction: A Cross-Cultural Correlation of Conflict Asymmetry, Hierarchy, and Degree of Polygyny," *Ethology and Sociobiology* 3, (1982): 218.
4. Francis Fukuyama, *The Origins of Political Order* (New York: Farrar, Straus, and Giroux, 2011), 233.
5. Fukuyama, *The Origins of Political Order*, 76.
6. Mounira M. Charrad, *States and Women's Rights: The Making of Postcolonial Tunisia, Algeria, and Morocco* (Berkeley: University of California Press, 2001), 55.
7. David Jacobson, *Of Virgins and Martyrs: Women and Sexuality in Global Conflict* (Baltimore, MD: Johns Hopkins University Press, 2013), 115–116. Clans differ according to the level and intensity of female subordination. For example, Barth notes among the Basseri tribe of Iran, women are given a meaningful measure of authority, but only in family matters. Fredrik Barth, *Nomads of South Persia: The Basseri Tribe of the Khamseh Confederacy* (Boston: Little, Brown, 1961).
8. Valerie Hudson and Andrea Den Boer, *Bare Branches: The Security Implications of Asia's Surplus Male Population* (Cambridge, MA: MIT Press, 2004).
9. Hudson and Den Boer, *Bare Branches*.
10. Hudson and Den Boer, *Bare Branches*.

11. William Graham Sumner, *Folkways* (New York: Dover, 1959), 309–310
12. Monica Das Gupta "Family Systems, Political Systems, and Asia's 'Missing Girls': The Construction of Son Preference and Its Unraveling" (World Bank, Washington, DC, December 2009), 20.
13. Valerie M. Hudson and Andrea Den Boer, "When a Boy's Life Is Worth More Than His Sister's," *Foreign Policy*, July 30, 2015. http://foreignpolicy.com/2015/07/30/when-a-boys-life-is-worth-more-than-his-sisters-sex-ratio/.
14. Andrea Den Boer and Valerie M. Hudson, "Patrilineality, Son Preference, and Sex Selection in South Korea and Vietnam," *Population and Development Review* 43, no. 1 (2017): 119–147.
15. Betzig, "Despotism and Differential Reproduction," 216.
16. Hudson and Den Boer, *Bare Branches*.
17. Lena Edlund et al., "Sex Ratios and Crime: Evidence from China's One-Child Policy," *Review of Economics and Statistics* 95, no. 5 (December 2013): 1520–1534."
18. Jean Dreze and Reetika Khera, "Crime, Gender, and Society in India: Insights from Homicide Data," *Population and Development Review* 26, no. 2 (June 2000): 335–352; see also Cheng Lu, "Excess of Marriageable Males and Violent Crime in China and South Korea, 1970–2008" (paper presented at the 2012 annual meeting of the Population Association of America, San Francisco, CA, May 3–5, 2012), http://paa2012.princeton.edu/abstracts/121243; see also Lisa Cameron, Xin Meng, and Dandan Zhang, "China's Sex Ratio and Crime: Behavioral Change or Financial Necessity?" IZA discussion paper no. 9747, Institute for the Study of Labor, February 2016), http://ftp.iza.org/dp9747.pdf.
19. Jonathan Gottschall, *The Rape of Troy: Evolution, Violence, and the World of Homer* (Cambridge: Cambridge University Press, 2008), 151; William T. Divale and Marvin Harris note that "demographic analysis of 160 band and village populations, censused prior to modern contact and while they still practiced warfare, shows an average sex ratio in the age group 14 and under of 128 boys per 100 girls." William T. Divale and Marvin Harris, "Population, Warfare, and the Male Supremacist Complex," *American Anthropologist* 78 (1976): 525.
20. Alan Taylor, "Rising Protests in China," *The Atlantic*, February 17, 2012, http://www.theatlantic.com/photo/2012/02/rising-protests-in-china/100247/.
21. Kevin O'Brien and Li Lianjiang, *Rightful Resistance in Rural China* (Cambridge: Cambridge University Press, 2006).
22. Eve Bower, "Report: Some Areas in China Under Martial Law After Protests," *CNN*, May 31, 2011, http://www.cnn.com/2011/WORLD/asiapcf/05/28/china.martial.law.
23. Allan Mazur and Alan Booth, "Testosterone and Dominance in Men," *Behavioral and Brain Science* 21, no. 3 (June 1998): 353–397. Furthermore, these characteristics may persist even after sex ratios have subsequently normalized. For example, Victoria Baranov, Ralph De Haas, and Pauline Grosjean have shown that areas in Australia that historically had the worst male-biased sex ratios in the early days of British colonization still to this day (when sex ratios are normal) experience greater violence, excessive alcohol consumption, and greater sex segregation by occupation. Victoria Baranov, Ralph De Haas, and Pauline Grosjean "Men: Roots and Consequences of Masculinity Norms," *SSRN*, June 12, 2018, https://papers.ssrn.com/sol3/papers.cfm?abstract_id=3185694.
24. Nic White, "'Gang Is Your Best Friend': African Apex Members Reveal What Life Is Like Inside the Notorious Melbourne Group," *Daily Mail*, May 1, 2017, http://www.dailymail.co.uk/news/article-4462746/Apex-members-reveal-life-like-inside-gang.html.
25. Hudson and Den Boer, *Bare Branches*, 208.

26. Daniel Little, *Understanding Peasant China* (New Haven, CT: Yale University Press, 1989), 209.

27. James L. Boone, "Parental Investment and Elite Family Structure in Preindustrial States: A Case Study of Late Medieval-Early Modern Portuguese Genealogies," *American Anthropologist* 88, no. 4 (December 1986): 859–878; 862, 868.

28. William Tucker, *Marriage and Civilization* (New York: Regnery, 2014), 83.

29. Joseph Henrich, Robert Boyd, and Peter J. Richerson, "The Puzzle of Monogamous Marriage," *Philosophical Transactions of the Royal Society* 367 (2012): 660.

30. Henrich et al., "The Puzzle of Monogamous Marriage," 660.

31. David Barash, *Out of Eden: The Surprising Consequences of Polygamy* (Oxford: Oxford University Press, 2016), 29.

32. Gerda Lerner has something interesting to say about Sparta: "[Sparta] expressed the concept that the bearing of children was as important a service to the state as the service of the warrior in a war, which allowed the inscription of the name of the deceased on a tomb only of a man who had died at war and of a woman who had died in childbirth." Gerda Lerner, *The Creation of Patriarchy* (New York: Oxford University Press, 1986), 203.

33. Tucker, *Marriage and Civilization*, 111.

34. Barash, *Out of Eden*, 112–113.

35. Tucker notes that while Western slavery emphasized capturing males who could perform hard labor, Islamic slavery emphasized female slavery, with female slaves outnumbering male slaves two-to-one, to provide access to women for lower class men who had been edged out of the marriage market by the elite's practice of polygyny. Tucker, *Marriage and Civilization*, 174.

36. Barash, *Out of Eden*, 38.

37. Barash, *Out of Eden*, 40.

38. Barash, *Out of Eden*, 45.

39. Esther Mokuwa et al., "Peasant Grievance and Insurgency in Sierra Leone: Judicial Serfdom as a Driver of Conflict," *African Affairs* 110, no. 440 (2011): 339–366.

40. Marvin Harris, "The Evolution of Human Gender Hierarchies," in *Sex and Gender Hierarchies*, ed. Barbara D. Miller (Cambridge: Cambridge University Press, 1993), 57–79; Satoshi Kanazawa, "Evolutionary Psychological Foundations of Civil Wars," *Journal of Politics* 71, no. 1 (January 2009): 25–34; Kristian Gleditsch et al., "Polygyny or Misogyny? Reexamining the 'First Law on Intergroup Conflict,'" *Journal of Politics* 73, no. 1 (January 2011): 265–270; Tim Krieger and Laura Renner, "A Cautionary Tale on Polygyny, Conflict, and Gender Inequality" (University of Freiburg discussion paper 2018–02, Wilfried-Guth-Stiftungsprofessor fur Ordnungs-und Wettbewerbspolitik, April 2018).

41. James L. Boone, "Noble Family Structure and Expanisionist Warfare in the Late Middle Ages: A Socioecological Approach," in *Rethinking Human Adaptation: Biological and Cultural Models*, ed. Rada Dyson-Hudson and Michael A. Little (Boulder, CO: Westview, 1983), 79–96.

42. Rebecca Nielsen, "Presentation on Sierra Leone Research" (WomanStats co-PI meeting, Provo, UT, July 10, 2017).

43. Ben Raffield and Mark Collard, "Male-Biased Operational Sex Ratios and the Viking Phenomenon: An Evolutionary Anthropological Perspective on Late Iron Age Scandinavian Raiding," *Evolution and Human Behavior* 38, no. 3 (2016): 315–324.

44. Gottschall, *The Rape of Troy*.

45. Jack Goody and Stanley J. Tambiah, *Bridewealth and Dowry*, Cambridge Papers in Social Anthropology (Cambridge: Cambridge University Press, 1974), 7.

46. Stephanie Coontz, *Marriage, A History* (New York: Penguin Books, 2005), 92, 94.
47. Krieger and Renner, "A Cautionary Tale on Polygyny, Conflict, and Gender Inequality."
48. Betzig, *Despotism and Differential Reproduction*.
49. Andrey Korotayev and Dmitri Bondarenko, "Polygyny and Democracy: A Cross-Cultural Comparison," *Cross-Cultural Research* 34, no. 1 (2000): 190–208.
50. Robert Wright, *The Moral Animal* (New York: Vintage, 1995), 98.
51. Rose McDermott and Jonathan Cowden, "Polygyny and Violence Against Women," *Emory Law Journal* 64, (2015): 1767–1814.
52. Richard D. Alexander et al., "Sexual Dimorphisms and Breeding Systems in Pinnipeds, Ungulates, Primates, and Humans," in *Evolutionary Biology and Human Behavior*, ed. Napoleon A. Chagnon and Wiliam Irons (North Scituate, MA: Duxbury Press, 1979), 423, 432–433.
53. Henrich et al., "The Puzzle of Monogamous Marriage," 657, 659–660.
54. Supreme Court of British Columbia, "Reference Re: Section 293 of the Criminal Code of Canada," 2011 BCSC 1588 (CanLII) (2011), para 499, https://www.canlii.org/en/bc/bcsc/doc/2011/2011bcsc1588/2011bcsc1588.html#.
55. Henrich et al., "The Puzzle of Monogamous Marriage," 657, 659–660.
56. Michèle Tertilt, "Polygyny, Fertility, and Savings," *Journal of Political Economy* 113, no. 6 (2005): 1365, http://tertilt.vwl.uni-mannheim.de/research/polygyny05.pdf.
57. Peter Turchin, *Ultra Society: How 10,000 Years of War Made Humans the Greatest Cooperators on Earth* (Chaplin, CT: Beresta Books, 2016), 228.
58. McDermott and Cowden, "Polygyny and Violence Against Women," 1767–1814.
59. Betzig, "Despotism and Differential Reproduction," 310.
60. Ann O'Neill, "Witnesses: Scallops for the Bishop, Toast for the Kids." *CNN*, April 6, 2016. https://www.cnn.com/2016/04/05/us/flds-secrets-warren-jeffs/index.html.
61. McDermott and Cowden, "Polygyny and Violence Against Women," 1810–1814.
62. Peggy Reeves Sanday, *Female Power and Male Dominance: On the Origins of Sexual Inequality* (Cambridge: Cambridge University Press, 1981), 209.
63. This subsection's discussion was adapted from Valerie M. Hudson and Hilary Matfess, "In Plain Sight: The Neglected Linkage Between Brideprice, Raiding, and Rebellion," *International Security* 42, no. 1 (Summer 2017): 7–40, doi:10.1162/ISEC_a_00289.
64. Matt Richmond and Flavia Krause-Jackson, "Cows-for-Brides Inflation Spurs Cattle Theft in South Sudan," *Bloomberg News*, July 25, 2011, http://www.bloomberg.com/news/articles/2011-07-26/cows-for-bride-inflation-spurs-cattle-theft-among-mundari-in-south-sudan.
65. Philip Thon Aleu and Parach Mach, "Risking One's Life to Be Able to Marry," *Development and Cooperation*, June 26, 2016, https://www.dandc.eu/en/article/bride-price-tradition-destructive-strong-strife-torn-south-sudan.
66. Marc Sommers and Stephanie Schwartz, "Dowry and Division" (USIP special report 295, U.S. Institute of Peace, November 2011), http://www.usip.org/sites/default/files/SR_295.pdf.
67. Scott Shane and Jo Becker, "A New Libya, with 'Very Little Time Left,'" *New York Times*, February 27, 2016, https://www.nytimes.com/2016/02/28/us/politics/libya-isis-hillary-clinton.html.
68. Heather Murdock, "'Delayed' Marriage Frustrates Middle East Youth," *Voice of America*, February 22, 2011, https://www.voanews.com/a/delayed-marriage-frustrates-middle-east-youth-116744384/172742.html.
69. Alexandra Tenny, personal communication, August 3, 2017.

70. Henrik Urdal, "A Clash of Generations? Youth Bulges and Political Violence," *International Studies Quarterly* 50, no. 3 (September 2006): 607–629; and Noah Bricker and Mark Foley, "The Effect of Youth Demographics on Violence: The Importance of the Labor Market," *International Journal of Conflict and Violence* 7, no. 1 (2013): 179–194; and Richard Cincotta, "Minority Youth Bulges and the Future of Intrastate Conflict," *New Security Beat*, October 13, 2011, https://s3.amazonaws.com/academia.edu.documents/32162413 /NSB_Cincotta_Minority_YB.pdf?AWSAccessKeyId=AKIAIWOWYYGZ2Y53UL3A &Expires=1521143853&Signature=3Z4Q5vYsNZKFiR6%2BOZD1ReHWGME %3D&response-content-disposition=inline%3B%20filename%3DMinority _Youth_Bulges_and_the_Future_of.pdf.

71. Hannes Weber, "Demography and Democracy: The Impact of Youth Cohort Size on Democratic Stability in the World." *Democratization* 20, no. 2 (2014): 335–357, http:// dx.doi.org/10.1080/13510347.2011.650916.

72. Weber, "Demography and Democracy," 344.

73. Weber, "Demography and Democracy," 348.

74. Murdock, " 'Delayed' Marriage Frustrates Middle East Youth."

75. Interestingly, a report by Nava Ashraf, Natalie Bau, Nathan Nunn, and Alessandra Voena found that increasing girls' education may raise brideprice in the community as the girls' value is perceived to have increased due to this extra investment. The observation of this unintended side-effect is not meant to discredit girls' education as a development objective, but it serves to highlight a situation in which girls' gains may actually feed other sources of female oppression, as well as marriage market obstruction. Nava Ashraf et al., "Brideprice and the Returns to Education for Women" (NBER working paper no. 22417, National Bureau of Economic Research, Cambridge, MA, July 21, 2015), http://www.nber.org/papers/w22417.

76. It is interesting that rebel and terrorist groups are eager to recruit men on the basis of increased marriage prospects, but that these married recruits then tend to become problematic for the group. For example, during the Huk Rebellion of the 1950s in the Philippines, Goodwin notes that married cadres suffered from what was called "await-ism," meaning they were less likely to put themselves forward in a fight because of loyalty to wives. Jeff Goodwin, "The Libidinal Constitution of a High-Risk Social Movement: Affectual Ties and Solidarity in the Huk Rebellion, 1946–1954," *American Sociological Review* 62, no. 1 (February 1997): 53–69. The Palestine Liberation Organization actually used this tendency to their advantage, offering payment of brideprice and marriage as a way to get its troublesome Black September subgroup out of action; once these men were married, and especially if they had young sons, they no longer wanted to be actively involved in terrorist activities. Bruce Hofman,"Gaza City: All You Need is Love," *The Atlantic*, December 2001. https://www.theatlantic.com/past/docs /issues/2001/12/hoffman.htm.

ISIS learned from this incident: it recruited foreign fighters by offering them marriage, but then to prevent what happened with Black September, they immediately forced the wives to go on Depo-Provera so that they would not get pregnant. Rukmini Callimachi, "To Maintain Supply of Sex Slaves, ISIS Pushes Birth Control," *New York Times*, March 12, 2016, https://www.nytimes.com/2016/03/13/world/middleeast /to-maintain-supply-of-sex-slaves-isis-pushes-birth-control.html. As soon as their husbands were killed in action, ISIS did not allow these women the religiously mandated three months of grieving, but rather married them off immediately to another foreign fighter. Alexis Henshaw of Duke University has also done some interesting work on "conjugal order" in rebel groups, noting how the employment of means such as forced abortions in the FARC (Revolutionary Armed Forces of Colombia—People's Army) were designed to simultaneously exploit male sexual interest while minimizing the threat to revolutionary zeal that might otherwise follow. Alexis Henshaw, "Conjugal Order in the Rebel Family: A Comparative View" (unpublished manuscript, January 17, 2018).

77. Diane Singerman, *The Economic Imperatives of Marriage: Emerging Practices and Identities among Youth in the Middle East* (Dubai: Wolfensohn Center for Development at the Dubai School of Government, 2007).

78. T. El-Khodary, "For War Widows, Hamas Recruits Army of Husbands," *New York Times*, October 31, 2008.

79. Siofra Brennan, "Here Come the Brides!" *Daily Mail*, February 6, 2017, http://www.dailymail.co.uk/femail/article-4197474/Couples-prepare-mass-wedding-Syria.html.

80. Keiligh Baker, "ISIS Offers Fighters $1500 Starter Home Bonus and a Free Honeymoon," *Daily Mail*, May 26, 2015, http://www.dailymail.co.uk/news/article-3098235/ISIS-offers-fighters-1-500-starter-home-bonus-free-honeymoon.html.

81. Ariel I. Ahram, "Sexual Violence and the Making of ISIS," *Survival* 57, no. 3 (2015): 57–78. Interestingly, as ISIS fell in 2017, women who had joined the group to marry began to tell some interesting tales about the foreign fighters. For example, in one interview, one Indonesian young woman named Rahma noted of her time with ISIS, "They [the foreign fighters] say they want to jihad for the sake of Allah, but what they want is only about women and sex." And another ISIS wife, named May, said the women in Raqqa "has been left shocked after being divorced by foreign fighters only three to four days or one month after marrying." Jillian Robinson, "Jihadi Speed-Dating," *Daily Mail*, July 17, 2017, http://www.dailymail.co.uk/news/article-4703426/ISIS-brides-reveal-reality-married-jihadi.html.

82. Hudson and Matfess, "In Plain Sight."

83. Hilary Matfess, "Here's Why Many People Join Boko Haram, Despite Its Notorious Violence," *Washington Post*, April 26, 2016, https://www.washingtonpost.com/news/monkey-cage/wp/2016/04/26/heres-why-so-many-people-join-boko-haram-despite-its-notorious-violence/.

84. Matfess, "Boko Haram is Enslaving Women, Making Them Join the War," *Newsweek*, February 8, 2016.

85. Human Rights Watch, "Nigeria: Boko Haram Abducts Women, Recruits Children," November 29, 2013, http:// www.hrw.org/fr/node/121029.

86. T. J. Raphael. "ISIS Uses Rape and Sexual Violence Against Women to Consolidate Its Power," *PRI*, August 14, 2015, https://www.pri.org/stories/2015-08-14/isis-uses-rape-and-sexual-violence-against-women-consolidate-its-power.

87. Vikas Bajaj and Lydia Polgreen, "Suspect Stirs Mumbai Court by Confessing," *New York Times*, July 20, 2009. http://www.nytimes.com/2009/07/21/world/asia/21india.html?_r=2.

88. Farea Al-Muslimi, "The Social Politics of Weddings in Yemen," *Al-Monitor*, November 20, 2013, http://www.al-monitor.com/pulse/originals/2013/11/yemen-weddings-politics-social-discrimination.html?utm_source=&utm_medium=email&utm_campaign=8603.

89. Al-Muslimi, "The Social Politics of Weddings in Yemen."

90. Agence France Presse, "Poor Celebrate at Mass Weddings in Algeria," *Gulf Times*, January 2, 2017, http://www.gulf-times.com/story/526653/Poor-celebrate-at-mass-weddings-in-Algeria; Majd Al-Waheidi, "Gaza Dating Site Matches Widows to Men Seeing Second (or Third) Wife," *New York Times*, June 4, 2017, https://www.nytimes.com/2017/06/04/world/middleeast/gaza-palestinians-hamas-wesal-polygamy.html; Kelly McLaughlin, "Hundreds of Fatherless Brides in India Tie the Knot as Diamond

Tycoon Funds Their Weddings in a Mass Celebration," *Daily Mail*, December 24, 2017, http://www.dailymail.co.uk/news/article-5210547/Hundreds-fatherless-brides-India -tie-knot.html.

91. Robert Lacey, *Inside the Kingdom: Kings, Clerics, Modernists, Terrorists, and the Struggle for Saudi Arabia* (New York: Penguin, 2010), 258.
92. Hudson and Matfess, "In Plain Sight."
93. Corry Elida, "Indonesia: Mass Wedding Provides Marriage and Birth Registration for Low Income Families," *Jakarta Post*, January 29, 2015, http://www.thejakartapost .com/news/2015/01/29/mass-wedding-delivers-birth-certificates.html; "Taiwan Ministry Turns Matchmaker to Boost Birth Rate," *BBC*, June 21, 2010, http://www.bbc.com/news /10364381;" Elahe Izadi, "The Potential Spouse Is Brought to You by the Islamic Republic of Iran," *Washington Post*, June 16, 2015, https://www.washingtonpost.com/news /soloish/wp/2015/06/16/this-potential-spouse-is-brought-to-you-by-the-islamic -republic-of-iran/?noredirect=on&utm_term=.31a564271628.
94. Michelle Moghtader, "Iranian Parliament Bans Vasectomies in Bid to Boost Birth Rate," *Reuters*, August 11, 2014, https://www.reuters.com/article/us-iran-population/iranian -parliament-bans-vasectomies-in-bid-to-boost-birth-rate-idUSKBN0GB15Z20140811.
95. Goody and Tambiah, *Bridewealth and Dowry*, 9.
96. Julia Adams, "Politics, Patriarchy and Frontiers of Historical Sociological Explanation," in *Political Power and Social Theory* 19 (2008): 289–294.
97. Boone, "Noble Family Structure and Expansionist Warfare," and Boone, "Parental Investment and Elite Family Structure."
98. Goody and Tambiah, *Bridewealth and Dowry*, 8–9.
99. Anthony Lopez, Rose McDermott, and Michael Bang Petersen. "States in Mind: Evolution, Coalitional Psychology, and International Politics," *International Security* 36, no. 2 (Fall 2011): 81, 82.
100. Goody and Tambiah, *Bridewealth and Dowry*, 10.
101. Singerman, *The Economic Imperatives of Marriage*.
102. Kirk Semple, "Big Weddings Bring Afghans Joy, and Debt," *New York Times*, January 14, 2008.
103. Semple, "Big Weddings Bring Afghans Joy, and Debt."
104. Michael Slackman, "Stifled, Egypt's Young Turn to Islamic Fervor," *New York Times*, February 17, 2008.
105. Sommers and Schwartz, "Dowry and Division."
106. Singerman, *The Economic Imperatives of Marriage*, 34.
107. Singerman, *The Economic Imperatives of Marriage*, 34.
108. Slackman, "Stifled, Egypt's Young Turn to Islamic Fervor."
109. Singerman, *The Economic Imperatives of Marriage*, 12.
110. Richmond and Krause-Jackson, "Cows-for-Brides Inflation."

6. The Effects of the Syndrome, Part Two: Human, Economic, and Environmental Security

1. Jack Goldstone et al., "A Global Model for Predicting Political Instability," *American Journal of Political Science* 54, no. 1 (January 2010): 190–208.
2. Edward Schatz, *Modern Clan Politics* (Seattle: University of Washington Press, 2004), 30.
3. Abdul Al Lily, *The Bro Code of Saudi Culture* (San Bernardino, CA: Al Lily, 2016), 117.

4. Afghan Women's Writing Project ("Zohra N."), "I Just Keep Delivering," July 10, 2014, http://awwproject.org/2014/07/i-just-keep-delivering/.

5. Afghan Women's Writing Project ("Arezoo"), "Whatever Men Want Is What Happens," July 10, 2014, http://awwproject.org/2014/07/whatever-men-want-is-what-happens/.

6. Alberto Alesina, Benedetta Brioschi, and Eliana La Ferrara, "Violence Against Women: A Cross-Cultural Analysis for Africa" (NBER working paper no. 21901, National Bureau of Economic Research, Cambridge, MA, January 2016), 16, http://www.nber.org/papers/w21901.

7. Malcolm Potts and Thomas Hayden, *Sex and War* (Dallas, TX: Benbella Books, 2008), 91.

8. Richard Cincotta, "Africa's Reluctant Fertility Transition," *Current History* (May 2011), 188–189.

9. Noah Bricker and Mark Foley, "The Effect of Youth Demographics on Violence," 190–191.

10. Noah Bricker and Mark Foley, "The Effect of Youth Demographics on Violence: The Importance of the Labor Market," *International Journal of Conflict and Violence 7*, no. 1 (2013): 181.

11. Peter Goldstein, "Population and Gender in the MENA: Reflections from PRB's Farzaneh Roudi," *Population Reference Bureau*, September 1, 2016, https://www.prb.org/population-gender-mena-reflections/.

12. United Nations Population Fund, "Motherhood in Childhood: Facing the Challenge of Adolescent Pregnancy," UNFPA State of World Population 2013, https://www.unfpa.org/sites/default/files/pub-pdf/EN-SWOP2013-final.pdf.

13. Rachel Vogelstein, *Ending Child Marriage: How Elevating the Status of Girls Advances U.S. Foreign Policy Objectives* (New York: Council on Foreign Relations, May 14, 2013), 13–15.

14. Lakshmi Puri, "Gender Inequalities Affect Health Outcomes and Must Be Addressed Accordingly," *UNWomen*, May 30, 2013, http://www.unwomen.org/en/news/stories/2013/5/lakshmi-puri-gender-inequalities-affect-health-outcomes-and-must-be-addressed-accordingly.

15. Vogelstein, *Ending Child Marriage*, 16.

16. Vogelstein, *Ending Child Marriage*, 16.

17. Lauren Wolfe, "Why Are So Many Women Dying from Ebola?" *Foreign Policy*, August 20, 2014, http://foreignpolicy.com/2014/08/20/why-are-so-many-women-dying-from-ebola/.

18. John Aglionby, "Four Times as Many Women Died in Tsunami," *The Guardian*. March 26, 2005, https://www.theguardian.com/society/2005/mar/26/internationalaidanddevelopment.indianoceantsunamidecember2004.

19. Isaiah Esipisu, "Men and Women, Farming Together, Can Eradicate Hunger," *Inter Press Service*, September 1, 2012, http://www.nationofchange.org/men-and-women-farming-together-can-eradicate-hunger-1346512517; see also "Eat Better? Let Women Do the Work . . .," *The Economist*, July 11, 2012, http://www.economist.com/blogs/graphicdetail/2012/07/global-food-security.

20. PeaceFM, "Mahama Charges African Governments to Empower Women for Increased Productivity," September 12, 2017, https://www.peacefmonline.com/pages/politics/politics/201709/327272.php.

21. Food and Agriculture Organization of the United Nations, "Closing the Gender Gap in Agriculture," March 7, 2011, http://www.fao.org/news/story/en/item/52011/icode/.

22. Zakia Salime, "Women and the Right to Land in Morocco: The Sulaliyyates Movement," in *Women and Gender in Middle East Politics* (The Project on Middle East Political Science, May 10, 2016), 35, https://pomeps.org/wp-content/uploads/2016/05/POMEPS_Studies_19_Gender_Web.pdf.

23. Landesa, "Women's Land Rights," Resources: Infographics, December 21, 2015, https://www.landesa.org/resources/womens-land-rights-and-the-sustainable-development-goals/; Yacob A. Zereyesus, "Women's Empowerment in Agriculture and Household-Level Health in Northern Ghana: A Capability Approach," *Journal of International Development* 29 (2017): 899–918; Yacob A. Zereyesus et al., "Does Women's Empowerment in Agriculture Matter for Children's Health Status? Insights from Northern Ghana," *Social Indicators Research* 132, no. 3 (2017): 1265–1280.

24. Stanley Sharaunga, Maxwell Mudhara, and Ayalneh Bogale, "The Impact of 'Women's Empowerment in Agriculture' On Household Vulnerability to Food Insecurity in the KwaZulu-Natal Province," *Forum for Development Studies* 42, no. 2 (2015): 218.

25. McKinsey Global Institute, "How Advancing Women's Equality Can Add $12 Trillion to Global Growth," *Institute Report*, September 2015, http://www.mckinsey.com/global-themes/employment-and-growth/how-advancing-womens-equality-can-add-12-trillion-to-global-growth.

26. Quentin Wodon and Benedicte de la Briere, "Unrealized Potential: The High Cost of Gender Inequality in Earnings" (The Cost of Gender Inequality Notes Series, World Bank, Washington, DC, 2018), https://openknowledge.worldbank.org/bitstream/handle/10986/29865/126579-Public-on-5-30-18-WorldBank-GenderInequality-Brief-v13.pdf?sequence=1&isAllowed=y.

27. Wodon and de la Briere, "Unrealized Potential," 2.

28. Sri Mulyani Indrawati, "Discriminating Against Women Keeps Countries Poorer," *World Bank Voices* (blog), September 10, 2015, http://blogs.worldbank.org/voices/discriminating-against-women-keeps-countries-poorer?CID=ECR_TT_worldbank_EN_EXT&utm_content=bufferfb296&utm_medium=social&utm_source=facebook.com&utm_campaign=buffer.

29. United Nations Population Fund, "Motherhood in Childhood."

30. Alesina et al., "Violence Against Women," 1.

31. Kaniz Siddique, "Domestic Violence Against Women: Cost to the Nation," CARE Bangladesh, June 2011, http://www.carebangladesh.org/publication/Publication_5421518.pdf.

32. Vogelstein, *Ending Child Marriage*, 18.

33. Jack Goody and Stanley J. Tambiah, *Bridewealth and Dowry*, Cambridge Papers in Social Anthropology (Cambridge: Cambridge University Press, 1974), 10.

34. James Foreman-Peck and Peng Zhou, "Late Marriage as a Contributor to the Industrial Revolution in England," *Economic History Review* 71, no. 4 (2018): 1073–1099.

35. Stephan Klasen, "Low Schooling for Girls, Slower Growth for All? Cross-Country Evidence on the Effect of Gender Inequality in Education on Economic Development," *World Bank Economic Review* 16, no. 3 (2002): 345–373.

36. Vogelstein, *Ending Child Marriage*, 17.

37. Barbara Hertz and Gene Sperling, "What Works in Girls' Education: Evidence and Policies from the Developing World," *Council on Foreign Relations*, 2004. https://www.cfr.org/report/what-works-girls-education.

38. Elizabeth M. King, *Educating Girls and Women: Investing in Development* (Washington, DC: World Bank, 1990).

39. United Nations Development Program, "The Human Development Index," UNDP Human Development Reports, http://hdr.undp.org/en/content/human-development-index-hdi.

40. Namsuk Kim and Pedro Conceicao, "The Economic Crisis, Violent Conflict, and Human Development," *International Journal of Peace Studies* 15, no. 1 (2010): 29–43, https://www.gmu.edu/programs/icar/ijps/vol15_1/KimConceicao15n1.pdf.

41. Douglass North, John Wallis, and Barry Weingast, *Violence and Social Orders* (Cambridge: Cambridge University Press, 2009); see also Schatz, *Modern Clan Politics*.
42. Joseph Henrich, Robert Boyd, and Peter J. Richerson, "The Puzzle of Monogamous Marriage," *Philosophical Transactions of the Royal Society* 367, (2012): 657–669.
43. Clare Castillejo, "Gender Inequality and State Fragility in the Sahel" (FRIDE policy brief no. 204, *Fundación para las Relaciones Internacionales y el Diálogo Exterior*, June 2015), 3.
44. Ruchi Kumar, " 'Oh, God, Please Let Me Die': Treating Women Who Have Set Themselves on Fire in Afghanistan," *The Guardian*, June 26, 2017, https://www.theguardian.com /global-development-professionals-network/2017/jun/26/oh-god-please-let-me-die -treating-women-who-have-set-themselves-on-fire-in-afghanistan.
45. Rachel Vogelstein, *Ending Child Marriage: How Elevating the Status of Girls Advances US Foreign Policy Objectives*, New York: Council on Foreign Relations, May 14, 2013, 1, 21–22.

7. The Effects by the Numbers: The Empirical Relationship Between the Syndrome and National Outcomes

1. Kristen R. Monroe, ed., *The Evils of Polygyny: Rose McDermott* (Ithaca, NY: Cornell University, 2018), 23.
2. We note that as we finished the editing of this volume in June 2019, Canada appointed its first ever ambassador for women, peace, and security: Jacqueline O'Neill. Perhaps countries such as Canada will be prepared to utilize these findings.
3. Unfortunately, there is no such variable on whether women's agricultural labor is considered important; perhaps there is too much subnational variation to successfully operationalize this concept, but we hope others will take up the challenge.
4. Andrea Den Boer and Valerie M. Hudson, "Patrilineality, Son Preference, and Sex Selection in South Korea and Vietnam," *Population and Development Review* 43, no. 1 (2017): 119–147.
5. Monica Das Gupta, "Family Systems, Political Systems, and Asia's 'Missing Girls': The Construction of Son Preference and Its Unraveling" (World Bank, Washington, DC, December 2009), 15–16.
6. Das Gupta, "Family Systems, Political Systems," 18–19.
7. Mary Hartman, *The Household and the Making of History: A Subversive View of the Western Past* (Cambridge: Cambridge University Press, 2004).
8. Louisa Chiang, personal communication with Valerie Hudson, October 24, 2016.
9. Den Boer and Hudson, "Patrilineality, Son Preference."
10. Das Gupta, "Family Systems, Political Systems," 19.
11. "South Korea's Fertility Rate Is the Lowest in the World," *The Economist*, June 30, 2018, https://www.economist.com/asia/2018/06/30/south-koreas-fertility-rate-is-the-lowest -in-the-world.
12. Valerie Hudson et al., *Sex and World Peace* (New York: Columbia University Press, 2012).
13. Das Gupta, "Family Systems, Political Systems," 17.
14. Peggy Reeves Sanday, *Female Power and Male Dominance: On the Origins of Sexual Inequality* (Cambridge: Cambridge University Press, 1981).
15. Rina Chandran, "Hunger, Child Marriage, Prostitution: India Drought Hurts Women, Low-Caste Dalits More," *Thomson Reuters*, May 23, 2016, http://news.trust.org/item /20160523133537-m9pde/.

16. Andrea Den Boer, Valerie M. Hudson, and Jenny Russell, "China's Mismatched Bookends: A Tale of Birth Sex Ratios in South Korea and Vietnam" (paper presented at the International Studies Association Annual Conference. New Orleans, LA, February 2015), 18–21.

17. Das Gupta, "Family Systems, Political Systems," 6.

18. Steven Erlanger, "In Unruly Gaza, Clans Compete in Power Void," *New York Times*, October 17, 2005, http://www.nytimes.com/2005/10/17/international/middleeast/17 https://www.marxists.org/archive/marx/works/download/pdf/origin_family.pdf mideast.html.

19. Erlanger, "In Unruly Gaza."

20. Erlanger, "In Unruly Gaza."

21. "World Risk Report," Bundnis Entwicklung Hilft, http://weltrisikobericht.de/english/.

22. Variables that we considered but that had to be dropped because of this stipulation included number of unique land borders, and two of the component parts of the aggregated fractionalization score (i.e., racial and linguistic fractionalization).

23. Syndrome/Urbanization 2015 (−.496, significance .000), Syndrome/Number of Land Neighbors (−.163, significance .031), Syndrome/Terrain 2014 (−.167, significance .028), Syndrome/Religious Fractionalization 2003 (−.016, significance .839), and Syndrome/ Ethnic Fractionalization 2003 (.520, significance .000). The Syndrome is positively and significantly associated with Ethnic Fractionalization, and negatively and significantly associated with Urbanization, both of which findings are in harmony with our theoretical framework.

24. World Bank, "World Development Indicators," 2015, http://databank.worldbank.org/data.

25. Samuel Huntington, *The Clash of Civilizations and the Remaking of World Order* (New York: Simon and Schuster, 1996).

26. It was necessary to collapse these three categories of Huntington's because of their very low N sizes, but we recognize the conceptual difficulties in doing so.

27. Donna Lee Bowen and Valerie M. Hudson, "Colonial Heritage Status Coding, 2017" Spreadsheet reproduced in appendix II of this volume.

28. Ikechi Mbeoji, "The Civilised Self and the Barbaric Other: Imperial Delusions of Order and the Challenges of Human Security," *Third World Quarterly* 27, no. 5 (2007): 855–869.

29. World Bank, "World Development Indicators," 2015; World Bank, "World Development Indicators," 2014, http://databank.worldbank.org/data.

30. Thomas Homer-Dixon, "On the Threshold: Environmental Changes as Causes of Acute Conflict," *International Security* 16, no. 1 (Fall 1991): 76–116; Steve Pickering, "Determinism in the Mountains: The Ongoing Belief in the Bellicosity of 'Mountain People,'" *The Economics of Peace and Security* 6, no. 2 (2011): 20–25; Stephen A. Emerson, "Desert Insurgency: Lessons from the Third Tuareg Rebellion." *Small Wars and Insurgencies* 22, no. 4 (2011): 669–687; Francis Fukuyama, *Political Order and Political Decay* (New York: Farrar, Straus, and Giroux, 2014).

31. Wikipedia, "List of Countries and Territories by Land Borders," 2018, https:// en.wikipedia.org/wiki/List_of_countries_and_territories_by_land_borders; Harvey Starr and G. Dale Thomas, "The Nature of Borders and International Conflict: Revisiting Hypotheses on Territory," *International Studies Quarterly* 49, no. 1 (March 2005): 123–139.

32. Harvey Starr and Benjamin Most, "Contagion and Border Effects on Contemporary African Conflict," *Comparative Political Studies* 16, no. 1 (1983): 92–117.

33. Alberto Alesina et al., "Fractionalization," *Journal of Economic Growth* 8, no. 2 (June 2013): 155–194.

34. James Fearon and David Laitin, "Ethnicity, Insurgency, and Civil War," *American Political Science Review* 97, no. 1 (2003): 75–90; Randall Blimes, "The Indirect Effect of Ethnic Heterogeneity on the Likelihood of Civil War Onset," *Journal of Conflict Resolution* 50, no. 4 (2006): 536–547.

35. Alesina, "Fractionalization," 155–194.

36. Jonathan Fox, "The Ride of Religious Nationalism and Conflict: Ethnic Conflict and Revolutionary Wars, 1945–2001," *Journal of Peace Research* 41, no. 6 (2004): 715–731; Mark Juergensmeyer, *Terror in the Mind of God: The Global Rise of Religious Violence*, 4th ed. (Oakland: University of California Press, 2017).

37. These nations are Central African Republic, Libya, Syria, and Vanuatu. Syria's imputation was actually 12.5, which was rounded up to 13 for input into the database to allow mapping to be possible.

38. We chose to use Freedom House rather than the Polity dataset because of its larger sample size.

39. Brynne Townley, "Women in Rwanda: The Truth About Gender Equality," *WomanStats* (blog), February 13, 2017, https://womanstats.wordpress.com/2018/02/13/women-in -rwanda-the-truth-about-gender-equality/.

40. Daniela Donno and Bruce Russett, "Islam, Authoritarianism, and Female Empowerment: What Are the Linkages?" *World Politics* 56 (July 2004): 582–607.

41. As mentioned earlier, the bivariate correlation between urbanization and GDP per capita PPP when that latter variable is *not* log transformed is .662 (p <.000).

42. Yu-Ming Liou and Paul Musgrave, "Oil, Autocratic Survival, and the Gendered Resource Curse: When Inefficient Policy Is Politically Expedient," *International Studies Quarterly* 60, no. 3 (2016): 440–456.

43. We also analyzed the variable Total Dependency Ratio. This ratio gives the ratio of the population between birth and ten years old plus those over sixty five, per one hundred population ages twenty to sixty-four. We excluded this variable from further analysis because it was too closely correlated with Total Fertility Rate.

44. Richard Cincotta, "Africa's Reluctant Fertility Transition," *Current History* (May 2011): 184–190.

45. Noah Bricker and Mark Foley, "The Effect of Youth Demographics on Violence: The Importance of the Labor Market," *International Journal of Conflict and Violence* 7, no. 1 (2013): 179–194.

46. Kate Manne, *Down Girl: The Logic of Misogyny* (Oxford: Oxford University Press, 2018).

47. Monroe, *The Evils of Polygyny*, 23. McDermott is making this comment with reference to her empirical results concerning polygyny, which is a subcomponent of the Syndrome.

48. Christine E. Bose, "Patterns of Global Gender Inequalities and Regional Gender Regimes," *Gender and Society* 29, no. 6 (December 2015): 767–791.

49. Khandis Blake, personal communication with Valerie Hudson, October 21, 2018.

8. Change: Historical Successes and Failures

1. Malcolm Potts and Thomas Hayden, *Sex and War* (Dallas, TX: Benbella Books, 2008), 25–26, 97, 301.

2. Anna Tornkvist, "Sweden Stands Out in Domestic Violence Study," *TheLocal.se*, March 5, 2014, http://www.thelocal.se/20140305/sweden-out-top-in-eu-domestic-violence -league.

3. We believe a second reservoir is the legacy of inequitable law disfavoring women, which teaches members of the society that women may be treated worse with justification. Notice, for example, how even in the Russia of 2019, a woman can be a sailor, but she is forbidden by law from being the captain of a commercial sea vessel.

4. Richard Wrangham and Dale Peterson, *Demonic Males: Apes and the Origins of Human Violence* (New York: Mariner Books, 1996), 125, 198–199.

5. Jack Weatherford, *Genghis Khan and the Making of the Modern World* (New York: Crown, 2004), 52–53.

6. Frederick Denny, "Ummah in the Constitution of Medina," *Journal of Near Eastern Studies* 36, no. 1 (January 1977): 39–47. http://www.jstor.org/stable/544125.

7. Edward Schatz, *Modern Clan Politics* (Seattle: University of Washington Press, 2004); Bassam Tibi, "The Simultaneity of the Unsimultaneous: Old Tribes and Imposed Nation-State in the Modern Middle East," in *Tribes and States Formation in the Middle East*, ed. Philip S. Khoury and Joseph Kostiner (Los Angeles: University of California Press, 1990), 127–152.

8. Kathleen Collins, "The Logic of Clan Politics: Evidence from the Central Asian Trajectories," *World Politics* 56, no. 2 (2004): 260.

9. Collins, "The Logic of Clan Politics," 245.

10. Mark S. Weiner, *The Rule of the Clan: What an Ancient Form of Social Organization Reveals About the Future of Individual Freedom* (New York: Farrar, Straus and Giroux, 2013), 129.

11. Weiner, *The Rule of the Clan*, 13.

12. David Jacobson, *Of Virgins and Martyrs: Women and Sexuality in Global Conflict* (Baltimore, MD: Johns Hopkins University Press, 2013), 198.

13. Jack Goody, *The European Family* (New York: Wiley-Blackwell, 2000), 10.

14. Goody, *The European Family*, 28–29.

15. Goody, *The European Family*, 51.

16. Goody, *The European Family*, 52.

17. Goody, *The European Family*, 44.

18. Potts and Hayden, *Sex and War*, 309. Note how crucial and how effective the role of Christianity proved, as noted by Korotayev and Bondarenko:

    > The total absence of the polygyny in the Christian part of the Circum-Mediterranean region (but not in its Moslem part) could be hardly explained by anything else but by the strict prohibition of the polygyny by the Christian Church . . . pre-Christian Germans, Celts, and Slavs were quite polygynous in the pre-Christian period. Hence, the formation of the zone of uninterrupted monogamy in Europe could be hardly attributed to anything but the Christianization.

    Andrey Korotayev and Dmitri Bondarenko, "Polygyny and Democracy: A Cross-Cultural Comparison," *Cross-Cultural Research* 34, no. 1 (2000): 204.

19. Avner Greif, "Family Structure, Institutions, and Growth: The Origins and Implications of Western Corporations," *American Economic Review* 96, no. 2 (2006): 308, 310, http://web.stanford.edu/~avner/Greif_Papers/2006%20AER%20Families%20and %20Corporations.pdf.

20. Greif, "Family Structure, Institutions, and Growth," 311.

21. Weiner points out that Muhammad attempted the same:

    > After he arrived in Medina, Muhammad brought the clans together for a historic agreement known as the Constitution of Medina, which united fractured elements of the political community under a common set of principles. In this

respect, the *shahadah* also contains an ideal of political organization that transcends tribalism. It imagines the early Islamic state that Muhammad and the first caliphs would forge amidst the Arabian tribes and that would enforce the new principles of Islamic law.

Once Muhammad had united the tribes (through the *riddah*, or wars of apostasy), this "channeled the power that the tribes of Arabia had previously used to fight amongst themselves," enabling expansion. But Weiner notes that some tribal elements remained essential to Islamic rule:

> In constructing the new Islamic state, Muhammad and his successors did more than simply honor particular tribal leaders whose alliances they sought. They used the tribal form itself for Islamic purposes. Lineage heads were actively incorporated into the apparatus of the new state. Military payroll was not distributed centrally but instead through clan elders, thus making duty to the Islamic state and duty to the clan one and the same. Tax agents were drawn from tribal ranks. (Weiner, *The Rule of the Clan*, 154, 155, 157).

22. Jack Goody, *The Development of Marriage and Family in Europe* (Cambridge: Cambridge University Press, 1983), 42.
23. The Church "rectified" the asymmetrical right to divorce by men and women by forbidding *everyone*—men and women—from divorcing. By the twelfth century, even nonconsummation of a marriage was no longer acceptable grounds for divorce.
24. Goody, *The Development of Marriage and Family in Europe*, 45–46.
25. Goody, *The Development of Marriage and Family in Europe*, 59, 67.
26. Goody, *The Development of Marriage and Family in Europe*, 155. The Church endeavored to prevent these lineages from arising among its own ranks through mandatory celibacy, and enforcing that rule was quite a struggle as well. Coontz notes that "not until 1139 did canon law completely forbid clerical marriage," and that before that time most clerics were married. Stephanie Coontz, *Marriage, A History* (New York: Penguin Books, 2005), 106.
27. Francis Fukuyama, *The Origins of Political Order* (New York: Farrar, Straus, and Giroux, 2011), 209.
28. Coontz, *Marriage, A History*, 101.
29. Coontz, *Marriage, A History*.
30. Goody, *The European Family*, 38.
31. Goody, *The European Family*, 52.
32. Also important to Goody is that in northwest Europe one often found "retirement contracts for the senior generation and public provision for the poor." Goody, *The European Family*, 106. This is important for diluting the need for sons to provide for elderly parents in a context in which sons are expected to amass greater wealth than daughters.
33. Goody, *The Development of Marriage and Family in Europe*, 95.
34. Fukuyama, *The Origins of Political Order*, 255.
35. Fukuyama, *The Origins of Political Order*, 253.
36. Fukuyama, *The Origins of Political Order*, 245.
37. Fukuyama, *The Origins of Political Order*, 231.
38. Fukuyama, *The Origins of Political Order*, 248, xiii.
39. Fukuyama, *The Origins of Political Order*, 247.
40. See also James Foreman-Peck and Peng Zhou, "Late Marriage as a Contributor to the Industrial Revolution in England," *Economic History Review* 71, no. 4 (2018): 1073–1099.

41. John Hajnal, "Two Kinds of Preindustrial Household Formation Systems," *Population and Development Review* 8 (1982): 476.
42. Mary Hartman dates later marriage in northwestern Europe at least as far back as the 1200s. She notes that in the 1600–1700s in England and France, the average age of marriage for women was twenty-five or twenty-six, and average age of marriage for men was twenty-seven or twenty-eight. Hartman, *The Household and the Making of History.*
43. John Hajnal, "European Marriage Patterns in Perspective: The Uniqueness of the European Pattern," in *Population in History*, ed. D. V. Glass and D. Eversley (London: Edward Arnold, 1965), 101–143.
44. Jack Goody and Stanley J. Tambiah, *Bridewealth and Dowry*, Cambridge Papers in Social Anthropology (Cambridge: Cambridge University Press, 1974), 37–38.
45. Goody and Tambiah, *Bridewealth and Dowry*, 54.
46. Hartman, *The Household and the Making of History.*
47. Goody and Tambiah, *Bridewealth and Dowry*, 10.
48. Jacobson, *Of Virgins and Martyrs*, 41, 43.
49. Fukuyama, *The Origins of Political Order*, 233.
50. Charlotte Stanford, "Women and the Building Trades in Henry VIII's England" (presentation to the Women's Studies Program, Brigham Young University, Provo, UT, September 14, 2017).
51. Hartman, *The Household and the Making of History*, 179, 192, 206, 215.
52. Fukuyama, *The Origins of Political Order*, 234.
53. Fukuyama, *The Origins of Political Order*, 235.
54. Greif, "Family Structure, Institutions, and Growth," 308.
55. Foreman-Peck and Zhou, "Late Marriage as a Contributor," 1073–1099.
56. Coontz, *Marriage, A History*, 114, 128.
57. Mark Dyble et al., "Sex Equality Can Explain the Unique Social Structure of Hunter-Gatherer Bands," *Science* 348, no. 6236 (2015): 796–798.
58. Hartman, *The Household and the Making of History*, 229.
59. Hartman, *The Household and the Making of History*, 229.
60. Hartman, *The Household and the Making of History*, 20.
61. Hartman, *The Household and the Making of History*, 221.
62. Hartman, *The Household and the Making of History*, 221, 222, 224, 227.
63. Hartman, *The Household and the Making of History*, 221.
64. Hartman, *The Household and the Making of History*, 194.
65. Hartman, *The Household and the Making of History*, 194.
66. Hartman, *The Household and the Making of History* 209, 210.
67. Hartman, *The Household and the Making of History* 270.
68. Goody, *The Development of Marriage and Family in Europe*, 155.
69. Fukuyama, *The Origins of Political Order*, 236.
70. Fukuyama, *The Origins of Political Order*, 239.
71. A less materially based variant of the idea that women are crucial postulates that romantic love between men and women is the key to dismantling the system and the Syndrome, or as Mark Weiner puts it, "love is the emblem of freedom." Weiner, *The Rule of the Clan*, 93. One can trace this from Jane Austen's *Pride and Prejudice* all the way to modern fiction, such as Derek Miller's *The Girl in Green*. His main character, Arwood Hobbes, explains in the middle of the Iraqi desert,

    The most significant of [Western] ideas? Romantic love. It is the most disruptive and transformative power in the history of the world. Terrorists are powerless against it. We support it, and they will lose. . . . Think of *Romeo and Juliet.*

"Two houses, both alike in dignity," we are first told. Why? Because the houses are the power, and dignity is the currency of that realm. We need to know this so we can understand that what keeps the lovers apart is not a higher justice but a higher power. And then here come these two children who defy and disrupt the underlying social order, and who die for their efforts because their humanity cannot survive in concert with that world. The moment Shakespeare makes our sympathies go to them, the system is overturned. Personal love is very disruptive to tribal thinking. And what of Juliet? A young woman? Romantic love empowered her to be equal to a man, to choose her own destiny, to make her own choices, to be in absolute control over her own body and her own heart. It is the first truly feminist story. It validated love, and fueled a revolution. These people, this ISIL, we should fight them, yes. We can bomb them, yes. But that's not a strategy for victory. This is a *guerra fria*. Victory lies in replacing their social order, which is why they are afraid, and they should be. And our secret weapon? It is not drones. Quite the opposite. It is women. We should free them, educate them, give them power—put a Juliet in every village. They will change the world. This is why Boko Haram is so afraid of the girls and abducts them, why the Taliban will not educate them, why ISIL murders those in Western clothes and who think freely. Women. They are how the West will win. They are how love will prevail.

Derek Miller, *The Girl in Green* (New York: Houghton Mifflin Harcourt, 2017), 246–247. We would say instead that it's not how "the West will win"—after all, *Romeo and Juliet* was set in the West. Rather, it is how the Syndrome is overthrown and the whole world wins.

72. Goody, *The European Family*, 62.
73. Jacobson, *Of Virgins and Martyrs*, 11, 12.
74. Jacobson, *Of Virgins and Martyrs*, 48.
75. Fukuyama, *The Origins of Political Order*, 241.
76. Fukuyama, *The Origins of Political Order*, 229, 21.
77. Adrienne Edgar, *Tribal Nation: The Making of Soviet Turkmenistan* (Princeton, NJ: Princeton University Press, 2004), 221.
78. Even universal health care made no difference. See discussion in Schatz, *Modern Clan Politics*, 53ff.
79. Edgar, *Tribal Nation*, 248.
80. Edgar, *Tribal Nation*, 248.
81. Edgar, *Tribal Nation*, 248.
82. Edgar, *Tribal Nation*, 249, 256.
83. Edgar, *Tribal Nation*; see also Adrienne Edgar, "Emancipation of the Unveiled: Turkmen Women Under Soviet Rule, 1924–29," *The Russian Review* 62 (January 2003): 132–49; Adrienne Edgar, "Bolshevism, Patriarchy, and the Nation: The Soviet 'Emancipation' of Muslim Women in Pan-Islamic Perspective," *Slavic Review* 65, no. 2(2006): 252–272; Adrienne Edgar, "Marriage, Modernity, and the 'Friendship of Nations': Interethnic Intimacy in Post-war Central Asia in Comparative Perspective," *Central Asian Survey* 26, no. 4 (2007): 581–599.
84. Gregory J. Massell, *The Surrogate Proletariat: Moslem Women and Revolutionary Strategies in Soviet Central Asia, 1919–1929* (Princeton, NJ: Princeton University Press, 1974), 201.
85. Sophia Wilson, "Human Rights and Law Enforcement in the Post-Soviet World: Or How and Why Judges and Police Bend the Law" (lecture, Brigham Young University, Provo, UT, November 12, 2010).

86. Elizabeth A. Constantine, "Practical Consequences of Soviet Policy and Ideology for Gender in Central Asia and Contemporary Reversal," in *Everyday Life in Central Asia: Past and Present*, ed. Jeff Shadeo and Russell Zanca (Bloomington: Indiana University Press, 2007), 115–126.

87. Edgar, "Bolshevism, Patriarchy, and the Nation," 255, 256.

88. Louise Grogan, "Patrilocality and Human Capital Formation: Evidence from Central Asia," *Economics of Transition* 15, no. 4 (2007): 685–705. Post-Soviet Central Asia is also experiencing an influx of Saudi money and Wahhabi missionaries, which we suggest also fuels regress on the rights women enjoyed as Soviet citizens; see Sadie Whitelocks, "The Soviet Times were Good," *Daily Mail*, June 30, 2017, http://www.dailymail.co.uk /travel/travel_news/article-4632216/Kyrgyzstan-local-reveals-life-good-USSR-rule.html.

89. Monica Das Gupta, "Family Systems, Political Systems, and Asia's 'Missing Girls': The Construction of Son Preference and Its Unraveling" (World Bank, Washington, DC, December 2009), 16.

90. Das Gupta, "Family Systems, Political Systems," 18.

91. Das Gupta, "Family Systems, Political Systems," 18.

92. Jie Fan, Thomas Heberer, and Wolfgang Taubmann, *Rural China: Economic and Social Change in the Late Twentieth Century* (New York: M. E. Sharpe, 2006), 258.

93. Geoffrey Murray, *China: The Next Superpower, Dilemmas in Change and Continuity* (New York: St Martin's Press, 1998), 146.

94. Fukuyama, *The Origins of Political Order*, 61.

95. Katherine Young, "Introduction," in *Today's Woman in World Religions*, ed. by Arvind Sharma (New York: State University of New York Press, 1994), 35.

96. Again, this is one of the reasons we focus not on patriarchy but on the Syndrome's components, which are the roots of patriarchy.

97. Das Gupta, "Family Systems, Political Systems," 17.

98. Andrea Den Boer and Valerie M. Hudson, "Patrilineality, Son Preference, and Sex Selection in South Korea and Vietnam," *Population and Development Review* 43, no. 1 (2017): 119–147.

99. Den Boer and Hudson, "Patrilineality, Son Preference"; the South Korean case study was adapted from this article.

100. Seung Gwon Kim et al., *The 2012 National Survey on Fertility, Family Health and Welfare* [in Korean] (Seoul: Korea Institute for Health and Social Affairs, 2012).

101. Sang-Hun Choe, "South Koreans Rethink Preference for Sons," *New York Times*, November 28, 2007, http://www.nytimes.com/2007/11/28/world/asia/28iht-sex.1.8509372 .html?_r=1&; also Sang-Hun Choe, "As Families Change, Korea's Elderly Are Turning to Suicide," *New York Times*, February 16, 2013, http://www.nytimes.com/2013/02/17 /world/asia/in-korea-changes-in-societyand-family-dynamics-drive-rise-in-elderly -suicides.html?pagewanted=all.

102. Daniel Goodkind, "Do Parents Prefer Sons in North Korea?" *Studies in Family Planning* 30, no.3 (September 1999): 212.

103. Youngsook Cho. 2000. "South Korea," in *The First CEDAW Impact Study*, ed. Marilou McPhedran, Susan Bazilli, Moana Erickson, and Andrew Byrnes, 187–202 (Toronto: York University Centre for Feminist Studies).

104. Uhn Cho, "Gender Inequality and Patriarchal Order Recontexualized," in *Contemporary South Korean Society: A Critical Perspective*, ed. Hee-Yeon Cho, Lawrence Surendra, and Hyo-Je Cho (London and New York: Routledge, 2013), 18–27.

105. Sanghui Nam, "The Women's Movement and the Transformation of the Family Law in South Korea. Interactions Between Local, National and Global Structures," *European Journal of East Asian Studies* 9, no. 1 (2010): 77.

106. Nam, "The Women's Movement."
107. Mi-Kyung Cho, "Recent Reform of Korean Family Law" (conference paper, Ajou University, Korea), http://www.law2.byu.edu/isfl/saltlakeconference/papers/isflpdfs/CHO.pdf.
108. Rosa Kim, "The Legacy of Institutionalized Gender Inequality in South Korea: The Family Law," *Boston College Third World Law Journal* 14, no. 1 (1994): 144–162, http://lawdigitalcommons.bc.edu/cgi/viewcontent.cgi?article=1269&context=twl.
109. Pil-Wha Chang and Eun-shil Kim, *Women's Experiences and Feminist Practices in South Korea* (Seoul, South Korea: Ewha Womans University Press, 2005).
110. Nam, "The Women's Movement ," 77.
111. Convention on the Elimination of All Forms of Discrimination Against Women, "Consideration of Reports Submitted Under Article 18 of the Convention on the Elimination of All Forms of Discrimination Against Women," *Sixth Periodic Report of States Parties: Republic of Korea*, CEDAW/C/KOR/6, March 5, 2007.
112. Seung Gwon Kim et al., *The 2003 National Survey on Fertility and Family Health* [in Korean] (Seoul: Korea Institute for Health and Social Affairs, 2004), Table 8–8. [김승권, 조애저, 김유경, 박세경, 이건우 (2003) 2003년 전국 출산력 및 가족보건 실태조사연구 보고서. 서울:한국보건사회연구원.]
113. Nam, "The Women's Movement," 77.
114. CEDAW, "Consideration of Reports Submitted Under Article 18."
115. CEDAW, "Consideration of Reports Submitted Under Article 18."
116. "Marital Rape," *Korea Times.* January 18, 2009, http://m.koreatimes.co.kr/pages/article.asp?newsIdx=38045.
117. Erin Hye-Won Kim and Philip J. Cook, "The Continuing Importance of Children in Relieving Elder Poverty: Evidence from Korea," *Ageing and Society* 31, no. 6 (2011): 953–976.
118. KOSTAT, *2005 Statistics on the Aged*, October 21, 2005, www.kostat.go.kr.
119. KOSTAT, *Statistics Korea, 2012 Statistics on the Aged*, September 27, 2012, www.kostat.go.kr. Evidence of shifting attitudes toward elder care can be found in the recent phenomenon of a ballooning elderly suicide rate in South Korea. Newspapers carry harrowing tales of elderly South Koreans who drained savings to facilitate children's success, expecting that the children would in turn care for their parents—only for the parents to find themselves abandoned. Choe, "South Koreans Rethink Preference for Sons."
120. KOSTAT, *Statistics Korea, Summary Results of 2014 Social Survey.* November 27, 2014, www.kostat.go.kr.
121. Woojin Chung and Monica Das Gupta, "The Decline of Son Preference in South Korea: The Roles of Development and Public Policy," *Population and Development Review* 33, no. 4 (2007): 757–783.
122. In 2006, 67 percent of those age sixty-five and over believed that it was the responsibility of family members to take care of the elderly, but that figure had dropped to 38 percent in 2010—the majority of elderly parents are now working to higher ages and have plans in place to ensure their economic well-being after retirement. KOSTAT, *Statistics Korea, 2011 Statistics on the Aged.*
123. Sung Yong Lee, "How did Son-Preference Disappear in Korea? Based on the Perspective of the Value of Children" (paper presented at the Sociology of Population Side Meeting Program, Busan, South Korea, 2013).
124. Lee, "How Did Son-Preference Disappear in Korea?"
125. Goody, *The Development of Marriage and Family in Europe*, 142.
126. Avraham Ebenstein, "Patrilocality and Missing Women," Hebrew University of Jerusalem, April 2014, 7, 20, http://in.bgu.ac.il/en/humsos/Econ/Documents/seminars/October%2030-2014.pdf.

127. Theodore D. Kemper, *Social Structure and Testosterone: Explorations of the Socio-Bio-Social Chain* (New Brunswick, NJ: Rutgers University Press, 1990), 4. Indeed, Kemper asserts this may happen not just socially, but physiologically. He states, "Women who are subordinated in their marriages, rarely winning victories in their familiar interactions and frequently defeated, will ordinarily have very low levels of T and when pregnant, will contribute very little placental T by which to affect female offspring. Hence, male dominance in marriage is likely to be associated with relatively less dominant [female] offspring" (164). He suggests that when women are no longer subordinated in marriage, they will produce more dominant female offspring than their foremothers; daughters who will be far less likely to acquiesce to the Syndrome. We find that a very interesting thought.

9. Conclusion: Contemporary Applications

1. William R. Rice, "Sexually Antagonistic Male Adaptation Triggered by Experimental Arrest of Female Evolution," *Nature* 381, (1996): 232–234.
2. Patricia Adair Gowaty, "Sexual Natures: How Feminism Changed Evolutionary Biology," *Signs: Journal of Women in Culture and Society* 28, no. 3 (2003): 63.
3. Gowaty, "Sexual Natures."
4. William R. Rice, "Dangerous Liaisons," *Proceedings of the National Academy of Sciences* 97 (2000): 12953–12955.
5. Richard Petts, Kevin Shafer, and Lee Essig, "Does Adherence to Masculine Norms Shape Fathering Behavior?" *Journal of Marriage and Family* 80, no. 3 (June 2018): 704–720.
6. Steven C. Caton, "Anthropological Theories of Tribe and State Formation in the Middle East: Ideology and the Semiotics of Power," in *Tribes and States Formation in the Middle East*, ed. Philip S. Khoury and Joseph Kostiner (Los Angeles: University of California Press, 1990), 82.
7. Allison Brysk, *The Struggle for Freedom from Fear: Contesting Violence Against Women at the Frontiers of Globalization* (New York: Oxford University Press, 2018).
8. David Jacobson, *Of Virgins and Martyrs: Women and Sexuality in Global Conflict.* (Baltimore, MD: Johns Hopkins University Press, 2013), 115. Note also that the Convention on the Elimination of All Forms of Discrimination Against Women (CEDAW) has been ratified by 189 nation-states. It's hard to see, then, how its principles concerning basic human rights for women could constitute cultural imperialism.
9. Kristen R. Monroe, ed., *The Evils of Polygyny: Rose McDermott* (Ithaca, NY: Cornell University, 2018), 93, 94.
10. Mark Weiner, *The Rule of the Clan: What an Ancient Form of Social Organization Reveals about the Future of Individual Freedom* (New York: Farrar, Straus and Giroux, 2013), 159.
11. Adrienne Edgar, *Tribal Nation: The Making of Soviet Turkmenistan* (Princeton, NJ: Princeton University Press, 2004), 260.
12. Gaia Pianigiani, "Breaking Up the Family as a Way to Break Up the Mob," *New York Times*, February 10, 2017, https://www.nytimes.com/2017/02/10/world/europe/breaking -up-the-family-as-a-way-to-break-up-the-mob.html.
13. Jordan Barnes, "Immigrant Children Born in Danish 'Ghettos' Will Be Separated from Their Families from the Age of One for 25 Hours per Week to Teach Them 'Danish Values' and the Language," *Daily Mail*, July 2, 2018, http://www.dailymail .co.uk/news/article-5909273/Immigrant-kids-Danish-ghettos-separated-families -age-ONE-25-hours-week.html.

14. Albania, Algeria, Angola, Argentina, Armenia, Azerbaijan, Barbados, Belize, Benin, Botswana, Brazil, Chad, Chile, Costa Rica, Democratic Republic of the Congo, Djibouti, Egypt, Equatorial Guinea, Eritrea, Ethiopia, Fiji, Gambia, Guatemala, Guinea, Guyana, India, Israel, Jordan, Kenya, Kyrgyzstan, Liberia, Madagascar, Malawi, Maldives, Mauritania, Morocco, Mozambique, Oman, Paraguay, Peru, Romania, Rwanda, Sierra Leone, South Korea, South Sudan, Tajikistan, Togo, Tunisia, Turkey, Turkmenistan, Vietnam, and Zimbabwe.

15. Bangladesh, Denmark, Ecuador, El Salvador, Georgia, Honduras, Norway, and Panama.

16. Hannah McNeish, "Malawi's Fearsome Chief, Terminator of Child Marriages," *Al-Jazeera*, May 16, 2016, https://www.aljazeera.com/indepth/features/2016/03/malawi-fearsome -chief-terminator-child-marriages-160316081809603.html; UNWomen, "Malawi Chief Annuls 330 Child Marriages," September 17, 2015, http://www.unwomen.org/en/news /stories/2015/9/malawi-chief-annuls-330-child-marriages; Sarah Ruiz-Grossman, "How This Female Chief Broke Up 850 Child Marriages in Malawi," *HuffPost*, April 1, 2016, https://www.huffingtonpost.com/entry/woman-chief-breaks-up-850-child-marriages -in-malawi_us_56fd51c2e4b0a06d580510da?ir=Good+News&).

17. USAID, "Ending Child Marriage and Meeting the Needs of Married Children: The USAID Vision for Action," 2012, https://www.usaid.gov/sites/default/files/documents /1870/USAID%20Ending%20Child%20Marriage%202012.pdf.

18. U.S. Department of State "Opening Statement on Global Efforts to End Child Marriage," by Ambassador Catherine M. Russell, September 14, 2016, https://2009-2017.state.gov /s/gwi/rls/rem/2016/261970.htm.

19. Rebecca Savransky, "State Department Cutting Language on Women's Rights Discrimination in Annual Report," *The Hill*, February 22, 2018, http://thehill.com/homenews /administration/375009-state-department-cutting-language-on-womens-rights -discrimination-in.

20. McDermott et al., "Attitudes Toward Polygyny: Experimental Evidence from Six Countries," in *The Evils of Polygyny: Rose McDermott*, ed. Kristen R. Monroe (Ithaca, NY: Cornell University, 2018), 97–122.

21. Monroe, *The Evils of Polygyny*.

22. Veronique Hertrich, "Is Polygamy Weakening? Diversity and Trends in Africa During the Past 50 Years," French Institute for Demographic Studies, http://paa2007.princeton .edu/papers/71630.

23. Monroe, *The Evils of Polygyny*, 22.

24. "Muslim Women Hail Triple Talaq Bill, Seek Ban on Polygamy," *Times of India*, December 29, 2017, https://timesofindia.indiatimes.com/india/muslim-women-hail -triple-talaq-bill-seek-ban-on-polygamy/articleshow/62298393.cms.

25. Anna Sussman, "Ugandan Adultery Law Curbs Effects of Polygamy," *Women's eNews*, June 24, 2007, https://womensenews.org/2007/06/ugandan-adultery-law-curbs-effects -polygamy/.

26. Anthony Ogbonna, "Law to Ban Polygamy: There's a Connection Between Polygamy, Poverty, and Terrorism—Emir of Kano," *Vanguard*, February 20, 2017, https://www .vanguardngr.com/2017/02/law-ban-polygamy-theres-connection-polygamy-poverty -terrorism-emir-kano/.

27. Catherine Sasman, "Polygamy to be Outlawed," *The Namibian*, April 12, 2012, https:// www.namibian.com.na/index.php?id=93899&page=archive-read.

28. Ogbonna, "Law to Ban Polygamy."

29. "The Link Between Polygamy and War," *The Economist*, December 19, 2017. https://www .economist.com/christmas-specials/2017/12/19/the-link-between-polygamy-and-war.

30. Punch, "Inheritance Sharing: Customary Law Fuelling Disharmony in Nigerian Families," May 19, 2016, http://punchng.com/inheritance-sharing-customary-laws-fuelling -disharmony-nigerian-families/.

31. Punch, "Inheritance Sharing."

32. Seung-Yun Oh et al., "The Decline of Polygyny: An Interpretation," Santa Fe Institute, 2017, https://sfi-edu.s3.amazonaws.com/sfi-edu/production/uploads/working_paper /pdf/2017-12-037-rev_fedae8.pdf.

33. "The Link Between Polygamy and War."

34. Oh et al., "The Decline of Polygyny"; Michèle Tertilt "Polygyny, Fertility, and Savings," *Journal of Political Economy* 113, no. 6 (2005): 1341–1371; Lena Edlund and Nils-Petter Lagerlöf, "Polygyny and Its Discontents: Paternal Age and Human Capital Accumulation," Columbia University Academic Commons, 2012, https://doi.org/10.7916/D8988GCB, https://academiccommons.columbia.edu/catalog/ac:155593.

35. United Nations Human Rights Committee, "General Comment No. 28: Equality of Rights Between Men and Women," Article 3 of the International Covenant on Civil and Political Rights, U.N. Doc. CCPR/C/21/Rev.1/Add.10 (2000), http://hrlibrary.umn.edu /gencomm/hrcom28.htm.

36. Vanessa Von Struensee, "The Contribution of Polygamy to Women's Oppression and Impoverishment," *Murdoch University Electronic Journal of Law*, 2005, http://www .austlii.edu.au/au/journals/MurUEJL/2005/2.html#Heading227.

37. UN Committee on the Elimination of Discrimination Against Women (CEDAW), *CEDAW General Recommendation No. 21: Equality in Marriage and Family Relations*, 1994. available at: http://www.refworld.org/docid/48abd52c0.html.

38. Supreme Court of British Columbia, "Reference Re: Section 293 of the Criminal Code of Canada, 2011 BCSC 1588 (CanLII) (2011), https://www.canlii.org/en/bc/bcsc/doc/2011 /2011bcsc1588/2011bcsc1588.html#.

39. Equality Now, "Ending Sex Discrimination in the Law," January 2015. https://www .equalitynow.org/sites/default/files/B+20_Report_EN.pdf.

40. Samy Magdy, "Egypt's Top Cleric Calls Polygamy 'Injustice,' Draws Debate," *US News and World Report*, March 3, 2019, https://www.usnews.com/news/world/articles/2019 -03-03/egypts-top-cleric-stirs-controversy-with-polygamy-remarks.

41. United Nations, "International Covenant on Economic, Social, and Cultural Rights," 1967. https://treaties.un.org/doc/Treaties/1976/01/19760103%2009-57%20PM/Ch_IV_03.pdf.

42. Hajanirina Arson et al., *Women, Land, and Corruption* (Berlin: Transparency International, 2018), 8–9.

43. World Bank, "Promoting Land Rights to Empower Rural Women and End Poverty," October 14, 2016, http://www.worldbank.org/en/news/feature/2016/10/14/promoting -land-rights-to-empower-rural-women-and-end-poverty.

44. Gayle Tzemach Lemmon, "Reforming Women's Property Rights in Afghanistan," *Council on Foreign Relations*, September 5, 2017, https://www.cfr.org/blog/reforming -womens-property-rights-afghanistan.

45. USAID, "Afghanistan: Land Reform in Afghanistan," LandLinks, https://www.land -links.org/project/land-reform-in-afghanistan/; Charles S. Clark, "USAID Faulted for Law Oversight of Afghan Land Reforms," *Government Executive*, February 9, 2017, https://www.govexec.com/defense/2017/02/usaid-faulted-lax-oversight-afghan-land -reforms/135258/.

46. Habitat for Humanity, "Level the Field: Ending Gender Inequality in Land Rights," 2016, https://www.habitat.org/multimedia/shelter-report-2016/; Giovarelli, Renee, and Elise Scalise, "Women's Land Tenure Framework for Analysis: Land Rights," Landesa,

March 21, 2013, https://s24756.pcdn.co/wp-content/uploads/Land_Rights_Framework _2013March.pdf.

47. Arson et al., *Women, Land, and Corruption*.

48. Lesley Newson and Peter J. Richerson. "Why Do People Become Modern? A Darwinian Explanation," *Population and Development Review* 35, no. 1 (2009): 117–58, doi:10.1111/j.1728-4457.2009.00263.x.

49. Valerie M. Hudson and Hilary Matfess, "In Plain Sight: The Neglected Linkage Between Brideprice, Raiding, and Rebellion," *International Security* 42, no. 1 (Summer 2017): 7–40, doi:10.1162/ISEC_a_00289.

50. Sara Sharratt, "Voices of Court Members," in *Sexual Violence as an International Crime: Interdisciplinary Approaches*, ed. Anne-Marie deBrouwer, Charlotte Ku, Renee G. Romkens, and L. J. van der Herik (Cambridge: Intersentia, 2013), 353–369.

51. *The Washington Post*, "All the Warning Signs Were There: Why Do We Keep Missing Them?" Opinion, *Washington Post*, February 15, 2018, https://www.washingtonpost .com/blogs/post-partisan/wp/2018/02/15/all-the-warning-signs-were-there-before -the-florida-shooting-why-do-we-keep-missing-them/?noredirect=on&utm_term =.7621221d6678.

52. Pamela Shifman and Salamishah Tillet, "To Stop Violence, Start at Home," *New York Times*, February 3, 2015, https://www.nytimes.com/2015/02/03/opinion/to-stop-violence -start-at-home.html?_r=0.

53. Izzy Ferris, "Men with Histories of Sexual Violence Are 'More Likely To Be Terrorists,' Top Lawyer Claims," *Daily Mail*, May 26, 2019, https://www.dailymail.co.uk/news/article -7073493/Men-histories-sexual-violence-likely-terrorists-lawyer-claims.html.

54. Bonita Meyersfield, "A Theory of Domestic Violence in International Law," *Yale Law School Legal Scholarship Repository*, 2016, http://digitalcommons.law.yale.edu/cgi/view content.cgi?article=1002&context=ylsd.

55. For example, the idea that one would ever draft mothers of young children for military service is ludicrously inhumane, we believe.

56. Jacobson, *Of Virgins and Martyrs*, 159.

57. Weiner, *The Rule of the Clan*, 38–39.

58. Andrew Higgins, "Norway Offers Migrants a Lesson in How to Treat Women," *New York Times*, December 19, 2015, https://www.nytimes.com/2015/12/20/world/europe /norway-offers-migrants-a-lesson-in-how-to-treat-women.html; Stephen Dziedzic and Henry Belot, "Australian Citizenship Law Changes Mean Migrants Will Face Tougher Tests," *ABC News*, April 19, 2017. http://www.abc.net.au/news/2017-04-20/migrants-to -face-tougher-tests-for-australian-citizenship/8456392.

59. Charlie Moore and Hannah Moore, "'Immigrants Should Blend In and Adopt Australian Values': Migrants to Undergo New Test About Forced Marriage, Genital Mutilation, and Freedom of Speech Before Being Granted Citizenship," *Daily Mail*, July 20, 2018, http://www.dailymail.co.uk/news/article-5972557/Migrants-undergo- Australian-Values-test-Alan-Tudge-says.html.

60. *The Economist*, "Europe Is Trying to Teach Its Gender Norms to Refugees," *The Economist*, October 15, 2016. https://www.economist.com/europe/2016/10/15/europe-is -trying-to-teach-its-gender-norms-to-refugees.

61. Valerie M. Hudson, "Europe's Man Problem," *Politico*, January 5, 2016, http://www .politico.com/magazine/story/2016/01/europe-refugees-migrant-crisis-men-213500.

62. Valerie M. Hudson, Donna Lee Bowen, and Perpetua Lynne Nielsen, "What Is the Relationship Between Inequity in Family Law and Violence Against Women? Approaching the Issue of Legal Enclaves," *Politics and Gender* 7, no. 4 (Winter 2012b): 453–492.

63. Monroe, *The Evils of Polygyny*.

64. "Migrant Child Brides Put Europe in a Spin," *BBC*, September 30, 2016, https://www.bbc
    .com/news/world-europe-37518289; Stephanie Linning, "Germany to Scrap 'Cultural
    Immunity' and Will No Longer Allows Migrants to Have Multiple Marriages or Child
    Brides," *Daily Mail*, June 15, 2016, http://www.dailymail.co.uk/news/article-3643411
    /Germany-scrap-cultural-immunity-no-longer-allow-migrants-multiple-marriages
    -child-brides.html.

65. Elaine Sciolino, "Britain Grapples with Role for Islamic Justice," *New York Times*,
    November 10, 2008, http://www.nytimes.com/2008/11/19/world/europe/19shariah.html.

66. Jacobson, *Of Virgins and Martyrs*, 107–108.

67. Hudson et al., "What Is the Relationship?"

68. Mounira M. Charrad, "Central and Local Patrimonialism: State-Building in Kin-Based
    Societies," *The Annals of the American Academy of Political and Social Science* 636, no. 1
    (July 2011): 49–68.

69. Interestingly, Tapper and Ahmed, respectively, make similar arguments, using the exam-
    ples of the Safavids and Pahlavis in Iran, and Ataturk in Turkey, and also noting that
    a tribe may try to become the state, such as with the Ottomans, the Qajars, and the
    Durrani. Richard Tapper, "Anthropologists, Historians, and Tribespeople on Tribe and
    State Formation in the Middle East," in *Tribes and States Formation in the Middle East*,
    ed. Philip S. Khoury and Joseph Kostiner (Los Angeles: University of California Press,
    1990), 48–73; and Akbar Ahmed, *The Thistle and the Drone: How America's War on Terror
    Became a Global War on Tribal Islam* (Washington, DC: Brookings Institution, 2013).

70. Charrad, "Central and Local Patrimonialism," 56.

71. Valerie M. Hudson and Rose McDermott, "Why Polygamy Is Bad for National
    Security," *Politico*, July 16, 2015, https://www.politico.com/magazine/story/2015/07
    /polygamy-national-security-putin-120234.

72. Richard Cincotta, "Africa's Reluctant Fertility Transition," *Current History* (May 2011): 190.

73. Andrzej Nowak et al., "The Evolutionary Basis of Honor Cultures," *Psychological Science*
    (2015): 10.

74. Valerie M. Hudson and Patricia Leidl, *The Hillary Doctrine: How Sex Came to Matter in
    American Foreign Policy* (New York: Columbia University Press, 2015).

75. Feriel Ben Mahmoud, *Feminism Insha'allah: The Story of Arab Feminism* (Java Films,
    February 23, 2015), https://vimeo.com/ondemand/feminists.

76. As we have seen throughout the volume, improving the situation of women can also
    make a long-term dictator vulnerable to overthrow, as the "bargain" of subordinating
    men to the leader while allowing all men to subordinate women is undone at that point.

77. Hudson and Leidl, *The Hillary Doctrine*.

78. Gloria Steinem, e-mail correspondence to Valerie M. Hudson, February 5, 2013.

79. This might, for example, have important consequences for U.S. support of the Kurdish
    PKK, who, in places such as Rojava, have insisted on a version of Sanday's diarchy. Male
    and female mayors must make decisions together, any decisions regarding women
    can only be made by women, and family/personal status law has changed drastically:
    "Women were immediately given the right to divorce, previously a right reserved to
    men; to inherit property on an equal basis with men; and to keep their children and
    their homes in a marital breakup. Gone were long-observed Shariah law provisions
    that gave a woman's testimony in court only half the weight of a man's." Rod Nordland,
    "Crackdown in Turkey Threatens a Haven of Gender Equality Built by Kurds," *New
    York Times*, December 7, 2016, https://www.nytimes.com/2016/12/07/world/middleeast
    /turkey-kurds-womens-rights.html," and Rod Nordland, "Women Are Free, and
    Armed, in Kurdish-Controlled Northern Syria," *New York Times*, February 24, 2018,

https://www.nytimes.com/2018/02/24/world/middleeast/syria-kurds-womens-rights
-gender-equality.html.

80. Hudson et al., *Sex and World Peace* (New York: Columbia University Press, 2012).

81. David Barash, *Out of Eden: The Surprising Consequences of Polygamy* (Oxford: Oxford University Press, 2016), 173.

82. Masud (Masud is listed as the "summarizer," not the author on the Sisters in Islam website) "Prophet Muhammad's Wife Aisha." We are also intrigued by the work of Noor, who argues that being raped is not a confession of *zina*. Azman Mohd Noor, "A Victim's Claim of Being Raped Is Neither a Confession to *Zina* Nor Committing *Qadhf* (Making False Accusation of *Zina*)," *Muslim World Journal of Human Rights* 8, no. 1 (2011): 1–20.

83. Carla Power, "Muslim Women Are Fighting to Redefine Islam as a Religion of Equality," *Time*, March 20, 2015, http://time.com/3751243/muslim-women-redefine-islam-feminism/.

84. Quoted in Rose McDermott and Jonathan Cowden, "Polygyny and Violence Against Women," *Emory Law Journal* 64, (2015): 1767–1814, 1777.

85. Lerner, *The Creation of Patriarchy*, 229.

86. Promundo: Health Masculinity, Gender Equity, https://promundoglobal.org.

87. We were thrilled to discover, while doing the final edits on this book, that Promundo was awarded the Luxembourg Peace Prize in June 2019.

88. Monroe, *The Evils of Polygyny*, 31.

89. Monroe, *The Evils of Polygyny*, 31.

90. Stephanie Coontz, *Marriage, A History* (New York: Penguin Books, 2005), 131.

91. Khandis Blake, Maleke Fourati, and Robert C. Brooks, "Who Suppresses Female Sexuality? An Examination of Support for Islamic Veiling in a Secular Muslim Democracy as a Function of Sex and Offspring Sex," *Evolution and Human Behavior* 39, no. 6 (2018): 632–638.

92. Natalie Angier, "In the Bonobo World, Female Camaraderie Prevails." *New York Times*, September 10, 2016, https://www.nytimes.com/2016/09/13/science/bonobos-apes-matriarchy.html.

93. James Fenske, "African Polygamy: Past and Present," *Journal of Development Economics* 117 (2015): 58–73.

94. Eve Bower, "New Protest Statement Builds in Iran—Men in Head Scarves," *CNN*, December 14, 2009, http://edition.cnn.com/2009/WORLD/meast/12/14/iran.headscarf.protest/.

95. Carole Pateman, *The Sexual Contract* (Stanford, CA: Stanford University Press, 1988), 232.

96. Nellie Peyton and Lamin Jahateh, "Gambia: Resurgence of FGM and Child Marriage, Formerly Banned, But Returning with New Political Leadership," *Thomson Reuters Foundation*, January 23, 2018. http://news.trust.org/item/20180123090036-m8b80/.

97. Caitlin Dewey, "Men Who Harass Women Online Are Quite Literally Losers, New Study Finds," *Washington Post*, July 20, 2015, https://www.washingtonpost.com/news/the-intersect/wp/2015/07/20/men-who-harass-women-online-are-quite-literally-losers-new-study-finds/?utm_term=.7eb86911f6c5.

98. We cannot help but remember what Andrew Natsios, USAID administrator during the George W. Bush administration, said to Hudson in an interview in 2013: "How is it a national security threat to the United States for women to be at a low status or whatever term you want to use? How is that a threat to American national security interests? I don't see how you can make that argument . . . National security is what's the threat of attack on the United States, during the Cold War or now because of terrorism. I don't see how the two are connected." This attitude is still quite prevalent in government circles even now, though most holding such views avoid the type of explicit disclosure Natsios offers here.

99. Monroe, *The Evils of Polygyny*, 102.
100. Jacobson, *Of Virgins and Martyrs*, 11.
101. Francis Fukuyama, *The Great Disruption: Human Nature and the Reconstitution of Social Order* (New York: Free Press, 1999), 220.
102. Malcolm Potts and Thomas Hayden, *Sex and War* (Dallas, TX: Benbella, 2008), 367.

Appendix I. Syndrome Scores for 176 Countries

1. Roger L. Worthington and Tiffany A. Whittaker, "Scale Development Research: A Content Analysis and Recommendations for Best Practices," *Counseling Psychologist* 34 (2006): 806–838.
2. Note that the Inequity in Family Law/Practice (IFL) scale has many subcomponents, some of which include Age of Marriage for Girls, Polygyny, and Inheritance as Wife. However, the IFL scale is much broader than those subcomponents and also includes information on laws and practices concerning Abortion, Marital Rape, Forced Marriage, and Divorce, which are not operationalized as being part of the Syndrome. This broader IFL scale is thus a good starting point for the Syndrome scale. Because we wish to accentuate the actual components of the Syndrome, we then look separately in the Syndrome scale algorithm at the scores for Age of Marriage for Girls and Polygyny as well as at the scale of Women's Property Rights in Law and Practice (of which Inheritance as a Wife is a subcomponent).

Appendix III. Testing the Effects: Methods and Extended Results Methodology

1. Christopher Achen, "Toward a New Political Methodology: Microfoundations and Art," *Annual Review of Political Science* 5 (June 2002): 423–450.
2. Phil Schrodt, "Seven Deadly Sins of Contemporary Quantitative Political Analysis," (unpublished manuscript, August 23, 2010), https://lcsr.hse.ru/data/2011/12/19/1261789486/Schrodt7SinsAPSA10.pdf.
3. The five variables excluded for N size reasons from the Political Stability and Governance dimension analysis were "Rule of Law 2016" from the World Justice Project, "Procedural Justice" from the Human Freedom Index, "Civil Justice" from the Human Freedom Index, "Criminal Justice" from the Human Freedom Index, and "Freedom of Associations" from the Human Freedom Index. Additionally, the variables "Index of Democracy" from the Economist Intelligence Unit (EIU), "Electoral Process and Pluralism" from EIU's Index of Democracy, and "Electoral Democracy Index" from the V-Dem 2017 Annual Report, were excluded because they were too highly correlated with the variable "Freedom House Index Political Rights 2016."
4. The five variables excluded for N size reasons from the Security and Conflict dimension were "Riots and Protests after Election" from the National Elections across Democracy and Autocracy from The Quality of Government Institute, "Military Expenditure Percentage of Central Government Expenditure" from the World Bank, "Crime Is Effectively Controlled" from World Justice Project, "Civil Conflict Is Effectively Limited" from the World Justice Project, and "People Do Not Resort to Violence to Redress Grievances" from the World Justice Project. The "International Organized Conflict"

variable from Human Freedom Index was excluded because it correlated too highly (>.9) with the "Intensity of Internal Conflicts" variable from Vision of Humanity.

5. The nine variables excluded for N size reasons from the Economic Performance dimension were "Poverty Ratio at \$1.90 per Day" from the World Bank, "Economic Output Strength" from Bertelsmann Stiftung's Transformation Index, "Unemployment Rate 2016–2017" from Global Economy, "Research and Development Expenditure" from the World Bank, "Prevalence of Undernourishment" from the Food and Agriculture Organization of the United Nations, "Depth of Food Deficit" from the Food and Agriculture Organization of the United Nations, "Human Capital Index Economy" from the World Economic Forum, "Population Living in Slums" from the World Bank, and "Global Innovation Index" from the Global Innovation Index. "Real Interest Rate" from the World Bank was excluded because of operationalization issues. "Economic Performance" from Bertelsmann was excluded because it was highly correlated with the "Economic Output Strength" variable from the Global Peace Index and also had the same N size as that variable. The "Unemployment Rate Male 2016" variable from the World Bank was excluded because it correlated too highly (>.9) with the "Unemployment Rate" variable from the World Bank.

6. Five factors were formed, but two of the factors combined variables that did not make sense to combine and so these were analyzed separately. These included a factor with (1) Final Consumption (log transformed) and (2) High Technology Exports as well as a factor with (1) Government Expenditure as Percentage of GDP and (2) Unemployment.

7. No variables were excluded for N size reasons from the Economic Rentierism dimension.

8. The variable excluded for N size reasons from the Health and Well-Being dimension was "Use of Modern Contraception by Married Women" from the Population Reference Bureau. "Mortality Rate for Communicable Disease" from the United Nations World Health Statistics was excluded because it was from 2008. "Percentage of Adults Ages Fifteen to Forty-Nine with HIV/AIDS" from the CIA *World Factbook* was excluded because it was highly correlated with the "Percentage of Population Between Fifteen and Forty-Nine with HIV" variable from the World Bank. "Life Expectancy at Birth for Males" from the World Health Organization was excluded because it was highly correlated with the "Life Expectancy" variable from the CIA *World Factbook*. "Mortality Under Five per One Thousand Live Births" from the World Bank was excluded because it was too highly correlated with the "Life Expectancy" variable from the CIA *World Factbook* and the "Infant Mortality Rate" variable from the World Bank. The "Percentage of Women Ages Fifteen to Nineteen Who Have Had Children or Are Currently Pregnant" variable from the World Bank was excluded because other variables already cover this data.

9. "Total Dependency Ratio" from the United Nations Development Program (UNDP), "Birth Rate Scale" from The WomanStats Project, and "Fertility Rates Ages Twenty to Twenty-Four" from UNDP were all excluded because they were each too highly correlated with "Total Fertility Rate" from the World Bank. In addition, the correlation between "Mother's Mean Age at First Birth" from the CIA *World Factbook* and "Median Age of Population" from the United Nations was also very high. Because "Mother's Mean Age at First Birth" is more in line with our theoretical framework, we excluded Median Age of Population. We also excluded "Mean Age of Childbearing" in favor of "Mother's Mean Age at First Birth" because we are more interested in the prevalence of child brides.

10. Noah Bricker and Mark Foley, "The Effect of Youth Demographics on Violence: The Importance of the Labor Market," *International Journal of Conflict and Violence* 7, no. 1 (2013): 179–194.

11. No variables were excluded for N size reasons from the Education of the Population dimension. The "Male Literacy Rate" and the "Female Literacy Rate" from the CIA *World Factbook* were excluded because they were too highly correlated with the World Bank literacy variables. The "Male Literacy Rate Ages Fifteen to Twenty-Four" from the World Bank was excluded because it was too highly correlated with the "Female Literacy Rate Ages Fifteen to Twenty-Four" variable from the World Bank. The "Gender Parity Index for Primary and Secondary Schools" variable from the World Bank was excluded because it was too highly correlated with the "Gender Parity Index for Secondary School" variable from the World Bank. The "Access to Advanced Education" variable from the Social Progress Index was excluded because it was too highly correlated with the "Average Years of Schooling" variable from the United Nations Development Program Human Development Reports. The "Overall Literacy Rate Difference Between Males and Females" variable, calculated as the difference between the CIA values for Male and Female literacy rates was excluded because it was too close conceptually with the "Male/Female Difference in Literacy Rates" variable from the World Bank and the "Discrepancy in Educational Attainment Between Males and Females" variable from The WomanStats Project.
12. We chose the indicator for secondary school rather than primary school because the N size for secondary school was larger.
13. The one variable excluded for N size reasons from the Social Progress dimension was "Population Living in Slums" from Bertelsmann Stiftung's Transformation Index. "Social Progress Index 2016" from the Social Progress Index (SPI) was excluded because it was correlated highly with "Human Development Index" and because we included subcomponents of SPI in the analysis.
14. No variables were excluded for N size reasons from the Environmental Protection dimension. "Environmental Health" from the Environmental Performance Index was excluded because it correlated too highly with the "Water and Sanitation" variable from the Environmental Performance Index.

BIBLIOGRAPHY

Abdelal, Rawi, Yoshiko Herrera, Alastair Iain Johnston, and Rose McDermott. "Identity as a Variable." *Perspectives on Politics* 4 no. 4 (2006): 695–711.

Acemoglu, Daron, and James Robinson. *Why Nations Fail: The Origins of Power, Prosperity, and Poverty.* New York: Crown, 2013.

Achen, Christopher. "Toward a New Political Methodology: Microfoundations and Art." *Annual Review of Political Science* 5 (June 2002): 423–450.

Adams, Brooke. "Teen Age Girl Talks of FLDS Wedding." *Salt Lake Tribune*, April 5, 2006. http://www.rickross.com/reference/polygamy/polygamy432.html.

Adams, Julia. "The Rule of the Father: Patriarchy and Patrimonialism in Early Modern Europe." In *Max Weber's Economy and Society: A Critical Companion*, edited by C. Camic, P. S. Gorski and D. M. Trubek, 237–266. Stanford, CA: Stanford University Press, 2005. http://sociology.yale.edu/sites/default/files/adams_rulefather.pdf.

Adams, Julia. "Politics, Patriarchy and Frontiers of Historical Sociological Explanation." *Political Power and Social Theory* 19 (2008): 289–294.

Afghan Women's Writing Project ("Nasima"). "The Herat Maternity Clinic." July 11, 2014. http://awwproject.org/2014/07/the-herat-maternity-clinic/.

Afghan Women's Writing Project ("Zohra N."). "I Just Keep Delivering." July 10, 2014, http://awwproject.org/2014/07/i-just-keep-delivering/.

Afghan Women's Writing Project ("Arezoo"). "Whatever Men Want Is What Happens." July 10, 2014. http://awwproject.org/2014/07/whatever-men-want-is-what-happens/.

Agacinski, Sylviane. *The Parity of the Sexes.* New York: Columbia University Press, 2001.

Agence France Presse. "Algeria Passes Law Banning Violence Against Women." *Al Arabiya*, March 6, 2015. http://english.alarabiya.net/en/News/africa/2015/03/06/Algeria-passes-law-banning-violence-against-women.html.

——. "Poor Celebrate at Mass Weddings in Algeria." *Gulf Times*, January 2, 2017. http://www.gulf-times.com/story/526653/Poor-celebrate-at-mass-weddings-in-Algeria.

Aglionby, John. "Four Times as Many Women Died in Tsunami." *The Guardian*, March 26, 2005. https://www.theguardian.com/society/2005/mar/26/internationalaidanddevelopment .indianoceantsunamidecember2004.

Ahmed, Akbar. *The Thistle and the Drone: How America's War on Terror Became a Global War on Tribal Islam*. Washington, DC: Brookings Institution, 2013.

Ahram, Ariel I. "Sexual and Ethnic Violence and the Construction of the Islamic State." Political Violence at a Glance, September 18, 2014. https://politicalviolenceataglance .org/2014/09/18/sexual-and-ethnic-violence-and-the-construction-of-the-islamic-state/.

——. "Sexual Violence and the Making of ISIS." *Survival* 57, no. 3 (2015): 57–78.

——. "Sexual Violence, Competitive State Building, and the Islamic State in Syria and Iraq." Unpublished manuscript, 2015.

Akese, Efia. "Reduce Dowry and Let's Marry." *The Mirror* (Ghana), September 12–18, 2014, https://www.graphic.com.gh/lifestyle/relationships/reduce-dowry-and-let-s-marry.html.

Alami, Aida. "A Loophole for Rapists Is Eliminated in Morocco." *New York Times*, January 23, 2014. https://www.nytimes.com/2014/01/24/world/africa/after-debate-moroccan-government -amends-rape-law.html.

Alesina, Alberto, Benedetta Brioschi, and Eliana La Ferrara. "Violence Against Women: A Cross-Cultural Analysis for Africa." NBER Working Paper No. 21901, National Bureau of Economic Research, Cambridge, MA, January 2016. http://www.nber.org/papers/w21901.

Alesina, Alberto, Arnaud Devleeschauwer, William Easterly, Sergio Kurlat, and Romain Wacziarg. "Fractionalization." *Journal of Economic Growth* 8, no. 2 (June 2013): 155–194.

Alesina, Aleberto, Paola Giuliano, and Nathan Nunn. "On the Origins of Gender Roles: Women and the Plough." *Quarterly Journal of Economics* 128, no. 2 (2013): 469–530.

Aleu, Philip Thon, and Parach Mach. "Risking One's Life to Be Able to Marry." Development and Cooperation, June 26, 2016. https://www.dandc.eu/en/article/bride-price-tradition -destructive-strong-strife-torn-south-sudan.

Alexander, Richard D. "Evolution, Culture, and Human Behavior: Some General Considerations." In *Natural Selection and Social Behavior*, edited by Richard D. Alexander and Donald W Tinkle, 509–520. New York: Chiron Press, 1981.

Alexander, Richard D., John L. Hoogland, Richard D. Howard, Katherine M. Noonan, and Paul W. Sherman. "Sexual Dimorphisms and Breeding Systems in Pinnipeds, Ungulates, Primates, and Humans." In *Evolutionary Biology and Human Behavior*, edited by Napoleon A. Chagnon and Wiliam Irons, 402–435. North Scituate, MA: Duxbury Press, 1979.

Ali, Obaid. " 'You Must Have a Gun to Stay Alive': Ghor, A Province with Three Governments." Afghanistan Analysts Network, August 4, 2013. http://www.afghanistan-analysts .org/you-must-have-a-gun-to-stay-alive-ghor-a-province-with-three-governments.

"All the Warning Signs Were There Before the Florida Shooting: Why Do We Keep Missing Them?" Opinion. *Washington Post*, February 15, 2018. https://www.washingtonpost.com /blogs/post-partisan/wp/2018/02/15/all-the-warning-signs-were-there-before-the -florida-shooting-why-do-we-keep-missing-them/?noredirect=on&utm_term =.7621221d6678.

Amara, Tarek. "Tunisian Women March for Equal Inheritance Rights." *Reuters*, March 10, 2018. https://www.reuters.com/article/us-tunisia-women/tunisian-women-march-for-equal -inheritance-rights-idUSKCN1GM0OT.

Anderlini, Jamil. "China: Blueprint for Reform Targets Corruption." *Financial Times*, November 26, 2013. http://www.ft.com/intl/cms/s/0/d4bd3de0-4fb6-11e3-b06e-00144feabdco .html#axzz2lnTmx4fF.

Anderson, Siwan. "The Economics of Dowry and Brideprice." *Journal of Economic Perspectives* 21, no. 4 (Fall 2007): 151–174. doi:10.1257/jep.21.4.151.

——. "Legal Origins and Female HIV." *American Economic Review* 108 no. 6 (2018): 1407–1439.

Anderson, Sulome. "Women Brutalized by ISIS." *Foreign Policy*, October 11, 2016. http://foreignpolicy.com/2016/10/11/women-survive-they-do-not-live-isis-islam-yazidi/.

Angier, Natalie. "In the Bonobo World, Female Camaraderie Prevails." *New York Times*, September 10, 2016. https://www.nytimes.com/2016/09/13/science/bonobos-apes-matriarchy.html.

Associated Press. "One Indian Woman Killed Every Hour Over Dowry." *Al Jazeera*, September 3, 2013. https://www.aljazeera.com/news/asia/2013/09/201393134051503366.html.

Apicella, Coren, Justin Carre, and Anna Dreber. "Testosterone and Financial Risk Taking: A Review." *Adaptive Human Behavior and Physiology* 1, no. 3 (2015): 358–385. doi:10.1007/s40750-014-0020-2.

Apicella, Coren, Anna Dreber, Benjamin Campbell, Peter Gray, Moshe Hoffman, Anthony Little. "Testosterone and Financial Risk Performance." *Evolution and Human Behavior* 29, no. 6 (208): 384–390. https://www.ehbonline.org/article/S1090-5138(08)00067-6/abstract.

Archer, John. "Testosterone and Human Aggression: An Evaluation of the Challenge Hypothesis." *Neuroscience and Biobehavioral Reviews* 30, no. 3 (2006): 319–345.

Arson, Hajanirina, et al. *Women, Land and Corruption: Resources for Practitioners and Policy-Makers*. Transparency International, March 8, 2018. https://www.transparency.org/whatwedo/publication/women_land_and_corruption_resources_for_practitioners_and_policy_makers.

Asal, Victor, Richard Legault, Ora Szekeley, and Jonathan Wilkenfeld. "Gender Ideologies and Forms of Contentious Mobilization in the Middle East." *Journal of Peace Research* 50, no. 3 (2013): 305–318.

Asal, Victor, Marcus Schulzke, and Amy Pate. "Why Do Some Organizations Kill While Others Do Not: An Examination of Middle Eastern Organizations." *Foreign Policy Analysis* 13, no. 4 (October 2017): 811–831. https://doi-org.ezproxy.library.tamu.edu/10.1111/fpa.12080.

Asfura-Heim, Patricio. "Tribal Customary Law and Legal Pluralism in al Anbar, Iraq." In *Customary Justice and the Rule of Law in War-Torn Societies*, edited by Deborah H. Isser. Washington, DC: United States Institute of Peace Press, 2011: 239–283.

Ashraf, Nava, Natalie Bau, Nathan Nunn, and Alessandrea Voena. "Brideprice and the Returns to Education for Women." NBER Working Paper No. 22417, National Bureau of Economic Research, Cambridge, MA, July 21, 2015. http://www.nber.org/papers/w22417.

Atuobi, Samuel Mondays. "Corruption and State Instability in West Africa: An Examination of Policy Options." Occasional Paper, Kofi Annan International Peacekeeping Training Center, December 2007. http://reliefweb.int/sites/reliefweb.int/files/resources/9BD8A1F729CEB5B8C125746C0049D740-kaiptc-dec2007.pdf.

Bajaj, Vikas, and Lydia Polgreen. "Suspect Stirs Mumbai Court by Confessing." *New York Times*, July 20, 2009. http://www.nytimes.com/2009/07/21/world/asia/21india.html?_r=2.

Baker, Keiligh. "ISIS Offers Fighters $1500 Starter Home Bonus and a Free Honeymoon." *Daily Mail*, May 26, 2015. http://www.dailymail.co.uk/news/article-3098235/ISIS-offers-fighters-1-500-starter-home-bonus-free-honeymoon.html.

Bakht, Natasha. "Family Arbitration Using Sharia Law: Examining Ontario's Arbitration Act and Its Impact on Women." *Muslim World Journal of Human Rights* 1, no. 7 (2004): 1–24.

Baradaran, Shima. "Eyinyani and Rape Among the Xhosa in South Africa." Honors Thesis, Department of Sociology, Brigham Young University, Provo, UT, February 2001.

Baranov, Victoria, Ralph De Haas, and Pauline Grosjean. "Men: Roots and Consequences of Masculinity Norms." *SSRN*, June 12, 2018. https://papers.ssrn.com/sol3/papers.cfm?abstract_id=3185694.

Barash, David P. *Out of Eden: The Surprising Consequences of Polygamy.* Oxford: Oxford University Press, 2016.

Barfield, Thomas. "Tribe and State Relations: The Inner Asian Perspective." In *Tribes and State Formation in the Middle East*, edited by Philip Khoury and Joseph Kostiner, 153–184. Berkeley: University of California Press, 1990.

——. *Afghanistan: A Cultural and Political History.* Princeton, NJ: Princeton University Press, 2010.

Barnes, Andrew E. *Making Headway: The Introduction of Western Civilization in Colonial Northern Nigeria.* Rochester, NY: University Rochester Press, 2009.

Barnes, Jordan. "Immigrant Children Born in Danish 'Ghettos' Will Be Separated from Their Families from the Age of One for 25 Hours per Week to Teach Them 'Danish Values' and the Language." *Daily Mail*, July 2, 2018. http://www.dailymail.co.uk/news/article-5909273/Immigrant-kids-Danish-ghettos-separated-families-age-ONE-25-hours-week.html.

Barth, Fredrik. *Nomads of South Persia: The Basseri Tribe of the Khamseh Confederacy.* Boston: Little, Brown, 1961.

Beck, Lois, "Tribes and the State 19th and 20th Century Iran." in *Tribes and State Formation in the Middle East* edited by Philip Khoury and Joseph Kostiner, 185–225. Berkeley: University of California Press, 1990.

Bendix, Reinhard. *Max Weber: An Intellectual Portrait.* New York: Simon and Schuster, 1961.

Benstead, Lindsay. "Conceptualizing and Measuring Patriarchy: The Importance of Feminist Theory." In *Women and Gender in Middle East Politics*, 8–12. The Project on Middle East Political Science, May 10, 2016. https://pomeps.org/wp-content/uploads/2016/05/POMEPS_Studies_19_Gender_Web.pdf.

——. "Why Quotas Are Needed to Achieve, Gender Equality." In *Women and Gender in Middle East Politics*, 55–57. The Project on Middle East Political Science, May 10, 2016. https://pomeps.org/wp-content/uploads/2016/05/POMEPS_Studies_19_Gender_Web.pdf.

Bentzen, Jeanet, Nicolai Kaarsen, and Asger Wingender. "Irrigation and Autocracy." *Journal of the European Economics* Association (June 29, 2016). https://onlinelibrary.wiley.com/doi/abs/10.1111/jeea.12173.

Betzig, Laura. "Despotism and Differential Reproduction: A Cross-Cultural Correlation of Conflict Asymmetry, Hierarchy, and Degree of Polygyny." *Ethology and Sociobiology* 3 (1982): 209–221.

——. *Despotism and Differential Reproduction: A Darwinian View of History.* New York: Aldine de Gruyter, 1986.

——. "Roman Polygyny." *Ethology and Sociology* 13 (1992): 309–349.

Bhat, P. N. Mari, and Shiva S. Halli. "Demography of Brideprice and Dowry: Causes and Consequences of the Indian Marriage Squeeze." *Population Studies* 53, no. 2 (1999): 129–149.

Bidgoli, Fae. "Iran, Yemen and the Plague of Forced Marriages: Millions of Girls Are Made to Become Child Brides." *New York Daily News*, November 28, 2010. http://www.nydailynews.com/opinion/iran-yemen-plague-forced-marriages-millions-girls-made-child-brides-article-1.456314.

"Big Money for Niger's Child Brides." *BBC*, May 30, 2014. https://ru-clip.com/video/bFCM4Jo4ToE/big-money-for-niger-s-child-brides-bbc-news.html.

Bill, James, and Robert Springborg. *Politics in the Middle East.* 5th ed. New York: Pearson, 2000.

Blake, Khandis, Maleke Fourati, and Robert C. Brooks. "Who Suppresses Female Sexuality? An Examination of Support for Islamic Veiling in a Secular Muslim Democracy as a Function of Sex and Offspring Sex." *Evolution and Human Behavior* 39, no. 6 (2018): 632–638. https://www.sciencedirect.com/science/article/pii/S109051381730363X.

Bjarnegard, Elin, Karen Brouneus, and Erik Melander. "Honor and Political Violence: Micro-Level Findings from a Survey in Thailand." *Journal of Peace Research* 546, no. 6 (2017): 748–761.

Bjarnegard, Elin, and Erik Melander. "Pacific Men: How the Feminist Gap Explains Hostility." *The Pacific Review* 30, no. 4 (2017): 478–493. doi:10.1080/09512748.2016.1264456.

Blaydes, Lisa, and Eric Chaney. "The Feudal Revolution and Europe's Rise: Political Divergence of the Christian West and the Muslim World Before 1500 CE." *American Political Science Review* 107, no. 1 (February 2013): doi:10.1017/S0003055412000561.

Blimes, Randall. "The Indirect Effect of Ethnic Heterogeneity on the Likelihood of Civil War Onset." *Journal of Conflict Resolution* 50, no. 4 (2006): 536–547.

Boone, James L. "Noble Family Structure and Expanisionist Warfare in the Late Middle Ages: A Socioecological Approach." In *Rethinking Human Adaptation: Biological and Cultural Models*, edited by Rada Dyson-Hudson and Michael A. Little, 79–96. Boulder, CO: Westview, 1983.

——. "Parental Investment and Elite Family Structure in Preindustrial States: A Case Study of Late Medieval-Early Modern Portuguese Genealogies." *American Anthropologist* 88, no. 4 (December 1986): 859–878.

Bose, Christine E. "Patterns of Global Gender Inequalities and Regional Gender Regimes." *Gender and Society* 29, no. 6 (December 2015): 767–791.

Bowen, Donna Lee, and Valerie M. Hudson. "Colonial Status Coding, 2017." Reproduced in appendix II of this volume.

Bowen, Donna Lee, Valerie M. Hudson, and Perpetua Lynne Nielsen. "State Fragility and Structural Gender Inequality in Family Law: An Empirical Investigation." *Laws* 4, no. 4 (2015): 654–672. doi:10.3390/laws4040654.

Bower, Eve. "New Protest Statement Builds in Iran—Men in Head Scarves." *CNN*, December 14, 2009. http://edition.cnn.com/2009/WORLD/meast/12/14/iran.headscarf.protest/.

——. "Report: Some Areas in China Under Martial Law After Protests." *CNN*, May 31, 2011. http://www.cnn.com/2011/WORLD/asiapcf/05/28/china.martial.law.

Braunstein, Elissa. "The Feminist Political Economy of the Rent-Seeking Society: An Investigation of Gender Inequality and Economic Growth." *Journal of Economic Issues*. 42 no. 4, December 2008): 959–979.

Brennan, Siofra. "Here Come the Brides!" *Daily Mail*, February 6, 2017. http://www.dailymail.co.uk/femail/article-4197474/Couples-prepare-mass-wedding-Syria.html.

Bricker, Noah, and Mark Foley. "The Effect of Youth Demographics on Violence: The Importance of the Labor Market." *International Journal of Conflict and Violence* 7, no. 1 (2013): 179–194.

"Brideprices in China Have Shot Up, Bending the Country's Society and Economy Out of Shape." *The Economist*, January 16, 2018. https://twitter.com/theeconomist/status/953388324835741701.

Brysk, Allison. *The Struggle for Freedom from Fear: Contesting Violence Against Women at the Frontiers of Globalization*. New York: Oxford University Press, 2018.

Burke, Dave. "The Women Who Beg to Be Whipped." *Daily Mail*, May 11, 2017. http://www.dailymail.co.uk/news/article-4494904/The-women-whipped-LOVE.html.

Butler, Christopher, Tali Gluch, and Neil J. Mitchell. "Security Forces and Sexual Violence." *Journal of Peace Research* 44, no. 6 (2007): 669–687.

Buzan, Barry. "What Is National Security in the Age of Globalisation?" Utenriksdepartementet, 2007. http://www.regjeringen.no/nb/dep/ud/kampanjer/refleks/innspill/sikkerhet/buzan.html?id=493187.

Callimachi, Rukmini. "To Maintain Supply of Sex Slaves, ISIS Pushes Birth Control." *New York Times*, March 12, 2016. https://www.nytimes.com/2016/03/13/world/middleeas t/to-maintain-supply-of-sex-slaves-isis-pushes-birth-control.html.

Cameron, Lisa, Xin Meng, and Dandan Zhang. "China's Sex Ratio and Crime: Behavioral Change or Financial Necessity?" IZA Discussion Paper No. 9747, Institute for the Study of Labor, February 2016. http://ftp.iza.org/dp9747.pdf.

Campbell, Anne. "Sex Differences in Direct Aggression: What Are the Psychological Mediators?" *Aggression and Violent Behavior* 11, no. 3 (2006): 237–264.

Caprioli, Mary. "Gendered Conflict." *Journal of Peace Research* 37 (2000): 51–68.

——. "Gender Equality and State Aggression: The Impact of Domestic Gender Equality on State First Use of Force." *International Interactions* 29, no. 3 (2003): 195–214.

——. "Democracy and Human Rights Versus Women's Security: A Contradiction?" *Security Dialogue: Special Issue Gender and Security* 35, no. 4 (2004): 411–428.

——. "Primed for Violence: The Role of Gender Inequality in Predicting Internal Conflict." *International Studies Quarterly* 49 (2005): 161–178.

Caprioli, Mary, and Mark A. Boyer. "Gender, Violence, and International Crisis." *Journal of Conflict Resolution* 45 (2001): 503–518.

Caprioli, Mary, Valerie M. Hudson, Rose McDermott, Bonnie Ballif-Spanvill, Chad F. Emmett, and S. Matthew Stearmer. "The WomanStats Project Database: Advancing an Empirical Research Agenda." *Journal of Peace Research* 46, no. 6 (November 2009): 1–13.

Caprioli, Mary, and Peter F. Trumbore. "Human Rights Rogues in Interstate Disputes, 1980–2001." *Journal of Peace Research* 43, no. 2 (2006): 131–148.

Carré, J. M., S. K. Putnam, and C. M. McCormick. "Testosterone Responses to Competition Predict Future Aggressive Behaviour at a Cost to Reward in Men." *Psychoneuroendocrinology* 34, no. 4 (2009): 561–570.

Castillejo, Clare. "Gender Inequality and State Fragility in the Sahel." FRIDE Policy Brief No. 204, *Fundación para las Relaciones Internacionales y el Diálogo Exterior*, June 2015. https://www.files.ethz.ch/isn/191893/Gender%20inequality%20and%20state%20fragil-ity%20in%20the%20Sahel.pdf

Caton, Steven C. "Anthropological Theories of Tribe and State Formation in the Middle East: Ideology and the Semiotics of Power." In *Tribes and States Formation in the Middle East*, edited by Philip S. Khoury and Joseph Kostiner. 74–108. Los Angeles: University of California Press, 1990.

Center for Reproductive Rights. *Legal Grounds: Reproductive and Sexual Rights in African Commonwealth Courts*. New York: Center for Reproductive Rights, 2005.

Centers for Disease Control and Prevention. "Sexual Violence: Risk and Protective Factors." https://www.cdc.gov/violenceprevention/sexualviolence/riskprotectivefactors.html.

Chakraborty, Tanika, and Sukkoo Kim. "Kinship Institutions and Sex Ratios in India." *Demography* 47, no. 4 (November 2010): 989–1012.

Chamberlain, Gethin. "South Sudan's Battle for Cattle Is Forcing Schoolgirls to Become Teenage Brides." *The Guardian*, June 8, 2017. https://www.theguardian.com/global -development/2017/jun/08/south-sudan-battle-for-cattle-is-forcing-schoolgirls-to-become -teenage-brides.

Chandran, Rina. "Hunger, Child Marriage, Prostitution: India Drought Hurts Women, Low-Caste Dalits More." *Thomson Reuters*, May 23, 2016. http://news.trust.org/item /20160523133537-m9pde/.

Chang, Pil-Wha, and Eun-shil Kim. *Women's Experiences and Feminist Practices in South Korea*. Seoul, South Korea: Ewha Womans University Press, 2005.

Chapais, Bernard. *Primeval Kinship*. Cambridge, MA: Harvard University Press, 2010.

Charrad, Mounira M. *States and Women's Rights: The Making of Postcolonial Tunisia, Algeria, and Morocco.* Berkeley: University of California Press, 2001.

——. "Central and Local Patrimonialism: State-Building in Kin-Based Societies." *Annals of the American Academy of Political and Social Science* 636, no. 1 (July 2011): 49–68.

Chayes, Sarah. *Thieves of State.* New York: Norton, 2016.

Chemaly, Soraya. "If You Don't Take Women's Harassment Seriously, You Don't Want to Understand the Problem." *HuffPost* (blog), January 27, 2016. https://www.huffingtonpost .com/soraya-chemaly/if-you-dont-take-womens-harassment-seriously-you-dont-want -to-understand-the-problem_b_9082952.html?utm_source=Alert-blogger&utm_medium =email&utm_campaign=Email%2BNotifications.

Cheng Lu. "Excess of Marriageable Males and Violent Crime in China and South Korea, 1970–2008." Paper presented at the 2012 Annual Meeting of the Population Association of America, San Francisco, CA, May 3–5, 2012. http://paa2012.princeton.edu/abstracts/121243.

China from the Inside, episode 2, "Women of the Country." Transcript. PBS. 2007. http://www .pbs.org/kqed/chinainside/pdf/pbschina-ep2.pdf.

Cho, Mi-Kyung. "Recent Reform of Korean Family Law." Conference Paper, Ajou University, Korea. https://docplayer.net/2354517-Recent-reform-of-korean-family-law-mi-kyung-cho -ajou-university-korea.html .

Cho, Uhn. "Gender Inequality and Patriarchal Order Recontexualized." In *Contemporary South Korean Society: A Critical Perspective*, edited by Hee-Yeon Cho, Lawrence Surendra and Hyo-Je Cho, 18–27. London and New York: Routledge, 2013.

Choe, Sang-Hun. "South Koreans Rethink Preference for Sons." *New York Times*, November 28, 2007. http://www.nytimes.com/2007/11/28/world/asia/28iht-sex.1.8509372.html?_r=1&.

——. "As Families Change, Korea's Elderly Are Turning to Suicide." *New York Times*, February 16, 2013. http://www.nytimes.com/2013/02/17/world/asia/in-korea-changes-in-societyand-family -dynamics-drive-rise-in-elderly-suicides.html?pagewanted=all.

Choi, Charles Q. "Ancient Human Sacrifice Victims Faced Slavery Before Death." *LiveScience*, June 16, 2017. https://www.livescience.com/59513-ancient-china-human-sacrifice-revealed .html.

Chung, Woojin, and Monica Das Gupta. "The Decline of Son Preference in South Korea: The Roles of Development and Public Policy." *Population and Development Review* 33, no. 4 (2007): 757–783.

Cincotta, Richard. "Africa's Reluctant Fertility Transition." *Current History* 110, no. 736 (May 2011): 184–190.

——. "Minority Youth Bulges and the Future of Intrastate Conflict." *New Security Beat*, October 13, 2011. https://s3.amazonaws.com/academia.edu.documents/32162413/NSB _Cincotta_Minority_YB.pdf?AWSAccessKeyId=AKIAIWOWYYGZ2Y53UL3 A&Expires=1521143853&Signature=3Z4Q5vYsNZKFiR6%2BOZD1ReHWGME %3D&response-content-disposition=inline%3B%20filename%3DMinority_Youth _Bulges_and_the_Future_of.pdf.

Clark, Charles S. "USAID Faulted for Law Oversight of Afghan Land Reforms." *Government Executive*, February 9, 2017. https://www.govexec.com/defense/2017/02/usaid-faulted-lax -oversight-afghan-land-reforms/135258/.

Coburn, Noah. *Bazaar Politics: Power and Pottery in an Afghan Market Town.* Stanford, CA: Stanford University Press, 2011.

Cockburn, Patrick. "Iraq Crisis: As ISIS Terror Spreads, Its Fighters Look for Wives." *The Independent*, June 21, 2014. https://www.independent.co.uk/news/world/middle-east /iraq-crisis-as-the-sunni-terror-spreads-its-fighters-look-for-wives-9554231.html?origin =internalSearch.

Cohen, Dara Kay. *Rape During Civil War*. Ithaca, NY: Cornell University Press, 2016.

Collins, Kathleen. "Clans, Pacts, and Politics in Central Asia." *Journal of Democracy* 13, no. 3 (2002): 137–152.

Collins, Kathleen. "The Political Role of Clans in Central Asia." *Comparative Politics* 35, no. 2 (2003): 171–90.

Collins, Kathleen. "The Logic of Clan Politics: Evidence from the Central Asian Trajectories." *World Politics* 56, no. 2 (2004): 224–261.

Collins, Kathleen. *Clan Politics and Regime Transition in Central Asia*. Cambridge: Cambridge University Press, 2006.

"Consanguineous Marriage: Keeping It All in the Family." *The Economist*, February 25, 2016. http://www.economist.com/news/middle-east-and-africa/21693632-marriage-between -close-relatives-much-too-common-keeping-it-family.

Constantine, Elizabeth A. "Practical Consequences of Soviet Policy and Ideology for Gender in Central Asia and Contemporary Reversal." In *Everyday Life in Central Asia: Past and Present*, edited by Jeff Shadeo and Russell Zanca, 115–126. Bloomington: Indiana University Press, 2007.

Convention on the Elimination of All Forms of Discrimination Against Women. "Consideration of Reports Submitted Under Article 18 of the Convention on the Elimination of All Forms of Discrimination Against Women." *Sixth Periodic Report of States Parties: Republic of Korea* CEDAW/C/KOR/6, March 5, 2007.

Coontz, Stephanie. *Marriage, A History*. New York: Penguin Books, 2005.

Court of Criminal Appeals of the State of Texas. Nos. 1460–01, 1461–01. April 3, 2002. https:// caselaw.findlaw.com/tx-court-of-criminal-appeals/1000114.html.

Crone, Patricia. "The Tribe and the State." In *States in History*, edited by John A. Hall, 48–77. Oxford: Basil Blackwell, 1986.

Cronk, Lee. "Low Socio-Economic Status and Female-Biased Parental Investment: The Mukogodo Example." *American Anthropologist* 91, no. 2 (June 1989): 414–429. https:// anthrosource.onlinelibrary.wiley.com/doi/abs/10.1525/aa.1989.91.2.02a00090.

Dafoe, Allan, and Devin Caughey. "Honor and War: Southern U.S. Presidents and the Effects of Concern for Reputation." *World Politics* 68, no. 2 (April 2016): 341–381.

Dalton, John T., and Tin Cheuk Leung. "Why Is Polygyny More Prevalent in Western Africa? An African Slave Trade Perspective." *Economic Development and Cultural Change* 62, no. 4 (July 2014): 599–632. http://www.jstor.org/stable/10.1086/676531.

Das Gupta, Monica. "Family Systems, Political Systems, and Asia's 'Missing Girls': The Construction of Son Preference and Its Unraveling." World Bank, Washington, DC, December 2009.

Dawsari, Nadwa al-. "Tribal Governance and Stability in Yemen." The Carnegie Papers, Middle East, Carnegie Endowment for International Peace, Washington, DC, April 2012. http://carnegieendowment.org/files/yemen_tribal_governance.pdf.

Dawson, Miles Melander. *The Ethics of Confucius*. 1915. Reproduced online. http://www .sacred-texts.com/cfu/eoc/eoc09.htm.

Divale, William T., and Marvin Harris. "Population, Warfare, and the Male Supremacist Complex." *American Anthropologist* 78 (1976): 521–538.

Den Boer, Andrea. "Son Preference, Sex Ratios, and Security in the South Caucasus." Unpublished paper, May 2017.

Den Boer, Andrea, and Valerie M. Hudson. "Patrilineality, Son Preference, and Sex Selection in South Korea and Vietnam." *Population and Development Review* 43, no. 1 (2017): 119–147. doi:10.1111/padr.12041; http://onlinelibrary.wiley.com/doi/10.1111/padr.12041/abstract.

Den Boer, Andrea, Valerie M. Hudson, and Jenny Russell, "China's Mismatched Bookends: A Tale of Birth Sex Ratios in South Korea and Vietnam." Paper presented at the International Studies Association Annual Conference, New Orleans, LA, February 5, 2015.

Denny, Frederick. "Ummah in the Constitution of Medina." *Journal of Near Eastern Studies* 36, no. 1 (January 1977): 39–47. http://www.jstor.org/stable/544125.

Dewey, Caitlin. "Men Who Harass Women Online Are Quite Literally Losers, New Study Finds." *Washington Post*, July 20, 2015. https://www.washingtonpost.com/news/the-intersect /wp/2015/07/20/men-who-harass-women-online-are-quite-literally-losers-new-study -finds/?utm_term=.7eb86911f6c5.

Divale, William and Marvin Harris. "Population, Warfare, and the Male Supremacist Complex." *American Anthropologist* 78, no. 3 (September 1976): 521–538. https://doi.org /10.1525/aa.1976.78.3.02a00020.

Donno, Daniela, and Bruce Russett. "Islam, Authoritarianism, and Female Empowerment: What Are the Linkages?" *World Politics* 56 (July 2004): 582–607.

Dresch, Paul. "Imams and Tribes: The Writing and Acting of History in Upper Yemen." In *Tribes and States Formation in the Middle East*, edited by Philip S. Khoury and Joseph Kostiner. 252–287. Los Angeles: University of California Press, 1990.

Dreze, Jean, and Reetika Khera. "Crime, Gender, and Society in India: Insights from Homicide Data." *Population and Development Review* 26, no. 2 (June 2000): 335–352.

Duthe, Geraldine, France Mesle, Jacques Vallin, Irina Baduraashvili, and Karine Kyumjyan. "High Sex Ratios at Birth in the Caucasus: Modern Technology to Satisfy Old Desires." *Population and Development Review* 38, no. 3 (2012): 487–501.

Dyble, Mark, G. Salali, N. Chaudhary, A. Page, D. Smith, J. Thompson, L. Vinicius, R. Mace, and A. Migliano. "Sex Equality Can Explain the Unique Social Structure of Hunter-Gatherer Bands." *Science* 348, no. 6236 (2015): 796–798.

Dziedzic, Stephen, and Henry Belot. "Australian Citizenship Law Changes Mean Migrants Will Face Tougher Tests." *ABC News*, April 19, 2017. http://www.abc.net.au/news/2017-04-20 /migrants-to-face-tougher-tests-for-australian-citizenship/8456392.

"Eat Better? Let Women Do the Work . . ." *The Economist.* July 11, 2012. http://www.economist .com/blogs/graphicdetail/2012/07/global-food-security.

Ebenstein, Avraham. "Patrilocality and Missing Women." Hebrew University of Jerusalem, April 2014. http://in.bgu.ac.il/en/humsos/Econ/Documents/seminars/October%2030-2014 .pdf.

Edgar, Adrienne. "Emancipation of the Unveiled: Turkmen Women Under Soviet Rule, 1924–29." *Russian Review* 62 (January 2003): 132–149.

——. "Marriage, Modernity, and the 'Friendship of Nations': Interethnic Intimacy in Post-war Central Asia in Comparative Perspective." *Central Asian Survey* 26, no. 4 (2007): 581–599.

——. *Tribal Nation: The Making of Soviet Turkmenistan.* Princeton, NJ: Princeton University Press, 2004.

——. "Bolshevism, Patriarchy, and the Nation: The Soviet 'Emancipation' of Muslim Women in Pan-Islamic Perspective." *Slavic Review* 65, no. 2 (2006): 252–272.

——. "Marriage, Modernity, and the 'Friendship of Nations': Interethnic Intimacy in Post-war Central Asia in Comparative Perspective." *Central Asian Survey* 26, no. 4 (2007): 581–599.

Edlund, Lena, and Nils-Petter Lagerlöf. "Polygyny and Its Discontents: Paternal Age and Human Capital Accumulation." Columbia University Academic Commons, 2012. https:// doi.org/10.7916/D8988GCB, https://academiccommons.columbia.edu/catalog/ac:155593.

Edlund, Lena, Hongbin Li, Junjian Yi, and Junsen Zhang. "Sex Ratios and Crime: Evidence from China's One-Child Policy." *Review of Economics and Statistics* 95, no. 5 (December 2013): 1520–1534. http://www.mitpressjournals.org/doi/abs/10.1162/REST_a_00356#.VsYFzRj7Ll4.

Eickelman, Dale. *The Middle East and Central Asia: An Anthropological Approach.* Upper Saddle River, NJ: Prentice Hall, 2002.

Elida, Corry. "Indonesia: Mass Wedding Provides Marriage and Birth Registration for Low Income Families." *Jakarta Post*, January 29, 2015. http://www.thejakartapost.com /news/2015/01/29/mass-wedding-delivers-birth-certificates.html.

Ellison, Marc. "Tales of a Child Bride: 'My Father Sold Me for 12 Cows.'" *Al Jazeera*, July 12, 2016. https://www.aljazeera.com/indepth/features/2016/07/tales-child-bride-father-sold -12-cows-160711100933281.html.

Elman, Service. *Origins of the State and Civilization*. New York: Norton, 1975.

Emerson, Stephen A. "Desert Insurgency: Lessons from the Third Tuareg Rebellion." *Small Wars and Insurgencies* 22, no. 4 (2011): 669–687.

Engels, Friedrich. *The Origins of Family, Private Property, and the State*. 1884. Marxist Internet Archive. Proofed and corrected 2010. https://www.marxists.org/archive/marx/works /download/pdf/origin_family.pdf.

"Equal Inheritance Rights: Next Battle for Morocco's Women." *North Africa Post*, March 23, 2018, http://northafricapost.com/22834-equal-inheritance-rights-next-battle-moroccos -women.html.

Equality Now. "Ending Sex Discrimination in the Law." January 2015. https://www.equalitynow .org/sites/default/files/B+20_Report_EN.pdf.

Erlanger, Steven. "In Unruly Gaza, Clans Compete in Power Void." *New York Times*, October 17, 2005. http://www.nytimes.com/2005/10/17/international/middleeast/17 https://www.marxists .org/archive/marx/works/download/pdf/origin_family.pdfmideast.html.

Ermakoff, Ivan. "Patrimonial Rise and Decline: The Strange Case of the Familial State." *Political Power and Social Theory* 19 (2008): 253–271.

——. "Patrimony and Collective Capacity: An Analytical Outline." *Annals of the American Academy of Political and Social Science* 636, no. 1 (2011): 182–203.

Esipisu, Isaiah. "Men and Women, Farming Together, Can Eradicate Hunger." *Inter Press Service*, September 1, 2012. http://www.nationofchange.org/men-and-women-farming -together-can-eradicate-hunger-1346512517.

"Europe Is Trying to Teach Its Gender Norms to Refugees." *The Economist*, October 15, 2016. https://www.economist.com/europe/2016/10/15/europe-is-trying-to-teach-its-gender -norms-to-refugees.

Fan, Jie, Thomas Heberer, and Wolfgang Taubmann. *Rural China: Economic and Social Change in the Late Twentieth Century*. New York: M. E. Sharpe, 2006.

Fearon, James, and David Laitin. "Ethnicity, Insurgency, and Civil War." *American Political Science Review* 97, no. 1 (2003): 75–90.

Fenske, James. "African Polygamy: Past and Present." *Journal of Development Economics* 117 (2015): 58–73.

Ferguson, Robert. "Health Minister 'Deeply Disturbed' by Report of 'Son Preference' Sex-Selective Abortions." *The Star*, April 12, 2016. https://www.thestar.com/news/queenspark /2016/04/12/health-minister-deeply-disturbed-by-report-son-preference-linked-to-sex -selective-abortions.html.

Ferris, Izzy. "Men with Histories of Sexual Violence Are 'More Likely To Be Terrorists' So Policy Should Monitor Them, Top Lawyer Claims." *Daily Mail*, May 26, 2019. https:// www.dailymail.co.uk/news/article-7073493/Men-histories-sexual-violence-likely-terrorists -lawyer-claims.html.

Fish, M. Steven. "Islam and Authoritarianism." *World Politics* 55, no. 1 (2002): 4–37.

Food and Agriculture Organization of the United Nations. "Closing the Gender Gap in Agriculture." March 7, 2011. http://www.fao.org/news/story/en/item/52011/icode/.

"Forced Marriages in Council of Europe Member States: A Comparative Study of Legislation and Political Initiatives." Council of Europe, 2005, https://eige.europa.eu/library /resource/aleph_eige000000879.

Foreman-Peck, James, and Peng Zhou. "Late Marriage as a Contributor to the Industrial Revolution in England." *Economic History Review* 71, no. 4 (2018): 1073–1099.

Foucault, Michel. *Power/Knowledge*. New York: Vintage, 1980.

Fournier, Pascale. "The Reception of Muslim Family Law in Western Liberal States." Paper written for the Canadian Council of Muslim Women, September 30, 2004. http://www.ccmw.com/documents/Pascalepaper.pdf.

Fox, Jonathan. "The Ride of Religious Nationalism and Conflict: Ethnic Conflict and Revolutionary Wars, 1945–2001." *Journal of Peace Research* 41, no. 6 (2004): 715–731.

Francis, Andrew M. "Sex Ratios and the Red Dragon: Using the Chinese Communist Revolution to Explore the Effect of the Sex Ratio on Women and Children in Taiwan." *Journal of Population Economics* 24, no. 3 (2011): 813–827.

Fukuyama, Francis. *The Great Disruption: Human Nature and the Reconstitution of Social Order*. New York: Free Press, 1999.

——. *The Origins of Political Order*. New York: Farrar, Straus, and Giroux, 2011.

——. *Political Order and Political Decay*. New York: Farrar, Straus, and Giroux, 2014.

Galeotti, Mark. "The Making of a Chechen Hitman." *Foreign Policy*, May 24, 2018. https://foreignpolicy.com/2018/05/24/the-making-of-a-chechen-hitman/.

Gat, Azar. *War in Human Civilization*. Oxford: Oxford University Press, 2006.

——. "So Why Do People Fight? Evolutionary Theory and the Causes of War." *European Journal of International Relations* 15, no. 4 (December 2009): 571–600.

——. *Nations: The Long History and Deep Roots of Ethnicity and Nationalism*. Cambridge: Cambridge University Press, 2013.

Gellner, Ernest. "Tribalism and the State in the Middle East." In *Tribes and States Formation in the Middle East*, edited by Philip S. Khoury and Joseph Kostiner, 109–126. Los Angeles: University of California Press, 1990.

Geniole, S. N., M. A. Busseri, and C. M. McCormick. "Testosterone Dynamics and Psychopathic Personality Traits Independently Predict Antagonistic Behavior Towards the Perceived Loser of a Competitive Interaction." *Hormones and Behavior* 64 (2013): 790–798.

Ghani, Ashraf, Michael Carnahan, and Clare Lockhart. "Stability, State Building and Development Assistance: An Outside Perspective." The Princeton Project on National Security, 2006. https://www.princeton.edu/ppns/papers/ghani.pdf.

Giovarelli, Renee, and Elise Scalise. "Women's Land Tenure Framework for Analysis: Land Rights." Landesa, March 21, 2013. https://s24756.pcdn.co/wp-content/uploads/Land_Rights_Framework_2013March.pdf.

Giovarelli, Renee, Beatrice Wamalwa, and Leslie Hannay. "Land Tenure, Property Rights, and Gender." LandLinks, U.S. Agency for International Development, August 16, 2013. https://www.land-links.org/issue-brief/land-tenure-property-rights-and-gender/.

Girls Not Brides. "Syrian Arab Republic." http://www.girlsnotbrides.org/child-marriage/syrian-arab-republic/.

Gleditsch, Kristian, Julian Wucherpfennig, Simon Hug, and Karina Reigstad. "Polygyny or Misogyny? Reexamining the 'First Law on Intergroup Conflict.' " *Journal of Politics* 73, no. 1 (January 2011): 265–270.

Glowacki, Luke, Alexander Isakov, Richard Wrangham, Rose McDermott, James Fowler, and Nicholas Christakis. "Formation of Raiding Parties for Intergroup Violence Is Mediated by Social Network Structure." *Proceedings of the National Academy of Sciences* 113, no. 43 (2016): 12114–12119. www.pnas.org/cgi/doi/10.1073/pnas.1610961113.

Goldstein, Joseph. "At Afghan Weddings, His Side, Her Side, and 600 Strangers." *New York Times*, April 18, 2015. https://www.nytimes.com/2015/04/19/world/asia/at-afghan-weddings-his-side-her-side-and-600-strangers.html.

Goldstein, Peter. "Population and Gender in the MENA: Reflections from PRB's Farzaneh Roudi." Population Reference Bureau, September 1, 2016. https://www.prb.org/population -gender-mena-reflections/.

Goldstone, Jack, Robert Bates, David Epstein, Ted Robert Gurr, Michael Lustik, Monty Marshall, Jay Ulfeder, and Mark Woodward. "A Global Model for Predicting Political Instability." *American Journal of Political Science* 54, no. 1 (January 2010): 190–208.

Goodkind, Daniel. "Do Parents Prefer Sons in North Korea?" *Studies in Family Planning* 30, no. 3 (September 1999): 212–218.

Goodwin, Jeff. "The Libidinal Constitution of a High-Risk Social Movement: Affectual Ties and Solidarity in the Huk Rebellion, 1946–1954." *American Sociological Review* 62, no. 1 (February 1997): 53–69.

Goody, Jack. *The Development of Marriage and Family in Europe.* Cambridge: Cambridge University Press, 1983.

——. *The European Family.* New York: Wiley-Blackwell, 2000.

Goody, Jack, and Stanley J. Tambiah. *Bridewealth and Dowry.* Cambridge Papers in Social Anthropology. Cambridge: Cambridge University Press, 1974.

Gottschall, Jonathan. *The Rape of Troy: Evolution, Violence, and the World of Homer.* Cambridge: Cambridge University Press, 2008.

Gowan, Annie. "An Indian Teen Was Raped by Her Father. Village Elders Had Her Whipped." *Washington Post,* May 9, 2016, https://www.washingtonpost.com/world/asia _pacific/an-indian-teenager-was-raped-by-her-father-village-elders-had-her-whipped /2016/05/09/f6d6c840-c531-11e5-8965-0607e0e265ce_story.html.

Gowaty, Patricia Adair. "Evolutionary Biology and Feminism." *Human Nature* 3 (1992): 217–249.

——, ed. *Feminism and Evolutionary Biology: Boundaries, Intersections, and Frontiers.* New York: Springer, 1997.

——. "Sexual Natures: How Feminism Changed Evolutionary Biology." *Signs: Journal of Women in Culture and Society* 28, no. 3 (2003): 901–921.

Gracia, Enrique, and Juan Merlo. "Intimate Partner Violence Against Women and the Nordic Paradox." *Social Science and Medicine* 157 (2016): 27–30. doi:10.1016/j.socscimed.2016.03.040.

Greif, Avner. "Family Structure, Institutions, and Growth: The Origins and Implications of Western Corporations." *American Economic Review* 96, no. 2 (2006): 308–312. http:// web.stanford.edu/~avner/Greif_Papers/2006%20AER%20Families%20and%20Corporations .pdf.

Grogan, Louise. "Patrilocality and Human Capital Formation: Evidence from Central Asia." *Economics of Transition* 15, no. 4 (2007): 685–705.

——. "Household Formation Rules and Female Labour Supply: Evidence from Post-Communist Countries." *Journal of Comparative Economics* 41, no. 4 (2013): 1167–1183.

Grund, Brigid. "Behavioral Ecology, Technology, and the Organization of Labor: How a Shift from Spear Thrower to Self Bow Exacerbates Social Disparities." *American Anthropologist* 119, no. 1 (2017): 104–119. https://anthrosource.onlinelibrary.wiley.com/doi/pdf/10.1111 /aman.12820.

Guilmoto, Christophe. "Sex-Ratio Imbalance in Asia: Trends, Consequences, and Policy Responses." United Nations Population Fund, 2007. https://www.unfpa.org/sites/default /files/resource-pdf/regional_analysis.pdf.

Habitat for Humanity. "Level the Field: Ending Gender Inequality in Land Rights." 2016. https://www.habitat.org/multimedia/shelter-report-2016/.

Hajnal, John. "European Marriage Patterns in Perspective: The Uniqueness of the European Pattern." In *Population in History,* edited D. V. Glass and D. Eversley, 101–143. London: Edward Arnold, 1965.

——. "Two Kinds of Preindustrial Household Formation Systems." *Population and Development Review* 8 (1982): 470–482.

Handwerk, Brian. "An Ancient, Brutal Massacre May Be the Earliest Evidence of War." *Smithsonian Magazine*, January 20, 2016. https://www.smithsonianmag.com/science-nature/ancient-brutal-massacre-may-be-earliest-evidence-war-180957884/.

Hannagan, Rebecca J. 2008. "Gendered Political Behavior: A Darwinian Feminist Approach." *Sex Roles* 59: 465–75.

Harari, Yuval Noah. *Sapiens: A Brief History of Humankind*. New York: Harper Perennial, 2018.

Harel-Shalev, Ayelet. "Policy Analysis Beyond Personal Law: Muslim Women's Rights in India." *Politics and Policy* 41, no. 3 (June 2013): 384–419.

Harris, Cameron, and Daniel James Milton. "Is Standing for Women a Stand Against Terrorism? Exploring the Connection Between Women's Rights and Terrorism." *Journal of Human Rights* 15, no. 1 (2016): 60–78. doi:10.1080/14754835.2015.1062722.

Harris, Marvin. "The Evolution of Human Gender Hierarchies." In *Sex and Gender Hierarchies*, edited by Barbara D. Miller, 57–79. Cambridge: Cambridge University Press, 1993.

Hart, David. "Clan, Lineage and the Feud in a Rifian Tribe [Aith Waryaghar, Morocco]." In *Peoples and Cultures of the Middle East*, edited by Louise Sweet. Garden City, NY: Natural History Press, 1970: 3–75.

Hartman, Mary. *The Household and the Making of History: A Subversive View of the Western Past*. Cambridge: Cambridge University Press, 2004.

Hatem, Mervat. "First Ladies and the (Re)Definition of the Authoritarian State in Egypt." In *Women and Gender in Middle East Politics*, 42–44. The Project on Middle East Political Science, 2016. https://pomeps.org/wp-content/uploads/2016/05/POMEPS_Studies_19_Gender_Web.pdf.

He Linlin, Yang Hai, and Lan Tianming. "Deeper Investigation: How Difficult Is It for Rural Men to Get Married?" *China Youth Daily*, February 25, 2016.

Henrich, Joseph, Robert Boyd, and Peter J. Richerson. "The Puzzle of Monogamous Marriage." *Philosophical Transactions of the Royal Society* 367 (2012): 657–669.

Henshaw, Alexis. "Conjugal Order in the Rebel Family: A Comparative View." Unpublished manuscript, January 17, 2018.

Hertrich, Veronique. "Is Polygamy Weakening? Diversity and Trends in Africa During the Past 50 Years." French Institute for Demographic Studies. http://paa2007.princeton.edu/papers/71630.

Herz, Barbara, and Gene Sperling. "What Works in Girls' Education: Evidence and Policies from the Developing World." Council on Foreign Relations, 2004. https://www.cfr.org/report/what-works-girls-education.

Higgins, Andrew. "Norway Offers Migrants a Lesson in How to Treat Women." *New York Times*, December 19, 2015. https://www.nytimes.com/2015/12/20/world/europe/norway-offers-migrants-a-lesson-in-how-to-treat-women.html.

Hill, Kari, and Harvey Langholtz. "Rehabilitation Programs for African Child Soldiers." *Peace Review* 15, no. 3(2003): 279–285.

Hofman, Bruce. "Gaza City: All You Need Is Love." *The Atlantic*, December 2001. https://www.theatlantic.com/past/docs/issues/2001/12/hoffman.htm.

Homer-Dixon, Thomas. "On the Threshold: Environmental Changes as Causes of Acute Conflict." *International Security* 16, no. 1 (Fall 1991): 76–116.

Htun, Mala, and Laurel Weldon. "Sex Equality in Family Law: Historical Legacies, Feminist Activism, and Religious Power in 70 Countries." World Development Report 2012, Gender Equality and Development, World Bank, April 11, 2011. http://siteresources.worldbank.org/INTWDR2012/Resources/7778105-1299699968583/7786210-1322671773271/Htun-Weldon-family-law-paper-april-11.pdf.

Hudson, Valerie M. "Europe's Man Problem." *Politico*, January 5, 2016. http://www.politico
.com/magazine/story/2016/01/europe-refugees-migrant-crisis-men-213500.

Hudson, Valerie M., Bonnie Ballif-Spanvill, Mary Caprioli, and Chad Emmett. *Sex and World
Peace*. New York: Columbia University Press, 2012.

Hudson, Valerie M., Donna Lee Bowen, and Perpetua Lynne Nielsen. "What Is the Relationship Between Inequity in Family Law and Violence Against Women? Approaching the
Issue of Legal Enclaves." *Politics and Gender* 7, no. 4 (Winter 2012): 453–492.

——. "Clan Governance and State Stability: The Relationship Between Female Subordination
and Political Order." *American Political Science Review* 109, no. 3 (August 2015): 535–555.

Hudson, Valerie M., Mary Caprioli, Bonnie Ballif-Spanvill, Rose McDermott, Chad F.
Emmett. "The Heart of the Matter: The Security of Women and the Security of States."
International Security 33, no. 3 (2008/2009): 7–45.

Hudson, Valerie M., and Andrea Den Boer. *Bare Branches: The Security Implications of Asia's
Surplus Male Population*. Cambridge, MA: MIT Press, 2004.

——. "When a Boy's Life Is Worth More Than His Sister's." *Foreign Policy*, July 30, 2015. http://
foreignpolicy.com/2015/07/30/when-a-boys-life-is-worth-more-than-his-sisters-sex-ratio/.

Hudson, Valerie M., and Patricia Leidl. *The Hillary Doctrine: How Sex Came to Matter in
American Foreign Policy*. New York: Columbia University Press, 2015.

Hudson, Valerie M., and Hilary Matfess. "In Plain Sight: The Neglected Linkage Between
Brideprice, Raiding, and Rebellion." *International Security* 42, no. 1 (Summer 2017): 7–40.
doi:10.1162/ISEC_a_00289.

Hudson, Valerie M., and Rose McDermott. "Why Polygamy Is Bad for National Security."
Politico, July 16, 2015. https://www.politico.com/magazine/story/2015/07/polygamy
-national-security-putin-120234.

"Human Rights Study Links Payment of Bride Price to Abuse of Women." *IRIN News*,
May 16 2006. http://www.irinnews.org/report/59032/tanzania-study-links-payment-bride
-price-abusewomen.

Human Rights Watch. "Nigeria: Boko Haram Abducts Women, Recruits Children." November 29,
2013. http:// www.hrw.org/fr/node/121029.

——. "Unequal and Unprotected: Women's Rights Under Lebanese Personal Status Laws."
2015. https://www.hrw.org/report/2015/01/19/unequal-and-unprotected/womens-rights
-under-lebanese-personal-status-laws.

Huntington, Samuel. *The Clash of Civilizations and the Remaking of World Order*. New York:
Simon and Schuster, 1996.

Husseini, Rana. "Honor Killings." PBS.org. http://www.pbs.org/speaktruthtopower/rana.html.

Hussin, Iza. "The Pursuit of the Perak Regalia: Islam, Law and the Politics of Authority in the
Colonial State." *Law and Social Inquiry* 32, no. 3 (2007): 759–788.

Hyde, Jesse. "Inside 'The Order,' One Mormon Cult's Secret Empire." *Rolling Stone*, June 15,
2011. https://www.rollingstone.com/culture/news/inside-the-order-one-mormon-cults
-secret-empire-20110615.

Ikels, Charlotte. *Filial Piety: A Practice and Discourse in Contemporary East Asia*. Stanford,
CA: Stanford University Press, 2004.

Indrawati, Sri Mulyani. "Discriminating Against Women Keeps Countries Poorer." *World
Bank Voices* (blog), September 10, 2015. http://blogs.worldbank.org/voices/discriminating
-against-women-keeps-countries-poorer?CID=ECR_TT_worldbank_EN_EXT&utm
_content=bufferfb296&utm_medium=social&utm_source=facebook.com&utm
_campaign=buffer.

Ingelhart, Ronald, and Pippa Norris. *Rising Tide: Gender Equality and Cultural Change
Around the World*. New York: Cambridge University Press, 2003.

International Center for Missing and Exploited Children. "Child Marriage in the Middle East and North Africa." White paper, 2013. https://www.icmec.org/wp-content/uploads /2015/10/Child_Marriage_in_the_MENA_Region.pdf.

International Monetary Fund. "Security, Stability Measures Needed to Fix Fragile States." IMF Survey Interview, March 29, 2013. https://www.imf.org/en/News/Articles/2015/09 /28/04/53/soint032913a.

Izadi, Elahe. "The Potential Spouse Is Brought to You by the Islamic Republic of Iran." *Washington Post*, June 16, 2015. https://www.washingtonpost.com/news/soloish/wp/2015 /06/16/this-potential-spouse-is-brought-to-you-by-the-islamic-republic-of-iran/?noredirect =on&utm_term=.31a564271628.

Jacobson, David. *Of Virgins and Martyrs: Women and Sexuality in Global Conflict*. Baltimore, MD: Johns Hopkins University Press, 2013.

Jacoby, Hanan G., and Ghazala Mansuri. "Watta Satta: Bride Exchange and Women's Welfare in Rural Pakistan." World Bank Development Research Working Paper No. 4126, World Bank, Washington, DC, 2007.

Jakobsen, Hilde. "How Violence Constitutes Order: Consent, Coercion, and Censure in Tanzania." *Violence Against Women* 24, no. 1 (2018): 45–65.

Jewkes, Rachel, Emma Fulu, Tim Roselli, and Claudia Garcia-Moreno. "Prevalence of and Factors Associated with Non-Partner Rape Perpetration: Findings from the UN Multi-Country Cross-Sectional Study on Men and Violence in Asia and the Pacific." *The Lancet* 1, no. 4 (October 2013): e208–e218. https://doi.org/10.1016/S2214-109X(13)70069-X; https://www.thelancet.com/journals/langlo/article/PIIS2214-109X(13)70069-X/fulltext.

Jiang, Quanbao, and Jesus Sanchez-Barricarte. "Brideprice in China: The Obstacle to 'Bare Branches' Seeking Marriage." *History of the Family* 17, no. 1. (2012): 2–15. https://doi.org /10.1080/1081602X.2011.640544.

Johnson, Chandra. "How a Stable Home Life Can Help Prevent Mass Violence." *Deseret News*, August 5, 2016. https://www.deseretnews.com/article/865659350/How-a-stable-home-life -can-help-prevent-mass-violence.html.

Johnson, Dominic, Rose McDermott, Emily S. Barrett, Jonathan Cowden, Richard W. Wrangham, Matthew H. McIntyre, and Stephen Peter Rosen. "Overconfidence in Wargames: Experimental Evidence on Expectations, Aggression, Gender, and Testosterone." *Proceedings of the Royal Society B* (June 20, 2006): 2513–2520.

Johnson, Dominic, and Bradley Thayer. "The Evolution of Offensive Realism." *Politics and the Life Sciences* 35, no. 1 (March 2016): 1–26. doi:10.1017/pls.2016.6.

Jones, Ann. *War Is Not Over When It's Over: Women Speak Out from the Ruins of War*. New York: Metropolitan Books, 2010.

Joseph, Suad. "Political Familism in Lebanon." *Annals of the American Academy of Political and Social Science* 636, no. 1 (2011): 150–163.

"Judge Tosses Convicted British Columbia Polygamists' Constitutional Challenge." CBC News, March 9, 2018. http://www.cbc.ca/news/canada/british-columbia/polygamy-conviction -bc-winston-blackmore-james-oler-1.4569158.

Juergensmeyer, Mark. *Terror in the Mind of God: The Global Rise of Religious Violence*. 4th ed. Oakland: University of California Press, 2017.

Kamchybekova, Aisuluu. Project Component Coordinator, Promotion of Women to Civil Service and Politics, United Nations Development Program. Interview by Carl Brinton, Original Language English, recorded in the WomanStats Database, August 25, 2009.

Kanazawa, Satoshi, "Evolutionary Psychological Foundations of Civil Wars." *Journal of Politics* 71, no. 1 (January 2009): 25–34.

Kandiyoti, Deniz. "Bargaining with Patriarchy." *Gender and Society* 2, no. 3 (1988): 274–290.

Kasumovic, Michael, and Jeffrey Kuznekoff. "Insights into Sexism: Male Status and Performance Moderates Female-Directed Hostile and Amicable Behavior." *PLOS One* 10, no. 9
(2015): e0138399. https://doi.org/10.1371/journal.pone.0131613; https://journals.plos.org
/plosone/article?id=10.1371/journal.pone.0131613.

Kaur, Ravi Inder. "Perception of Female University Students Towards Their Inheritance Rights."
International Journal of Research in Humanities, Arts, and Literature 6, no. 2 (February 2018):
109–118.

Keenan, Jillian. "The Blood Cries Out." *Foreign Policy*, March 27, 2015. http://foreignpolicy.
com/2015/03/27/the-blood-cries-out-burundi-land-conflict.

Kemper, Theodore D. *Social Structure and Testosterone: Explorations of the Socio-Bio-Social
Chain*. New Brunswick, NJ: Rutgers University Press, 1990.

Khodary, T. el-. "For War Widows, Hamas Recruits Army of Husbands." *New York Times*,
October 31, 2008, https://www.nytimes.com/2008/10/31/world/middleeast/31gaza.html.

Kilcullen, David. "Anatomy of a Tribal Revolt." *Small Wars Journal*, 2007. http://smallwars
journal.com/blog/anatomy-of-a-tribal-revolt.

Kim, Erin Hye-Won, and Philip J. Cook. "The Continuing Importance of Children in Relieving Elder Poverty: Evidence from Korea." *Ageing and Society* 31, no. 6 (2011): 953–976.

Kim, Namsuk, and Pedro Conceicao. "The Economic Crisis, Violent Conflict, and Human
Development." *International Journal of Peace Studies* 15, no. 1 (2010): 29–43. https://www
.gmu.edu/programs/icar/ijps/vol15_1/KimConceicao15n1.pdf.

Kim, Rosa. "The Legacy of Institutionalized Gender Inequality in South Korea: The Family
Law." *Boston College Third World Law Journal* 14, no. 1 (1994): 144–162. http://lawdigital
commons.bc.edu/cgi/viewcontent.cgi?article=1269&context=twlj.

Kim, Seung Gwon, Ae Cho Cho, Yu Kyong Kim, Se Kyong Pak, and Kon Wu Yi. *The 2003
National Survey on Fertility and Family Health*. [In Korean.] Seoul: Korea Institute for
Health and Social Affairs, 2004. [김승권, 조애저, 김유경, 박세경, 이건우 (2003) 2003
년 전국 출산력 및 가족보건 실태조사연구 보고서. 서울:한국보건사회연구원.]

Kim, Seung Gwon, et al. *The 2012 National Survey on Fertility, Family Health and Welfare*.
[In Korean.] Seoul: Korea Institute for Health and Social Affairs, 2012.

King, Diane E., and Linda Stone. "Lineal Masculinity: Gendered Memory Within Patriliny."
American Ethnologist 37, no. 2 (2010): 323–336.

King, Elizabeth M. *Educating Girls and Women: Investing in Development*. Washington, DC:
World Bank, 1990.

Kirkpatrick, David. "Saudi Arabia Arrests 11 Princes." *New York Times*, November 4, 2017.
https://www.nytimes.com/2017/11/04/world/middleeast/saudi-arabia-waleed-bin-talal.
html.

——. "Saudi Crown Prince's Mass Purge Upends a Longstanding System." *New York Times*,
November 5, 2017. https://www.nytimes.com/2017/11/05/world/middleeast/saudi-crown
-prince-purge.html.

Klasen, Stephan. "Low Schooling for Girls, Slower Growth for All? Cross-Country Evidence
on the Effect of Gender Inequality in Education on Economic Development." *World Bank
Economic Review* 16, no. 3 (2002): 345–373. doi:10.1093/wber/lhf004.

Klausen, Jytte. *The Islamic Challenge: Politics and Religion in Western Europe*. Oxford: Oxford
University Press, 2005.

Korotayev, Andrey. "Form of Marriage, Sexual Division of Labor, and Postmarital Residence
in Cross-Cultural Perspective: A Reconsideration." *Journal of Anthropological Research* 59,
no. 1 (2003): 69–89. https://www.jstor.org/stable/3631445.

Korotayev, Andrey, and Dmitri Bondarenko. "Polygyny and Democracy: A Cross-Cultural
Comparison." *Cross-Cultural Research* 34, no. 1 (2000): 190–208.

KOSTAT. *2005 Statistics on the Aged*. October 21, 2005. www.kostat.go.kr.
——. *Social Survey (Health and Family)*. December 9, 2008. www.kostat.go.kr.
——. *Statistics Korea, 2012 Statistics on the Aged*. September 27, 2012. www.kostat.go.kr.
——. *Statistics Korea, Summary Results of 2014 Social Survey*. November 27, 2014. www.kostat.go.kr.
Kostiner, Joseph. "Transforming Dualities: Tribe and State Formation in Saudi Arabia." In *Tribes and States Formation in the Middle East*, edited by Philip S. Khoury and Joseph Kostiner, 226–251. Los Angeles: University of California Press, 1990.
Knipper, Corina, Alissa Mittnik, K. Massy, C. Kociumaka, I. Kucukkalipci, M. Maus, F. Wittenborn, S. Metz, A. Staskiewicz, J. Krause, and Philipp Stockhammer. "Female Exogamy and Gene Pool Diversification at the Transition from the Final Neolithic to the Early Bronze Age in Central Europe." *Proceedings of the National Academy of Sciences of the United States of America* (2017): 1–6. doi:10.1073/pnas.1706355114.
Krieger, Tim, and Laura Renner. "A Cautionary Tale on Polygyny, Conflict, and Gender Inequality." University of Freiburg Discussion Paper 2018–02, Wilfried-Guth-Stiftungs professor fur Ordnungs-und Wettbewerbspolitik, April 2018.
Kumar, Ruchi. "'Oh, God, Please Let Me Die': Treating Women Who Have Set Themselves on Fire in Afghanistan." *The Guardian*, June 26, 2017. https://www.theguardian.com /global-development-professionals-network/2017/jun/26/oh-god-please-let-me-die -treating-women-who-have-set-themselves-on-fire-in-afghanistan.
Lacey, Robert. *Inside the Kingdom: Kings, Clerics, Modernists, Terrorists, and the Struggle for Saudi Arabia*. New York: Penguin, 2010.
Lancaster, William. *The Rwala Bedouin Today*. Prospect Heights, IL: Waveland Press, 1997.
Landesa. "Women's Land Rights." Resources: Infographics, December 21, 2015. https://www .landesa.org/resources/womens-land-rights-and-the-sustainable-development-goals/.
Lapidus, Ira. "Tribes and State Formation in Islamic History." In *Tribes and States Formation in the Middle East*, edited by Philip S. Khoury and Joseph Kostiner, 25–47. Los Angeles: University of California Press, 1990.
Lee, Sung Yong. "How Did Son-Preference Disappear in Korea? Based on the Perspective of the Value of Children." Paper presented at the Sociology of Population Side Meeting Program, Busan, South Korea, 2013.
Lemmon, Gayle Tzemach. "Reforming Women's Property Rights in Afghanistan." Council on Foreign Relations, September 5, 2017. https://www.cfr.org/blog/reforming-womens -property-rights-afghanistan.
Lerner, Gerda. *The Creation of Patriarchy*. New York: Oxford University Press, 1986.
Lily, Abdul Al. *The Bro Code of Saudi Culture*. San Bernardino, CA: Al Lily, 2016.
Lindholm, Charles. *Generosity and Jealousy: The Swat Pukhtun of Northern Pakistan*. New York: Columbia University Press, 1982.
Linning, Stephanie. "Germany to Scrap 'Cultural Immunity' and Will No Longer Allows Migrants to Have Multiple Marriages or Child Brides." *Daily Mail*, June 15, 2016. http://www.dailymail.co.uk/news/article-3643411/Germany-scrap-cultural-immunity -no-longer-allow-migrants-multiple-marriages-child-brides.html.
Little, Daniel. *Understanding Peasant China*. New Haven, CT: Yale University Press, 1989.
Liou, Yu-Ming, and Paul Musgrave. "Oil, Autocratic Survival, and the Gendered Resource Curse: When Inefficient Policy Is Politically Expedient." *International Studies Quarterly* 60, no. 3 (2016): 440–456. doi:10.1093/isq/sqw021.
Liptak, Adam. "When God and the Law Don't Square." *New York Times*, February 17, 2008. https://www.nytimes.com/2008/02/17/weekinreview/17liptak.html.
Litvinova, Daria. "If He Beats You, It Means He Loves You." *Moscow Times*, August 5, 2016. https:// www.themoscowtimes.com/2016/08/05/if-he-beats-you-it-means-he-loves-you-a54866.

Lopez, Anthony, Rose McDermott, and Michael Bang Petersen. "States in Mind: Evolution, Coalitional Psychology, and International Politics." *International Security* 36, no. 2 (Fall 2011): 48–83.

Lu, Cheng. "Excess of Marriageable Males and Violent Crime in China and South Korea, 1970–2008." Paper presented at the 2012 Annual Meeting of the Population Association of America, San Francisco, CA, May 3–5, 2012. http://paa2012.princeton.edu /abstracts/121243.

Magdy, Samy. "Egypt's Top Cleric Calls Polygamy 'Injustice,' Draws Debate." *US News and World Report*, March 3, 2019. https://www.usnews.com/news/world/articles/2019-03-03 /egypts-top-cleric-stirs-controversy-with-polygamy-remarks.

Mahmoud, Feriel Ben. *Feminism Insha'allah: The Story of Arab Feminism*. Java Films, February 23, 2015. https://vimeo.com/ondemand/feminists.

Maier, Charles S. "Peace and Security for the 1990s." Unpublished paper for the MacArthur Fellowship Program, Washington, DC: Social Science Research Council. June 12, 1990.

Maine, Henry. *Ancient Law: Its Connection with the Early History of Society and its Relation to Modern Ideas*. Tucson: University of Arizona Press, 1986.

Maisel, Sebastian. "The Resurgent Tribal Agenda in Saudi Arabia." Issue Paper No. 5, The Arab Gulf States Institute in Washington, 2015.

Malm, Sara. "Girls as Young as Three Are Being Married Off in Yemen as Starving Families Try to Ensure They Have One Less Mouth to Feed and Use Dowry Payments to Buy Themselves Food." *Daily Mail*, March 4, 2019. https://www.dailymail.co.uk/news/article -6768425/Girls-young-THREE-married-Yemen-Oxfam-claims.html.

Manne, Kate. *Down Girl: The Logic of Misogyny*. Oxford: Oxford University Press, 2018.

Manson, Joseph H., Richard W. Wrangham, James L. Boone, Bernard Chapais, R. I. M. Dunbar, Carol R. Ember, William Irons, L. F. Marchant, W. C. McGrew, Toshisada Nishida, James D. Paterson, Eric Alden Smith, Craig B. Stanford. and Carol M. Worthman. "Intergroup Aggression in Chimpanzees and Humans" [and Comments and Replies] Author(s)." *Current Anthropology* 32, no. 4 (August–October 1991): 369–390.

Margan, Max. "I'll Slit Your Throat and Put a Bullet to Your Brain." *Daily Mail Australia*, January 29, 2017. http://www.dailymail.co.uk/news/article-4169084/Boy-abused-mother -thought-normal.html.

"Marital Rape," *Korea Times*, January 18, 2009, http://m.koreatimes.co.kr/pages/article. asp?newsIdx=38045.

Marshall, Monty G., and Donna Ramsey. "Gender Empowerment and the Willingness of States to Use Force." Unpublished research paper, Center for Systemic Peace, 1999. http:// www.members.aol.com/CSPmgm/.

Massell, Gregory J. *The Surrogate Proletariat: Moslem Women and Revolutionary Strategies in Soviet Central Asia, 1919–1929* (p. 201). Princeton, NJ: Princeton University Press, 1974.

Masud, Muhammad Khalid, comp. "Prophet Muhammad's Wife Aisha: How Old Was She at the Time of Her Marriage?" Sisters in Isla. https://www.sistersinislam.org.my/comment. php?comment.news.997.

Matfess, Hilary. "Boko Haram Is Enslaving Women, Making Them Join the War." *Newsweek*, February 8, 2016.

——. "Here's Why Many People Join Boko Haram, Despite Its Notorious Violence." *Washington Post*, April 26, 2016. https://www.washingtonpost.com/news/monkey-cage/wp/2016/04/26 /heres-why-so-many-people-join-boko-haram-despite-its-notorious-violence/.

Mattison, Siobhan. "Economic Impacts of Tourism and Erosion of the Visiting System Among the Mosuo of Lugu Lake." *Asia Pacific Journal of Anthropology* 11, no. 2 (2010): 159–176.

Mattison, Siobhan, Bret Beheim, Bridget Chak, and Peter Buston. "Offspring Sex Preferences Among Patrilineal and Matrilineal Mosuo in Southwest China Revealed by Differences in Parity Progression." *Royal Society Open Science* 3 (2016): 160526. http://dx.doi.org/10.1098/rsos.160526.

Mayer, Ann Elizabeth. "Reform of Personal Status Laws in North Africa: A Problem of Islamic or Mediterranean Laws?" *Middle East Journal* 49, no. 3 (1995): 432–446.

Mazur, Allan, and Alan Booth. "Testosterone and Dominance in Men." *Behavioral and Brain Science* 21, no. 3 (June 1998): 353–397.

Mbeoji, Ikechi. "The Civilised Self and the Barbaric Other: Imperial Delusions of Order and the Challenges of Human Security." *Third World Quarterly* 27, no. 5 (2007): 855–869.

McCreery, John L. "Women's Property Rights and Dowry in China and South Asia." *Ethnology* 15, no. 2 (1976): 163–174.

McDermott, Rose, and Jonathan Cowden. "Polygyny and Violence Against Women." *Emory Law Journal* 64 (2015): 1767–1814.

McDermott, Rose, Michael Dickerson, Steve Fish, Danielle Lussier, and Jonathan Cowden. "Attitudes Toward Polygyny: Experimental Evidence from Six Countries." In *The Evils of Polygyny: Rose McDermott*, edited by Kristen R. Monroe, 97–122. Ithaca, NY: Cornell University, 2018.

McDermott, Rose, Anthony C. Lopez, and Peter K. Hatemi. "'Blunt Not the Heat, Enrage It': The Psychology of Revenge and Deterrence." *Texas National Security Review*, October 24, 2017. https://tnsr.org/2017/10/blunt-not-heart-enrage-psychology-revenge-deterrence/.

McKinsey Global Institute. "How Advancing Women's Equality Can Add $12 Trillion to Global Growth." *Institute Report*, September 2015. http://www.mckinsey.com/global-themes/employment-and-growth/how-advancing-womens-equality-can-add-12-trillion-to-global-growth.

McLaughlin, Kelly. "Hundreds of Fatherless Brides in India Tie the Knot as Diamond Tycoon Funds Their Weddings in a Mass Celebration." *Daily Mail*, December 24, 2017. http://www.dailymail.co.uk/news/article-5210547/Hundreds-fatherless-brides-India-tie-knot.html.

McNeish, Hannah. "Malawi's Fearsome Chief, Terminator of Child Marriages." *Al-Jazeera*, May 16, 2016. https://www.aljazeera.com/indepth/features/2016/03/malawi-fearsome-chief-terminator-child-marriages-160316081809603.html.

Mearsheimer, John. *The Tragedy of Great Power Politics.* New York: Norton, 2003.

Meintjes, Sheila, Anu Pillay, and Meredeth Turshen. "There Is No Aftermath for Women." In *The Aftermath: Women in Post-Conflict Transformation*, edited Sheila Meintjes, Anu Pullay, and Meredeth Turshen, 3–17. New York: Zed Books 2001.

Melander, Erik. "Gender Equality and Interstate Armed Conflict." *International Studies Quarterly* 49, no. 4 (2005): 695–714.

——. "The Masculine Peace." In *Debating the East Asian Peace*, edited Elin Bjarnegard and Joakim Kreutz, 200–219. Copenhagen: NIAS Press, 2017.

Meyersfield, Bonita. "A Theory of Domestic Violence in International Law." Yale Law School Legal Scholarship Repository, 2016. http://digitalcommons.law.yale.edu/cgi/viewcontent.cgi?article=1002&context=ylsd.

Mies, Maria. "Social Origins of the Sexual Division of Labor." In *Women: The Last Colony*, edited by Maria Mies, Veronika Bennholdt-Thomsen, and Claudia Von Werlhof, 67–95. London: Zed Books, 1988.

Migiro, Katy. "More Child Marriage in Drought-Hit Ethiopia with Risk of 'Full-Blown' Disaster." *Thomson Reuters News*, December 11, 2015. http://news.trust.org//item/20151211164911-qtgz4/?source=dpMostPopular.

"Migrant Child Brides Put Europe in a Spin." *BBC*, September 30, 2016. https://www.bbc .com/news/world-europe-37518289.

Mill, John Stuart. *The Subjection of Women*. 1861. Reprint, Lexington, KY: [publisher unknown], 2013. Page references are to the 2013 edition.

Miller, Barbara Diane. "The Anthropology of Sex and Gender Hierarchies." In *Sex and Gender Hierarchies*, edited by Barbara D. Miller, 3–31. Cambridge: Cambridge University Press, 1993.

Miller, Derek. *The Girl in Green*. New York: Houghton Mifflin Harcourt, 2017.

Miller, Flagg. *The Moral Resonance of Arab Media: Audiocassette Poetry and Culture in Yemen*. Harvard Middle East Monograph Series, Cambridge, MA: Harvard University Press, 2007.

Mitchell, Jerry. "Most Dangerous Time for Battered Women? When They Leave." *Clarion-Ledger*, January 28, 2017. http://www.clarionledger.com/story/news/2017/01/28/most -dangerous-time-for-battered-women-is-when-they-leave-jerry-mitchell/96955552/.

Moffett, Helen. "Sexual Violence, Civil Society, and the New Constitution." In *Women's Activism in South Africa: Working Across Divides*, edited by Hannah Evelyn Britton, Jennifer Natalie Fish, and Sheila Meintjes, 155–184. Scottsville, South Africa: University of KwaZulu–Natal Press, 2007.

Moghadam, Valentine. *Gender and National Identity*. New York: Zed Books, 1996.

Moghtader, Michelle. "Iranian Parliament Bans Vasectomies in Bid to Boost Birth Rate." *Reuters*, August 11, 2014. https://www.reuters.com/article/us-iran-population/iranian -parliament-bans-vasectomies-in-bid-to-boost-birth-rate-idUSKBN0GB15Z20140811.

Mokuwa, Esther, Maarten Voors, Erwin Bulte, and Paul Richards. "Peasant Grievance and Insurgency in Sierra Leone: Judicial Serfdom as a Driver of Conflict." *African Affairs* 110, no. 440 (2011): 339–366.

Monroe, Kristen R., ed. *The Evils of Polygyny: Rose McDermott*. Ithaca, NY: Cornell University, 2018.

Moore, Charlie, and Hannah Moore. " 'Immigrants Should Blend In and Adopt Australian Values': Migrants to Undergo New Test About Forced Marriage, Genital Mutilation, and Freedom of Speech Before Being Granted Citizenship." *Daily Mail*, July 20, 2018. http:// www.dailymail.co.uk/news/article-5972557/Migrants-undergo-Australian-Values-test -Alan-Tudge-says.html.

Morgan Robin. *The Demon Lover*. New York: Washington Square Press, 2001.

"Morocco OKs Law Against Violence on Women, Wives Excluded." ANSAMed, February 15, 2018. http://www.ansamed.info/ansamed/en/news/sections/politics/2018/02/15/morocco -oks-law-against-violence-on-women-wives-excluded_8114f746-2c38-41ec-a783 -60388b1d031a.html.

Morris, Lulu. "Witch Hunting in Papua New Guinea." *National Geographic*, April 12, 2017. http://www.nationalgeographic.com.au/people/witch-hunting-in-papua-new-guinea .aspx.

Murdock, Heather. "'Delayed' Marriage Frustrates Middle East Youth." *Voice of America*, February 22, 2011. https://www.voanews.com/a/delayed-marriage-frustrates-middle-east -youth-116744384/172742.html.

Murray, Geoffrey. *China: The Next Superpower, Dilemmas in Change and Continuity*. New York: St Martin's Press, 1998.

"Muslim Women Hail Triple Talaq Bill, Seek Ban on Polygamy." *Times of India*, December 29, 2017. https://timesofindia.indiatimes.com/india/muslim-women-hail-triple-talaq-bill -seek-ban-on-polygamy/articleshow/62298393.cms.

Muslimi, Farea al-. "The Social Politics of Weddings in Yemen." *Al-Monitor*, November 20, 2013. http://www.al-monitor.com/pulse/originals/2013/11/yemen-weddings-politics-social -discrimination.html?utm_source=&utm_medium=email&utm_campaign=8603.

Muzhary, Fazal. "The Bride Price: The Afghan Tradition of Paying for Wives." *Afghanistan Analysts Network*, October 25, 2016. https://www.afghanistan-analysts.org/the-bride-price -the-afghan-tradition-of-paying-for-wives/.

Naili, Hajer. "Iraq Women's Shelter Responds to Growing Crisis." *Women's E-News*, June 19, 2014. https://womensenews.org/2014/06/iraq-womens-shelter-responds-growing-crisis/.

Najibullah, Farangis, and Mahmudjon Rahmatzoda. "Not Austere Enough: Tajik Authorities Seize Wedding Feast." *RadioFreeEurope*, September 19, 2017. https://www.rferl.org/a /tajikistan-wedding-feast-confiscated/28745090.html.

Nam, Sanghui. "The Women's Movement and the Transformation of the Family Law in South Korea. Interactions Between Local, National and Global Structures." *European Journal of East Asian Studies* 9, no. 1 (2010): 77.

Nanda, Priya, Abhishek Gautam, Ravi Verma, Aarushi Khanna, N. Khan, Nizamuddin Brahme, Shobhana Boyle, and Sanjay Kumar. *Study on Masculinity, Intimate Partner Violence and Son Preference in India*. New Delhi: International Center for Research on Women, 2014.

Narayan, Deepa. "India's Abuse of Women Is the Biggest Human Rights Violation on Earth." *The Guardian*, April 27, 2018. https://www.theguardian.com/commentisfree/2018/apr/27 /india-abuse-women-human-rights-rape-girls.

Newson, Lesley, and Peter J. Richerson. "Why Do People Become Modern? A Darwinian Explanation." *Population and Development Review* 35, no. 1 (2009): 117–158. doi:10.1111/j.1728 -4457.2009.00263.x.

Nielsen. Rebecca. "Presentation on Sierra Leone Research," WomanStats co-PI meeting, Provo, UT, July 10, 2017.

Niles, Chris. "UNICEF Strives to Help Papua New Guinea Break Cycle of Violence." UNICEF, August 14, 2008. https://www.unicef.org/infobycountry/papuang_45211.html.

Noor, Azman Mohd. "A Victim's Claim of Being Raped Is Neither a Confession to *Zina* Nor Committing *Qadhf* (Making False Accusation of *Zina*)." *Muslim World Journal of Human Rights* 8, no. 1 (2011): 1–20. doi:10.2202/1554-4419.1174.

Nordland, Rod. "Crackdown in Turkey Threatens a Haven of Gender Equality Built by Kurds." *New York Times*, December 7, 2016. https://www.nytimes.com/2016/12/07/world /middleeast/turkey-kurds-womens-rights.html.

——. "Women Are Free, and Armed, in Kurdish-Controlled Northern Syria." *New York Times*, February 24, 2018. https://www.nytimes.com/2018/02/24/world/middleeast/syria -kurds-womens-rights-gender-equality.html.

Norris, Pippa, and Ronald Inglehart. "The True Clash of Civilizations." *Foreign Policy* 135 (March–April 2003): 62–70. http://www.foreignpolicy.com/story/cms.php?story_id =16&page=0.

North, Douglass, John Wallis, and Barry Weingast. *Violence and Social Orders*. 2009. Reprint, Cambridge: Cambridge University Press, 2013.

Nowak, Andrzej, Michele Gelfand, Wojciech Borkowski, Dov Cohen, and Ivan Hernandez. "The Evolutionary Basis of Honor Cultures." *Psychological Science* (2015): 1–13. doi:10.1177/ 0956797615602860.

O'Brien, A. J. "Female Infanticide in the Punjab," *Folklore* 19, no. 3 (1908): 261–275.

O'Brien, Kevin, and Li Lianjiang. *Rightful Resistance in Rural China*. Cambridge: Cambridge University Press, 2006.

O'Neill, Ann. "Witnesses: Scallops for the Bishop, Toast for the Kids." *CNN*, April 6, 2016. https://www.cnn.com/2016/04/05/us/flds-secrets-warren-jeffs/index.html.

Offen, Karen. *European Feminisms: A Political History 1700–1950*. Stanford, CA: Stanford University Press, 2000.

Ogbonna, Anthony. "Law to Ban Polygamy: There's a Connection Between Polygamy, Poverty, and Terrorism—Emir of Kano." *Vanguard*, February 20, 2017. https://www.vanguardngr.com/2017/02/law-ban-polygamy-theres-connection-polygamy-poverty-terrorism-emir-kano/.

Oh, Seung-Yun, Cody T. Ross, Monique B. Mulder, and Samuel Bowles. "The Decline of Polygyny: An Interpretation." SFI Working Paper 2017-12-037, Santa Fe Institute, 2017. https://sfi-edu.s3.amazonaws.com/sfi-edu/production/uploads/working_paper/pdf/2017-12-037-rev_fedae8.pdf.

Okin, Susan Moller. "Inequalities Between the Sexes in Different Cultural Contexts." In *Women, Culture, and Development*, edited by Martha Nussbaum and Jonathon Glover, 274–297. Oxford: Clarendon Press, 1995.

Olalde, Inigo, et al. "The Genomic History of the Iberian Peninsula Over the Past 8000 Years." *Science* 363, no. 6432 (2019): 1230–1234. doi:10.1126/science.aav4040; http://science.sciencemag.org/content/363/6432/1230.

Palmstierna, Markel, Anna Frangou, Anna Wallette, and Robin Dunbar. "Family Counts: Deciding When to Murder Among the Icelandic Vikings." *Evolution and Human Behavior* 38, no. 2 (2017): 175–180. http://dx.doi.org/10.1016/j.evolhumbehav.2016.09.001.

Pateman, Carole. *The Sexual Contract*. Stanford, CA: Stanford University Press, 1988.

Patterson, Gerald R. "A Comparison of Models for Interstate War and for Individual Violence." *Perspectives on Psychological Science* 3, no. 3 (2008): 203–223.

Pearl, David S. *Islamic Family Law and Its Reception by the Courts in England*. Islamic Legal Studies Program, Harvard Law School, Occasional Publications 1, 2000.

PeaceFM. "Mahama Charges African Governments to Empower Women for Increased Productivity." September 12, 2017. https://www.peacefmonline.com/pages/politics/politics/201709/327272.php.

Peterson, J. E. "Tribes and Politics in Eastern Arabia." *Middle East Journal* 31, no. 3 (Summer 1977): 297–312.

Petts, Richard, Kevin Shafer, and Lee Essig. "Does Adherence to Masculine Norms Shape Fathering Behavior?" *Journal of Marriage and Family* 80, no. 3 (June 2018): 704–720.

Peyton, Nellie, and Lamin Jahateh. "Gambia: Resurgence of FGM and Child Marriage, Formerly Banned, But Returning with New Political Leadership." Thomson Reuters Foundation, January 23, 2018. http://news.trust.org/item/20180123090036-m8b8o/.

Pianigiani, Gaia. "Breaking Up the Family as a Way to Break Up the Mob." *New York Times*, February 10, 2017. https://www.nytimes.com/2017/02/10/world/europe/breaking-up-the-family-as-a-way-to-break-up-the-mob.html.

Pickering, Steve. "Determinism in the Mountains: The Ongoing Belief in the Bellicosity of 'Mountain People,' " *The Economics of Peace and Security* 6, no. 2 (2011): 20–25.

Piper, Elizabeth. "Putin's Daughter and Russia's Second-Generation Elite." *Japan Times*, November 12, 2015. https://www.japantimes.co.jp/news/2015/11/12/world/putins-daughter-russias-second-generation-elite/#.WvB9IiOZNZo.

Polk, Sam. "How Wall Street Bro Talk Keeps Women Down." *New York Times*, July 7, 2016. https://www.nytimes.com/2016/07/10/opinion/sunday/how-wall-street-bro-talk-keeps-women-down.html.

Potts, Malcolm, and Thomas Hayden. *Sex and War*. Dallas, TX: Benbella Books, 2008.

Pound, N., Martin Daly, and Margo Wilson. "There's No Contest: Human Sex Differences Are Sexually Selected." *Behavioral and Brain Sciences* 32, no. 3/4 (2009): 286–287.

Power, Carla. "Muslim Women Are Fighting to Redefine Islam as a Religion of Equality." *Time*, March 20, 2015. http://time.com/3751243/muslim-women-redefine-islam-feminism/.

Prensa Latina. "Child Marriage, Growing Phenomenon in Latin America and the Caribbean." April 9, 2018. http://www.plenglish.com/index.php?o=rn&id=26907&SEO=child-marriage -growing-phenomenon-in-latin-america-and-the-caribbean.

Promundo: Health Masculinity, Gender Equity, https://promundoglobal.org.

Punch. "Inheritance Sharing: Customary Law Fuelling Disharmony in Nigerian Families." May 19, 2016. http://punchng.com/inheritance-sharing-customary-laws-fuelling-disharmony -nigerian-families/.

Puri, Lakshmi. "Gender Inequalities Affect Health Outcomes and Must Be Addressed Accordingly." UNWomen, May 30, 2013. http://www.unwomen.org/en/news/stories/2013/5 /lakshmi-puri-gender-inequalities-affect-health-outcomes-and-must-be-addressed -accordingly.

Raffield, Ben, and Mark Collard. "Male-Biased Operational Sex Ratios and the Viking Phenomenon: An Evolutionary Anthropological Perspective on Late Iron Age Scandinavian Raiding." *Evolution and Human Behavior* 38, no. 3 (2016): 315–324. doi:10.1016/j. evolhumbehav.2016.10.013.

Rahman, Shaikh Azizur. "'We Decide to Take a Stand': Why Some Indian Families are Returning Dowries." *The Guardian*, June 5, 2017. https://www.theguardian.com/global -development/2017/jun/05/take-a-stand-indian-families-returning-dowries-dahez-roko -abhiyan-campaign.

Raphael, T. J. "ISIS Uses Rape and Sexual Violence Against Women to Consolidate Its Power." *PRI*, August 14, 2015. https://www.pri.org/stories/2015-08-14/isis-uses-rape-and -sexual-violence-against-women-consolidate-its-power.

Raphelson, Samantha. "Countries Around the World Move to Repeal 'Marry Your Rapist' Laws." NPR, August 9, 2017. https://www.npr.org/2017/08/09/542468265/countries-around -the-world-move-to-repeal-marry-your-rapist-laws.

Rasheed, Madawi Al-, and Loulouwa Al-Rasheed. "The Politics of Encapsulation: Saudi Policy Towards Tribal and Religious Opposition." *Middle Eastern Studies* 32, no. 1 (1996): 96–119. doi:10.1080/00263209608701093.

Rees, Susan, Mohammed Mohsin, Alvin Tay, R. Thorpe, S. Murray, E. Savio, M. Fonseca, Wietse Tol, and Derrick Silove. "Associations Between Brideprice Obligations and Women's Anger, Symptoms of Mental Distress, Poverty, Spouse and Family Conflict, and Preoccupations with Injustice in Conflict-Affected Timor-Leste." *British Medical Journal-Global Health*, May 26, 2016. http://gh.bmj.com/content/1/1/e000025.info.

Rees, Susan, Mohammed Mohsin, Alvin Tay, Elisa Soares, Natalino Tam, Zelia da Costa, Wietse Tol, and Derrick Silove. "Associations Between Brideprice Stress and Intimate Partner Violence Amongst Pregnant Women in Timor-Leste." *Globalization and Health* 13, no. 66. (2017). https://doi.org/10.1186/s12992-017-0291-z.

Regan, Patrick M., and Aida Paskeviciute. "Women's Access to Politics and Peaceful States." *Journal of Peace Research* 40 (2003): 287–302.

Reich, Wilhelm. *The Mass Psychology of Fascism*. 3rd ed. New York: Farrar, Straus and Giroux, 1980.

Reid, Sue. "The Tragic Truth About Cousin Marriages." *Daily Mail*, July 6, 2018. http://www .dailymail.co.uk/news/article-5927581/The-tragic-truth-cousin-marriages.html.

Reiter, Dan. "The Positivist Study of Gender and International Relations." *Journal of Conflict Resolution* 59, no. 7 (2015): 1301–1326.

Rice, William R. "Sexually Antagonistic Male Adaptations Triggered by Experimental Arrest of Female Evolution." *Nature* 381 (1996): 232–234. doi:10.1038/381232a0.

——. "Dangerous Liaisons." *Proceedings of the National Academy of Sciences* 97 (2000): 12953–12955.

Richmond, Matt, and Flavia Krause-Jackson. "Cows-for-Brides Inflation Spurs Cattle Theft in South Sudan." *Bloomberg News*, July 25, 2011. http://www.bloomberg.com/news/articles /2011-07-26/cows-for-bride-inflation-spurs-cattle-theft-among-mundari-in-south-sudan.

Rizvi, Narjis, Kauser S. Khan, and Babar T. Shaikh. "Gender: Shaping Personality, Lives, and Health of Women in Pakistan." *BMC Women's Health* 14, no. 53. (2014): https:// doi.org/10.1186/1472-6874-14-53.

Robinson, Jillian. "Jihadi Speed-Dating." *Daily Mail*, July 17, 2017. http://www.dailymail.co.uk /news/article-4703426/ISIS-brides-reveal-reality-married-jihadi.html.

Romm, Joseph J. *Defining National Security: The Nonmilitary Aspects*. Pew Project on America's Task in a Changed World (Pew Project Series), Council on Foreign Relations, Washington, DC, 1993.

Rosen, Stephen. *War and Human Nature*. Princeton, NJ: Princeton University Press, 2005.

Rosenberg, Tina. "Letting (Some of) India's Women Own Land." *New York Times*, March 22, 2016. https://opinionator.blogs.nytimes.com/2016/03/22/letting-some-of-indias-women-own-land/.

Rudolph, Susanne H., and Lloyd Rudolph. "Living with Difference in India." *Political Quarterly* 71, Suppl. 1 (2000): 20–38.

Ruiz-Grossman, Sarah. "How This Female Chief Broke Up 850 Child Marriages in Malawi." *HuffPost*, April 1, 2016. https://www.huffingtonpost.com/entry/woman-chief-breaks-up -850-child-marriages-in-malawi_us_56fd51c2e4b0a06d580510da?ir=Good+News&).

Sabbe, Alexia, Halima Oulami, Wahiba Zekraoui, Halima Hikmat, Marleen Temmerman, and Els Leye. "Determinants of Child and Forced Marriage in Morocco: Stakeholder Per-spectives on Health, Policies, and Human Rights." *BMC International Health and Human Rights* 13, no. 4 (2013): 43–53. https://doi.org/10.1186/1472-698X-13-43.

Sakkaf, Nasser al-. "Hard Times Drive Down Price of Marriage in War-Torn Taiz." *Middle East Eye*, January 26, 2016. http://www.middleeasteye.net/news/hard-times-drive-down -price-marriage-war-torn-taiz-1067666593.

Salime, Zakia "Women and the Right to Land in Morocco: The Sulaliyyates Movement." In *Women and Gender in Middle East Politics*, 35–37. The Project on Middle East Political Science, May 10, 2016. https://pomeps.org/wp-content/uploads/2016/05/POMEPS_Studies _19_Gender_Web.pdf.

Sanday, Peggy Reeves. *Female Power and Male Dominance: On the Origins of Sexual Inequality*. Cambridge: Cambridge University Press, 1981.

——. "The Socio-Cultural Context of Rape: A Cross-Cultural Study." *Journal of Social Issues* 37, no. 4 (1981): 5–27.

——. *Fraternity Gang Rape: Sex, Brotherhood, and Privilege on Campus*. 1990. Reprint, New York: New York University Press, 2007.

——. *Women at the Center: Life in a Modern Matriarchy*. Ithaca, NY: Cornell University Press, 2003.

Sasman, Catherine. "Polygamy to be Outlawed." *The Namibian*, April 12, 2012. https://www .namibian.com.na/index.php?id=93899&page=archive-read.

Save the Children. *Too Young to Wed, The Growing Problem of Child Marriages Among Syrian Refugees in Jordan*. 2014. https://www.savethechildren.org.uk/sites/default/files /images/Too_Young_to_Wed.pdf.

Savransky, Rebecca. "State Department Cutting Language on Women's Rights Discrimi-nation in Annual Report." *The Hill*, February 22, 2018. http://thehill.com/homenews /administration/375009-state-department-cutting-language-on-womens-rights -discrimination-in.

Schatz, Edward. *Modern Clan Politics*. Seattle: University of Washington Press, 2004.

Scheidel, Walter. *The Great Leveler: Violence and the History of Inequality from the Stone Age to the Twenty-First Century*. Princeton, NJ: Princeton University Press, 2017.

Schemm, Paul. "Climate Change Threatens an Ancient Way of Life in Ethiopia." *Washington Post*, July 18, 2017. https://www.washingtonpost.com/world/africa/climate-change-threatens -an-ancient-way-of-life-in-ethiopia/2017/07/16/c2726a4e-658c-11e7-94ab-5b1f0ff459df _story.html?utm_term=.f668774506c7.

Schlegel, Alice, and Rohn Eloul. "Marriage Transactions: Labor, Property, Status." *American Anthropologist* 90, no. 2 (1988): 290–309. doi:10.1525/aa.1988.90.2.02a00030.

Schnoebelen, Jill. "Witchcraft Allegations, Refugee Protection, and Human Rights: A Review of the Evidence." UNHCR Research Paper No. 169, United Nations High Commissioner for Refugees, January 2009. http://www.unhcr.org/afr/4981ca712.pdf.

Schulthies, Becky. Personal communication with author Bowen, 2009.

Schrodt, Phil. "Seven Deadly Sins of Contemporary Quantitative Political Analysis." Unpublished manuscript, August 23, 2010. https://lcsr.hse.ru/data/2011/12/19/1261789486 /Schrodt7SinsAPSA10.pdf.

Schwartz, Christopher, and Alisher Khamidov. "Kyrgyzstan: Corrupt, Anarchic—and Stable?" *The Diplomat*, August 16, 2016. https://thediplomat.com/2016/08/kyrgyzstan-corrupt-anarchic -and-stable/?utm_source=Active+Subscribers&utm_campaign=152b4b5b10-MR _08182016&utm_medium=email&utm_term=0_35c49cbd51-152b4b5b10-64183517.

Sciolino, Elaine. "Britain Grapples with Role for Islamic Justice." *New York Times*, November 10, 2008. http://www.nytimes.com/2008/11/19/world/europe/19shariah.html.

Scott, Joan Wallach. "Gender: A Useful Category of Historical Analysis." *American Historical Review* 91, no. 5 (1986): 1053–1075.

Seidensticker, Robert. "Christianity Becomes an African Religion, Islam Overtakes Christianity, and Other Upcoming Changes." *Patheos*, May 11, 2015. http://www.patheos.com /blogs/crossexamined/2015/05/christianity-becomes-an-african-religion-islam-overtakes -christianityand-other-upcoming-changes/.

Sell, Aaron, John Tooby, Leda Cosmides, and Gordon H. Orians. "Formidability and the Logic of Human Anger." *Proceedings of the National Academy of Sciences of the United States of America* 106, no. 35 (Sep. 1, 2009): 15073–15078.

Semple, Kirk. "Big Weddings Bring Afghans Joy, and Debt." *New York Times*, January 14, 2008.

Shane, Scott, and Jo Becker. "A New Libya, with 'Very Little Time Left.'" *New York Times*, February 27, 2016. https://www.nytimes.com/2016/02/28/us/politics/libya-isis-hillary-clinton .html.

Sharaungaa, Stanley, Maxwell Mudharab, and Ayalneh Bogalec. "The Impact of 'Women's Empowerment in Agriculture' On Household Vulnerability to Food Insecurity in the KwaZulu-Natal Province." *Forum for Development Studies* 42, no. 2 (2015): 195–223.

Sharratt, Sara. "Voices of Court Members." In *Sexual Violence as an International Crime: Interdisciplinary Approaches*, edited by Anne-Marie deBrouwer, Charlotte Ku, Renee G. Romkens, and L. J. van der Herik, 353–69. Cambridge: Intersentia, 2013.

Sherman, Howard. *How Society Makes Itself: The Evolution of Political and Economic Institutions.* New York: M. E. Sharpe, 2005.

Shifman, Pamela, and Salamishah Tillet. "To Stop Violence, Start at Home." *New York Times*, February 3, 2015. https://www.nytimes.com/2015/02/03/opinion/to-stop-violence-start-at -home.html?_r=0.

Siddique, Kaniz. "Domestic Violence Against Women: Cost to the Nation," CARE Bangladesh, June 2011, http://www.carebangladesh.org/publication/Publication_5421518.pdf.

Sikora, Martin, et al. "Ancient Genomes Show Social and Reproductive Behavior of Early Upper Paleolithic Foragers." *Science*, October 5, 2017. doi:10.1126/science.aao1807; http:// science.sciencemag.org/content/early/2017/10/04/science.aao1807.

Sinclair, Stephanie. "Interview/Documenting Child Marriage for Over a Decade—And Still Going." *National Geographic*, September 14, 2015. https://www.nationalgeographic .com/photography/proof/2015/09/14/documenting-child-marriage-for-over-a-decade -and-still-going/.

Singerman, Diane. *The Economic Imperatives of Marriage: Emerging Practices and Identities Among Youth in the Middle East*. Dubai: Wolfensohn Center for Development at the Dubai School of Government, 2007.

——. "The Economic Imperatives of Marriage: Emerging Practices and Identities Among Youth in the Middle East." Working Paper No. 6, Middle East Youth Initiative, Washington, DC, September 2007.

Skidmore, David. "Understanding Chinese President's Xi's Anti-Corruption Campaign." *The Conversation*, October 27, 2017. https://theconversation.com/understanding-chinese -president-xis-anti-corruption-campaign-86396.

Slackman, Michael. "Stifled, Egypt's Young Turn to Islamic Fervor." *New York Times*, February 17, 2008. https://www.nytimes.com/2008/02/17/world/middleeast/17youth.html.

Smith, Anthony D. *The Ethnic Origins of Nations*. New York: Wiley-Blackwell, 1991.

Smuts, Barbara. "Male Aggression Against Women: An Evolutionary Perspective." *Human Nature* 3, no. 1 (1992): 1–44.

——. "The Evolutionary Origins of Patriarchy." *Human Nature* 6, no. 1 (1995): 1–32.

Sobek, David, M. Rodwan Abouharb, and Christopher G. Ingram. "The Human Rights Peace: How the Respect for Human Rights at Home Leads to Peace Abroad." *Journal of Politics* 68, no. 3 (2006): 519–529.

Solnit, Rebecca. *Men Explain Things to Me*. Chicago: Haymarket, 2014.

——. *The Mother of All Questions*. Chicago: Haymarket, 2017.

Sommers, Marc, and Stephanie Schwartz. "Dowry and Division." USIP Special Report 295, U.S. Institute of Peace, Washington, DC, November 2011. http://www.usip.org/sites/default /files/SR_295.pdf.

"South Korea's Fertility Rate Is the Lowest in the World." *The Economist*, June 30, 2018. https://www .economist.com/asia/2018/06/30/south-koreas-fertility-rate-is-the-lowest-in-the-world.

Stanford, Charlotte. "Women and the Building Trades in Henry VIII's England." Paper presented to the Women's Studies Program, Brigham Young University, Provo, UT, September 14, 2017.

Starr, Harvey, and Benjamin Most. "Contagion and Border Effects on Contemporary African Conflict." *Comparative Political Studies* 16, no. 1 (1983): 92–117.

Starr, Harvey, and G. Dale Thomas. "The Nature of Borders and International Conflict: Revisiting Hypotheses on Territory." *International Studies Quarterly* 49, no.1 (March 2005): 123–139.

Strauss, Bernard. "Genetic Counseling for Thalassemia in the Islamic Republic of Iran." *Perspectives in Biology and Medicine* 52, no. 3 (Summer 2009): 364–376.

Stritof, Bob, and Sheri Stritof. "Marriage Laws in the US by Age—U.S. Teen Marriage License Laws." The Spruce. June 27, 2019. http://marriage.about.com/cs/teenmarriage/a/teenus _5.htm.

Sudani, Thaier al-. "Iraq: Islamist MPs Propose a Change in the Personal Status Law That Would Allow Child Marriages." *Al Monitor*, November 17, 2017, https://www.al-monitor .com/pulse/originals/2017/11/iraq-personal-status-law-child-marriage.html?utm_campaign =20171117&utm_source=sailthru&utm_medium=email&utm_term=Daily%20Newsletter.

Sumner, William Graham. *Folkways*. New York: Dover, 1959.

Supreme Court of British Columbia. Reference Re: Section 293 of the Criminal Code of Canada, 2011 BCSC 1588 (CanLII). (2011). https://www.canlii.org/en/bc/bcsc/doc/2011 /2011bcsc1588/2011bcsc1588.html#.

Sussman, Anna. "Ugandan Adultery Law Curbs Effects of Polygamy." *Women's eNews*, June 24, 2007. https://womensenews.org/2007/06/ugandan-adultery-law-curbs-effects -polygamy/.

Symons, Emma-Kate. "Morocco's Indigenous Amazigh Women Unite Against Islamists and Arab Elites." *New York Times*, March 24, 2016. http://nytlive.nytimes.com/womenin theworld/2016/03/24/matriarchal-traditions-in-north-africa-under-threat-from-islamists -and-arab-elites/.

Tadmouri, Ghazi, Pratibha Nair, Tasneem Obeid, Mahmoud Al Ali, Najib Al Khaja, and Hanan Hamamy. "Consanguinity and Reproductive Health Among Arabs." *Reproductive Health* 6, no. 17 (October 2009): http://www.reproductive-health-journal.com /content/6/1/17.

"Taiwan Ministry Turns Matchmaker to Boost Birth Rate." *BBC*, June 21, 2010. http://www .bbc.com/news/10364381.

Tapper, Richard. "Anthropologists, Historians, and Tribespeople on Tribe and State Formation in the Middle East." In *Tribes and States Formation in the Middle East*, edited by Philip S. Khoury and Joseph Kostiner, 48–73. Los Angeles: University of California Press, 1990.

Taylor, Alan. "Rising Protests in China." *The Atlantic*, February 17, 2012. http://www.theatlantic .com/photo/2012/02/rising-protests-in-china/100247/.

Tertilt, Michèle. "Polygyny, Fertility, and Savings." *Journal of Political Economy* 113, no. 6 (2005): 1341–1371. http://tertilt.vwl.uni-mannheim.de/research/polygyny05.pdf.

"The Link Between Polygamy and War." *The Economist.* December 19, 2017. https://www .economist.com/christmas-specials/2017/12/19/the-link-between-polygamy-and-war.

Tibi, Bassam. "The Simultaneity of the Unsimultaneous: Old Tribes and Imposed Nation-State in the Modern Middle East." In *Tribes and States Formation in the Middle East*, edited by Philip S. Khoury and Joseph Kostiner, 127–152. Los Angeles: University of California Press, 1990.

Tohidi, Nayereh. "Soviet in Public, Azeri in Private: Gender, Islam, and Nationality in Soviet and Post-Soviet Azerbaijan." *Women's Studies International Forum* 19, no. 1–2 (1996): 111–123.

Tornkvist, Anna. "Sweden Stands Out in Domestic Violence Study." *TheLocal.se*, March 5, 2014. http://www.thelocal.se/20140305/sweden-out-top-in-eu-domestic-violence-league.

Townley, Brynne. "Women in Rwanda: The Truth About Gender Equality." *WomanStats* (blog), February 13, 2017. https://womanstats.wordpress.com/2018/02/13/women-in-rwanda -the-truth-about-gender-equality/.

Tucker, William. *Marriage and Civilization.* New York: Regnery, 2014.

Turchin, Peter. *War and Peace and War: The Rise and Fall of Empires.* New York: Plume, 2007.

——. *Ultra Society: How 10,000 Years of War Made Humans the Greatest Cooperators on Earth.* Chaplin, CT: Beresta Books, 2016.

"Uganda Brideprice Refund Outlawed by Top Judges." *BBC*, August 6, 2015. http://www.bbc .com/news/world-africa-33800840.

United Nations. "International Covenant on Economic, Social, and Cultural Rights." 1967. https://treaties.un.org/doc/Treaties/1976/01/19760103%2009-57%20PM/Ch_IV_03.pdf.

——. "Declaration on the Rights of Persons Belonging to National or Ethnic, Religious and Linguistic Minorities." A/RES/47/135, 1992. http://www.un.org/documents/ga/res/47 /a47r135.htm.

United Nations Children's Fund. "Early Marriage: A Harmful Traditional Practice." UNICEF, 2005. http://www.unicef.org/ publications/files/Early Marriage 12.lo.pdf.

United Nations Committee on the Elimination of Discrimination Against Women (CEDAW), *CEDAW General Recommendation No. 21: Equality in Marriage and Family Relations*, 1994. http://www.refworld.org/docid/48abd52co.html.

United Nations Development Program. "The Human Development Index." UNDP Human Development Reports. http://hdr.undp.org/en/content/human-development-index-hdi.

United Nations Development Program, Regional Bureau for Arab States. *Arab Human Development Report 2004: Towards Freedom in the Arab World*, New York: United Nations Development Program, 2005.

United Nations Economic and Social Council (ECOSOC). "Civil and Political Rights, Including the Question of Religious Intolerance." E/CN.4/2002/73/Add.2, April 23, 2009. http://www.wunrn.com/un_study/english.pdf.

United Nations Entity for Gender Equality and the Empowerment of Women. "Malawi Chief Annuls 330 Child Marriages." UNWomen, September 17, 2015. http://www.unwomen.org /en/news/stories/2015/9/malawi-chief-annuls-330-child-marriages.

United Nations Human Rights Committee. "General Comment No. 28: Equality of Rights Between Men and Women." Article 3 of the International Covenant on Civil and Political Rights, U.N. Doc. CCPR/C/21/Rev.1/Add.10 2000. http://hrlibrary.umn.edu/gencomm /hrcom28.htm.

United Nations Human Rights Council. "'I Lost My Dignity': Sexual and Gender-Based Violence in the Syrian Arab Republic." A/HRC/37/CRP.3, March 8, 2018. http://www .ohchr.org/Documents/HRBodies/HRCouncil/CoISyria/A-HRC-37-CRP-3.pdf.

United Nations Population Fund. "Motherhood in Childhood: Facing the Challenge of Adolescent Pregnancy." UNFPA State of World Population, 2013. https://www.unfpa.org /sites/default/files/pub-pdf/EN-SWOP2013-final.pdf.

U.S. Agency for International Development. "Afghanistan: Land Reform in Afghanistan." LandLinks. https://www.land-links.org/project/land-reform-in-afghanistan/.

——. "Ending Child Marriage and Meeting the Needs of Married Children: The USAID Vision for Action." 2012. https://www.usaid.gov/sites/default/files/documents/1870/USAID%20Ending %20Child%20Marriage%202012.pdf.

U.S. Department of State. "India: International Religious Freedom Report." 2007. http://www .state.gov/g/drl/rls/irf/2007/90228.htm.

——. "Country Report on Human Rights: Rwanda." 2007. https://www.state.gov/j/drl/rls /hrrpt/2007/100499.htm.

——. "Opening Statement on Global Efforts to End Child Marriage by Ambassador Catherine M. Russell. September 14, 2016. https://2009-2017.state.gov/s/gwi/rls/rem/2016/261970 .htm.

Urdal, Henrik. "A Clash of Generations? Youth Bulges and Political Violence." *International Studies Quarterly* 50, no. 3 (September 2006): 607–629.

Velitchkova, Ana. "World Culture, Uncoupling, Institutional Logics, and Recoupling: Practices and Self-Identification as Institutional Microfoundations of Political Violence." *Sociological Forum* 30, no. 3 (2015): 698–720.

Vogelstein, Rachel. *Ending Child Marriage: How Elevating the Status of Girls Advances U.S. Foreign Policy Objectives.* New York: Council on Foreign Relations, May 14, 2013.

Von Struensee, Vanessa. "The Contribution of Polygamy to Women's Oppression and Impoverishment." *Murdoch University Electronic Journal of Law*, 2005. http://www.austlii.edu .au/au/journals/MurUEJL/2005/2.html#Heading227.

Vonasch, Andrew, Tania Reynolds, Bo Winegard, and Roy Baumeister. "Death Before Dishonor: Incurring Costs to Protect Moral Reputation." *Social Psychological and Personality Science*, July 21, 2017. http://journals.sagepub.com/doi/pdf/10.1177/1948550617720271.

Wagner, John D., Mark V. Flinn, and Barry G. England. "Hormonal Response to Competition Among Male Coalitions." *Evolution and Human Behavior* 23, no. 6 (November 2002): 437–442.

Waheidi, Majd al-. "Gaza Dating Site Matches Widows to Men Seeing Second (or Third) Wife." *New York Times*, June 4, 2017. https://www.nytimes.com/2017/06/04/world/middleeast /gaza-palestinians-hamas-wesal-polygamy.html.

Walter, Barbara. *Reputation and Civil War: Why Separatist Conflicts Are So Violent*. Cambridge: Cambridge University Press, 2009.

Waring, Marilyn. *Counting for Nothing: What Men Value and What Women Are Worth*. Toronto: University of Toronto Press, 1999.

Warner, James M., and D. A. Campbell. "Supply Response in an Agrarian Economy with Nonsymmetric Gender Relations." *World Development* 28, no. 7 (2000): 1327–1340.

Weatherford, Jack. *Genghis Khan and the Making of the Modern World*. New York: Crown, 2004.

Weber, Hannes. "Demography and Democracy: The Impact of Youth Cohort Size on Democratic Stability in the World." *Democratization* 20, no. 2 (2014): 335–357. http://dx.doi.org /10.1080/13510347.2011.650916.

Weiner, Mark S. *The Rule of the Clan: What an Ancient Form of Social Organization Reveals About the Future of Individual Freedom*. New York: Farrar, Straus and Giroux, 2013.

Weiner, Scott. "Rethinking Patriarchy and Kinship in Arab Gulf States." in *Women and Gender in Middle East Politics*, 13–16. The Project on Middle East Political Science, 2016. https:// pomeps.org/wp-content/uploads/2016/05/POMEPS_Studies_19_Gender_Web.pdf.

White, Nic. "'Gang is Your Best Friend': African Apex Members Reveal What Life Is Like Inside the Notorious Melbourne Group." *Daily Mail*, May 1, 2017. http://www.dailymail .co.uk/news/article-4462746/Apex-members-reveal-life-like-inside-gang.html.

Whitfield, Charles L, Robert Anda, Shanta Dube, and Vincent Felliti. "Violent Childhood Experiences and the Risk of Intimate Partner Violence in Adults." *Journal of Interpersonal Violence* 18, no. 2 (2003): 166–185. https://doi.org/10.1177/0886260502238733.

Whitelocks, Sadie. "The Soviet Times Were Good." *Daily Mail*, June 30, 2017. http://www .dailymail.co.uk/travel/travel_news/article-4632216/Kyrgyzstan-local-reveals-life-good -USSR-rule.html.

Wikipedia. "List of Countries and Territories by Land Borders." 2018. https://en.wikipedia .org/wiki/List_of_countries_and_territories_by_land_borders.

Wilson, Sophia. "Human Rights and Law Enforcement in the Post-Soviet World: Or How and Why Judges and Police Bend the Law." Lecture, Brigham Young University, Provo, UT, November 12, 2010.

Wilson, Margo, and Martin Daly. "Competitiveness, Risk Taking, and Violence: The Young Male Syndrome." *Ethology and Sociobiology* 6, no. 1 (1985): 59–73.

Wilson, Margo, Martin Daly, and Joanna Scheib. "Femicide: An Evolutionary Psychological Perspective." In *Feminism and Evolutionary Biology: Boundaries, Intersections, and Frontiers*, edited by Patricia Adair Gowaty, 431–465. New York: Chapman and Hall, 1997.

Wodon, Quentin. "Child Marriage, Family Law, and Religion." *Review of Faith and International Affairs* 13, no. 3 (2015): https://www.tandfonline.com/doi/full/10.1080/15570274.2015.1075761.

Wodon, Quentin, and Benedicte de la Briere. "Unrealized Potential: The High Cost of Gender Inequality in Earnings." The Cost of Gender Inequality Notes Series, World Bank, Washington, DC, 2018. https://openknowledge.worldbank.org/bitstream/handle /10986/29865/126579-Public-on-5-30-18-WorldBank-GenderInequality-Brief-v13.pdf? sequence=1&isAllowed=y.

Wolfe, Lauren. "Why Are So Many Women Dying from Ebola?" *Foreign Policy*, August 20, 2014. http://foreignpolicy.com/2014/08/20/why-are-so-many-women-dying-from-ebola/.

Wood, Reed, and Mark Ramirez. "Exploring the Microfoundations of the Gender Equality Peace Hypothesis." *International Studies Review* 20, no. 3 (2018): 345–367. https://doi.org /10.1093/isr/vix016.

World Bank. "Gender Equality and Development." *World Development Report*, 2011. https://siteresources.worldbank.org/INTWDR2012/Resources/7778105-1299699968583/7786210-1315936222006/Complete-Report.pdf.

——. "World Development Indicators." 2014. http://databank.worldbank.org/data.

——. "World Development Indicators." 2015. http://databank.worldbank.org/data.

——. "Promoting Land Rights to Empower Rural Women and End Poverty." October 14, 2016. http://www.worldbank.org/en/news/feature/2016/10/14/promoting-land-rights-to-empower-rural-women-and-end-poverty.

World Health Organization. "Violence Against Women." November 29, 2017. http://www.who.int/en/news-room/fact-sheets/detail/violence-against-women.

"World Risk Report." Bundnis Entwicklung Hilft. http://weltrisikobericht.de/english/.

Worthington, Roger L., and Tiffany A. Whittaker. "Scale Development Research: A Content Analysis and Recommendations for Best Practices." *Counseling Psychologist* 34 (2006): 806–838.

Wrangham, Richard, and Dale Peterson. *Demonic Males: Apes and the Origins of Human Violence*. New York: Mariner Books, 1996.

Wright, Robert. *The Moral Animal*. New York: Vintage, 1995.

Wrong, Michela. *It's Our Turn to Eat: The Story of a Kenyan Whistle-Blower*. New York: Harper Perennial, 2010.

Wulfhorst, Ellen. "Violence Is the Biggest Challenge Facing Women, Says Top Women's Rights Advocate." *Thomson Reuters*, March 6, 2017. http://news.trust.org/item/20170306050632-czatd/.

Yin, Steph. "In South Asian Social Castes, a Living Lab for Genetic Disease." *New York Times*, July 17, 2017. https://www.nytimes.com/2017/07/17/health/india-south-asia-castes-genetics-diseases.html.

Young, Katherine. "Introduction." In *Today's Woman in World Religions*, edited by Arvind Sharma, 1–37. New York: State University of New York Press, 1994.

Youssef, Nour. "Two Paths for Yemen's War-Scarred Children: Combat, or Marriage." *New York Times*, October 9, 2017. https://www.nytimes.com/2017/10/09/world/middleeast/yemen-war-children.html.

Yuray, Mark. "Mannerbund 101." *Social Matter*, February 23, 2016. https://www.socialmatter.net/2016/02/23/mannerbund-101/.

Yuval-Davis, Nira. *Gender and Nation*. New York: Sage, 1997.

Zahel, Nadia. "Beaten and Tortured for 24 Years to Pay for Her Father's Mistake." *HuffPost*, 2017. https://testkitchen.huffingtonpost.com/saharspeaks/#nadiazahel/.

Zeng, Tian Chen, Alan Aw, and Marcus Feldman (2018) "Cultural Hitchhiking and Competition Between Patrilineal Kin Groups Explain the Post-Neolithic Y-Chromosome Bottleneck." *Nature Communications*, May 25, 2018. https://www.nature.com/articles/s41467-018-04375-6.

Zereyesus, Yacob A. "Women's Empowerment in Agriculture and Household-Level Health in Northern Ghana: A Capability Approach." *Journal of International Development* 29 (2017): 899–918. doi:10.1002/jid.3307.

Zereyesus, Yacob A., Vincent Amanor-Boadu, Kara L. Ross, and Aleksan Shanoyan. "Does Women's Empowerment in Agriculture Matter for Children's Health Status? Insights from Northern Ghana." *Social Indicators Research* 132, no. 3 (2017): 1265–1280. doi:10.1007/s11205-016-1328-z.

Zweynert, Astrid. "Misinterpreting Islamic Law Robs Muslim Women of Land: Experts." *Reuters*, March 1, 2018. https://www.reuters.com/article/us-women-landrights-inheritance/misinterpreting-islamic-law-robs-muslim-women-of-land-experts-idUSKCN1GD56W.

INDEX

Page numbers in *italics* refer to figures and tables.

abandonment, 32

abortion, sex-selective, 43, 45, 60, 71–74; masculinized sex ratios and, 146–49; one-child policy and, 333

Abouharb, Rodwan, 115

Absence of Violent Terrorism and Freedom of Domestic Movement Factor, 414

Access to Basic Knowledge, 264, 268–70, 453

Access to Improved Water, 241, 254

Access to Information and Communications, 265, 270–71, 454

Adams, Brooke, 36

Adams, John, 49

Adams, Julia, 120, 162, 500n71, 530n128

adultery, 83, 90, 319–20

Afghanistan: birth rates, 169; brideprice and wedding costs, 60–63, 158–59, 163–64; child marriage, 78; corruption, 132–33; empowerment of women, 1; patrilineal/fraternal kinship networks, 3, 50; son preference, 71; Soviet invasion of, 367–68; violence in, 137; women's property rights, 356–57

Africa, Sub-Saharan: brideprice, 58, 163; clan governance, 25; customary law, 85–86; food security, 171; polygyny, 44–45, 65, 67, 156; sex ratios, 149; Syndrome societies, 54.

See also East Africa; West Africa; *specific countries*

African Charter on the Rights and Welfare of the Child, 350

African Union, 357

Agacinski, Sylviane, 14–15

age of marriage: birth rates and, 168–70; brideprice and, 63–64, 163; democracy and, 324–26; devaluation of daughters and, 43; effects on women and girls, 76–78; exigency and, 141–42; laws on, 83, 85–86; low, 74–79, 119; map of, *75*; neolocal marriage and, 174, 322–23; power differentials and, 171; as Syndrome variable, 4, 52. *See also* child marriage

Aggregated Civilization Identification, 185–86

aggression, 36

agnatic kinship groups, 3–4, 28, 40, 62, 80, 315, 502n77

agricultural sector, 171–72, 506n115, 506n118, 517n145

Ahmed, Akbar, 137, 556n69

Ahram, Ariel, 99, 120, 139, 522n236

AIDS, 170–71

Air Pollution Factor, 296, 299–301, 470, 472

Albania: democracy and, 82; masculinized sex ratio, 72, 74; Syndrome scale score, *344*